Liezi (列子)
World of Delusions

(Full Chinese text and translation, analysis and appreciation)

Jingwei (景維)

jjingwei11@gmail.com

Singapore
February 2021
This is a self-published monograph.
A full Chinese text presentation, translation and study of the *Liezi (列子)*

Title Availability:
Worldwide (order online)
Print-on-demand (POD) by Lightning Source, UK
Distribution through Ingram International
Espresso Book Machine
Amazon.com
The Book Depository.co.uk *(with free delivery worldwide)*

Publication Data

Disclaimer:
Every precaution has been taken in the preparation of this monograph.
The publisher and author apologize for any errors or omissions that may remain.
The publisher and author assume no liability whatsoever, for damages suffer from its usage.
Copyright © 2020
All rights reserved.
Copying is allowed for individual private use.
Copying is *not* allowed for commercial trade.

Self-Published by Jingwei (景維)
email: jjingwei11@gmail.com
Title Availability:
Worldwide (order online)
Print-on-demand (POD) by Lightning Source, UK
Distribution through Ingram International
The Book Depository.co.uk (with free delivery worldwide)
Espresso Book Machine
Amazon.com
List price: SGD$30.00

National Library Board, Singapore Cataloguing in publication Data
Name(s): Jingwei, 1945-
Title: Liezi : world of delusions : a complete translation and appreciation of Liezi / Jingwei.
Description: [Singapore] : Jingwei, 2021. | Includes bibliographical references.
Identifier(s): OCN 1201296901 | ISBN 978-981-14-8572-5 (paperback)
Subject(s): LCSH: Liezi, active 4th century B.C. Liezi--Criticism, Textual. | Taoist philosophy. | Philosophy, Chinese.
Classification: DDC 181.114--dc23

Jingwei Publishing (self-publisher)
Cover design: The ancient city of Bianliang (汴梁, 清明上河圖)(purchased online ~SD30/-)

Printer: Ultra Supplies, Singapore
First Print: 10 copies, November 2020
Print-on-demand (POD) by Lightning Source UK Ltd.
Paperback: B&W 156 x 234mm
Page Count: 350
Weight: 550g (approx.)

Liezi: World of Delusions

Dedicated to the Curiosity of all Humanity

天问 曰：	**Heaven Queries** Says: "
遂古之初，	Distant Ancient-era Its Beginning,
谁传道之？	Who Transmits Narrates It ?
上下未形，	Above (Heaven) Below (Earth) Prior Formation,
何由考之？	How Ever Verify It ?
冥昭瞢闇，	Night Day, in Dim Confusion
谁能极之？	Who Able Details It ?
冯翼惟象，	By Wings Of Imagination
何以识之？	How To Know It ?
明明闇闇，	Day Day, Night Night
惟时何为？	This Timing, What Purpose ?
阴阳三合，	Yin Yang, 3rd in Union
何本何化？	Which Original, Which Transformation ?
圜则九重，	Heaven Circumscribes 9 Layers,
孰营度之？	Who Manages, Measures It ?
惟兹何功，	This Construct, Whose Credit,
孰初作之？	Who First Made It ?
斡维焉系，	Pivotal String, How Secured,
天极焉加？	Heaven's Limit How Installed ?
八柱何当，	8 Pillars, How Supporting,
东南何亏？	East South, Why Lacking ?
九天之际，	9 Heavens Their Boundaries,
安放安属？	How Placed, How Connecting ?
隅隈多有，	Corners Coves, Many Existing,
谁知其数？	Who Knows Their Numbers ?
天何所沓？	Heaven Why So Many (layers) ?
十二焉分？	12 (2-hourly periods) How Divided ?
日月安属？	Sun Moon, How Connected ?
列星安陈？	Parade Stars, How Display ?
出自汤谷，	Emerges (Sun) From Tang Gu,
次于蒙汜。	Sets At Meng Creek.
自明及晦，	From Morning Till Evening,
所行几里？	Distance Travel, What Mileage ?
夜光何德，	Night Light (Moon), What Virtue,
死则又育？	Wane Then Grows Again ?

Qu Yuan (c.350 BC), the first famous poet of China, was a senior minister of the state of Chu.
He was in charge of ritual celebrations in the honors of Heaven, the Gods and Spirits.
However, being a thinker scholar, he was never superstitious as reflected in the poem above.
In Heaven, he wondered how sun and moon are related, how the myriad of stars are displayed.
On Earth, he asked why the land mass is lacking in the China Sea compared to the north-west.
Heaven Queries has ~1560 Chinese characters, uniquely dedicated to fielding queries (>150).
His questions admirably revealed his curiosity in the Universe and thirst for knowledge.

Liezi: World of Delusions

Life in the ancient city of Bianjing (汴京)
(artist: Zhang Zeduan, c.1085-1145. court artist.Northern Sung Dynasty)
(宋画家张择端. 清明上河圖)

Liezi: World of Delusions

SYNOPSIS

Liezi (c.450-375BC), Laozi and Zhuangzi are the 3 pillars of philosophical Daoism.
A lesser known philosopher among the trio, we have seen few translations of his work.
He was first introduced by Zhuangzi, described as having the ability to 'ride on wind'.
Since then Liezi has been mis-interpreted as transcendental, seeding religious Daoism.
But on the contrary, natural Daoism is anti-transcendence, honest and down to earth !

Liezi:World of Delusion, translates the ancient *"Liezi"* in its entirety.
Full Chinese Text presentation and English translation of all 8 chapters.
Includes herein are analysis of his thinking on life and death, destiny and freedom, ...
Heavenly Signs (ch.1 天瑞): Explores Origin of the Universe, Humanity and Nature.
Like postulating the self-Creator, achieving longevity, to timing & harvesting of nature.
Huangdi (ch.2 黃帝): Explores forms of Government, exposes Sorcery, and 'No Dao'.
Like Huangdi's dream, Liezi 'ride on wind', God-like sorcerer, to Elder catching cicada.
King Mu of Zhou (ch.3 周穆王): Narratives on Illusions, Dreams, Realities, Emotions.
Like King Mu's astro-travels, Woodcutter's lost deer, Yanren's emotional home return.
Zhongni (Confucius, ch.4 仲尼): Examines what is Sagehood, Sages, Philosophies.
Like Confucius teaches flexibility, Hermit Nankuazi talks to win, Gongsunlong's logic.
Tang's Queries (ch.5 汤问): Limits of Heaven and Earth, Limits of human arts /skills.
Like Kuafu chased the sun, Exchanging hearts to balance, Zaofu learned charioteering.
Effort or Destiny (ch.6 力命): That shapes the march of events, success and failure.
Like Beigonzi thick in Virtue thin in Destiny, and Yiwu's inevitable denial of Baoshu.
Yangzhu (ch.7 杨朱): Covering his thoughts on life, death, humanity and Hedonism.
"No need to lose a hair to save the world; Enjoy life, not be shackled by convention."
Charming talks (ch.8 說符): Miscellaneous narratives, revealing human delusions.
Like Liberating doves, better to ban catching; Disaster fell from Heaven; Axe-thief.

Liezi narratives/stories are imaginative yet refreshingly simple, morally enlightening.
Kuafu Chased Sun (夸父追日), *Yugong Moved Mountains (愚公移山)*, are well known.
And Liezi's logic is simple: "Nothing creates nothing; outside of limits, no limit".
Liezi exposes sorcery, illusions and delusions, and repeatedly says there is 'No Dao'.
Liezi advises constant meditation on 'thinking no right/wrong, speaking no good/evil'.
Life is short, not be shackled with convention, to enjoy life with *no intrusion on others*.
Naturally, Liezi believes in Effort for success, and lets Destiny to account for failures !
Liezi rejects transcendentals and such, saying 'Dao' cannot be acquired and possessed.
Liezi teaches natural Daoism, his charming stories are all reflective of human society.
We read Liezi, take note of our Delusional failings, and self-cultivate for the better.
Like Duke Wen, the tale of flirting man turned him back to defend his borders. (ch.8.7)
Liezi's tales also give amusement, joy, yet more provoking thoughts and moral insights.
The Book of Lieh-tzu (A.C. Graham, 1990)
"Lieh-tzu stories, vivid, lively, full of marvels, often humorous, guilelessly simple."

Liezi: World of Delusions

PREFACE
Since retirement from my research job in 2007, I have written and self-published 2 books.
The *Laozi: Quest for the Ultimate Reality* (ISBN 978-981-07-3758-0), nonfiction, October 2012.
And the *Yijing: Wisdom of 4 Sages* (ISBN 978-981-14-0204-3), nonfiction, March 2019.
In total I have donated more than 300 copies to individuals and institutional libraries, worldwide.
The Congress Library, the Diet Library, Tsinghua University, U. of Pittsburgh, UC Berkeley, ...
The *Laozi* is listed among the "Indie Books Worth Discovering", 15 May 2017, *Kirkus Reviews*.
Available Print-on-demand (POD) by Lightning Source Inc, Amazon.com, other online stores.

*Kuafu Chased Sun (*夸父追日*)*, *Qiren Worried Sky A-falling (*杞人忧天*)*, are well known stories.
*Yugong Moved Mountains (*愚公移山*)* is taught in primary classes, and they come from *Liezi*.
Liezi (c.450-375BC) together with Laozi and Zhuangzi, are the 3 pillars of philosophical Daoism.
Liezi is the lesser known philosopher among the trio, thus there are few translations into English.
Liezi was first referred to by *Zhuangzi (ch.1)*, described as having the ability to 'ride on wind'.
And after Zhuangzi, philosophical Daoism had developed into religious Daoism in China.
Thus the *Liezi* of 8 chapters was often annotated and translated with a tendency towards fantasy.

I find Liezi's narratives and stories simple, engaging, entertaining and enlightening.
And often, Liezi's logic is simple: "Nothing creates nothing; outside of limits, no limit".
In fact, Liezi exposes sorcery, illusions and delusions, and repeatedly says there is 'No Dao'.
Liezi advises constant meditation on 'thinking no right/wrong, speaking no good/evil'.
Life is short, not to be shackled with convention, and to enjoy life without intruding on others.
Liezi believes in Effort for success, leaving Destiny to account for failures!
Liezi was not delusional that he can 'ride on wind', but diligently cultivated his natural Daoism.
Contrary to the impression gained from most written materials, Liezi is pragmatic, not mystical.
Liezi rejects transcendence, enlightening us with vivid stories, revealing our failings/Delusions.

Lieh-tzu *(Pinyin Liezi, Micropedia, Encyclopedia Britannica, 2002.)*
"As in earlier Taoist classics, emphasis in the Lieh-tzu centres on the mysterious Tao (Way) of Taoism, a great unknowable cosmic reality of incessant change to which human life should conform... Such 'fatalism' implies a life of radical 'self-interest' (a new development in Taoism), according to which a person should not sacrifice so much as a single hair of his head for the benefit of others."

Aim of Study:
Contrary to Britannica, to present *Liezi text* in the positive light that Liezi himself has intended.
This study presents the Full Chinese text of *Liezi* (all 8 chapters) and the English translation.
Analysis and appreciation of Liezi's thinking on topics like destiny, freedom, life and death.
The title chosen for this work is:
Liezi: World of Delusions (Full Chinese text and English translation, analysis and appreciation)

Contents

1	**Title Page**
2	**Publication Data**
3	**Dedication**
4	***illustration:*** Life in the ancient city of Bianjing (汴京)
5	**Synopsis**
6	**Preface**
7	**Contents**
9	**Introduction**
10	*illustration: Source of Liezi in Chinese Text for translation (Ye, 2016)*
11	*Liezi*
14	*Design of this study*
15	**Liezi (列子) Translation and Appreciation**
16	*Chapter 1. Heavenly Signs (天瑞)*
44	*Chapter 2. Huangdi (黃帝)*
94	*Chapter 3. King Mu of Zhou (周穆王)*
117	*Chapter 4. Zhongni (Confucius, 仲尼)*
150	*Chapter 5. Tang's Queries (汤问)*
193	*Chapter 6. Effort or Destiny (力命)*
222	*Chapter 7. Yangzhu (杨朱)*
261	*Chapter 8. Charming Talks (說符)*
316	**Discussion**
317	*Authorship and Dating*
318	*Is Liezi a mystic ?*
319	*Is Liezi a scientific ?*
320	*On Life Purpose*
321	*On Death and After*
322	*Natural Daoism*
323	*All Lives Matter*
324	*Humanity, Birds and Animals*
325	*Awareness, Dreams and Minds*
326	*Confucius and Sagehood*
327	*Liezi and Confucians*
328	*Effort and Destiny*
329	*Yangzhu (杨朱, c.395-335BC)*
330	*World of Delusions*
331	*Leadership*
332	*Freedom*
333	*Concept of 'Dao'*

334	**Conclusions**
	All Lives Matters
	Effort or Destiny
	Enjoy life
	Government for the People
	Know your Delusions
	Minds, Dreams and Emotions
	Natural Daoism
	Queries and Curiosity
	Reject Tanscendentals
	Selfless Duties
	Strive for Excellence
339	**Looking Ahead**
340	**After Thoughts**
341	**Universal Basic Income (UBI)**
342	**Bibliographies** *Publications in English*
343	*Publications in Chinese*
344	**Appendices**
345	*Acknowledgements*
346	*List of Important Dates*
347	*Glossary*
348	*Self-Publishing*
349	*Copyrights and Disclaimer*
350	*Back-cover*

Introduction

10.   illustration: Source of Liezi in Chinese Text for translation (Ye, 2016)

11.   Liezi

12.   Studies on Liezi

13.   The 8 chapters of Liezi

14.   Design of study, Style of writing

乱迷惑呢？背上你的粮食，不如趁早回家去吧。"

燕人生于燕，长于楚，及老而还本国。

过晋国，同行者诳之，指城曰："此燕国之城。"其人愀然变容。指社曰①："此若里之社。"乃喟然而叹。指舍曰："此若先人之庐。"乃涓然而泣②。指垄曰："此若先人之冢。"其人哭不自禁。同行者哑然大笑③，曰："予昔绐若④，此晋国耳。"其人大惭。

及至燕，真见燕国之城社，真见先人之庐冢，悲心更微。

【注释】
① 社：祭祀社神的地方，俗称"土地庙"。
② 涓然：慢慢流泪的样子。
③ 哑然：形容笑声。
④ 绐（dài）：哄骗。

【译文】
有个燕国人在燕国出生，在楚国长大，到年老时回到燕国去。

路过晋国时，同行的人诳骗他，指着城墙说："这是燕国的城墙。"那个人听了，凄怆地改变了面容。同行的人指着土地庙说："这是你家乡的土地庙。"那个人听了，感慨地长叹。同行的人指着房舍说："这是你祖先的房子。"那个人于是涓然泪下。同行的人指着坟墓说："这是你祖宗的

Sample source of Liezi in Chinese Text for translation (Ye, 2016)
(Yanren's Home Return, chapter 3.9)

Introduction

Liezi

Chinese folklores and tales are often used in primary school to instill good values and conduct.
Example like *Kuafu Chased Sun (夸父追日)*, an heroic effort to find out where the sun set daily.
Like *Qiren Worried Sky Falling (杞人忧天)*, a query on why the sun, moon and stars not falling.
Like *Stupid Grandpa Moved Mountains (愚公移山)*, a stoic determination to remove obstacles.
Like *No Action Not Like A Thief (无為而不窃铁者)*, a study of prejudice common in society.
But even today, most of us do not know that these wonderful stories come from the *Liezi* text.

Liezi (c.450-375 BC) was named Yukou (御寇), resided in Zheng, in early Warring States Period.
Zhuangzi (c.369-286BC) made many references to Liezi, and *Zhuangzi* has a chapter called Liezi.
Sima Qian (司馬迁, c.145-87BC) a historian has listed Laozi, Zhuangzi, but no mention of Liezi!
Liu Xiang (刘向, 77-6BC) in his *Liezi new book catalogue* (列子新书目录) listed 8 chapters.

However the authenticity of the *Liezi* text has long been questioned by scholars and rightly so.
Inclusion of Gongsunlong (公孙龙 c.320-250BC) who came after Liezi, attested to this (ch.4.13).
And that Zhang Zhan (張湛, 317-420AD) of Eastern Jin Period, had purportedly fabricated *Liezi*.
But there are also those who insisted that the book was a product initiated before the Qin Dynasty.
Before late insertions and additions by individuals who came after to edit and annotate the book.
Nonetheless, as the 20th century scholar Qian Zhongshu (錢钟書, 1910-1998) pointed out, quote:
"Even if the Liezi is truly a fabrication, we may not diminish the Liezi but respect Zhang Zhan."

Zhuangzi's first reference to Liezi was his 'Joy, riding on wind for 15 days'. (*Zhuangzi*, ch.1)
This seems to set the tone in interpreting Liezi, and development towards religious Daoism.
Emperor Xuanzong (Tang) designated the *Liezi* as 'Classic of Perfect Emptiness (沖虛真经)'.
Britannica (2002) says the *Liezi* emphasis centers on the mysterious Dao, a cosmic reality.
Coutinho (2020) says it is noteworthy that the *Liezi* stands out as more apparently metaphysical.

The *Laozi*, the *Liezi* and the *Zhuangzi*, have been hailed as the '3 pillars of Daoism'.
There have been many translations of *Laozi* and *Zhuangzi* into English and other languages.
Liezi, little known even in China, has fewer translations and is almost unknown in the West.
As an atheist, not believing in the supernatural, I find Liezi pragmatic as Laozi (Jingwei, 2012).
I believe my approach has given me a new perspective of Liezi that I like to share with readers.
Attempts at explaining the origin of the universe and creation of all matters are rather primitive.
But most narratives in fables and discussions are rather refreshing, engaging and enlightening.
The 139 sections in 8 chapters are revealing of human faults; in pride, prejudice and selfishness.
To reflect on such awareness, the title chosen for this study is: *"Liezi: World of Delusions"*.

Introduction

Studies on Liezi

Since the dawn of time, thinking humans have been pondering on the origin of the universe. Laozi was the first to postulate 'Dao' as the primal creator of all matters in his book, *Daodijing*. Many people take 'Dao' to be real, and wish to 'possess' it for its supposed 'supernatural power'. The *Liezi* seems an extension of Laozi's quest for the Ultimate Reality or 'Dao' (Jingwei, 2012). Through characters in the text, Liezi insistently says there is no 'Dao' energy or magic. (ch.2) Thus it is ironic that many people today read Liezi as promoting metaphysics and transcendence.

Lieh-tzu *(Pinyin Liezi, Micropedia, Encyclopedia Britannica, 2002.)*
"As in earlier Taoist classics, emphasis in the Lieh-tzu centres on the mysterious Tao (Way) of Taoism, a great unknowable cosmic reality of incessant change to which human life should conform…The 'Yang Chu' chapter of the classic gives the Lieh-tzu a particular interest, for this chapter acknowledges the futility of challenging the immutable and irresistable Tao; it concludes that all man can look forward to in this life is sex, music, physical beauty, and material abundance, and even these goals are not always satisfied. Such 'fatalism' implies a life of radical 'self-interest' (a new development in Taoism), according to which a person should not sacrifice so much as a single hair of his head for the benefit of others."

Liezi *(Internet Encyclopedia of Philosophy. Steve Coutinho, Muhlenberg College. viewed 2020.)*
"It is noteworthy that the *Liezi* stands out as more apparently metaphysical than the cosmologically oriented texts of the Zhou and Han dynasties (such as the *Laozi*, *ZhongYong*, and the *Xici* of the *Yijing*)."

The Book of Lieh-tzu *(AC Graham transl. 1960.Columbia U. Press, NY, p.II)*
"The Taoist, it will already be clear, cannot be a philosopher, in the Western sense, establishing his case by rational argument; he can only guide us in the direction of the Way by aphorisms, poetry and parable."
"The strength of Lieh-tzu is in its stories, vivid, lively, full of marvels, often humorous, to all outward appearances guilelessly simple."

Liezi: World of Delusions *(This study, 2020)*
Indeed, Liezi's legendary fables and stories are captivatingly simple, stimulating for thoughts. Liezi is more exciting in his revelation of delusions in human society, rather than his cosmology. And is apparently in favor of daoist virtues, rather than encouraging metaphysics, transcendence. Hopefully this monograph can provide some positivity to counter the negativity that is prevailing. The full Chinese text is presented with English translation that the general population can enjoy.

We human creatures are much troubled by the unknown after death, constantly seeking solace. Thus we are more willing to believe that there is a supernatural power out there to help us. Even today, we have no proper explanation for the existence of the universe, and purpose of life. Liezi, like Laozi are the rare individuals who are rational thinkers seeking for true understanding. Full of imaginative descriptions, their writings basically teach logical and rational thinking. They merely postulate the primal 'Dao' for initiation of the universe and creation of all matters. 'Dao' may not be acquired for selfish gain, but we may emulate its many perceived attributes.
Liezi's Daoism is humility, unselfish, enjoy life, work for success, accept Destiny after events.

Introduction

The 8 chapters of *Liezi*

There are 139 sections in total, organised loosely into 8 chapters under various themes.
The majority of 5 chapters are named after legendary emperors and renown sages.

Heavenly Signs (ch.1 天瑞): Explores Origin of the Universe, Humanity and Nature.
Like postulating the self-Creator, achieving longevity, to timing and harvesting nature.
Huangdi (ch.2 黄帝): Explores forms of Government, exposes Sorcery, and saying 'No Dao'.
Like Huangdi's dream, Liezi 'ride on wind', God-like sorcerer, to an Elder catching cicada.
King Mu of Zhou (ch.3 周穆王): Narratives on Illusions, Dreams, Realities, and Emotions.
Like King Mu's astro-travels, Woodcutter's lost deer, to Yanren's emotional return.
Zhongni (Confucius, ch.4 仲尼): Examines what is Sagehood, Sages and their Philosophies.
Like Confucius teaching Flexibility, Hermit Nankuazi talking to win, and Gongsunlong's Logic.
Tang's Queries (ch.5 汤问): Discusses Limits of Heaven and Earth, Limits of arts and skills.
Like Kuafu chased the sun, Exchanging hearts to balance, and Zaofu learned charioteering.
Effort or Destiny (ch.6 力命): That shape the march of events, determine success and failure.
Like Beigonzi thick in Virtue thin in Destiny, and Yiwu's inevitable denial of Baoshu.
Yangzhu (ch.7 杨朱): Covering his thoughts on life, death, humanity and Hedonism.
Like: "Nobody needs lose a hair to save the world", "Enjoy life, not be shackled by convention."
Charming talks (ch.8 說符): Miscellaneous narratives, revealing human prejudices, delusions.
Like: Liberation of Doves, better to ban catching; Disaster fell from Heaven; Axe-thief.

Liezi's simple logic: Self-Creator unselfishly created the universe, not by design, but naturally so.
Liezi exposes sorcery, illusions and delusions, repeatedly says there is 'no Dao', no superpower.
Advises us to be aware of states of realities and dreams, know their connections, have no fear.
Liezi advises meditation on 'thinking no right/wrong, speaking no good/evil' for self-cultivation,
Ever inquisitive in thinking, to explore the limits in science, in all spheres of human activities.
Naturally, Liezi believes in Effort for success, and Destiny to account for failures after events !
Life is short, not shackled by conventions, to enjoy life, hedonism without intrusion on others.
Lastly see the miscellaneous reflections of our pride, prejudice and delusions, and to self-correct.
Each of the 139 sections may give us something to think about and to look at our world anew!

Yangzhu (ch.7 杨朱) seems to promote hedonism, and apparently it is odd he is included here.
It has been interpreted that Yangzhu was not willing to lose a single hair to save the world !
But what Yangzhu had said is, "When nobody needs to lose a single hair, the world is ordered !"

人人不损一毫，	Each Person Not (needed) to Lose 1 Hair, (ch.7.10.10)
人人不利天下，	Each Person Not (needed) to Benefit The World,
天下治矣。"	The World is Ordered indeed."

Yangzhu is a conscientious hedonist who wished everybody could enjoy life, without exceptions.

Introduction

Design of study
This monograph is a complete translation, analysis and appreciation of the Liezi.
Introduction
Liezi
The 8 chapters of Liezi
Design of study, Style in writing.
Presentation of the 8 chapters
Chapter introduction.
Each section:
  The original Chinese text printed in full (from Ye, 2016).
  The English verbatim translation printed in the next column on the same line.
  Liezi Text Narrative, a concise rewrite of the English translation for easy reading.
  Comments, author's analysis and appreciation of the narrative, to crystallize thoughts.
Chapter summary.
Discussion
Authorship and dating
Liezi's thoughts on destiny, freedom, life, death,... (total 17 topics)
Conclusions:
Looking Forward
After Thoughts
Universal Basic Income (UBI)
Bibliographies
English, Chinese
Appendices:
Acknowledgement
List of important dates
Glossary
Self-Publishing, Copyrights, Disclaimers.

Style in Writing
A near verbatim English translation of the Chinese characters is done to better capture the *Liezi*. Main English words for verbatim translation begin with a Capital letter, not conjunction words. Chinese style construct of sentences is adopted, short phrases separated with commas for clarity. And English words needed to clarify implied meaning, to assist comprehension are bracketed. Translation done over 2 years, different words of close meaning are used in different sections. No attempt is made for uniformity as together the differences may give a broader perspective. Shorter and simpler English words are favored when meaning and spirit are not compromised. All sentences are constructed so as to confine to a single line for easy reading.

Liezi: World of Delusions
Aims: To achieve a down-to-earth translation of the ancient *Liezi* in its entirety, all 8 chapters. Presentation of a perspective of *Liezi* that all readers can easily relate, enjoy and apply.

Liezi (列子)
Translation and Appreciation

Chapter 1. Heavenly Signs (天瑞)

Introduction

1.01 Self-Creator (有生不生)

1.02 All Matters Transform Alive (万物化生)

1.03 All Selfless These Duties (皆无为之职)

1.04 Hundred Years Skull (百岁髑髅)

1.05 Spirit Body parted, Am I Still Existing？(精神离形, 我尚何存？)

1.06 Human's 4 big transformations (人生大化有四)

1.07 The 3 Joys of Rongqiqi (荣启期之三乐)

1.08 The Centurion Linlei (百岁林类)

1.09 Zigong Weary of Learning (子贡倦于学)

1.10 Liezi Values Emptiness (列子贵虚)

1.11 Heaven Earth Close Changes (天地密移)

1.12 Qiren's Worries (杞人忧天)

1.13 Can Dao Be Possessed？(道可得而有乎？)

1.14 Robbing Heaven Earth (盗天地之时利)

Summary

Chapter 1. Heavenly Signs (天瑞)

Introduction

This first chapter focuses on exploring creation of the Universe, Nature and Life.
Teaches Human learning and adaptation to Nature to achieve Longevity and Prosperity.

Beginning with the primal Self-Creator, postulated to initiate creation of the Universe.
With the Self-Transformer, postulated to help further transformation of the myriad things and life.
Thus appearance of Heaven, Earth, Sage and all matters with specific duties, all selfless actions.
The 100-year skull left Liezi no delusion, that humans are inside the transformations of nature.
After death when the spirit disperses in Heaven and the body returns to Earth, do 'I' still exist ?
After the 4 stages of human life, Baby growth, Youth vitality, Old-age leisure, total rest in Death.
Two paths to longevity are revealed with Rongqiqi's 3 joys and hermit Linlei's lack of desires.
Zigong's weariness teaches us the truth of life, there is truly no rest till death and burial.
The subtle changes of nature and our insensitivity, thus let's be mindful of the advance of old age.
Qiren's worry of the sky falling does warn of the real possibility of our destruction (by meteors).
Liezi suggests, better to practice quietude and humility; for love of 'emptiness' is only empty talk.
Liezi refutes any possession of 'Dao'; as we cannot not die and do not even 'Possess' our body.
Lietzi teaches we may 'rob' (harvesting) nature; but 'criminal' to take the possessions of others.

Chapter 1. Heavenly Signs (天瑞)

1.1 有生不生 | 1.1 Self-Creator

01	子列子居郑圃，	Teacher Liezi Resided Zhengpu (region),
02	四十年人无识者。	Forty Years People Not Know Him.
03	国君卿大夫眂之，	State King Senior Ministers Saw Him,
04	犹众庶也。	Like The Commoners that's.
05	国不足，将嫁于卫。	State In Famine, About Migrating To Wei (state).
06	弟子曰："先生往无反期，	Disciples Said: "Teacher Going-off No Return Date,
07	弟子敢有所谒；	Disciples Dare Have Reason to Implore;
08	先生将何以教？	Teacher With What To Teach us ?
09	先生不闻壶丘子林之言乎？"	Teacher Not Heard Huqiuzilin His Words, right ?"
10	子列子笑曰："壶子何言哉？	Teacher Liezi Laughing Said: "Huqiu Said What, O' ?
11	虽然，夫子尝语伯昏瞀人，	Though, Teacher Often Conversed with Bohun Maoren,
12	吾侧闻之，试以告女。	Aside I heard him, Try To Tell You.
13	**其言曰：有生不生，**	**His Words Said: Has Creator Not-Created (self-Creator)**
14	有化不化。	Has Transformer Not-Transformed (self-Transformer).
15	不生者能生生，	Not-Created Entity Able to Create the Created,
16	不化者能化化。	Not-Transformed Able to Transform the Transformed.
17	生者不能不生，	The Created Can Not, Not Create,
18	化者不能不化，	The Transformed Can Not, Not Transform,
19	故常生常化。	Thus Constant Creation Constant Transformation.
20	常生常化者，	The Constant Creator Constant Transformer,
21	无时不生，无时不化。	No Time Not Creating, No Time Not Transforming.
22	阴阳尔，四时尔，	Yin Yang Thus, 4 Seasons Thus,
23	不生者疑独，不化者往复。	Self-Creator Focus Unique, Self-Transformed Recycles.
24	往复其际不可终，	Recycles The Boundaries Can Not End,
25	疑独其道不可穷。	Focus Unique The 'Dao' Can Not be Depleted.
26	《黄帝书》曰：	*Huangdi Text* Said:
27	'谷神不死，	'Valley-Spirit (of fertility) Never Die,
28	是谓玄牝。	Is Called Primal Female.
29	玄牝之门，	Primal Female Its Doorway,
30	是谓天地之根。	Is Called Foundation of Heaven and Earth.
31	绵绵若存，	Softly Continuously Like Existing (not existing),
32	用之不勤。'	Use It Not Depleting.'
33	故生物者不生，	Thus Creator of Matters Not Created,
34	化物者不化。	Transformer of Matters Not Transformed.
35	自生自化，自形自色，	Self Created Self Transformed, Self Formed Self Colored,
36	自智自力，自消自息。	Self Knowledge Self Action, Self Death, Self Life.
37	谓之生化、形色、	Call These Creation Transformation, Forms Color,
38	智力、消息者，	Knowledge Actions, Death Life Entities,
39	非也。"	No, that's." (all self naturally, not by design)

1.1 Self-Creator

Liezi Text Narrative
For forty years, Liezi resided in Zhengpu like a commoner with no recognition by king, nobles.L4
About to migrate to Wei with no return-date, disciples implored to learn of his wisdom. L9
Laughing, Liezi told of hearing Huqiuzi's talk of the Self-Creator and Self-Transformer. L14
Self-Creator able to create the created; Self-Transformer can transform the transformed. L16
The created cannot not create (more), the transformed cannot not transform (more). L18
Hence constant creations and constant transformations at all times. L21
Yin Yang, Self-Creator uniquely focuses; like four seasons, Self-Transformer recycles. L23
Recycling the boundaries no end, uniquely focuses, the 'Dao' cannot be depleted. L25
Huangdi Text said: 'Valley-spirit (of fertility) never die, is said to be the primal female. L28
Primal female's doorway is said to be the foundation of Heaven and Earth. L30
Softly continuously existing (not existing), is used without being depleted.' L32
Creator of matters, itself not been created; L33
Transformer of matters, itself not been transformed. L34
Self-create, self-transform, self-form, self-color, self-will, self-action, self-died, self-live. L36
Calling it creation, transformation, form, color, intellect, action, death, and life by design. L38
No, not at all." L39

Comments:
1.1 Self-Creator
Liezi lived anonymously in Zhengpu for 40 years, with no attention from the king and ministers. Because of famine he left for Wei with no return date and his disciples implored for his wisdom.
He narrated the concept of self-Creator self-transformer from his fictitious teacher Huqiuzilin.
Self-creator must create with Yin Yang; Self-Transformer must transform like four-seasons cycles.
Those created constantly create, those transformed constantly transform, naturally not by design.

26	《黄帝书》曰：	*Huangdi Text* Said:
27	'谷神不死，	'Valley-spirit (of fertility) never die,
28	是谓玄牝。	Is said to be the primal female.
29	玄牝之门，	Primal female's doorway,
30	是谓天地之根。	Is said to be the foundation of Heaven and Earth.
31	绵绵若存，	Softly continuously like existing (not existing),
32	用之不勤。'	Is used without being depleted.'

This passage is an exact replica of Laozi's *Daodejing* Chapter 6 (Jingwei, 2012).
Liezi's idea of the universe creation seems a continuation from Laozi's conception of 'Dao'.
And Transformation of all things is an extension of *Yijing's* concept of 'Changes'(Jingwei, 2018).
The ancient Chinese had not been able to conceive a super-being in the creation of the universe.
They are happy to observe nature and advise that we pay attention and act with respect to nature.

These 3 ancient texts, (Yijing, Laozi, Liezi), are uniquely in unison with a godless universe.
A Primal Self-Creator, cannot not create and transform all things naturally, not by design !

Chapter 1. Heavenly Signs (天瑞)

1.2 万物化生 | 1.2 All Matters Transform Alive

01 子列子曰：	Teacher Liezi Said:
02 "昔者圣人因阴阳	"Past Sage Person With Yin Yang
03 　以统天地。	For Presiding over Heaven Earth.
04 夫有形者生于无形，	O' Has-Form Entity Created From No-Form,
05 则天地安从生？	Then Heaven Earth How Where-from Created ?
06 故曰：有太易，有太初，	Hence Says: Has Primal Yi, Has Primal Initial,
07 有太始，有太素。	Has Primal Beginning, Has Primal Simple.
08 太易者，未见气也：	Primal Yi Entity, Not Seen Air that's:
09 太初者，气之始也；	Primal Initial Entity, The Beginning of Air that's;
10 太始者，形之始也；	Primal Beginning Entity, The Beginning of Form that's;
11 太素者，质之始也。	Primal Simple Entity, The Beginning of Character that's.
12 气形质具而未相离，	Air Form Character Complete But Not Mutually Separate
13 故曰浑沦。	Hence Call-it Whirly-Bubbly (*whirlpool*).
14 浑沦者，言万物	Whirly-Bubbly that's, Says All Matters
15 　相浑沦而未相离也。	Mutual Whirly-Bubbly And Not Mutually Separate.
16 视之不见，听之不闻，	Look at It Not See, Listen to It Not Hear,
17 循之不得，故曰易也。	Follow It Not Possible, Hence Call Yi that's.
18 易无形埒，易变而为一，	Yi No Form Boundary, Yi Transformed And Be One,
19 一变而为七，七变而为九。	One Transformed And Be 7, 7 Transformed And Be 9.
20 九变者，穷也，	9 Transformed Entity, Limit that's (*highest number 9*),
21 乃复变而为一。	Then Again Transformed And Be One (*cycling-back*).
22 一者，形变之始也。	One Entity, The Beginning of Form Transforming that's.
23 清轻者上为天，	Clear Light Matters rise Up Be Heaven,
24 浊重者下为地，	Muddy Heavy Matters fall Below Be Earth,
25 冲和气者为人；	Mixing Harmony Air Entity Be Human;
26 故天地含精，	Thus Heaven Earth Contain Essence,
27 *万物化生。"*	***All Matters Transform Alive."***

1.2 All Matters Transform Alive

Liezi Text Narrative
Liezi said: "Ancient sages presided over Heaven and Earth with Yin and Yang interaction. L1-3
The Has-Form created from No-Form, then how and where-from Heaven Earth created?" L5
Well, there were 4 stages, the Primal Yi, Primal Initial, Primal Beginning and Primal Simple. L7
Primal Yi stage is Air Not Seen (invisible), Primal Initial is the stage of Air formation. L9
Primal Beginning stage is having Forms and Primal Simple stage is having Character. L11
Matters complete with Air, Form and Character not yet separated in a *galactic spiral*. L13
Matters complete with Air, Form and Character not yet separated, call-it Hunlun (浑沦). L15
Matters unseen, unheard, cannot be grasped, cannot follow (invisible), hence call-it Yi (易). L17
Yi (易) has no form, transformed and be One; One transformed be 7; 7 transformed and be 9. L19
This 9-Transformed limited (*highest number 9*), then transformed back to be One (*recycling*). L21
This One, the Beginning of Form transformation. L22
Light Matters Rise-up to form Heaven and Heavy Matters Drop-below to form the Earth. L24
Medium harmonious Air Matters harmoniously combine to form Human Beings. L25
Heaven Earth Containing Essence (Yin Yang energies) for the transformation of Life." L27

Comments:
1.2 All Matters Transform Alive
The above is a motley description of the early stages in the creation of the universe by Liezi.
A primitive attempt at visualizing the universe formation, stepwise from nothing to complexity.
Heaven Earth, male female, day and night, life death; dualism is a clear sign in our daily life .
Dualism gives rise to the Yin Yang concept, two opposing negative energy and positive energy.
The ancients see Yin Yang in all matters, and the need to balance them to achieve harmony.
Why the transformation of Yi from Nothing to One, to 7, then to 9 and back to One, is baffling!
Prominence of 7 may be related to the 7 stars in every quarter of Heaven, total 28 stars (28星宿).
Lining stars with moon phases, prominence of 7 is today seen in our 7-day week solar calendar.
The highest number limit is 9 on the finger-tips as 10 is considered a number too full to be good.
A return to One is natural and is the beginning of form transformations.
Light matters rising up to form Heaven and heavy matters falling below to form Earth.
Mixing harmonious air matters that combined to form Human Beings between Heaven Earth.
Thus Heaven and Earth contain essence (Yin Yang energies) and matters transform alive.
Liezi seems to flesh out ideas in 'Yijing' about the creation of the universe (Jingwei, 2018)
Like Self-Creator of 1.1, Yi also creates all things of the universe naturally and not by design.

Liezi is proposing the concept of a universe and life, arising gradually naturally, not by design.

Chapter 1. Heavenly Signs (天瑞)

1.3 皆无为之职	**1.3 All Selfless These Duties**
01 子列子曰：	Teacher Liezi Said:
02 "天地无全功，	"Heaven Earth Not All Mighty
03 圣人无全能，	Sage Person Not All Rounder
04 万物无全用。	All Matters Not All Capable
05 故天职生覆，	Hence Heaven's Duties to Create and Protect
06 地职形载，	Earth's Duties to Form and Support
07 圣职教化，	Sage's Duties to Teach and Enlighten,
08 物职所宜。	Matters' Duties for Purposes Intended
09 然则天有所短，	Naturally Then Heaven Has Its Short (weakness).
10 地有所长，	Earth Has Its Long (strength).
11 圣有所否，	Sage Has His Defects,
12 物有所通。	Matters Have Their Connectivity.
13 何则？	What Rules ?
14 生覆者不能形载，	Creator Protector Entity Not Able to Form and Support,
15 形载者不能教化，	Form Support Entity Not Able to Teach and Enlighten,
16 教化者不能违所宜，	Teach Enlighten Entity Not Able Oppose Its Purpose,
17 宜定者不出所位。	Purpose Intended Entity Not Exceeding Its Position.
18 故天地之道，非阴则阳；	Hence Heaven Earth Their Ways, Not Yin Then Yang;
19 圣人之教，非仁则义；	Sage Person His Teaching, Not Humanity Then Justice;
20 万物之宜，非柔则刚：	All Matters Their Suitability, Not Soft Then Hard:
21 此皆随所宜而不能	This All Follow Whatever Suitable And Not Allow
22 　出所位者也。	Exceeding Whatever The Position, that's.
23 故有生者，有生生者；	Hence Has Created Entity, Has Creator of The Created;
24 有形者，有形形者；	Has Form Entity, Has Form-creator of The Formed;
25 有声者，有声声者；	Has Sound Entity, Has Sound-creator of The Sound;
26 有色者，有色色者；	Has Color Entity, Has Color-creator of The Color;
27 有味者，有味味者。	Has Taste Entity, Has Taste-creator of The Taste.
28 生之所生者死矣，	Creator, Its Whatever Created Entity Died that's,
29 而生生者未尝终；	But Creator of the Created Entity Never Ever End;
30 形之所形者实矣，	Form-creator, Its Whatever Formed Entity Solid that's
31 而形形者未尝有；	But Form-creator of the Formed Entity Never Ever Have;
32 声之所声者闻矣，	Sound-creator, Its Whatever Sounded Entity Heard that's,
33 而声声者未尝发；	But Sound-creator of Sounded Entity Never Ever Issued;
34 色之所色者彰矣，	Color-creator, Its Colored Entity Displayed that's,
35 而色色者未尝显；	But Color-creator of Colored Entity Never Ever Show;
36 味之所味者尝矣，	Taste-creator, Whatever Taste Entity Tasted that's
37 而味味者未尝呈：	But Taste-creator of Taste Entity Never Ever Present:
38 **皆无为之职也。**	***All Selfless These Duties that's.***
39 能阴能阳，能柔能刚，	Can Yin Can Yang, Can Soft Can Hard,
40 能短能长，能圆能方，	Can Short Can Long, Can Round Can Square,
41 能生能死，能暑能凉，	Can Live Can Die, Can Hot Can Cold,

1.3 All Selfless Duties

42	能浮能沉，能宫能商，	Can Float Can Sink, Can be Tone1 Can be Tone2,
43	能出能没，能玄能黄，	Can Emerge Can Submerge, Can Black Can Yellow,
44	能甘能苦，能膻能香。	Can Sweet Can Bitter, Can Stink Can Fragrant.
45	无知也，无能也；	Not Knowing that's, Not Able that's;
46	而无不知也，而无不能也。"	But Not Not-Knowing that's, But Not Not Able that's."

Liezi Text Narrative
Heaven Earth not all-mighty, Sage person not all-rounder, All Matters not all-useful. L4
Heaven's duties are to create and protect, Earth's duties are to form and support. L6
Sage's duties are to teach and enlighten, Matters' duties are for Purposes Intended. L8
Heaven has its weakness Earth has its strength; Sage has defects, Matters have interactions. L12
Reasons? As Heaven is not able to form and support, Earth is not able to teach and enlighten. L15
Sage is unable to oppose being a teacher; Matters not exceed positions of intended purposes. L17
Hence Heaven Earth their Ways, Yin or Yang; Sage's teaching, Humanity or Justice; L19
All Matters' suitability, Soft or Hard; All follow, are not allowed to exceed their positions. L22
Hence the Created has Creator, Form has Form-creator, Sound has Sound-creator. L25
Color has Color-creator and Taste has Taste-creator. L27
The Created died but the Creator never perish; Form is solid but Form-creator is formless; L31
Sound heard but Sound-creator not forth-coming; Color displayed but Color-creator not seen; L35
Taste tasted but Taste-creator not present. L37
All Selfless These Duties by the creators (all natural occurrences). L38
The Self-Creator can be:
Yin /Yang, soft /hard, short /long, round /square, alive /dead, hot /cold; L41
float /sink, Tone1 /Tone2, emerge /submerge, black /yellow, sweet /bitter, stink /fragrant. L44
Self-Creator is selfless, unaware, with no self-display, created everything naturally! L45
All knowing and all capable, the Self-Creator created all things in the universe. L46

Comments:
1.3 All Selfless Duties
Heaven creates, protects; Earth forms, supports; Sage teaches, enlightens;
All Matters have been created for specific purposes that may not to be exceeded.
Heaven cannot support, Earth cannot teach, i.e. all Matters have their own specific duties.
Heaven and Earth have their Ways balancing Yin /Yang and Sage teaching Humanity and Justice.
Matters achieving compatibility with Soft /Hard, and All are to keep their positions in harmony.
Life created is perishable, but the Creator never died with continuous creation of generations.
Sound heard expires, but the Creator never expired with continuous production of sound.
The Creator (of Life, Sound, Form, Color, Taste) is Imperishable, Invisible, Formless and Selfless.
Self-Creator is everything, Yin /Yang, soft /hard, short /long, round /square, alive /dead;
Hot /cold, float /sink, tone1 /tone2, emerge /submerge, black /yellow, sweet /bitter, stink/fragrant.
All knowing and capable and selfless, not self-aware, no self-display, all actions are naturally so.
This section extends the previous 2 sections with more attributes of the selfless Self-Creator.

Self-Creator, selfless duties in the creation of the universe, self-unaware and no self-display.

Chapter 1. Heavenly Signs (天瑞)

1.4 百岁髑髅   1.4 100-Year Dead-man Skull

01	子列子适卫，食于道，	Teacher Liezi Went to Wei, Eating By Way-side,
02	*从者见百岁髑髅，*	***Followers Saw 100 Years Dead-man Skull.***
03	攓蓬而指，	Brushing-off Grass-debris And Pointing,
04	顾谓弟子百丰曰：	Attention To Disciple Baifeng Said:
05	"唯予与彼知	"Only I With Him (skull) Knowing
06	而未尝生未尝死也。	Have Not Ever Lived, Not Ever Died that's
07	此过养乎？	This (death) Really Sadness, Yes/no ?
08	此过欢乎？	This (life) Really Happiness, Yes/no ?
09	种有几：若蛙为鹑，	Species Have Intricacies: Like Frogs Become Quails,
10	得水为𦭝，	Have Water Become Ji-grass,
11	得水土之际，	Have Water Soil In Between,
12	则为娃嫔之衣。	Then Become Carpet Of Green Moss.
13	生于陵屯，则为陵舄。	Growing On High-Ground Dry, Then Become Plantain.
14	陵舄得郁栖，则为乌足。	Plantain Have Manure Soil, Then Become Black-foot.
15	乌足之根为蛴螬，	Black-foot (grass) Its roots Become Grubs (insect larvae),
16	其叶为蝴蝶。	Its Leaves Become Butterflies.
17	蝴蝶胥也，	Butterflies Shortly That's,
18	化而为虫，	Transformed And BecomeWorms,
19	生灶下，其状若脱，	Growing at Stove Bottom, Their Forms Like Moulting,
20	其名曰鸲掇，	The Name Call-it Qu Duo (worms),
21	鸲掇千日化而为鸟，	Qu Duo in 1000 days Transformed And Become Birds,
22	其名曰乾馀骨。	The Name Call-it Gan Yu Gu.
23	乾馀骨之沫为斯弥。	Gan Yu Gu, Their Saliva Become Si Mi (worms).
24	斯弥为食醯颐辂。	Si Mi Become Vinegar Feeding Shen Lu (mayflies).
25	食醯颐辂	Vinegar Feeding Shen Lu
26	生乎食醯黄軦，	Born Of Vinegar Feeding Yellow Kuang (worms)
27	食醯黄軦生乎九猷。	Vinegar Feeding Yellow Kuang Born Of JiuYou (worms).
28	九猷生乎瞀芮，	Jiu You Born of Mao Rui (flies)
29	瞀芮生乎腐蠸，	Mao Rui Born Of Rotten Quan (melon beetle)
30	羊肝化为地皋，	Goat Liver Transformed to Be Ground Gao (a grass),
31	马血之为转邻也，	Horse Blood, It Be Transform Phosphorus that's,
32	人血之为野火也。	Human Blood, It Be WildFire that's (corpse-forest)
33	鹞之为鹯，	Eagles, They Be Zhan (bird of prey)
34	鹯之为布谷，	Zhan, They Be Cuckoos,
35	布谷久复为鹞也。	Cuckoos Long-time Back to Be Eagles that's.
36	燕之为蛤也，	Swallows, It Be Clams that's,
37	田鼠之为鹑也，	Field mice, It Be Quails that's,
38	朽瓜之为鱼也，	Rotten Melons, It Be Fish that's,
39	老韭之为苋也。	Old Leeks, It Be Chives that's
40	老羭之为猨也，	Old Mother-goats, It Be Monkeys that's,

23

1.4 Liezi and the Dead-man Skull

41	鱼卵之为虫。	Fish Eggs, They Become Worms.
42	亶爰之兽,	Dan Yuan (mountain), Its Animals,
43	自孕而生,曰类。	Self Pregnant And Reproduced, Call-it Lei.
44	河泽之鸟视而生曰鶂。	River Wetland, Its Birds Stared Reproduced Call-it Yi.
45	纯雌其名大腰,	Purely Females, The Name Big-Waist (turtles),
46	纯雄其名稚蜂。	Purely Males, The Name Small-waist Wasps.
47	思士不妻而感,	Lovesick Males No Wifes But Affectionating,
48	思女不夫而孕。	Lovesick Females No Husbands But Pregnant.
49	后稷生乎巨迹,	Hou Ji Born Of Big Foot-print,
50	伊尹生乎空桑。	Yi Yin Born Of Hollow Mulberry-tree.
51	厥昭生乎湿,	Jue Yan (locust) Born Of Wetland,
52	醯鸡生乎酒。	Xi Ji (small flies) Born Of Wine.
53	羊奚比乎不笋,	Alpaca Grass Neighbor of No Bamboo-shoot,
54	久竹生青宁,	Old Bamboo Produced Qing Ning (worms),
55	青宁生程,	Qing Ning Give-birth to Cheng (leopard),
56	程生马,	Leopard Give-Birth to Horse,
57	马生人。	Horse Give-Birth to Human.
58	人久入于机。	Human Long-after Enter Into Ji (Primal-source).
59	万物皆出于机,	All Matters Always Emerging From Ji (Primal-source),
60	皆入于机。"	Always Entering Into Ji (Primal-source, or Yi, or Dao !)."

[Xu:机123主發謂之機; 主105鐙中火主也; 鐙295錠也,中置燭故謂之鐙]

Liezi Text Narrative

Liezi on his way to Wei, eating by the wayside, his followers spy a 100-yr skull. L2
Brushing off debris and pointing to it, Liezi addressed his disciple Baifeng said: L4
"Only I with him (skull) know truly that we have not lived and we have not died! L6
Is death really sadness and is life really happiness ? L8
Species have intricacies, like frogs turn into quail, and have water become Ji grass. L10
Have water and soil become a carpet of moss, growing on high dry ground become plantain. L13
Plantain with manure soil become blackfoot grass whose roots become grubs, insect larvae. L15
Its leaves become butterflies that shortly turn into worms, grow, moult at bottom of the stove. L19
These worms are named Qu Duo, which transform in 1000 days into birds called Gan Yu Gu. L22
Saliva of Gan Yu Gu become Si Mi worms that turn into vinegar feeding Shen Lu (mayflies). L24
Mayflies arise from vinegar feeding yellow Kuang (worms) that arise from Jiu You worms. L27
Jiu You arise from MaoRui flies that arise from Rotten Quan (melon beetle). L29
Goat liver transforms into ground Gao (grass), horse blood transforms into Phosphorus. L31
Human blood turns into wild-fire (abandoned corpses in the forest produce methane gas). L32
Eagle becomes a Zhan, that turns into a cuckoo, that reverts to eagle after long-time. L35
Swallows become clams, field mice become quails, rotten melons become fish. L38
Old leeks become chives, old mother-goats become monkeys, fish eggs become worms. L41
Called Lei, animals from Dan Yuan mountain can have self-pregnancy and reproduce. L43
Called Yi, birds from river wetland can just stare at each other and reproduce. L44

1.4 Liezi and the Dead-man Skull

Big waist turtles are all males and small-waist wasps are all females. L46
Lovesick males without wives emotional, lovesick females without husbands are pregnant. L48
Hou Ji (ancestor of Shang) conceived when mother stepped on foot-print of Heavenly King. L49
Yi Yin (minister of Zhou) was recovered from the hollow of a mulberry tree after a flood. L50
Jue Yan (locust) arises from wetland, Xi Ji (small flies) arise from wine. L52
Alpaca grass associated with old bamboo (produced no shoots) but Qing Ning (worms). L54
Qing Ning gave birth to leopards that in turn gave birth to horses that gave birth to humans. L57
*Humans after long-time die and enter back into Ji (i.e. primal-source, or Yi, or Dao of Laozi). L58
Matters are always born of Ji, always expire and return back to Ji, the primal-source." L60*

Comments:
1.4 Liezi and the Dead-man Skull
"Qing Ning gave birth to leopards that in turn gave birth to horses that gave birth to humans."
Most of the above are nonsensical, and can only be regarded as corruptions by pseudo-daoists.
Such nonsensical corruption has also been inserted in *The Yijing* (pp. 258, Jingwei 2018).

Ji is primal-source, is nature, is like Yi of the *Yijing*, is like Dao described in Laozi's *Daodejing*.
Skull causes Liezi to reflect on after-death, and he sees no significance of personal existence.
Thus he philosophizes that we should neither be happy to live or sad to die.
Occurrences and transformations he describes of nature seems *bizarre* but not all are groundless!
Frog lay eggs that hatched tadpoles, that swim like fish, that morph into frogs that hop on land.
Metamorphosis of caterpillar worm into a butterfly, of beetles and flies eggs lay in rotten fruits.
Wild fire ignites when methane gas gets released from human corpses abandoned in forests.
And certain birds are known to deposit their eggs in the nests of other species to hatch for them!
Mother wasp poisoned a beetle, laid eggs inside, and paralyzed beetle turned into a nest of wasps.
The common earthworm is a bisexual animal, and a hive of bees has only a single female queen.
Bamboo produces bamboo-shoots for years, then dies after flowering and production of seeds.
Legends: Hou Yi (Shang) was conceived when mother stepped into the foot-print of Heaven King.
Yi Yin (Zhou) was retrieved from a hollow mulberry, his mother's transformation after death.
Liezi concludes that including humans, all that emerge from nature return back to nature.

Liezi saw the skull, had no delusion, that humans are also inside the transformations of nature.

Chapter 1. Heavenly Signs (天瑞)

1.5 精神离形，我尚何存？   1.5 Spirit Body Parted, Am I Still Existing ?

01	《黄帝书》曰：	*Huangdi Text* Said:
02	"形动不生形而生影，	"Form Act Not to Produce Form But Produce Shadow,
03	声动不生声而生响，	Sound Act Not to Produce Sound But Produce Echo,
04	无动不生无而生有。"	Nothing Act Not Produce Nothing But Produce Things."
05	形，必终者也；	Form, Inevitably an Ending Entity that's;
06	天地终乎？	Heaven Earth Ending, Yes/No ?
07	与我偕终。	With I, All Ending.
08	终进乎？	Ending Advance, Yes/No ?
09	不知也。	Not Knowing that's.
10	道终乎本无始，	Dao Ending O' Originally No Beginning,
11	进乎本不久。	Advancing O' Originally Not Everlasting.
12	有生则复于不生，	Has Life Then Revert To No Life,
13	有形则复于无形。	Has Form Then Revert To No Form.
14	不生者，非本不生者；	Lifeless Entity, Not Originally Lifeless Entity;
15	无形者，非本无形者也。	Formless Entity, Not Originally Formless Entity that's.
16	生者，理之必终者也。	Life Entity, By Reason Inevitably an Ending Entity that's.
17	终者不得不终，	Ending Entity Not Able to Not End,
18	亦如生者之不得不生。	Also Like Life Entity, It's Not Able to Not Live.
19	而欲恒其生，	But Wishing Everlasting Its Life,
20	画其终，惑于数也。	Planning Its Ending, Confusing The Numbers that's.
21	精神者，天之分；	Spirit Entity, Heaven Its Part;
22	骨骸者，地之分。	Skeleton Entity, Earth Its Part.
23	属天清而散，	Affiliate with Heaven, Clear And Dispersing,
24	属地浊而聚。	Affiliate with Earth, Turbid And Concentrating.
25	精神离形，	Spirit Separate from Form,
26	各归其真，	Each Return to Its Truth,
27	故谓之鬼。	Hence Call It Devil.
28	鬼，归也，归其真宅。	Devil, Return that's, Return to Its Truth Abode.
29	黄帝曰：	Huangdi Said:
30	*"精神入其门，*	***"Spirit Enters Its Door (in Heaven),***
31	*骨骸反其根，*	***Skeleton Returns to Its Root (on Earth),***
32	*我尚何存？"*	***Am I Still Existing ?"***

1.5 Spirit Body Parted, Am I Still Existing ?

Liezi Text Narrative
Book of Huangdi, " Form produces Shadow, Sound produces Echo, Nothing produces Thing." L4
Form must end; Will Heaven Earth end? With I, all must end. L7
Ended then advanced (life after death) ? Not knowing. L9
Dao ending what originally has no beginning, advanced what is originally not Everlasting. L11
What has Life will die and be lifeless, what has Form will disintegrate and be formless. L13
In Death, what is lifeless originally has Life, what is formless originally has Form. 15
Life naturally must die, and Death is inevitable just like the inevitable creation of Life. L18
But then wishing Eternal-life, planning to avoid death, just confusing numbers in natural law. L20
Spirit our Heavenly part is clear and dispersing; Skeleton our Earthly part is turbid, dense. L24
Call it Devil, Spirit and Form parted in death, each return its true abode of Heaven or Earth. L28
Huangdi said,*"When Spirit enters its door, Skeleton reverts to its roots, Am I Still Existing ?" L32*

Comments:
1.5 Spirit Body parted, Am I Still Existing ?
Spirit and Body are separate entities; are liken to Form/Shadow, Sound/Echo and Nothing/Thing.
Life-forms must die, Heaven and Earth will end, and with I the individual, all must come to end.
Dao, with no Beginning and no Ending, with the inevitable creation of life and inevitable death.
As the devil, Spirit disperses in Heaven and Body returns to Earth, does the individual still exist?

In death when Spirit and Body have separated, that the individual still exists is questioned ?

27

Chapter 1. Heavenly Signs (天瑞)

1.6 人生大化有四   1.6 Human's 4 big transformations

01 人自生至终，	***Human From Birth Till Death,***
02 大化有四：	***Big Transformations Have 4***
03 婴孩也，少壮也，	Baby Child that's, Youth Strength that's,
04 老耄也，死亡也。	Old Feeble that's, Death Loss that's.
05 其在婴孩，气专志一，	That In Baby Child, Breath Focus Will Singular,
06 和之至也；	Harmony Is Here that's;
07 物不伤焉，德莫加焉。	Matters Not Harming that's, Virtues (full) Not Adding.
08 其在少壮，则血气飘溢，	That In Youth Prime, Then Blood Breath Rise Spilling,
09 欲虑充起，物所攻焉，	Desires Worries Charge Up, Matters That Attack that's,
10 德故衰焉。	Virtues Thus Decline that's.
11 其在老耄，则欲虑柔焉，	That In Old Feeble, Then Desires Worries Soften that's,
12 体将休焉，物莫先焉；	Body Start to Rest that's, Matters Not Contesting that's;
13 虽未及婴孩之全，	Though Not Comparable to Baby Child As Wholesome,
14 方于少壮，闲矣。	Contrast With Prime of Youth, Leisurely indeed.
15 其在死亡也，则之于息焉，	That In Death Loss that's, Then It Is Extinct that's,
16 反其极矣。	Revert to Its Extreme indeed.

Liezi Text Narrative

Humans, 4 big changes from birth till death, namely childhood, manhood, old-age, death. L4
Baby child innocent, focus, all virtuous and harmonious hence outside matters will not harm. L7
Manhood vitality, charge with desires and worries, outside matters attack and virtues decline. L10
Old-age, desires and worries lessen, body weaken and outside matters will not contest. L12
Not wholesome as Child in its innocence, but is leisurely in contrast to the vigor of youth. L14
Death and gone, that is complete rest and peaceful return to the extreme of nature. L16

Comments:
1.6 Human's 4 big transformations

Childhood harmony, Manhood vitality contests, Old-age leisure, then return to nature in Death.
A complete and concise description of the human condition through the 4-stages cycle of life.

Grow-up in harmony, lessen desires worries, enjoy old-age, peaceful return to nature in death.

Chapter 1. Heavenly Signs (天瑞)

1.7 荣启期之三乐　　1.7 The 3 Joys of Rongqiqi

01	孔子游于太山，	Kongzi when Touring At Mount Tai,
02	**见荣启期行乎郕之野，**	***Saw Rongqiqi Walking About Countryside Of Cheng,***
03	鹿裘带索，	Deer-skin Coat and Belt,
04	鼓琴而歌。	Playing the Zither And Singing.
05	孔子问曰：	Kongzi Asking, Said:
06	"先生所以乐，何也？"	"Senior's Reason For Joy, What that's ?"
07	对曰：	Responding Said:
08	"吾乐甚多。	" My Joys Very Many.
09	天生万物，唯人为贵。	Heaven Creating All Matters, Only Humans Are Noble.
10	而吾得为人，	And I Able Be Human,
11	是一乐也。	This Joy No. 1 that's.
12	男女之别，	Male Female The Difference,
13	男尊女卑，	Man Honor Female Humble
14	故以男为贵，	Thus As Male Be Honored,
15	吾既得为男矣，	I Since Able Be Male indeed,
16	是二乐也。	This Joy No. 2 that's.
17	人生有不见日月，	Has Human Life Not Seen Sun Moon,
18	不免襁褓者，	Person Not Free of Swaddling Clothes (early death),
19	吾既已行年九十矣，	I Since Already Through 90 Years indeed,
20	**是三乐也。**	***This Joy No. 3 that's.***
21	贫者士之常也，	This Poverty, Is Common of Scholar that's,
22	死者人之终也，	This Death, Is End of Humans that's,
23	处常得终，	Living Regularly Till End,
24	当何忧哉？"	Now What Worry, Right ?"
25	孔子曰：	Kongzi Said:
26	"善乎？	"Fine O' ?
27	能自宽者也。"	Person Able Self Accommodating that's."

1.7 The 3 Joys of Rongqiqi

Liezi Text Narrative
Kongzi while touring Mt Tai, chanced upon Rongqiqi walking the countryside at Cheng. L2
Attired in a deer-skin coat and belt, he was singing along happily playing on the zither. L4
Kongzi then asked: "Senior, what is the reason for your Joy ?" L6
The response was, "My Joys are very many. L8
Heaven creates All Matters, and only humans are noble. L09
And I am born a Human, this is No.1 Joy. L11
Male and Female are different in that Male is honored and Female is debased. L13
Since I am born a Male, this is No.2 Joy. L16
Some never see the sun and moon, dying prematurely in their swaddling clothes. L18
I have been through 90 years of living, and so this is No.3 Joy, Longevity. L20
Poverty is common among Scholars and Death is the ultimate End of everybody. L22
Living the common poverty of a Scholar until Death in ripe old age, what is there to worry." L24
Kongzi said: "Fine Isn't it ! Person is able to be accommodating with himself. L27

Comments:
1.7 The 3 Joys of Rongqiqi
Kongzi chanced upon Rongqiqi walking about the countryside in a deer-skin coat and belt.
Playing the zither and singing along happily, Rongqiqi was a poor scholar not in high office.
Query on the reasons for his joy, he counted at least 3 blessings that he enjoyed.
Firstly, born a Human, the noblest above all living things.
Secondly, born a Male who enjoyed honor and respect above that of a Female.
Thirdly, enjoyed Longevity and lived to a ripe old age of 90 and beyond.
Rongqiqi accepted the common poverty of a scholar, and was happy with no worries.
Kongzi complimented him as a person who was able to be at peace with himself.

Count our blessings, at peace with self, and happy with no worries to achieve longevity.

Chapter 1. Heavenly Signs (天瑞)

1.8 百岁林类	**1.8 The Centurion Linlei**
01 *林类年且百岁，*	***Linlei in Years Was a Centurion,***
02 底春被裘，	Time of Spring Wearing Coat,
03 拾遗穗于故畦，	Picking Left-over Wheat On Harvested Field,
04 并歌并进。	Simultaneously Singing and Progressing.
05 孔子适卫，望之于野。	Kongzi Went to Wei, Spied Him In the Countryside.
06 顾谓弟子曰：	Turning to Talk with Disciples Said:
07 "彼叟可与言者，	"That old Man, a Person to Talk With,
08 试往讯之！"	Try Go Communicate with Him !"
09 子贡请行。	Zigong Step-up to Go.
10 逆之垄端，面之而叹曰：	Confronted Him at Field End, Faced Him, Sighing Said:
11 "先生曾不悔乎，	" Senior Ever Not Regretting That's,
12 而行歌拾穗？"	And Singing Along while Picking Wheat ?"
13 林类行不留。	Linlei Moving on Not Delaying.
14 歌不辍。	Singing Not Pausing.
15 子贡叩之不已，	Zigong Enquired of Him None Stop,
16 乃仰而应曰：	Then Looked up And Responding Said:
17 "吾何悔邪？"	" I, What Regrets Are There ?"
18 子贡曰：	Zigong Said:
19 "先生少不勤行，	"Senior, Not Industrious when Young,
20　长不竞时，	Grown-up, has Not stand the Test of Time,
21 老无妻子，死期将至，	Old with No Wife, Time of Death is Coming Soon,
22 亦有何乐而拾穗行歌乎？"	Then Have What Joy Picking Wheat And Sing Along ?"
23 林类笑曰：	Linlei Laughing, Said:
24 "吾之所以为乐，	"I, The Reasons For Being Happy,
25 人皆有之，	Every Person Has Them,
26 而反以为忧。	But in Contrast They Cause Worries to others.
27 少不勤行，	No Industrious Action when Young,
28 长不竞时，	Grown-up, Not standing the Test of Time,
29 故能寿若此。	Hence Capable of Longevity Like This.
30 老无妻子，死期将至，	Old Without Wife, Time of Death Soon Coming,
31 故能乐若此。"	Hence Able be Happy Like This."
32 子贡曰：	Zigong Said:
33 "寿者人之情，	"Longevity That's What People Wish,
34 死者人之恶。	Death That's What People Abhor.
35 子以死为乐，何也？"	Senior Taking Death As Joy, Why That's ?"
36 林类曰：	Linlei Said:
37 "死之与生，一往一反。	Death And Life, One Going-forth One Returning.
38 故死于是者，	Thus Death To This Person here,
39 安知不生于彼？	How to Know it's Not Birth Over There ?
40 故吾知其不相若矣？	Hence do I Know Life/Death Not Mutually Alike indeed?
41 吾又安知	And How am I to Know

1.8 The Centurion Linlei

42	营营而求生非惑乎？	Struggling To Survive is Not a Delusion Is-it-not ?"
43	亦又安知，吾今之死，	Also Again How to Know, I My Death Now,
44	不愈昔之生乎？"	Not Better than The Life of Yesterday Is-it-not ?"
45	子贡闻之，不喻其意，	Zigong Hearing This, Not Understanding His Meaning,
46	还以告夫子。	Returned To Inform Teacher (Kongzi).
47	夫子曰：	Teacher Said:
48	"吾知其可与言，果然；	"I Know He Can be Talked With, As Expected;
49	然彼得之而不尽者也。"	Though He Has It But Not the Complete Thing that'

Liezi Text Narrative

Spring, centurion Linlei wore a coat, picked left-over wheat in the field, singing as he went. L4
Kongzi while in Wei saw him in the countryside; and turning to disciples said: L4
"We can talk to this old man; go, try to communicate with him." L8
Zigong step-up to go, approached Linlei at end of field, faced him and sighing, said: L10
"Senior not ever regretting singing along, while picking left-over wheat ?" L12
Linlei kept moving without delay, and his singing never paused. L14
Zigong enquired of him repeatedly before he looked up to ask: "What regrets do I have ?" L17
Zigong said: "Senior not industrious when young, and as a man not meeting the Test of Time.L20
Now old without wife and death coming soon, yet singing along picking left-over wheat ?" L22
Linlei laughing said: "My reasons for being joyous, everybody has them too. L25
But instead these same reasons cause worries in others. L26
Not industrious when young, as a man not standing the test of time, hence I enjoy Longevity. L29
Now old with no wife and time of Death coming soon, hence I am happy with no Worries." L31
Zigong said: "Longevity is what people wish and Death is what people abhor. L34
But Senior is Happy with Death, why is that ?" L35
Linlei said: "Life and Death is just a matter of Coming and Going. L37
Hence when a person dies here, who knows the person is not reborn over there ? L39
Hence am I to know these events are not mutually complementary ? L40
And how am I to know struggling to survive is not a Delusion that's ? L42
Again how am I to know my Death now is not better than the Life of yesterday. ?" L44
Zigong on hearing this and not understanding his meaning, returned to his Teacher. L46
Teacher said: "I know He is a person we can communicate with, and it is true; L48
However his enlightenment is not the complete thing." L49

Comments:

1.8 The Centurion Linlei

With no achievement in life, now old with no wife but imminent death, generally we are sad.
On the contrary, these are the very reasons that make the hermit and centurion Linlei, happy!
With no commitments of life, he suffered no stress and hence was able to have Joy and Longevity.
With no wife but imminent death to relieve his century old body, he was happy with no worries.
Life and Death is a matter of coming and going, and not sure if death here is not birth over there.
Not sure if struggling to survive is not a Delusion, not sure if Death is better than Life yesterday.
A hermit's life is not everybody's cup of tea, hence Kongzi said his enlightenment is incomplete.

The reasons that made the hermit Linlei happy, are the same that can make others worry ! L26

Chapter 1. Heavenly Signs (天瑞)

1.9 子贡倦于学   1.9 Zigong Weary of Learning

01 子贡倦于学，	***Zigong Weary Of Learning,***
02 告仲尼曰：	Informing Zhongni (alias of Kongzi) Said:
03 "愿有所息。"	"Wish to Have Some Rest."
04 仲尼曰：	Zhongni Said:
05 "生无所息。"	"Life, Not For Resting."
06 子贡曰：	Zigong Said:
07 "然则赐息无所乎？"	"So Then Ci (alias, Zigong) Rest has No Place True ?"
08 仲尼曰：	Zhongni Said:
09 "有焉耳，望其圹，	"Have Indeed That's, Look over That Field,
10 皋如也，宰如也，	Tall Like that's, Burial-ground Like that's,
11 坟如也，鬲如也，	Cemetery Like that's, Tomb Like that's,
12 则知所息矣。"	Then Know Places for Resting, that's."
13 子贡曰：	Zigong Said:
14 "大哉死乎！	"Greatness Indeed is Death, Is-it-not !
15 君子息焉，小人伏焉。"	Gentleman Rested that's, Small Person Buried that's."
16 仲尼曰：	Zhongni Said:
17 "赐！汝知之矣。	"Ci ! You Know This that's.
18 人胥知生之乐，	People All Know The Joy of Life,
19 未知生之苦；	Not Knowing The Bitterness of Life;
20 知老之惫，	Know The Weariness of Old-age,
21 未知老之佚；	Not Knowing The Leisure of Old-age;
22 知死之恶，	Know Fear Of Death,
23 未知死之息也。	Not Knowing RIP of Death that's.
24 晏子曰：	Yanzi Said:
25 '善哉，古之有死也！	'Goodness Gracious, Ancients They Had Death, that's !
26 仁者息焉，	Kind Person Rested that's,
27 不仁者伏焉。'	Not Kind Person Buried, that's.'
28 死也者，德之徼也。	Death Entity that's, Homing The Virtues that's.
29 古者谓死人为归人。	*The Ancients Called Dead People As Returnee People.*
30 夫言死人为归人，	O' Calling Dead People As Returnee People,
31 则生人为行人矣。	Then Living People As Traveller People that's.
32 行而不知归，	Travel And Not Know Returning,
33 失家者也。	Person Lost Home that's.
34 一人失家，一世非之；	One Person Lost Home, One Society Faulting Him;
35 天下失家，莫知非焉。	Whole World Lost Home, None Know Faulting that's.
36 有人去乡土，	Has a Person Left Village Ground,
37 离六亲、废家业，	Separated from 6 Kinships, Abandoned Family Business,
38 游于四方而不归者，	Travelled The 4 Regions And Person Not Returning,
39 何人哉？	Who is such a Person indeed ?
40 世必谓之为狂荡之人矣。	Society Certain Call Him Wild Loafer Of A Person that's.
41 又有人钟贤世，	Also Has Person Focused on Civil Society,
42 矜巧能，修名誉，	Valued Skills and Abilities, Cultivated Name Reputation,

1.9 Zigong Weary of Learning

43	夸张于世	Boastful Exaggerated (conduct) In Society
44	而不知已者，	And Person Not Knowing when to Stop,
45	亦何人哉？	Again Who is such a Person indeed ?
46	世必以为智谋之士。	Society Certain To Regard As Wise Planner Scholar.
47	此二者，胥失者也。	These 2 Persons, Both Persons have Faults that's.
48	而世与一不与一，	But Society Approve of One, Not Approve of the Other,
49	唯圣人知所与，	Only Sage Person Knows What to Appreciate,
50	知所去。"	Knows What to Discard."

Liezi Text Narrative

Zigong was weary of learning, told Zhongni (alias, Kongzi) he wished to have some Rest. L3
Zhongni said: "Life, not for Resting." L5
Zigong said: " So then Ci (alias of Zigong) has no place to Rest Is-it-not ? L7
Zhongni said: "Have indeed, look over to that field, the Tall structures, the Burial-ground. L10
The Cemetery and the Tombs, then you know the places for Resting that's." L12
Zigong said: "Greatness be for Death, Is-it-not ! L14
Gentleman be Rested, Small Person be Buried that's." L15
Zhongni said: "Ci ! Now you know what Rest means, that's. L17
People all know the Joy of Living and not know the Bitterness of Living; L19
Know the Weariness of Old-age and not the Leisure of Old-age; L21
Know the Evil of Death and not the Rest-in-peace of Death that's." L23
Yanzi said: 'Goodness indeed, the Ancients have Death that's ! L25
Kind people be rested, and not kind people be buried, that's .' L27
Death entity the Return-home of Virtues, hence the ancients call Dead person a Returnee. L29
And O' calling Dead person a returnee, and then calling Live person a Traveler that's. L31
Traveling and not knowing how to Return, a person lost his home, that's. L33
One person lost home, society faulted him; the whole society lost homes, faulting unknown. L35
A person left village ground, separated from 6 kinships, and abandoned family business; L37
Traveling the 4 corners of the world and not returning; Who is such a person ? L39
Society certain to call him a wild loafer person that's. L40
Another person focused on civil society, valued skills, abilities, cultivated name reputation; L42
Boastful Exaggerated conduct in society, not knowing when to stop; Who is such a person ? L45
Society certain to regard him as a wise planner scholar. L46
These 2 persons, both have faults; but society approves of one and disapprove of the other. L48
And only the Sage person knows what to appreciate and what to discard. L50

Comments:

1.9 Zigong Weary of Learning

Zigong wished some rest, but Zhongni said no rest for the living, only final rest at the cemetery.
Living, people know the joy not the bitterness; Old-age, people know the weariness not leisure.
People know the Evil of Death and not the Rest-in-peace of Death; What a Revelation !
The ancients called a dead person, a Returnee; and living person, a Traveler.
Society disapproves of wild loafer who leaves home, abandons family never to return.
Society approves of wise planner scholar who stays, makes his reputation with boastful conduct.
A loafer who doesn't return diminishes a society, whereas a stayer scholar grows a society.

Chapter 1. Heavenly Signs (天瑞)

1.10 列子贵虚   1.10 Liezi Values Emptiness

01	或谓子列子曰：	People Asking Liezi Said:
02	*"子奚贵虚？"*	*"Teacher, Why Value Emptiness ?"*
03	列子曰：	Liezi Said:
04	"虚者无贵也。"	"Emptiness Entity No Value that's"
05	子列子曰：	Teacher Liezi Said:
06	"非其名也，	"Unimportant The Name that's,
07	莫如静，莫如虚。	Not Better than Quietude, Not Better than Humility.
08	静也虚也，	Quietude that's, Humility that's,
09	得其居矣；	Enter The Abode (of Dao) that's;
10	取也与也，	Taking that's Giving that's,
11	失其所矣。	Lost The Abode (of Dao) indeed.
12	事之破𥗨	Destruction Of Affairs
13	而后有舞仁义者，	And After Has Dance of Kindness Justice,
14	弗能复也。"	Not Able to Revert, that's."

Liezi Text Narrative
People asking Liezi, said: "Teacher, why value Emptiness ?" L2
Liezi said: " Emptiness itself is emptiness, therefore has no value." L4
Liezi said: " The name is not important, better to have Quietude and Humility. L7
Achieve Quietude and Humility to enter the anchorage of 'Dao' that's; L9
Living in the confusion of Giving and Taking, we lost the anchorage of 'Dao' indeed. L11
When Affairs are ruined, the dance of Kindness and Justice will not revert the damage. L14

Comments:
1.10 Liezi Values Emptiness
Liezi said, Emptiness is emptiness, with no value in proclaiming, the name is not important. Better option is to practice quietude and humility (of emptiness) to enter the abode of 'Daoism'.
Living in the confusion of giving and taking, we lose living in 'Dao', ruining matters.

Emptiness, name has no value; better to practice quietude humility to enter the abode of 'Dao'.

Chapter 1. Heavenly Signs (天瑞)

1.11 天地密移	**1.11 Heaven Earth Close Changes**
01 粥熊曰：	Zhouxiong Said:
02 "运转亡已，	"Moving Turning None Stop,
03 天地密移，	***Heaven Earth Close Changes,***
04 畴觉之哉?	Who Feels Them (changes) indeed ?
05 故物损于彼者盈于此，	Thus Matters Lost Over There Are Surplus Over Here,
06 成于此者亏于彼。	The Completion Over Here is Depletion Over There.
07 损盈成亏，	Loss Surplus Completion Depletion,
08 随世随死。	Anytime Occuring Anytime Expiring
09 往来相接，	Come and Go Mutually Connecting,
10 间不可省，	Intervals Not Be Detected,
11 畴觉之哉?	Who Feels Them (changes) indeed ?
12 凡一气不顿进，	Every 1 Air (breath) Not Suddenly Increase,
13 一形不顿亏；	One Form Not Suddenly Depleted;
14 亦不觉其成，	Also Not Feel The Completion,
15 亦不觉其亏。	Also Not Feel The Depletion.
16 亦如人自世至老，	Also Like Person From Birth Till Old-age,
17 貌色智态，	Look Color Wisdom Condition,
18 亡日不异；	No Day Not Different;
19 皮肤爪发，	Cover-Skins Claws Hairs,
20 随世随落，	Anytime Growing Anytime Drop-off,
21 非婴孩时有停	Not (since) Baby Child Time Has Paused
22 　而不易也。	And Not Changing that's.
23 间不可觉，	Intervals Not Able to Feel,
24 俟至后知。"	Wait Till Afterward then Know."

Liezi Text Narrative
Zhouxiong said, "Revolving non-stop, Heaven Earth close changes, who feels them ? " L4
Hence matters lost there and surplus here, completion here and depletion there. L6
Loss, surplus, completion, depletion, anytime happening anytime expiring. L8
Come and go mutually connecting, intervals not detectable, who feels these changes ? L11
Every one breath no sudden increase no feeling, one form no sudden depletion no feeling. L15
Like humans from birth till old-age, condition of look color wisdom, no day not different. L18
Skins/claws/hairs anytime growing/drop-off, since baby's time no pause of such changes. L22
Intervals (small changes non-stop) not felt till afterwards." L24

Comments:
1.11 Heaven Earth Close Changes
Zhouxiong said, "No one feels the close continuous changes of Heaven and Earth."
The gradual darkening from day to night, and the blending of springtime into summer days.
All matters, their loss, surplus, completion, depletion, happening anytime expiring anytime.
Come and go they are connected, like flooding here and less water there causing drought.
We feel sudden changes; like sudden deep breath of air, depletion of forms in an earthquake.
We don't feel small daily changes; like humans from baby till old-age, changes never pause.

Knowing our insensitivity, we ought to be mindful of small changes, the approach of old-age.

Chapter 1. Heavenly Signs (天瑞)

1.12 杞人忧天　　　　1.12 Qiren's Worries

01 杞国有人忧天地崩坠，	***Qi State Had Person Worried Collapse of Heaven Earth.***
02 身亡所寄，废寝食者；	Body Lost Support Place, Person Cannot Eat Sleep;
03 又有忧彼之所忧者，	Also Had Person Who Worry For That Worrying Person,
04 因往晓之，曰：	Hence Went to Inform Him, Said:
05 "天，积气耳，亡处亡气。	"Heaven, Mass of Air That's, No Place No Air.
06 若屈伸呼吸，	Like Bending Stretching Exhale Inhale,
07 终日在天中行止，	Whole Day In the Midst of Heaven, Walking Pausing,
08 奈何忧崩坠乎？"	Then Why Worry about Collapsing Right ?"
09 其人曰：	The Person Said:
10 "天果积气，	"Heaven Really Accumulated Air,
11 日月星宿，不当坠耶？"	Sun Moon Abode of Stars, Should Not Fall Is-it-not ?"
12 晓之者曰：	Person Informing Him Said:
13 "日月星宿，	"Sun Moon Abode of Stars,
14 亦积气中之有光耀者；	Also Mass of Air, Among Them They Have Bright Light;
15 只使坠，	Even Enable to Fall,
16 亦不能有所中伤。"	Also Not Possible to Have Injury In Air."
17 其人曰：	The Person Said:
18 "奈地坏何？"	"Earth Breakup Then How ?"
19 晓者曰：	Informing Person Said:
20 "地积块耳，充塞四虚，	"Earth, Mass Pieces that's, Filling Blocking the 4 Voids,
21 亡处亡块。	No Place No such Pieces.
22 若躇步跐蹈，	Like Pacing Stepping Jumping Dancing,
23 终日在地上行止，	Whole Day On Earth Surface Walking Pausing,
24 奈何忧其坏？"	Why Then Worry Earth's Breaking-up ?"
25 其人舍然大喜，	The Person Relieved Naturally, Very Happy,
26 晓之者亦舍然大喜。	The Telling Person Also Relieved Naturally, Very Happy.
27 长庐子闻而笑曰：	Zhangluzi Heard And Laughing, Said:
28 "虹蜺也，云雾也，	Rainbow that's, Clouds and Mist that's
29 风雨也，四时也，	Wind and Rain that's, 4 Seasons that's,
30 此积气之成乎天者也。	This Mass of Air Form Of The Heaven that's.
31 山岳也，河海也，	Hills and Mountains that's, Rivers and Seas that's,
32 金石也，火木也，	Metals and Rocks that's , Fire and Wood that's
33 此积形之成乎地者也。	These Amassing Forms That Completed The Earth that's.
34 知积气也，知积块也，	Know Amassing of Air, Know Amassing of Pieces that's,
35 奚谓不坏？	Why Say No Breakup ?
36 夫天地，空中之一细物，	O' Heaven Earth, A Small Matter In the Void (universe)
37 有中之最巨者。	In our Material world, It is the Largest Thing.
38 难终难穷，此固然矣；	Hard to End Hard to Deplete, This Firmly Natural that's;
39 难测难识，此固然矣。	Hard to Measure Hard to Know, It's Surely Natural that's.
40 忧其坏者，诚为大远；	Person Worry It's Breakup, Truly This is Far Away.
41 言其不坏者，亦为未是。	Person Said Will Not Break-up, Also may Not Be Right.
41 天地不得不坏，	Heaven Earth Not Possible Not to Break-up,

37

1.12 Qiren's Worries

42 则会归于坏。	Hence Will Return To the Broken.
43 遇其坏时，奚为不忧哉？"	Meeting The Breakup Time, Why Not Be Worry, True ?"
44 子列子闻而笑曰：	Teacher Liezi Heard And Laughing, Said:
45 "言天地坏者亦谬，	"Person Talks of Heaven-Earth's Breakup Also Wrong,
46 言天地不坏者亦谬。	Person Talks of Heaven-Earth's No Breakup Also Wrong.
47 坏与不坏，吾所不能知也。	Breakup And Not Breakup, I Not Able to Know that's.
48 虽然，彼一也，此一也。	Although, That One (breakup), This One (no breakup).
49 故生不知死，死不知生；	As Alive Not know Death, Death Not Know Alive;
50 来不知去，去不知来。	Coming Not Know Going, Going Not Know Coming.
51 坏与不坏，吾何容心哉？"	Broken And Not Broken, Why Do I Keep at Heart. ?"

Liezi Text Narrative

Qiren (person of Qi) lost sleep/appetite worrying collapse of Heaven Earth, loss of support. L2
A person worrying for him went to him, said: "Heaven, just a mass of air, air is everywhere. L5
Like bending/stretching exhale /inhale, all day activities inside Heaven, so why worry ? L8
Qiren said: "If Heaven is really a mass of Air, Sun Moon Stars shouldn't be falling too ?" L11
Informer said: "Sun Moon Star are also masses of air, among them some shining bright; L14
And even if they fall, it is also not possible to suffer injury in the air." L16
Qiren said: "When Earth breaks down, then how ?"
Informer said: "Earth, mass of solids that fill and block the 4 voids, solids are everywhere. L21
Stepping Jumping Dancing, all day activities on the surface of Earth, so what's the worry ?" L24
Qiren on hearing this is naturally relieved and immensely happy; and so is the informer. L26
Zhangluzi said: "Rainbows, clouds, wind, rain, 4 seasons, the air masses make-up Heaven. L30
Mountains hills rivers seas metal rock fire wood, these amass forms to make-up the Earth. L33
Know Heaven is amassing air and Earth is amassing solid, so why say no break-down ? L35
Heaven Earth, small in void of the universe, but are the largest things in our material world. L37
Universe and world, certainly hard to know the end, the limit; hard to study to understand. L39
Their collapse is truly too far away for worry; but not true to say they may not be broken. L41
Heaven Earth not possible not to break-up; when breakup time arrives, shouldn't we worry ?"L43
Liezi laughing, said: "Talks that Heaven Earth may break or may not break, are wrong. L46
Say that one is broken, this one is not broken, I am not able to know that's. L48
Life knows not death, death knows not life; present knows not past, past knows not present. L50
The world will collapse or will not collapse, why should I keep at heart and worry, right ?" L51

Comments:

1.12 Qiren's Worries

Qiren (person of Qi) worried Heaven and Earth may collapse and he had nowhere to stand.
To allay his fears, a friend said the Heaven, sun moon stars are masses of air and not hurting.
The friend is largely correct as the sun and stars are gaseous masses, but the moon is solid.
Zhangluzi noted the immensity of the void (universe), and the smallness of our Heaven-Earth.
Rightly he expected a final breakup but the collapse of our world is too far away for worries.
Our universe is of unfathomable vastness and our sun will burn out, albeit after billions of years.
*Liezi does not know if Heaven Earth will collapse, but knows vice versa life does not know death.
And vice versa the past does not know the present, hence Liezi will not keep worries in his heart !*

But Heaven, like collapsing when meteors hit earth, so we ought to worry about the big ones !

Chapter 1. Heavenly Signs (天瑞)

1.13 道可得而有乎？ 1.13 Can Dao Be Possessed ?

01	舜问乎烝曰：	Shun Asked His Minister Said:
02	"道可得而有乎？"	*"Dao Possible to Acquire And Possess, True ?"*
03	曰："汝身非汝有也，	Said: "Your Body Not Your Possession that's,
04	汝何得有夫道？"	You However Acquire and Possess O' Dao ?"
05	舜曰："吾身非吾有，	Shun Said: "My Body Not My Possession,
06	孰有之哉？"	Who Possesses It Then ?"
07	曰："是天地之委形也。	Said: "This Heaven-Earth The Entrusting of Form that's.
08	生非汝有，	Life Not Your Possession,
09	是天地之委和也。	This Heaven-Earth The Entrusting of Harmony that's.
10	性命非汝有，	Nature-Fate Not Your Possession,
11	是天地之委顺也。	This Heaven-Earth The Entrusting of Accord that's.
12	孙子非汝有，	Grand Children Not Your Possession,
13	是天地之委蜕也。	This Heaven-Earth The Entrusting of Molt(rejuvenation).
14	故行不知所往，	Hence Traveling, Not Knowing Where to Go,
15	处不知所持，	Staying, Not Knowing What to Guard,
16	食不知所以。	Eating, Not Knowing for What Purpose.
17	天地强阳，气也，	Heaven Earth Strong Yang, Air that's,
18	又胡可得而有邪？"	So How Possible to Acquire And to Possess, Right ?"

Liezi Text Narrative

Shun asked his minister: " Dao can be acquired and be possessed ?" L2
Minister said: "Your body is not your possession, how will you acquire and possess Dao ?" L4
Shun said: "My body not my possession, then who possesses it ?" L6
Minister said: "Heaven Earth entrusting you with Form (body); L7
You have no Life, Heaven Earth entrusting you with Life through Harmony (of Yin Yang) L9
You have no Spirit-Life, Heaven Earth entrusting you with Accord (of nature) L11
Your grandchildren not your possession, Heaven-Earth entrusting you with Procreation. L13
Traveling knows not where to go, staying knows not what to guard, eating knows no purpose. 16
Heaven-Earth Fiery Sun, air that's, so how is it possible to acquire and possess Dao, Right ?" L18

Comments:
1.13 Can Dao Be Possessed ?
Shun, a legendary ruler of ancient China, asked his minister if he can possess Dao.
He had many subjects, hence was surprised to hear that he doesn't even possess his own body !
Who possesses it, he asked ?
The reply was, Heaven-Earth and fiery Sun just entrusting us with a body, nature and procreation.
We cannot stop ageing, we cannot not die, we know not why we are here, where we are going !

Even our body, spirit and destiny are not in our control, so possession of Dao is a Delusion.

Chapter 1. Heavenly Signs (天瑞)

1.14 盗天地之时利   1.14 Robbing Heaven Earth

01	齐之国氏大富，	Mr Guo of Qi (state) Greatly Wealthy,
02	宋之向氏大贫；	Mr Xiang of Song (state) Greatly Poor;
03	自宋之齐，请其术。	From Song to Qi, Asking for The Know-how.
04	国氏告之曰：	Mr Guo Informing Him, Said:
05	"吾善为盗。	"I am Good At Robbing.
06	始吾为盗也，一年而给，	Starting In My Robbing that's, First Year Only Surviving,
07	二年而足，三年大穰。	2nd Year Then Sufficient, 3rd Year Greatly Prosperous
08	自此以往，施及州闾。"	Since Then And Forward, Beneficial To Neighborhood."
09	向氏大喜，	Mr Xiang Greatly Happy,
10	喻其为盗之言，	Hearing The Words Of Know-how In Robbing,
11	而不喻其为盗之道，	But Not Hearing The Principle For Robbing,
12	遂逾垣凿室，	Went Scaling Walls Breaking Houses,
13	手目所及，亡不探也。	Whatever Seen Reachable by Hands, None Not Taking.
14	未及时，以赃获罪，	Before Long Time, Caught Red-handed Got Conviction,
15	没其先居之财。	Confiscated Of His Previously Acquired Possessions.
16	向氏以国氏之谬己也，	Mr Xiang Believed Mr Guo Had Lied to Him that's,
17	往而怨之。	Went To Complain about It.
18	国氏曰：	Mr Guo Said:
19	"若为盗若何？"	"Like In Robbing Like How ?"
20	向氏言其状。	Mr Xiang Narrated His Conditions.
21	国氏曰：	Mr Guo Said:
22	"嘻！若失为盗之道	"Hee! Like Lost The Principle Of Robbing
23	至此乎？	Reaching This (state) Is-it-not ?
24	今将告若矣。	Now Will Inform You indeed.
25	吾闻天有时，地有利。	I Hear Heaven Have Timing, Earth Has Resources.
26	**吾盗天地之时利，**	***I Rob Heaven Earth, The Timing and Resources,***
27	云雨之滂润，	Cloud and Rain, Their Irrigation and Nourishment,
28	山泽之产育，	Mountain and Wetland, Their Production and Growth
29	以生吾禾，殖吾稼，	To Grow My Grains, Produce My Crops,
30	筑吾垣，建吾舍，	Erect My Walls, Build My House,
31	陆盗禽兽，	Robbing Birds and Animals on Land,
32	水盗鱼鳖，	Robbing Fish and Turtle from Water,
33	亡非盗也。	None Not Robbing that's.
34	夫禾稼、土木、	O' Grains and Crops, Soil and Wood,
35	禽兽、鱼鳖，	Birds and Animals, Fish and Turtle
36	皆天之所生，	All Are Products Of Heaven,
37	岂吾之所有？	How can They Be My Possessions ?
38	然吾盗天而亡殃。	Naturally I Rob Heaven And have No Misfortune.
39	夫金玉珍宝，	O' Gold, Jade, Pearls and Treasure,
40	谷帛财货，	Grains, Silk, Money and Goods,

40

1.14 Robbing Heaven Earth

41	人之所聚，	Whatever The People Accumulate,
42	岂天之所与？	How can They Be Heaven Given ?
43	若盗之而获罪，	Like Robbing Them (people) And Get Convicted,
44	孰怨哉？"	Who be Blame, Right ?"
45	向氏大惑，	Mr Xiang Greatly Confused,
46	以为国氏之重罔己也，	Believed That Mr Guo Was Seriously Deceiving Him,
47	过东郭先生问焉。	Went to Senior Dongguo to Ask the Reason.
48	东郭先生曰：	Senior Dongguo (respected hermit) Said:
49	"若一身庸非盗乎？	"Like Your Body Simply put, Not From Robbing ?
50	盗阴阳之和以成若生，	Robbing of Yin Yang The Harmony To Create Like Life,
51	载若形；	Holding Like Form (body);
52	况外物而非盗哉？	Moreover External Matters Which Not from Robbing ?
53	诚然，天地万物不相离也；	Truly, Heaven Earth All Matters Vis.a.vis Not separate;
54	仞而有之，皆惑也。	Rob And Possess Them, All Delusional that's.
55	国氏之盗，公道也，	Mr Guo's Robbing, Public Way (from nature) that's,
56	故亡殃；	Hence No Misfortune;
57	若之盗，私心也，	Like Your Robbing, Private Heart (selfish) that's,
58	故得罪。	Hence Get Conviction.
59	有公私者，亦盗也；	Is Public Person Privatize, Also is Robbing that's;
60	亡公私者，亦盗也。	Not Public Person Privatize, Also is Robbing that's.
61	公公私私，	Publicize the Public, Privatize the Private,
62	天地之德。	The Virtues of Heaven Earth.
63	知天地之德者，	People Knowing Virtues Of Heaven Earth,
64	孰为盗邪？	Who Are Robbers, that's ?
65	孰为不盗邪？"	Who Aren't Robbers that's ?"

Liezi Text Narrative

Mr Guo of Qi was very rich and Mr Xiang of Song was very poor; L2
From Song to Qi, Xiang went over to consult Guo on his know-how. L3
Kuo informing him, said: "I am good at robbing, starting the first year, I manage to survive. L6
Second year sufficient, 3rd year prosperous, and from then beneficial to the neighborhood." L8
Xiang was happy to learn Guo's words on robbing but did not learn the principle for robbing. L11
He went scaling walls, break-homes, taking whatever he saw and can lay his hands on. L13
Before long he was caught red-handed, convicted, even his own possessions got confiscated. L15
Xiang believed Guo had lied to him and went to complain about it. L17
Guo said: "So how is it like in your robbing ?" ; and Xiang narrated his experience. L20
Guo said: "Hee! like you lost the principle of robbing for reaching this state is-it-not ? L23
Now I shall inform you. I hear that Heaven has timing and Earth has resources. L25
I rob Heaven Earth of timing and resources, clouds rain of their irrigation nourishment. L27
Mountains wetlands of their products and growth, to grow my grains and crops. L29
To erect my walls and build my house, robbing land of birds, animals and sea of fish turtles. L32
None of these actions are not 'robbing' of Heaven and Earth. L33
O' grains, crops, soil, wood, birds, animals and fish turtles. L35
All are products of Heaven, so how can they be my own possession ? L37

1.14 Robbing Heaven Earth

Naturally I rob Heaven and have no misfortune. L38
O' but gold jade and precious treasure, grains silk and money goods. L40
These are accumulated by people, not given by Heaven is-it-not ? 42
Like robbing them and getting convicted, then who is to be blamed, indeed ?" L44
Xiang, greatly confused and believing that Guo deceived him, went to ask Senior Dongguo. L47
Dongguo (respected hermit) said: "Is-it-not that your ordinary body comes from robbing ? L49
Robbing from the harmony of Yin Yang for the creation of life and formation of the body.. L51
Moreover which external matters are not robbed (from Heaven Earth) ? L52
Truly, Heaven Earth all matters vis-a-vis not separate, rob and possess them all delusional. L54
Guo's robbing from Heaven and Earth, Public Way (from nature) hence no misfortune. L56
You are robbing from people their Private properties hence get conviction (being selfish). L58
Of public nature, privatizing is also robbing; of private persons, privatizing is also robbing. L60
Publicise the public and privatize the private, these are virtues of Heaven Earth. L62
Know the virtues of Heaven Earth, know who are robbers and who are not robbers, right ?" L64

Comments:
1.14 Robbing Heaven Earth
The above narrative describes dramatically in detail who are truly robbers and who are not !
Simply put, when you go fishing by the river and take some fish, the river will not object.
No one else will object too as he or she can also do likewise, freely go fishing by the river.
This robbing of nature does no harm to the environment or harm anybody, hence not criminal.
In contrast, one cannot go to a privately owned pond and go fishing there without paying a fee.
The owner spends money and effort there, hence it is selfish and criminal to avoid paying fees.
Among the hills, a person brings home a precious stone, and the hills have no objection.
No one else will object too as he or she can also do likewise, walking the hills in search of stones.
This robbing of nature does no harm to the environment or hurt anybody, hence not criminal.
However one cannot take the precious stone from the hands of the finder on his way home.
The finder will contest it and your robbing him by force is certainly selfish and criminal.
Reason is simple, if you're finder, will you allow someone to take the stone from your hands ?

Taking from nature or from others, robbing or not, we know in our hearts if we are selfish.

Liezi: World of Delusions

Chapter 1. Heavenly Signs (天瑞)

Summary

1.01 **Self-Creator (有生不生)**: describes a self-existing creator, not unlike Laozi's 'Dao'.
And a Self-Transformer, cannot not create the universe naturally and without design.

1.02 **Creation of the Universe(万物化生)**: describes the early formation stages of the universe.
Concepts of *Yin*, *Yang* and *Yi* from *Yijing* are used to transform the myriad things and life.

1.03 **All Selfless These Duties (皆无为之职)**: in the creation of all things, creators never die.
And Heaven creates, Earth supports, Sage teaches, all matters have their specific duties.

1.04 **Hundred Years Skull (百岁髑髅)**: shows humans are parts of all natural transformations.
And all Lives that emerge in nature, all the transformations, all must return back to nature.

1.05 **Spirit Body parted, Am I Still Existing ? (精神离形, 我尚何存？)**: indeed has ended.
Spirit dispersed in Heaven, body returned to Earth, the combined entity 'I' ceased to exist.

1.06 **Human's 4 big transformations (人生大化有四)**: childhood, youth, old-age and death.
Childhood harmony, youth contesting vitality, old-age leisure and total rest in death.

1.07 **The 3 Joys of Rongqiqi (荣启期之三乐)**: born a human, a male and no premature death.
In Spite of poverty, Rongqiqi counted his blessings to remain happy and achieved longevity.

1.08 **The Centurion Linlei (百岁林类)**: happy as a hermit with no stress of life commitments.
With no wife, Linlei held imminent death may transform for something better elsewhere.

1.09 **Zigong Weary of Learning (子贡倦于学)**: seems like no place to rest but the cemetery!
The ancients welcome death, calling dead people, returnees; and living people, travellers.

1.10 **Liezi Values Emptiness (列子贵虚)**: but Liezi says Emptiness has no value, name only.
Living the confusion of give and take! Better to practice quietude and humility of Daoism.

1.11 **Heaven Earth Close Changes (天地密移)**: recognised our insensitivity to natural changes.
Subtle daily changes, the growth of childhood to decline of old age, never pause a moment.

1.12 **Qiren Worried Sky A-falling (杞人忧天)**: opens discussion and understanding of nature.
Liezi says let's not worry too much, as the past knows not the present, life knows not death.

1.13 **Can 'Dao' Be Possessed ? (道可得而有乎 ?)**: No, possession of 'Dao' a delusion.
We cannot not die, so we do not even possess our body, and know where we are going!

1.14 **Robbing Heaven Earth (盗天地之时利)**: Is not criminal, like harvesting fish from the sea.
Whereas taking things from people's private homes is selfish, criminal and punishable.

This chapter speculates on the origin of the universe and human adaptation to live with nature.

Chapter 2.   Huangdi (黄帝)

Introduction

2.1 Reign of Huangdi (黄帝即位)

2.2 Spirit On the Mountain (山上有神人)

2.3 Return Riding On Wind (乘风而归)

2.4 Drunkard Fall from Carriage (醉者坠于车)

2.5 Liezi's Archery (列御寇射)

2.6 Not Dare Play with Water Fire Again (水火岂复可近)

2.7 Liangyang Keeping Tigers (梁鸯养虎)

2.8 Ferry-man Handled Boat God-like (津人操舟若神)

2.9 Live By Water, Safe By Water (长于水而安于水0)

2.10 Hunchback Elder Catching Cicada (佝偻者承蜩)

2.11 Starling Birds (沤鸟)

2.12 Strange Man Not Know Fire Rock (奇人不知火石)

2.13 God-like Sorcerer (神巫)

2.14 Liezi, I Fear (列子吾惊)

2.15 Yangzhu Contesting Seat (杨朱争席)

2.16 Beauty's Self-beautiful (其美者自美)

2.17 Ever Triumph Call-it Gentleness (常胜之道曰柔)

2.18 Birds Animals Human Like-minded (禽兽未必无人心)

2.19 Morning 3 Evening 4 (朝三而暮四)

2.20 Jishengzi Raised Fighting Cock (纪渻子养斗鸡)

2.21 Huiang Debated King Kang of Song (惠盎见宋康王)

Summary

Chapter 2. Huangdi (黄帝)

Introduction:

Huangdi (c. 2599 BC), the legendary Yellow Emperor, First ancestor of the Chinese people. Narratives here reveal ideal governments and expose sorcery and claims of 'having Dao'.

Huangdi dreamt of an ideal government of non-interference, he relaxed and citizens were happy. Or living with a good spirit who protects with good weather, good harvest, no fear, no sufferings. Liezi said, mediated 9 years thinking of no evil enlightened, *not* enabling him to 'ride on wind'. Falling drunkard has no fear thus less injury, has no sorcery tricks like entry into water and fire. Narrating his failure to shoot on the edge of a cliff, Liezi shows his humiliation and humility.
"I have no Dao", Shangqiukai declared and did not dare to play with water and fire again.
Liangyang shared methods on keeping tigers, no life food, just mindful of their needs and habits.
Ferryman had no fear of water, thus god-like; poker players are clumsy when the stakes are high.
"I have no Dao", the swimmer declared; born happy in the hill, growth safe by water, just destiny.
"I have Dao", the elder said; 'Dao' of months of practice and patience picking cicada off trees.
Starling birds were alerted to danger, sensing the boy's ill intent to catch them for his father.
Fictitious man from rocks-fire exposes Zixia's claim of Confucius capability, duke's gullibility.
Fictitious Huzi with his 'Dao' drove the God-like sorcerer away and Liezi home to feed the pigs.
Liezi was fearful his fame might catch the king's attention, yet amassed lots of disciples at home.
Yangzhu was receptive of Laozi's admonition, shed his arrogance, and enjoyed companionship.
Beautiful wife's self-importance demanded attention instead of being helpful, hence disliked.
Triumph of Gentleness is an ancient idea, assumes the superiority of others, causes no misfortune.
Birds, animals, humans are like-minded for survival, have similar instincts for kindness and evil.
Morning 3 evening 4, such tactical offerings fool nobody, not even the monkeys; first, take more.
Jishengzi raised fighting cock, a satire on the training of swordsmen, turning them into 'zombies'.
Huiang debated and convinced King Kang to embrace kindness and justice for his government.

Chapter 2. Huangdi (黄帝)

2.1 黄帝即位 | 2.1 Reign of Huangdi

01 黄帝即位十有五年，	***Huangdi Ascended Throne Ten Plus 5 Years,***
02 喜天下戴己，	Happy The citizenry Support Self,
03 养正命，	Support Positive Life (living it up)
04 娱耳目，供鼻口，	Entertaining Ears Eyes, Serving Nose Mouth,
05 焦然肌色皯黣，	Worrying Naturally as Skin Color turned Dry Darken,
06 昏然五情爽惑。	Dulling Naturally 5 Feelings, Very Delusional.
07 又十有五年，	Again Ten Plus 5 Years,
08 忧天下之不治，	Worrying That Citizenry Not Well-managed,
09 竭聪明，进智力，	Exhausting Intellect Wisdom, Advancing Clever Effort,
10 营百姓，	Administrating the Citizenry,
11 焦然肌色皯黣，	Worrying Naturally as Skin Color turned Dry Darken,
12 昏然五情爽惑。	Dulling Naturally 5 Feelings, Very Delusional.
13 黄帝乃喟然赞曰：	Huangdi Hence Loudly Sighed and Lamenting Said:
14 "朕之过淫矣。	" Zheng (self) My Over Indulgence that's.
15 养一己其患如此，	Supporting Self Alone, The Danger Such as This,
16 治万物其患如此。"	Governing All Matters, The Danger Such as This."
17 于是放万机，舍宫寝，	Hence Put-down All Duties, Abandoned Palace Abode,
18 去直侍，彻钟悬。	Dismissed Direct Servants, Dismantled Hanging-Bells.
19 减厨膳，	Reduced Kitchen Food,
20 退而闲居大庭之馆，	Retired, Lived Leisurely in Guest-house Of Great Hall,
21 斋心服形，	Clarified Thoughts Relaxed Body,
22 三月不亲政事。	3 Months No Administrative Duties in Person.
23 昼寝而梦，	Daytime Slept And Dreamt,
24 游于华胥氏之国。	Touring The State Of Huaxushi.
25 华胥氏之国在弇州之西，	State Of Huaxu Clan, Position West of Yan Zhou,
26 台州之北，	North Of Tai Zhou,
27 不知斯齐国几千万里；	Not Known From Qi State Tens Of Millions Miles;
28 盖非舟车足力之所及，	Also No Boats, Carts, Leg Effort By Which to Reach.
29 神游而已。	Spiritual Travel That Was.
30 其国无帅长，自然而已。	The State No Teacher, Elder, Self Naturally That Is.
31 其民无嗜欲，自然而已。	The Citizens No Cravings Desires, Naturally So That Is.
32 不知乐生，不知恶死，	Not Knowing Joy of Life, Not Knowing Fear of Death,
33 故无夭殇；	Hence No Premature Death;
34 不知亲己，不知疏物，	Not Known Loving Self, Not Known Rejecting Others,
35 故无爱憎；	Hence No Love and Hate;
36 不知背逆，不知向顺，	Not Known Conflict Behind, Not Known Frontal Accord,
37 故无利害；	Hence No Gain Loss;
38 都无所爱惜，	Also No Whatever for Love and Sympathy,
39 都无所畏忌。	Also No Whatever to Fear and Avoid.
40 入水不溺，入火不热。	Enter Water Not Drown, Enter Fire Not Hot.

2.1 Reign of Huangdi

41	斫挞无伤痛,	Chopped Whipped No Injury no Pain,
42	指擿无痟痒。	Finger Pinched No Bruising no Itch.
43	乘空如履实,	Riding Air Like Stepping on Solid,
44	寝虚若处床。	Sleeping on Emptiness Like Position in Bed.
45	云雾不硋其视,	Clouds Mists Not Blocking The Vision,
46	雷霆不乱其听,	Thunder Rolling Not Disturbing The Hearing,
47	美恶不滑其心,	Beauty Beastly Not Lubricating The Heart (feelings).
48	山谷不踬其步,	Mountains Valleys Not Tripping The Steps,
49	神行而已。	Spiritual Walking That Is.
50	黄帝既寤, 怡然自得,	Huangdi Then Awoke, Joyful Naturally Self Contented,
51	召天老、力牧、太山稽,	Convening Tianlao, Limu, Taishanji (ministers),
52	告之, 曰: "朕闲居三月,	Informed Them, Said: "I Stay Rested for 3 Months,
53	斋心服形,	Cleared Heart Tamed Form (rested mind and body),
54	思有以养身治物之道,	Thought Of Ways That Nourished Body Managed Affairs,
55	弗获其术。	Not Attained The Technique.
56	疲而睡, 所梦若此。	Tired and slept, The Dream Like This.
57	今知至道	Now Know the Ultimate Way
58	不可以情求矣。	Not Able To Request as Desired indeed.
58	朕知之矣!	I Know It indeed !
59	朕得之矣!	I Get It indeed !
60	而不能以告若矣。"	And Not Able To Tell Likeness, indeed."
61	又二十有八年,	Again Twenty Plus 8 Years,
62	天下大治,	The World Greatly Administered,
63	几若华胥氏之国,	Almost Like State Of Huaxushi,
64	而帝登假,	And Huangdi Ascension up Heaven,
65	百姓号之,	Citizenry Lamented for Him,
66	二百余年不辍。	Two Hundreds More Years, None Stop.

Liezi Text Narrative

Huangdi as emperor, the first 15 years was happy enjoying life fully with citizens' support. L3
Indulging all senses till haggard in skin condition, dull in 5 feelings, and mind delusional. L6
Next 15 years worrying for citizenry well-being, made exhaustive intellectual clever efforts. L9
Working hard for citizens, again till haggard in skin, dull in feelings, and mind delusional. L12
Huangdi sighing said: "My indulgence or administration efforts both caused much suffering." L16
Hence abandoned all duties, palaces, dismissed servants, dismantled musical hanging-bells. L18
Ate less, retired to idleness out of court, clarified mind relaxed body, 3 months not working. L22

Daytime slept and dreamt touring the state of Huaxushi which was west of Yanzhou. L25
North of Taizhou, from Qi tens of million miles, not reachable by boats, carts and walking. L28
Spirited there, he found the state had no commander, citizens had no desires, all natural. L31
Not known the joy of Life, not known the fear of death, hence no premature death; L33
Not known loving of self, not known rejection of others, hence had no love, no hate. L35
Not known conflict, not known accordance, hence no gain, no loss; L37

2.1 Reign of Huangdi

None whatsoever to love and sympathize, none whatsoever to fear and avoid. L39
Entered water not drown, entered fire not hot; whipped no injury, finger pinched no bruise. L42
Riding air like stepping on solid, sleeping on emptiness like lying in bed. L44
Clouds and mists not blocking vision, rolling thunder not disturbing the hearing; L46
Beauty and evil do not affect feelings, mountains valleys not tripping steps, spiritual walk. L49

Then Huangdi awoke joyful and contented; convened ministers Tianlao, Limu and Taishanji. L51
Informing them said: "I had idled for 3 months, clarified the mind and rested the body. L53
Thinking of ways to nourish my body and to manage the affairs of state, but to no avail. L55
Tired, slept and dreamt like this; Now knows the ultimate way, not be requested as desired. L57
I know it ! I get it ! But not able to tell it indeed." L60
Another 28 years and the world was well administered, almost like the state of Huaxushi. L63
Huangdi ascended up Heaven, and citizens grieved him for the next 200 years and more. L66

Comments:
2.1 Reign of Huangdi

First 15 years after ascension, Huangdi was happy, enjoyed life with citizens' full support.
However indulging all senses made him haggard in skin condition, dull in feelings and mind.
Next 15 years, worrying for citizens' well-being, he was equally exhausted with the efforts.
Hence he abandoned all duties, dismissed his servants, ate less, relaxed and rested for 3 months.

One day he ***dreamt*** touring the state of Huaxushi, situated tens of million miles to the Northwest.
He found citizens had no leader, no desires, no joy of life, no fear of death, no premature death.
No self loving, no rejection of others thus no hatred; no conflict agreement, thus no gain no loss.
No love no sympathy thus no fear; no drowning no burn, no whipping injury no pinching bruise.
Riding in air, sleeping on emptiness, mists not blocking views, thunder not disturbing hearing.
Beauty and evil not affecting feelings, mountains valleys not blocking steps, all naturally so !

Huangdi awoke joyous and declared to his ministers that he had found it, the 'Dao' to rule.
Narrative suggests that Huangdi was inspired by the state of Huaxushi that needed no leader.
He led with no interference for the next 28 years, and citizens grieved his death for 200 years.
None interference is the highest level of a ruler as ranked by Laozi, chapter 17 (Jingwei, 2012).

| 太上，下知有之 | Great ruler, people know it exist |
| 其次，亲而誉之 | The next best, love and praised it |

Non-interference is better than expansionism, enlisting citizens for wars and building palaces.

Chapter 2. Huangdi (黄帝)

2.2 山上有神人   2.2 Spirit On the Mountain Top

01	列姑射山在海河洲中，	Mount Liegushe On Island In River Delta,
02	*山上有神人焉，*	***Mountain Top Has Spirit Person that's,***
03	吸风饮露，不食五谷；	Breathe Wind Drink Dew, Not Eat 5 Grains;
04	心如渊泉，形如处女；	Heart Like Depth of Spring, Form Like Virgin Girl;
05	不偎不爱，仙圣为之臣；	Not Friendly Not Loving, Spirits Sages Are Her Subjects;
06	不畏不怒，愿悫为之使；	Not Bearish No Anger, Willing Honestly Do Her Bidding;
07	不施不惠，而物自足；	Not Giving No Favor, And Materials Self Sufficient;
08	不聚不敛，而已无愆。	Not Amassing No Restrain, And So No Transgression.
09	阴阳常调，日月常明，	Yin Yang Forever Attune, Sun Moon Forever Shine,
10	四时常若，风雨常均，	4 Seasons Forever Normal, Wind Rain Forever Balance,
11	字育常时，年谷常丰；	Procreation Ever Timely, Yearly Harvest Ever Plentiful.
12	而土无札伤，人无夭恶，	And Land No Epidemic, People No Premature Death,
13	物无疵疠，鬼无灵响焉。	Matters No Terrible Disease, Devils Not Effective that's.

Leizi Text Narrative

Liegushe Mount on the river delta, Spirit person breathe wind, drink dew, eat no grains. L3
Heart like spring depth, form like a virgin; not friendly, not loving, spirits, sages as her subjects.L5
Not fierce, no anger, honest people do her bidding; not giving no favor, material self sufficient.L7
No amassing no restrain so no transgression; Yin Yang forever attune, Sun Moon ever shine. L9
4 seasons ever normal, wind rain ever balance; procreation timely, annual harvest plentiful. L11
No epidemic on land, no premature death; no terrible diseases, devils not effective that's. L13

Comments:
2.2 Spirit On the Mountain Top
This narrative beautifully describes the magical, fairyland experience of life with a Spirit person.
Her benevolent influence extends over the land, good weather, harvest aplenty, and no epidemic.

An ancient imagination of utopian living without suffering, in the world of the good Spirit !

Chapter 2. Huangdi (黄帝)

2.3 乘风而归   2.3 Return Riding On Wind

01	列子师老商氏，	Liezi Studied under Laoshangshi,
02	友伯高子，	Friend of Bogaozi,
03	进二子之道，	Master The Way of Both Seniors,
04	**乘风而归。**	***Riding Wind On Return.***
05	尹生闻之，从列子居，	Yinsheng Heard This, Followed Liezi and Stayed,
06	数月不省舍。	Few Months Not Visited Home.
07	因间请蕲其术者，	Seeking Chance to Implore For The Technique,
08	十反而十不告。	Ten Times And Ten times Not Informed.
09	尹生怼而请辞，	Yinsheng Hated this And Asked to Retire,
10	列子又不命。	Liezi Again No Response.
11	尹生退，数月，	Yinsheng Retired, Several Months later,
12	意不已，又往从之。	Wish Not Passed, Again Went to Follow Him.
13	列子曰：	Liezi Said:
14	"汝何去来之频？"	"You, Why Come and Go So Frequently ?"
15	尹生曰：	Yinsheng Said:
16	"曩章戴有请于子，	"Formerly Times Again Requested Of Teacher,
17	子不我告，固有憾于子。	Teacher Not Tell Me, Hence Angry With Teacher.
18	今复脱然，是以又来。"	Now Again Relieved at Ease, Therefore Come Again."
19	列子曰：	Liezi Said:
20	"曩吾以汝为达，	"Formerly I Believed You Are Enlightened,
21	今汝之鄙至此乎。	Now You Are Ignoble To this Extent indeed.
22	姬！	Sit !
23	将告汝所学于夫子者矣。	Will Tell You Whatever Learned From my Teacher.
24	自吾之事夫子， 友若人也，	Since I Served My Teacher, Also This Friend that's,
25	三年之后，	3 Years And After,
26	心不敢念是非，	Heart Not Dared Think of Right /Wrong,
27	口不敢言利害，	Mouth Not Dared Speak of Good /Evil,
28	始得夫子一眄而已。	Then Started to Gain from Teacher A Side-glance Only.
29	五年之后，	5 Years And After,
30	心庚念是非，	Heart Never Think Right /Wrong,
31	口庚言利害，	Mouth Never Speak Good /Evil,
32	夫子始一解颜而笑。	Teacher Started to show A Relieved Face and Laughed.
33	七年之后，从心之所念，	7 Years And After, From Heart All The Thoughts,
34	庚无是非；	Certainly No Right or Wrong;
35	从口之所言，	From Mouth Whatever Is Spoken,
36	庚无利害，	Certainly No Good or Evil,
37	夫子始一引吾并席而坐。	Teacher Started To Allow Me to Sit Together on Mat.
38	九年之后，	9 Years And After,
39	横心之所念，	Unbridle Heart Whatever The Thoughts,
40	横口之所言，	Unbridle Mouth Whatever The Speech,

50

2.3 Return Riding On Wind

41	亦不知我之是非利害欤，	Also Not Know My Own Right Wrong, Good or Evil,
42	亦不知彼之是非利害欤；	Also Not Know Others' Right Wrong, Good or Evil;
43	亦不知夫子之为我师，	Also Not Know Teacher Has Been My Tutor,
44	若人之为我友：	That Person Has Been My Friend:
45	内外进矣。	Inside Outside all Enter ('Dao') that's.
46	而后眼如耳，耳如鼻，	And Afterwards Eyes Like Ears, Ears Like Nose,
47	鼻如口，无不同也。	Nose Like Mouth, None Not Same that's.
48	心凝形释，骨肉都融；	Heart Focused Form Freed, Bones Flesh All Fusion;
49	不觉形之所倚，	Not Feeling Whatever That Form (body) Upon rested,
50	足之所履，	Whatever That Feet Step-upon,
51	随风东西，	Following Wind to East to West,
52	犹木叶干壳。	Like Wood Leaves Dry Shells.
53	竟不知风乘我邪？	Somehow Not Know If Wind is Riding on Me ?
54	我乘风乎？	Or I am Riding on Wind ?
55	今女居先生之门，	Now You Residing Under Senior's Tutelage,
56	曾未浃时，	Has Not been Long Time,
57	而怼憾者再三。	And Hating Regretting That's Time and Again.
58	女之片体将气所不受，	Your Whole Body, Air However Will Not Accept,
59	汝之一节将地所不载。	Your Each Limb, Earth However Will Not Support.
60	履虚乘风，	Stepping on Emptiness, Riding on Wind,
61	其可几乎？"	Can That be Expected, Right ?"
62	尹生甚怍，屏息良久，	Yinsheng Most Ashamed, Held Breath Long Time,
63	不敢复言。	Not Dared Speak Again.

Leizi Text Narrative

Liezi under his teacher Laoshangshi and friend Bogaozi, mastered the 'Dao' of both seniors. L3
Yinsheng heard of Liezi's Return Riding on Wind, and decided to go live-in to serve Liezi. L5
Few months had not visited his home, just waiting to ask Liezi for the art of 'Riding on Wind'. L7
Asked 10 times with no response, Yinsheng angered, begged to retire, Liezi remained silent. L10
Yinsheng retired, few months later, still wishing to 'Ride on Wind', again went back to Liezi. L12
Liezi said: " Why did you come and go so frequently ?" L14
Yinsheng said: "Formerly, many times requested, Teacher had not taught me, thus angered. L17
Now anger relieved and returned to normal, therefore come back again" L18
Liezi said: "Formerly I believed you were enlightened but now you are ignoble to this extent. L21
Sit ! Will tell you whatever learned from my Teacher since serving him and my friend. L24
After 3 years, heart not dare think of Right or Wrong, mouth not dare speak of Good or Evil. L27
Then only gained a side-glance from Teacher. L28
After 5 years, the heart never thinks of Right or Wrong, mouth never speaks of Good or Evil. L31
Then Teacher first broke countenance and smiled. L32
After 7 years, from heart all thoughts, no Right no Wrong, mouth speaks no Good no Evil. L36
Then Teacher first time allowed me to sit and to share his mat with him. L37
After 9 years, unbridle all thoughts from heart, unbridle all words from mouth. L40
Also not knowing my own Right or Wrong, Good or Evil and also that of others. L42

2.3 Return Riding On Wind

Also not knowing the Teacher has been my tutor and that person has been my friend. L44
Inside and Outside, all immersed in 'Dao', that's. L45
Thereafter, eyes like ears, ears like nose, nose like mouth, all same (functionality) that's. L47
Heart focus Body set-free, bones and flesh all in fusion, not feeling what body is lying upon. L49
Where feet stepping upon, following Wind to East to West, like wood leaves dry shells. L52
Somehow not knowing whether 'Wind is riding on me', or 'me riding on Wind' ? L54
Now you are under my tutelage, and in a short period have anger and regrets time and again. L57
Your whole body however air will not accept, your limbs however Earth will not support. L 59
Stepping on Emptiness Riding Wind, how can you expect that, right ?" L61
Yinsheng felt most ashamed, held his breath for a long time, and dared not speak again. L63

Comments:
2.3 Return Riding On Wind

It was said, Liezi had attained 'Dao' from Laoshangshi, and had returned 'Riding on Wind'.
Yinsheng had this delusional wish to learn the art of 'Riding on Wind', so went to stay with Liezi.
He left in anger when Liezi refused to teach him anything, only to return a few months later.
Liezi scolded him for being ignoble to this extent and sat him down to listen to his experience.
In 3 years, not dare think of right/wrong, not dare speak of good/evil, the teacher gave a glance.
In 5 years, never thought of right/wrong, never spoke of good/evil, the teacher only gave a smile.
In 7 years, all thoughts no right/wrong, spoke no good/evil, the teacher allowed me to share mat.
In 9 years, inside and outside all immersed in 'Dao', no more concept of right/wrong, good/evil,

So, it is all about meditating on Right and Wrong, Good and Evil, and for 9 years, not easy !
Relieved of these concepts of self and of others, we shall feel absolutely free in mind and body.
*The feeling of 'Riding on Wind' is real, for when happy and carefree, the spring is in every step.
Liezi is certainly not delusional that 'Riding On Wind' is a reality, for he also says:*

竟不知风乘我邪?   Somehow Not Know If Wind is Riding on Me ? L53
我乘风乎?   Or I am Riding on Wind ? L54

Unselfish we can think no wrong, speak no evil, and the world can 'Ride on Wind' together.

Chapter 2. Huangdi (*黄帝*)

2.4 醉者坠于车   2.4 Drunkard's Fall from Carriage

01	列子问关尹曰：	Liezi Asked Guanyin Said:
02	"至人潜行不空，	"Dao-attained Person Moving in Water Not suffocate,
03	蹈火不热，	Dancing in Fire Not Hot,
04	行乎万物之上而不慄。	Moving On Top Of All Matters And Not Afraid.
05	请问何以至于此？"	Beg to Ask How To Reach To this Level ?"
06	关尹曰："是纯气之守也，	Guanyin Said: "It's Pure Air To Guard, that's,
07	非智巧果敢之列。	Not Clever Skills and Bravery These Kinds (of tricks).
08	姬！鱼语女。	Sit ! I Tell You.
09	凡有貌像声色者，	All Those Having Look Image Sound Color,
10	皆物也。	All Matters that's (materialism).
11	物与物何以相远也？	Matter And Matter Why Mutually so Far-apart that's ?
12	夫奚足以至乎先？	O' How Enough To Reach the Primal-state ?
13	是色而已。	It's Color Only that's (materialism corrupt).
14	则物之造乎不形，	As Matter Its Creation By the Formless (Dao),
15	而止乎无所化。	And Limited By the Non-transformed (Dao).
16	夫得是而穷之者，	Thus Person Who Attained It (Dao) and Fully,
17	焉得而正焉？	How Able To Correct, that's ?
18	彼将处乎不深之度，	He Will Dwell In Not Depth Of Measure (Dao),
19	而藏乎无端之纪，	And Hide In The Era with No Ends (Dao),
20	游乎万物之所终始。	Moving In The Beginning and Ending Of All Matters.
21	壹其性，养其气，	Unifies His Desires, Nourishes His life-Breath,
22	含其德，	Embraces His Virtues,
23	以通乎物之所造。	To Connect O' The Creator Of Matters.
24	夫若是者，其天守全，	O' Person Like This, The Heaven Guard Totally,
25	其神无郤，物奚自入焉？	His Spirit No Cracks, How Matters Self Enter, that's ?
26	**夫醉者之坠于车也，**	**Like Drunken Person His Fall From Carriage that's**
27	虽疾不死。	Though Injured Not Dead.
28	骨节与人同，	Bones Joints Similar To People (others),
29	而犯害与人异，	But Injury Suffered Different From People (others),
30	其神全也。	His Spirit Wholesome, that's.
31	乘亦弗知也，坠亦弗知也。	Riding Also Not Know, Fallen Also Not Know that's.
32	死生惊惧不入乎其胸，	Life Death Shock Fear Not Entering Into His Chest,
33	是故遻物而不慴。	Therefore Encounters Matter And Not Fear.
34	彼得全于酒而犹若是，	He Gets Preserved With Liquor And So Like This,
35	而况得全于天乎？	Then More so Gets Preserved By Heaven Right ?
36	圣人藏于天，	Sage Person Stores (spirit) In Heaven,
37	故物莫之能伤也。"	Thus Matters None Can Harm Him that's."

2.4 Drunkard's Fall from Carriage

Leizi Text Narrative
Liezi, asking Guanyin, said: "Dao-attained person not suffocate in water, not hot in fire. L3.
Moving on top of all matters, not afraid; beg to ask how to attain such a level ?" L5
Guanyin said: "It is primal-Air retained, that's not clever skills (or tricks) or bravery. L7
Sit! I shall tell you; all those having looks, images, sound, color, all are matters, that's. L10
Matters, how can they be so different ? Why not be able to reach primal-state ? L12
It is all due to materialism that's. L13
Creator of all matters, Dao attained the formless state and forever imperishable condition. L15
Person who has attained Dao fully, how can outside matters affect him, that's ? L17
He dwells in the depth of Dao, the era without ends, the beginning and end of all matters. L20
He unifies his desires, nourishes his life-Breath, embraces his virtues to connect with Dao. L23
Person like this has no cracks in spirit, Heaven protects, so how can outside matters affect? L25
Like a drunkard fallen from a carriage, though injured but not dead. L27
Bones and joints similar to other people yet injuries different, as wholesome in spirit. L30
Unaware of riding or falling, life/death does not enter his mind, thus encounters no fear. L33
His preservation by liquor is like this, so what more if protection is from Heaven, right? L35
Sage person keeps the spirit in Heaven, hence outside matters cannot harm him, that's." L37

Comments:
2.4 Drunkard's Fall from Carriage
Liezi asked Guanyin how a Dao-attained person cannot be suffocated in water and burn in fire.
Guanyin said: "It is retaining the primal-air (purity), not some clever skills or tricks and bravery.
It is the materialism of looks, images, sound and color, such materialism that draw us apart.
Returning to the timeless depth of Dao, the daoist reduces desires and embraces his virtues.
Such a person has no crack in character, evil cannot enter, relaxed hence Heaven protects.
Like the drunkard fallen from the carriage, got hurt but will not die.
Relaxed in spirit, unaware of riding or falling, he has no fear to tense up and break his joints."

Guanyin, the legendary guard at the border-pass, who had asked Laozi to write the *Daodejing*.
Hundreds of years later, Liezi couldn't have met Guanyin to ask about phenomena of daoism.
Here, Liezi merely invokes the authority of Guanyin to fight the rampant con-artists of his time.
Even today, pseudo-daoists claim supernatural power to mislead the gullibles for material gains,
Categorically Guanyin denied 'skills and bravery' in claims of not getting hurt in water and fire.
非智巧果敢之列。　　　　Not Clever Skills and Bravery These Kinds (of tricks). L7

Be good daoists, reduce desires, conserve energy, keep virtues and Heaven will protect.

Chapter 2. Huangdi (黄帝)

2.5 列御寇射   2.5 Liezi Displayed Shooting

01	*列御寇为伯昏无人射，*	*Lieyukou Shooting (display) For Bohunwuren,*
02	引之盈贯，	Pulled Bow Fully Maximumly,
03	措杯水其肘上，发之，	Placed Cup of Water On Fore-arm Above, Shot It,
04	镝矢复沓，	Dysprosium Arrow Again Repeatedly,
05	方矢复寓。	Just Shot Again Resided (put on next arrow).
06	当是时也，犹象人也。	At That Time that's, Like Wood-curved Person that's.
07	伯昏无人曰：	Bohunwuren Said:
08	"是射之射，	"This Shooting Is Shooting (exhibition),
09	非不射之射也。	Not The Shooting of Non-Shooting (true) that's.
10	当与汝登高山，	Ought to Climb High Mountain With You,
11	履危石，	Standing on Precarious Rock (cliff-hanger),
12	临百仞之渊，	Fronting The 100 Meter Abyss,
13	若能射乎？"	Like Can Shoot or Not ?"
14	于是无人遂登高山，	Therefore Wuren Proceeded to Climb High Mountain,
15	履危石，	Standing on Precarious Rock (cliff-hanger),
16	临百仞之渊，	Upon 100 Meters Of Abyss,
17	背逡巡，足二分垂在外。	Back Padding, Foot 2/3 Hanging On Outside.
18	揖御寇而进之。	Greeting Yukou And Requesting Him (to shoot).
19	御寇伏地，	Yukou Prostrated on Ground,
20	汗流至踵。	Sweat Drained To Heels.
21	伯昏无人曰：	Bohunwuren Said:
22	"夫至人者，	"O' That Dao-attained Person,
23	上窥青天，	Above, Peering into Green Heaven
24	下潜黄泉，	Below, Exploring Yellow Spring (Hell),
25	挥斥八极，	Commanding Challenging the 8 Limits (universe),,
26	神气不变。	Spirit Air Not Changed.
27	今汝怵然有恂目之志，	Now You Have Fiercely Natural Honest Display Of Will,
28	尔于中也殆矣夫！"	But In This (shooting), Dangerously (inept) Indeed O' !"

2.5 Liezi Displayed Shooting

Liezi Text Narrative
Lieyukou (Liezi) displayed shooting for his friend, Bohunwuren. L1
With a cup of water placed on his forearm, opened the bow to the fullest and started shooting. L3
Dysprosium arrows in quick succession he shot, momentarily still, like a wood-carved person. L6
Bohunwuren said: "This is a shooting exhibition, not non-shooting (shooting real in battle). L9
Climb high mountain, stand on cliff-hanger rock, facing 100 meter abyss, can you shoot ?" L13
Wuren proceeded to climb high mountain, stood on cliff-hanger rock, facing 100 meter abyss. L16
Back-padded till ⅔ of feet hanging outside the cliff, bowed to Yukou, inviting him to shoot. L18
Seeing this, Yukou prostrated on the ground with sweat streaming down to his heels. L20
Bohunwuren said: "Dao-attained Person, above peers into Heaven, below explores Hell. L24
Commands and challenges the 8 limits of the universe, his spirited air never changed. L26
You have a fiercely honest display of Will, but in shooting you are dangerously inept !" L28

Comments:
2.5 Liezi Displayed Shooting
 Liezi is delusional of his skill and did a shooting exhibition for his friend, Bohunwuren.
With a cup of water on his forearm, he shot repeatedly, steady like a wooden carved person.
Wuren said this was exhibition shooting, and proceeded to lead Liezi up a high mountain.
Upon a 100 meter abyss, he back-padded till ⅔ of feet hanging off the cliff, and bowed to Liezi.
Invited to shoot in a cliff position, Liezi prostrated on the ground, sweat draining to his heels.
A daoist may peer into Heaven above and explores Hell below, and his spirited air never changes.
Thus Liezi may have a fiercely honest display of Will, but in shooting he was truly inept.
Fearless, bravery in archery is also important, as in a battle one is also at the receiving end !

Showing himself in the worst of light, Liezi truly has humility, and not above self-criticism.

2.6 吾亡道

2.6 I Have No 'Dao'

01	范氏有子曰子华，	Clan of Fan Had Son Called Zihua,
02	善养私名，	Good in Keeping Private Names (talented persons),
03	举国服之；	Whole State Submitted to Him;
04	有宠于晋君，	Had Favors With King of Jin (state);
05	不仕而居三卿之右。	Not an Official Yet Position To Right of 3 top Ministers.
06	目所偏视，	Whoever his Eyes Inclined to Look,
07	晋国爵之；	State of Jin made Whoever a Lord;
08	口所偏肥，	Whoever his Mouth Inclined to Criticize,
09	晋国黜之。	State of Jin will Down-grade the Person.
10	游其庭者侔于朝。	Milling around His Court, People Equal To Royal Court.
11	子华使其侠客	Zihua Made His Heroic Guests
12	以智鄙相攻，	Mutually Fighting With Talents and Bravery
13	疆弱相凌。	Strong and Weak Mutually Contesting.
14	虽伤破于前，	Although In Front of Injuries Broken-bones,
15	不用介意。	Nothing to Worry About.
16	终日夜以此为戏乐，	Whole Day Night With These For Entertainment,
17	国殆成俗。	State Endangered, Became a Tradition.
18	禾生、子伯、范氏之上客。	Daoshen, Zibo, Were Clan of Fan Top Guests.
19	出行，经坰外，	Out Travelling, Through Country Outside,
20	宿于田更商丘开之舍。	Stayed At The Abode of Old Farmer Shangqiukai.
21	中夜，禾生、子伯二人	Middle of Night, Daoshen, Zibo Both Persons
22	相与言子华之名势，	Conversing On The Reputation and Power of Zihua,
23	能使存者亡，	Able to Cause Survivor Person to Die,
24	亡者存；	Condemned Person to Live;
25	富者贫，贫者富。	Rich Person Poor, Poor Person Wealthy.
26	商丘开先窘于饥寒，	Shangqiukai had Past Distresses In Hunger Cold,
27	潜于牖北听之。	Hidden At Window North, Listening In.
28	因假粮荷畚之	Hence with Borrowed Food in Basket Carried to
29	子华之门。	The Door of Zihua.
30	子华之门徒皆世族也，	The Disciples of Zihua, All Clan Members that's,
31	缟衣乘轩，缓步阔视。	Silk Attired, Rode Carriage, Relaxed Walk, Proud Looks.
32	顾见商丘开年老力弱，	Turned and Saw Shangqiukai, Old Age, Weak Strength,
33	面目黎黑，	Face and Eyes Dark like Commoner,
34	衣冠不检，	Attired in Head-dress Not Ordered,
35	莫不眲之。	None Not Despised Him.
36	既而狎侮欺诒，	Thus Then Harassed, Insulted, Bullied, Scammed,
37	攩挶挨抌，	Hammered, Pushed, Punched, Back-hitting.
38	亡所不为。	None Whatever Not Do.
39	商丘开常无愠容，	Shangqiukai Consistently No Angry Expression,
40	而诸客之技单，	Then These Guests Their Tricks Thin-out,
41	惫于戏笑。	Exhausted At Plays and Laughs.
42	遂与商丘开俱乘高台，	Proceeded With Shangqiukai, All Mounted High Stage,

2.6 I Have No 'Dao'

43	于众中漫言曰：	Among The Crowd Chorus Calling Said:
44	"有能自投下者，	"Person Has Ability to Cast Himself Down,
45	赏百金。"	Award 100 Gold."
46	众皆竞应。	Crowd All Compete to Respond (pretending).
47	商丘开以为信然，	Shangqiukai Believed This Be True,
48	遂先投下，形若飞鸟，	Proceeded First to Jump Down, Form Like Flying Bird,
49	扬于地，骬<骨几>骨无(石为)。	Floating Onto Ground, Flesh and Bones No Injury.
50	范氏之党以为偶然，	Gang of the Clan of Fan Took This to Be Coincidental,
51	未讵怪也。	Not Hugely Surprised that's.
52	因复指河曲之淫隈曰：	Thus Again Pointing to Deep Pool at River Bend Said:
53	"彼中有宝珠，泳可得也。"	"There-In Has Precious Pearl, Swim, Able to Get, that's."
54	商丘开复从而泳之。	Shangqiukai Again Obeyed And Swam for It.
55	既出，果得珠焉。	Then Emerged, Successfully Attained Pearl indeed.
56	众昉同疑。	Crowd Began to Wonder Alike.
57	子华昉令	Zihua Started the Order
58	豫肉食衣帛之次。	Awarding The Status Of Meat Meal Silk Clothes.
59	俄而范氏之藏大火。	Shortly Then Stores of The Clan of Fan on Big Fire.
60	子华曰：	Zihua Said:
61	"若能入火取绵者，	"Like Person Able to Enter Fire to Retrieve Silk,
62	从所得多少赏若。"	Like whatever Retrieved, Get More or Less Reward."
63	商丘开往无难色，	Shangqiukai Ventured With No Color of Difficulty,
64	入火往还，	Entered Fire Back and Forth,
65	埃不漫，身不焦。	Soot Not Staining, Body Not Burn.
66	范氏之党以为有道，	Gang of Clan Fan Took This like Having 'Dao' (power),
67	乃共谢之曰：	Hence Together Thanked Him, Said:
68	"吾不知子之有道而诞子，	"We Not Know That Teacher Has 'Dao' And Bullied You,
69	吾不知子之神人而辱子。	We Not Know Teacher Is God-Person And Insulted You.
70	子其愚我也，子其聋我也，	Teacher We Are Stupid, Teacher We Are Deaf that's,
71	子其盲我也，敢问其道。"	Teacher We Are Blind that's, Dare Ask Your 'Dao'."
72	**商丘开曰："吾亡道。**	***Shangqiukai Said: "I have No 'Dao'.***
73	虽吾之心，亦不知所以。	Although In My Heart, Also Not Know What Happened.
74	虽然，有一于此，	Although, Has This One Here,
75	试与子言之。	With You Try Tell It.
76	曩子二客之宿吾舍也，	Earlier Teacher's 2 Guests, They Stay-in My Abode that's,
77	闻誉范氏之势，	Heard them Praising Power of The Clan of Fan,
78	能使存者亡，亡者存；	Able to Cause Live Person to Die, Dead Person to Live;
79	富者贫，贫者富。	Rich Person Poor, Poor Person Rich.
80	吾诚之无二心，	I Honestly believe These with No Doubt,
81	故不远而来。	And Hence Came Despite the Distance.
82	及来，	When Here,
83	以子党之言皆实也，	Regard The Words of Teacher's Gang are All True that's.
84	唯恐诚之之不至，	Only Worry That My Sincerity Not Maximized,
85	行之之不及，	That My Efforts Not Enough,
86	不知形体之所措，	Not Know My Body Form Where Place,

58

2.6 I Have No 'Dao'

87	利害之所存也。	The Loss and Gain (interests) Where Keep that's.
88	心一而已。	That's, Only One Heart (thought).
89	物亡迕者，如斯而已。	Matters Not Affect me, And Just Like This.
90	今昉知子党之诞我，	Now Begin to Know That Teacher's Gang Fooling Me,
91	我内藏猜虑，外矜观听，	I, Inside Store Doubt Worry, Outside Value Sight Hearing,
92	追幸昔日之不焦溺也，	Remember Fortune Of Former Days Not Burnt Drowned,
93	怛然内热。	Shock Naturally Inside and Hot.
94	惕然震悸矣。	Alerted Naturally Terrifying Fear indeed.
95	水火岂复可近哉？"	Water Fire Dare Again Be Near, Possible?"
96	自此之后，	Since Then and Ever After,
97	范氏门徒路遇乞儿马医，	Disciples of Fan Met Beggars, Horse Medics on Road,
98	弗敢辱也，	Not Dared to Humiliate that's,
99	必下车而揖之。	Certain to Alight Carriage And to Greet Them.
100	宰我闻之，以告仲尼。	Zaiwo Heard This, Hence Informed Zhongni (Confucius).
101	仲尼曰：	Zhongni Said:
102	"汝弗知乎？	"You Not Know O'?
103	夫至信之人，	That with Absolute Believing Such Person,
104	可以感物也。	Possible To Influence Matters, that's.
105	动天地，感鬼神，	Moving Heaven Earth, Influencing Devil Spirit,
106	横六合，而无逆者，	Person Traversing the 6 Directions, And No Opposition,
107	岂但履危险，	Not Only Treading Danger,
108	入水火而已哉？	Entering Water Fire, Only These?
109	商丘开信伪物犹不逆，	Shangqiukai Faith in False Matters, Also Not be Oppose,
110	况彼我皆诚哉？	Whatmore You and I are All Sincerity, Right?
111	小子识之！"	Young Man Take-note of This!"

Liezi Text Narrative

Zihua son of Clan Fan, supported a 'think tank' of talents, and everyone submitted to him; L3
King of Jin favored him, and though not an official, his status is higher than top 3 ministers. L5
Whoever he looked favorably, king made a lord; whoever he spoke ill would be down-graded. L9
His attendees rival the royal court; Zihua made his guests contested in talents and bravery. L12
The strong and weak mutually fight, not worry in the presence of injuries and broken bones. L15
Having this kind of entertainment day and night, detrimental to good traditions of the state. L17
Zihua's top guests Daoshen, Zibo; on travel faraway, stayed in abode of farmer Shangqiukai. L20
Mid-night, Daoshen and Zibo were both conversing on the reputation and power of Zihua. L22
Had power to cause the living to die, the condemned to live; rich be poor, and poor be rich. L25
Shangqiukai with previous experience of hunger cold, hid at the north window and listened. L27
Hence he borrowed some food, carried them in a basket, and came to the door of Zihua. L29
Disciples of Zihua were clan members, attired in silk, rode carriages, relaxed, looking proud. L31
They saw Shangqiukai, an old farmer, a commoner with dark face, attired head-dress shabby. L34
None not despised him, and then harassed, insulted, bullied and scammed him. L36
Hammered, pushed, punched his back and so on, Shangqiukai never expressed any anger. L39
These guests, having no more tricks, next mounted a high stage with Shangqiukai. L42
The crowd chorus said: "Person who will cast himself down, be awarded 100 gold. L45

2.6 I Have No 'Dao'

The crowd pretended to respond, but Shangqiukai believed and he jumped first like a bird. L48
Floated to ground with no injury, the guests took this as co-incidental, not hugely surprised. L51
Next, pointing to a deep pool at the river bend said, "There is precious pearl, swim to get it." L53
Shangqiukai obeyed, swam for it, emerged with the pearl and the crowd began to wonder. L56
Then Zihua gave the order, starting him on the higher status for meat meals and silk attires. L58
Shortly the store was on fire and Zihua said, "Person able to enter the fire to retrieve silk. L61
The more retrieved the higher the reward."; Shangqiukai went in with no sign of difficulty. L63
Entered fire back and forth, with no staining from soot and body not burnt. L65
Gang of Fan clan now believed Shangqiukai had the power of 'Dao', thanked him, said: L67
"We know not Sir had 'Dao' and bullied; we know not Sir is a God-person and insulted. L69
Sir regard us as stupid, deaf and blind that's, but may we enquire of your power of 'Dao'." L71
Shangqiukai said, "I have no 'Dao'. From my heart, I also know not what has happened. L73
Although what has happened here, I shall try to tell you. L75
Earlier, Teacher's 2 guests stayed in my abode, and I heard them praising the power of Zihua. L77
The power to cause the living to die and the condemned to live; rich be poor, the poor be rich. L79
I honestly have no doubt, hence borrowed some food and came despite the distance. L81
On arrival, I took words of Teacher-gang as truths, only worried my sincerity was not enough. L85
Know not where my body was placed, and where my thoughts of loss and gain were kept . L87
With only one heart (mind), outside matters did not affect me, that was all to it. L89
I know Teacher-gang fooled me, with doubts and worries I am now affected by sight, hearing. L91
Recalling formerly not drowned or burnt, so now naturally shocked and hot inside. L93
Alerted naturally with terrifying fear inside, now dare I be near water and fire again, right ?" L95
Thereafter, disciples of Clan Fan meeting with beggars or horse-medics, dared not humiliate. L98
But certain to alight from carriage and to greet them with respect. L99
Zaiwo (disciple of Confucius) heard this and informed Zhongni (Confucius) who said: L101
"Don't You know? That person with absolute faith can influence matters that's. L104
Moves Heaven Earth, influences devils spirits, traverses the 6 directions with no resistance. L106
And not just only treading danger, entering water and fire, right ? L108
Shangqiukai's faith in false matters, not opposed, what more so than with our sincerity ? L110
Young man take-note of this !" L111

Comments:
2.6 I Have No 'Dao'
Zihua in his court, supported many talents and fighters who contested daily for his entertainment.
King of Jin favored him, hence his power can cause the condemned to live and the rich be poor.
Shangqiukai who had experienced hunger and cold heard this, and came to Zihua from afar.
An old shabby farmer, he was despised, bullied and scammed, but he never expressed any anger.
He survived a jump from a high platform for 100 gold, swam a deep pool to get a precious pearl.
Elevated to status of a meat-eating guest, he next helped Zihua retrieved silk from a store on fire.
His torturers believing he had power of the 'Dao' begged his forgiveness and asked to share it.
Shangqiukai said: "I have no 'Dao'. Now alerted, I had fear inside, how dare I do it again ?"
Through the mouth of Shengqiukai, Liezi says there is no supernatural power in 'Dao'.
Indeed today, all 'supernatural powers' are science based and can be explained.
The atom bomb that can flatten a whole city, the computer that instantly accesses the world.
Liezi is not a mystic and has no delusion that 'Dao' cannot confer supernatural power.

2.7 养虎之法

01 周宣王之牧正	Head of Husbandry of King Xuan of Zhou
02 　有役人梁鸯者,	Had Person, Servant Liangyang,
03 能养野禽兽,	Able to Keep Wild Birds Animals,
04 委食于园庭之内,	Dispensing Food Inside The Garden Compound,
05 虽虎狼雕鹗之类,	Though Tigers Wolves Vultures Eagles These Kinds,
06 无不柔驯者。	None That were Not Gentle and Trained.
07 雄雌在前,	Male Female In Front,
08 孳尾成群,	Breeding Tails (coupling), Creating Crowds (youngsters)
09 异类杂居,	Different Species Mixed Living (together)
10 不相搏噬也。	Not Mutually Fighting Biting that's.
11 王虑其术终于其身,	King Concerned His Skills will End With His Person,
12 令毛丘园传之。	Ordered Maoqiuyuan to Understudy Him.
13 梁鸯曰:	Liangyang Said:
14 "鸯, 贱役也,	"Yang (Liangyang), Lowly Servant that's,
15 何术以告尔?	What Skills To Inform You ?
16 惧王之谓隐于尔也,	Afraid King May Say Hiding (skills) From You, that's,
17 且一言我养虎之法。	***So Just Talk of My Methods Keeping Tigers.***
18 凡顺之则喜,	Ordinarily Accord with Them Then Happy,
19 逆之则怒,	Oppose Them Then Angry,
20 此有血气者之性也。	This The Nature of Those With Blood and Breath that's.
21 然喜怒岂妄发哉?	Naturally How can Joy Anger Just Explode, right ?
22 皆逆之所犯也。	All That Cause Them, Opposition that's.
23 夫食虎者,	O' Person Feeding Tigers,
24 不敢以生物与之,	Not Dare Give Them With Life Food,
25 为其杀之之怒也;	Because Of The Anger in Killing Life-food that's;
26 不敢以全物与之,	Not Dare to Give Them With Whole Food ,
27 为其碎之之怒也。	Because Of The Anger in Tearing Food that's.
28 时其饥饱,	Timing Their Hunger and Fullness,
29 达其怒心。	Accord with Their Anger Heart (feelings).
30 虎之与人异类,	Tigers Their Difference With Human Kind,
31 而媚养己者, 顺也;	So Loving Own Feeder Person, Accordance that's;
32 故其杀之, 逆也。	Thus Its Killing Feeder, Opposition that's.
33 然则吾岂敢	Naturally Then I Not Dare
34 　逆之使怒哉?	Oppose Them Causing Anger, right ?
35 亦不顺之使喜也。	Also Not Accord with Them to Cause Joy that's,
36 夫喜之复也必怒,	O' make Them Happy, The Revere Surely is Anger,
37 怒之复也常喜,	Anger Them, The Reverse that's Always Happy,
38 皆不中也。	All Not Proper that's.
39 今吾心无逆顺者也,	Now in My Heart, No Opposition no Accordance that's,
40 则鸟兽之视吾,	Then Birds and Animals Their Eyeing Me,
41 犹其侪也。	Like Their Own kind that's.

42 故游吾园者，	Hence Those Roaming in My Garden,
43 不思高林旷泽；	Not Thinking of High Forest, Broad Wetland;
44 寝吾庭者，	Those Living in My Courtyard,
45 不愿深山幽谷，	Not Wishing Deep Mountains, Dark Valleys,
46 理使然也。"	Reasons Enable Naturally, that's."

Liezi Text Narrative

King Xuan of Zhou, his head of husbandry, had Liangyang who kept wild birds and animals. L3
In the garden, feeding tigers wolves vultures eagles such kinds, and all were gentle and tamed. L6
Male Female coupling in front, breeding crossing tails and creating crowds of youngsters. L8
Different species mixing, living together, not mutually fighting or biting that's. L10
King, concerned that his skill died with him, ordered Maoqiuyuan to learn to succeed him. L12
Liangyang said: "Yang (self), lowly servant, what skills have I to inform you ? L15
Afraid that the King says I am hiding my skills, let's talk of my methods in keeping tigers. L17
They are happy with accordance, and angry with opposition; this is the nature of blood-life. L20
How can joy and anger just blow-up, right ? It is all because of opposition to them, that's. L22
O' person feeding tigers, not dare to give them life-food, as killing life-food anger them; L25
Not dare to give them whole food because of the anger in tearing food that's. L27
Mindful of timing their hunger and fullness, accord with their heart feeling of anger. L29
Tigers and humans are different in kinds. L30
Tigers loving their feeder, accordance that's; tigers killing the feeder, opposition that's. L32
Naturally then I do not dare to oppose them causing anger, right ? L34
Also not according to them to cause over-joy, as reverse of over-joy is surely anger. L36
Pampering or making them angry, all these are not proper that's. 38
My heart has no opposition or accordance, birds and animals see me as their own kind. L41
Hence those roaming in my garden, not thinking of high forest and broad wetland; L43
Living in my courtyard, no wish for deep mountains, dark valleys, reasonably naturally so." L45

Comments:
2.7 Methods Keeping Tigers

Liangyang kept wild birds and animals in his garden, all gentle and tamed with no fighting.
Tigers, wolves, vultures, eagles and such kinds, all living together and breeding together.
King Xuan, concerned his skill would die with him, ordered Maoqiuyuan to learn from him.
Liangyang: "King may say I am hiding my skills, so let's talk of my methods in keeping tigers.
That person feeding tigers does not dare to give them life-food, for killing life-food angers them.
That person does not dare to give them whole food because of the anger in tearing food that's.
Mindful of the timing of their hunger and fullness, accord with their heart feeling of wellness.
Tigers loving their feeder, accordance that's; tigers killing the feeder, opposition that's.
Pampering them causes over-joy, the reverse is surely anger, so all these are not proper, that's.
Thus my heart has no opposition or accordance, birds and animals see me as their own kind."
Through Liangyang, Liezi narrates methods in keeping tigers, the natural way to tame the wild.

Liezi explains the nature of taming the wild, so as to dispel delusion in the supernatural.

2.8 津人操舟若神

2.8 Ferry-man Handle Boat God-like

01	颜回问乎仲尼曰：	Yanhui Asked Of Zhongni (Confucius) Said:
02	"吾尝济乎觞深之渊矣，	"I Make The Crossing Of Deep-pool Shangshen that's,
03	***津人操舟若神。***	***Ferry Man Handle Boat Like God.***
04	吾问焉，曰：	I Asked Why, Said:
05	'操舟可学邪？'	'Handling Boat Possible to Learn, is-it-not ?'
06	曰：'可。	Said: 'Possible.
07	能游者可教也，	Person Able to Swim Possible to Teach that's,
08	善游者数能。	Person Good in Swimming Quick to Learn.
09	乃若夫没人，	Also Like The Diver Person,
10	则未尝见舟而谡操之者也。'	Then Not Yet Seen Boat And Person Ready to Handle It.'
11	吾问焉，而不告。	I Asked Why, And Not Telling.
12	敢问何谓也？"	Beg to Ask What Reason that's?"
13	仲尼曰：	Zhongni Said:
14	"嘻！吾与若玩其文也久矣，	"Yi！I And You Play The Text That's Long-time indeed,
15	而未达其实，	But Not Attain The Solid (in practice),
16	而固且道与。	And Yet Let's Speak of This.
17	能游者可教也，	Person Able to Swim Possible to Teach that's,
18	轻水也；	Thinks lightly of Water that's;
19	善游者之数能也，	Person Good in Swimming Quick to Learn that's,
20	忘水也。	Unaware of Water that's.
21	乃若夫没人之未尝见舟也	Also Like The Diver Person He Not Yet Seen Boat that's
22	而谡操之也，	And Ready to Handle It that's,
23	彼视渊若陵，	He Sees Deep-pool Like Hill-mound,
24	视舟之覆犹其车却也。	See Capsized Boat Like That Cart Roll-back that's.
25	覆却万物方陈乎前	Capsize Roll-back All Matters Present Displayed In Front
26	而不得入其舍。	These are not Able to Enter His Consciousness.
27	恶往而不暇？	How can he Proceed And Not be Leisurely ?
28	以瓦抠者巧，	Person Betting With Tile, Skillful,
29	以钩抠者惮，	Person Betting With Copper-belt, Fearful,
30	以黄金钩抠者惛。	Person Betting With Gold-belt, Slow-witted.
31	巧一也，而有所矜，	Skills One (same) that's, But Has That Restrain,
32	则重外也。	Because Outside Weighed-heavy that's.
33	凡重外者拙内。"	Person All Weighed-heavy Outside, Clumsy Inside."

2.8 Ferry-man Handle Boat God-like

Liezi Text Narrative
Yanhui asking Zhongni (Confucius) said: L1
"Crossing the Shangshen pool, the ferry person handled boat god-like. L3
Wondering, I said: 'Handling boats, possible to learn, is-it-not ?' L5
And he said: 'Possible. L6
Person able to swim is able to learn; a person good in swimming quickly learns. L8
Also the diver person prior to seeing a boat is ready to handle it.' L10
I asked why and he was not telling; so may I ask what is the reason, that's ?" L12
Zhongni said: "Yi! We have played with text longtime, but yet to reach the practical stage. L15
Let's speak further on this; a person able to swim, thinks lightly of water, so can be taught. L18
Person good at swimming is unaware of water, hence quick to learn that's. L20
A diver is ready to handle the boat prior to seeing it because he sees a deep-pool like a hill. L23
He sees a capsized boat like a cart rolling back L24
Capsize, roll-back, all matters presently displayed in front, will not enter his consciousness. L26
How can he not proceed to take matters leisurely in his stride, right ? L27
Person betting with titles skillful; betting with copper-belt fearful; betting with gold-belt, dull. L30
One skill that's, but is restrained by whatever outside that weighs heavy on the mind. L32
All that weigh heavy outside, the person will be clumsy inside. L33

Comments:
2.8 Ferry-man Handle Boat God-like
Ferry man was right that good swimmers can learn fast and a diver needn't even learn!
Surprised, Yanhui asked Zhongni who explained that a good swimmer is not aware of water.
The diver sees a deep-pool like a hill-mound, capsized boat like a back-rolling cart, not serious.
With greater ability in water and no fear of drowning, they have greater capacity handling boats.
On the betting table, a poker player is skillful when the stake is low and pressure of losing low.
When the stake is raised, the poor man becomes clumsy whereas the rich can stay calm.
The condition outside weighs heavy on the mind inside, naturally affecting performance.
Priority is having the ability and capacity to relieve pressure on the mind for good results.

Liezi is not delusional about god-like performances, offering sensible reasons and explanations.

Chapter 2. Huangdi (黄帝)

2.9 长于水而安于水   2.9 Live By Water, Safe By Water

01	孔子观于吕梁，	Kongzi Sight-seeing At Luliang,
02	悬水三十仞，流沫三十里，	Water-Fall 30 Meters, Rapids Foaming 30 Miles,
03	鼋鼍鱼鳖	Sea-turtle Lizard Fish Turtle,
04	之所不能游也。	Where They were Not Able to Swim that's.
05	见一丈夫游之，	Saw One Elder Man Swimming There,
06	以为有苦而欲死者也，	Thinking Person Had Trouble And Wished Death that's,
07	使弟子并流而承之。	Asked Disciples Parallel Flow To Support Him.
08	数百步而出，	Few Hundred Steps Then Emerged,
09	被发行歌，	Flowing Hairs Moving along Singing,
10	而游于棠行。	And Swimming By the River Side.
11	孔子从而问之，	Kongzi Followed And Asked Him,
12	曰："吕梁悬水三十仞，	Said: "Luliang Water-Fall 30 Meters,
13	流沫三十里，	Rapids Foaming 30 Miles,
14	鼋鼍鱼鳖所不能游，	Sea-turtle Lizard Fish Turtle, Where Not Able to Swim,
15	向吾见子道之，	Just then I Saw Sir Crossing It,
16	以为有苦而欲死者，	Thinking You were Having Problem And Wishing Death,
17	使弟子并流将承子。	Asked Disciples Parallel Flow To Support Sir.
18	子出而被发行歌，	Sir Emerged And with Flowing Hair Walking Singing,
19	吾以子为鬼也。	I Suspected Sir Is Devil that's.
20	察子，则人也。	Examined Sir, Is Human that's.
21	请问蹈水有道乎？"	May Ask, Treading Water Has 'Dao' Is-it-not ?"
22	曰："亡，吾无道。	Said: "No, I have No 'Dao'.
23	吾始乎故，	I Started At Origin,
24	长乎性，成乎命。	Growth By Nature, Completed In Destiny,
25	与脐俱入，与汩偕出。	All Entered Into the Whirlpool, All Out With the Spring.
26	从水之道而不为私焉，	Followed Water's Way And Not Do Private (way) that's,
27	此吾所以道之也。"	This Was How I Crossed It, that's."
28	孔子曰："何谓始乎故，	Kongzi Said: "Why Call-it Started At Origin,
29	长乎性，成乎命也？"	Growth By Nature, Completed In Destiny that's ?"
30	曰："吾生于陵安于陵，故也；	Said: "I was Born In Hill Safe In Hill, Origin that's;
31	***长乎水而安于水，性也；***	***Growth By Water And Safe By Water, Nature that's;***
32	不知吾所以然而然，命也。"	I Am But Not Know Why I Am, Destiny, that's."

2.9 Live By Water, Safe By Water

Liezi Text Narrative
Kongzi sight-seeing at Luliang where a 30 meter Water-Fall made rapids up to for 30 miles. L2.
Where even sea-turtles, water-lizards, fish and turtles cannot swim, that's. L4
Then spy an elder man swimming there, and suspected he might be troubled, wishing death. L6
Kongzi asked disciples to follow the flow to help, then he surfaced after a few hundred steps. L8
With hairs flowing he swam down by the river, moving along singing. L10
Kongzi followed to ask him, saying: "Luliang water-fall 30 meters, making rapids 30 miles. L13
Where sea-turtle, water lizard, fish turtle cannot swim, but just then saw you Sir, crossing it. L15
Suspecting that you had problems and wished death, so asked disciples to help you Sir. L17
Sir emerged with hairs flowing, moving along singing, I thought Sir is a ghost that's. L19
On examination Sir is human, hence may I ask if you have 'Dao' treading water there ?" L21
Said: " No, I have no 'Dao'; I started at Origin, Growth by Nature, Completed in Destiny. L24
All entered the whirlpool, all out with the spring, followed water's way, not my own. L26
This was how I crossed the rapids." L27
Kongzi said: "Why call-it Started at Origin, Growth by Nature, Complete in Destiny that's?" L29
Said: "I was born in the hills safe in the hills, Origin that's; L30
Live by water safe by water, Nature that's; I am and not know why I am, Destiny that's." L32

Comments:
2.9 Live By Water, Safe By Water
At Luliang, there was a 30 meter waterfall that made rapids up to 30 miles.
Kongzi and his disciples saw an elder man swimming there, where fish and turtles cannot swim.
Concerned that the man was troubled and seeking death, they followed him along the river bank.
Man surfaced after a few hundred steps, with hair flowing and singing along down the river.
Kongzi followed him, saying: "Sir is human, may I ask if you have 'Dao' treading water there ?"
Said: " No, I have no 'Dao'; I started at Origin, Growth by Nature, Completed in Destiny."
The swimmer of Luliang was able to shoot rapids not because of the supernatural power of 'Dao'.
As he explained, it was the natural ability of the daoist to adapt to conditions wherever he was.
Born in the hills he was happy with the hills; growing-up by water, he was safe with the flow.
He was what he was, cannot explain why, accept his destiny, at peace with himself and the world.
True daoists like Liezi accept nature and destiny, have no delusion about the superpower of 'Dao'.
Only pseudo-daoists are delusional, ever hoping to attain the power of 'Dao' to perform miracles!
Confucians must have been laughing at delusional pseudo-daoists since before the time of Laozi.
This is reflected by Kongzi asking the swimmer if he has the 'Dao' to survive crossing the rapids!

True daoists are not delusional about the power of 'Dao', as feats are just natural phenomena.

Chapter 2. Huangdi (黃帝)

2.10 佝偻者承蜩　　2.10 Hunchback Elder Catching Cicada

01	仲尼适楚，出于林中，	Zhongni went to Chu, Appeared In Forrest Center,
02	***见佝偻者承蜩，***	***Saw Rickety Hunchback Person Catching Cicada,***
03	犹掇之也。	Like Picking Them that's.
04	仲尼曰：	Zhongni said:
05	"子巧乎！有道邪？"	"Sir Skillful Indeed ! Have 'Dao' right ?"
06	曰："我有道也。	Said: " I Have 'Dao' that's.
07	五六月，	Five Six Months (practice),
08	累垸二而不坠，	Pile-up 2 Sticky-balls And Not Fall-off,
09	则失者锱铢；	Then Failure Chance Very Small;
10	累三而不坠，	Pile-up 3 Sticky-balls And Not Fall-off,
11	则失者十一；	Then Failure Chance 1 out of Ten;
12	累五而不坠，犹掇之也。	Pile-up 5 And Not Fall-off, Like Picking Them that's.
13	吾处也若橛株驹，	I Stand that's Like Upright Tree Trunk,
14	吾执臂若槁木之枝。	I Hold Arms Like The Branch of Withered Tree.
15	虽天地之大，	Though in The Vastness of Heaven Earth,
16	万物之多，	The Multitude of All Matters,
17	而唯蜩翼之知。	But Only The Cicada's Wings Aware.
18	吾不反不侧，	I Not Reverse (distracted) Not Side-way (distracted)
19	不以万物易蜩之翼，	Not With Any Matter Replaces The Cicada's Wings,
20	何为而不得？"	What Reason Thus Not Attainable ?"
21	孔子顾谓弟子曰：	Kongzi Turned, Speaking to Disciples, Said:
22	"用志不分，	"Use of Will (power) Not divided,
23	乃凝于神。	That's the Focus Of Attention.
24	其佝偻丈人之谓乎！"	The Words of Rickety Hunchback Elder Person, indeed !"
25	丈人曰："汝逢衣徒也，	Elder Man Said: " You Member of Broad Attire, that's,
26	亦何知问是乎？	Also How Know to Ask of This, is-it-not ?"
27	修汝所以，	Revise Your Whatever For (discipline),
28	而后载言其上。"	And Then Come to Speak of The Above."

67

2.10 Hunchback Elder Catching Cicada

Liezi Text Narrative
In the forest of Chu, Zhongni saw a hunchback-elder catching Cicadas, like just picking. L3
Zhongni said: "Sir skillful indeed, You have 'Dao' is-is-not ?" L5
Said: "I have 'Dao' that's. L6
Practiced 5 to 6 months with 2 sticky-balls attached without falling, failure rate is small. L9
Attached 3 sticky-balls to the bamboo-rod without falling, chance of failure is one in ten. L11
Attached 5 sticky-balls without falling off, catching cicada is like just picking them off trees. L12
I stand motionless like an upright tree trunk, my arms still, like branches of a withered tree. L14
Heaven and Earth are vast, multitude of all matters, the only thing I know is the cicada wings. L17
Not distracted from the back, sides, nothing replaces the cicada's wings, so how can I fail ?" L20
Kongzi to his disciples, said: "Use of will power undivided, so says hunchback elder, right !" L24
Elder said: "You are members of broad-attire (scholars), why do you want to ask this ?" L26
Revise your whatever discipline, then come again to discuss the above, catching cicada." L28

Comments:
2.10 Hunchback Elder Catching Cicada
In the forest of Chu State, Zhongni (Confucius) saw an elder easily 'picking' cicadas off trees.
Zhongni said: "Sir skillful indeed, You have 'Dao' is-is-not ?"
Elder said yes, 6 months practice with 2 to 5 sticky-balls attached to bamboo-rod without falling.
Stood like a tree trunk, arms like withered branches, and focused unperturbed on cicada's wings.
Kongzi to his disciples, said: "Use of will power undivided, so says hunchback elder, right !"
Hunchback elder rebuked Kongzi and company, as scholars with empty talk and discussion only.
Catching cicada is not just empty talk of will power undivided, but adaptation and hard practices.
This narrative again suggests animosity between daoism and confucianism since early times.

Elder's 'picking' cicadas off trees is through long practices, not just will power undivided.

Chapter 2. Huangdi (黃帝)

2.11 沤鸟　　　　　2.11 Starling Birds

01	海上之人有好沤鸟者，	Among People By the Sea Had Starling Lover Person.
02	每旦之海上，	Very Morning On The Sea,
03	从沤鸟游，	Followed Starling Birds in Play,
04	沤鸟之至者百住而不止。	The Starlings That Came 100 Numbers And No Less.
05	其父曰：	The Father Said:
06	"吾闻沤鸟皆从汝游，	"I Heard Starling Birds All Follow You in Play,
07	汝取来，吾玩之。"	You Bring Here, I Play with Them."
08	明日之海上，	Next Day Above The Sea,
09	**沤鸟舞而不下也。**	***Starling Birds Dancing But Not Coming Down that's.***
10	故曰：	Hence Sayings:
11	至言去言，	Ultimate Words Discard Words,
12	至为无为。	Ultimate Action Unselfish Action
13	齐智之所知，则浅矣。	The Common Wisdom That is Known, Is Shallow indeed.

Liezi Text Narrative

Among people by the sea was a starling lover who played with them every morning by the sea. L3
The starling birds that came were no less than 100 in numbers. L4
The father said: "I heard starlings follow you in play, you bring here and I play with them." L7
Next day above the sea, starlings danced but none came down. L9
Hence sayings: ultimate speech is no speech, ultimate action is unselfish action. L12
The common knowledge that we know and see is shallow indeed. L13

Comments:
2.11 Starling Birds

Hundreds of starlings came and the starling-lover played with them every morning by the sea.
The father heard this and requested that he bring some starlings home for him to play.
Next day the starlings danced above the sea as usual, but none came down to play with him.
Starlings in the wild are ever sensitive to the danger of being captured, and kept their distance.
The starling-lover subtly changed demeanor is quite clear to the starlings as to his ill intention.

Living in civilised society, we have lost much of our natural sensitivity to immediate danger.
And the common things that we know and see are often shallow and need our closer attention.

In fact, we ought to be alert to the rampant fake news that are in our media and internet today.

2.12 奇人不知火石

2.12 Strange Man Not Know Fire Rock

01	赵襄子率徒十万，	Zhaoxiangzi Led 100 Thousands (army),
02	狩于中山，藉芿燔林，	Hunting In Zhongshan, Trampled Grass Burned Forest,
03	扇赫百里，	Fanning, Glowing 100 Miles (fire),
04	有一人从石壁中出，	There Was Person Emerged From Among Wall of Rocks,
05	随烟烬上下，	Up and Down Following the Smoking Ember,
06	众谓鬼物。	Crowd Called it Devil Matter.
07	火过，徐行而出，	Fire Over, Slowly Walking And Emerged,
08	若无所经涉者，	Like Person Not Experienced Whatever had Happened,
09	襄子怪而留之，	Xiangzi Bewildered And Detained Him,
10	徐而察之：	Gently In Examining Him:
11	形色七窍，人也；	Form, Color, 7 Orifices (facial), all Human that's;
12	气息音声，人也。	Air, Breath, Sound, Voice, all Human that's.
13	问奚道而处石？	Asked What 'Dao' To Stay in Rocks?
14	奚道而入火？	What 'Dao' To Enter Fire?
15	其人曰：	The Person Said:
16	**"奚物而谓石？**	**"What Matter Is Called Rocks?**
17	**奚物而谓火？"**	**What Matter Is Called Fire?"**
18	襄子曰：	Xiangzi Said:
19	"而向之所出者，石也；	"Just Now That Which Emerged From, Rocks that's;
20	而向之所涉者，火也。"	Just Now That Which Immersed In, Fire that's."
21	其人曰："不知也。"	The Person Said: "Not Knowing that's."
22	魏文侯闻之，问子夏曰：	Duke Weiwen Heard This, Asked Zixia Said:
23	"彼何人哉？"	"Who Was That Person?"
24	子夏曰：	Zixia Said:
25	"以商所闻夫子之言，	"By What Shang (alias) Heard of Teacher's Words,
26	和者大同于物，	Harmonious Person has Great Common With Matters,
27	物无得伤阂者，	Person that Matters Not Able to Hurt,
28	游金石，蹈水火，	Moving in Metal Rocks, Stepping in Water Fire,
29	皆可也。"	All Possible that's."
30	文侯曰：	Duke Wen Said:
31	"吾子奚不为之？"	"My Sir, Why (you) Not Do This?"
32	子夏曰：	Zixia (disciple of Kongzi) Said:
33	"刳心去智，商未之能。	"Cut Heart Exhaust Talent, Shang Yet Be Enable.
34	虽然，试语之有暇矣。"	Although, Has Leisure Trying to Speak of This, that's."
35	文侯曰："夫子奚不为之？"	Duke Wen Said: "Why Teacher (Kongzi) Not Do This?"
36	子夏曰：	Zixia Said:
37	*"夫子能之而能不为者也。"*	*"Teacher Able To, But Able to Not Do (restrained) that's."*
38	文侯大说。	Duke Wen was Very Happy.

2.12 Strange Man Not Know Fire Rock

Liezi Text Narrative
Zhaoxiangxi and 100 thousands, hunting in Zhongshan, burnt forest to flush out animals. L2
Fire fanning, glowing 100 miles, a person emerged from the rocks and smoke. L5
Crowd called it Devil matter; and the person walked out, like having no experience of the fire. L8
Xiangzi bewildered detained him, examined him; form color with 7 orifices (facial), Human! L11
Air-breath sound voice, all human that's. L12
Xiangzi asked, "what power of 'Dao' to stay in Rocks; what power of 'Dao' to enter Fire ?" L14
The person said: " What matter is called Rocks ? What matter is called Fire ?" L17
Xiangzi said: "Just now that which you emerged from, Rocks; that which immersed in, Fire. L20
The person said: "Not knowing that's." L21
Duke Weiwen heard this, then asking Zixia (Kongzi's disciple) said: "Who was that person ?" L23
Zixia said: "This is what I, Shang (alias), had heard from the words of my Teacher (Kongzi). L25
Person of Harmony has great common with matters, hence matters not able to injure him. L27
Person moving in metal rocks, stepping into water fire, all are possible and safe that's." L29
Duke Wen asked: "My Sir, why you not do this ?" L31
Zixia said: "Cut my heart and exhaust my talent, Shang will not be able to do this. L33
Although I have the leisure to try speaking of this, that's." L34
Duke Wen asked: "Why Teacher (Kongzi) not do this ?" L35
Zixia said: "Teacher able to, but also able not to do this (restrained, not to show-off) that's." L37
Duke Wen was very happy. L38

Comments:
2.12 Strange Man Not Know Fire Rock
Zhaoxiangzi and his 100 thousands strong army, burnt forest to flush out animals for his hunt!
This narrative is a life-size satirical dig on the extravagance of the rich and powerful at that time.
Appearance of a stranger who knew not rocks and fire is another satirical dig on confucianism.
Zixia remembered Kongzi's words, Harmony can unite matters, so fire cannot injure the stranger!
Zixian even claimed that Kongzi had the power of the stranger, but not showing, out of humility!
Here Zixia is guilty of over-stating the goodness and power of the concept of Harmony.
Pseudo-daoists and confucians alike are often guilty of erring on the power of their concepts.
Duke Wen was happy with Zixia's answer, showing ignorance and gullibility of the ruling class.

Liezi's satires alienate confucians who black-out his work, until rediscovered by Zhuangzi.

Chapter 2. Huangdi (黄帝)

2.13 神巫　　　　　2.13 God-like Sorcerer

01 有神巫自齐来处于郑，	*Had God-like Sorcerer From Qi Came Stay In Zheng*
02 命曰季咸，	Name Called Jixian,
03 知人死生存亡，	Knew People's Survival Death,
04 祸福寿夭，	Fortune Misfortune Longevity Short-lived,
05 期以岁月旬日,如神。	Predicted With Year Month Week Day, Like God,
06 郑人见之，皆避而走。	People of Zheng Saw Him, All Avoiding And Walk-away.
07 列子见之而心醉，	Liezi Saw Him And Heart Drunken (totally captivated),
08 而归以告壶丘子，曰：	Then Returned To Tell Huqiuzi, Said:
09 "始吾以夫子之道为至矣，	"Beginning I Took Teacher's 'Dao' to Be the Ultimate,
10 则又有至焉者矣。"	Then Again Has This Ultimate Attained Person that's."
11 壶子曰："吾与汝无其文，	Huqiuzi Said: "I Teach You Only The Superficial,
12 未既其实，而固得道与？	Prior to The Solid, So Sure Has 'Dao' been Given ?
13 众雌而无雄，	All Females And No Males,
14 而又奚卵焉？	Then How Else Eggs (fertilized) that's ?
15 而以道与世抗，	And With 'Dao' (superficial) Contesting With World,
16 必信矣，	Certain to Believe (sorcerer) that's,
17 夫故使人得而相汝。	O' Thus Enable Person to Attain And Read You.
18 尝试与来，以予示之。"	Try a Test Come With (him), To Get Revelation of Him."
19 明日，列子与之见壶子。	Next Day, Liezi came With Sorcerer to See Huzi.
20 出而谓列子曰："嘻！	Emerged (sorcerer) To Tell Liezi Said: "Ci !
21 子之先生死矣，弗活矣，	Sir Your Teacher Dying Indeed, Not to Live indeed,
22 不可以旬数矣。	Not More Than 10-days Number indeed.
23 吾见怪焉，见湿灰焉。"	I Saw Strange Whatever, Saw Wet Ashes indeed."
24 列子入，涕泣沾襟，以告壶子。	Liezi Entered, Wept Sobbed Wetting Lapels, To Tell Huzi.
25 壶子曰："向吾示之以地文，	Huzi Said: "Just then I Showed Him The Earth Signs,
26 罪乎不誫不止，	O' Criminally, No Action No Stopping (all still),
27 是殆见吾杜德几也。	He Only Saw My Blocked Life Energy that's.
28 尝又与来！"	Try Again Come With (him) !"
29 明日，又与之见壶子，	Next Day, Again With Sorcerer to See Huzi,
30 出而谓列子曰："幸矣！	Emerged (sorcerer) To Tell Liezi Said: "Fortunate indeed!
31 子之先生遇我也，有瘳矣。	Sir YourTeacher Met Me that's, Has Healing indeed.
32 灰然有生矣，	Ashes Ignited Has Life indeed,
33 吾见杜权矣。"	I Saw Blockage Changes indeed."
34 列子入告壶子。	Liezi Entered to Inform Huzi.
35 壶子曰：	Huzi Said:
36 "向吾示之以天壤，	"Just now I Showed Him The Heaven Soil-bed,
37 名实不入，而机发于踵，	Name Solid Not Enter, And Energy Starts From Heels,
38 此为杜权。	This Is Blockage Changes.
39 是殆见吾善者几也。	He Only Saw My Goodness Energy that's.
40 尝又与来！"	Try Again Come With (him) !"

72

2.13 God-like Sorcerer

41	明日，又与之见壶子，	Next Day, Again With Sorcerer to See Huzi,
42	出而谓列子曰：	Emerged (sorcerer) To Tell Liezi Said:
43	"子之先生坐不斋，	"Sir Your Teacher, Sitting Not Ordered,
44	吾无得而相焉。	I am Not Able To Assess indeed.
45	试斋，将且复相之。"	Try Fasting, Will Then Again Assess Him."
46	列子入告壶子。	Liezi Entered to Inform Huzi.
47	壶子曰：	Huzi Said:
48	"向吾示之以太冲莫(目关)，	"Just now I Showed Him The Primal Void Unfathomed,
49	是殆见吾衡气几也。	He Only Saw My Balanced Breath Energy that's.
50	鲵旋之潘为渊，	Whales Circled Its Churning As Fjord,
51	止水之潘为渊，	Still Water Its Churning As Fjord,
52	流水之潘为渊，	Flowing Water Its Churning As Fjord,
53	滥水之潘为渊，	Up-surging Water Its Churning As Fjord,
54	沃水之潘为渊，	Down-flowing Water Its Churning As Fjord,
55	氿水之潘为渊，	Lateral-surging Water Its Churning As Fjord,
56	雍水之潘为渊，	Return-flowing Water Its Churning As Fjord,
57	汧水之潘为渊，	Spring-Pool Water Its Churning As Fjord,
58	肥水之潘为渊，	Confluent Water Its Churning As Fjord,
59	是为九渊焉。	These Are 9 Fjords indeed.
60	尝又与来！"	Try Again Come With (him) !"
61	明日，又与之见壶子。	Next Day, Again With Sorcerer to See Huzi.
62	立未定，自失而走。	Stood Not Stable, Self Lost And Walked-off.
63	壶子曰："追之！"	Huzi Said: "Chase Him !"
64	列子追之而不及，	Liezi Chased Him But Not Reaching,
65	反以报壶子，	Returned To Report to Huzi,
66	曰："已灭矣，	Said: "Already Vanished indeed,
67	已失矣，吾不及也。"	Already Lost indeed, I Cannot Reached, that's."
68	壶子曰：	Huzi Said:
69	"向吾示之以未始出吾宗。	"Just What I Showed Him, Not Issued From My 'Origin'.
70	吾与之虚而猗移，	I Gave Him the Empty And Fantasy Movements,
71	不知其谁何，	Not Knowing The Whoever and However,
72	因以为茅靡，	Thus Suspecting Like Thatch-Grass Wind-blown
73	因以为波流，	Thus Suspecting Like Waves Flowing-along,
74	故逃也。"	Hence Run-away that's."
75	然后列子自以为	Then Afterwards Liezi Self Like Feeling
76	未始学而归，	Prior Starting to Learn Then Returned,
77	三年不出，	Three Years Not Appearing (in public),
78	为其妻爨，	Helped The Wife in Cooking,
79	食豨如食人，	Feeding Pigs Like Feeding People (with respect),
80	于事无亲，	With Affairs No Concern,
81	雕琢复朴，	Discarded Adornment Returned to Modesty,
82	块然独以其形立，	Dead-wood Like, Alone Was His Form Standing,
83	忩然而封戎，	Confused Naturally And Blocked Guarded,
84	壹以是终。	One ('Dao'), Like This Ended.

2.13 God-like Sorcerer

Liezi Text Narrative
There had been a god-like sorcerer named Jixian who came from Qi to stay in Zheng. L2
He predicted with god-like accuracy the exact date of people's life, death, fortune, misfortune. L5
People of Zheng feared and walked away to avoid him, but Liezi was captivated by him. L7
Liezi returned to Huqiuzi, said: "I take Teacher's 'Dao' as ultimate, but Jixian is ultimate! " L10
Huzi said: "I teach you only the superficial prior to the solid, have you attained the 'Dao'? L12
All females and no males then how else to produce fertilized eggs, that's ? L14
With superficial 'Dao' to confront sorcerer, certain to believe and allowing him to read you. L17
Try to come with him, I shall reveal him; the next day Lietzi came with sorcerer to see Huzi. L19
Sorcerer emerged to tell Liezi said: "Xi! Sir your teacher is dying, not to live beyond 10 days. L22
I saw strange things, I saw wet ashes indeed." L23
Liezi entered weeping to tell Huzi; and Huzi said: "Just then I showed him signs of Earth. L25
O' criminally no action no stopping (all still), he only saw my blocked life energy that's. L27
Try again to come with him !"; the next day Liezi came again with the sorcerer to see Huzi. L29
Sorcerer emerged to tell Liezi says: "Fortune indeed ! Sir, your teacher met me, has a cure. L31
Ashes ignited, has life and I see the blockage has changed indeed." L33
Liezi entered to inform Huzi; and Huzi said: "Just then I showed him the soil-bed of Heaven. L36
Fame and wealth not corrupting, and with blockage changed, life-energy started from heels. L38
He was only seeing my energy of goodness, that's; Try again to come with him !" L40
Next day, Liezi came again with sorcerer; the sorcerer emerged to tell Liezi said: L42
"Sir your teacher's sitting is not ordered, I am not able to assess; try fasting to assess again." L45
Liezi entered to inform Huzi; Huzi said: "I just showed him the Primal Void unfathomed. L48
He is only seeing my balanced breath of energy, that's; like whales circling churning as fjord. L50
Like still water, churning as fjord; like flowing water, churning as fjord. L52
Like up-surging, churning as fjord; like down-flowing water, churning as fjord. L54
Like lateral-surging water, churning as fjord; like return-flowing water, churning as fjord. L56
Like spring-pool water, churning as fjord; like confluent water, churning as fjord. L58
These are 9 fjords indeed; try again to come with him !" L60
Liezi came again with the sorcerer to see Huzi; before standing stable, the sorcerer bolted. L62
Huzi said: "Chase him !"; Liezi chased him but did not reach, and returned to report to Huzi. L65
Said: "Already vanished indeed, already lost indeed, I cannot reach him that's." L67
Huzi said: "Just now I showed him but not revealing my original 'Dao'. L69
I gave him the empty and fantasy movements, so he did not know who or whatever. L71
He suspected, like thatch-grass wind-blown, like waves flowing-along, hence run-away. L74
And then, Liezi self feeling not having started to learn and attain 'Dao', returned. L76
Three years not seen in public, helped wife in cooking, feeding pigs like people, with respect. L79
Not concerned with affairs, discarded adornment, returned to modesty. L81
Stood alone like dead-wood, blocked all world's confusion and be one with 'Dao' till the end. L84

2.13 God-like Sorcerer

Comments:
2.13 God-like Sorcerer
Sorcerer Jixian from Zheng could predict with god-like accuracy, the date of people's death.
People feared him but Liezi was captivated by him, and returned to tell his teacher, Huiqiuzi.
Huzi said Liezi had only learned the superficial 'Dao', hence had allowed the sorcerer to read him.
Huzi asked Liezi to bring the sorcerer so that he could be revealed; next day Liezi came with him,
Sorcerer emerged to say he saw wet ashes, and that Liezi's teacher would die in 10 days.
Liezti wept but Huzi explained that he showed sorcerer stillness of Earth, and blocked life energy.
Huzi asked Liezi to bring the sorcerer again;
Next day, the sorcerer emerged saying ashes ignited, had life and that the blockage had changed.
Huzi explained that he showed the sorcerer soil-bed of Heaven, life-energy started from the heels.
Next day, the sorcerer emerged saying the teacher's sitting unruly, to assess again after fasting.
Huzi explained the sorcerer saw his Primal Void unfathomed and his balanced breath of energy.
And the formation of the 9 fjords; again asked Liezi to bring the sorcerer the next day to see him.
The sorcerer came, took one look and bolted; Liezi chased but was unable to bring him back.
Huzi explained he had not shown his true 'Dao' but emptiness and fantasy like wind-blown grass.
The sorcerer not knowing who or whatever, panicked and ran away.
Now Liezi himself felt he had not even started to learn 'Dao', let alone attain it.
He returned to help his wife with cooking and feeding the pigs like feeding people, with respect.
No ambition with public affairs, discarding all aggrandisement and returning to modest living.
After 3 years of self cultivation, he truly attained one with 'Dao', wooden-like and peaceful !

Liezi has shown that 'Dao' is all fantasy, and a return to respect and modesty is the best policy.
There are evil pseudo-daoists who go around victimizing the innocents with prediction of evils.
They strike terror in the hearts of the weak thus often making their predictions self-fulfilling.
Through god-like Jixian, Liezi mercilessly exposes them in great detail with his Teacher's 'Dao'.
It is said, Huqiuzi (or Huzi) is likely a fictitious character that Liezi introduces as his Teacher!

True Daoism is not prediction of fortune or misfortune, but a return to modesty and respect.

Chapter 2. Huangdi (黄帝)

2.14 列子吾惊

2.14 Liezi Is Fearful

01	子列子之齐，中道而反，	Teacher Liezi To Qi, Half Way And Turn-back,
02	遇伯昏瞀人。	Met Bohunmaoren.
03	伯昏瞀人曰：	Bohunmaoren said:
04	"奚方而反？"	"Why, Direction Is Backward ?"
05	**曰："吾惊焉。"**	***Said: "I am Fearful indeed."***
06	"恶乎惊？"	"Frightfully O' Fearful ?
07	"吾食于十浆，而五浆先馈。"	"I Ate At 10 Soup-shops, And 5 Shops First Offered."
08	伯昏瞀人曰：	Bohunmaoren said:
09	"若是，则汝何为惊已？"	"Truly So, Then You, What Reason So Fearful ?"
10	曰："夫内诚不解，	Said: "O' my Inner Honesty Not Released,
11	形谍成光，	Formed Secretly and Came to Light,
12	以外镇人心，	To Outwardly Commanding People's Heart,
13	使人轻乎贵老，	Making People Easily O' Respect me as Elder,
14	而(敫韭)其所患。	And Bring-on Whatever The Misfortune.
15	夫浆人特为食羹之货，	O' Soup People Thus Prepare Food Soup Such Goods,
16	多余之赢；	More Extra For Profit;
17	其为利也薄，	Their Action for Gain Is Thin,
18	其为权也轻，	Their Action of Authority Is Light,
19	而犹若是。	And Still Like This (so respectful of me).
20	而况万乘之主，	And Whatmore The Master of 10,000 Chariots (king),
21	身劳于国，	Body Labors For State,
22	而智尽于事；	And Talent Devotes To Affairs (of state);
23	彼将任我以事，	He (king) Will Appoint Me With Duties (of state),
24	***而效我以功，吾是以惊。"***	***To Enlist Me With Praise, I Am Therefore Fearful."***
25	伯昏瞀人曰：	Bohunmaoren said:
26	"善哉观乎！	"Goodness Indeed, Discerning O' !
27	汝处己，人将保汝矣。"	You Stay Safe, People Will Protect You, that's."
28	无几何而往，	Not Too Long after He Go-forth (Bohunmaoren),
29	则户外之履满矣。	Then Outside House, The Footwears Full (many) indeed.
30	伯昏瞀人北面而立，	Bohunmaoren Faced North And Standing,
31	敦杖蹙之乎颐，	Held Stick On Chin Creasing It,
32	立有间，不言而出。	Stood Some Time, No Words And Left.
33	宾者以告列子。	Guest Person With this Informed Liezi.
34	列子提屦徒跣而走，	Liezi Carried Footwears, And Walked Barefooted,
35	暨乎门，问曰：	Reached The Door, Asking Said:
36	"先生既来，	"Teacher Already Here,
37	曾不废药乎？"	Why No Prescription (of teaching) O' ?"
38	曰："已矣。	Said: "Already Done.
39	吾固告汝曰：	I have Previously Informed You Said:
40	人将保汝，果保汝矣。	People Will Protect You, Really do Protect You indeed.
41	非汝能使人保汝，	Not that You Able to Make People Protect You,

2.14 Liezi Is Fearful

42	而汝不能使人无汝保也,	But You Not Able Make People, Not to Protect You that's,
43	而焉用之感也?	Hence Where Needed This Sensing that's ?
44	感豫出异。	Advance Sensing Emerges Special.
45	且必有感也,	Thus Sure to Have Effects (on others) that's,
46	摇而本身,	Shaken (effects) Back to Own Self,
47	又无谓也。	Also No Comment (purpose) that's.
48	与汝游者,	Those Travelling With You,
49	莫汝告也。	None Inform You (mistakes) that's.
50	彼所小言,	Their Whatever Small Talks,
51	尽人毒也。	All Poisons of People that's.
52	莫觉莫悟,	No Awareness No Realization,
53	何相孰也。"	How Mutually Beneficial that's."

Liezi Text Narrative

Teacher Liezi went to Qi and turned back half-way, meeting with Bohunmaoren. L2
Bohunmaoren said: " Why, direction backward ?" L4
Liezi said: "I am fearful indeed."; Bohunmaoren said: "Why so fearful ?" L6
Liezi says: "I ate at 10 soup-shops, and 5 giving me offers first." L7
Bohunmaoren said: "Truly so, then why are you fearful, for what ?" L09
Liezi said: "O' my inner goodness not control and show outwardly, thus burdening people. L12
Making people oblige to respect as an Elder, and so this may bring me misfortune. L14
Those people make soup food to earn a living; their profit is small and their authority light. L18
 Still they are respectful of me, then what about the master of 10,000 chariots, the king. L20
King labors with state affairs, and exhausts himself with affairs of state. L22
Hence he will appoint me for duties and responsibilities, therefore I am fearful. L24
Bohunmaoren said: "O' Goodness, you are discerning, people will protect you. L27
Not too long after, Bohunmaoren returned and saw many footwears outside Liezi's place. L29
Bohunmaoren stood facing north, with chin creasing on his stick. L31
After standing for a while thus, he left without a word. L32
A guest saw this, and informed Liezi who came running out bare-footed. L34
On reaching the door, Liezi asked: "Teacher already here, why not give me some advice ?" L37
Bohunmaoren said: "Already done. I previously informed you that people will protect you. L40
You make people protect you, but are not able to make people, not to protect you that's. L42
So what is the use of your revelation to others that's ? Your revelation that you are special. L44
Also sure to have effects on others and then gets reflected back on your ego, that's. L46
So what is the purpose of it all; those traveling with you, none will tell you your faults. L49
Their whatever small talk is all poison to people, that's. L51
No awareness, no realization, mutually not beneficial to anybody that's. L53

Comments:
2.14 Liezi Is Fearful
On his way to Qi, 5 of 10 soup-shop keepers treated Liezi with great deference with offerings.
Liezi realised that his reputation had traveled, and the king of Qi may enlist him into government.
He turned back in fear as he fully realised that celebrity status is a double edged sword.
Serving the king is like sleeping beside a tiger, and misfortune may come upon him any time!
He met Bohunmaoren who understood him and commended saying the people will protect him.
However, a short time later on return, he saw lots of footwears outside the house of Liezi.
He leaned on his stick, faced north like a subject looking up to the king, pondered a while and left.
On report Liezi chased out bare-footed, calling to the teacher to stay and to give him some advice.
Bohunmaoren said he had advised, but Liezi cannot not show his talents, and people liked him.
He elaborated that people and their small talks are poisons, and will not tell him his faults.
No awareness, no realisation, hence beneficial to nobody.

Bohunmaoren is right in his concerns, but his hermetic life does benefit nobody but himself !
Liezi is right about sharing his talents with others but ought be careful of his own safety and life.

If Liezi has not done what he had done, we may not benefit from his thoughts and writing.

Chapter 2. Huangdi (黄帝)

2.15 杨朱争席   2.15 Yangzhu Contesting Seat

01	杨朱南之沛，	Yangzhu Went South To Pei (place),
02	老聃西游于秦。	Old Dan (Laozi) Travelled West To Qin (state).
03	邀于郊。	Appointment At the Outskirt.
04	至梁而遇老子。	Reaching Liang And Met Laozi.
05	老子中道仰天而叹曰：	Half Way Laozi Look-up to Heaven And Sighing Said:
06	"始以汝为可教，	"Initially, Believed You Are Possible be Taught,
07	今不可教也。"	Now seems Not Possible to Teach, that's."
08	杨朱不答。	Yangzhu Not Answering.
09	至舍，进涫漱巾栉，	Arrived at Inn, Entered, Cleaned-up with Towel Comb,
10	脱履户外，	Outside Abode, Took off Footwears,
11	膝行而前，	Knelt Then Moved Forward (on knees),
12	曰："向者夫子仰天而叹曰：	Said: "Just Now Teacher Look-up to Heaven And Sighed:
13	'始以汝为可教，	'Initially, Believed You Are Possible be Taught,
14	今不可教。'	Now seems Not Possible to Teach.'
15	弟子欲请夫子辞，	Disciple Wishes To Hear Teacher's Words,
16	行不闲，是以不敢。	On-road No Leisure, Therefore Not Dared (to ask).
17	今夫子闲矣，请问其过。"	Now Teacher has Leisure, may ask for my faults."
18	老子曰：	Laozi Said:
19	"而睢睢而盱盱，	"Like Looking Proud, Like Looking Up,
20	而谁与居？	So Who will Stay With (you) ?
21	大白若辱，	Great White (innocence) Like Guilty,
22	盛德若不足。"	Abundant of Virtues Like Not Enough."
23	杨朱蹴然变容曰：	Yangzhu, Suddenly Countenance Changed Said:
24	"敬闻命矣！"	"Respectfully Hear your Order indeed !"
25	其往也，舍迎将家，	Yangzhu in the Past, Everybody in Inn Welcomed him,
26	公执席，妻执巾栉，	The Man Held Seat, Wife Held Towel Comb,
27	舍者避席，炀者避灶。	Inn People all Left Seats, Kitchen People Left Stoves.
28	其反也，	These all Reversed, that's,
29	**舍者与之争席矣。**	**Inn People all Contesting Seats With Him, that's.**

2.15 Yangzhu Contesting Seat

Liezi Text Narrative
Yangzhu went south to Pei and Laozi travelled west to Qin, agreeing to meet at the outskirts. L3
At Liang they met-up, and half way Laozi looked up to Heaven and sighing said: L5
"Initially I believed you are teachable, but now it's not possible that's." L7
Yangzhu did not answer; Arrived at the Inn, entered, cleaned-up and washed-up. L9
Leaving footwears outside the room, Yangzhu knelt then moved forward on his knees. L11
Said: "Just now Teacher Look-up to Heaven and sighed, said: L12
 'Initially believed you are possible to be taught, now seems not possible to teach.' L14
Disciple wishes to hear the Teacher's words, but on-road no leisure therefore dared not ask. L16
Now Teacher has leisure that's, please, what are my faults ?" L17
Laozi said: "Like looking-proud, like looking-up, so who will be close to you ? L20
With Great White (innocence) still like guilty, with Abundant Virtues still like not enough." L22
Yangzhu's countenance suddenly changed and said: "Respectfully I hear your Teaching." L24
In the past, everybody in the inn welcomed him, man held his seat, wife readied towel comb. L26
Others in the inn left their seats in respect and kitchen staff stopped cooking to welcome him. L27
On return, people in the inn dared to contest him for seats as his arrogance had all gone. L29

Comments:
2.15 Yangzhu Contesting Seats
Yangzhu and Laozi had previously agreed to meet and they met at the outskirts of Liang.
On the way, Laozi sighing said: "Initially I believed you are teachable, but now it seems not so."
Yangzhu did not answer, and they proceeded to the Inn, entered, cleaned-up and washed-up.
Then Yangzhu went to Laozi, left footwear outside, knelt, and moved forward on his knees, said:
"Now Teacher has leisure that's, please tell me what are my faults ?"
Laozi said: "Like looking proud and arrogant, driving people away.
Have great innocence still like guilty, with abundant virtues still like not enough."
This teaching came as a revelation to Yangzhu who was delusional of his own greatness.
In the past, people in the inn gave up their seats in respect and fear when Yangzhu came in.
Now on return, people in the inn dared to contest him for seats as his arrogance had all gone.
This narrative dramatizes Laozi's teaching in Daodejing:
大白若辱，广德若不足　　　Great Innocence Like Guilty, Broad Virtue Like Not Enough
(Laozi, *Daodejing* ch.41, Jingwei 2012)

"Great innocence like guilty, abundant virtues like not enough", a revelation for Yangzhu.

Chapter 2. Huangdi (黄帝)

2.16 其美者自美   2.16 Beauty's Self-beautiful

01	杨朱过宋，	Yangzhu Passing through state of Song,
02	东之于逆旅。	To The East Stayed in Travellers Inn.
03	逆旅人有妾二人，	Travellers Inn Owner Had Concubines 2 Persons,
04	其一人美，	One of Them Beautiful Person,
05	其一人恶；	One of Them Ugly Person;
06	恶乾贵而美者贱。	Ugly one Favored Respected, But Beautiful one Debased.
07	杨子问其故。	Yangzi Asked The Reason.
08	逆旅小子对曰：	Travellers Inn Owner Replying Said:
09	**"其美者自美，**	**" The Beautiful Person Self Beautiful,**
10	吾不知其美也；	I Don't Know Her Beauty that's;
11	其恶者自恶，	The Ugly Person Self Ugly,
12	吾不知其恶也。"	I Don't Know Her Ugliness that's."
13	杨子曰：	Yangzi said:
14	"弟子记之！	"Disciples Remember This !
15	行贤而去自贤之行，	Action Virtuous, To Discard The Self Virtuous Action,
16	安往而不爱哉！"	Go anywhere And How Not be Loved Indeed !"

Liezi Text Narrative
Yangzhu, passing through Song, stayed in Travellers Inn to the east. L2
The Travellers Inn owner had 2 concubines, one beautiful and one ugly. L5
Ugly one was favored and respected, but the beautiful one was frowned upon. L6
Yangzi asked the reason and Travellers Inn owner replying said: L8
"The beautiful person, self-regarded as beautiful but I not know her beauty that's; L10
The ugly person, self-regarded as ugly, but I do not know her ugliness, that's. L12
Yangzi said: "Disciples remember this ! L14
Action virtuous, to discard the self virtuous action (not claim credit). L15
Go anywhere and how not to be loved indeed !" L16

Comments:
2.16 Beauty's Self-beautiful
On the way to Song, Yangzhu met a Travellers Inn owner who had 2 concubines.
He liked the ugly one and disliked the beautiful one; and Yangzhu asked him for the reason.
Owner said he knew not the beauty in the beautiful, or the ugliness in the ugly one !
The beautiful one was thinking that her beauty was everything, may be lazy and was disliked.
The ugly one was not delusional, her ugliness did not prevent her giving her best hence favored.
Thus Yangzi told disciples to discard the delusion of being self-virtuous and be loved everywhere.
This narrative is also reflective of Laozi's phrase:
上德，不德，是爲有德   High Virtue, Not Claiming Virtue, Hence Has Virtue
(Laozi, *Daodejing* ch.38, Jingwei 2012)

It is delusional to claim being virtuous for a good deed, as we ought to do good.

2.17 常胜之道曰柔 | 2.17 Ever Triumph Call-it Gentleness

01 天下有常胜之道，	The World Has The Way to Ever Triumph,
02 有不常胜之道。	Has The Way to Not Ever Triumph.
03 ***常胜之道曰柔，***	***The Way to Ever Triumph Call-it Gentleness,***
04 常不胜之道曰强。	The Way to Not Ever Triumph Call-it Strength.
05 二者亦知，	Both Concept Easy to Know.
06 而人未之知。	But People May Not Know.
07 故上古之言：	Hence Most Ancients, Their Words:
08 强，先不己若者；	Strength, First (think) People (inferior) Not Like Self;
09 柔，先出于己者。	Gentleness, First (think) People Superior To Self.
10 先不己若者，	First (think) People (inferior) Not Like Self,
11 至于若己，	Wait Till Like Self,
12 则殆矣。	Then Misfortune indeed.
13 先出于己者，	First (think) People Superior To Self,
14 亡所殆矣。	No Such Misfortune indeed.
15 以此胜一身若徒，	With This to Triumph Whole Life Like a Disciple,
16 以此任天下若徒，	With This to Serve The World Like a Disciple,
17 谓不胜而自胜，	Call-it No Triumph But Self Triumph,
18 不任而自任也。	No Service But Self Served that's.
19 粥子曰：	Yuzi Says:
20 "欲刚，必以柔守之；	"Wish be Tough, Must With Gentleness Guard It;
21 欲强，必以弱保之。	Wish be Strong, Must With Weakness Protect It.
22 积于柔必刚，	Accumulate By Gentleness, Certain be Tough,
23 积于弱必强。	Accumulate By Weakness, Certain be Strong.
24 观其所积，	Observe The Whatever Accumulation,
25 以知祸福之乡。	To Know The Home of Fortune or Misfortune.
26 强胜不若己，	Strength to Triumph over Not Like Self (inferior),
27 至于若己者刚；	Until Person Like Self then Hard (problem);
28 柔胜出于己者，	Gentleness to Triumph over People Superior To Self,
29 其力不可量。"	The Power Not Possible to Measure."
30 老聃曰：	Old Dan Says:
31 "兵强则灭，	"Army Strong Then Extinguish,
32 木强则折。	Wood Strong Then Break.
33 柔弱者生之徒，	The Gentleness Weakness, Path Of Survival,
34 坚强者死之徒。"	The Tough Strong, Path Of Death."

2.17 Ever Triumph Call-it Gentleness

Liezi Text Narrative
The World has the way to forever triumph, and way to forever not triumph. L2
The way to forever triumph call-it Gentleness; way to forever not triumph call-it Strength. L4
Both concepts are easy to know, but yet people may not know. L6
Hence the most ancients have words: L7
Strength is, first think others inferior to self; Gentleness is, first think others superior to self. L9
First think others inferior to self, when others catch up, no longer inferior, then misfortune. L12
First think others superior to self, then no such misfortune indeed. L14
Be a disciple of this concept for life, be a disciple of this concept to serve the World. L16
This is called no triumph but triumph of Self, not serving but Self serving that's.
Yuzi says: "Wish to be Tough, guard with gentleness; to be Strong, protect with weakness. L21
Accumulated by gentleness certain to triumph, accumulated by weakness certain be strong. L23
Observe whatever the accumulation is to know the home of fortune or misfortune. L25
Strength triumphs over a person inferior, when the person improves like self, danger that's. L27
Gentleness triumphs over a person superior to self, then the power not possible to measure." L29
Old Dan (Laozi, *Daodejing* ch.76) says: L30
"Army strong then be destroyed, wood strong then be broken. L32
Gentleness and weakness are paths to survival, toughness and strength are paths to death." L34

Comments:
2.17 Ever Triumph Call-it Gentleness
Triumph by gentleness is everlasting whereas triumph by strength is not everlasting.
These 2 concepts are easy to know yet few do, hence they are emphasized here by 3 authorities.
The most ancients says: the gentle first thinks others are superior and adapt, so no misfortune.
The strong first thinks others are inferior, then when others catch-up with him, misfortune.
Yuzi says: "Wishing toughness, guard with gentleness; wishing strength, protect with weakness.
Gentleness triumphs over a person superior to self, then the power not possible to measure".
Old Dan (Laozi, Daodejing ch.76) says: "Army strong extinguish, wood strong break.
Gentleness and weakness are paths to survival, toughness and strength are paths to death."

It seems that the triumph of gentleness over strength is the most ancient of ideas.

Chapter 2. Huangdi (黄帝)

2.18 禽兽未必无人心   2.18 Birds Animals Human Like-minded

01	状不必童，而智童；	Form (body) No Need be Same But Mind be Same;
02	智不必童，而状童。	Mind No Need be Same But Form be Same.
03	圣人取童智而遗童状，	The Sage Takes Same Mind But Discards Same Form,
04	众人近童状而疏童智。	People Close to the Same Form But Distant Same Mind.
05	状与我童者，近而爱之；	The Form (body) Same With Me, get Close And Love It;
06	状与我异者，疏而畏之。	The Form (body) Different From Me, Distant and Fear It.
07	有七尺之骸，手足之异，	Has Body of 7 Feet, Hands Feet Are Different,
08	戴发含齿，	Crown with Hair Possess Teeth,
09	倚而趣者，谓之人；	Which Stand And Walk, Call Them Humans;
10	而人未必无兽心。	And Humans Not Necessary No Animal Heart (feeling).
11	虽有兽心，	Though Has Animal Heart (feeling evil),
12	以状而见亲矣。	As Form (human) Thus See Love indeed.
13	傅翼戴角，	Attached with Wings Wearing Horns,
14	分牙布爪，	Baring Teeth. Extending Claws,
15	仰飞伏走，谓之禽兽；	Soaring Flight, Crawl, Walk, Call Them Birds Animals;
16	而禽兽未必无人心。	And Birds Animals Not Certain No Human Heart (love).
17	虽有人心，	Although Has Human Heart (feeling kindness),
18	以状而见疏矣。	As Form (not similar) Thus See Distance indeed.
19	庖牺氏、女娲氏、	Paoxishi, Nuwashi,
20	神农氏、夏后氏，	Shennongshi, Xiahoushi,
21	蛇身人面，牛首虎鼻：	Snake Body Human Face, Bull Head, Tiger Nose:
22	此有非人之状，	Here Had The Forms of Non Human,
23	而有大圣之德。	But Had The Virtues of Great Sage.
24	夏桀、殷纣、	Jie of Xia (dynasty), Zhou of Yin (dynasty),
25	鲁桓、楚穆，	Huan of Lu (state), Mu of Chu (state),
26	状貌七窍，皆同于人，	Form, Face 7 Orifices, All Similar To Human,
27	而有禽兽之心。	But Had The Heart (feeling evil) of Birds Animals.
28	而众人守一状	And Masses of Human Fix on One Form (human only)
29	以求至智，未可几也。	To Find Absolute Wisdom, No Possible Chance that's.
30	黄帝与炎帝战于阪泉之野，	Huangdi With Yandi Battled In Banquan At Countryside,
31	帅熊、罴、狼、豹、貙、	Commanding Bear, Huge-bear, Wolf, Leopard, Wild-cat,
32	虎为前驱，雕、鹖、	Tiger As Advance Guard, Vulture, Pheasant,
33	鹰、鸢为旗帜，	Eagle, Glede As Standards Bearers,
34	此以力使禽兽者也。	This Was With Force Directing Birds Animals that's.
35	尧使夔典乐，	Yao Command Kui (minister for) Classics and Music,
36	击石拊石，百兽率舞；	Struck Stone Beat Stone, 100 Animals Led in Dancing;
37	《箫韶》九成，凤皇来仪，	*Xiaoshao* 9 Verses, Phoenix in Pair Came to Celebrate,
38	此以声致禽兽者也。	This Was With Music Reaching out to Birds Animals.
39	然则禽兽之心，	Naturally Then Birds Animals Their Hearts (feeling),
40	奚为异人？	How Be Different from Humans ?
41	形音与人异，	Form (body) Sound With Human Different,

84

2.18 Birds Animals Human Like-minded

42	而不知接之之道焉。	And Not Know The Way to Connect with Them, indeed.
43	圣人无所不知,	Sage Person None Whatever Not Know,
44	无所不通,	None Whatever Not Connected,
45	故得引而使之焉。	Hence Able to Lead And Direct Them indeed.
46	**禽兽之智有自然与人童者,**	**Birds Animals Naturally Have Mind Same Like Human,**
47	其齐欲摄生,	They Together Wish Survival and Life,
48	亦不假智于人也。	Also No Less Mindful Than Human that's.
49	牝牡相偶,	Female Male Mutual Pairing,
50	母子相亲,	Mother Child Mutual Love,
51	避平依险,	Avoid Flat (open area) Adhere Danger (protective place),
52	违寒就温;	Defy Cold Incline to Warmth;
53	居则有群,	Staying Then Have Groups,
54	行则有列;	Moving Then Have Orders;
55	小者居内,	Small Members Stay Inside,
56	壮者居外;	Strong Members Stay Outside;
57	饮则相携,	Drinking Then Mutually Helping,
58	食则鸣群。	Feeding Then Calling the Herd.
59	太古之时,	Most Ancient Of Times,
60	则与人同处,	Then With Human Stayed Together,
61	与人并行。	With Human Parallel Travelling.
62	帝王之时,	The Times of Tribal-leaders and Kings,
63	始惊骇散乱矣。	Began to Alarm and Fear, Scattered in Confusion that's.
64	逮于末世,	Caught (eaten) In Later Era,
65	隐伏逃窜,	Hiding Evading Fleeing Tunneling,
66	以避患害。	To Avoid Danger Death.
67	今东方介氏之国,	Now East Region The State of Clan of Jie,
68	其国人数数	The State People Some Numbers
69	解六畜之语者,	Who Comprehended Language Of the 6 Domesticated,
70	盖偏知之所得,	That's The Acquisition Of Unilateral Knowledge
71	太古神圣之人,	People Of the Most Ancient Spiritual Sage
72	备知万物情态,	Knowledge Store of All Matters, Conditions, Feelings.
73	悉解异类音声。	Knew, Understood Different Kinds, their Tone and Sound.
74	会而聚之, 训而受之,	Assembled And Gathered Them, Trained Bestowed Them
75	同于人民。	Same As People Citizens.
76	故先会鬼神魑魅,	Hence First Met Devils, Spirits, Elves, Monsters,
77	次达八方人民,	Next Extended in 8 Directions to People Citizen,
78	末聚禽兽虫蛾。	Finally Gathered Birds, Animals, Worms, Insects.
79	言血气之类,	Of Speech Blood Breath, These Kinds,
80	心智不殊远也。	Hearts and Minds Not Far Different that's.
81	神圣知其如此,	Spirit-Sage Knew It Like This,
82	故其所教训者	Hence That Whatever Taught and Trained
83	无所遗逸焉。	None Whatsoever Lost or Left-behind indeed.

2.18 Birds Animals Human Like-minded

Liezi Text Narrative

Form (body) no need be same but mind be same: or mind no need be same but body same. L2
Sage accepts the same mind, but discards the same form; L3
People like the same form, but distance the same mind. L4
Form similar to me, engage and love it; form different from me, to distant and fear. L6
Body of 7 feet, hands feet are different with a crown of hair and possessing teeth. L8
That stand and walk, call them humans; and humans not necessary have no animal feelings. L10
Though he has animal feelings but has human form, thus we see love and engage. L12
Attached with wings, wearing horns, baring teeth and extending claws. L14
Soaring flight, crawl walk, call them birds and animals; they too can have human feelings. L16
May have human feelings, birds and animals are different forms, we still keep our distance. L18
Paoxishi, Nuwashi, Shennongshi, Xiahoushi, snake body human face, bull head, tiger nose: L21
These legendary figures have forms of non human but have the virtues of great sages. L23
Evils like Jie of Xia dynasty, Zhou of Yin dynasty, Huan of Lu state and Mu of Chu state. L25
Their heads had 7 orifices, faces similar to humans, yet they had hearts of animals. L27
The masses acquiring one form (human) to find absolute wisdom, no possible chance that's. L29
Huangdi battled Yandi at the countryside in Banquan, commanding bears wolves leopard. L31
Tigers as advance guards, vultures, pheasants, eagles and hawks as standard bearers. L33
This was with force directing birds and animals that's. L34
Yao commanded Kui (minister for music), led 100 animals dancing to beats on stone. L36
Flute playing 9 verses of *Xiaoshao,* and Phoenix in pairs came to join in the celebration. L37
This was with music reaching out to birds and animals. L38
Naturally then birds animals their heart (feelings), how are they different from humans ? L40
Forms sounds different from humans and we do not know how to connect with them that's. L42
Sage person, none whatsoever not know, none not connecting, attracted and directed them. L45
Birds animals have minds the same as humans, all wishing survival, thus no less mindful. L48
Female male pairing, mother child mutual love, avoid flat stick to danger area for protection .L51
Defy cold keep warmth, staying in groups, moving in orders, small inside, strong outside. L56
Join in drinking, call the herd for feeding; most ancient of times stayed together with humans.L61
In the times of tribal leaders and kings, then they began to fear and scattered in confusion. L63
Caught and eaten in later eras, they hide, evade, flee, and tunnel to avoid danger and death. L66
The clan of Jie in the east region, some people comprehen language of the 6 domesticated. L69
That's the acquisition of unilateral knowledge by the most ancient spiritual sages. L71
Knowledge of all matters and conditions, they knew, understood the sound of foreign kinds. L73
Assembled them, trained and bestowed care on birds and animals, same as with citizens. L75
Hence first met devils spirits elves monsters, next extended to human citizens in 8 directions. L77
Finally gathered birds, animals, worms and insects. L78
All kinds that have speech, blood breath, their hearts and minds not far different that's. L80
Spiritual Sage knew this, hence whatever teaching and training, none lost or left behind. L83

2.18 Birds Animals Human Like-minded

Comments:
2.18 Birds Animals Human Like-minded
Forms similar, we engage and love; forms different, we distant and fear them.
Humans with hands and feet different, a crown of hair, stand and walk, may have animal feelings.
Evils like Jie of Xia dynasty, Zhou of Yin dynasty, Huan of Lu state and Mu of Chu state.
They were humans with the cruelty of animals, thus the human form has no absolute wisdom.
Paoxishi, Nuwashi, Shennongshi, Xiahoushi, with snake body, human face, bull head, tiger nose.
These legendary figures have forms of non human but have the virtues of great sages.
Birds and animals are of different forms but may have human feelings.
Huangdi battled Yandi at the countryside in Banquan, commanding bears wolves leopard.
This was with force directing birds and animals, with eagles and hawks as standard bearers.
Yao commanded Kui (minister for music), led 100 animals dancing to beats on stone.
This was with music reaching out to birds and animals, and Phoenix in pairs came to celebrate.

Birds, animals, human-beings are like-minded, all wishing survival, thus are no less mindful.
Female and male pairing, mother and child have mutual love, avoiding open space to be safe.
Defy cold keep warm, staying in groups moving in orders, the small inside the strong outside.
Drink together, calling the herd to feed; in ancient times staying, travelling together with humans.
Later in the times of tribal leaders, they scattered in confusion to evade being caught and eaten.
Liezi is practically saying we human beings are also but one kind among the birds and animals !
And admittedly humans are capable of having the cruelty of wild animals at times, killing others!

We humans are one kind among birds and animals, and we have no monopoly of wisdom.

Chapter 2. Huangdi (黄帝)

2.19 朝三而暮四 | 2.19 Morning 3 Evening 4

01	宋有狙公者，	Song Had Monkey-keeper Elder Person ,
02	爱狙，	Loved Monkey,
03	养之成群。	Raising Them In Droves.
04	能解狙之意，	Able to Understand Monkeys' Wishes,
05	狙亦得公之心。	Monkeys Also Understood the Elder's Heart (feeling).
06	损其家口，充狙之欲。	Deficited His Family Ration to Satisfy Monkeys' Needs.
07	俄而匮焉，将限其食。	Shortly Then Lacking that's, Needed to Limit Their Feed.
08	恐众狙之不驯于己也，	Fearing Monkey Crowd Not Submissive To Self that;s,
09	先诳之曰：	Initially Lying to Them Said:
10	"与若芧，	"Giving Chestnuts Like,
11	***朝三而暮四，足乎？"***	***Morning 3 Then Evening 4, Enough Right ?"***
12	众狙皆起而怒。	Monkey Crowd All Rising In Anger.
13	俄而曰：	Shortly Then Said:
14	"与若芧，	"Giving Chestnuts Like,
15	朝四而暮三，足乎？"	Morning 4 Then Evening 3, Enough Right ?"
16	众狙皆伏而喜。	Monkey Crowd All Prostrated And Happy.
17	物之以能鄙相笼，	All Matters By Ability Lowliness Mutually Constrained,
18	皆犹此也。	All Originated Here that's.
19	圣人以智笼群愚，	Sage Person With Smartness Constrained Stupid Masses,
20	亦犹狙公之	Also Like Monkey-keeper Elder's (smartness)
21	以智笼众狙也。	With Smartness Constrained the Monkey Crowd that's.
22	名实不亏，	Name and Reality Not Deficient (no difference),
23	使其喜怒哉！	Caused Them to be Joyous or Angry, Amazing!

Liezi Text Narrative

State of Song had a monkey-keeper elder who loved monkeys, raising them in droves. L3
Able to understand monkeys' wishes; and monkeys also able to fathom elder's feelings. L5
Elder rationed his family to feed monkeys; shortly, difficult time so needed to limit their feed. L7
Fearing monkey crowd may not be submissive, initially lied to them said: L9
"Giving chestnuts, like morning 3 and then evening 4, enough right ?" L11
Monkey crowd all rising in anger; shortly then said: L13
"Giving chestnuts like morning 4 and then evening 3, enough right ?" L15
Monkey crowd all prostrated in happiness. L16
All matters by ability, lowly tactics mutually constrained and in checks, starting this way. L18
Sage with smartness constrained the stupid masses, like elder in constraining his monkeys. L21
In name and in reality no difference, yet causes them to be joyous or angry, amazing ! L23

Comments:
2.19 Morning 3 Evening 4

Upon hard times, Elder of Song needed to ration his monkeys' feed to 7 chestnuts per day.
Morning 3 evening 4, or morning 4 evening 3; the 2 schedules are with the same 7 chestnuts.
Accepting one but not the other schedule, this is a satire Liezi uses to mock the stupid masses.
Or, Liezi tries to enlighten the masses to the tactical manipulations often practiced by authority !
But there seems a slight advantage in early acquisition of 4, and less worry for 3 in the evening !
Maybe the monkeys and the masses are not all that stupid as perceive most times, is-it-not ?

Chapter 2. Huangdi (黄帝)

2.20 纪渻子养斗鸡　　2.20 Jishengzi Raising Fighting Cock

01 纪渻子为周宣王	*Jishengzi Helped King Xuan of Zhou*
02 　养斗鸡，	*　Raised Fighting Cock.*
03 十日而问：	Ten days Then Asked:
04 "鸡可斗已乎？"	"Cock Can Fight Already, Is-it-not ?"
05 曰："未也，	Said: "Not Yet,
06 方虚骄而恃气。"	Just Airy Proud And Self Important."
07 十日又问。	Ten days Again Asked.
08 曰："未也，	Said: "Not Yet,
09 犹应影响。"	Still Responding to Shadows, Sounds."
10 十日又问。	Ten days Again Asked.
11 曰："未也，	Said: "Not Yet,
12 犹疾视而盛气。"	Still Darting Stares And Full of Air."
13 十日又问。	Ten days Again Asked.
14 曰："几矣。	Said: "Almost Ready.
15 鸡虽有鸣者，	Cock, though Have Others Crowing,
16 已无变矣。	Already No Changes that's.
17 望之似木鸡矣，	Look At It Like Wooden Cock indeed,
18 其德全矣。	Its Virtues Completed that's.
19 异鸡无敢应者，	Other Cocks Not One Dares to Respond,
20 反走耳。"	Turn and Walk (away) that's."

Liezi Text Narrative
Jishengzi helped King Xuan of Zhou to raise his fighting cock. L2
Ten days then asked: "Cock ready to fight yet, is-it-not ?" L4
Said: "Not yet, just airy, proud and self important." L6
Ten days then asked; said: "Not yet, still responding to shadows and sounds." L9
Ten days again asked; said: "Not yet, still darting stares and full of air." L12
Ten days again asked; said: "Almost ready. L14
Though others crowing, cock already shows no change. L16
Look at it like wooden cock indeed, its virtues complete indeed. L18
Other cocks, not one dared to challenge, all turn and walk away, that's." L20
Comments:
2.20 Jishengzi Raising Fighting Cock
In the era of Liezi, courts of kings and nobles welcomed talented people and good swordsmen. With much bloodshed, they contested with each other to win glory and wealth (Liezi 2.6 L12). Thus many young men aspired to be good swordsmen to earn a good living, respect and fame. Their training and conditioning often turned them into zombie-like persons, devoid of feelings.
It was supposed that a lack of emotion is an added advantage in fighting for the highest honor !
Jishengzi is a fictitious character Liezi uses in this narrative, a satirical exposure of this fallacy.

Even to be the best swordsman, turning into a wooden person is not a good proposition.

Chapter 2. Huangdi (黄帝)

2.21 惠盎见宋康王   2.21 Huiang Debated King Kang of Song

01	惠盎见宋康王。	Huiang Met King Kang of Song.
02	康王蹀足謦欬,	King Kang Paused Foot, Lightly Coughed
03	疾言曰:	Impatiently Speaking Said:
04	"寡人之所说者,	"Lonely Me Am Happy With Person,
05	勇有力也,	Brave, Has Strength that's,
06	不说为仁义者也。	Not Happy with a Person Being Kind, Righteous that's,
07	客将何以教寡人?"	Guest, With What To Teach Lonely Me ?"
08	惠盎对曰:	Huiang Responding Said:
09	"臣有道于此,	"Subject Has 'Dao' In Here,
10	使人虽勇, 刺之不入,	Causes Person Though Brave, Pierces Him Not Through,
11	虽有力, 击之弗中。	Though Has Strength, Strikes Him Not Hitting.
12	大王独无意邪?"	Great King Alone No Interest, Sure ?"
13	宋王曰:"善,	King of Song Said: "Good,
14	此寡人之所欲闻也。"	This Is What Lonely Me Desires to Hear, that's."
15	惠盎曰:"夫刺之不入,	Huiang Said: "O' Pierces Him Not Through,
16	击之不中, 此犹辱也。	Strikes Him Not Hitting, This Like Insulting that's.
17	臣有道于此,	Subject Has 'Dao' In Here,
18	使人虽有勇, 弗敢刺,	Causes Person Though Has Bravery, Not Dared to Pierce,
19	虽有力, 弗敢击。	Though Has Strength, Not Dared to Strike.
20	夫弗敢, 非无其志也。	O' Not Dared, Not Hasn't The Will that's.
21	臣有道于此,	Subject Has 'Dao' In Here,
22	使人本无其志也。	Causing a Person Basically has No Such Will, that's.
23	夫无其志也,	O' No Such Will that's,
24	未有爱利之心也。	Not Having The Heart to Love Benefits, that's.
25	臣有道于此,	Subject Has 'Dao' In Here,
26	使天下丈夫女子	Causes in The World, Men and Women
27	莫不驩然皆欲爱利之。	None Not Excited, All Wishing to Love, to Benefit Him.
28	此其贤于勇有力也,	This Is Superior To Bravery, Having Strength that's,
29	四累之上也。	Top of the Four Levels (mentioned) that's.
30	大王独无意邪?"	Great King Alone No Interest, Sure ?"
31	宋王曰:	King of Song: "Good,
32	"此寡人之所欲得也。"	This Is What Lonely Me Desires to Hear, that's."
33	惠盎对曰:	Huiang Responding Said:
34	"孔墨是已。	"Kong (Confucius), Mo (Mozi) That's.
35	孔丘, 墨翟无地而为君,	Kongqiu, Modi are Not Land-owner But Are Monarchal,
36	无官而为长;	No Official-status But Are Leaders;
37	天下丈夫女子莫不延颈	The World, Men and Women None Not Extend Neck
38	举踵而愿安利之。	Lift Heels And Wish Be Comforted, Benefited .
39	今大王, 万乘之主也,	Now Great King, Master of 10,000 Chariots that's,
40	诚有其志,	Honestly Has The Will,
41	则四竟之内皆得其利矣。	Then Within The 4 Regions, Has All The Advantages.

2.21 Huiang Debated King Kang of Song

42	其贤于孔，	In Virtues more Than Kong (Confucius),
43	墨也远矣。"	Far-ahead of Mo (Mozi) that's."
44	宋王无以应。	King of Song had Nothing To Respond.
45	惠盎趋而出。	Huiang Hurried To Exit.
46	宋王谓左右曰：	King of Song Addressing Left Right Said:
47	"辩矣，	" Debater, Indeed,"
48	**客之以说服寡人也！"**	***Guest, With This Speech Convinced Lonely Me that's !***

Liezi Text Narrative

Huiang met King Kang of Song who paused, coughed and speaking impatiently said: L3
"Lonely Me happy with a person brave with strength, and not a kind and righteous person. L6
My guest, what have you to teach Lonely Me ?" L7
Huiang responding said: "Subject has 'Dao' here; L9
Causes a brave person to pierce but not penetrate, has strength to strike but not hitting. L11
And Great King, you alone have no interest, is this true ?" L12
King of Song said: "Good, this is what Lonely Me desires to hear that's." L14
Huiang said: "O' piercing not through, striking not hit, this is insulting that's. L16
Subject has 'Dao' here, causing a person who has bravery but not dare to pierce. L18
Though has strength but dare not strike; O' not dare, not hasn't the will that's. L20
Subject has 'Dao' here, causing a person basically to have no such will, that's. L22
O' no such will that's, not having the heart to love benefits (not greedy) that's. L24
Subject has 'Dao' here, causing men and women, all excited, wishing to love and benefit. L27
This is superior to bravery and having strength that's, and top of the 4 levels mentioned. L29
Great King, you alone have no interest, is this true ?" L30
King of Song said: "Good, this is what Lonely Me desires to hear that's." L32
Huiang responding said: "Kong (sage Kongzi) Mo (sage Mozi) that's. L34
Kongqiu (alias), Modi (alias) have no land but are monarchal. L35
No official status but are leaders, L36
Men and women, none not strain neck lift heels wishing to be comforted, be benefited. L38
Now Great King, master of 10,000 chariots and honestly has the will. L40
Then has all the advantages within the 4 regions of the state, virtues far exceed Kongzi Mozi. L4
King of Song had nothing to respond; Huiang hurried out to exit. L45
King of Song to the left/right said, " Debater indeed, Guest has convinced Lonely Me !"L48

Comments:
2.21 Huiang Debated King Kang of Song

Huiang is a celebrity debater in the period of the Warring States, Eastern Zhou Dynasty.
King Kang is all for a person with bravery and strength, not a person of benevolence and justice.
King of Song met with Huiang and challenged his guest to teach him on this matter.
Leading King step by step, Huiang lay out 4 levels of his 'Dao' to counter bravery and strength.
Firstly, his 'Dao' can prevent penetration when pierced and avoid being hit when struck.
Secondly, his 'Dao' causes a person, not dared to pierce and not dared strike him.
Thirdly, better still his 'Dao' causes a person basically to have no such will to pierce and strike.
Lastly, his 'Dao' causes men and women of the world to love and benefit him.
This is top of the 4 levels mentioned above, and superior to having bravery and strength.
The levels are: The enemy (1) cannot penetrate, (2) not dare, (3) no will, (4) turn loving (best).

'Dao' preaches kindness and justice, so men and women of the world are comforted, benefited.
This 'Dao' in practice is seen in the conduct of the 2 sages, Kongzi and Mozi.
They have no land but are monarchal; they have no official status but are leaders.
Men and women, none not strain their necks, lift heels to see them, wishing comfort and benefit.
Huiang challenged King Kang to do likewise with all the advantages he had within his kingdom.
Not to further embarrass the king, Huiang hurriedly left.
Thoroughly convinced, King Kang to attendants left and right said, "Debater, indeed !"

So Huiang won the debate, kindness and righteousness are superior to bravery and strength.

Liezi: World of Delusions

Chapter 2. Huangdi (黄帝)
Summary:
2.1 **Reign of Huangdi (黄帝即位)**: Emperor initially suffered over indulgent, then overworked.
   Dreamt of a happy land with no leader, he practiced non-interference and citizens loved him.
2.2 **Spirit On the Mountain (山上有神人)**: Good spirit controlled good weather, good harvest.
   People can live with no restraint, no fear, no disease, no early death, an imaginary utopia.
2.3 **Returned 'Riding On Wind' (乘风而归)**: Liezi meditated 9 years, thought/spoke no evil.
   He returned unselfish, enlightened; said truth is, 'Riding on wind' or 'Wind riding on me' ?
2.4 **Drunkard Fall from Carriage (醉者坠于车)**: Drunk, no fear, not tense up and break joints.
   Reduced desires, drunk in virtues, evils cannot enter, a daoist is relaxed and Heaven protects.
2.5 **Liezi's Exhibition Archery (列御寇射)**: Liezi unable to exhibit on the edge of a high cliff.
   In danger like in battle when one is also the target, real shooting demands more courage.
2.6 **Not Dare Play with Water Fire Again (水火岂复可近)**: Shangqiukai: "I have no Dao".
   After being alerted to the danger of fire and water, he truly cannot enter fire and water at will.
2.7 **Liangyang Kept Tigers (梁鸯养虎)**: Liangyang shared thoughts, methods taming the wild.
   No life food, mindful of the habits and needs of tigers, and not pampering or angering them.
2.8 **Ferry-man Handle Boat God-like (津人操舟若神)**: Ferryman says: "A swimmer can learn.
   A good swimmer can learn fast and a diver can even handle a ferry prior to training."
2.9 **Live By Water, Safe By Water (长于水而安于水)**: This swimmer says: "I have no Dao.
   Born in the hill, happy with the hill; growth by water, safe by water; all naturally so, destiny.
2.10 **Hunchback Elder Catching Cicada (佝偻者承蜩)**: Easily like just picking off the trees.
   He has no 'Dao', just after months of practice starting with 2, progressing to 5 sticky-balls.
2.11 **Starling Birds (沤鸟)**: in the wild are constantly alert to the danger of being capture.
   Thus are sensitive to boy's subtle changes, now with intention to catch them for his father.
2.12 **Strange Man Not Know Fire Rock (奇人不知火石)**: A fictitious satire on gullibility.
   Duke was happy when Zixia said that Confucius can enter rock and fire, only not showing !
2.13 **God-like Sorcerer (神巫)**: Jixian can predict death to the day, and people avoided him.
   Huzi with his 'Dao' exposed the sorcerer, drove him away and Liezi home to feed the pigs.
2.14 **Liezi Was Fearful (列子吾惊)**: that his fame might cause the king to enlist him for duties.
   Yet later, Bohunmaoren re-visit, found that he had amassed a huge following at his place.
2.15 **Yangzhu Contesting Seats (杨朱争席)**: Laozi's admonition was a relevation to Yangzhu.
   On return, his air of arrogance was gone, and he enjoyed more companionship with others.
2.16 **Beauty's Self-beautiful (其美者自美)**: demanded more attention instead of helping more.
   Thus the inn-keeper preferred the ugly concubine who had no distraction but to work hard.
2.17 **Ever Triumph Call-it Gentleness (常胜之道曰柔)**: The most ancient of ideas.
   Gentleness thinks of others as superior, to learn from, thus no challenge and no misfortune.
2.18 **Birds Animals Human Like-minded (禽兽未必无人心)**: Initially all lifes lived together.
   For survival, all animals and humans have similar instincts for kindness and selfishness.
2.19 **Morning 3 Evening 4 (朝三而暮四)**: tactical offerings of the same total amount of nuts.
   Rest assured to have received the larger ration earlier, the monkeys' choice is actually wise.
2.20 **Jishengzi Raised Fighting Cock (纪渻子养斗鸡)**: is a satire on the training of swordsmen.
   Liezi hated the bloodshed, hoping to stop them by depicting them like wooden cocks.
2.21 **Huiang Debated King Kang of Song (惠盎见宋康王)**: King favored bravery and strength.
   Huiang debated and succeeded in winning him around to embrace kindness and justice.
This chapter exposes sorcery, and the fallacy of claiming the power of 'Dao' in human feats.

Chapter 3. King Mu of Zhou (周穆王)

Introduction

3.1 King Mu of Zhou (周穆王)

3.2 Budding Illusionist (学幻)

3.3 Awake Dreaming (觉梦)

3.4 Dreamlands (古莽之国)

3.5 Wishing Winner Takes All ? (欲觉梦兼之?)

3.6 Dividing Deer in Dreams (复梦分人鹿)

3.7 Memory Lost (病忘)

3.8 Delusion Sickness (迷罔之疾)

3.9 Yanren's Home Return (燕人还本国)

Summary

Chapter 3. King Mu of Zhou (周穆王)

Introduction:

King Mu of Zhou (c.976-922) was the 5th king of the Western Zhou dynasty at its height.
Here, narratives are on illusions, dreams and realities, loss of memory and emotional needs.

A sorcerer helped King Mu to enjoy astro-travels, leaving his citizens to prosper in peace.
Laochengzi meditated to become an illusionist who never displayed or passed on his 'skills'!
Know the 8 signs of awareness, the 6 states of dreams, their interactions, and not be alarmed.
Three States at odds, Middle is regular, Gumang regards dreams as true, Fuluo is always awake!
After a hard day, Yinshi and his stoic servant exchanged roles and experience in dreams at night.
A woodcutter lost his deer for day-dreaming and recovered half his deer for night dreaming!
Huazi enjoyed carefree life on loss of memory, and was angry to recover memory of unhappiness!
Satire of a son having delusion seeing white as black, and Laozi's challenge that he may be right!
Satire of Yanren and friends who drained his emotion with false information before he was home.

3.1 周穆王

01 周穆王时，
02 西极之国有化人来，
03 入水火，贯金石；
04 反山川，移城邑；
05 乘虚不坠，触实不硋。
06 千变万化，
07 不可穷极。
08 既已变物之形，
09 又且易人之虑。
10 穆王敬之若神，
11 事之若君。
12 推路寝以居之，
13 引三牲以进之，
14 选女乐以娱之。
15 化人以为王之宫室
16 　卑陋而不可处，
17 王之厨馔腥蝼而不可飨，
18 王之嫔御膻恶而不可亲。
19 穆王乃为之改筑。
20 土木之功，
21 赭垩之色，无遗巧焉。
22 五府为虚，而台始成。
23 其高千仞，临终南之上，
24 号曰中天之台。
25 简郑，卫之处子
　　娥媌靡曼者，
26 施芳泽，正蛾眉，
27 设笄珥，衣阿锡。
28 曳齐纨。
29 粉白黛黑，佩玉环。
30 杂芷若以满之，
31 奏《承云》，《六莹》、
32 《九韶》，《晨露》以乐之。
33 月月献玉衣，
34 旦旦荐玉食。
35 化人犹不舍然，
36 不得已而临之。
37 居亡几何，谒王同游。
38 王执化人之袪，
39 腾而上者，中天乃止。

3.1 King Mu of Zhou

Time of King Mu of Zhou,
From Extreme West Country Came Sorcerer Person,
Entered Fire Water, Penetrated Metal Rocks;
Inverted Mountains and Rivers, Moved Cities and Places;
Sat on Emptiness Not Fall, Touched on Solid Not Block.
Thousand Changes 10-thousand Transformations,
Not Possible to Exhaust the Extremes.
As Ready to Change The Form of Materials,
Also Able to Change The Thoughts of People.
King Mu Respected Him Like God,
Served Him Like a King.
Put out Travel-Palace To Accommodate Him,
Brought 3 Animals (sacrificials) To Offer Him,
Select Female Musicians to Entertain Him.
Sorcerer Person Regarded King's Palaces
　Lowly Scanty And Not Suitable for Living,
King's Kitchen Food, Fishy, Ants-smell And Not Edible,
King's Concubines Goat Smelly And Not Lovable.
King Mu Then For Him Built Alternatives.
Earth-works Wood-works, Their Intricate-carving,
Red, White These Colors, No Lack of Art indeed.
Five Coffers Were Emptied, Only Then Tower Done.
Its Height 1000 Meters, Upon Mount Zhongnan Above,
Name Call-it, Tower of Zhongtian (Heaven Centre).
Selected Virgin Girls From Zheng and Wei (states)
　Those Beautiful Slender, Seductive, Gentle,
Put-on Perfume Lotion, Corrected Beautiful Brows,
Set Hairpins Ear-rings, Clothes of Fine-cloth from A'.
Trailing Fine-robes from Qi (state).
White Powder Dye Black, Adorned with Jade Rings
Mixed Zhi Ruo (fragrant plants) To Satisfy Him,
Played "Chengyun", "Liuying",
"Jiushao", "Chenlu" (music) To Entertain Him.
Month after Month, Offering 'Jaded' Clothing,
Day after Day Presenting 'Jaded' Food.
Sorcerer Person Still Not Satisfied,
Not Able to be Otherwise, Then Stayed In (Tower).
Residing Not Too Long, Asked King to Travel Together.
King Held Sorcerer Person His Sleeve,
Rising And Upward Then, Centre Heaven Then Stopped.

3.1 King Mu of Zhou

40	暨及化人之宫。	Thus Arrived at The Sorcerer's Palace.
41	化人之宫构以金银，	Sorcerer Person, His Palace Built With Gold and Silver,
42	络以珠玉；	Networked With Pearls and Jade;
43	出云雨之上	Emerged Above The Cloud Rain
44	而不知下之据，	And Not Know What SupportingBelow,
45	望之若屯云焉。	Looking at It Like an Accumulation of Clouds that's.
46	耳目所观听，	Ears and Eyes Whatever Seen and Heard,
47	鼻口所纳尝，	Nose and Mouth Whatever Received and Tasted,
48	皆非人间之有。	All Not Found in The Human Sphere (of experiences).
49	王实以为清都、紫微、	King Believed These Were Qingdou, Ziwei,
50	钧天、广乐，	Juntian, Guangle, (palaces of Heaven)
51	帝之所居。	Emperor (of Heaven) His Place of Residence.
52	王俯而视之，	King Look-down And Saw Them (his own palaces)
53	其宫榭若累块积苏焉。	His Palaces Pavilions Like Heaps of Soil, Piles of Grass.
54	王自以居数十年	King Believed He Had Resided Tens of Years,
55	不思其国也。	Not Longing for Own State that's.
56	化人复谒王同游，	Sorcerer Person Again Asked King to Travel Together,
57	所及之处，	The Places Wherever Arrived,
58	仰不见日月，	Look-up Not See Sun or Moon,
59	俯不见河海。	Look-down Not See Rivers or Seas.
60	光影所照，	Lights and Shadows, Wherever Shone,
61	王目眩不能得视；	King's Eyes Dizzy Not Able to See;
62	音响所来，	Sounds and Echoes, Wherever From,
63	王耳乱不能得听。	King's Ears Confused, Not Able to Listen.
64	百骸六藏，	Hundred of Joints, the 6 Internal-organs,
65	悸而不凝。	Throbbing And Not Coordinated.
66	意迷精丧，	Senses Confused, Concentration Lost,
67	请化人求还。	Appealed to the Sorcerer Person, Requesting Return.
68	化人移之，	Sorcerer Person Pushed Him,
69	王若殒虚焉。	King Like Falling into Emptiness that's.
70	既寤，	Then Awoke,
71	所坐犹向者之处，	Where Sitting Still The Place Just Then,
72	侍御犹向者之人。	Imperial Servants Still The People Just Then.
73	视其前，	Looking In Front,
74	则酒未清，肴未晞。	Then Wine Not Cleared, Food Not Dried.
75	王问所从来。	King Asked Where (himself) Came From.
76	左右曰：	Left and Right Said:
77	"王默存耳。"	"King Silently Existing, that's."
78	由此穆王自失者	From Then King Mu Lost Himself that's
79	三月而复。	3 Months Then Recovered.
80	更问化人。	Again Asked the Sorcerer Person.
81	化人曰：	Sorcerer Person Said:

3.1 King Mu of Zhou

82	"吾与王神游也，	"I With King Spirit-traveling that's,
83	形奚动哉?	Body, Why Move, is-it-not ?"
84	且曩之所居，	Also Formerly That Wherever Resided,
85	奚异王之宫?	How Different from The King's Palace ?
86	曩之所游，	Formerly That Wherever Travelled,
87	奚异王之囿?	How Different From King's Garden ?
88	王闲恒有，	King Accustomed to Permanent Possessions,
89	疑暂亡。	Doubtful of Temporal Nothingness.
90	变化之极，	Changes and Transformation Their Extremes,
91	徐疾之间，	Slowly Quickly In Timing,
92	可尽模哉? "	How to Completely Capture (understand), is-it-not ?"
93	王大悦。	King Greatly Joyous.
94	不恤国事，	Not Concerned with State's Affairs,
95	不乐臣妾，	Not Enjoyed Subjects and Concubines,
96	肆意远游。	Unbridled Attention on Far-away Travels.
97	命驾八骏之乘，	Ordered to Drive The 8-Horses carriages,
98	右服骅骝而左绿耳，	Right Anchor Hualiu And Left Luer (name of horses),
99	右骖赤骥而左白仪，	Right Flank Chiji And Left Baiyi,
100	主车则造父为御，	Master (King's) Carriage, Then Zaofu As Driver,
101	离舄为右;	Liguo on The Right;
102	次车之乘，	Sub-Carriage The Occupancy,
103	右服渠黄而左逾轮，	Right Anchor Quhuang And Left Yulun,
104	左骖盗骊而右山子，	Left Flank Daoli And Right Shanzi,
105	柏夭主车，	Baiyao as carriage master,
106	参百为御，奔戎为右。	Canbai as driver, Benrong on the right.
107	驰驱千里，	Driving and moving thousand miles,
108	至于巨蒐氏之国。	Arriving At The State of Jusoushi.
109	巨蒐氏乃献	Jusoushi Then Offered
110	白鹄之血以饮王，	The Blood of White Swan For King's Drink,
111	具牛马之湩以洗王之足，	Collected Milk Of Cow and Horse To Wash King's feet,
112	及二乘之人。	Together With People of the 2 Carriages.
113	已饮而行，	Already Drank Then Move-on,
114	遂宿于昆仑之阿，	Continuing Slept At Foot of Kunlun (mountain),
115	赤水之阳。	Chishui (river) on the North Bank.
116	别日升昆仑之丘，	Next Day Climbed The Hills of Kunlun (mountain),
117	以观黄帝之宫，	To Visit The Palace of Huangdi,
118	而封之以诒后世。	And Tablet-written This To Bequeath Later Generations.
119	遂宾于西王母，	Continuing, be Guests To West King's Mother,
120	觞于瑶池之上。	Drank At The Yaochi Lake Above.
121	西王母为王谣，	West King's Mother Sang a Ballad For King,
122	王和之，	King Harmonized with Her,
123	其辞哀焉。	The Wording Sorrowful indeed.
124	西观日之所入。	Westward to Observe Sun Where It Set.
125	一日行万里。	One Day Travelled 10,000 Miles.

3.1 King Mu of Zhou

126 王乃叹曰：	King Then Sighing, Said:
127 "於乎！	"Yu' O' !
128 予一人不盈于德	To A Person Not Filled With Virtues
129 而谐于乐，	But Only Happy in Merriment,
130 后世其追数吾过乎！"	Generations After They Counted Up My Faults, O' !"
131 穆王几神人哉！	King Mu, Almost God-like Person, Amazing !
132 能穷当身之乐，	Able to Exhaust a Life-Time of Merry-making,
133 犹百年乃徂，	Till a 100 Years Then Died,
134 世以为登假焉。	Society Believed He Ascended Fairyland, that's.

Liezi Text Narrative
In the time of King Mu (Zhou), from the extreme west came a sorcerer person. L2
He could go through water fire, metal rocks, inverted mountain rivers, moved cities places. L4
Ride emptiness not falling, not blocked by solid matters, thousand of changes, no end. L7
As could change the forms of material, so also could change the minds of people. L9
King Mu respected him like god, served him like king. L11
Housed him in the summer palace, sacrificial feast offerings, female musicians to entertain. L14
Sorcerer regarded King's palace lowly and scanty not for living-in. L16
King's kitchen food fishy smell of ants not edible, concubines smell of goats not lovable. L18
King built alternatives, earth-work wood with intricate-carving, artful red white color. L21
All coffers emptied, tower name 'Centre of Heaven' rose 1000 meters on Mount Zhongnan. L24
Selected virgins from Zheng and Wei, those beauties all slender, seductive and gentle. L25
Perfume lotion, corrected beautiful brows, wearing hair-pin ear-rings, fine-dresses from A'. L27
Trailing fine-robes from Qi, white powdered face, dyed black brows, adorned jaded rings. L29
Mixed fragrant plants to satisfy sorcerer, played "Chengyun", "Liuying", "Jiushao" music. L32
Month after month offering jaded clothing, day after day presenting 'jaded' food. L34
The Sorcerer was still not satisfied, but nevertheless stayed in the Tower. L36
Not too long, asked King to travel together; King held his sleeve, rose to the Heaven Centre. L39
Thus arriving at sorcerer's palace which was built with gold silver, network with pearls jade. L42
Emerged above cloud rain, not knowing what support below, looked like accumulated clouds. L45
Ears heard, eyes seen, nose received, mouth tasted, all not of human experience. L48
King honestly believed it's Qingdou, Ziwei, Juntian, Guangle, palaces of the King of Heaven. L51
King looked down and saw his own palaces, pavilions like heap of soil and piles of grass. L53
King believed had resided for ten years in heavenly palace and not longing for own state. L55
Sorcerer again asked King to travel, all places arrived, looked up, saw no sun, no moon. L58
Looked down, no rivers, no seas, lights shadows wherever shone, King's dizzy not seeing. L61
Sounds echoes wherever from, King 's ears confused not able to listen. L63
Hundred of joints and the 6 internal-organs, throbbing and not coordinating. L65
Senses confused, concentration lost, so appealed to the sorcerer to return. L67
Sorcerer pushed King and King like falling down through emptiness. L69
Then awoke, still sitting at the original place, the imperial servant still the same people. L72
Looking in front, the wine not cleared, the food not dried. L74
King asked where he came from, and left right said: "King silently sitting that's." L77
From then King Mu lost himself for 3 months before recovering, again asked sorcerer. L80

3.1 King Mu of Zhou

Sorcerer said: "I and King traveled in spirit, so bodies had not moved, is-it-not ? L83
Also formerly wherever resided how different from King's palace ? L85
Formerly wherever traveled, how different from King's garden ? L87
King accustomed to permanent possession, doubtful of temporal nothingness. L89
Changes transformation extremes, slowly quickly how to completely understand is-it-not ?" L92
King greatly joyous; not concerned of state, not enjoy concubines, for unbridle traveling afar. L96
Ordered driving the 8 horses and carriages, right anchor Hualiu and left Luer (horses name). L98
Right Flank Chiji and left Baiyi, master car Zaofu as driver and Liguo on the right. L101
The sub-car carriage, right anchor Quhuang and left Yulun, left flank Daoli, right Shanzi. L104
Baiyao as car master, Canbai as driver, Benrong on the right. L106
Driving, moving a thousand miles, arriving at the state of Jusoushi. L108
Jusoushi offered blood of white swan as drink, milk of cow and horse to wash King's feet. L111
People of both carriages all drank then continued on, and slept at the foot of Mount Kunlun. L114
On the north bank of Chishui river; next day, they climbed the hills of Mount Kunlun. L106
Visited the palace of Huangdi and tablet-written this event to bequeath to later generations. L118
Continued to be guests to King Mother of the West, and drinking at Lake Yaochi above. L120
King Mother of the West sang a ballad, King harmonized her in response, the lyrics sad. L123
Then westward to observe where the Sun set, 10,000 miles a day. L125
King then sighing exclaimed: "Yu' O' ! L127
Not filled with virtues, only enjoyed merriments, generations after will count my faults !" L130
King Mu was almost god-like O' ! Spent a life-time merry-making and lived to 100 years. L133
Society all believed he had ascended up to fairyland, that's. L134

Comments:
3.1 King Mu of Zhou

Liezi exposed the danger of the sorcerer who was able to go through rocks, moved mountains.
The sorcerer was able to cause King Mu to empty his coffers in trying to satisfy his wishes.
The sorcerer was able to hypnotize King Mu, bringing him on a 'tour' of the Heavenly Kingdom.
Was able to convince King Mu to abandon his state and concubines for meditative spirit-travels.
Here the result was not bad as King Mu was able to enjoy his fantasy world for a hundred years.
At the same time his subjects were not disturb and were able to live in peace for a hundred years.
When he died citizens had not faulted him, merely believed he was god ascended into Heaven,

Liezi's description of King Mu's spirit-travels with sorcerer is highly imaginative and graphic.
With such fantasy descriptions, Liezi may be guilty of developing spiritual Daoism himself!
However Liezi is clearly not Delusional himself, merely wishing to expose sorcery.

Liezi seems to approve of King Mu enjoying his own life without disturbing his subjects.

Chapter 3. King Mu of Zhou (周穆王)

3.2 学幻   3.2 Budding Illusionist

01 老成子学幻于尹文先生,	*Laochengzi Learned Illusion With Yuwen Senior,*
02 三年不告。	Three Years Not Taught.
03 老成子请其过而求退。	Laochengzi Asked His Faults And Wished to Quit.
04 尹文先生揖而进之于室,	Yuwen Senior Bowed And Invited Him Into Study.
05 屏左右而与之言曰:	Calling-off left /right Then Speaking With Him Said:
06 "昔老聃之徂西也,	"Formerly, Laodan on His Journey Westward that's,
07 顾而告予曰:有生之气,	Turned And Informing Me Said: Has The Breath of Life,
08 有形之状,尽幻也。	Has The Condition of Form, All Illusions that's.
09 造化之所始,	Creation Transformation Their Whatever Beginning,
10 阴阳之所变者,	Yin Yang Their Whatever Products of Changes
11 谓之生,谓之死。	Call It Life, Call It Death.
12 穷数达变,	Exhaust the Numbers Attain the Changes,
13 因形移易者,	Because of Form Shifting and Changing that's
14 谓之化,谓之幻。	Call It Fantasy, Call It Illusion.
15 造物者其巧妙,其功深,	Creator of Matters, Its Art Subtle, Its Power Deep,
16 固难穷难终。	Hence Difficult to Exhaust, Difficult to End.
17 因形者其巧显,其功浅,	Because of The Form, Its Art Shows, Its Power Shallow,
18 故随起随灭。	Hence Following Its Rise, It Extinguished.
19 知幻化	Know Fantasy Transformation,
20 之不异生死也,	They are Not Different from Life and Death that's,
21 始可与学幻矣。	Can Start to Learn to be Illusionist indeed.
22 吾与汝亦幻也,	I With You Also are Illusions that's,
23 奚须学哉?"	Why the Need to Learn (be illusionist), is-it-not ?"
24 老成子归,	Laochengzi Returned,
25 用尹文先生之言深思三月,	With Yuwen Senior's Words, Deep thought for 3 Months,
26 遂能存亡自在,	Then Able to Live, to Die (in appearance) at Will,
27 幡校四时;	Changing and Adapting to the 4 Seasons;
28 冬起雷,夏造冰;	Winter Raising Thunder, Summer Making Ice;
29 飞者走,走者飞。	Those Flying to walk, Those Walking to Fly.
30 终身不箸其术,	Till Death, Not Show-off his Skills,
31 故世莫传焉。	Hence in Society, None Transfer (his skills) that's.
32 子列子曰:"善为化者,	Teacher Liezi Said: "Whoever Good At Illusion,
33 其道密庸,其功同人。	His Way Secretly Used, His Success Like Commoner.
34 五帝之德,三王之功,	Five Emperors Their Virtues, 3 Kings Their Successes,
35 未必尽智勇之力,	Not Necessary All are Efforts of Intelligence and Bravery,
36 或由化而成。	Maybe By Fantasy To Complete.
37 孰测之哉?"	Who Checks This, is-it-not ?"

3.2 Budding Illusionist

Liezi Text Narrative
Laochengzi learned the illusion with Yuwen Senior; for 3 years was not taught anything. L2
He asked what his faults were and wished to quit; Yuwen bowed, invited him into his study. L4
Calling off others confided to him said: "In the past, before Laozi started journey to the west.L6
He turned to inform me saying: has the breath of life, has the form of condition, all illusions. L8
Creation Transformation that started and Yin Yang that changed, call-it Life call-it Death. L11
Exhaust the numbers attain the changes, following form shifting and changing. L13
Call-it Transformation call-it Illusions. L14
Creator of Matters, its art subtlety, its power deep, hence difficult to exhaust to end. L16
That follows form, its device exposes, its power shallow, hence following its rise it demised. L19
Know Illusion Transformation not different from Life Death, then start to learn illusions.' L21
"I am with you also illusions that's, then why the need to learn to be an illusionist is-it-not?" L23

Laochengzi returned, then using Yuwen Senoir's words, deep thinking for 3 months. L25
Then able to take survival loss, self-at-easy, changes adapted to the 4 seasons. L27
In winter raised thunder, summer made ice, made those flying walk, those walking fly. L29
Till death did not show-off his skills, hence in society none can transfer his skills. L31
Liezi said: "Person good at illusions, his ways secretly used, his success like a commoner. L33
Five emperors' virtues and 3 kings' successes, not all efforts of intelligence and bravery. L35
Maybe their stories are completed by fantasizing, and who is to check the facts, is-it-not?" L36

Comments:
3.2 Budding Illusionist
Liezi brings in Laozi and Yuwen and their purported sayings to present the topic, Illusions of life.
Know Life and Death are illusions, You and I are also illusions, thus no need to go learn illusions.
He exposes the falsity of illusions as the illusionist practice secretly, skill or no skill, not transfer.
He doubts the ancient emperors, kings, whose virtues and successes could be legendary, illusions.
For he asks, "who is to check on the facts, is-it-not?"

The 'Big Bang', the universe (limited or unlimited), multiverses are also hypothetical thoughts.

Chapter 3. King Mu of Zhou (周穆王)

3.3 觉梦 | 3.3 Awake, Dreams

01	觉有八徵，梦有六候。	*Awake Has 8 Signs, Dream Has 6 States.*
02	奚谓八徵？	What Are the 8 Signs ?
03	一曰故，二曰为，	1 Call-it Affairs, 2 Call-it Action,
04	三曰得，四曰丧，	3 Call-it Success, 4 Call-it Lost,
05	五曰哀，六曰乐，	5 Call-it Sad, 6 Call-it Joy,
06	七曰生，八曰死。	7 Call-it Life, 8 Call-it Death.
07	此者八徵，形所接也。	These Are 8 Signs, Forms That Connect that's.
08	奚谓六候？	What Are the 6 States ?
09	一曰正梦，二曰愕梦，	1 Call-it Normal Dream, 2 Call-it Startle Dream,
10	三曰思梦，四曰寤梦，	3 Call-it Thought Dream, 4 Call-it Awaken Dream,
11	五曰喜梦，六曰惧梦。	5 Call-it Happy Dream, 6 Call-it Fear Dream,
12	此六者，神所交也。	These 6 Dreams, Meeting Of Spirits that's.
13	不识感变之所起者，	Not Know The Rising Cause of Feeling Changes,
14	事至则惑其所由然；	Affair Arrived Then Confused The Reason That Causes;
15	识感变之所起者，	Know The Rising Cause of Feeling Changes,
16	事至则知其所由然。	Affair Arrived Then Know the Reason That Causes.
17	知其所由然，	Know The Reason That Causes,
18	则无所怛。	Then No Whatever Fear.
19	一体之盈虚消息，	One Body Its Fulfilling Emptying Vanishing Resting,
20	皆通于天地，	All Connecting With Heaven and Earth,
21	应于物类。	Accord With Matter Kind.
22	故阴气壮，	Hence Yin (negative) Breath Strong,
23	则梦涉大水而恐惧；	Then Dream Venturing Big River, Alarming Terrifying;
24	阳气壮，	Yang (positive) Breath Strong,
25	则梦涉大火而燔爇；	Then Dream Venturing Big Fire Got Heated and Burnt;
26	阴阳俱壮，	Yin Yang Both Strong,
27	则梦生杀。	Then Dream Fighting for Survival.
28	甚饱则梦与，	Very Full Then Dream of Giving,
29	甚饥则梦取。	Very Hungry Then Dream of Taking.
30	是以以浮虚为疾者，	Thus Person Regards Drifting Emptiness As Sickness,
31	则梦扬；	Then Dream Uplifting;
32	以沈实为疾者，	Person Regards Sinking Solid As Illness,
33	则梦溺。	Then Dream of Drowning.
34	藉带而寝，	Pressed by Robes In Sleep,
35	则梦蛇；	Then Dream of Snake;
36	飞鸟衔发，	Flying Bird Pecking Hairs,
37	则梦飞。	Then Dream of Flying.
38	将阴梦火，	Getting Yin (cold) Dream of Fire,
39	将疾梦食。	Getting Sick Dreams of Food.
40	饮酒者忧，	Person Drinking Wine, Worried,
41	歌舞者哭。	Person Singing, Dancing, Cried.

3.3 Awake, Dreams

42 子列子曰：	Teacher Liezi Said:
43 "神遇为梦，形接为事。	"Spirits Meet Are Dreams, Forms Connect Are Affairs.
44 故昼想夜梦，神形所遇。	Thus Day Think Night Dream, Spirit Form They Meet.
45 故神凝者想梦自消。	Thus The Spirit Concentrate, Thought Dream Self Expire.
46 信觉不语，信梦不达，	Truly Awake No Words, True Dream No Connection,
47 物化之往来者也。	Matters Transformation Their Coming Going that's.
48 古之真人，其觉自忘，	Pure People Of Antiquity, Their Feeling Self Lost,
49 其寝不梦，几虚语哉？"	Their Sleep No Dream, Are Empty Words, Is-it-so ?"

Liezi Text Narrative
Person Awake has 8 Signs, in Dream has 6 States, and what are the 8 Signs ? L2
Call-it: 1 Affair, 2 Action, 3 Success, 4 Lost, 5 Sad, 6 Joy, 7 Life, 8 Death. L6
These 8 Signs are forms that connect that's; and what are the 6 States ? L8
Call-it: 1 Normal Dream, 2 Startle Dream, 3 Thought Dream, 4 Awaken Dream, L10
Call-it: 5 Happy Dream 6 Fear Dream; these 6 Dreams, meeting of Spirits that's. L12
Not knowing the initial cause of feeling changes, affair arrives then confuse for the reason; L14
Know the initial cause of feeling changes, affair arrives then know the reason. L16
Know the reason that causes, then no whatever fear. L18
One body, its fulfilling emptying vanishing resting, all connect with Heaven Earth, Matters. L21
Hence Yin (negative) Breath strong, then dream venturing big river, Alarming terrifying. L23
Yang (positive) Breath strong, then dream venturing big fire getting Hot and burnt. L25
Yin Yang both strong, then dream fighting for Survival. L27
Very full then dream of Giving, very hungry then dream of Taking. L29
Thus a person regards drifting emptiness as sickness then dreams of Uplifting. L31
Person regards sinking solid as illness, then dreams of Drowning. L33
Pressed by sleeping-robes then dream of Snake; has bird pecked hairs, dream of Flying. L37
Getting Yin (cold) dream of Fire, getting sick dream of Food. L39
Person drinks wine is Worried, a person singing and dancing is Crying (sad). L41
Teacher Liezi said: "Spirits meeting are Dreams, forms connecting are Affairs. L43
Day think night dream, spirit meeting form; thus spirit focus, thought dream self expire. L45
Truly awake no words, true dream no connection, matters transforming coming going that's. L47
Pure people of antiquity, their feeling Selfless, sleep dreamless, are these empty words ?" L49

Comments:
3.3 Awake, Dreams
Awake, we experience 8 signs, affair, action, success, loss, sadness, joy, life and death.
Dream, we experience 6 states, normal, startle, thought, awaking-light, joy and fear.
Our daily thoughts and experiences will affect our sleep and dreams, spirits forms connected.
Knowing the reasons for our feeling changes then we are not alarmed.
Liezi says pure people of antiquity their feeling selfless, no personal problems hence sleep well.
Lee Kuan Yew says problems don't go away, so have a good sleep to awake fresh to tackle them.

A rested mind is cleared to better see solutions in problems, so just relax and take a break.

Chapter 3. King Mu of Zhou (周穆王)

| 3.4 古莽之国 | 3.4 **Dreamlands** |

01 西极之南隅有国焉，　　　Extreme West And South Corner Has State that's,
02 不知境界之所接，　　　　Not Know Boundary Lines Where They Connect,
03 **名古莽之国。**　　　　　**Named State of Gumangzhi.**
04 阴阳之气所不交，　　　　Yin Yang These Air Where Not Interact,
05 故寒暑亡辨；　　　　　　Hence Winter Summer Not Differentiate;
06 日月之光所不照，　　　　Sun Moon Their Light Where Not Shine,
07 故昼夜亡辨。　　　　　　Hence Day Night Not Differentiate.
08 其民不食不衣而多眠。　　The Citizen Not Eating Not Dressing But More Sleep.
09 五旬一觉，　　　　　　　Five Xun (10-days) One Awakening,
10 以梦中所为者实，　　　　Regards In Dream Whatever The Action is Solid (true),
11 觉之所见者妄。　　　　　Awake, That Whatever Seen is Fantasy (untrue).
12 四海之齐，　　　　　　　Four Seas The Centre,
13 谓中央之国，　　　　　　Call-it State of Center Middle,
14 跨河南北，　　　　　　　Astride Yellow River South North,
15 越岱东西，　　　　　　　Over Mount Tai East West,
16 万有余里。　　　　　　　10,000 And More Miles.
17 其阴阳之审度，　　　　　The Yin Yang Their Correct Measure,
18 故一寒一暑；　　　　　　Hence One Cold (winter) One Hot (summer);
19 昏明之分察，　　　　　　Darkness Brightness Their Separate Observation,
20 故一昼一夜。　　　　　　Hence One Day One Night.
21 其民有智有愚。　　　　　The Citizens Have Cleverness Have Stupidity.
22 万物滋殖，　　　　　　　All Matters Luxuriantly Propagating,
23 才艺多方。　　　　　　　Talents Artistry Multi Facets.
24 有君臣相临，　　　　　　Have King Minister Mutually Consulting,
25 礼法相持。　　　　　　　Etiquette Laws Mutually Supporting.
26 其所云为不可称计。　　　All Those Sayings Actions Not Able Mention Count.
27 一觉一寐，　　　　　　　One Awake One Sleep,
28 以为觉之所为者实，　　　Regards That Awake Whatever Actions, That's Solid,
29 梦之所见者妄。　　　　　Dreaming Its Whatever Seen, That's Fantasy.
30 东极之北隅有国，　　　　Extreme East And North Corner Has State,
31 曰阜落之国。　　　　　　Call-it State Of Fuluo.
32 其土气常燠，　　　　　　The Soil Air Always Hot-inside (volcanic!),
33 日月馀光之照，　　　　　Sun Moon Residual Light That Shine,
34 其土不生嘉苗。　　　　　The Soil Not Grow Good Crops.
35 其民食草根木实，　　　　The Citizen Eat Grass Tree-roots Fruits,
36 不知火食。　　　　　　　Not Know Fire-cooked Food.
37 性刚悍，　　　　　　　　Nature Tough Fierce,
38 强弱相藉，　　　　　　　Strong Weak Mutually Contesting,
39 贵胜而不尚义；　　　　　Value Victory And Not Favor Justice;
40 多驰步，　　　　　　　　More Travel Tracking,
41 少休息，　　　　　　　　Less Stopping Resting,
42 常觉而不眠。　　　　　　Always Awake And Not Sleep

3.4 Dreamlands

Liezi Text Narrative
Extreme west south corner, where boundary lines are unknown, is state name Gumang. L3
Where Yin Yang their energies are not interacting, hence winter summer are not differentiated. L5
Where the sun moon their light did not shine, hence day night not differentiated. L7
The citizens not eating, not dressing but more Sleeping, 5 times 10-days one Awakening. L9
Regard whatever action done in Dream as true and whatever seen while Awake as untrue. L11

Surrounded by 4 seas, call-it Center Middle state, astride Yellow River to the south and north; L14
Extending across Mount Tai to the east west, for more than 10,000 miles. L16
The Yin Yang in right measure, hence one cold (winter) one hot (summer); L18
Darkness Brightness their separate observation, hence one day and one night. L20
The citizens, some have cleverness and some are stupid. L21
All matters luxuriant and propagating, there are multi-talents and multifacet artistry. L23
Have the king and minister in consultation, with etiquette and laws mutually supporting. L25
All those sayings, actions not able to mention or count. L26
Awake or Sleep, regard action while Awake is true, and whatever seen in Dream is untrue. L29

Extreme east north corner, has state call-it State of Fuluo. L31
The soil air is always hot inside (volcano!), sun moon residual light, not growing good crops. L34
The citizens eat grass tree-roots fruits, not knowing fire-cooked food. L36
Tough fierce nature, strong and weak mutual contesting, value victory not favor justice. L39
More travelling tracking, less stopping resting, always awake and not sleepy. L42

Comments:
3.4 Dreamlands
At the extreme west south corner, Gumang citizens experience no clear day/night, winter/summer.
Sleep 50 days one awakening, they regard action in Dream as true, what is seen awake as untrue.
Surrounded by 4 seas, Middle state citizens have regular day/night, winter/summer, law and order.
With regular awake/sleep patterns regard action while awake as true, that seen in Dream as untrue.
At the extreme north, Fuluo citizens have minimal sun/moon light, no crops, no cooked food.
Tracking incessantly, always awake with no sleep, they are fierce, value victory not value justice.
These many descriptions seem bizarre but to a certain extent are not impossible phenomena.
Bears are known to hibernate for months in winter, deep-jungle natives go naked eating raw meat.
Liezi from the privileged Middle Kingdom, makes no comparison, speaks no ill of others.
He seems satisfied to ascribe differences to weather and geography of the land, not to the people.
Liezi displays of understanding and tolerance in treatment of people of other states, is exemplary.

For world peace, we can take a lesson from Liezi in mutual understanding and tolerance.

Chapter 3. King Mu of Zhou (周穆王)

3.5 欲觉梦兼之？   3.5 Wishing Winner Takes All ?

01	周之尹氏大治产，	Mr Yin of Zhou administered Big Business,
02	其下趣役者	Those Scurrying Laborers Under Him
03	侵晨昏而弗息。	Continued Day Night With No Rest.
04	有老役夫，筋力竭矣，	Had Old Servant Man, Sinewy Strength Exhausted,
05	而使之弥勤。	But still Used Him Fully Frequently.
06	昼则呻呼而即事，	Daily Then Groaning Hard-breathing to Finish Tasks,
07	夜则昏惫而熟寐。	Nightly Then Dull Tired Hence Slumber Sleep.
08	精神荒散，	Spirit Mind Bewildered Scattered,
09	昔昔梦为国君。	Night after Night Dreaming As King of State.
10	居人民之上，	Positioned On Top of Citizens,
11	总一国之事。	Controlled All The Affairs of State.
12	游燕宫观，	Touring the Gardens Dining in the Palaces,
13	恣意所欲，	Unrestrained Wished Whatever Desires
14	其乐无比。	His Joy No Comparison.
15	觉则复役。	Awoke Then Returned to Toiling.
16	人有慰喻其勤者，	People Had Comforting Regards of His Industry that's,
17	役夫曰：	Servant Person Said:
18	"人生百年，	"People Living 100 Years,
19	昼夜各分。	Day Night Separately Divided (equal).
20	吾昼为仆虏，苦则苦矣；	I Daily As Servant Prisoner, Suffer And Suffer indeed;
21	夜为人君，其乐无比。	Nightly As People's King, The Joy No Comparison.
22	何所怨哉？"	What Reason to Complain Is-it-not ?"
23	尹氏心营世事，	Mr Yin Heart on Managing World Affairs,
24	虑钟家业，	Worries Devoted to Family Business,
25	心形俱疲，	Heart Body Totally Tired,
26	夜亦昏惫而寐。	Nightly Also Dull Tired Then Sleep.
27	昔昔梦为人仆，	Night after Night Dreaming As Somebody's Servant,
28	趋走作役，	Rushing About Working as Laborer,
29	无不为也；	None Not Doing (all tasks) that's;
30	数骂杖挞，	Berated Scolding Stick Beating,
31	无不至也。	None Not Received that's.
32	眠中哼呓呻呼，	In Sleep Dream-talking Groaning Hard-breathing,
33	彻旦息焉。	Until Dawn then Stop indeed.
34	尹氏病之，以访其友。	Mr Yin Sick of This, So Visited His Friend.
35	友曰：	Friend Said:
36	"若位足荣身，	"Like Position Enough for Self Honor,
37	资财有余，	Resource Wealth Have Excess,
38	胜人远矣。	Far Superior to Others that's.
39	夜梦为仆，	Nightly Dream of Being Servant,
40	苦逸之复，	Suffering and Leisure Their Reversal,

107

3.5 Wishing Winner Takes All ?

41 数之常也。	This Natural Accounting that's.
42 若欲觉梦兼之,	***Like Desiring Awake Dream Having Both,***
43 岂可得邪？"	How Possible Be Attained Is-it-not ?"
44 尹氏闻其友言,	Mr Yin Heard His Friend's Words,
45 宽其役夫之程,	Relaxing His Servant Man's Works,
46 减己思虑之事,	Reduces Thinking Worrying Of Own Affairs
47 疾并少间。	Sufferings Together Slightly Relieve.

Liezi Text Narrative
Mr Yin of Zhou managed big business, servants under him labored day and night with no rest. L3
There was an old servant all sinewy and exhausted, but still used him fully, frequently. L5
Daily groaning to finish tasks, nightly mind and body tired out went into slumber sleep, L7
Spirit thoughts bewildered and scattered, nightly dreaming as king of the state. L9
Positioned on top of citizens, controlling all affairs of state. L11
Touring the garden, dining in the palaces, his joy knew no comparison. L14
Awoke then back to toiling; people comforted and commended him regarding his industry. L16
Servant person said: "People living 100 years, day and night separately divided (equal). L19
I daily as a servant prisoner, suffering; nightly as people's king, joy had no comparison. L21
So what reason to complain, is-it-not ?" L22

Mr Yin heartedly managed world affairs, and worries concentrated on the family business. L24
Heart Body totally tired, nightly also mind dull and body exhausted, went to sleep. L26
Nightly dreaming as someone's servant, rushing about as laborer, working on all tasks. L29
Berated, scolding, beating with the stick, none not had been received that's. L31
In sleep, dream-talking, groaning, hard-breathing until dawn then stopped indeed. L33
Mr Yin sick of this, went to visit his friend; and his friend said: L35
"Like position enough to win honor, resource wealth has excess far superior to others. L38
Nightly dreams of being a servant, suffering the reverse of leisure, this is natural accounting. L41
Desiring to have it good both ways, awake and in dream, how possible to attain, is-it-not ?" L43
Mr Yin heard his friend's words, and lightened his servant man's workload. L45
Reduced thinking and worrying of own affairs, and all suffering together slightly relieved. L47

Comments:
3.5 Wishing Winner Takes All ?
Old servant had a stoic philosophy, accepting his fate, working hard in the day without complaint.
Master of his suffering in the day, he remained a master of contentment at night and slept well.
Yin had a desire philosophy of greed, ever maximizing profit from his subordinates mercilessly.
Servant to his desires in the day, he remained a servant to his worries at night, did not sleep well.
Friend's words enlightened him to lessen loads on servants and himself, together less suffering.
Generally when one works hard, one is rewarded with a good appetite and enjoyment of food.
When one is lazy and does not work, one is punished with no appetite and no enjoyment of food.

Nature is fair and winners cannot take all, for there is payback time when we take more.

Chapter 3. King Mu of Zhou (周穆王)

3.6 复梦分人鹿 — 3.6 Dividing Deer of Dreams

01	郑人有薪于野者，	Person from Zheng Getting Firewood From Countryside,
02	遇骇鹿，	Encountered Startle Deer,
03	御而击之，毙之。	Chased And Struck It, Killed It.
04	恐人见之也，	Afraid Others See It that's,
05	遽而藏诸隍中，	Quickly Then Hid All In a Ditch (dry),
06	覆之以蕉，	Covered It With Leaves-branches,
07	不胜其喜。	His Joy Not Surpassed.
08	俄而遗其所藏之处，	Shortly Then Forgot The Place Where Hidden,
09	遂以为梦焉。	Satisfy It Was a Dream indeed.
10	顺途而咏其事。	And Along the Way Chanting This Matter.
11	傍人有闻者，	Those Nearby a Person Had Heard,
12	用其言而取之。	Using His Words And Collected It (deer).
13	既归，告其室人曰：	When Returned (home), Told His Wife Said:
14	"向薪者梦得鹿	"Just then Woodcutter Dreamt Got a Deer,
15	而不知其处；	But Not Know The Place;
16	吾今得之，彼直真梦者矣。"	I Now Got It, He Made a Real Dream indeed."
17	室人曰：	House Person (wife) Said:
18	"若将是梦见薪者	"Like You Dream Seeing Woodcutter
19	之得鹿邪？	Who Got Deer Is-it-not ?
20	讵有薪者邪？	How Has Woodcutter Is-it-not ?
21	今真得鹿，	Now Really Got Deer,
22	是若之梦真邪？"	Is Like Your Dream is Real Is-it-not ?"
23	夫曰："吾据得鹿，	Husband Said: "I Evidently Got Deer,
24	何用知彼梦我梦邪？"	Why Need to Know His Dream or My Dream Is-it-not ?"
25	薪者之归，不厌失鹿，	Woodcutter His Return (home), Not Willing Lost Deer,
26	其夜真梦藏之之处，	That Night Really Dreamt Hiding It The Place,
27	又梦得之之主。	Also Dreamt Got It The Owner.
28	爽旦，案所梦而寻得之。	Early Dawn, According What Dreamt Found and Got It.
29	遂讼而争之，	Then Litigation And Contesting It,
30	归之士师。	Referred It to the Scholar Judge.
31	士师曰：	Scholar Judge Said:
32	"若初真得鹿，妄谓之梦；	"Like Initially, Really Got Deer, Rashly Called It Dream;
33	真梦得鹿，妄谓之实。	Really Dreamt Got Deer, Rashly Called It True.
34	彼真取若鹿，而与若争鹿。	He Really Got The Deer, And With Him Contest Deer.
35	室人又谓梦认人鹿，	Wife Also Call-it Dream Recognition of Person Deer,
36	无人得鹿。	No Person Got Deer.
37	今据有此鹿，请二分之。"	Now Evidently Has This Deer, Please Divide It by 2."
38	以闻郑君。	With This Informed King of Zheng (state).
39	郑君曰："嘻！	King of Zheng Said: " Hee !
40	士师将复梦分人鹿乎？"	*Scholar Judge Is Dividing Person's Deer in a Dream ?"*
41	访之国相。	Visited The State Senior Minister.

3.6 Dividing Deer of Dreams

42 国相曰：	Senior Minister Said:
43 "梦与不梦，	"Dream And No Dream,
44 臣所不能辨也。	What Subject Not Able to Differentiate that's.
45 欲辨觉梦，	Wishing to Differentiate Awake or Dream,
46 唯黄帝孔丘。	Only Huangdi (Yellow Emperor) Kongqiu (Confucius).
47 今亡黄帝孔丘，	Now Demised and Huangdi Kongqiu,
48 孰辨之哉?	Who can Differentiate This Is-it-not ?
49 且恂士师之言可也。"	Then Tentatively Accept Scholar Judge's Words that's."

Liezi Text Narrative

Person of Zheng collecting firewood from the countryside, startled a deer, chased and killed it. L3
Afraid others see it, quickly hid all in a dry ditch, covered it with leaves branches, overjoyed. L7
Shortly then forgot the place where it was hidden, so satisfied that it was just a dream. L9
Along the way chanting this matter, and a person among the passers-by heard him. L11
According to his words found the deer and collected it; returned home, told his wife said: L13
"Just then a woodcutter dreamt obtaining a deer and not know the place; L15
I now got it, so he did have a real dream indeed." L16
House person (wife) said: "Like you dreamt seeing a woodcutter got a deer is-it-not ? L19
How has this woodcutter is-it-not ? Now really got deer, is like your dream is real is-it-not ?"L22
Husband said: "I evidently got a deer, why do I need to know his dream or my dream, right?"L24
Woodcutter on his return (home), not willing to lose deer, that night dreamt of hiding place. L26
Also dreamt of the owner who got deer; early dawn, according to dream, found the person. L28
Then in litigation, contesting for return of the deer, so referred to scholar-judge. L30

Scholar judge said: "Like initially, really got deer, and rashly called it a dream; L32
Dreamt of getting deer, rashly called it True; collector really got it and now contested deer. L34
Wife also called it dream recognition of person and deer and nobody got deer. L36
Now evidently has this deer, please divide it by 2." L37
Informed, King of Zheng, said, "Hee ! scholar judge again in a dream divides deer persons ?" L40
Consulted, senior minister of state said, "Dream or no dream, subject unable to differentiate. L44
Wishing to differentiate awake or dream, only the Yellow Emperor, Confucius, was capable. L46
Now Huangdi (Yellow Emperor) Kongqui (Confucius) are demised, who can differentiate ? L48
Thus tentatively accept scholar judge's words, that's." L49

Comments:
3.6 Dividing Deer of Dreams

Woodcutter encountered deer, killed it, hid it and forgot his hiding place, thought it all a dream.
Unwilling to lose deer, he dreamt of the man who got it, and did find the man.
Wife said the man got the deer in his dream and so there was no real person who got the deer.
Hearing accounts of dreams of 2 parties, third party scholar-judge is certainly confused!
But the deer is evidently here and real, so scholar-judge suggested dividing deer for both parties.

Litigation cases are doubts and confusions, so it is fair that the winner should not take all.

Chapter 3. King Mu of Zhou (周穆王)

3.7 病忘	3.7 Memory Lost
01 宋阳里华子中年病忘，	*Song-era, Yangli Huazi at Middle Age Lost Memory,*
02 朝取而夕忘，	Morning Taken and Night Forgotten,
03 夕与而朝忘；	Night Given And Morning Forgotten;
04 在途则忘行，	On Road Then Forgotten Go-where,
05 在室而忘坐；	At Home Then Forgotten to Sit;
06 今不识先，	Now Not Remember Past,
07 后不识今。	Afterwards Not Remember Present.
08 阖室毒之。	Thus Whole Family Suffered.
09 谒史而卜之，弗占；	Visited Official For His Divination, Not Revealing;
10 谒巫而祷之，弗禁；	Visited Sorcerer For His Blessing, No Containment;
11 谒医而攻之，弗已。	Visited Doctor For His Treatment, Not Resolved.
12 鲁有儒生	Lu (state) Has Confucian Scholar
13 　自媒能治之，	Self Promotion Able to Cure Him.
14 华子之妻子以居产之半	Huazi's wife With Half of Residential Estate (value)
15 　请其方。	Pay for The Cure.
16 儒生曰：	Confucian Scholar Said:
17 "此固非卦兆之所占，	"This Surely Not Hexagram Sign That Can Divine,
18 非祈请之所祷，	Not Prayer Beseech That Can Bless,
19 非药石之所攻。	Not Medicine Stone That Can Treat.
20 吾试化其心，变其虑，	I Try Resolve His Heart (feelings), Change His Worries,
21 庶几其瘳乎！"	Ordinarily can Anticipate His Healing O' !"
22 于是试露之，而求衣；	That Was Try Exposing Him, And he asked Clothing;
23 饥之，而求食；	Starving Him, And he asked for Food;
24 幽之，而求明。	Kept Him in the Dark, And he asked for Light.
25 儒生欣然告其子曰：	Confucian Scholar Joyous Informing The Son Said:
26 "疾可已也。	"Illness Can be Cured that's.
27 然吾之方密，	But My Treatment Is Secret,
28 传世不以告人。	Transferred Generations, Not Disclosed To Others.
29 试屏左右，	Try Dismiss Left Right (all people),
30 独与居室七日。"	Stay Alone In-house With him 7 Days."
31 从之。	Agreed to This.
32 莫知其所施为也，	Not Know What He Applied or Did that's,
33 而积年之疾一朝都除。	And The Illness Chronic for Years, All Gone in One Day.
34 华子既悟，乃大怒，	Huazi With Realization, Thereupon Greatly Angered,
35 黜妻罚子，	Expelled Wife Punished Son,
36 操戈逐儒生。	Grasped Axe to Chase-out Confucian Scholar.
37 宋人执而问其以。	People of Song Held And Asked Him Why.
38 华子曰：	Huazi Said:
39 "曩吾忘也，	"Formerly I Forgetful that's,
40 荡荡然	Swinging Free Naturally
41 　不觉天地之有无。	Not Feeling If Heaven Earth Have or Have-not.
42 今顿识既往，	Now Instantly Know The Past,

3.7 Memory Lost

43	数十年来存亡、	Several Tens of Year Along Life/Death,
44	得失、哀乐、好恶，	Gain /loss, Sadness /Happiness, Good /Evil,
45	扰扰万绪起矣。	Troubling Troubling 10,000 Clues Arise indeed.
46	吾恐将来之存亡、	I Fear The Coming Future Of Survival Death,
47	得失、哀乐、	Gain /Loss, Sadness /Happiness,
48	好恶之乱吾心如此也，	Good /Evil They Confuse My Heart Like This that's,
49	须臾之忘，	A Moment Of Forgetfulness,
50	可复得乎？"	Possible to Have Again, right ?
51	子贡闻而怪之，	Zigong Heard And Surprise of It,
52	以告孔子。	With-it Informed Kongzi (Confucius).
53	孔子曰：	Kongzi Said:
54	"此非汝所及乎！"	"This Not You That can Attain O' !"
55	顾谓颜回纪之。	Turned and Asked Yanhui to Record It.

Liezi Text Narrative

Song era, Yangli Huazi at middle age, memory lost, morning taken, night forgotten. L2
Night given morning forgotten; on the road forgotten to go-where, in house forgotten to sit L4
Now not remember the past, afterwards not remember the present; the whole family suffered. L8
Visited official diviner not revealing, visited sorcerer for blessing no containment of illness. L10
Visited doctor for treatment, not resolved; L11
Confucian Scholar from State of Lu, self promoting, able to cure him. L13
Huazi's wife was willing to pay half the residential estate value for the cure. L15
The confucian scholar said, "This surely has no Hexagram sign that can forecast. L17
Not prayer beseech that can bless, not medical powder that can treat. L19
I try resolving his heart (feelings), change his worries, ordinarily can expect his healing O' !" L21
That was exposing him, and he asked for clothing; starving him, and he asked for food; L23
Kept him in the dark , and he asked for light. L24
The confucian scholar joyously informed the son said: "Illness can be cured that's. L26
But my treatment is secret, transmitted for generations, not disclosed to others. L28.
Try to dismiss left right (all people), will stay alone in-house with him for 7 days." L30
Family agreed; Not knew what he applied or did, and chronic illness all gone in a day. L33
Huazi now remembered, thereupon greatly angered; expelled wife and punished son. L35
Grasp axe to chase-out confucian scholar; people of Song held him to ask why. L37
Huazi said, "Formerly I forgetful that's, swinging free naturally not feeling have or have-not.L41
Now instantly knows the past, tens of years of existence/death, gain/loss, sad/joy, good/evil. L44
Troubling troubling 10,000 clues arise indeed; I fear the coming future of survival/death. L46
Gain/loss, sadness/happiness, good/evil, they confuse my heart like this, that's; L48
A moment of forgetfulness, possible to have again, yes/no ?" L50
Zigong heard and was surprised, went to inform Kongzi (Confucius). L52
Confucius said: "This is not what you can comprehend right !" L54
Then turned and asked Yanhui to record this. L55

Comments:
3.7 Memory Lost
Middle-aged Huazi lost memory, on the road forgot where to go etc., the whole family suffered.
A confucian scholar cured him, was angry, expelled wife, punished son, and chased out scholar.
With memory now, he suffered again years of gain/loss, sadness/joy, good/evil, fear of the future.
Troubled life of a confucian with worries contrasts with the blissful daoist with no worries !

Chapter 3. King Mu of Zhou (周穆王)

3.8 迷罔之疾   3.8 Delusion Sickness

01	秦人逄氏有子，	Person of Qin (state), Mr Pang Had Son,
02	少而惠，	Young And Kindly,
03	**及壮而有迷罔之疾。**	***Till Prime age Then Had Delusion Sickness.***
04	闻歌以为哭，	Hearing Song Regarded As Crying,
05	视白以为黑，	Seeing White Regarded As Black,
06	飨香以为朽，	Smelling Fragrant Regarded As Stinky,
07	尝甘以为苦，	Tasting Sweet Regarded As Bitter,
08	行非以为是：	Conduct Evil Regarded As Correct:
09	意之所之，	His Ideas His Reasons,
10	天地、四方，	Heaven Earth, 4 Regions,
11	水火、寒暑，	Water Fire, Winter Summer,
12	无不倒错者焉。	None That was Not Incorrect Reverted indeed.
13	杨氏告其父曰：	Mr Yang Informed His Father Said:
14	"鲁之君子多术艺，	"Lu's Gentleman has Many Tricks and Arts,
15	将能已乎？	Will be Able to Cure him O' ?
16	汝奚不访焉？"	You Why Not go Visit, that's ?"
17	其父之鲁，过陈，	The Father Went to Lu (state), Passing Chen (state)
18	遇老聃，	Encountered Laodan (Laozi)
19	因告其子之证。	Hence Informed of His Son's Sickness.
20	老聃曰：	Laodan (Laozi) Said:
21	"汝庸知汝子之迷乎？	"How You Know Your Son's Delusion, right ?
22	今天下之人	Today The World's People
23	皆惑于是非，	All Confuse in Right /Wrong,
24	昏于利害。	Dull In Gain /Loss.
25	同疾者多，	Many People Similar Sickness,
26	固莫有觉者。	Hence None Who Has Awareness.
27	且一身之迷不足倾一家，	And 1 Person's Delusion Not Enough to Upset 1 Family,
28	一家之迷不足倾一乡，	1 Family's Delusion Not Enough to Upset 1 Village,
29	一乡之迷不足倾一国，	1 Village's Delusion Not Enough to Upset 1 State,
30	一国之迷不足倾天下。	1 State's Delusion Not Enough to Upset The World.
31	天下尽迷，孰倾之哉？	The World All Delusional, Who is to Upset It, right ?
32	向使天下之人	If Make The World's People
33	其心尽如汝子，	Their Hearts All Like Your Son,
34	汝则反迷矣。	You Then in Contrast is Delusion indeed.
35	哀乐、声色、臭味、是非，	Sad /Joy, Sound /Color, Smell /Taste, Right /Wrong,
36	孰能正之？	Who Able to Correct These ?
37	且吾之此言未必非迷，	And I These Words of Mine Not Certain Not Delusion,
38	而况鲁之君子迷之邮者，	And Further Lu's Gentleman Delusion Is More So,
39	焉能解人之迷哉？	How Able to Relieve People's Delusion is-it-not ?
40	荣汝之粮，	Carry Your Own Rations,
41	不若遄归也。"	Might as well Hurry Home that's."

3.8 Delusion Sickness

Liezi Text Narrative
Person of Qin, Mr Pang had a son, young kindly till prime age then had Delusion sickness. L3
Heard singing as crying, saw white as black, smelled fragrant as stinky, tasted sweet as bitter. L17
Regarded evil conducts as correct; his ideas, reasons, Heaven/Earth, 4 regions, water /fire. L10
Winter /summer, none that's not incorrect and reverted indeed. L12
Mr Yang informed his father: "State of Lu, the gentleman there has many arts and tricks. L14
Sure able to cure him, right ? So why don't you go visit to consult him ?" L16
The father went to the state of Lu, passing the state of Chen, encountered Laodan (Laozi). L18
Hence informed Laodan of his son's illness. L19
Laodan (Laozi) said, "How do you know your son's Delusion is true or false ? L21
Today, the world's people are all confused about Right /Wrong, all dull in Gain /Loss. L24
Many people have similar sickness, thus none has awareness of this problem. L26
1 person's Delusion, not enough to upset a family, 1 family's Delusion cannot upset a village. L28
1 village's Delusion, not enough to upset the state, 1 state's Delusion cannot upset the world. L30
The world all Delusional, then who is to resolve this Delusion is-it-not ? L31
If the world's people, their hearts all like your son, then you are the Delusional one indeed. L34
Sadness /joy, sound /color, smell/taste, right /wrong, who is able to standardize these ? L36
Furthermore these words of mine are not certain that are not Delusion too. L37
Lu's gentleman who is more confused, how does he resolve people's Delusion, that's ?" L39
So might as well carry your rations, and hurry home, that's."

Comments:
3.8 Delusion Sickness
Liezi again pitches the philosophy of daoist Laozi against the confucian gentleman of Lu state.
Who is to set the standard of right /wrong, sadness /joy, sound /color, smell /taste ?
Who says driving on the left is correct and driving on the right is wrong ?
Durians prohibited on public transports are fine, but many of us do love the smell of durians !
Now we know some are born color blind, with different taste buds etc., we can be different.
However evil conduct cannot be tolerated and must be contained with reasonable laws and orders.
Rioters in Hongkong are criminals in vandalism, for others too have rights to common properties.

Confused behaviors may be tolerated, but not denying the equal and lawful rights of others.

Chapter 3. King Mu of Zhou (周穆王)

3.9 还本国 — 3.9 Home Return

01	燕人生于燕，	Yanren (person of Yan) Born In Yan (state),
02	长于楚，	Grow-up In Chu (state),
03	**及老而还本国。**	**When Old And Returning to Own State.**
04	过晋国，	Crossing State of Jin,
05	同行者诳之，	The Fellow Traveller Lied to Him,
06	指城曰：	Pointing at City-wall Said:
07	"此燕国之城。"	"This The City-wall of Yan State"
08	其人愀然变容。	The Person Changed Countenance Naturally Sorrowful.
09	指社曰：	Pointing at Temple Said:
10	"此若里之社。"	"This Like The Temple of Village."
11	乃喟然而叹。	Thereupon Naturally Mournful And Sighed.
12	指舍曰：	Pointing At House Said:
13	"此若先人之庐。"	"This Like The Abodes of Ancestors."
14	乃涓然而泣。	Thereupon Naturally Wept And Sobbed.
15	指垄曰：	Pointing at Cemetery Said:
16	"此若先人之冢。"	"This Like The Tombs of Ancestors."
17	其人哭不自禁。	The Person Cried Uncontrollably.
18	同行者哑然大笑，	The Fellow Traveller Naturally Speechless in Big Laugh,
19	曰："予昔绐若，	Said: "Just Given is Like Deceiving,
20	此晋国耳。"	This State of Jin That's."
21	其人大惭。	The Person Greatly Ashamed.
22	及至燕，	Then Arrived at Yan (state)
23	真见燕国之城社，	Truly Saw State of Yan's City-wall and Temple,
24	真见先人之庐冢，	Truly Saw the Cemetery and Tombs of Ancestors,
25	悲心更微。	Griefs of Heart further weaken.

Liezi Text Narrative

Yanren was born in the state of Yan, grow-up in Chu, and when old returned to own state. L3
Crossing the state of Jin, fellow traveller lied to him and pointing to the city-wall said: L6
"This the city-wall of the state of Yan"; Yanren changed countenance naturally sorrowfully. L8
Pointing at the temple said, "This the village temple"; thereupon naturally mournfully sighed. L11
Pointing at the house said, "These the abodes of ancestors."; thereupon he wept and sobbed. L14
Pointing at the cemetery said, " These the tombs of ancestors."; Yanren cried uncontrollably. L17
Fellow traveller laughingly said: "Just been deceiving you, this is the State of Jin." L20
Yanren was greatly ashamed, then upon arrival at the State of Jin. L22
Truly looking at Yan's city-wall and temple, truly looking at cemetery tombs of ancestors. L24
Yanren's griefs of heart further weaken. L25

Comments:

3.9 Home Return

With this narrative Liezi shows us that our emotions and realities are separate entities.
Warns us that our feelings can so easily be manipulated with false information close to our heart.
Realities and emotions are separate entities; false information close to heart easily deceives.

Chapter 3. King Mu of Zhou (周穆王)

Summary:

3.1 **King Mu of Zhou (周穆王):** worshipped a sorcerer of immense power like moving cities.
   He enjoyed a hundred years of astro-travels until death, leaving his citizens to live in peace.

3.2 **Budding Illusionist (学幻):** Yuwen said, "You and I are illusions, thus no need to learn."
   Laochengzi meditated on these words, became an 'illusionist' but never showed his skills!

3.3 **Awake Dreaming (觉梦):** There are 8 signs of awareness in life and 6 states of dreams.
   Daily life experience affects our dreams, thus knowing the reasons we are not alarmed.

3.4 **Dreamlands (古莽之国):** Liezi descriptions of Gumang State, Middle State, Fuluo State.
   Day/night differences caused more, regular or no sleep and different perceptions of reality.

3.5 **Wishing Winner Takes All ? (欲觉梦兼之?):** Narrative was on Yinshi and his stoic servant.
   After daily labor, the stoic elder enjoyed his sleep; while selfish Yinshi labored in his sleep.

3.6 **Dividing Deer of Dreams (复梦分人鹿):** Woodcutter forgot where he hid the deer he killed.
   Dreamed of the man who recovered it, sued for its return, and was awarded half of it.

3.7 **Memory Lost (病忘):** Huazi with memory lost was living the carefree life of a daoist.
   A confucian cured him, and with past memory of anxieties, he expelled his wife and son.

3.8 **Delusion Sickness (迷罔之疾):** Satire of a son having delusion, regarding white as black.
   On the way to Lu, father met Laozi who said the son may be right and we are all wrong !

3.9 **Home Return (还本国):** Highly emotional, Yanren was tricked by friends.
   All his emotional lockups were released on the way, so had little left for his true home town.

This chapter examines illusion of realities and dreams; and delusion of realities and emotions.

Chapter 4. Zhongni (仲尼, Confucius)

Introduction

4.1 Zhongni (Confucius) (仲尼)

4.2 My State Has Sage Person (吾国有圣人)

4.3 Qiu A Sage ? (丘圣者欤?)

4.4 Why Serve Teacher (Kongzi) ? (何为事夫子?)

4.5 Nankuazi (the Loner) (南郭子):

4.6 Liezi Learning (子列子学)

4.7 Liezi Loved To Travel (子列子好游)

4.8 Longshu, I Have Illness (龙叔吾有疾)

4.9 Yangzhu Sang Yangzhu Cried (杨朱而歌而哭)

4.10 Matters Not At Limit, Not Return (物不至者则不反)

4.11 How Differ From Dogs And Pigs ? (奚异犬豕之类乎?)

4.12 The Strength of Gongyibo (公仪伯以力)

4.13 Gongsunlong (公孙龙)

4.14 Yao Administration (尧治天下)

4.15 Guanyinxi (关尹喜)

Summary

Chapter 4. Zhongni (仲尼, Confucius)

Introduction:

Zhongni (Confucius) (551-479 BC), philosopher, Spring Autumn Period, Zhou Dynasty, China. Here in this 4th chapter, narratives are on sagehood, sages and their philosophies.

Zhongni was happy with Heaven, accepted destiny, had no worry, but still worried for society.
Kangcangzi denied power to hear with eyes, to see with ears; merely sensitive to danger if any.
Confucius not a sage, just a highly learned person and the 3 kings, 5 sovereigns, just good men.
Confucius was revered as a teacher, for he had all talents, not the best but able to teach flexibility.
Nankuazi (hermit) whom Liezi visited with 40 disciples, only talked with the last one, and to win.
Liezi meditated 9 years thinking no right/wrong, was liberated with no desires and light in steps.
Huqiuzi admonished Liezi, total travel also included travel inside self to examine changes there.
Longshu, with no desire for titles was ill, had 1 heart orifice blocked, thus sagehood not released.
Yangzhu sang for Jiliang and cried for Suiwu; normal or unfortunate, deaths accorded with 'Dao'.
'Matters not at limit, not return', a tenet that gives hope in the worst of situations, not a delusion.
'How differ from dogs and pigs', a tenet that chastises dependents who do not work to contribute.
Gongyibo was a frail man, couldn't bear weight, but well known for his ability to use strength.
Gongsunlong, a logician, like 'a white horse is a white horse, not a black horse, not a horse'.
Yao, a sage emperor, his legendary abdication to Shun was lauded, 'a peaceful transfer of power.'
Guanyinxi: "Enlightened, not selfish, but has no knowledge and no ability, is not a true Daoist".

4.1 仲尼

01 仲尼闲居，
02 子贡入侍，而有忧色。
03 子贡不敢问，出告颜回。
04 颜回援琴而歌。
05 孔子闻之，果召回入，
06 问曰："若奚独乐？"
07 回曰："夫子奚独忧？"
08 孔子曰："先言尔志。"
09 曰："吾昔闻之夫子曰
10 '乐天知命故不忧'，
11 回所以乐也。"
12 孔子愀然有间曰：
13 "有是言哉？
14 汝之意失矣。
15 此吾昔日之言尔，
16 请以今言为正也。
17 汝徒知乐天
18 　知命之无忧，
19 未知乐天知命
20 　有忧之大。
21 今告若其实：
22 修一身，任穷达，
23 知去来之非我，
24 亡变乱于心虑，
25 尔之所谓乐天
26 　知命之无忧也。
27 曩吾修《诗》
28 　《书》，正礼乐，
29 将以治天下，
30 遗来世；
31 非但修一身，治鲁国而已。
32 而鲁之君臣日失其序，
33 仁义益衰，
34 情性益薄。
35 此道不行一国与当年，
36 其如天下与来世矣？
37 吾始知《诗》《书》
38 礼乐无救于治乱，
39 而未知所以革之之方。
40 此乐天知命者之所忧。

4.1 Zhongni (Confucius)

Zhongni Leisurely at Home,
Zigong Entered to Serve, But Had Look Worrying
Zigong Not Dared Asked, Exited and Informed Yanhui.
Yanhui Played String-instrument And Sang.
Kongzi Heard It, Expectedly Called Hui (Yanhui) In,
Asking Said: "Like Why Alone Happy ?"
Hui (Yanhui) Said: " Teacher Why Alone Worrying ?"
Kongzi Said: "First Speak Your Will."
Said: "I formerly heard This,Teacher Said
　'Happy with Heaven Knows Destiny Thus No Worry',
Hui (Yanhui) Is Why Happy that's."
Kongzi Sadly Naturally Paused Said:
"Have Said This Indeed ?
Your Understanding is Incorrect that's.
This My Former Days Words to You,
Please Take Present Words As Correct that's.
You Disciples Know Happy with Heaven
　Know Destiny And No Worries.
Not Know Happy with Heaven Know Destiny
　Has Worry That's Big.
Now Telling Like The Truth:
Culture One Self, Regardless Poverty Attainment,
Know Going Coming These Not Mine (to control),
Forget Changes Turmoils Of Heart Concerns,
This Whatever You Call Happy with Heaven
　Know Destiny And No Worries.
Formerly I Updated 《Book of Poems》
　《Book of History》, Standardized Etiquette Music.
With Which to Govern The World,
Bequeath Coming Generations;
Not Only Cultivate One Self, Manages Lu State Only.
And Lu's King Ministers Daily Lost The Orders,
Benevolence Justice Increasingly Decline,
Love Emotion Increasingly Thinning.
This 'Dao' Not Apply In One State At Present,
How to Like The World And Coming Generations that's ?
I Begin to Know 《Book of Poems》《Book of History》
Etiquette Music No Salvation For Managing Turmoils,
And Not Know What The Method To Improve Them.
This Happy Heaven Knows Destiny, Person His Worry.

4.1 Zhongni (Confucius)

41	虽然，吾得之矣。	Although, I Attained It, already.
42	夫乐而知者，	O' Person Happy And Knows,
43	非古人之所谓乐知也。	Not What Ancient People Call Happy Knowing, that's.
44	无乐无知，是真乐真知；	Not Happy Not Knowing, Is Real Happy Real Knowing;
45	故无所不乐，	Thus None Whatever Not Happy,
46	无所不知，	None Whatever Not Know,
47	无所不忧，无所不为。	None Whatever Not Worry, None Whatever Not Do.
48	《诗》《书》	《Book of Poems》《Book of History》,
49	礼乐，	Etiquette Music.
50	何弃之有？	Why Have to Abandon Them ?
51	革之何为？"	Improve Them For What ?"
52	颜回北面拜手，曰：	Yanhui Facing North, Prayer Palms (together), Said:
53	"回亦得之矣。"	"Hui (Yanhui) Also Attained This indeed."
54	出告子贡。	Exited to Inform Zigong.
55	子贡茫然自失，	Zigong Naturally Confused, Self Lost,
56	归家淫思七日，	Returned Home Seriously Thought for 7 Days.
57	不寝不食，	Not Sleeping Not Eating,
58	以至骨立。	Until Like Standing Bones.
59	颜回重往喻之，	Yanhui Again Went to Explain It,
60	乃反丘门，	Then Returned to Door (tutelage) of Qui,
61	弦歌诵书，	Music Song Reciting Books,
62	终身不辍。	Whole Life Not Interrupted.

Liezi Text Narrative

Zhongni (Confucius) sat leisurely at home looking worried when Zigong entered to serve. L2
Zigong not asking, exited to inform Yanhui who then played a string instrument and sang. L4
Kongzi Heard It, and expectedly called Yanhui in, asking, said: "Like why happy all alone ?" L6
Yanhui said: " Teacher why alone worrying ?"; Kongzi said: "First speak your will." L8
Said: "I formerly heard This , Teacher said, 'Happy with Heaven, knows destiny, no worry'. L10
This is why Yanhui is happy, that's." L11
Kongzi, sadly paused, said: "Have I said that ? Your understanding is incorrect that's. L14
Those are my former days' words to you. Please take the present words as correct, that's. L16
You disciples know, Happy with Heaven, know destiny and have no worries. L18
But not knowing happy with Heaven, knowing destiny and having worries that are big. L20
Now like telling the truth: To cultivate oneself, regardless of poverty/attainment. L22
Knowing these going/coming not mine, forget changes/turmoil/concerns in our hearts. L24
This whatever you call, happy with Heaven, know destiny and no worries. L26
Formerly I updated 《Book of Poems》《Book of History》, standardized Etiquette Music. L28
With which to govern the world, bequeath to coming generations. L30
Not only to cultivate oneself, and also for managing State of Lu. L31
But Lu's king and ministers daily lost the orders, benevolence justice increasingly declined. L33
And love, emotion increasingly thinning; this 'Dao' hasn't applied in one state at present. L35
How then to apply it to the rest of the world and coming generations, that's ? L36
I Begin to Know 《Book of Poems》《Book of History》 L37

4.1 Zhongni (Confucius)

Etiquette Music, these no salvation for turmoils, not know what method for improvement. L39
This person happy with Heaven, knows destiny, his worries. L40
Although I attained it (happy with Heaven, knows destiny) already L41
O' person happy and knows, not what ancient people called happy knowing, that's. L43
Not happy not know is real happy real knowing; thus none whatever not happy not know. L46
None whatever not worry, none whatever not do. L47
　《Book of Poems》《Book of History》, Etiquette Music, why have to abandon them ? L50
Improve them for what ?" L51
Yanhui facing north, prayer palms (together) said: "Hui (Yanhui) also attained this indeed." L53
Exited to inform Zigong who naturally confused and felt totally self-lost. L55
Returned home, seriously thought for 7 days, not sleeping, not eating, till like standing bones. L58
Yanhui again went to explain it, then Zigong returned to the tutelage of Qui (Confucius). L60
And thus Zigong, with music and song, reciting books till whole life no more interruption. L62

Comments:
4.1 Zhongni (Confucius)
One of the tenets of Confucianism is happy with Heaven, accept destiny and have no worries.
This narrative shows that Confucius himself failed to attain it completely because he worried.
Confucius had attained 'enlightenment', but he worried for his state and the generations after.
Practice of the 5 classics that he had updated, had not been adopted even in his own state of Lu.
Thus less chance of the classics for salvation in turmoils of other states and coming generations.

Then Confucius came around to accepting the ideals of daoist self existence and being happy.
"Etiquette, Music, why have to abandon them ?; Improve them for what ?"
Truly, the individual's will has never been asked before being thrust upon this world.
The daoist has not agreed to any great mission to save others, the states and the world !
Daoists are happy with nature's (Heaven) provisions, live freely but with no intrusion on others.
When things do not turn out as he wishes, accepts his fate and destiny, so daoist has no worries !
Daoist is not selfish as he takes no advantage of others, just responsible for self and environment.

Happy with nature, accepts destiny, Daoist not worry; Confucians worry to save the world.

Chapter 4. Zhongni (仲尼, Confucius)

4.2 吾国有圣人　　4.2 My State Has Sage Person

01	陈大夫聘鲁，	Minister of Chen (state) Visited Lu (state),
02	私见叔孙氏。	Privately Meeting Mr Shusun.
03	**叔孙氏曰："吾国有圣人。"**	**Mr Shusun Said: "My State Has a Sage Person."**
04	曰："非孔丘邪？"	Said: "Not Kongqiu, right ?"
05	曰："是也。"	Said: "Yes that's."
06	"何以知其圣乎？"	"How Else to Know His Sagehood True-or-not ?"
07	叔孙氏曰："吾常闻之颜回，	Mr Shusun Said: "I Often Heard From Yanhui,
08	曰：'孔丘能废心而用形。'"	Said: "Kongqiu Able Discard Heart And Use Form."
09	陈大夫曰：	Minister of Chen Said:
10	**"吾国亦有圣人，**	***"My State Also Has Sage Person,***
11	子弗知乎？"	Sir Not Knowing, right ?"
12	曰："圣人孰谓？"	Said: "Sage Person How Calling ?"
13	曰："老聃之弟子	Said: "The Disciple of Laodan (Laozi)
14	有亢仓之者，	Has Person Kangcangzi,
15	得聃之道，	Attains The 'Dao' of Dan (Laozi)
16	能以耳视而目听。"	Able With Ears to See And Eyes to Listen."
17	鲁侯闻之大惊，	Duke of Lu Heard This Greatly Surprise,
18	使上卿厚礼而致之。	Asked Senior Minister Go to Him With Great Gifts.
19	亢仓子应聘而至。	Kangcangzi Responded to Appointment And Arrived.
20	鲁侯卑辞请问之。	Duke Lu with Humble Words Begged to Ask Him.
21	亢仓子曰：	Kangcangzi Said:
22	"传之者妄。	"Person Transmitting It (information) is Mistaken.
23	我能视听不用耳目，	I Able to See Listen Not Using Ears Eyes,
24	不能易耳目之用。"	Not Able Exchange Ears Eyes Their Usage."
25	鲁侯曰：	Duke of Lu Said:
26	"此增异矣。	"This Increases the Strangeness indeed.
27	其道奈何？	The 'Dao' How Is it ?
28	寡人终愿闻之。"	Lonely Me Certainly Wishes to Hear It."
29	亢仓子曰：	Kangcangzi Said:
30	"我体合于心，	"My Body Union With Heart,
31	心合于气，	Heart Union With Breath,
32	气合于神，	Breath Union With Spirit,
33	神合于无。	Spirit Union With Nothingness.
34	其有介然之有，	It's Having Matters Of Natural Domain,
35	唯然之音，	The Sound of All Nature,
36	虽远在八荒之外，	Though Far-away In the 8 Wilderness And Beyond,
37	近在眉睫之内，	Nearby On the Eye Lashes And Inside,
38	来干我者，我必知之。	That Coming to Disturb Me, I am Certain to Know It.
39	乃不知是我七孔	Then Not Know Is My 7 Orifices (ears eye nose mouth)
40	四支之所觉，	4 Limbs Whatever Their Feelings,
41	心腹六脏之知，	Heart Stomach 6 Organs Their Knowing,

122

4.2 My State Has Sage Person

42	其自知而已矣。"	This Just Self Knowing Only indeed."
43	鲁侯大悦。	Duke of Lu Greatly Please.
44	他日以告仲尼，	Next Day With-which Informed Zhongni (Confucius),
45	仲尼笑而不答。	Zhongni Laughed And Not Answer.

Liezi Text Narrative
The Minister from the state of Chen visited the State of Lu, privately met with Mr. Shusun. L2
Shusun: "My state has a sage person."; minister: "Is-it-not Kongqiu (Confucius) ?" L4
Shusun said: "Yes that's."; minister asked: "How else to know his sagehood is true-or-not ?" L6
Shusun said: "I often heard from Yanhui, said: 'Kongqiu able discard (heart) and use (form).'" L8
State of Chen, Minister said: "My state also has a sage person, Sir not knowing, right ?" L11
Shusun Said: "Sage person, how calling ?"; minister said: "Kangcangzi, disciple of Laodan. L14
Who has attained the 'Dao' of Laodan (Laozi), able to see with ears, to listen with eyes." L16
Duke of Lu heard this, greatly surprised, asked senior minister to go see him with great gifts. L18

Kangcangzi responded to invitation and arrived; Duke of Lu humbly pleased to consult him.L20
Kangcangzi said: "The person who has transmitted this (information) is wrong. L22
I am able to see and listen not using ears, eyes, NOT able to exchange ears, eyes, their usage. L24
Duke of Lu said: "This increases the strangeness indeed. L26
How does this 'Dao' work? Lonely Me certainly wishes to hear more of it." L28
Kangcangzi said: "My body union with heart, that union with breath, that union with spirit. L32
Spirit in union with nothingness; The matters of natural domain, sound of all nature. L35
Though far-away in the 8 wilderness and beyond, or nearby on the inside of the eye-lashes. L37
That is coming to disturb me, I am certain to know it. L38
Then not knowing if it is my 7 orifices (ears eyes nose mouth), or the 4 limbs their feelings. L40
Heart stomach, inside the 6 organs, their knowing, or just self knowing only indeed." L42
Duke Lu, greatly pleased, informed Zhongni (Confucius) the next day. L44
Zhongni just laughed and did not answer. L45

Comments:
4.2 My State Has Sage Person
Of the sage of Lu, Yanhui said: "Kongqiu able to discard heart feeling and to use form."
Of the sage of Chen, minister said: "Kangcangzi is able to see with ears and listen with eyes."
It seems a common sickness to exaggerate when information is transmitted, especially of sages.
Kangcangzi admitted to the Duke of Lu, truly not able to switch usage of ears and eyes.
But he said that matters or sound from afar or nearby coming to disturb, he can feel somehow!

Hearing this, the unscrupulous dramatize, exaggerate with fantasy to get blow-up for attention.
Whereas as a person of high calibre, Kangcangzi was merely more sensitive to his environment.
Hence Kongzi just laughed and did not reply.

Sages are high calibre, sensitive to their environment, not true to have supernatural powers.

Chapter 4. Zhongni (仲尼, Confucius)

4.3 丘圣者欤?   4.3 Qiu A Sage ?

01	商太宰见孔子，曰：	Shang Senior Minister Met Kongzi, Said:
02	**"丘圣者欤？"**	**"Qiu (Confucius) Sage Person, Is-it-not ?"**
03	孔子曰：	Kongzi (Confucius) Said:
04	"圣则丘何敢，	"Sage Then Qiu (Confucius) How Dare (claiming),
05	然则丘博学多识者也。"	But Then Qiu is All Studies Much Knowledge Person."
06	商太宰曰：	Shang Senior Minister Said:
07	"三王圣者欤？"	"3 Kings are Sage Persons, Is-it-not ?"
08	孔子曰：	Kongzi Said:
09	"三王善任智勇者，	"3 Kings Good at Appointing Talented Brave People,
10	圣则丘弗知。"	Sages they are Then Qiu Knows Not."
11	曰："五帝圣者欤？"	Said: "5 Emperors are Sage Persons, Is-it-not ?"
12	孔子曰：	Kongzi Said:
13	"五帝善任仁义者，	"5 Emperors Good at Appointing Kind Upright People,
14	圣则丘弗知。"	Sages they are, Then Qiu Knows Not."
15	曰："三皇圣者欤？"	Said: "3 Sovereigns are Sages Persons, Is-it-not ?"
16	孔子曰：	Kongzi Said:
17	"三皇善任因时者，	"3 Sovereigns Good Appointing, Time Accorded People,
18	圣则丘弗知。"	Sages they are, Then Qiu Knows Not."
19	商太宰大骇，	Shang Senior Minister Greatly Surprise,
20	曰："然则孰者为圣？"	Said: "But Then What Person can Be Sage ?"
21	孔子动容有间，曰：	Kongzi Countenance Changed, After Awhile, Said:
22	"西方之人有圣者焉，	"People Of The West Have Sage Person indeed,
23	不治而不乱，	No Administrating But No Disorder,
24	不言而自信，	Not Speaking But Naturally wins Confidence,
25	不化而自行，	No Teaching But Naturally Pervades (teaching)
26	荡荡乎民无能名焉。	Swinging Freely That's Citizens Can Not Name indeed.
27	丘疑其为圣。	Qiu Suspect He is Sage.
28	弗知真为圣欤？	Not Know Truly A Sage indeed ?"
29	真不圣欤？"	Truly Not A Sage indeed ?"
30	商太宰嘿然心计曰：	Shang Senior Minister Quietly Heart Thinking Said:
31	"孔丘欺我哉！"	"Kongqiu is Bullying Me, right !"

4.3 Qiu A Sage ?

Liezi Text Narrative
Shang senior minister met Kongzi, said: "Qiu (Kongzi) a sage person, is-it-not ?" L2
Kongzi said: "Qiu a sage, not dare to claim, but then Qiu is studied and knowledgeable." L5
Shang senior minister said: "The 3 Kings (of Xia Shang Zhou dynasties), are they sages ?" L7
Kongzi said: "3 Kings are good, deploying talented brave people; are they sages I know not."L10
Said: "5 Emperors (Huangdi, Dizhuanxu, Diku, Diyao, Dishun), are they sages ?" L11
Kongzi said: "5 Emperors are good, using kind upright people; are they sages I know not ?" L14
Said: "3 Sovereigns (Suirenshi, Fuxishi, Shennongshi), are they sages ?" L15
Kongzi said: "3 Sovereigns good using time accorded people; are they sages Qiu knows not."L18
Shang senior minister, greatly surprised, said: "But then what person can be sage ?" L20

Kongzi countenance changed, paused for a while, and said: "People of the west have sage. L22
Does no administration but no disorder; not speaking but naturally wins confidence. L24
No teaching but naturally teachings pervaded; flowing free that's, citizens cannot name why. L26
Qiu suspects he is a sage; but does not know he is truly a sage or truly not a sage ?" L28
Shang senior minister quietly thinking said: "Kongqiu is deceiving me, right !" L31

Comments:
4.3 Qiu A Sage ?
When asked, Kongzi dared not claim to be a sage himself.
The 3 ancient sovereigns, 5 prehistoric emperors, 3 kings of historic dynasties too are not sages.
This assessment of past revered rulers of China by Kongzi left Shang senior minister baffled.
Then who can be a sage ?
A person in the west who governs not but has no disorder, who teaches not but teachings pervade.
Kongzi suspects he is a sage, but confused as to whether he is truly a sage or truly not a sage ?

The great ancient rulers are not sages, as their influences are limited to regions and time periods.
But teachings of Daoism and Confucianism have been transmitted down the centuries to this day.

Laozi and Kongzi are sages, their teachings pervade today promoting harmony, world peace.

Chapter 4. Zhongni (仲尼, Confucius)

4.4 何为事夫子?   4.4 Why Serve Teacher (Kongzi) ?

01 子夏问孔子曰: Zixia Asking Kongzi Said:
02 "颜回之为人奚若?"   "Yanhui, He As a Person How Like ?"
03 子曰:"回之仁贤于丘也。"   Teacher Said: "Hui's Kindness Better Than Qiu that's."
04 曰:"子贡之为人奚若?"   Said: "Zigong, He As a Person How Like ?"
05 子曰:"赐之辨贤于丘也。"   Teacher Said: "Ci's Debate Better Than Qiu that's."
06 曰:"子路之为人奚若?"   Said: "Zilu, He As a Person How Like ?"
07 子曰:"由之勇贤于丘也。"   Teacher Said: "You His Bravery Better Than Qiu that's."
08 曰:"子张之为人奚若?"   Said: "Zizhang, He As a Person How Like ?"
09 子曰:"师之庄贤于丘也。"   Teacher Said: "Shi's Solemnity Better Than Qiu."
10 子夏避席而问曰: Zixia Left Mat (stand in respect) And Asking, Said:
11 "然则四子者   "But Then 4 Disciple Persons,
     何为事夫子?"   **Serve Teacher What For ?"**
12 曰:"居!吾语汝。   Said: "Sit ! I Tell You.
13 夫回能仁而不能反,   That's Hui Able be Kind But Not Able be Flexible,
14 赐能辨而不能讷,   Ci Able to Debate But Not Able be Quiet,
15 由能勇而不能怯,   You Able be Brave But Not Able be Afraid,
16 师能庄而不能同。   Shi Able be Solemn But Not Able be Comrade
17 兼四子之有以易吾,   All 4 Scholars, Their Talents In Exchange for Mine,
18 吾弗许也。   I Not Accept that's.
19 此其所以事吾而不贰也。"   This Is the Reason For Serving Me And Not Another."

Liezi Text Narrative

Zixia asking Kongzi said: "Yanhui, as a person how like ?" L2
Teacher said: "Hui (Yanhui), his kindness is better than Qiu (Kongzi) that's. L3
Said: "Zigong, as a person how like ?" The teacher said: "Ci debates better than Qiu, that's." L5
Said: "Zilu, as a person how like ?"; teacher said: "You, bravery is better than Qiu that's." L7
Said: "Zizhang, as a person how like ?"; the teacher said: "Shi's solemnity is better than Qiu." L9
Zixia stood up in respect, said: "But then the 4 disciples serve the teacher for what ?" L11
Said: "Sit, I shall tell you, that's, Hui able be kind but not able to be flexible. L13
Ci able to debate but not able to be quiet; You, able to be brave but not able to be afraid. L15
Shi is able to be solemn but not able to be comrade. L16
All 4 disciples, their talents in exchange for mine, I will not accept, that's. L18
This is the reason for wishing to serve me and not others." L19

Comments:

4.4 Why Serve Teacher (Kongzi) ?

Zixia asked Kongzi's assessment of his 4 top disciples, to know why these people serve Kongzi.
Kongzi said: "Yanhui in kindness is better than Qiu but not able to be flexible."
Kongzi said: "Zigong in debate is superior to Qiu but knows not when to be quiet."
Kongzi said: "Zilu is braver than Qiu but not able to be afraid and step back when necessary."
Kongzi said: "Zizhang is more solemn than Qiu but not able to enjoy comradeship with others."
These people have specific talents but also serious inflexibilities, thus need to learn from Kongzi.

Special talent is great but when practiced with inflexibilities may be disadvantaged.

Chapter 4. Zhongni (仲尼, Confucius)

4.5 南郭子 | 4.5 Nankuazi (the Loner)

01	子列子既师壶丘子林，	Teacher Liezi Was Tutored by Huqiuzilin,
02	友伯昏瞀人，乃居南郭。	Friend of Baihunwuren, Was Residing at Nanguo
03	从之处者，	His Followers People Staying,
04	日数而不及。	Daily Count And Not Possible (numerous).
05	虽然，子列子亦微焉，	Nevertheless, Teacher Liezi Also Finely-balanced that's,
06	朝朝相与辨，无不闻。	Daily Mutually Debating, None Not Heard (of him).
07	***而与南郭子连墙二十年，***	***And With Nankuazi Shared Wall 20 Years (neighbors),***
08	不相谒请；	No Mutual Visiting Consulting;
09	相遇于道，	Mutually Meeting On the Way,
10	目若不相见者。	That's Eyes Like Not Mutually Seeing that's.
11	门之徒役以为子列子	His Disciples Servants Thinking Teacher Liezi
12	与南郭子有敌不疑。	With Nankuazin No Doubt Has Rivalry.
13	有自楚来者，问子列子曰：	Person Coming From Chu, Asking Teacher Liezi Said:
14	"先生与南郭子奚敌？"	"Teacher With Nankuazi Why As Rivals ?"
15	子列子曰："南郭子貌充心虚，	Teacher Liezi said: "Nankuazi Looks Solid, Heart Empty,
16	耳无闻，目无见，口无言，	Ears Not Hearing, Eyes Not Seeing, Mouth Not Talking,
17	心无知，形无惕。	Heart Not Knowing, Form (body) Not Alert.
18	往将奚为？	Going-forth (visit him) Then What is the Purpose ?
19	虽然，试与汝偕往。"	Nevertheless, Try With You All to Go (see him)."
20	阅弟子四十人同行。	Selected Disciples 40 Persons, Went Together.
21	见南郭子，果若欺魄焉，	Saw Nankuazi, Really Like Earthen Figurine indeed,
22	而不可与接。	And Not Able With which to Connect.
23	顾视子列子，	Turning (Nankuazi) to Look at Teacher Liezi,
24	形神不相偶，	Body and Spirit No Mutual Meeting,
25	而不可与群。	And Not Able With which to have Comradeship.
26	南郭子俄而指子列子	Nankuazi Just then And Pointing to Teacher Liezi
27	之弟子末行者与言，	His Disciple, Person At Last Line And Spoke,
28	衎衎然若专直	Joyous Naturally Like Focused, Directed
29	而在雄者。	And like Person In Command.
30	子列子之徒骇之。	Teacher Liezi, His Disciples in Awe of Him.
31	反舍，咸有疑色。	Returned to Residence, All Have Puzzled Countenance.
32	子列子曰："得意者无言，	Liezi said: "Person With Understanding No Talk,
33	进知者亦无言，	Person with Advance Knowing Also No Talk.
34	用无言为言亦言，	Using No Talk As Talking Also Talking,
35	无知为知亦知。	No Knowledge As Knowing Also Knowing.
36	无言与不言，	No Talk And Not Talking,
37	无知与不知，	No Knowledge And Not Knowing,
38	亦言亦知。	Also Talking Also Knowing.
39	亦无所不言，	Also No Whatever Not Talking,
40	亦无所不知；	Also No Whatever Not Knowing;
41	亦无所言，亦无所知。	Also No Whatever Talk, Also No Whatever Knowledge.
42	如斯而已。	And Only Like This.
43	汝奚妄骇哉？"	Why are You all Confused and Afraid Is-it-not ?"

4.5 Nankuazi (the Loner)

Liezi Text Narrative
Teacher Liezi was tutored by Huqiuzilin, friend of Bohunmaoren, and residing at Nanguo. L2
Staying with him, day in day out his followers were numerous and cannot be counted. L4
Nevertheless, teacher Liezi was fine-tuned, with daily mutual debating, none not heard of him. L6
Staying next door with Nankuazi for 20 years, they had no mutual visiting and consulting. L8
Mutually meeting on the way, their eyes are like, not mutually seeing each other. L10
His disciples and servants were all thinking that Liezi, Nankuazi undoubtedly were rivals. L12
Person from the State of Chu asking Liezi said: "Teacher and Nankuazi, why are rivals." L14
Liezi said: "Nankuazi looks solid, heart empty, ears not hear, eyes not see, mouth not talk. L16
Heart not knowing, body not alert, then what is the purpose to go visiting him ? L18
Nevertheless, I can try to go see him with you."; selected 40 among disciples to go together. L20
On seeing Nankuazi, really like an earthen figurine, and with whom not able to connect. L22
Turning to look at Liezi, body and spirit, no mutual meeting, not able to have comradeship. L25
Nankuazi just then pointed to Liezi's disciple, the person at the last line and spoke. L27
Joyous naturally like focused and directed, like a person in command must win in argument. L29
Liezi's disciples, all in awe of him (Nankuazi), on return to residence, all have puzzled looks.L31
Liezi said: "Person with understanding no talk, person with advanced knowledge also no talk.L33
Using no talk as talking also is talking, no knowledge as knowing also is knowing. L35
No talk and not talking, no knowledge and not knowing, are also talking and knowing. L38
Also no whatever not talking, also no whatever not knowing; L40
Also no whatever talk, also no whatever knowledge; and only just like this. L42
Why are you all so confused so afraid, is-it-not ?" L43

Comments:
4.5 Nankuazi (the Loner)
Liezi was very sociable with many disciples and many visitors daily, hence well known.
Nankuazi was his next door neighbor for 20 years and they never spoke or communicated!
People suspect they were bitter rivals and a person from the State of Chu asked Liezi, why?
With 40 disciples in attendance, Liezi paid a visit and found himself ignored.
They found Nankuazi really looking like an earthen figurine and incommunicable !
Nankuazi chose to address a disciple in the last line with focused talk aiming to win !
Disciples all awed and returned confused and puzzled.
Liezi explained in great tortuous length why it's alright, talking or not talking, etc., ..
No talks and not talking, no knowledge and not knowing, are also talking and knowing.
In short, like no answer is still an answer, that's a negative response !

Nankuazi with advanced knowledge also little talk is alright, as he did no harm.

Chapter 4. Zhongni (仲尼, Confucius)

4.6 子列子学 | 4.6 Liezi Learning

01 子列子学也，三年之后，	*Teacher Liezi Learning that's, 3 Years Thereafter,*
02 心不敢念是非，	Heart Not Dared Think of Right or Wrong,
03 口不敢言利害，	Mouth Not Dare Speak of Gain or Loss,
04 始得老商一眄而已。	First Got Laoshang's 1 Glance And That's it.
05 五年之后，	Five Years Thereafter,
06 心更念是非，	Heart (mind) Never Think of Right or Wrong,
07 口更言利害，	Mouth Never Speak of Gain or Loss.
08 老商始一解颜而笑。	Laoshang First Time Countenance Relieved And Smile.
09 七年之后，	Seven Years Thereafter,
10 从心之所念，	Followed The Heart (mind) Whatever Thought,
11 更无是非；	Furthermore No Right or Wrong;
12 从口之所言，	Followed The Mouth Whatever Spoken,
13 更无利害，	Furthermore No Gain or Loss,
14 夫子始一引吾并席而坐。	Teacher Started First Let Me Together Sat On Mat.
15 九年之后，	Nine Years Thereafter,
16 横心之所念，	Unbridled Heart (mind) Whatever The Thought,
17 横口之所言，	Unbridled Mouth Whatever The Speech,
18 亦不知我之是非利害欤，	Also Not Know My Right/Wrong Gain/Loss that's,
19 亦不知彼之是非利害欤，	Also Not Know Others' Right/Wrong Gain/Loss that's,
20 外内进矣。	Outward Inward Progress that's.
21 而后眼如耳，耳如鼻，	And Afterwards Eyes Like Ears, Ears Like Nose,
22 鼻如口，口无不同。	Nose Like Mouth, Mouth None Not Similar.
23 心凝形释，	Heart Focused Form Set-free,
24 骨肉都融；	Bones Flesh All Melt-together;
25 不觉形之所倚，	Not Feeling Whatever Supported The Form (body),
26 足之所履，	Whatever The Feet Step-on,
27 心之所念，	Whatever The Heart (mind) Thought,
28 言之所藏。	Whatever Hidden In Speech.
29 如斯而已。	Like This And that's That.
30 则理无所隐矣。	Then Reasonably None Whatever Secrets that's.

4.6 Liezi Learning

Liezi Text Narrative
Liezi, after learning 3 years, heart (mind) not dared think of Right or Wrong. L2
Mouth not dared speak of Gain or Loss, then only got the first glance from Laoshang. L4
After 5 years, the mind never thinks of Right/Wrong, mouth never speaks of Gain/Loss. L7
Then Laoshang's countenance first time relieved and laughed. L8
After 7 years, followed whatever the mind thought, furthermore no Right /Wrong; L11
Whatever the mouth spoke, no more Gain/Loss; then the teacher first time let me sat on mat. L14
After 9 years, unbridled heart (mind) whatever thought, unbridled mouth whatever speech. L17
Not knowing my Right/Wrong Gain/Loss; also not knowing others' Right/Wrong Gain/Loss. L19
Outside inside progressed that's; then afterwards eyes like ears, ears like nose. L21
Nose like mouth, mouth none not similar; heart focused form (body) set-free. L23
Bones flesh all melt-together, not feeling whatever supported the form (body). L25
Whatever the feet stepped-on, whatever the heart (mind) thought, whatever hidden in speech. L28
Just like this that's; then reasonably none whatever can be secrets that's. L30

Comments:
4.6 Liezi Learning
This narrative is almost a complete repeat of section Liezi 2.3 before and has been commented on.
Liezi spent 9 long years meditating in Right/Wrong Gain/Loss under guidance.
At the end he was fully liberated in body and mind, no more burden with any desires.
He was light in steps and in speech nothing to hide, feeling a free man totally.
"Bones flesh all melt-together, not feeling whatever supports the form (body)."
Like in walking, we are not aware of muscles and bones working to keep our balance.
Like a fish swimming freely, it is not even aware of the surrounding water !

Liezi is just feeling good and light, not describing the supernatural power of daoist meditation !

Chapter 4. Zhongni (仲尼, Confucius)

4.7 子列子好游	**4.7 Liezi Loved To Travel**
01 初，子列子好游。	*Early, Teacher Liezi Loved Travelling.*
02 壶丘子曰：	Huqiuzi Said:
03 "御寇好游，	"Yukou Loves Travelling,
04 游何所好？"	Travel, Why and What Good ?"
05 列子曰：	Liezi Said:
06 "游之乐所玩无故。	"Travels Its Joy, Whatever Enjoy Never Old (state).
07 人之游也，	People's Travels that's,
08 观其所见；	Observe Whatever They See;
09 我之游也，	My Own Travels that's,
10 观之所变。	Observe Whatever The Changes.
11 游乎游乎！	Travelling O' Travelling O'!
12 未有能辨其游者。"	There's None Who Is Discerning In Travels."
13 壶丘子曰：	Huqiuzi Said:
14 "御寇之游固与人同欤，	"Yukou His Travels Sure Similar With Others that's,
15 而曰固与人异欤？	But Said Certainly Different With Others that's ?
16 凡所见，	All That are Observed,
17 亦恒见其变。	Also Always Observe Their Changes.
18 玩彼物之无故，	Enjoying Outside Matters Not Their Old (state),
19 不知我亦无故。	Not Knowing Self Also Not Old (state).
20 务外游，	Working on Outside Travels,
21 不知务内观。	Not Know Working on Inside Observation.
22 外游者，	Person Outside Travelling,
23 求备于物；	Requiring Preparedness Of Matters (outside);
24 内观者，	Person Inward Observing,
25 取足于身。	Attain Completeness From Self.
26 取足于身，	Attain Completeness From Self,
27 游之至也；	Travels, Its Totality that's
28 求备于物，	Requiring Preparedness of Matters (outside),
29 游之不至也。"	Travels, Not Its Totality that's."
30 于是列子终身不出，	Henceforth Liezi Life-long Not Out (travelling),
31 自以为不知游。	Suspecting Self Not Know Travelling.
32 壶丘子曰：	Huqiuzi Said:
33 "游其至乎！	"Travelling, Its Totality That's !
34 至游者，不知所适；	Total Traveller Person, Not Know Wherever Going;
35 至观者，不知所眡。	Total Observer Person, Not Know Whatever Seeing.
36 物物皆游矣，	All Matters All Travelling that's,
37 物物皆观矣，	All Matters All Observing that's,
38 是我之所谓游，	This Is What I Call Travelling,
39 是我之所谓观也。	This Is What I Call Observing, that's.
40 故曰：游其至矣乎！	Hence Said: Travelling Its Totality O' that's !
41 游其至矣乎！"	Travelling Its Totality O' that's !"

4.7 Liezi Loves To Travel

Liezi Text Narrative
Earlier, teacher Liezi loved travelling. L1
Huqiuzi Said: "Yukou loves travelling, so why and what good is travelling ?" L4
Liezi said: "Travelling its joy, whatever enjoyed never old states. L6
People's travels, observe whatever they see; my travels, observe whatever changes that's. L10
Travelling O' travelling O' ! ; there's none who is more discerning in travels." L12
Huqiuzi said: "Yukou, his travels are similar to others but why say different from others ? L15
All that are observed, also always observe their changes. L17
Enjoying outside matters not their old states, not knowing their own self also not old state. L19
Working on outside travels, not knowing working on inside observation. L21
Person outside travelling, requires preparedness of matters outside; L23
Person inside observing, attains completeness from self. L25
Attain completeness from self, travels its totality that's. L27
Requiring preparedness of matters outside, travelling not its totality that's." L29
Henceforth Liezi life-long not out travelling, suspecting self not know travelling. L31.
Huqiuzi said: "Travelling its totality, that's ! L33
Total traveller person, not know wherever going; not know whatever seeing. L35
All matters all travelling that's, all matters all observing that's. L37
This is what I call travelling, this is what I call observing that's. L39
Hence said: "Travelling its totality O' that's ! Travelling its totality O' that's !" L41

Comments:
4.7 Liezi Loved To Travel
Huqiuzi is absolutely correct that the totality of travelling is:
"All matters all travelling that's, all matters all observing that's."
When travelling, we observe the locals and the locals observe us !

We must not just know what changes in others but also know what changes in ourselves.
Travelling a two-way process, be mindful of our behavior and not be the 'ugly' ones.

Chapter 4. Zhongni (仲尼, Confucius)

4.8 龙叔吾有疾	**4.8 Longshu, I Have Illness**

01 龙叔谓文挚曰：	Longshu Speaking to Wenzhi Said:
02 "子之术微矣。	"Sir, Your Skill (medical) Fine-tuned indeed.
03 吾有疾，子能已乎？"	*I Have illness, Sir Able to Cure Is-it-not ?"*
04 文挚曰："唯命所听。	Wenzhi Said: "Your Order is My Command.
05 然先言子所病之证。"	Naturally First Say The Symptoms Of Your Illness."
06 龙叔曰：	Longshu Said:
07 "吾乡誉不以为荣，	"My Village is Praised Not Regard As Honorable,
08 国毁不以为辱；	State Destroyed Not Regard As Humiliating;
09 得而不喜，失而弗忧；	Success And Not Happy, Loss And Not Worry;
10 视生如死；	Look at the Living Like the Dead;
11 视富如贫；	Look at the Wealthy Like the Poor;
12 视人如豕；	Look at People Like the Pigs;
13 视吾如人。	Look at Self Like another Person..
14 处吾之家，	Staying in My Own Home,
15 如逆旅之舍；	Like Putting-up in Traveller's Inn;
16 观吾之乡，	Looking at My Own Village,
17 如戎蛮之国。	Like The Warring Uncivilized State.
18 凡此众疾，	All These Many Sicknesses,
19 爵赏不能劝，	Noble-title Award Not Be Tempted,
20 刑罚不能威，	Torture Punishment Not Be Threatened,
21 盛衰、利害不能易，	Prosperity Decline, Gain Loss Not Be Changed,
22 哀乐不能移。	Sadness Joy Not Be Moved..
23 固不可事国君，	Hence Not Possible to Serve King of State,
24 交亲友，	Interact with Relatives and Friends,
25 御妻子，制仆隶。	Handle The Wife, Control Servants and Slaves.
26 此奚疾哉？	This, What Illness That's ?
27 奚方能已之乎？"	What Method Able to Cure It O' ?"
28 文挚乃命龙叔背明而立，	Wenzhi Then Ordered Longshu to Stand, Back to Light,
29 文挚自后向明而望之。	Wenzhi From Behind Facing Light And Looked at Him.
30 既而曰："嘻！	Done And Said: "Hee !
31 吾见子之心矣，	I See Sir Your Heart that's,
32 方寸之地虚矣。	The Square Inch Area (heart) is Empty that's.
33 几圣人也！	Almost like a Sage Person that's !
34 子心六孔流通，	Sir's Heart 6 Orifices Flowing Freely,
35 一孔不达。	One Orifice Not Yet.
36 今以圣智为疾者，	Now Person Regards Virtues of Sage As Illness
37 或由此乎！	Maybe Originates Here Is-it-not !
38 非吾浅术所能已也。"	Not My Shallow Skill That is Able to Cure, that's."

4.8 Longshu, I Have Illness

Liezi Text Narrative
Longshu speaking to Wenzhi said: "Sir, you have medical methods fine-tuned. L2
I have an illness, Sir, able to cure it, right ?" L3
Wenzhi said: "Your order is my command; naturally first say the symptoms of your illness." L5
Longshu said: "My village is praised not regard as honorable, state destroyed not humiliating; L8
Success not happy, loss not worry, look at the living like dead, look at the wealthy like poor. L11
Look at people like pigs, look at self like another person, stay at home like in travellers' inn. L15
Look at my own home-state like the warring barbarian state. L17
All these many illnesses, noble-title awards not be tempted. L19
Torture punishment not be threatened, prosperity decline gain/loss not be affected. L21
Sadness/Joy not be Moved. L22
Thus, it is not possible to serve the King of state, interact with relatives and friends. L24
Handle wife, control servants and slaves. L25
This, what illness that's ? What method is able to cure that's ?" L27

Wenzhi then ordered Longshu to stand, his back to the light. L28
Wenzhi came from behind, facing the light and looked at him. L29
Then said: "Hee ! I see Sir your heart that's, the square inch heart area is empty that's. L32
Almost like that of a Sage person that's ! L33
Sir's heart, 6 orifices free flowing, but one orifice not yet. L35
Now a person regards virtues of sage as illness, maybe originating from here, is-it-not ! L37
Not my shallow skill that is able to cure, that's." L38

Comments:
4.8 Longshu, I Have Illness
Legends have it that the heart of a sage has 7 orifices, clear and free flowing.
Wenzhi observed Longshu in the light and his heart showed 6 orifices cleared, 1 not yet.
Title awards not tempted, torture punishment not threatened, gain loss not affected.
These are virtues of a sage and Longshu had them, and so is near sagehood !
His inability to feel honor, humiliation, happiness, worry, sadness, and joy is inhuman.
He was illusional seeing the living as dead, wealthy as poor and people as pigs.
He was dis-functional, not able to serve the king, no interaction with family and friends.
His virtues of sagehood cannot be released, blocked like the 7th orifice of his heart.
He is very sick, probably with obsessive development of his virtues to insensitivities ?

With this satire, Leizi warns of the over-cultivation of virtues with disastrous consequences.

Chapter 4. Zhongni (仲尼, Confucius)

4.9 杨朱而歌而哭   4.9 Yangzhu Sang Yangzhu Cried

01	无所由而常生者，	No Whatever Origin And Ever Existing Entity,
02	道也。	'Dao' that's
03	由生而生，	Origin Life And Living,
04	故虽终而不亡，常也。	Thus Though Ends But Not Loss, Normal that's.
05	由生而亡，不幸也。	Origin Life And Died, Un-Fortunate that's.
06	有所由而常死者，	Has The Origin And Ever Death Entity,
07	亦道也。	Also 'Dao' that's.
08	由死而死，	Origin Death And Died,
09	故虽未终而自亡者，	Thus Though No Ending But Self Died Person,
10	亦常也。	Also Normal that's.
11	由死而生，幸也。	Origin Death And Living, Fortunate that's.
12	故无用而生谓之道，	Thus No Use And Living Call It 'Dao',
13	用道得终谓之常；	Use 'Dao' Attain Ending Call It Norm;
14	有所用而死者亦谓之道，	Has The Usage And Death Entity, Also Call It 'Dao',
15	用道而得死者亦谓之常。	Use 'Dao' And Get Death Entity, Also Call It Norm.
16	*季梁之死，*	*Jiliang His Death,*
17	*杨朱望其门而歌。*	*Yangzhu Looked at His Door And Sang.*
18	*随梧之死，*	*Suiwu His Death,*
19	*杨朱抚其尸而哭。*	*Yangzhu Embraced His Corpse And Cried,*
20	隶人之生，	Common People Their Life,
21	隶人之死，	Common People Their Death,
22	众人且歌，众人且哭。	The People They Sang, The People They Cried.

Liezi Text Narrative
No Origin but Ever-existing entity, 'Dao' that's. L2
Origin Life and living, though died but not Loss (has future generations), normal that's. L4
Origin Life and died, un-fortunate that's. L5
Has the Origin and ever Dead entity, also 'Dao' that's. L7
Origin Death and died, though no end but self-died (born dead), also normal that's. L10
Origin Death and living, fortunate that's. L11
Thus no use and living call it 'Dao', use 'Dao' and attained living till death, call it Norm; L13
Jiliang died, Yangzhu looked at his door and sang; L17
Suiwu died, Yangzhu embraced his corpse and cried. L19
Common people their living, common people their death; L21
Common people they sang, common people they cried. L22

Comments:
4.9 Yangzhu Sang Yangzhu Cried
Narrative claims that 'Dao' itself has no origin but is the origin of life and death.
Born alive, lives and dies, has off-springs so 'lives' on; born alive and died, unfortunate that's.
Born death, also norm in 'Dao' that's; born 'death' but saved, continued to live, fortunate that's.
Common people living or dead, sing or cry as Yangzhu has shown, call it the Norm.
Thus 'useful' or 'useless', people living till death, all in accord with 'Dao', with no bias.

Chapter 4. Zhongni (仲尼, Confucius)

4.10 物不至者则不反   4.10 Matters At Limit, Return

01	目将眇者，	Eyes Going Blind That's,
02	先睹秋毫；	First See Autumn Down (micro feather);
03	耳将聋者，	Ears Going Deaf That's,
04	先闻蚋飞；	First Hear Gnat Fly;
05	口将爽者，	Mouth Going Tasteless That's,
06	先辨淄渑；	First Differentiates (water) of river Zi, river Mian;
07	鼻将窒者，	Noses Going to Block That's,
08	先觉焦朽；	First Smell Burnt Rot;
09	体将僵者，	Body Going Stiff That's,
10	先亟犇佚；	First Lightly Run Easily;
11	心将迷者，	Heart Going Confused That's,
12	先识是非：	First Knows Right Wrong:
13	故物不至者则不反。	**Thus Matters Not at Extreme That's Then Not Return.**

Liezi Text Narrative
Before Eyes go blind, person sees autumn down (sight fine); L2
Before Ears go deaf, person hears gnat fly (hearing fine); L4
Before Mouth goes tasteless, person differentiates water of river Zi and river Mian; L6
Before Nose is blocked, person smells burnt rot; L8
Before Body is stiffened, person runs lightly easily; L10
Before Heart goes confused, person knows right wrong: L12
Thus matters not at extreme that's, then not return.

Comments:
4.10 Matters At Limit, Return
Before Spring we experience the severity of Winter.
Before the Rebellion people suffer the greatest of oppression.
The above tenet seems correct, that matters not at extreme then not return.
*But then often we should nip things in the bud before progression to the extremes and **No return**.*
Take care of our health and protect our senses, for their deterioration is natural and has No return.

We should be precautionary and not have the Delusion that things must get worse to get better!

Chapter 4. Zhongni (仲尼, Confucius)

4.11 奚异犬豕之类乎？   4.11 How Differ From Dogs And Pigs ?

01	郑之圃泽多贤，	Puze of Deng (state) Many Virtuous-talented,
02	东里多才。	Dongli Many Multi-talented.
03	圃泽之役有伯丰子者，	Among Puze Disciples Had Person Bofengzi,
04	行过东里，遇邓析。	Passage Passed Dongli, Met Dengxi.
05	邓析顾其徒而笑曰：	Dengxi Eyed Disciples And Laughing, Said:
06	"为若舞彼来者，	"Do Like Dance (have fun) with The Coming People,
07	奚若？"	How About ?"
08	其徒曰："所愿知也。"	His Disciples Said: "That Wish to Know that's"
09	邓析谓伯丰子曰：	Dengxi Speaking to Bofengzi Said:
10	"汝知养养之义乎？	"You Know Keeping Feeding Its Meaning Is-it-not ?
11	受人养而不能自养者，	Receive Others Feed And Not Able Self Sustain People,
12	犬豕之类也；	Dogs Pigs Those Kinds that's;
13	养物而物为我用者，	Feeding Animals And Animals For My Use That's,
14	人之力也。	People's Labor that's.
15	使汝之徒食而饱，	Enable You Your Disciples Feeding And Full,
16	衣而息，	Clothe and Rest,
17	执政之功也。	Present Government Their Credits that's.
18	长幼群聚	Old Young Crowd Gathered
19	而为牢藉庖厨之物，	And Be Corral Fenced, Materials For Kitchen,
20	**奚异犬豕之类乎？"**	***How Different from Dogs Pigs Those Kinds Is-it-not ?"***
21	伯丰子不应。	Bofengzi No Response.
22	伯丰子之从者越次而进曰：	Bofengzi's Follower Passed Over And Offering Said:
23	"大夫不闻	"Senior Minister Not Hear
24	齐鲁之多机乎？	States of Qi and Lu Many Skill-talents Is-it-not ?
25	有善治土木者，	Has People Good at Managing Soil Wood,
26	有善治金革者，	Has People Good at Managing Metal Leather,
27	有善治声乐者，	Has People Good at Managing Sound Music,
28	有善治书数者，	Has People Good at Managing Books Mathematics
29	有善治军旅者，	Has People Good at Managing Army Campaigns,
30	有善治宗庙者，	Has People Good at Managing Ancestral Temples
31	群才备也。	Crowd of Talents all Available that's.
32	而无相位者，	And No Person Relatively Position (higher),
33	无能相使者。	No Person Able to Order Another (no governing).
34	而位之者无知，	And Person Position (higher) than Them No Knowledge,
35	使之者无能，	Person Ordering Them No Ability,
36	而知之与能为之使焉。	Those Know It And Able to Do It, they Order that's.
37	执政者，乃吾之所使；	Present Governing Person, Is Whom I Am Ordering;
38	子奚矜焉？"	Sir, Why so Proud that's?"
39	邓析无以应，	Dengxi Nothing To Response,
40	目其徒而退。	Eyed His Disciples And Retreated.

4.11 How Differ From Dogs And Pigs ?

Liezi Text Narrative
Puze region of Deng State had many virtuous-talents and Dongli region, many multi-talented. L2
A disciple of Liezi from Puze, Bofengzi was travelling past Dongli one day and met Dengxi. L4
Dengxi eyed his disciples laughing, said: "Do like to have fun with the person, how about ?" L7
His disciples said: "This we wish to know that's"; L8
Dengxi speaking to Bofengzi said: "You know the meaning of keeping feeding, is-it-not ?" L10
Receive others' feed and not able to self sustain people, are like dogs pigs, that kind that's; L12
Keeping animals and animals are for my use, that's people's efforts. L14
Enabling you and disciples to be fed, clothed and rested is credit of the present government. L17
Old and young crowded together and be fenced-in waiting for food from the kitchen, L19
How different are you from the dogs and pigs kind, that's ?" Bofengzi did not respond. L21

Bofengzi's follower then went forward and offering said: L22
"The Senior Minister has not heard states of QI and Lu has many artisans is-it-not ?" L24
Has people who are good at managing soil wood, people good at managing metal leather. L26
Has people who are good at playing sound music, people good at books mathematics. L28
Has people who are good at leading army campaigns, people good in rites ancestral temples. L30
Crowd of talents all available that's, and none in higher position ordering one another. L33
Now a person in a higher position has no knowledge, the person ordering them has no ability. L35
Therefore those who know it and are able to do it, they are ordering that's. L36
Person in the governing position should be the one I am ordering; Sir, why so proud that's ?" L38
Dengxi had nothing to respond, eyed his disciples and retreated. L40

Comments:
4.11 How Differ From Dogs And Pigs ?
Narrative shows the rivalry between Liezi and Dengxi of the Law and Order tradition.
Dengxi, senior minister suggests disciples of Liezi cannot sustained by themselves.
Hence are like dogs and pigs, awaiting to be fed and clothed by the governing authority.
This debasing tactic by calling rivals dogs and pigs, has been much quoted thereafter.
Liezi's disciple retorts that the person of authority has no knowledge and no skill abilities.
Government is just an administrative authority for serving artisans and citizens below.
Civil servants are to manage the wealth and products created by citizens, for citizens.
37 执政者，乃吾之所使；   Present Governing Person, Is Whom I Am Ordering;
This suggestion of Liezi has rarely been quoted if ever, thereafter,

Indeed, the government is a good servant but a bad master.

4.12 公仪伯以力 — 4.12 The Strength of Gongyibo

01	公仪伯以力闻诸侯，	*Gongyibo For Strength Renowned Among the Lords,*
02	堂谿公言之于周宣王，	Donxigong Told This To King Xuan of Zhou,
03	王备礼以聘之。	King Prepared Gifts To Engage Him.
04	公仪伯至；	Gongyibo Arrived;
05	观形，懦夫也。	Present Form, a Weak Man that's.
06	宣王心惑而疑曰：	King Xuan Heart-felt Confused And Doubtful, Said:
07	"女之力何如？"	"You Your Strength How Like ?"
08	公仪伯曰：	Gongyibo Said:
09	"臣之力能折	"Subject-me My Strength Able to Break
10	春螽之股，	Spring Grasshopper Its Thigh,
11	堪秋蝉之翼。"	Puncture Autumn Cicada Its Wing."
12	王作色曰：	King Changed Countenance Said:
13	"吾之力者能裂犀兕之革，	"I My Strength That's to Tear Rhino Its Skin,
14	曳九牛之尾，犹憾其弱。	Tow 9 Bulls Their Tails, Still Regrets It's Weak.
15	女折春螽之股，	You Break Spring Grasshopper Its Thigh,
16	堪秋蝉之翼，	Bears Autumn Cicada Its Wing,
17	而力闻天下，何也？"	And Strength Renown World Wide, Why that's ?"
18	公仪伯长息退席，曰：	Gongyibo Long Sigh Left Seat, Said:
19	"善哉王之问也！	"Good Indeed King Your Query that's !
20	臣敢以实对。	Subject-me Dares With Truth to Respond.
21	臣之师有商丘子者，	Subject-me My Teacher Shangqiuxi Person,
22	力无敌于天下，	Strength No Rival In The World,
23	而六亲不知，	And the 6 Relatives Not Know,
24	以未尝用其力故也。	Reason Is Never Try Using His Strength that's.
25	臣以死事之。	Subject-me Dead-fast to Serve Him.
26	乃告臣曰：	Then he Informed Subject-me, Said:
27	'人欲见其所不见，	' People Wish Seeing Whatever Not Visible,
28	视人所不窥；	Seeing Whatever People Cannot See;
29	欲得其所不得，	Wish Attaining Whatever Cannot Attainable,
30	修人所不为。	Cultivate Whatever People Cannot Perform.
31	故学视者先见舆薪，	Thus Person Training Sight First Look at Cart of Fagot,
32	学听者先闻撞钟。	Person Training Hearing First Hear the Striking Bells.
33	夫有易于内者无难于外。	O' Person Has it Easy Inside, No Difficulty Outside.
34	于外无难，	As Outside No Difficulty,
35	故名不出其一家。'	Thus Name (fame) Not Out This One Family.'
36	今臣之名闻于诸侯，	Now Subject-me My Name Renowned Among the Lords,
37	是臣违师之教，	This Subject-me Violates Teacher His Teaching,
38	显臣之能者也。	By showing-off Subject-me My Ability that's.
39	然则臣之名	Naturally Then Subject-me My Reputation
40	不以负其力者也，	Not For Having The Strength Entity that's,
41	以能用其力者也；	For The Ability to Use The Strength that's;
42	不犹愈于负其力者乎？"	This Even Better Than Bearing The Weight, Is-it-not ?"

4.12 The Strength of Gongyibo

Liezi Text Narrative
Dongxigong to King Xuan of Zhou, 'Gongyibo was renowned for strength among the lords.' L2
King prepared gifts to engage him and Gongyibo arrived; present form, a weak man that'. L5
King Xuann felt confused and doubtful, said: "You your strength, how like ?" L7
Gongyibo said: "Subject-me, my strength is able to break a spring grasshopper's thigh. L10
Puncture autumn cicada its wing." L11
King's countenance changed. said: "I my strength that's able to tear rhino skin. L13.
Tow 9 bulls by their tails, and still regret my strength is weak. L14
You are only able to break spring grasshopper its thigh, puncture autumn cicada its wing. l16
And yet your strength is renowned world-wide, why is that ?" L17
Gongyibo with a long sigh left his seat and standing with respect , said: L18
"Very well, King your query that's ! Subject-me dares answer truthfully. L20
Subject-me, my teacher Shangqiuxi, a person whose strength is un-rival in the World. L22
And his 5 relatives know not; reason is never try using his strength, that's. L24
Subject-me deadfast to serve him; then only he informed subject-me, said: L26
'People wish to see whatever is not visible, seeing whatever others cannot see. L28
Wishing to attain whatever not attainable, cultivate whatever others cannot perform. L30
Thus person training sight, first looked at cart of fagot. L31
 Training to hear, first hear the striking of bells. L32
O' person has it easy internally, has no difficulty outside. L33
As outside no difficulty, thus name (fame) not out his one family (remains unknown).' L35
Now subject-me my name renowned among the lords, that's. L36
I have violated my teacher's teaching by showing off, subject-me my ability that's. L38
Actually my reputation is not for having the strength, but for the ability to use strength that's. L41
This is even better than being able to bear heavy weight, is-it-not ?" L42

Comments:
4.12 The Strength of Kongyibuo
 Shangqiuxi had strength un-rival in the world, never showed it thus unknown outside the family.
Gongyibo with dead-fast devotion to this teacher, was able to get the secret of his 'strength'.
Gongyibo violated his teacher's teaching, show-off strength and was renowned among the lords.
Thus inviting attention from a curious king who was very strong and wished to know more.
A frail man Gongyibo, could only break the thigh of a grasshopper, puncture a cicada's wing.
He explained that he does not have the strength to bear loads, but was able to use 'strength'.
So he probably has knowledge of levers and pulleys, thus has great 'strength' for heavy works.

Able to use strength, able to teach others to use strength, better than have strength, right ?

Chapter 4. Zhongni (仲尼, Confucius)

4.13 公孙龙　　　　　4.13 Gongsunlong

01	中山公子牟者，	Prince Mou of Zhongshan Person,
02	魏国之贤公子也。	The Virtuous Prince of the State of Wei that's.
03	好与贤人游，	Loved to Travel with Virtuous-talented People,
04	不恤国事；	Not Concerned of State Affairs;
05	**而悦赵人公孙龙。**	***And Delighted in Gongsunlong, Person of Zhao (state).***
06	乐正子舆之徒笑之。	Lezhengziyu and His Disciples Laughed at Him.
07	公子牟曰：	Prince Mou Said:
08	"子何笑牟	"Sir Why Laugh at Mou
09	之悦公孙龙也？"	My Delight in Gongsunlong that's?"
10	子舆曰：	Ziyu (Lezhengziyu) Said:
11	"公孙龙之为人也，	"Gongsunlong He As a Person that's,
12	行无师，学无友，	Actions No Teacher, Learning No Friend,
13	佞给而不中，	Eloquent But Not Center (illogical),
14	漫衍而无家，	Unrestrained Diffuse And No Family (discipline),
15	好怪而妄言。	Loves the Strange And Speaks the Preposterous.
16	欲惑人之心，屈人之口，	Wishes Confuse People's Heart, Bend People's Mouth,
17	与韩檀等肄之。"	With Hantan and Gang Practicing It."
18	公子牟变容曰：	Prince Mou Countenance Changing, Said:
19	"何子状公孙龙之过欤？	"Why Sir Criticizes Gongsunlong So Excessive as Such?
20	请闻其实。"	Please to Hear The Truth."
21	子舆曰：	Ziyu Said:
22	"吾笑龙之诒孔穿，	"I Laugh at Gongsunlong His Deceiving Kongchuan,
23	言·善射者能	Said, 'Good at Shooting Person Able to
24	令后镞中前括，	Cause Back Arrowhead Centered at Front's (arrow) Tail,
25	发发相及，	Shot after Shot Mutually on Target,
26	矢矢相属；	Arrow after Arrow Mutually Connected;
27	前矢造准而无绝落，	Front Arrow Hit Target And None Drop Off,
28	后矢之括犹衔弦，	Last Arrow Its Tail Still On Bow-string,
29	视之若一焉。'	Looking at It Like One (line) indeed.'
30	孔穿骇之。	Kongchuan Astonished by This.
31	龙曰：'此未其妙者。	Long (Gongsunlong) Said: 'This Not The Most Amazing.
32	逢蒙之弟子曰鸿超，	Fengmeng His Disciple Call Hongchao,
33	怒其妻而怖之。	Angry With Wife And Terrorized Her.
34	引乌号之弓，	Pull The Bow of Wuhao (Huangdi's bow)
35	綦卫之箭，射其目。	Arrow from Qiwei, Shot Her Eye.
36	矢来注眸子而眶不睫，	Arrow Came Centered on Pupil And Eyelash Not Blink,
37	矢隧地而尘不扬。'	Arrow Fell to the Ground And Dust Not Fly.'
38	是岂智者之言与？"	This Not Virtuous-talented Person His Words is-it-not?"
39	公子牟曰：	Prince Mou Said:
40	"智者之言固非	"Clever Person His Words Sure Not
41	愚者之所晓。	Stupid Person Who Can Understand.

42	後鏃中前括，	Arrowhead Behind Centered Front Arrowtail,
43	钧後于前。	Balanced Back To Front.
44	矢注眸子而睫不睫，	Arrow Aim at Pupil And Eyelashes Not Blink,
45	尽矢之势也。	Terminal, Arrow Its Motion that's.
46	子何疑焉？"	Sir Why the Doubts, indeed?"
47	乐正子舆曰：	Lezhengziyu Said:
48	"子，龙之徒，	"Sir, Long's Disciple,
49	焉得不饰其阙？	How Able Not to Adorn His Faults?
50	吾又言其尤者。	I Again Say His Greater Hilarity.
51	龙诳魏王曰：	Long Lied to King of Wei, Said:
52	'有意不心。	'Has Desires Not Heart' (feelings).
53	有指不至。	Has Description Not Absolute.
54	有物不尽。	Has Matters No Ending.
55	有影不移。	Has Shadow Not Shifting.
56	发引千钧。	Hairs Lifting 1000 Weights.
57	白马非马。	White Horse Not Horse.
58	孤犊未尝有母。'	Orphan Cow Not Ever Has Mother.'
59	其负类反伦，	His Negative Kinds Contradicting Arguments,
60	不可胜言也。"	Not Possible to Completely Narrate, that's."
61	公子牟曰：	Prince Mou Said:
62	"子不谕至言	"Sir, Not Understand Great Sayings
63	而以为尤也，	And Regard them As Worrisome that's,
64	尤其在子矣。	Worrisome Is With you Sir indeed.
65	夫无意则心同。	O' No Desires Than Heart (wishes) Same.
66	无指则皆至。	No Directive Than All Agreed.
67	尽物者常有。	Division of Matter That's, Always Has (no ending).
68	影不移者，说在改也。	That Shadow Not Shifting, Says It's Correcting that's.
69	发引千钧，势至等也。	Hair Leads 1000Weights, Force Absolute Balanced that's.
70	白马非马，形名离也。	White Horse Not Horse, Form Name Separated that's.
71	孤犊未尝有母，	Orphan Cow Never Has Mother,
72	非孤犊也。"	Not Orphan Cow otherwise, that's."
73	乐正子舆曰：	Lezhengziyu Said:
74	"子以公孙龙之鸣皆条也。	"Sir, With Gongsunlong His Talks All in Order that's.
75	设令发于余窍，	Suppose Let Shot From (His) Orifice (fart),
76	子亦将承之。"	Sir Also Will Accept It."
77	公子牟默然良久，	Prince Mou Silent Naturally Long While,
78	告退，曰：	Bidding Farewell, Said:
79	"请待余曰，更谒子论。"	"Please Wait Some Days, Sure Visit Sir for Debate."

4.13 Gongsunlong

Liezi Text Narrative
Prince Mou of Zhongshan, this person was the virtuous prince of the state of Wei that's. L2
Loved to keep company with virtuous-talented people, and not concerned with state affairs. L4
Delighted in Gongsunlong of Zhao (state); Lezhengziyu and disciples laughed at him. L6
Prince Mou said: "Sir, why laugh at Mou, my delight in Gongsunlong that's?" L9
Ziyu (Lezhengziyu) said: "Gongsunlong as person, actions no teacher, learning no friends. L12
Eloquent but no center (illogical), unrestrained diffused with no discipline of thoughts. L14
Loves the strange and speaks the preposterous. L15
Wishes to confuse people's feelings, distorts people's words, practices with Hantan's gang. L17
Prince Mou countenance changed, said: "Why Sir critical of Gongsunlong's faults as such? L19
Pleased to hear the truth." Ziyu said: "I laugh at Gongsunlong, he deceived Kongchuan. L22
Said 'Good at shooting person able to cause back arrowheads centered at the front arrowtails. L24
Shot after shot mutually on target, arrow after arrow mutually like connected; L26
Front arrow hit target and none dropped off, last arrow its tail still on bow-string. L28
All looking like in one straight line indeed.' And Kongchuan was in awe with him. L30
Long (Gongsunlong) said: 'This is not the most amazing. L31
Fengmeng's disciple called Hongchao, who was angry with wife, tried to terrorize her. L33
Pull the bow Wuhao (Huangdi's bow), and with an arrow from Qiwei shoot at her eye. L35
Arrow centered on the pupil, eyelash untouch, arrow fell on the ground, dust not stirred.' L37
How can these be the words of a virtuous-talented person, is-it-not?" L38
Prince Mou said: "Virtuous-talented person, his words surely not a stupid person can know. L41
Arrowhead of arrow behind, centered on front arrowtail, balanced from back to front. L43
Coming arrow aimed at pupil and eyelash not blink, arrow's motion terminated just in time. L45
Sir why all the doubts, indeed?" L46
Lezhengziyi said: "Sir is a disciple of Long, how is it possible not to cover-up his fallacies? L49
I again say his greater absurdity; Long hilariously to King of Wei, said: L51
'Has desires not feelings of heart, has description not absolute, has matters no ending. L54
Shadow don't move, hairs lift 1000 weights, white horse not horse, orphan cow no mother.' L58
His negative kinds and reverse arguments, not possible to completely narrate that's." L60
Prince Mou said: "Sir not understand great sayings and regard them as worrisome that's. L63
Worries are on you Sir, indeed; no selfish desires then everybody's heart wishes all the same. L65
No selfish directives then all are agreed; halving of matters that's, always have remainder. L67
Shadow not moving, say it is correcting; hairs lift 1000 weights, force absolutely balanced. L69
White horse not horse, form name separated; orphan cow no mother, else not orphan cow." L72
Lezhengziyu said: "Sir regards Gongsunlong's utterances all reasonable that's. L74
Supposedly getting shots from anus (farts), Sir will also accept them." L76
Prince Mou naturally silent for a long while, then bidding farewell, said: L78
"Please wait for some days, then will visit Sir for more debate." L79

Comments:
4.13 Gongsunlong
Gongsunlong (c.325-250 BC), State of Zhao, teacher and writer of the Warring State Period.
A prominent member of the School of Names (Logicians) among ancient Chinese philosophers. Most of his writings are lost but have been referenced in the writing of Liezi and Zhuangzi. Gongsunlong came after Liezi (c.450-375 BC), hence is a corrupt insertion into *Liezi* by scholars.

有意不心。 'Has Desires Not Heart (feelings). L52
Wishes and desires often are corrupted by selfish thinking, only true heart feelings remain pure.
有指不至。 Has Description Not Absolute. L53
Descriptions of things and events may be made, but at best are partial and incomplete.
有物不尽。 Has Matters No Ending. L54
Matters are divided with no end, like a man, organs, cells, molecules, atoms, neutrons, quarks, ….
有影不移。 Has Shadow Not Shifting. L55
Shadow does not move when the object that casts it stay-put.
发引千钧。 Hairs Lifting 1000 Weight. L56
A person may be lifted by his hairs; bundles of fine steel 'threads' are used to suspend bridges.
白马非马。 White Horse Not Horse. L57
A white horse is not a black horse, the color 'white' and object 'horse' are separate entities .

Gongsunlong's words often sound bizarre at first encounter but can withstand closer examination. He is not out to dazzle but to invite in-depth consideration and study of all matters and affairs.

Gongsunlong's critical thinking helps to advance our understanding of nature and the world.

Chapter 4. Zhongni (仲尼, Confucius)

4.14 尧治天下　　　　4.14 Yao Administration

01	*尧治天下五十年，*	*Yao Administered The World 50 Years,*
02	不知天下治欤，	Not Know The World Managed Already,
03	不治欤？	Not Managed Already ?
04	不知亿兆	Not Know Millions Trillions
05	之愿戴己欤？	Citizens' Wish to Support Self Still?
06	不愿戴己欤？	Not Wishing to Support Self Still ?
07	顾问左右，	Looking to Ask Left Right,
08	左右不知。	Left Right Not Know.
09	问外朝，	Asked Outer Court,
10	外朝不知。	Outer Court Not Know,
11	问在野，	Asked The Wilderness (citizens),
12	在野不知。	The Wilderness Not Know,
13	尧乃微服游于康衢，	Yao Then Plain-cloth Tour On the Cross-roads,
14	闻儿童谣曰：	Heard Little Children Ballad, Said:
15	"立我蒸民，	"Nurturing My Many Citizens,
16	莫匪尔极。	None Not Your Absolute (virtues).
17	不识不知，	Not Recognising Not Knowing,
18	顺帝之则。"	Emperor Shun His Regulations."
19	尧喜问曰：	Yao Happy and Asking, Said:
20	"谁教尔为此言？"	"Who Teaches You With These Words ?"
21	童儿曰：	Little Boy Said:
22	"我闻之大夫。"	"I Hear It from a Great Scholar."
23	问大夫，	Ask Great Scholar,
24	大夫曰：	Great Scholar Said:
25	"古诗也。"	"Ancient Poem that's"
26	尧还宫，	Yao Returned to Palace,
27	召舜，	Summoned Shun,
28	因禅以天下。	Reason, to Abdicate The World.
29	舜不辞而受之。	Shun Not Decline But Accepted It.

4.14 Yao Administration

Liezi Text Narrative
Yao administered the world 50 years, not knowing if the world managed or not managed ? L3
Not know if the millions trillions of citizens' wish to support self still, or not support self ? L6
Looking to ask left and right, left and right not know. L8
Asked outer court and outer court know not; asked citizens in the wilderness, not know. L12
Yao then in plain-cloth went on tour on the cross-roads, and heard children's ballad, said: L14
"Nurturing my many citizens, none not with your absolute virtues. L16
Not recognising not knowing, Emperor Shun his regulations." L18
Yao feeling happy, and asking said: "Who teaches you with these words ?" L20
Little boy said: 'I heard it from the great scholar." L22
Asked the great scholar, and the great scholar said: "Ancient Poem that's." L25
Yao returned to his palace and summoned Shun; reason, to abdicate his power to the latter. L28
Shun without initial polite declining, accepted the kingship. L29

Comments:
4.14 Yao Administration
Emperor Yao, after 50 years on the throne, was old and looking for a successor.
Yao heard praises of Shun's virtues in the ballad recited by children among the citizens.
In good faith he summoned Shun, and happily appointed the latter as his successor.
He is not concerned with retaining power but rather to continue the nurture of citizens.

Yao's unselfish abdication and the peaceful transfer of power to Shun is lauded to this day.

Chapter 4. Zhongni (仲尼, Confucius)

4.15 真知真能   4.15 True Knowledge True Capability

01	关尹喜曰：	Guanyin Happily Said:
02	"在己无居，	"In Self No Position (no bias, unselfish),
03	形物其著。	Forms and Matters Their Clarity (showing).
04	其动若水，	'Dao' Flow Like Water (conforming),
05	其静若镜，	'Dao' Silent Like Mirror (reflecting),
06	其应若响。	'Dao' Respond Like Echo (authentic).
07	故其道若物者也。	Thus The 'Dao' Like The Matters that's.
08	物自违道，	Matters Self Contradict 'Dao'
09	道不违物。	'Dao' Not Contradict Matters.
10	善若道者，	Person Good Like 'Dao',
11	亦不用耳，	Also Not Using Ears,
12	亦不用目，	Also Not Using Eyes,
13	亦不用力，	Also Not Using Strength,
14	亦不用心。	Also Not Using Heart.
15	欲若道而用	Wishing Like 'Dao' And Using
16	视听形智以求之，	Sight, Hearing, Form, Cleverness To Acquire it ('Dao')
17	弗当矣。	Not Appropriate indeed.
18	瞻之在前，	Seeing It In Front,
19	忽焉在后；	Suddenly It's At the Back;
20	用之弥满六虚，	Use It Filling Up the 6 Voids (up, down, 4 directions),
21	废之莫知其所。	Abandon It Not Know Its Whereabout.
22	亦非有心者所能得远，	Also Not, Person Has Wish, Then Can Distant 'Dao',
23	亦非无心者所能得近。	Also Not, Person No Wish, Then Can Close to 'Dao'.
24	唯默而得之	Only Silence Will Attain It ('Dao')
25	而性成之者得之。	And Person With Complete Nature, Gets It ('Dao').
26	知而忘情，	Knows And Forget Emotion,
27	能而不为，	Capable And Not Selfish,
28	**真知真能也。**	***True Knowledge True Capability that's.***
29	发无知，何能情？	Initiates with No Knowledge, How Able to Love ?
30	发不能，何能为？	Initiates with No Capability, How Able to Achieve ?
31	聚块也，积尘也，	Collected Pieces that's, Accumulated Dust that's,
32	虽无为而非理也。	Although Not Selfish But Not Reasonable that's."

147

4.15 True Knowledge True Capability

Liezi Text Narrative
Guanyin happily said: "In self no position (no bias), forms matters outside all clarity show. L3
'Dao' like flowing water conforms, like silent mirror reflects, like responding echo, authentic. L6
Thus 'Dao' like the matters that's; matters may contradict 'Dao'; 'Dao' not contradict matters. L9
Person good like 'Dao', also not use ears, not use eyes, not use strength, not use heart. L14
Wishing like 'Dao' to use sight, hearing, form, cleverness to acquire 'Dao', not appropriate. L17
Looking at it ('Dao') in front, suddenly it's at the back. L19
'Dao', fill up the 6 voids (up, down, 4 directions); abandon, not knowing its where-about. L21
No person wishing, can get to distant 'Dao'; no person not wishing, can get close to 'Dao'. L23
Only silence will attain it ('Dao'), and the person completed in nature will get it ('Dao'). L25
Knows and forgets prejudice, capable and not selfish, true knowledge and true capability. L28
Initiates with no knowledge, how able to love ? L29
Initiates with no ability, how able to achieve ? L30
Collected pieces and accumulated dust that's, although not selfish but not reasonable that's."L32

Comments:
4.15 True Knowledge True Capability
Guanyin, enlightened declares "person pure at heart, sees clarity in all forms and matters".
Like the flowing water conforming, the silent mirror reflecting, and echo authentic response.
Knowledge with no prejudice, is true knowledge; capable and unselfish, is true ability.
But with no knowledge to love, no ability to perform, people are like collected pieces and dust.

Guanyin was purportedly the guard at the frontier pass, who asked Laozi to write the *Daodejing*.
Through Guanyin, Liezi indicates that his concept of 'Dao' is an extension of Laozi's 'Dao'.

Enlightened and not selfish, but has no knowledge, no ability, is not a true display of 'Daoism'.

Chapter 4. Zhongni (仲尼, Confucius)

Summary

4.1 Zhongni (Confucius) (仲尼): Happy with Heaven, accept destiny and have no worry. . Though liberated himself, Confucius worried for the wish to liberate the world and society.

4.2 My State Has Sage Person (吾国有圣人): Able to hear with eyes and to see with ears ! Kangcangzi said, "No, mis-information."; eg. sages highly alert but no supernatural power.

4.3 Qiu A Sage ? (丘圣者欤?): Confucius claimed no sagehood, just a highly learned person. The 3 kings and 5 sovereigns were kind and just doing their duties, thus also were not sages.

4.4 Why Serve Teacher (Kongzi) ? (何为事夫子?): Disciples were the best in specific talents. Teacher Confucius was not the best, but had many talents and was able to teach flexibilities.

4.5 Nankuazi (the Hermit) (南郭子): A neighbor, Liezi brought 40 disciples for first visit. He spoke only to the last disciple in line and just aiming to win; this is why he is a loner.

4.6 Liezi Learning (子列子学): For 9 years, thinking no right/wrong, speaking no good/evil. Fully liberated, mind not burden with desires, body light in steps, speech nothing to hide.

4.7 Liezi Loved To Travel (子列子好游): To observe changes in the outside world and society. Huqiuzi instructed, to also observe changes inside ourselves, then travelling is complete.

4.8 Longshu, I Have Illness (龙叔吾有疾): Titles not tempting, Longshu was near sagehood. Wenzhi saw 1 of 7 heart orifices blocked, sagehood not released, so feeling self not self !

4.9 Yangzhu Sang Yangzhu Cried (杨朱而歌而哭): Jiliang died, he sang; Suiwu died, he cried. Born and live, normal, we sing; born and died, unfortunate, we cry; all in accord with 'Dao'.

4.10 Matters Not At Limit, Not Return (物不至者则不反): Like before going blind, see best! A belief that gives hope in the worst of situations, not a delusion that things only get better.

4.11 How Differ From Dogs And Pigs ? (奚异犬豕之类乎?): Dengxi debasing Bofengzi. His disciple countered saying daoists were artisans and service citizens earning their keeps.

4.12 The Strength of Gongyibo (公仪伯以力闻): King Xuan doubted him, as physique small. He cannot bear weight, but better, he had the ability to use strength, and to teach others.

4.13 Gongsunlong (公孙龙): (c.325-250BC) A philosopher of the School of Names, China. His many logics are like, 'a white horse is a white horse, not a black horse, not any horse.'

4.14 Yao Administration (尧治天下): Yao (c.2,350BC), one of 5 legendary emperors, China. His legendary abdication and peaceful transfer of powder to Shun, was lauded to this day.

4.15 Guanyinxi (关尹喜): The legendary guard who requested Laozi to write the Daodejing. Enlightened and not selfish, but has no knowledge, no ability, is not a true Daoist.

This chapter describes what makes a person, a sage, a human, a hermit, a confucian, a daoist.

Chapter 5.　Tang's Queries (汤问)

Introduction

5.1　Tang's Queries (汤问)

5.2　Yukong (Stupid Grandpa) (愚公)

5.3　Kuafu Chased The Sun (夸父追日)

5.4　Outside Of Sagehood (非圣人之所通)

5.5　An Absurd State (谬之一国)

5.6　Different States Different Traditions (为俗未足为异)

5.7　Kongzi Cannot Decide (孔子不能决)

5.8　Fairness (均)

5.9　Change of Hearts (换汝之心)

5.10　Three Years No Music (三年不成章):

5.11　Lingering 3 Days Above Rafter (绕梁三日)

5.12　Soulmates In Music (伯牙, 钟子期)

5.13　The Artificial Performer (所造能倡者)

5.14　Ancient Archers (古之善射者)

5.15　Zaofu Learned Charioteering (造父习御)

5.16　Laidan Schemed Revenge (来丹谋报仇)

5.17　Overly Self-Confident (果于自信)

Summary

Chapter 5. Tang's Queries (汤問)

Introduction:

Tang (1670-1587 BC) was the founder king of the Shang Dynasty (1,600-1,066 BC). China.
Narratives here query the origin and limits of Heaven, on Earth and the universe beyond.
Queries with legends exploring the formation of lands, mountains, seas and where the sun set.
Queries with discussion, into the nature of sagehood, uniformity, balance and fairness.
Queries, exploring the limits of achievement in music, automation, archery and charioteering.

Tang queried his minister on the origin and limits of the universe, in Heaven and on Earth.
Xiage: "Nothing creates nothing, outside limits no limits", and gushed legends on Earth creations.
Can Yukong succeed, the old man who wished to move mountains that blocked his way to town ?
Kuafu chased the Sun to query where the sun set, and legend said he died turning into an oasis.
Yu: "all creations through gods"; Xiage: "creations of 'Dao' self natural", raising more queries.
Liezi called the State of Zhongbei an absurd state; an exploration of a legendary utopian state.
Narrative of ancient customs like eating the first born for more children, abandoning parents !
Is the Sun nearer to Earth in the morning or at noon, a query that Confucious cannot answer !
From hairs' uniformity for strength, Zhanhe's fancy balance in fishing, to fairness for governing.
Bianque tried to balance Gonghu and Qiying opposite temperaments by exchanging their hearts !
Shiwen's exploration for feeling in music lasted 3 years, then only achieved after a short break.
Hane's singing lingered 3 days after she left, and left a legacy that people at Yong Gate cherished.
Boya played well and Zhongziqi listened well; they are the legendary perfect soulmates in music.
The artificial performer winked at court ladies, automation perfect that almost cost Yanshi's life.
Archers: Feiwei surpassed his teacher; his student Jichang tried to surpass him by killing him !
Zaofu learned charioteering with the legendary Tadoushi; firstly trained to walk on raised piles.
Laidan avenged his father by 'killing' Heiluan with a 'virtual' sword that passed with no blood !
The Prince didn't believe the Kunyu sword, firewash-cloth; arrogance stopped his learning.

5.1 汤问

01 殷汤问于夏革曰：
02 "古初有物乎？"
03 夏革曰：
04 "古初无物，
05 今恶得物？
06 后之人将谓今之无物，
07 可乎？"
08 殷汤曰：
09 "然则物无先后乎？"
10 夏革曰：
11 "物之终始，
12 初无极已。
13 始或为终，终或为始，
14 恶知其纪？
15 然自物之外，自事之先，
16 朕所不知也。"
17 殷汤曰：
18 "然则上下八方
19 　有极尽乎？"
20 革曰："不知也。"
21 汤固问。
22 革曰："无则无极，有则有尽；
23 朕何以知之？
24 然无极之外复无无极，
25 无尽之中复无无尽。
26 无极复无无极，
27 无尽复无无尽。
28 朕以是知其无极无尽也，
29 而不知其有极有尽也。"
30 汤又问曰：
31 "四海之外奚有？"
32 革曰："犹齐州也。"
33 汤曰："汝奚以实之？"
34 革曰：
35 "朕东行至营，人民犹是也。
36 问营之东，复犹营也。
37 西行至豳，人民犹是也。
38 问豳之西，复犹豳也。
39 朕以是知四海、四荒、
40 四极之不异是也。

5.1 Tang's Queries

Tang of Yin To Xiage Asking, Said:
"Ancient Beginning Has Matters or Not ?"
Xiage Said:
"Ancient Initially No Matters,
Today How to Acquire Matters ?
The People After us Say, Today There's No Matters,
Posssible or Not ?
Tang of Yin Said:
"But Then Matters No Before / After (sequence), True ?"
Xiage Said:
"Matters Their Ending Beginning,
Initially No Limiting Finishing.
Beginning May Be Ending, Ending May Be Beginning,
Hard Knowing The Order ?
But Then Outside Of Matters, From Affairs Their Past,
Whatever, I Know Not that's"
Tang of Yin Said:
"But Then Above Below, the 8 Regions
　Have Limits Ends or Not ?"
Ge (Xiage) Said: "Not Knowing that's."
Tang Persistently Asking.
Ge Said: "No Then No Limit, Has Then Has Ending;
How Would I Know It ?
Naturally No Limit, Its Outside Again No, No Limit,
No End, It's Inside Again No, No End.
No Limit Again No, No Limit,
No End Again No, No End.
I Therefore Know The No Limit No End that's,
And Not Know The Have Limit Have End that's."
Tang Again Asking, Said:
" 4 Seas, The Outside Whatever Have ?"
Ge Said: "Like the Central Continent (China) that's."
Tang Said: "How Can You Confirm This ?"
Ge Said:
"I Went East To Ying, Citizens Like Similar, that's.
Asked about East Of Ying, Again Like Ying that's.
Went West To Bin, Citizens Like Similar, that's.
Asked about West of Bin, Again Like Bin that's.
I Therefore Know 4 Seas, 4 Wildernesses,
4 Limits They No Difference That's that.

5.1 Tang's Queries

41	故大小相含，	Thus Big Small Mutually Inclusive,
42	无穷极也。	No Ending Limit that's.
43	含万物者，	That Inclusive of All Matters,
44	亦如含天地。	Also Like Inclusive of Heaven Earth.
45	含万物也故不穷，	Inclusive of All Matters that's Thus No Ending,
46	含天地也故无极。	Inclusive of Heaven Earth that's Thus No Limit.
47	朕亦焉知天地之表	Also How I Know Heaven Earth Their Appearance
48	不有大天地者乎？	Not Having That Bigger than Heaven Earth, True ?
49	亦吾所不知也。	That Also I Know Not, that's.
50	然则天地亦物也。	But Then Heaven, Earth Also Matters, that's.
51	物有不足，	Matters Have Not Enough,
52	故昔者女娲氏	Thus Past Person Nuwashi
53	炼五色石以补其阙；	Refined 5-Colored Stone To Patch-up The Deficiency;
54	断鳌之足以立四极。	Cut Turtle Its 4 Legs To Hold-up the 4 Limits.
55	其后共工氏与颛顼	After That, Gonggongshi And Zhuanxu
56	争为帝，	Contested to Be Emperor,
57	怒而触不周之山，	Angry Then Crashed Buzhou The Mountain,
58	折天柱，绝地维；	Broke Pillar of Heaven, Severed Rope of Earth;
59	故天倾西北，	Thus Heaven Inclined West North,
60	日月星辰就焉；	Sun Moon Stars Followed that's;
61	地不满东南，	Earth Not Full in the East South,
62	故百川水潦归焉。"	Thus 100 Rivers Water Flowing Back that's."
63	汤又问："物有巨细乎？	Tang Again Asked: "Matters Have Huge Small, True ?
64	有修短乎？有同异乎？"	Has Long Short, True? Has Similarity Difference, True?"
65	革曰：	Ge Said:
66	"渤海之东不知几亿万里，	"Bo Sea To East Not Know Few Trillion Miles,
67	有大壑焉，实惟无底之谷，	Has Huge Gully that's, Truly Is A No Bottom Valley,
68	其下无底，名曰归墟。	Its Beneath No Bottom, Name Call-it Guixu.
69	八纮九野之水，	8 Faraways 9 Wilderness (earth) Their Water,
70	天汉之流，	Heaven Milky-way Their Streams,
71	莫不注之，而无增无减焉。	None Not Pour In, Yet No Increase No Decrease that's.
72	其中有五山焉：	In There Have 5 Mountains that's"
73	一曰岱舆，二曰员峤，	1 Call-it Daiyu, 2 Call-it Yuanqiao,
74	三曰方壶，四曰瀛洲，	3 Call-it Fanghu, 4 Call-it Yingzhou
75	五曰蓬莱。	5 Call-it Penglai.
76	其山高	The Mountains High
77	下周旋三万里，	Below Circumference Circle 30 Thousand Miles,
78	其顶平处九千里。	The Peak Flat Area 9 Thousand Miles.
79	山之中间相去七万里，	Mountain Centers Mutually Apart 70 Thousand Miles.
80	以为邻居焉。	To Be a Neighborly Situation that's.
81	其上台观皆金玉，	On Top, Viewing Tower All Gold and Jade,
82	其上禽兽皆纯缟。	On Top, Birds Animals All Pure White-covering.
83	珠玕之树皆丛生，	Trees of Pearls Gems All Grow in Clusters,
84	华实皆有滋味，	Flowers Fruits All Are Nutritious Fragrant,

5.1 Tang's Queries

85	食之皆不老不死。	Eating Them All No-growing Old No Death.
86	所居之人皆仙圣之种；	The People Residing There, All Are Fairies Sages Kinds;
87	一日一夕飞相往来者，	One Day One Night Mutually Flying Back/ Forth People,
88	不可数焉。	Not Able to Count indeed.
89	而五山之根无所连著，	And 5 Mountains' Roots No Whatever Connecting With,
90	常随潮波上下往还，	Often Follow Tides Waves Up Down Forward Backward,
91	不得暂峙焉。	Not Able to Momentarily Pause indeed.
92	仙圣毒之，诉之于帝。	Fairies Sages Hated It, Complained This To the Emperor.
93	帝恐流于西极，	Emperor Fear (mountains) Flowing To West End,
94	失群仙圣之居，	Crowd of Fairies Sages Lost Their Abodes,
95	乃命禺彊使巨鳌十五	Thus Ordered Rhujiang to Make 15 Huge Turtles
96	举首而戴之。	Hold-up their Heads To Support Them (mountains).
97	迭为三番，	Alternate As 3 Batches,
98	六万岁一交焉。	60 Thousands Years One Change-over that's.
99	五山始峙而不动。	Five Mountains Then Stable Not Moving.
100	而龙伯之国有大人，	And Kingdom of Longbo Has Huge Person,
101	举足不盈数步	Raised Foot Not Fully Few Steps
102	而暨五山之所，	And Arrived At Whereabout of 5 Mountains,
103	一钓而连六鳌，	One Hook And Connected 6 Turtles,
104	合负而趣，	Together Carried And Hurried back,
105	归其国，	Returned to His Kingdom,
106	灼其骨以数焉。	Scorched The Bones (turtle) For Divination that's.
107	于是岱舆，员峤	Therefore Daiyu, Yuanqiao
108	二山流于北极，	2 Mountains Floated To North Pole,
109	沈于大海，	Submerged Into Big Sea,
110	仙圣之播迁者	Fairies Sages Their Dispersing Migrating People
111	巨亿计。	Counting Greatly in Billions.
112	帝凭怒，	Emperor Very Angry,
113	侵减龙伯之国使厄。	Slowly Reduced Kingdom of Longbo, Made Smaller.
114	侵小龙伯之民使短。	Slowly Diminished Citizens of Longbo, Made Shorter.
115	至伏羲神农时，	Till Time of Fuxi Shennong,
116	其国人犹数十丈。	The Kingdom's People Still Several Tens of Yards.
117	从中州以东四十万里	From Central Continent To East 400 Thousand Miles
118	得僬侥国，	Reaching Kingdom of Qiaojiao.
119	人长一尺五寸。	People's Height 1 Foot 5 Inches.
120	东北极有人名曰诤人，	East North End Has People Name Call Zheng People,
121	长九寸。	Height 9 Inches.
122	荆之南有冥灵者，	South of Jing (place) Has Mingling Trees,
123	以五百岁为春，	With 500 Years As a Spring,
124	五百岁为秋。	500 Years As an Autumn.
125	上古有大椿者，	Most Ancient Has Dachun Trees,
126	以八千岁为春，	With 8 Thousand Years As a Spring,

5.1 Tang's Queries

127	八千岁为秋。	8 Thousands Years As an Autumn.
128	朽壤之上有菌芝者，	Rotten Soil On Top Has Bacteria Entity,
129	生于朝，死于晦。	Born At Dawn, Die At Nightfall.
130	春夏之月有蠓蚋者，	The Month of Spring Summer Has Midges Gnats Entities,
131	因雨而生，见阳而死。	Because of Rain And Live, See the Sun And Die.
132	终北之北有溟海者，	North of North Pole Has Dark Sea Entity,
133	天池也，有鱼焉。	Pond of Heaven, Has Fish that's.
134	其广数千里，	Its Width Few Thousand Miles,
135	其长称焉，其名为鲲。	Its Length Matching that's, Its Name Is Kun.
136	有鸟焉，其名为鹏，	Has Bird that's, Its Name Is Peng,
137	翼若垂天之云，其体称焉。	Wings Hang Like Heaven's Clouds, Its Body Matching.
138	世岂知有此物哉？	World How Know Has This Thing True ?
139	大禹行而见之，	Great Yu Travelled And Saw It,
140	伯益知而名之，	Boyi Knew And Named It,
141	夷坚闻而志之。	Yijian Heard And Recorded It.
142	江浦之间生麽虫，	River Side That Space Living Tiny Insects,
143	其名曰焦螟，	The Name Call Jiaoming,
144	群飞而集于蚊睫，	Swarm Flying And Assembled On Fly's Eyelash,
145	弗相触也。	Not Mutually Contacting that's.
146	栖宿去来，蚊弗觉也。	Perching Roosting Coming Going, Flies Not Aware that's.
147	离朱子羽方昼拭眦扬眉而望之，	Lizhu, Ziyu Noon Day Eyes Rub Open-wide And Look,
148	弗见其形；	Not See Their Forms;
149	𩠉俞师旷方夜	Zhiyu, Shikuang Deep Night
150	擿耳俯首而听之，	Clear Ears Bend Head And Listen to Them,
151	弗闻其声。	Not Hear Their Sound.
152	唯黄帝与容成子	Only Huangdi And Rongchengzi
153	居空峒之上，	Staying On Top of Kongdong (mountain),
154	同斋三月，	Together Fasting 3 Months,
155	心死形废；	Heart (feelings) Dead (calm) Form Wasted (quiet);
156	徐以神视，	Slowly With Spiritual Looking,
157	块然见之，	Massively Suddenly Seeing Them,
158	若嵩山之阿；	Like Songshan (mountain) Its Body;
159	徐以气听，	Slowly With Air (breath) Listening,
160	砰然闻之，	Explosive Suddenly Hearing Them,
161	若雷霆之声。	Like ThunderBolts The Sound.
162	吴楚之国有大木焉，	Kingdoms of Wu and Chu Have Big Trees indeed,
163	其名为櫾，	The Name Is You,
164	碧树而冬生，实丹而味酸。	Green Tree And Winter Alive, Fruits Red and Taste Sour.
165	食其皮汁，已愤厥之疾。	Eating Its Skin and Juice, Cure Anger Resentment Illness
166	齐州珍之，	Qizhou (place) Value It,
167	渡淮而北，	Crossing Huai (river) And North,
168	而化为枳焉。	And Transform As Orange that's.
169	鸲鹆不逾济，	Mynah Bird Not Go-beyond Ji (river).

5.1 Queries of Tang

170	貉逾汶则死矣。	Fox Go-beyond Wen (river) Then Die indeed.
171	地气然也。	Earth Air (different) Naturally that's.
172	虽然，形气异也，	Although, Form Air Different that's,
173	性钧已，无相易已。	Nature Balance Already, No Mutual Changing Already.
174	生皆全已，	Living (conditions) All Complete Already,
175	分皆足已。	Adaptation All Enough Already.
176	吾何以识其巨细？	I, How To Know The Big and Small ?
177	何以识其修短？	How To Know The Long and Short ?
178	何以识其同异哉？"	How To Know The Similarity and Difference ?"

Liezi Text Narrative

Tang (founder king Shang Dynasty) of Yin (place name) to Xiage (minister) asking, said: L1
"Ancient beginning has matters or not ?" L2
Xiage said: "Ancient initially no matters, today how to acquire matters ?" L5
The people after us may say we have no matters today, possible or not ?" L7
Tang of Yin said: "But then matters have no before or after sequence, true ?" L9
Xiage said: "Matters their ending beginning, initially no limiting finishing. L12
Beginning may be ending or vice versa, so difficult to know the order ? L14
But then, from outside of matters, from the past of affairs, whatever, I know not that's." L16
Tang of Yin said: "But then above and below, the 8 regions have limits/ends or not ?" L19
Xiage said: "Not knowing that's; Tang persisted in asking. L21
Ge (Xiage) said: "No order, no limit; has order has an end; how can I know this ? L23
Naturally, No-Limit its outside again has no 'no-limit', No-End its inside also no 'no end'. L25
No-Limit again no 'no-limit, No-End again no 'no-end'. L27
Therefore I know the No-Limit No-End that's, and not know the have-limit have-end that's. L29
Tang again asking, said: "4 seas, the outside, whatever have ?" L31
Ge said: "Like Central Continent (China) that's."; Tang said: "How can you confirm this ?" L33
Ge said "I went East to Ying, citizens are similar; asked about East of Ying, like Ying that's. L36
Went West to Bin, citizens are similar; asked about West of Bin, again are like Bin that's. L38
Thus I know the 4 Seas, 4 Wilderness, 4 Limits and beyond, there are no differences that's. L40
Therefore Big Small mutually inclusive, No-Endings No-Limits that's. L42
That is inclusive of all matters, also like inclusive of Heaven and Earth. L44
Inclusive of all matters that's thus no endings, inclusive of Heaven Earth that's thus no limits.L46
How do I know the look of Heaven Earth as there is none bigger than Heaven Earth, true ? L48
That also I know not; but then Heaven and Earth are also matters that's. L50
Matters may be deficient, hence ancestor Nuwashi refined 5-color stone to patch deficiency. L53
Cut turtle's 4 Legs to hold up (Heaven) at the 4 Limits on Earth. L54
Later, contesting Zhuanxu to be emperor, Gonggongshi he crashed Buzhou Mt. in anger. L56
Broke the Pillar of Heaven and severed the Rope of Earth from anchorage. L58
Thus the Heaven inclined towards West North, and sun moon stars all shifted that way, that's.L60
No Earth filling (seas) in the East South, and there the 100 rivers flowing to return that's. L62
Tang again asked: "Matters have Big/Small, have Long/Short, Similarity/Difference, true ?" L64
Ge said: "East of Bo Sea, trillions of miles away has a huge gully, truly a bottomless valley. L67
Beneath it no bottom, name call-it Guixu. L68

5.1 Queries of Tang

From 8 great-belts and 9 wilderness their water, and Heaven Milky-way their streams; L70
None not pouring in, yet no increase or decrease that's (sea level). L71
On the sea are 5 mountains that's: 1.Daiyu, 2.Yuanqiao, 3.Fanghu, 4.Yingzhou, 5.Penglai. L75
The mountains are high, and below the surrounding circumference is 30 thousand miles. L77
The top flat area 9 thousand miles, mountain neighbors are 70 thousand miles apart, that's. L80
On top, viewing towers are all gold and jade, birds and animals all pure white skins feathers. L82
Trees of pearls and gems all grow in clusters, all flowers, fruits are nutritious and fragrant. L84
Eating them (elixir), all not grow old and not die; all residents are kind of fairies and Sages. L86
Days and nights, people mutually flying back and forth visiting, numbers not able to count. L88
Roots of 5 mountains are not secure, with tidal waves up down back forth, not a moment still. L91
Fairies Sages hated this and complained to the Emperor of Heaven. L92
The Emperor feared mountains would flow to the west end, fairies, sages lost their abodes. L94
Thus he ordered Rhujiang to make 15 huge turtles raise their heads to support mountains. L96
Alternate as 3 batches, 60 thousands years one change-over, then 5 mountains not moving. L99

The Kingdom of Longbo had a huge person who with a few steps arrived at 5 mountains. L102
One hook and fish-off 6 turtles, hurried back to kingdom, scorched bones for divination. L106
Thus Daiyu Yuanqiao the two mountains flowed to the North Pole, submerged in a big sea. L109
Fairies, Sages, people dispersing and migrating, counted in hundreds of millions. L111
The Emperor was angry, made the Longbo Kingdom smaller, and the citizens shorter. L114
At the time of Fuxi Shennong, the kingdom's people were still several tens of yards tall. L116
Central Continent to East 400,000 miles was Qiaojiao Kingdom, people only 5 inches tall. L119
East North End had people named Zheng People, height 9 inches. L121
South of Jing (place) had a Mingling tree, 500 years a spring, 500 years an autumn. L124
Most ancient Era had Dachun Tree, 8 thousand years a Spring, 8 thousand years an Autumn. L127
On top of the rotten soil were bacteria entities, born at dawn, and died at nightfall. L129
Months of Spring Summer had midges gnats, with Rain came alive, see Sun will die. L131
North of the North Pole, a dark sea called Pond of Heaven, had a Fish that's. L133
The Fish's width was thousands miles, its length comparable that's, and name was Kun. L135
Had Bird that's, its name was Peng, wings hang like Heaven's clouds, its body matching. L137
How the World knows these things is-it-not ? L138
Great Yu travelled and saw them, Boyi knew and named them, Yijian heard, recorded them. L141
The river-side lived tiny insects, named Jiaoming, swarming assembled on fly's eyelashes. L144
Not mutually in contact that's, perching roosting coming/going and flying unaware that's. L146
Lizhu and Ziyu at noon, eyes rubbed open-wide, looking and not seeing their forms. L148
Zhiyu and Shikuang at midnight, ears cleared, head bent to listen, not hearing their sound. L151
Huangdi and Rongchengzi, on top of Mt Kongdong fasted 3 months, felt dead calm, quiet. L155
Slowly like a divine sighting, saw them suddenly massive like the waist of Mt Songshan; L158
Slowly like listening to air, suddenly explosively heard them like the thunderbolt sound. L161
Kingdoms of Wu and Chu have big trees indeed, the name is You. L163
Evergreen trees alive in Winter, fruits red taste sour, eat skin juice can cure anger agitation, L165
Qizhou (place) values it, but after crossing Huai (river) and north, transform as orange. L168
Mynah birds not go beyond Ji River, fox beyond Wen River will die, eco system not right. L171
Though the eco systems are different, natural balance already, no mutually changing over. L173

5.1 Tang's Queries

Living conditions all completed already, adaptation all enough already. L175
I, how to know the Big or Small ?; how to know the Long and Short ? L177
I, how to know, the similarity and the difference ?" L178

Comments:
5.1 Tang's Queries
Tang of Yin, founder king of Shang Dynasty, queried minister Xiage on nature, the universe.
On if ancient origin has matters, Xiage: 'yes'; else have no matters now, nothing creates nothing.
On, if above below, 8 regions of the universe have limits, Xiage: 'no limit, outside also no limits'.
On what's there outside the 4 seas, Xiage: 'To East or West and beyond, people are like us here.'
Ge (Xiage) said not knowing things bigger than Heaven Earth, then went on narrating legends.
Nuwashi refined 5 colored stones to patch the sky, cut the turtle's 4 legs to hold up Heaven.
Contested with Zhuanxu, Gonggongshi crashed Mt. Buzhou in anger, broke pillar of Heaven.
Thus Heaven inclined towards West North where sun moon stars shifted and were clearly seen.
Then where no Earth filled the East South, the 100 rivers flow in forming the south seas there.

Interested for more, Tang further queried if matters have big/small, long/short, similar/different ?
Excitedly Xiage gushed: "East of Bo Sea, trillions miles away, there is the huge gully Guixu.
From 8 belts 9 wilderness and Milky-way, waters pour in, yet no increase or decrease of sea level.
On the sea were 5 high mountains, 30 thousand miles circumference, 70 thousand miles apart.
On flat-top 9 thousand miles, fairies sages live in towers of gold jade, birds animals pure white.
Trees of pearls, flowers fragrant, fruits nutritious, elixir to residents who never grow old and die.
Mountains may flow west with waves, so Rhujian made 15 huge turtles raise heads to support.
A Giant of Longbo Kingdom came in a few steps, fish off 6 turtles, Daiyu Yuanqiao submerged.
Emperor of Heaven was angry, reducing the Longbo area and citizens' height to yards only.
Central to East was Qiaojiao's people, 5 inches short ; East North End, Zheng people 9 inches.
The ancient Dachun tree lives 8 thousand years a Spring, 8 thousand years an Autumn.
In the months of Spring Summer, midges and gnats with rain come alive, and die on sunrise.
North of the Pole, the Pond of Heaven had Kun, a fish thousand miles wide, length to match.
Had Peng, a bird with wings hanging like Heaven's clouds, with its body matching.
Purportedly the Great Yu saw them in travels, Boyi knew and named them, Yijian recorded them.
On the river-side lived tiny insects Jiaoming assembled on fly's eyelashes and flies not aware.
Lizhu and Ziyu sharp-sighted cannot see their forms; Zhiyu and Shikuang cannot hear their sound.
Huangdi and Rongchengzi, on top of Mt Kongdong fasted 3 months, felt dead calm and quiet.
Saw them suddenly massive like waist of Mt Songshan; heard them suddenly like thunderbolts.
Wu and Chu areas have evergreens You, fruits red taste sour, skins juice can cure anger agitation.
Qizhou area people value them, but after crossing Huai river and north, transformed into orange.
Mynahs do not go beyond Ji River, nor fox beyond Wen River, as the eco systems are not right.
Though the eco systems are different, natural balances already established, so no crossing over.
Xiage by logic deduced the presence of matters at the beginning and that the universe is infinite.
Traveling from Central continent to the east/west and beyond, he saw people are all the same.
The rest are legends by the ancients and ancestors like Great Yu, Boyi, Yijian who made records."
Hence Xiage truly and honestly ended his long narrative declaring vehemently:
"How am I to know the Big or Small, the Long and Short, the similarity and difference, that's ?"
Tang's queries, human curiosities enable studies, better knowledge of our universe each day.

Chapter 5. Tang's Queries (汤问)

5.2 愚公   5.2 Yukong (Stupid Grandpa)

01	太形、王屋二山，	Taixing, Wangwu 2 Mountains,
02	方七百里，高万仞。	Area 700 Miles, Height 10-thousand Meters.
03	本在冀州之南，	Basically On Jizhou Its South,
04	河阳之北。	Heyang Its North.
05	***北山愚公者，***	***North Hill Yukong Person,***
06	***年且九十，***	***Age About 90,***
07	面山而居。	And Resided Facing Hill.
08	惩山北之塞，	Suffering Block to North of Mountain,
09	出入之迂也，	Exiting Entering The Roundabout that's,
10	聚室而谋，曰：	Gathering Family And Planning, Said:
11	"吾与汝毕力平险，	"I With You Exhaust Strength to Flatten Blockade,
12	指通豫南，	Directly Through to South of Yu (Yuzhou),
13	达于汉阴，	Reaching To Yin (south) of Han (river),
14	可乎？"	Possible or Not ?"
15	杂然相许。	Miscellaneous Naturally Mutually Agreed.
16	其妻献疑曰：	The Wife Offered Doubts Said:
17	"以君之力，	"With 'Lord' Your Strength,
18	曾不能损魁父之丘，	Already Not Able to Decrease Kuifu The Hill,
19	如太形王屋何？	Like Taixing Wangwu How possible ?
20	且焉置土石？"	Also Where to Dispose of Soil Stones ?"
21	杂曰：	Miscellaneous Said:
22	"投诸渤海之尾，	"Cast Into Bo Sea Its End,
23	隐土之北。"	Hermits (abodes) Their North."
24	遂率子孙荷担者三夫，	Then Led Son Grandson Load Carriers 3 Men,
25	叩石垦壤，	Knock Stone Dig Soil,
26	箕畚运于渤海之尾。	Bamboo Basket Transport To The End of Bo Sea.
27	邻人京城氏之孀妻有遗男，	Neighbor Jingchengshi His Widow Had Bequeathed Boy
28	始龀，跳往助之。	Just Teething, Jumping Forward to Help Him.
29	寒暑易节，始一反焉。	Winter Summer Changed Seasons, First One Return only.
30	河曲智叟笑而止之，曰：	Wise Elder of River Bend Laughingly Stopped Him, Said:
31	"甚矣汝之不惠！	"Very Indeed You Have No Kindness !
32	以残年馀力，	With Waning Years and Residual Strength
33	曾不能悔山之一毛，	Already Not Able Reduce Mountain's One Grass,
34	其如土石何？"	With the Like of Soil Stones, How ?"
35	北山愚公长息曰：	Yukong of North Mountain with Long Sigh, Said:
36	"汝心之固，固不可彻，	"Your Heart The Hardness, Hardness Not Able to Pierce,
37	曾不若孀妻弱子。	Certainly Not Comparable to Widow's Weak Son.
38	虽我之死，有子存焉。	Though I Shall die, Have Son Living that's.
39	子又生孙，孙又生子；	Son Again Begets Grandson, Grandson Will Begets Son;
40	子又有子，子又有孙：	Son Again Has Son, Son Again Has Grandson:
41	子子孙孙，无穷匮也，	Sons Grandsons, No End Lacking that's,

5.2 Yukong (Stupid Grandpa)

42	而山不加增，	But Mountain No Adding Increasing,
43	何苦而不平？"	Why Worry Mountain Not Flattened ?
44	河曲智叟亡以应。	Wise Elder from River Bend at Lost To Respond.
45	操蛇之神闻之，	The Snake-Player Spirit Heard This,
46	惧其不已也，	Afraid Their Never Ending (dig) that's,
47	告之于帝。	Report This To the Emperor (of Heaven).
48	帝感其诚，	Emperor Empathized His Honesty,
49	命夸蛾氏二子负二山，	Ordered Kuaeshi's 2 Sons to Carry the 2 Mountains
50	一厝朔东，一厝雍南。	One to Place East of Shuo, One to Place South of Yong.
51	自此冀之南、汉之阴，	Since Then South of Ji, South of Han (river),
52	无陇断焉。	No Blocking Off that's.

Liezi Text Narrative

Taixing Wangwu 2 mountains, area 700 miles, height 10 thousand meters. L2
Basically on Jizhou south and Heyang north. L4
Yukong of North Hill, age 90, resided facing the hill. L7
Suffered blockade to the north of the hill, needed to go roundabout in and out of the house. L9
Gathering family and planning, said: "I with you to exhaust strength to flatten the blockade; L11
Directly through to the south of Yuzhou, to reach south of the Han river, possible or not ?" L14
All members chorused in agreement, but the wife offered doubts, said: L16
"With 'lord' your strength, already not able to decrease one bit of Kuifu the small hill; L18
How possible like Mt Taixing and Mt Wangwu, and also where to dispose of soil and stones. L20
All members said: "Cast into Bo Sea at its end, and north of the abodes of hermits." L23
Then leading son and grandson, 3 who can carry loads, breaking stones and digging soil. L25
And transporting in bamboo baskets to the end of Bo Sea. L26
Neighbor Jingchengshi's widow, had a son who was teething, who jumped forward to help. L28
And the first return-trip only, took the whole winter to summer, 3 seasons to complete. L29
Wise elder of River Bend laughingly stopped him, said: "You are very unkind indeed ! L31
With waning years, residual strength, not able to reduce mountain of one tuft of grass; L33
How to with rocks and soil ?"; Yukong of North Mountain with a long sigh, said: L35
"The hardness of your heart not able to break, surely not comparable to the widow's son. L37
Though I shall die, have son living that's; son begets grandson and grandson begets own son; L39
Son again has a son who has grandson, sons and grandsons, no ending no lacking that's. L41
However mountain no adding no increasing, so why worry mountain not be flattened ?" L43
Wise elder from River Bend was at a loss to respond. L44
Snake-player 'god' heard this, feared the digging never ending, reported it to the Emperor. L47
The Emperor felt Yugong's honesty, ordered Kuaeshi's 2 sons to carry off the 2 mountains. L49
One to deposit East of Shuo, one to place South of Yong. L50
Since then, South of Ji and South of Han river, no more block-off that's. L52

Comments:

5.2 Yukong (Stupid Grandpa)

Yukong or stupid grandpa is a fable story long been included in Chinese primary school textbook.
Yukong is fictitious but has been long lauded as a symbol of strength for overcoming obstacles.
Yukong is eco friendly, casting soil and stones into the far end of the Bo Sea.
Yukong is considerate of others, disposing of rubbles north of the abodes of hermits.
Even the 'gods' feared his no-end digging, and decided to remove the mountains overnight !
Beside a symbol of strength to overcome obstacles, Yugong is also eco friendly and neighborly.

Chapter 5. Tang's Queries (汤問)

5.3 夸父追日   5.3 Kuafu Chased The Sun

01	夸父不量力，	*Kuafu did Not Assessed own Strength,*
02	欲追日影，	*Desired to Chase Sun's Shadow,*
03	逐之于隅谷之际。	Chased It To The Boundary of Yugu.
04	渴欲得饮，	Thirsty, Desired to Get Drinks,
05	赴饮河渭。	Went to Drink at He (Yellow River) Wei (river).
06	河渭不足，	He (Yellow River) Wei (river) Not Enough,
07	将走北饮大泽。	About to Walk North to Drink Daze (Great Lake)
08	未至，	Prior Arriving,
09	道渴而死。	Wayside, Thirst And Died.
10	弃其杖，	Abandoned His Staff,
11	尸膏肉所浸，	That Soaked up Corpse's Oil Meat,
12	生邓林。	Grew into a Peach Forest.
13	邓林弥广数千里焉。	Peach Forest Fully Widely, Few Thousands Miles that's.

Liezi Text Narrative
Kuafu, not aware of his own strength, desired to chase Sun's shadow. L2
Chased it to the boundary of Yugu; thirsty, desired to get drinks. L4
Went to drink from the Yellow River and the Wei River, which were not enough. L6
Then walked north to drink the Daze (great lake); prior to arriving thirst and died by the way. L9
His abandoned staff that soaked up his corpse's oil and meat, grew into a peach forest. L12
Peach Garden was wide, extending a few thousand miles indeed. L13

Comments:
5.3 Kuafu Chased The Sun
Narrative first appeared in the ancient book, *Mountains and Seas Classic (山海經 c.2,200BC)*.
Word for word identical except for the first line, missing in the older text !
Again like Yugong, Kuafu has long been included in Chinese primary school books..
Both the bravery and stupidity of Kuafu are highlighted for daring to challenge the burning Sun !

The ancient Chinese believed the Heaven was a round dome, covering over the square flat Earth.
Daily the sun rises in the east and sets in the west; the sun comes down somewhere in the west !
Out of curiosity, some brave hearts went to the west in search of the truth in this matter.
Almost none return, but over the centuries a few did return to tell tales of deaths, deserts, oases.
Tales into a legend, that a Kaufu went after the sun, thirst to death and turned into a forest (oasis).

Kuafu chased the sun is a legend celebrating the human spirit in seeking answers to queries.

Chapter 5. Tang's Queries (汤问)

5.4 其道自然，	5.4 The 'Dao' Self Natural,
01 大禹曰：	Great Yu Said:
02 "六合之间，	"6 Quarters The Spaces,
03 四海之内，	4 Seas The Inside,
04 照之以日月，	Shine It With Sun Moon,
05 经之以星辰，	Traverse With Stars and Lights
06 纪之以四时，	Order It With 4 Seasons,
07 要之以太岁。	Limit It With Jupiter (12-year cycle).
08 神灵所生，	Gods Spirits Their Creations (all matter),
09 其物异形；	The Matters Diverse in Forms,
10 或夭或寿，	Maybe Short-lived Maybe Long-lived,
11 唯圣人能通其道。"	Only a Sage Person Able to Connect The 'Dao' "
12 夏革曰：	Xiage Said:
13 "然则亦有	"But Then Also Has
14 　不待神灵而生，	Not Dependent on God Spirit And be Created,
15 不待阴阳而形，	Not Dependent on Yin Yang And be Formed,
16 不待日月而明，	Not Dependent on Sun Moon And be Lighted,
17 不待杀戮而夭，	Not Dependent on Concerted Killing And be Dead,
18 不待将迎而寿，	Not Dependent on Greeting And be Long-lived,
19 不待五谷而食，	Not Dependent on 5 Cereals And be Fed,
20 不待缯纩而衣，	Not Dependent on Silk Cotton And be Clothed,
21 不待舟车而行。	Not Dependent on Boat Carriage For Travel.
22 *其道自然，*	***The Dao Self Natural,***
23 非圣人之所通也。"	Not Sage Person He However Enabled, that's."

Liezi Text Narrative

The Great Yu said: "Space in the 6 quarters (up down 4 direction), within the 4 seas; L3
The sun and moon shine, the stars and lights traverse, ordered passage of 4 seasons;. L6
The 12 yearly limited cycle of Jupiter, Gods/Spirits their creations of matters, diverse in form; L9
Maybe short-lived, maybe long-lived, only a Sage person able to connect with the 'Dao'." L11
Xiage Said: "But then also has, not dependent on Gods Spirits and be created; L14
Not dependent on Yin Yang and be formed, not dependent on Sun Moon and be lighted; L16
Not dependent on riot killing and be dead, not dependent on goodwill and be long-lived; L18
Not dependent on 5 cereals and be fed, not dependent on silk cotton and be clothed; L20
Not dependent on boats or carriages for travel; the 'Dao' is self natural. L22
Not what the Sage person enabled that's." L23

Comments:
5.4 The 'Dao' Self Natural,
Emperor Yu (c. 22nd - 21st century BC), ruler of ancient China, who tamed the great Deluge.
He said all things were created by gods and spirits, and facilitated by the Sage person.
Xiage the minister, not willing to contradict his Emperor directly, suggests:
Also have matters not created by gods and spirits, not facilitated by Sage person;
The 'Dao' is self natural.
Truly we know not the first creation, but all matters naturally progressed till this day.

Chapter 5. Tang's Queries (汤问)

5.5 谬之一国	**5.5 An Absurd State**
01 禹之治水土也，	Yu, His Managing Water Soil that's,
02 迷而失途涂，	Confused And Lost Way,
03 谬之一国。	***Of An Absurd State.***
04 滨北海之北，	Coast of North Sea to the North,
05 不知距齐州几千万里，	Not Known Distance from State of Qi Millions of Miles,
06 其国名曰终北，	The State Name Called Zhongbei (End North),
07 不知际畔之所齐限。	Not Knowing Where Its Edge Shore Together Limited.
08 无风雨霜露，	No Wind Rain Frost Dew,
09 不生鸟兽、	No Living Birds Animals,
10 虫鱼、草木之类。	Insects Fish, Grass Woods These Kinds.
11 四方悉平，	Four Direction Entirely Flat,
12 周以乔陟。	Surrounded With Tall Ranges (mountains).
13 当国之中有山，	Right Centre Of State Had Mountain,
14 山名壶领，	Mountain Named Huling (Mt. Pitcher),
15 状若甒甄。	Form Like a Small-mouth Pitcher.
16 顶有口，状若员环，	Top Had Mouth, Form Like Round Ring,
17 名曰滋穴。	Name Called Zixue (Nutrient Cave).
18 有水涌出，	Had Water Gushing Out,
19 名曰神瀵，	Name Called Shenfen (Spirit-Liquor),
20 臭过兰椒，	Fragrant Exceeding Lan-grass Pepper-flower,
21 味过醪醴。	Taste Exceeding Mashed and Sweet-wine.
22 一源分为四埒，	One Spring Divided As 4 Streams,
23 注于山下。	PouringTo Mountain Foot.
24 经营一国，	Managed Caring One State,
25 亡不悉遍。	No Loss Reaching Everywhere.
26 土气和，	Soil Atmosphere Harmonized,
27 亡札厉。	No Epidemic Experienced,
28 人性婉而从物，	Human Nature Gentle And Accorded Matters,
29 不竞不争。	No Contesting No Fighting.
30 柔心而弱骨，	Gentle Heart And Weak Bones,
31 不骄不忌；	Not Proud Not Envious;
32 长幼侪居，	Elders Youngsters Peerless Living (together),
33 不君不臣；	No King No Subjects;
34 男女杂游，	Males Females Mixed in Play,
35 不媒不聘；	No Match-makers No Betrothal;
36 缘水而居，	Alongside Water And Residing,
37 不耕不稼。	No Ploughing No Planting.
38 土气温适，	Soil Atmosphere Warm Suitably,
39 不织不衣；	No Weaving No Clothing;
40 百年而死，	Hundred Years Then Died,
41 不夭不病。	No Premature-death, No Sickness.

5.5 *An Absurd State*

42	其民孳阜亡数,	The Citizens Breeding Prolific No Counts (countless),
43	有喜乐,	Had Joy Happiness,
44	亡衰老哀苦。	No Declining Old-age or Grief of Suffering
45	其俗好声,	They Traditionally Loved Music,
46	相携而迭谣,	Holding-hands Together With Alternating Singing,
47	终日不辍音。	Whole Day Not Pausing Music.
48	饥惓则饮神（氵粪）,	Hungry Tired Then Drank Shenfen (spirit-liquor)
49	力志和平。	Strength Will Harmonized and Calm.
50	过则醉,	Exceeded Became Drunk,
51	经旬乃醒。	Past 10-days Then Awaken.
52	沐浴神瀵,	Bathing With Spirit-liquor,
53	肤色脂泽,	Skin Color Well-oiled Moisturized
54	香气经旬乃歇。	Fragrant Air Past 10-days Then Dissipated.
55	周穆王北游过其国,	King Mu of Zhou, North Tour Past That State,
56	三年忘归。	Three Years Forgot to Return.
57	既反周室,	After Return to Palace of Zhou,
58	慕其国,	Admiration for That State,
59	怊然自失。	Openly Like Self Lost.
60	不进酒肉,	Not Drinking Wine eating Meat,
61	不召嫔御者,	Not Calling Concubines Servants People,
62	数月乃复。	Several Months Then Recovered.
63	管仲勉	Guanzhong (chief minister) Encouraged
64	齐桓公因游辽口,	Duke Huan of Qi (state) On Touring Liaokou,
65	俱之其国,	To Include That State (Zhongbei, absurd state).
66	几克举,	Almost Beginning Tour,
67	隰朋谏曰：	Xipeng (minister) Admonished, Said:
68	"君舍齐国之广,	"King Abandon State of Qi Its Immensity,
69	人民之众,	The Multitude of Citizens,
70	山川之观,	Mountains Rivers Their Beauty,
71	殖物之阜,	Growth Matters The Abundance,
72	礼义之盛,	Etiquette Rites The Grandiosity,
73	章服之美；	Fineries Clothings Their Beauty;
74	妖靡盈庭,	Palace Full of Bewitching Concubines.
75	忠良满朝。	Court Full of Loyal (officials) Great (generals),
76	肆咤则徒卒百万,	Random Call And Million Soldiers (respond),
77	视抈则诸侯从命,	Issue Command Then All the Lords Obey Orders,
78	亦奚羡于彼	So Why Admiration For That (faraway state)
79	而弃齐国之社稷,	And Abandon State of Qi Its Temples and Citizens,
80	从戎夷之国乎？	To Follow Militant Barbarians Their State that's ?
81	此仲父之耄,	This is Father Zhong's (Guanzhong) Old-age (delusion),
82	奈何从之？"	Whatever Reason to Agree with Him ?"
83	桓公乃止,	Duke Huan Hence Stopped,
84	以隰朋之言告管仲。	With Xipeng's Words Informed Guanzhong.
85	仲曰：	Zhong Said:

5.5 *An Absurd State*

86 "此固非朋之所及也。	"This Certainly Not Peng's Ability to Know that's.
87 臣恐彼国	Subject-me Afraid That State
88 　之不可知之也。	It's (I) Not Able to Know that's.
89 齐国之富奚恋?	State of Qi, Its Prosperity Why Feel-attached ?
90 隰朋之言奚顾? "	Xipeng's Words Why Border ?"

Liezi Text Narrative

Yu, in his travels while managing the great deluge, lost his way into a state of Absurdity. L3
On the coast north of the North Sea, millions of miles away from the State of Qi; L5
The state named Zhongbei (North End), does not know where the edges, shores were limited. L7
No wind, rain, frost, dew, no living birds, animals or insects, fish, grass, woods, these kinds. L10
Four directions entirely flat, surrounded with tall mountain ranges. L12
Centre of the state was mountain Huling (Mt. Pitcher), formed like a small-mouthed pitcher. L15
Mountain top had a mouth, formed like a round ring named Zixue (Nutrient Cave). L17
Had water gushing out, the spring was named Shenfen (Spirit-liquor). L19
Fragrant exceeding Lan-grass pepper-flower, taste exceeding mashed and sweet-wine. L21
One spring was divided into 4 mountain streams, running down to the foot of the mountain. L23
Managing and caring for the whole state, water reaching everywhere not missing a corner. L25
Soil air harmonized, no epidemic record, human nature gentle and accorded with all matters. L28
No contesting no fighting, gentle heart and weak bones, not proud no envy; L31
Young and old peerless living together, no king no subjects; L33
Males females mixed in play, no match-makers no betrothal; L35
Residing alongside water-way, no ploughing no planting; L37
Soil air suitably warm, no weaving no clothing; L39
Died after a 100 years, no premature death no sickness; L41
The citizens' breeding prolific in countless number, had joy happiness; L43
No declining old-age or grief of suffering, they traditionally love music. L45
Holding-hands together with alternating singing, the whole day no pausing of music. L47
Hungry tired then drank Shenfen (Spirit-liquor), strength thoughts harmonized and calm. L49
Exceeded in drinking then became drunk, and needed to pass 10-days before waking up. L51
Bathing with Shenfen, skin color well-oiled and moisturized, fragrance 10-days to dissipate. L54
King Mu of Zhou, touring past that state, 3 years forgot to return. L56
After returning to the palace of Zhou, admiration for North End made him to openly self-lost.L59
No wine or meat, no call for concubines or servants, several months then recovered. L62
Guanzhong (chief minister) encouraged Duke Huan of Qi, on tour of Liaokou, L64
To include Zhongbei (absurd state); tour almost to begin when Xipeng(minister) admonished. L67
Said: "King abandon state of Qi its immensity, the multitude of citizens; L69
Beauty of mountains, rivers, abundance of growth matters, the grandiosity of etiquette rites. L72
Beautiful fineries clothings, palace full of bewitching concubines; L74
Courts of loyal officials and great generals, random call and a million soldiers respond. L76
Issue command then all the lords obey orders, so why admire that faraway state; L78
And abandon the state of Qi, its temples and citizens, to follow militant barbarians that's. L80
This Father Zhong's (Guanzhong) delusion in old-age, so what reason to agree with him ?" L82
Duke Huan hence stopped the tour, and with Xipeng's words informed Guanzhong. L84
Zhong said: "This certainly is not Peng's ability to know that's. L86
Subject-me is afraid that I will never get to know that state of Zhongbei (North End) that's. L88
State of Qi, its prosperity, why feel attached ? Xipeng's words, why bother ?" L90

165

5.5 An Absurd State

Comments:
5.5 An Absurd State
Emperor Yu (c.22-21st century BC), a Chinese legendary hero who had tamed the Great Deluge.
Legend has it that when managing the Deluge, Yu in travels was lost in the state of Zhongbei.
Zhongbei was millions of miles from the State of Qi, in the North End, north of the North sea.
Zhongbei (North End), on the coast of North Sea had no wind rain, frost dew, no birds animals !
Entirely flat, surrounded by tall mountain range, at centre Mt. Huling like a pitcher
With hole on top named Zixue (Nutrient Cave), gushing Shenfen (Spirit-liquor).
Which people drank when hungry and tired, fragrant and tasted like sweet wine.
When drunk, it took 10 days to recover; Shenfen bath gave moisturized skin, fragrant for 10 days.
Weather warm, residing along the water-way, no ploughing, no planting, no weaving, no clothing.
Gentle people, no contests, no fighting, no envy; young old together, peerless, no king /subjects.
Males females mixed in play, no match-makers, breeding prolific, had fun, happy, loved music.
Singing the whole day with no pause, no declining into old-age, no suffering and no grief.
No premature death or sickness, and lived to 100 years.
Is the above utopia ? No, that is the delusion of pseudo-daoists !
A true daoist, Liezi says:
" 谬之一国。　　 *Of An Absurd State. L03*

Legend has it that King Mu of Zhou (c.~3,000 BC) on tour, went to stay in Zhongbei for 3 years.
On return, he lost himself for several months, no drink, not eating, no concubines and no servants.
Guanzhong wished Duke Huan of Qi (c. ~2,600 BC) to include Zhongbei in his tour of the north.
However he missed the chance to visit Zhongbei as Xipeng succeeded in discouraging the Duke.
Guanzhong in old age is more inclined to not contest, to have the peace and quiet of daoism.
Hence he criticised Duke Huan for his attachment to the prosperity of Qi.
And Xipeng for lack of ability to know and appreciate the peace and enjoyment of daoism.

Liezi exposes the delusional utopian pseudo-daoism with this legendary state of Zhongbei.

Chapter 5. Tang's Queries (汤問)

5.6 为俗未足为异   5.6 Different States Different Traditions

01	南国之人祝发而裸；	South State, The People Shaved Hairs Were Naked;
02	北国之人鞨巾而裘；	North State, The People Turban Cloth And Jacketed;
03	中国之人冠冕而裳。	Centre State, The People Cap Crown And Dressed.
04	九土所资，或农或商，	9 Lands All Resources, Or Agriculture Or Commerce,
05	或田或渔，	Or Farming Or Fishing,
06	如冬裘夏葛，	Like Winter Jacket Summer Linen,
07	水舟陆车，默而得之，	Water Boat Land Carriage, Quietly These Are Attained,
08	性而成之。	Naturally They Are Formed.
09	越之东有辄沐之国，	East of Yue State There's The State of Zhemu,
10	其长子生，则鲜而食之，	The Elder Son Born, Then Offer To Be Consumed,
11	谓之宜弟。	Called This Facilitating more Brothers.
12	其大父死，	The GrandFather Died,
13	负其大母而弃之，	Carry The GrandMother For Abandoning Her,
14	曰："鬼妻不可以同居处。"	Said: "Devil Wife Not Allow To Stay at the Same Place."
15	楚之南有炎人之国，	South of Chu State There's The State of Yanren,
16	其亲戚死，	The Parents Died,
17	刳其肉而弃之，	Shaved The Muscles And Discarded Them,
18	然后埋其骨，	Then Afterward Buried The Bones,
19	乃成为孝子。	Then Considered to Be a Filial Son.
20	秦之西有仪渠之国者，	West of Qin State There's The State of Yiqu
21	其亲戚死，	The Parents Died,
22	聚柴积而焚之。	Gathered Wood Together And Burnt Them.
23	燻则烟上，	Fumigating Then Smoke Rising,
24	谓之登遐，	Called This Ascending Faraway (Heaven),
25	然后成为孝子。	Then Afterward Considered to Be Filial Son.
26	此上以为政，	These, Above (authority) Used As Governance
27	**下以为俗，**	**Below (subjects) Used As Traditions,**
28	**而未足为异也。**	**Then Not Enough Be Different (surprised) that's.**

5.6 Different States Different Traditions

Liezi Text Narrative
Southern states, people shaved hairs and naked; northern states, people turbaned jacketed; L2
Central states, people crown caps and dressed. L3
The 9 lands all resources, or agriculture or commerce; or farming or fishing; L5
Like winter/jacket summer/linen-cloth, water/boat land/carriage, all quietly attained, formed. L8
East of Yue State there was the State of Zhemu. l9
The first born son was offered to be consumed, believing this will bring more brothers! L11
The grandfather died, then grandmother will be carried away and be abandoned. L13
Said: " Devil wife not allowed to stay together at the same place." L14
South of Chu State there's the State of Yanren. L15
When the parents died, they shaved off the muscles and discarded them. L17
Then buried the bones and then afterwards be considered filial sons. L19
West of Qin State there's the State of Yiqu. L20
When parents died, they gathered woods in piles and burnt the corpses. L22
Fumigating, then the smoke rising, called it ascending Heaven, then be considered filial sons. L25
These practices, above authority used as governance and subjects below used as traditions. L27
Hence we shall not be surprised at these differences in customs. L28

Comments:
5.6 Different States Different Traditions
People of different states in the north south or central, had very diverse customs and traditions.
Liezi has not been surprised, for they are formed quietly, naturally in the various communities.

However in our modern world today, we surely do not condon certain customs that are barbaric.
Like offering the first born to be consumed, believing this practice will bring more brothers.
Like carrying away the surviving grandparent to be abandoned to die alone, away from home.
Still we ought to understand and respect the community preference for treating their deceased.
Like land burial, cremation sea-burial, cremation stored, Tibetan Heaven burial feed to vultures,...

Humanity first, then we ought to understand and respect customs and practices of others.

Chapter 5. Tang's Queries (汤问)

5.7 孔子不能决　　5.7 Kongzi Cannot Decide

01 孔子东游，	Kongzi Eastern Tour,
02 见两小儿辩斗。	Saw 2 Small Children Debating Contesting.
03 问其故。	Asked The Reason.
04 一儿曰：	One Child Said:
05 "我以日始出时去人近，	" I Think Sun First Emerges Nearer To People,
06 而日中时远也。"	And Sun MidDay is Further, that's."
07 一儿以日初出远，	One Child Thought Sun First Emerges Is Further,
08 而日中时近也。	And Sun MidDay is Nearer that's.
09 一儿曰：	One Child Said:
10 "日初出大如车盖，	" Sun First Emerges Big Like Carriage Cover,
11 及日中，则如盘盂，	Till Sun at Zenith, Then Like Dish Cup,
12 此不为远者小	That's Things Further are Smaller
13 　而近者大乎？"	And Things Nearer are Bigger, is-it-not ?"
14 一儿曰：	One Child Said:
15 "日初出沧沧凉凉，	"Sun First Emerges Cold and Cool,
16 及其日中如探汤，	Till The Sun at Zenith, Like Tasting Soup,
17 此不为近者热	That's Things Nearer are Hot
18 　而远者凉乎？"	And Things Further are Cold is-it-not ?"
19 *孔子不能决也。*	*Kongzi Not Able to Decide that's.*
20 两小儿笑曰：	Two Little Children Laughing, Said:
21 "孰为汝多知乎？"	"Who Says You're Very Knowledgeable ?"

Liezi Text Narrative
Kongzi on eastern tour, saw 2 small children debating and asked for the reason. L3
One child said: "I think Sun first emerges nearer to people and Sun midday is further, that's. L6
One child thought Sun first emerges further and Sun midday is nearer that's. L8
One child said: "Sun first emerges big like a carriage cover, till Sun at zenith, then like a dish. L11
That's things further are smaller and things nearer are bigger, is-it-not ?" L13
One child said: "Sun first emerges cold and cool, till the Sun at zenith like tasting soup. L16
That's things nearer are hot and things further are cold. is-it-not ?" L18
Kongzi was not able to decide, that's. L19
The two little children laughing, said: " Who says you're very knowledgeable ?" L21

Comments:
5.7 Kongzi Cannot Decide
One child said, "Morning Sun looks big thus is nearer; Noon Sun looks smaller thus is further !"
One child said, "Morning Sun feels cool hence further; Noon Sun feels hot hence nearer !"
On hearing their debate, Kongzi cannot decide who is right and the children laughingly say:
"Who says you're very knowledgeable ?"
In this narrative, Liezi light-heartedly reminds us that the Sage also does not know everything.
But then, the whole wide world believed that above Heaven is round, and below Earth is flat.

Today, children find answers on the internet as all information is in the 'Cloud'.

Chapter 5. Tang's Queries (汤問)

5.8 均 | 5.8 Fairness

01 均，	*Fairness (balance, uniformity, even distribution)*
02 天下之至理也，	Heaven Beneath (the world) The Most Logical that's,
03 连于形物亦然。	Connecting To Form and Matter Also Natural.
04 均发均县，	Uniform Hairs Evenly Suspending,
05 轻重而发绝，	Light or Heavy And Hairs Broke,
06 发不均也。	Hairs Not Evenly-distributed that's.
07 均也，	Uniformity that's,
08 其绝也莫绝。	That Breaks That's Won't be Broken.
09 人以为不然，	People Think This Not Natural,
10 自有知其然者也。	Also Have People Know This is Natural that's.
11 詹何以独茧丝为纶，	Zhanhe With Single Silk Thread As Line,
12 芒针为钩，	Awn (bristly fibre on head of oat) Needle As Hook,
13 荆筱为竿，	Bramble Bamboo As Rod,
14 剖粒为饵，	Halved Rice-grain As Bait,
15 引盈车之鱼	Caught Cart Load Of Fish
16 　于百仞之渊、	From Pool-depth of 100 Meters,
17 汩流之中，	From Centre of Rapid Flow,
18 纶不绝，	Thread Not Broken
19 钩不伸，	Hook Not Straightened,
20 竿不挠。	Rod Not Bended.
21 楚王闻而异之，	King of Chu (state) Heard And Was Surprised
22 召问其故。	Invited And Asked the Reason.
23 詹何曰：	Zhanhe Said:
24 "臣闻先大夫之言，	"Subject-me Heard Past Scholar His Words,
25 蒲且子之弋也，	Puqiezi His Arrow-string (attached arrow) that's,
26 弱弓纤缴，	Weak Bow Thin String ,
27 乘风振之，	Aided by Wind Shot It,
28 连双鸧于青云之际。	Connecting 2 Starlings in Clouds At Edge of Heaven.
29 用心专，	Usage of Heart (mind) Focused,
30 动手均也。	Hands Motion Balanced that's.
31 臣因其事，	Subject-me Because of This Story,
32 放而学钓，	Abandoned (everything) To Learn Fishing.
33 五年始尽其道。	Five Years Then Mastered The 'Dao' (the way, the skill).
34 当臣之临河持竿，	When Subject-me Come-on River Holding Rod,
35 心无杂虑，	Heart (mind) No Miscellaneous Worries,
36 唯鱼之念；	Only Fish In Mind;
37 投纶沉钩，	Throw-in Line Sinking Hook,
38 手无轻重，	Hands Not Light or Heavy.
39 物莫能乱。	Matters Not Able to Confuse.
40 鱼见臣之钩饵，	Fish Seeing Subject-me My Hook and Bait,
41 犹沉埃聚沫，	Like Sinking Dust Gathering Bubbles.
42 吞之不疑。	Swallow Them Without Doubt.

Chapter 5. Tang's Queries (汤问)

43	所以能以弱制强，	Therefore Able With the Weak Triumph-over the Strong,
44	以轻致重也。	With the Light Attaining the Heavy that's.
45	大王治国诚能若此，	Great King Governing State Truly Able be Like This,
46	则天下	Then Heaven Beneath (the world)
47	可运于一握，	Possible to Play In One's Hand,
48	将亦奚事哉？"	Then Whatever Else Matters Is-it-not ? "
49	楚王曰："善。"	King of Chu Said: "Very Good."

Liezi Text Narrative
Fairness (balance, uniformity, even distribution), the most logical beneath Heaven, that's. L2
Naturally also applicable to forms and matters. L3
Uniform hairs evenly suspending light or heavy weight and hairs break, hairs not uniform. L6
Uniformity that's, enabling what can break, will not be broken. L8
People think this is not naturally so, but there will be people who know this is natural, that's. L10
Zhanhe with single silk thread as line, awn (bristly fibre from head of oat) as hook; L12
Bramble bamboo as rod, halved rice grain as bait, caught a cart load of fish; L15
From the depth of the pool and centre of rapid flow; L17
Thread not broken, hook not straightened, and rod not bended. L20
King of Chu (state) heard and was surprised, thus invited Zhanhe and asked for the reason. L22
Zhanhe said: "Subject-me heard from a past scholar, that Puqiezi's arrow (string attached). L25
Weak bow thin string (arrow attached), aided by wind shot through 2 starlings in the clouds. L28
With heart and mind focused, and hands motion balanced L30
Subject-me because of this story, abandoned everything to learn fishing. L32
Five years later, Zhanhe mastered the art. L33
When subject-me comes to the river holding rod, I have no worries, only fish in mind. L36
Throw-in the line, sink the hook, hands not light or heavy, all matters not able to confuse me. L39
Fish see my hook and bait like sinking dust gathered bubbles, swallow them without a doubt. L42
Thus able with the weak to triumph-over the strong, with the light attaining the heavy that's." L44
Great King's government if truly like this, then possible to control the world in one's hand. L47
Then whatever else does not matter, is-it-not ?" L48
King of Chu (state) said: "Very good." L49

Comments:
5.8 Fairness
Fairness, balance and fair distribution of wealth among people are the most logical.
Same with material, like uniformity, even distribution of stress and force in buildings and bridges.
People think this is not naturally so, but there will be people who know this is natural, that's.

Fantasy narratives: Puqiezi's weak bow thin string-attached arrow shooting 2 starlings at once.
And Zhanhe caught a cart load of fish with a single silk thread line, awn hook and rice grain bait.
Liezi merely uses these stories to catch the attention of King of Chu (state) and other rulers.
To enlighten them on the great utility of the concept of fairness and even distribution of interest.
That with fairness practice in government, they can control the world with one hand.
And that nothing else matters, right ?
Fairness is lacking in the world today, as 1% of people control the combined wealth of the rest !

Chapter 5. Tang's Queries (汤問)

5.9 换汝之心　　　　5.9 Change of Hearts

01 鲁公扈，赵齐婴二人有疾，	Lugonghu, Zhaoqiying 2 Persons Had Sickness,
02 同请扁鹊求治，	Together Invited Bianque Requesting Treatment,
03 扁鹊治之。	Bianque Treated Them.
04 既同愈。	Then Together Recovered.
05 谓公扈，齐婴曰：	Speaking to Gonghu, Qiying Said:
06 "汝曩之所疾，	"Formerly That Sickness Of Yours,
07 自外而干府藏者，	From Outside, That Which Injured Internal Organs,
08 固药石之所已。	Thus Herbs Medicinal-minerals That Enable Cure.
09 今有偕生之疾，	Now Has Inherited Born Sickness,
10 与体偕长，	Which Accompany Body in Growth,
11 今为汝攻之，何如？"	Now to Help You Correct Them, How About ?"
12 二人曰：	Two Persons Said:
13 "愿先闻其验。"	"Wishing First to Hear The Diagnosis."
14 扁鹊谓公扈曰：	Bianque Speaking to Gonghu said:
15 "汝志强而气弱，	"Your Will Strong But Breath Weak,
16 故足于谋而寡于断。	Thus Enough In Planning But Lacking in Decision.
17 齐婴志弱而气强，	Qiying's Will Weak But Breath Strong,
18 故少于虑	Hence Lacking In Worrying (planning)
19 　而伤于专。	But Hurting In Focus (decision).
20 若换汝之心，	***If Exchange Your two Hearts,***
21 则均于善矣。"	Then Equalize Towards Goodness Indeed."
22 扁鹊遂饮二人毒酒，	Bianque Let the 2 Persons Drank Poison Wine,
23 迷死三日，	Fainted Dead 3 Days,
24 剖胸探心，	Cut-open Chests Took Hearts,
25 易而置之；	Exchanged And Placed Them;
26 投以神药，	Put-on With 'God' Medicine,
27 既悟如初。	Then Awoken Like Beginning.
28 二人辞归。	Two Persons took Leave and Returned.
29 于是公扈反齐婴之室，	Then Gonghu Returned to Qiying's Home,
30 而有其妻子；	And There was The Wife;
31 妻子弗识。	The Wife No Recognition.
32 齐婴亦反公扈之室，	Qiying Also Return to Gonghu's Home,
33 有其妻子	There was The Wife
34 妻子亦弗识。	Wife Also No Recognition.
35 二室因相与讼，	Two Families had Cause and Both Went for Litigation.
36 求辨于扁鹊。	Requested Identification From Bianque.
37 扁鹊辨其所由，	Bianque Identified What The Cause was,
38 讼乃已。	Litigation Thus Past.

5.9 Change of Hearts

Liezi Text Narrative
Lugonghu and Zhaoqiying both were ill and together went to Bianque requesting treatment. L2
Bianque treated them and both recovered. L4
Bianque, speaking to Gonghu and Qiying, said: "Formerly that sickness of yours. L6
Causes from outside affecting internal organs, thus treatable with herbs and medical minerals. L8
Now you are born with inherited sickness which accompanies your body growth. L10
And to help you correct them, how about ?" L11
These 2 persons said: "First wishing to hear the examination results." L13
Bianque speaking to Gonghu said: "Your Will is strong but your Breath is weak. L15
Thus you are strong in planning but lacking in decision and implementation L16
Qiying's Will is weak but Breath is strong, thus less worry in plan, but exertive in action. L19
If we exchange your two hearts, then will balance your temperaments towards goodness." L21
Bianque let both of them drink poisoned wine so that they fainted dead for 3 days. L23
He then opened their chests, took their hearts, interchanged and placed them back. L25
Then applied with 'god' medicine, both persons awoken and were as good as prior operation. L27
Gonghu and Qiying both took leave and returned home separately. L28
Then Gonghu returned to Qiying's house, and the wife there had no recognition of him. L31
Qiying also returned to Gonghu's house, and the wife there had no recognition of him. L34
The two families had reason to go for litigation, thus requested identification from Bianque. L36
Bianque identified the cause, and thus terminated the litigation. L38

Comments:
5.9 Change of Hearts
Lugonghu and Zhaoqiying were both taken ill, treated by Bianque and recovered.
Bianque explained, illness caused by outside factors on internal organs, herbs medicine effective.
But inborn traits and deficiencies accompany our body growth, thus not treatable with medicine.
Like Lugonghu, strong in Will but weak in Breath, hence good in planning, lacking in decision.
Like Zhaoqiying, weak in Will but strong in Breath, hence short in planning, exertive in action.
Bianque suggested balancing the opposite temperaments for good, he can interchange their hearts.
Both were willing, so Bianque did the operation, gave poison wine to drug them 'dead' for 3 days.
Opened their chests, inter-changed their hearts, applied 'god' medicine to revive them as normal.
Then each 'followed the heart' and went back home to where the heart 'belonged'!
The wifes cannot recognize their own husbands and they went to Bianque in litigation.
Bianque explained the cause of the identification problem and ended the litigation.

Liezi uses this fictitious narrative to dramatize the difficulty of changing one's entrenched traits.
To the uninitiated, fictitious narratives often lead to fantasy of what a daoist or Daoism can do.
The unscrupulous capitalize on the imagination of the gullibles, and give Daoism a bad name.

In-born traits are entrenched, so literally we need a 'change of heart' for correction.

5.10 三年不成章

01 瓠巴鼓琴而鸟舞鱼跃，
02 郑师文闻之，
03 弃家从师襄游。
04 柱指钧弦，
05 三年不成章。
06 师襄曰：
07 "子可以归矣。"
08 师文舍其琴，叹曰：
09 "文非弦之不能钧，
10 非章之不能成。
11 文所存者不在弦，
12 所志者不在声。
13 内不得于心，
14 外不应于器，
15 故不敢发手而动弦。
16 且小假之，以观其后。"
17 无几何，复见师襄。
18 师襄曰："子之琴何如？"
19 师文曰：
20 "得之矣。请尝试之。"
21 于是当春而叩商弦
22 　以召南吕，
23 凉风忽至，草木成实。
24 及秋而叩角弦，
25 以激夹钟，
26 温风徐回，草木发荣。
27 当夏而叩羽弦以召黄钟，
28 霜雪交下，
29 川池暴沍。
30 及冬而叩徵弦以激蕤宾，
31 阳光炽烈，坚冰立散。
32 将终，命宫而总四弦，
33 则景风翔，庆云浮，
34 甘露降，澧泉涌。
35 师襄乃抚心高蹈曰：
36 "微矣子之弹也！
37 虽师旷之清角，
38 邹衍之吹律，
39 亡以加之。
40 彼将挟琴执管
41 　而从子之后耳。"

5.10 Three Years No Music

Paoba Played Zither And Birds Danced Fish Spring,
Shiwen of Zheng State Heard This,
Left Home to Follow Shixiang on Tour (learning).
Fingering on Bar-scale Harmonizing Strings,
3 Years Music Not Formed.
Shixiang Said:
"Sir Is Allowed to Return that's."
Shiwen Abandon The Zither, Sighing Said:
"Wen, Not That String Not Able Harmonize,
Not That Music Not Able to Attain.
Wen, That Which Exists Not On the Strings,
That Which Aspires Not On the Sound.
Inward Not Attain With Heart,
Outward Not Resonate With Instrument,
Hence Not Dare Move Hand To Hit Strings.
Have A Little Break, To Observe What Follows."
Not Much Longer, Again Visited Shixiang.
Shixiang Said: "Sir Your Zither, How About ?"
Shiwen Said:
"Attained It indeed. Please to Try Playing It."
Then At Spring And Hitting the Shang String
　To Call for Nanlui (tune),
Cool Wind Suddenly Arrived, Grass Trees Bear Fruits.
Till Autumn And Hitting the Jao String,
To Excite Jiazhong (tune)
Wet Wind Slowly Return, Grass Trees Sprout Prosperity.
At Summer To Hit Yue String To Call Huangzhong tune,
Frost Snow Alternating Falling,
Rivers Ponds Sudden Frozen.
Till Winter To Hit Zheng String To Arouse Ruibin (tune),
Sun Shine Glowing Fierce, Hard Ice Instantly Disperse.
Towards End, Command Gong To Assemble all 4 Strings,
Then Landscape Wind Flying, Prosperity Clouds Floating,
Sweet Dew Descending, Li Spring Surging.
Shixiang Then Touched Heart, High Dancing Said:
"Finest Indeed Sir, Your Playing that's !
Though Shikuang His Solo Jiao (tune)
Zouyan His Piping Tune,
None Can Exceed This (performance).
They Shall be Carrying Zither Holding Flute
　To Follow Behind You Sir, that's."

Chapter 5. Tang's Queries (汤問)

Liezi Text Narrative
When Paoba (an ancient musician) played the zither, birds danced and fishes jumped with joy. L1
Shiwen of Zheng on hearing this left home to follow Shixiang on tour, learning music. L3
Fingering on the scale bar and harmonizing strings, 3 years of learning produced no music. L5
Shixiang Said: "Sir is allowed to return home that's." L7
Shiwen down zither sighing said: "Not that Wen not able to harmonize string, to make music. L10
My mind and thoughts are not on the string, my aspiration is not on the sound. L12
Inwardly not attune with heart, and outwardly not resonating with instrument; L14
Thus hands dare not move to strike strings; let rest from practice to observe what follows." L16
Before long, again visited Shixiang who said: "Sir, your zither playing, how about now?" L18
Shiwen said: "Have it indeed. Please let me try playing it." L20
It's Spring time, then hitting the Shang string to call up the Nanlui tune. L22
Cool wind suddenly arrived, grass and trees bear fruits. L23
Come Autumn time, then hitting the Jao string to excite the Jiazhong tune. L25
Warm winds slowly return, grass and trees sprouting prosperity. L26
Come Summer time, then hit the Yue string to call up the Huangzhong tune. L27
Frost snow alternative falling, rivers and ponds suddenly freeze. L29
Come Winter time, then hitting the Zheng string to arouse the Ruibin tune. L30
Sun shines glowing fierce, hard ice instantly disperse. L31
Coming to the end, then commanding the Gong string to assemble all the other 4 strings. L32
The gentle breeze rises, prosperity clouds afloat, sweet dew descend, spring of Li gushing. L34
Shixiang touched the heart, danced a jig, and said: "Finest indeed Sir. You're playing that's ! L36
Even Shikuang with his solo Jiao tune and Zouyan with his piping tune cannot exceed this. L39
They shall be carrying the zither holding the flute, and follow behind you Sir, that's." L41

Comments:
5.10 Three Years No Music
Hearing that Paoba's music gave joy even to birds fishes, Shiwen went to study under Shixiang,
Fingering on the scale and harmonizing the strings, Shiwen still cannot play after 3 years.
Had technicality precision but no heart feelings on strings nor aspiration on the sound production.
Teacher advised him to return home and take a break.
Before long, he came back to Shixiang and did a demonstration performance.

He hit the Shang string, called the Nanlui tune of Spring, cool wind arrived, and trees bear fruits.
Hit the Jao string, excited the Jiazhong tune of Autumn, warm wind return, and trees sprouting.
Hit the Yue string, called the Huangzhong tune of Summer, frost snow, rivers and ponds frozen.
Hit the Zheng string, aroused the Ruibin tune of Winter, sun shine glowing fierce, hard ice melted.
Coming to the ending, hit the command Gong string to assemble all the other 4 strings.
Gentle breeze arose, prosperity clouds flowing, sweet dew descending, spring of Li spouting.
This performance so touched his heart that Shixiang jumped up danced a jig, declaring:
"Finest Sir, playing surpassed Shikuang and Zouyan. They are willing to follow behind you."

Soul of music is expressions of the notes and sounds, not just technical accuracy and purity.

175

Chapter 5. Tang's Queries (汤問)

5.11 餘音绕梁欐	5.11 Music, 3 Days in Rafter

01	薛谭学讴于秦青，	Xuetan Learned Ballad-singing With Qinqing
02	未穷青之技，	Before Mastery of Qing's Skill,
03	自谓尽之；	Self Thinking had Completed It already;
04	遂辞归。	Then took Leave to Return.
05	秦青弗止。	Qinqing Not Stopping him.
06	饯于郊衢，	Farewell At Countryside Crossroad,
07	抚节悲歌，	Clapping Bamboo-instrument Singing Sadly,
08	声振林木，	Voice Shaking the Forest Trees,
09	响遏行云。	Sound Stopping the Moving Clouds.
10	薛谭乃谢求反，	Xuetan Hence Thanked teacher and Requested to Return,
11	终身不敢言归。	Whole Life Not Daring to Talk about Returning again.
12	秦青顾谓其友曰：	Qinqing Turning to Talk to His Friend, Said:
13	"昔韩娥东之齐，	"Past-time, Hane went East To Qi (state),
14	匮粮，过雍门，	Short of Food, Passing Yong (city) Gate,
15	鬻歌假食。	Peddling Songs Exchanging for Food.
16	***既去而餘音绕梁欐，***	***Then Left And Remnant Sound Lingered Rafter (above),***
17	三日不绝，	3 Days Not Lost,
18	左右以其人弗去。	Left Right Thinking The Person had Not Left.
19	过逆旅，	Passing Travellers' Inn,
20	逆旅人辱之。	People at Travellers' Inn Insulted Her.
21	韩娥因曼声哀哭，	Hane Therefore in Drawn-out Voice Sorrowfully Cried,
22	一里老幼悲愁，	One Mile radius Old and Young all Sad and Unhappy,
23	垂涕相对，	Runny Nose Facing Each other,
24	三日不食。	3 Days Not Eating.
25	遽而追之。	Hastened To Chase Her.
26	娥还，	Hane Returned,
27	复为曼声长歌，	Again With Drawn Voice Open-up Singing,
28	一里老幼	One Mile radius Old and Young
29	喜跃抃舞，	Joyous Jumping and Tap Dancing,
30	弗能自禁，	Not Able to Self Regulate,
31	忘向之悲也。	Forgetting The Past Sadness, that's.
32	乃厚赂发之。	Then with Many Gifts Sent Her on.
33	故雍门之人	Thus The People of Yong (city) Door
34	至今善歌哭，	Till Now Good at Sorrowful Singing,
35	放娥之遗声。"	Continuing Hane Her Voice Legacy.

176

5.11 Music, 3 Days in Rafter

Liezi Text Narrative
Xuetan was learning ballad singing with Qinqing; shortly he thought he had mastered the skill. L3
Thus he took leave to return, and Qinqing bid him farewell at the countryside crossroad. L6
Clapping bamboo-plates, singing sadly, his voice shook forest trees, stopped passing clouds. L9
Xuetan hence thanked his teacher, requested to stay on, never dare to talk of leaving again. L11.
Qinqing to a friend, said: "In the past, Hane at Yong Gate of Qi, peddled singing for food. L15
Remnant sound lingered above the rafter for 3 days, and people thought she had not left. L18
In a travellers' inn, people insulted her, and Hane sorrowfully cried in a long-drawn voice. L21
One mile radius, old and young all sad with runny noses facing each other, 3 days not eating. L24
They hastened to chase, and Hane returned, opened up to sing again with a long-drawn voice. L27
One mile radius, old and young all joyous, tap-dancing wildly, forgetting past sadness, that's. L31.
They sent her on with many gifts. L32
To this day people at Yong Gate of Qi State are good at the sorrowful singing style. L34
They have inherited the legacy of Hane's voice. L35

Comments:
5.11 Music, 3 Days in Rafter
The impatient Xuetan took leave to return shortly after started singing under Qinqing's tutelage.
The latter subtly showed up Xuetan's deficiency in a farewell party at the cross-roads in the forest.
With beat from bamboo-plates he sang sadly, his voice shook forest trees, stopped passing clouds.
Xuetan realised his mistake, thanked Qiqing, requested to stay and never again talk of leaving.

Qinqing shared a narrative on the higher standard in singing, achieved by the **legendary** Hane.
At Yong Gate of Qi, Hane peddled songs, and people still 'hear' her 3 days after she had left.
The inn people insulted her, and she sang so sadly, people young and old, cannot eat for 3 days.
They hastened to recall her, and she opened up singing to the joyous dance of all people.
The people at Yong Gate inherited the legacy of Hane and are good at singing in her voice.
Today, "Lingering 3 days in the rafter" (绕梁三日) is the idiom for the highest praise in singing.

The height of achievement in singing is leaving a legacy in style and voice that people cherish.

Chapter 5. Tang's Queries (汤問)

5.12 伯牙, 钟子期 | 5.12 Soulmates In Music

01	*伯牙善鼓琴,*	***Boya Good In Playing Zither,***
02	*钟子期善听。*	***Zhongziqi Good In Listening.***
03	伯牙鼓琴,	Boya Playing Zither,
04	志在登高山。	Aspiration On Climbing High Mountain.
05	钟子期曰:"善哉!	Zhongziqi Said: "Good Grace !
06	峨峨兮若泰山!"	Lofty Lofty Xi' Like Mount Tai !"
07	志在流水,	Aspiration On Flowing Water,
08	钟子期曰:"善哉!	Zhongziqi Said: "Goodness Gracious !
09	洋洋兮若江河!"	Merry Merrily Xi' Like Yangzijiang Huangho (rivers) !"
10	伯牙所念,	Boya Whatever Thinking,
11	钟子期必得之。	Zhongziqi Certain to Get It.
12	伯牙游于泰山之阴,	Boya Touring To The North of Mount Tai
13	卒逢暴雨,	Suddenly Meeting Torrential Rain,
14	止于岩下;	Sheltering Beneath A Rock;
15	心悲,	Heart feeling Sad,
16	乃援琴而鼓之。	So Fetched Zither And Played It.
17	初为霖雨之操,	Initially Do The Drill of Torrential Rain
18	更造崩山之音。	Further Making The Sound of Collapsing Mountain.
19	曲每奏,	Melody on Each Playing,
20	钟子期辄穷其趣。	Zhongziqi Always Got The Interesting point.
21	伯牙乃舍琴而叹曰:	Boya Then Put-away Zither And Sighing, Said:
22	"善哉,善哉!	"Good Grace, Good Grace !
23	子之听夫!	Sir Your Listening O' !
24	志想象犹吾心也。	Aspiration Thinking Like My Heart feelings that's.
25	吾于何逃声哉?"	My heart Sounds How To Escape from you, that's ?"

Liezi Text Narrative

Boya was good at playing zither, Zhongziqi was good at listening. L2
Boya playing zither, aspiration on climbing high mountains. L4
Zhongziqi said: "Good Grace ! Lofty Lofty Xi' Like Mount Tai !" L6
Aspiration on flowing water. L7
Zhongziqi said: "Good Grace! Merry merrily like the Yangzijiang Huangho rivers !" L9
Boya, thinking whatever, Hongziqi was certain to get it. L11
Boya, touring to the north of Mount Tai, suddenly met with torrential rain. L13
Sheltering beneath a rock and heart feeling sad, took the zither and played it. L16
Initially, the drill of torrential rain, further made the sound of a collapsing mountain. L18
Each melody on playing, Zhongziqi always got the interesting point. 20
Boya then put away zither and, sighing, said : "Good Grace, Good Grace ! L22
Sir, your listening O' ! Aspiration thinking is like my heart's feelings that's. L24
How can the sound of my heart escape your listening, that's ?" L25

Comments:
5.12 Soulmates In Music
A legendary player of the zither, Boya can express all his feelings and thoughts through music.
A legendary listener, Zhongziqi is able to know Boya's feelings and thoughts through his music.
In Chinese culture, this narrative sets Boya and Zhongziqi as legendary soulmates in music.

Chapter 5. Tang's Queries (汤问)

5.13 所造能倡者   5.13 The Artificial Performer

01	周穆王西巡狩，	King Mu of Zhou Western Tour of Hunting,
02	越昆仑，不至弇山。	Over Kunlun (mountain), Not Reaching Mount Yan.
03	反还，未及中国，	Returned Back, Not Reaching Center State (China),
04	道有献工人名偃师，	Said Crafts Person Named Yanshi, Had Offer,
05	穆王荐之，问曰：	King Mu Received Him, Asking Said:
06	"若有何能？"	"Like Having What Ability ?"
07	偃师曰：	Yanshi Said:
08	"臣唯命所试。	"Subject-me Only your Order Whatever will Try.
09	然臣已有所造，	But then Subject-me Already Have That Made,
10	愿王先观之。"	Wishing King to First Observe It."
11	穆王曰：	King Mu Said:
12	"日以俱来，	"Day after Then Bring them All,
13	吾与若俱观之。"	I and You Together Watch Them."
14	越日偃师谒见王。	Next Day Yanshi Called to See the King.
15	王荐之，曰：	King Received Him, Said:
16	"若与偕来者何人耶？"	"You With a Person Accompanying Who is That ?"
17	对曰：	Responding Said:
18	***"臣之所造能倡者。"***	***"Subject-me My Artificial Able Performer."***
19	穆王惊视之，	King Mu Astonished Looking at It,
20	趣步俯仰，信人也。	Quick Steps Stooping Looking-up, Truly Human that's.
21	巧夫鎮其颐，则歌合律；	CraftsPerson Touch Its Face, Then Sang In Tune;
22	捧其手，则舞应节。	Raise Its Hand, Then Dancing to Beat.
23	千变万化，	Thousand Changes 10 Thousands Transformations,
24	惟意所适。	Following at Will As Pleased.
25	王以为实人也，	King Believed it Be Real Human that's,
26	与盛姬内御	With Favored Concubines Inner Court-attendants
27	并观之。	Together Watching It.
28	技将终，	Performance Nearing the End,
29	倡者瞬其目而招王	Performer Blink Its Eyes To Teasing King
30	之左右侍妾。	His Concubines Servants on Left and Right.
31	王大怒，立欲诛偃师。	King was Very Angry, Instantly Wished to Kill Yanshi.
32	偃师大慑，	Yanshi Greatly Alarmed,
33	立剖散倡者以示王，	Instantly Break-up, Scattered Performer To Show King,
34	皆傅会革、	All Sorts and Collection of Leather,
35	木、胶、漆、白、	Wood, Gum, Lacquer, white,
36	黑、丹、青之所为。	Black, Red, Green, Of These Makeup.
37	王谛料之，	King Closely Examined Them,
38	内则肝、胆、心、肺、	Inside Are Liver, Gall, Heart, Lung,
39	脾、肾、肠、胃，	Spleen, Kidney, Intestine, Stomach,
40	外则筋骨、支节、皮毛、	Outside Are Tendon Bones, Limps Joints,

5.13 The Artificial Performer

41	齿发，皆假物也，	Teeth Hair, All False Materials that's,
42	而无不毕具者。	And None Not Completely Equipped that's.
43	合会复如初见。	Combined Together Back Like First Seen.
44	王试废其心，	King Tried Removed The Heart,
45	则口不能言；	Then Mouth Not Able to Speak;
46	废其肝，则目不能视；	Removed The Liver, Then Eyes Not Able to See;
47	废其肾，则足不能步。	Removed The Kidney, Then Legs Not Able to Walk.
48	穆王始悦而叹曰：	King Mu Then Happy And Sighing Said:
49	"人之巧乃可与造化者	"Human's Craft Is Able With The Creator
50	同功乎？"	of Similar Success It-is-not ?"
51	诏贰车载之以归。	Called 2 Carriages to Carry Them For Home.
52	夫班输之云梯，	O' Banshu His 'Cloud Ladder',
53	墨翟之飞鸢，	Modi His 'Flying Yuan' (bird),
54	自谓能之极也。	Self Declared The Extreme of Capabilities that's.
55	弟子东门贾禽滑厘	Disciples Dongmenjia Qinhuali
56	闻偃师之巧以告二子，	Heard The Craft of Yanshi And Told their 2 Teachers,
57	二子终身不敢语艺，	Two Teachers Whole Life Not Dare Speak of Craft,
58	而时执规矩。	And Always Hold to Rulers Squares (carpentry tools)

Liezi Text Narrative

King Mu of Zhou western tour of hunting, over Mount Kunlun, not yet reaching Mt Yan. L2
On return before reaching Center State (China), informed craftsman Yanshi had offered. L4
King Mu received him asking, said: "Like having what skills ?" L6
Yanshu said: "Subject-me will try your order whatever. L8
But then subject-me already had this made, and wished King to see it first. L10
King Mu said: "Day after, bring them all, I and you together to watch them." L13
Next day Yanshi called to see the King. L14
King on receiving him, said: "You with a person accompanying, who is that ?" L16
Responding said: "Subject-me my artificial, capable performer." L18
King Mu astonished looking at it, quick steps, stooping, looking-up, truly human that's. L20
Craft Person touched its face then sang in tune; raised its hand then danced to beat. L22
Thousand changes 10 thousands transformations, following at will as pleased. L24
King believed it to be a real human and watched together with concubines, court attendants. L27
Performance nearing the end, performer winked, teasing King's concubines left and right. L30
King was very angry, instantly wished to kill Yanshi who was greatly alarmed. L32
Yanshi immediately break-up and scattered the performer to show King. L33
All sorts, a collection of leather, wood, gum, lacquer, white, black, red, green, such makeup. L36
King examined them, inside are liver, gall, heart, lung, spleen, kidney, intestine, stomach. L39
Outside are tendon bones, limps joints, teeth hair, all false materials that's. L41
And none not completely equipped that's; combined together and back like first seen. L43
King tried removed the heart then mouth not able to speak; L45
Removed the liver then eyes not able to see; removed the kidney then legs not able to walk. L47
King Mu then joyous and sighing said: L48
"Human's craft is comparable to that of the creator, of similar success is-it-not ?" L50

180

5.13 The Artificial Performer

Then called for 2 carriages to carry them back home. L51
O' Banshu his 'cloud ladder' (for attack) and Modi his 'flying yuan' (artificial bird); L53
Their self-acclaimed 'the extreme of capabilities' that's. L54
Disciples Dongmenjia, Qinhuali heard of Yanshi's craft, and went to inform their teachers. L56
Thereafter, the 2 teachers dared not speak of craft and just hold on to their rulers and squares. L58

Comments:
5.13 The Artificial Performer
Yanshi was a legendary craftsman of ancient era.
King Mu watched Artificial Performer taking quick steps, stooping, looking-up, truly human-like.
Yanshi touched its face and it sang in tune, raised its hand and it danced to beat.
Towards the end of performance, it even winked at the concubines and consorts of King Mu.
It was all so real that King Mu believed what he saw and wanted to kill Yanshi in his rage.
Alarmed, Yanshi immediately dismantled the performer to show the King the real things.
A collection of leather, wood, gum, lacquer, white, black, red, green, such makeup.
When combined and put back together, it looked like when first seen.
Examining it, King Mu removed heart, mouth can't speak; removed kidney, legs can't walk.
Joyous, King Mu lauded that human craftsmanship is comparable to the Creator, is-this-not !

Banshu (鲁班 Luban c.2,500BC) acknowledged pioneer craftsman of the Spring Autumn Period.
Reputedly he built the 'Cloud Ladder' famously effective for breaching city walls in attacks.
Modi (墨子, Mozi c.2,500BC) was also a renowned craftsman of his time.
Reputedly, he built the wooden 'Flying Yuan' that can remain aloft for 3 days.
However these achievements are certainly not comparable to Yanshi's Artificial Performer.
Liezi has raised the bar of craftsmanship to a higher level with this narrative.
But today, with the assistance of computer chips, our robots are fast surpassing his standards !

With the Artificial Performer, Liezi dampens craftsmen's delusion of self-acclaimed greatness.

5.14 古之善射者

01 甘蝇，古之善射者，
02 彀弓而兽伏鸟下。
03 弟子名飞卫，
04 学射于甘蝇，
05 而巧过其师。
06 纪昌者，又学射于飞卫。
07 飞卫曰：
08 "尔先学不瞬，
09 而后可言射矣。"
10 纪昌归，
11 偃卧其妻之机下，
12 以目承牵挺。
13 二年之后，
14 虽锥末倒眦，
15 而不瞬也。
16 以告飞卫。
17 飞卫曰：
18 "未也，必学视而后可。
19 视小如大，视微如著，
20 而后告我。"
21 昌以氂悬虱于牖。
22 南面而望之。
23 旬日之间，浸大也；
24 三年之后，如车轮焉。
25 以睹余物，皆丘山也。
26 乃以燕角之弧、
27 朔蓬之簳射之，
28 贯虱之心，而悬不绝。
29 以告飞卫。
30 飞卫高蹈拊膺曰：
31 "汝得之矣！"
32 纪昌既尽卫之术，
33 计天下之敌己者，
34 一人而已；
35 乃谋杀飞卫。
36 相遇于野，
37 二人交射；
38 中路矢锋相触，
39 而坠于地，而尘不扬。
40 飞卫之矢先穷。

5.14 Ancient Archers

Ganying, The Good Archer of Ancient time,
Fully-extended Bow Then Animals Prostrate Birds Down.
Disciple Named Feiwei,
Learned Shooting With Ganying,
And Skill Exceeded The Teacher.
Person Jichang, Then Learned Shooting With Feiwei.
Feiwei Said:
"You First Learn to Not Wink,
Then After Can Speak of Shooting that's."
Jichang returned,
Lying Face-up Under His Wife's Loom,
With Eyes Following Stepping Lead.
Two Years Afterward,
Though Cone End (sharp) Reaching Eye-ring,
And Not Wink that's.
And so Informed Feiwei.
Feiwei Said:
"Not Yet, Must Learn Seeing And Then Can learn.
Seeing Small Like Big, Seeing Tiny Like Prominent,
And Then Inform Me."
Chang (Jichang) with Hair Suspending a Lice At Window.
South Facing Looking at It.
A Period of 10 Days, Gradually Big that's;
3 Years Afterward, Like the Wheel of Carriage indeed.
Then Looked at Other Things, All Mound Hills that's.
Then With Bow of Horn From Yan (state),
Stalk (arrow) of Grass Shot It,
Piercing Lice Its Heart, And Suspending-hair Not Break.
And so Informed Feiwei.
Feiwei Danced a Jig Patting Chest Said:
"You Mastered It that's !"
Jichang Already Mastered Wei's Skill,
Assessing, TheWorld Person who can Oppose Me
1 Person And Only;
Hence Planning to Kill Feiwei.
Mutually Meeting At Countryside,
2 Persons Cross Shooting
Middle of Road Arrow Points Mutually Contact,
And Fell To Ground, And Dust Not Raise.
Feiwei's Arrows First Exhausted.

5.14 Ancient SharpShooters

41	纪昌遗一矢；既发，	Jichang still Left 1 Arrow; Already Shot,
42	飞卫以棘刺之端扞之，	Feiwei With Thistle Thorn Its Tip Defended It,
43	而无差焉。	And No Miss indeed.
44	于是二子泣而投弓，	Therefore 2 Scholars Wept silently And Cast the Bows,
45	相拜于涂，	Mutually Swearing On Site,
46	请为父子。	Engaged As Father and Son.
47	剋臂以誓，	Tattooed on Arms As Oath,
48	不得告术于人。	Not Allow to Teach Skill To Others,

Liezi Text Narrative
Ganying, fine archer of ancient time, extended bow and animals prostrated, birds lay low. L2
Disciple named Feiwei learned shooting with Ganying, and his skill exceeded his teacher. L5
Jichang in turn learned shooting with Feiwei. L6
Feiwei said: "You first learn to not wink, then can speak of shooting that's." L9
Jichang returned, lying face-up under his wife's loom, eyes following the stepping lead. L12
After 2 years, though the cone tip coming up and eyes not wink, went to inform Feiwei. L16
Feiwei said: "Not yet, must learn seeing and then can learn shooting. L18
Seeing small like big, seeing tiny like prominent, then inform me." L20
Chang (Jichang) with hair suspending a lice at the window, south facing and looking at it. L22
In a10-day period, it gradually became bigger that's; 3 years later, like a wheel of carriage. L24
Then looking at other things, all mound hill size that's. L25
Then with a bow of horn from the State of Yan, an arrow-stalk of Shupik-grass shot it. L27
Piercing lice's heart and suspending hair not broken; so informed Feiwei. L29
Feiwei danced a ji, thumping chest and said: "You have mastered it that's !"
Jichang already mastered Wei's skill; realising only 1 person in the world can oppose him. L34
Hence planned to kill Feiwei. L35
Mutually meeting in the countryside, 2 persons cross-shooting at each other. L37
Middle of the road, arrow points mutually contacted, fell to the ground, and no dust raised. L39
Feiwei's arrows first exhausted, Jichang still left with 1 arrow and already shot out. L41
Feiwei with thistle thorn its tip defended it and no miss indeed. L43
Therefore the 2 scholars weep silently, cast down their bows and swore on site. L45
To engage henceforth as father and son; tattooed on arms as oath, not to teach skill to others. L48
Comments:
5.14 Ancient SharpShooters
Ganying, Feiwei and Jichang are legendary sharpshooters in archery.
Feiwei learned shooting from Ganying, and surpassed the teacher in skill, and all is well.
Jichang learned shooting from Feiwei, and having mastered the skill, planned to kill the teacher !
Feiwei with his little additional skill defended himself successfully.
Both adversaries touched by the incident, engaged as father and son, swore not to teach others.
Two stories from this narrative.
Firstly, skill can be improved, like Feiwei surpassing his teacher Ganying.
Secondly, teaching martial arts is dangerous, so choose your virtuous students wisely !

We never stop self-improvement, else be surpassed or be threatened (Hexagram 1,Yijing).

Chapter 5. Tang's Queries (汤問)

5.15 造父习御   5.15 Zaofu Learned Charioteering

01	造父之师曰泰豆氏。	Zaofu His Teacher Called Taidoushi.
02	***造父之始从习御也,***	***Zaofu, He Starting To Learn Charioteering that's,***
03	执礼甚卑,	Observed Etiquette Very Humbly,
04	泰豆三年不告。	Taidou 3 Years No Teaching.
05	造父执礼愈谨,	Zaofu Observed Etiquette More Diligently,
06	乃告之曰:	Then Informed Him Said:
07	"古诗言:	"Ancient Poem Says:
08	'良弓之子,	'Good Bow-maker His Son,
09	必先为箕,	Must First Make Bamboo-tray,
10	良冶之子,	Good Blacksmith His Son,
11	必先为裘。'	Must First Make Leather-jacket.'
12	汝先观吾趣。	You First Observe My Brisk-walk.
13	趣如吾,	Walk Like Me,
14	然后六辔可持,	Naturally Afterwards 6 Reins Able to Hold,
15	六马可御。"	6 Horses Able to Drive."
16	造父曰:	Zaofu Said:
17	"唯命所从。"	"Your Orders Whatever, will Follow."
18	泰豆乃立木为途,	Taidou Then Stood-up Wood-piles As Path,
19	仅可容足;	Just Enough to Accomodate a Foot;
20	计步而置。	Estimated Step-width And Setting.
21	履之而行。	Stepping on Them and Moving onward.
22	趣走往还,	Brisk Walk Forward and Backward,
23	无跌失也。	No Miss and Fall that's.
24	造父学之,	Zaofu The Student,
25	三日尽其巧。	3 Days Mastered The Skill.
26	泰豆叹曰:	Taidou Sighing Said:
27	"子何其敏也?	"Sir, What The Agility that's ?
28	得之捷乎!	Attained It so Quickly O' !
29	凡所御者, 亦如此也。	All Who Ever Drive, Also Like This that's.
30	曩汝之行, 得之于足,	Just now Your Movement, Getting It On Foot,
31	应之于心。	Responding It At Heart.
32	推于御也,	Pushing (understanding) To Charioteering that's,
33	齐辑乎辔衔之际,	Line-up Horses With Reins And Bits Combination,
34	而急缓乎唇吻之和,	And Fast/Slow speed With Lips Mouth Harmony (calls)
35	正度乎胸臆之中,	Correct Judgement Filling The Chest Centre,
36	而执节乎掌握之间。	Then Grasp The Rhythm Within Hand Held reins.
37	内得于中心,	Inwardly Feel-it At Center of Heart,
38	而外合于马志,	And Outwardly Accord With Horses' Will,
39	是故能进退履绳	Thus Able Forward/Backward like Treading Tight-Rope
40	而旋曲中规矩,	And Turning Curving Right on Ruler Square (precision)
41	取道致远而气力有余,	Take Path To Faraway And Breath Strength Have Excess,

5.15 Zaofu Learns Charioteering

42	诚得其术也。	Truly Attained The Skill that's.
43	得之于衔，应之于辔；	Attaining It At Bits, Responding It At Reins;
44	得之于辔，应之于手；	Attaining It At Reins, Responding It At Hands;
45	得之于手，应之于心。	Attaining It At Hands, Responding It At Heart.
46	则不以目视，不以策驱；	Then Not With Eyes Seeing, Not With Whip to Drive;
47	心闲体正，六辔不乱，	Heart at Ease Body Upright, 6 Reins Not Confused,
48	而二十四蹄所投无差；	And 24 Hoofs Wherever Put No Mistakes;
49	回旋进退，	Turning Curving Forward Backward,
50	莫不中节。	None Not Right and Regulated.
51	然后舆轮之外可使无馀辙，	And Then Chariot, Outside Can Enable No Extra Track,
52	马蹄之外可使无馀地；	Horses' Hoofs, Outside Can Enable No Extra Ground;
53	未尝觉山谷之险，	No Experience Feeling The Danger of Mountain Valley,
54	原隰之夷，视之一也。	Dryland Wetland Its Safety, See It As One that's (same).
55	吾术穷矣。	My Skills Completely Here.
56	汝其识之！"	You Remember It All !"

***Liezi* Text Narrative**

Zaofu started to learn charioteering with his teacher, named Taidoushi. L1
He observed etiquette very humbly, but Taidou did not teached for 3 years. L4
Zaofu observed etiquette even more diligently, then Taidoushi started teaching him, said: L6
"Ancient poem says: 'Good bow maker, his son must first make bamboo-tray; L9
Good blacksmith, his son must first make a leather-jacket.'; You first observe my brisk-walk. L12
Brisk-walk like me, naturally afterward able to hold 6 reins and able to drive 6 horses." L15
Zaofu said: "Your orders whatever, are my commands." L17
Taidou then stood-up wood-poles as path, size just enough to accomodate a foot; L19
Setting wood-poles apart at estimated step-width, stepping on them in all movements. L21
Brisk-walking forward and backward with no mistakes and no falls that's. L23
Zaofu, the student mastered the skill in 3 days. L25
Taidou sighing said: "Sir, what agility that's ? Learned it so quickly O' ! L28
All people, whoever had driven were also like this, that's. L29
Just now your movement (on poles), is doing it on foot with resonance at heart. L31
Pushing this understanding to charioteering, line-up horses with reins and bits combination; L33
Fast and slow speed that's, with lips and mouth calling in harmony; L34
With correct judgement filling the chest, and grasping the rhythm within hand-held reins. L36
Inwardly feeling it at the center of heart, and outwardly in accord with horses' will. L38
Thus able to go forward and backward like on tightrope, turning curving with precisions. L40
Taking path to faraway distance, and horses still have excess strength, this is truly the skill. L42
Attain it with bits, responding to it at reins; attain it with reins, responding to it at hands; L44
Attain it with hands, responding to it at heart. L45
Then not with eyes for seeing, not with whip for driving; L46
Heart at ease, body upright, all 6 reins not confused and 24 hoofs, no mistakes wherever put. L48
Turning curving forward backward, none not right, not regulated. L50
Then outside chariot can have no extra track, outside horses' hoofs can have no extra ground; L52
Then will not experience the danger of mountains and valleys. L53
As safety on dryland and wetland, will all be seen as one and the same that's. L54
Here are all my skills and you will remember them all !" L56

5.15 Zaofu Learns Charioteering

Comments:
5.15 Zaofu Learns Charioteering
Zaofu and Taidoushi were both legendary charioteers of their time.
Zaofu observed etiquette very humbly when he started charioteering under Taidoushi's tutelage.
But Taidou did not teach him for 3 years and Zaofu observed etiquette even more diligently.
Assured that Zaofu was a very patient and humble person, Taidou then started his teaching.

Ancient poem said: "A good bow-maker first trained his son to make bamboo-trays.
And a good blacksmith let his son make a leather-jacket."
So Taidou first trained Zaofu to brisk walk like himself, on a path made of raised piles.
The tops of piles were foot size in area and setting step-width apart to form a precarious path.
Taidou showed the way, walking briskly forward and backward with no misses and no falls.
Zaofu, the student was able to master the skill in 3 days and earned the praise of his teacher.

Thus trained, the driver is stable on rough terrain, feet balanced, heart at ease, no fear of falling.
The confident driver then is able to line up the horses with reins and bits combination.
With harmonious calls regulating the fast and slow speed, grasping the rhythm within held reins.
Inwardly feeling control at heart and outwardly in accord with the 6 horses' will.
With no strain to see with eyes, and no whipping to drive, the team had excess strength to go far.
Heart relaxed, body upright, all 6 reins not confused, and 24 hoofs no mistakes wherever placed.
Not stressed by the danger of mountains valleys, and dryland wetland are seen as one, i.e. same.

Humility, patience and diligence helped Zaofu to gain trust and learned his skill very quickly.

5.16 来丹谋报仇 — 5.16 Laidan Scheming Revenge

01	魏黑卵以昵嫌	Heiluan Of Wei (state) Because of Private Quarrel
02	杀丘邴章。	Killed Qiubingzhang.
03	丘邴章之子	Qiubingzhang His Son
04	**　来丹谋报父之仇。**	**Laidan Planned to Revenge Father's Death.**
05	丹气甚猛，形甚露，	Dan Anger Very Fierce, Body Most Exposed (bones),
06	计粒而食，顺风而趋。	Counting Grains For Food, Following Wind Be Moved.
07	虽怒，不能称兵以报之。	Though Angry, Not Able to Raise Weapon To Revenge It.
08	耻假力于人，	Ashamed to Using Efforts Of Others,
09	誓手剑以屠黑卵。	Vowed to Hand-held Sword To Kill Heiluan.
10	黑卵悍志绝众，	Heiluan Fierce Will Exceeding the Masses,
11	九抗百夫，	Ninth time Resisting 100 Men (very brave),
12	节骨皮肉，	Joints Bones Skin Muscle,
13	非人类也。	Not Human Kind that's (very tough).
14	延颈承刀，	Extended Neck to Block Knife,
15	披胸受矢，	Exposed Chest to Receive Arrow,
16	铓锷摧屈，	Sharp-tip Blade Piercing Slashing,
17	而体无痕挞。	And Body No Trace of Scars
18	负其材力，	Loaded with His Wealth Strength,
19	视来丹犹雏鷇也。	Saw Laidan Like Baby Bird, that's.
20	来丹之友申他曰：	Laidan His Friend Shengta Said:
21	"子怨黑卵至矣，	"Sir Hates Heiluan Extremely indeed,
22	黑卵之易子过矣，	Heiluan His Belittling You Excessively indeed,
23	将奚谋焉？"	Then What Planning That's ?"
24	来丹垂涕曰：	Laidan Dripping with Runny-nose Said:
25	"愿子为我谋。"	"Wish Sir Help Me to Plan."
26	申他曰：	Shenta Said:
27	"吾闻卫孔周其祖	"I Heard Kongzhou of Wei State, His Ancestor
28	得殷帝之宝剑，	Received From Emperor of Yin Wonder Sword,
29	一童子服之，	A Child Boy Wearing It,
30	却三军之众，	Can Resist 3 Armies Of Men,
31	奚不请焉？"	Why Not Request For-it ?"
32	来丹遂适卫，	Laidan Hence Went to Wei,
33	见孔周，	Seeing Kongzhou,
34	执仆御之礼，	Observed The Etiquette of Slave Servant,
35	请先纳妻子，	Request (Kongzhou) First to Accept His Wife Children,
36	后言所欲。	Afterward then Speak of Desire.
37	孔周曰：	Kongzhou Said:
38	"吾有三剑，	" I have 3 Swords,
39	唯子所译；	For Sir To Choose;
40	皆不能杀人，	All Not Able to Kill People,
41	且先言其状。	Now Firstly to Speak of Their Conditions.

5.16 Laidan Scheming Revenge

42	一曰含光，	1: Call-it Hanguang (Conceal-light),
43	视之不可见，	Look at It Not Able to See,
44	运之不知有。	Using It Not Knowing its Presence.
45	其所触也，	Whatever It Contact that's,
46	泯然无际，	Submerge Naturally No Boundary,
47	经物而物不觉。	Pass-through Matter and Matter Not Aware.
48	二曰承影，	2: Call-it Chengying (Support-shadow),
49	将旦昧爽之交，	Approaching Dawn Dim Bright The Crossover,
50	日夕昏明之际，	Day Night Dark Light The Boundary,
51	北面而察之，	North Facing And Inspecting It,
52	淡淡焉若有物存，	Pale and Light that's Like Having Matters Existing,
53	莫识其状。	Not Knowing Its Condition.
54	其所触也，	Whatever It Contact that's,
55	窃窃然有声，	Furtively naturally Have Sound,
56	经物而物不疾也。	Pass-through Matter And Matter No Pain, that's.
57	三曰宵练，	3. Call-it Xiaolian (Night-practice),
58	方昼则见影而不见光，	All Day Then See Shadow And Not See Light,
59	方夜见光而不见形。	All Night See Light And Not See Form.
60	其触物也，	It Contact Matter that's,
61	騞然而过，	Quickly Naturally And Passed,
62	随过随合，	Following Passage Following Join-up,
63	觉疾而不血刃焉。	Feel Pain But No Blood on Blade That's.
64	此三宝者，	These 3 Treasured Items,
65	传之十三世矣，	They have Passed-on 13 Generations Already,
66	而无施于事。	And Not Use In Affairs.
67	匣而藏之，	Boxed And Stored Them,
68	未尝启封。"	Not Ever Open the Sealing."
69	来丹曰：	Laidan Said:
70	"虽然，吾必请其下者。"	"Nevertheless, I Must Request for The Low (last) Item."
71	孔周乃归其妻子，	Kongzhou Then Returned His Wife and Children,
72	与斋七日。	With him Fasted for 7 Days.
73	晏阴之间，	Quietly Dimly In Between,
74	跪而授其下剑，	Kneeling To Bestow Him The Low Sword,
75	来丹再拜受之以归。	Laidan Close-palms (salute) Accepting It And Returned.
76	来丹遂执剑从黑卵。	LaidanThen Held Sword, Followed Heiluan.
77	时黑卵之醉偃于牖下，	Timely, Heiluan Was Drunk Supine Below The Window.
78	自颈至腰三斩之。	From Neck Till Waist 3 times Cutting Him.
79	黑卵不觉。	Heiluan No Awareness.
80	来丹以黑卵之死，	Laidan Believing Heiluan Was Dead,
81	趣而退。	Quick In Retreat.
82	遇黑卵之子于门，	Meeting Heiluan His Son At the Door,
83	击之三下，如投虚。	Striked Him 3 Strokes, Like Casting Emptiness.
84	黑卵之子方笑曰：	Heiluan His Son All Laughing Said:
85	"汝何蚩而三招予？"	"You Why Ignorant And 3 Beckonings of Me ?"

5.16 Laidan Scheming Revenge

86	来丹知剑之不能杀人也，	Laidan Knew Sword It's Not Able to Kill People that's,
87	叹而归。	Sighed And Returned.
88	黑卵既醒，怒其妻曰：	Heiluan When Awoke, Angry With Wife Said:
89	"醉而露我，	"Drunk And Exposed Me,
90	使人嗌疾而腰急。"	Caused Me Sore Throat And Waist Pain."
91	其子曰：	His Son Said:
92	"畴昔来丹之来。	"Just Then Laidan He Came.
93	遇我于门，三招我，	Met Me At Door, 3 times Beckoning Me,
94	亦使我体疾而支强，	Also Caused Me Body Ache And Limbs Stiff,
95	彼其厌我哉！"	Laidan His Sorcery on Me is-it-not !"

Liezi Text Narrative

Heiluan of Wei State Killed Qiubingzhang because of a private quarrel. L2
And his son Laidan wished to avenge his father's death. L4
Laidan's anger was fierce but body weak with exposed bones. L5
A few grains for food, wind can blow him away, though angry cannot lift a weapon to avenge. L7
Ashamed to use the efforts of others, avowed to kill Heiluan with his own hand-held sword. L9
Heiluan's fierce will and bravery exceeded the masses, 9 times resisting 100 men. L11
Very tough Joints bones skin and muscle, not of the human kind that's. L13
Extended neck to challenge knife, exposed chest to arrow, piercing slashing leave no scars. L17
Loaded with wealth and strength, he saw Laidan harmless like a baby bird in its nest, that's. L19
Laidan's Friend Shenta Said: "Sir hates Heiluan to the extreme. L21
And Heiluan, his belittling you is excessive, so what are you planning to do ?" L23
Laidan, very unhappy with dripping runny-nose said: "Wishing Sir, you help me to plan." L25
Shenta said "I heard Kongzhou of Wei, his ancestor had from Emperor of Yin wonder sword. L28
A child boy wearing it can resist 3 armies of men; why not request from him ?" L31
Laidan hence went to the State of Wei, and seeing Kongzhou observed the etiquette of slaves. L34
Requested that Kongzhou first accept his wife and children before speaking of his desire. L36
Kongzhou said: "I have 3 swords for you to choose, but all are not able to kill people. L40
But firstly to speak of their conditions. L41
1: Call-it Hanguang (Conceal-light), look at it not seen, use it not know its presence. L44
Whatever it contacts, submerge naturally no boundary, pass-through matter, matter not aware. L47
2: Call-it Chengying (Support-shadow), dawning, dim bright light crossing-over; L49
Day and night at the boundary of dark and light, north facing and inspecting it; L51
Pale and light that's like having matters existing, but not knowing its condition. L53
Whatever it contacts, furtively naturally has sound, passes through matter, matter no pain. L56
3: Call-it Xiaolian (Night-practice), all day see shadow not light, all night see light not form. L59
It contacted matter, quickly passed, joined-up instantly, felt pain but no blood on the blade. L63
These 3 treasures had passed on for 13 generations already and not been used in affairs. L66
Boxed and stored, the sealing never opened." L68
Laidan said: "Nevertheless, I must request for the low (last) item." L
Kongzhou then returned his wife and children, and with Laidan fasted for 7 days. L72
Quietly and dimly in between, kneeling to bestow Laidan with the low (last) sword. L74
Laidan close-palms signed in a thankful response, accepting it and returned. L75

5.16 Laidan Scheming Revenge

Laidan then held the sword, followed Heiluan, found him drunk lying beneath the window. L77
From neck to the waist, cut him 3 times, and Heiluan had no awareness. L79
Laidan, believing Heiluan was dead, hurried in retreat. L81
Meeting Heiluan's son at the door, struck him 3 strokes, like striking in emptiness. L83
Heiluan's son then laughing, said: "Are you ignorant with 3 times beckoning at me ?" L85
Laidan knew the sword was not able to kill people, and sighing returned. L87
Heiluan when awoke, was angry with his wife and said: "I am drunk and you exposed me. L89
Caused me to have sore throat and waist pain." L90
His son said: "Just then Laidan came and met me at the door, beckoning me 3 times. L93
Also caused my body ache and limbs stiff, he played sorcery on me, is-it-not !" L95

Comments:
5.16 Laidan Scheming Revenge
Heiluan killed Qiubingzhang because of a private quarrel and the son Laidan seeked revenge.
Laidan was fierce, but eating a few grains for food, he was so thin that he could be blown away.
Delusional, he vowed to kill Heiluan by himself but was too weak to lift a weapon to do so.
Heiluan was able to fight 100 men, and joints, bones, skin, muscles were not of the human kind.
Knife slashed neck and arrow pierced chest left no scars, he regarded Laidan as just a baby bird.
Friend Shenta saw that Laidan was so sadly bullied, and so suggested he go to Kongzhou in Wei.
For Kongzhou had a wonder sword that a child carrying it could resist 3 armies of men.

Laidan took the etiquette of the slave, offering his wife and children to Kongzhou before asking.
Kongzhou said he had 3 swords for Laidan to choose, but all of them are not able to kill people.
1. Conceal-light, not seen with no matter, on contact pass-through matter, matter not aware.
2. Support-shadow, pale with matter existing, in contact has sound, pass-through matter, no pain.
3. Night-practice, day-shadow night-light, in contact quickly passed, closed, has pain no blood.
These swords had been passed down for 13 generations already, boxed and sealed but never open.
Laidan chose the 3rd one that can inflict pain, then Kongzhou kindly returned his family to him.
Kongzhou fasted 7 days with Laidan to calm him for non-violence before handing him the sword.

Laidan found Heiluan drunk lying beneath the window, and cut him 3 times from neck to waist.
Heiluan had no awareness, and Laidan, believing him dead, hurried in retreat.
Met the son at the door and struck him 3 times, prompting the latter to ask why beckoned 3 times.
Then Heiluan awoke to scold his wife for leaving him out to suffer a sore throat and waist pain.
And the son said that Laidan had came, played sorcery on him causing body ache and stiff limbs!
Laidan knew he was delusional about killing Heiluan, accepted the fact with a sigh and returned.

Daoism is against killing, the wonder sword is no sorcery but to liberate Laidan of his delusion.

Chapter 5. Tang's Queries (汤問)

5.17 果于自信   5.17 Overly Self-Confident

01 周穆王大征西戎，	King Mu of Zhou Great Campaign in West Rong (tribe)
02 西戎献锟铻之剑，	West Rong (tribe) Offered The Kunyu Sword,
03 火浣之布。	The Fire-Washable Cloth (asbestos).
04 其剑长尺有咫，	That Sword, Length More Than Foot,
05 练钢赤刃，	Processed Steel Pure Blade,
06 用之切玉如切泥焉。	Use It, Cutting Jade Like Cutting Mud that's.
07 火浣之布，	The Fire-washable Cloth,
08 浣之必投于火；	Washing It Must Cast Into Fire;
09 布则火色，	Cloth Then Color of Fire;
10 垢则布色；	Dirt Then Color of Cloth;
11 出火而振之，	Out of Fire And Shake It,
12 皓然疑乎雪。	Bright Naturally Condensed Like Snow.
13 皇子以为无此物，	The Prince Believed No Such Materials,
14 传之者妄。	People Transmitting It, Absurd.
15 萧叔曰：	Xiaoshu Said:
16 "皇子果于自信，	***"The Prince Certainly Over Self Confident,***
17 果于诬理哉！"	***Dare Be Not Rational is-it-not !"***

Liezi Text Narrative
King Mu of Zhou had a great campaign against the Rong tribe in the west. L1
The West Rong tribe offered the famous Kunyu Sword, a rare Fire-washable Cloth (asbestos). L3
The Sword was more than a foot long, of processed steel, pure blade cut Jade like cutting mud. L6
The Fire-washable cloth, to wash, cast it into fire till red hot, then shake to dislodged the dirt. L12
The Prince did not believe these items existed, and said it was absurd to transmit such ideas. L14
Xiaoshu said: "The Prince is overly self-confident, and certainly not rational, is-it-not !" L17

Comments:
5.17 Overly Self-Confident
The Kunyu Sword of steel cut jade like mud and the Fire-washable Cloth is cleansed by fire !
The Prince did not believe in their existence, and said people were absurd to transmit such ideas.
Indeed these were very rare items that few like Xiaoshu, had the privilege to see at that time.
Hence Xiaoshu confidently criticized the Prince for being irrational and overly self-confident.

We are reminded not to be overly confident, dismiss things off-hand, and be humble to learn.

Liezi: World of Delusions

Chapter 5. Tang's Queries (汤问)

Summary

5.1 Tang's Queries (汤问): The origin and limits on Earth, in Heaven, and the universe beyond.
And his minister gushed with legends of the formation of lands, mountains and seas.

5.2 Yukong (Stupid Grandpa) (愚公): Legend of an old man's wish to move mountains.
He said success assured, as mountains don't grow, but we have many future generations.

5.3 Kuafu Chasing The Sun (夸父追日): To query where the sun might go down at night.
Legend has it that he died in the desert, transforming into an oasis for future generations.

5.4 'Dao' Self Natural (*道自然*): Yu said all creations through gods, spirits, and sages.
Xiage said, had independent creations, 'Dao' is natural, raising more queries to be answered.

5.5 An Absurd State (谬之一国): This was Liezi's description of the State of Zhongbei.
With no rain, no animals, all play, no work, etc., this is an exploration of a legendary utopia !

5.6 Different States Different Traditions (为俗未足为异): Bizarre ancient customs revealed.
Like eating the first born, abandoning parents to die and such, were based on superstitions.

5.7 Kongzi Cannot Decide (孔子不能决): Is the Sun nearer to Earth at noon or in the morning?
A satire on confucians' for the lack of attention in science, concentration only on social issues.

5.8 Uniformity (Fairness) (均): Hairs of steel with uniformity are used for suspending bridges.
Zhanhe's bizarre balance in fishing was to show the king, fairness is good for government.

5.9 Change of Hearts (换汝之心): Gonghu and Qiying were opposite in temperament.
Bianque exchanged their hearts to balance for them; result, unrecognition by the families !

5.10 Three Years No Music (三年不成章): Shiwen played music for 3 years with no feelings.
 After a break, he played with such gusto, able to summon up feelings of the 4 seasons.

5.11 Lingered 3 Days Above Rafter (绕梁三日): Hane's singing was still there after she left.
Her singing also left a legacy in style and voice, that the people still cherished at Yong Gate.

5.12 Soulmates In Music (伯牙, 钟子期): Zhongziqi and Boya were legends in music.
Zhongziqi was able to appreciate the feelings and thoughts of Boya, when the latter played.

5.13 The Artificial Performer (所造能倡者): He winked at the court ladies after he performed.
King was outraged, and to avoid being killed, Yanshi dismantled him (it) to show his parts.

5.14 Ancient Archers (古之善射者): Ganying taught Feiwei, and Feiwei taught Jichang.
Then Jichang tried to kill his teacher to be first, and Feiwei defended with a reserved stroke.

5.15 Zaofu Learned Charioteering (造父习御): Training was with the legendary Tadoushi.
First to train body balance by walking briskly on raised piles (foot-size) without falling.

5.16 Laidan Scheming Revenge (来丹谋报仇): To avenge his father's death by Heiluan.
Laidan loaned Kongzhou's 'virtual' sword that passed with no blood, and 'killed' Heiluan.

5.17 Overly Self-Confident (果于自信): Arrogance denying further exploration and learning.
Prince said it is absurd to believe the existence of the Kunyu sword and the fire-washcloth.

This chapter query limits in the universe, in human activities like music, automation, others.

Chapter 6. Effort or Destiny (力命)

Introduction

6.1 Effort or Destiny (力命)

6.2 Thick in Virtue, Thin in Destiny (厚于德，薄于命)

6.3 The Inevitable Denial (不得不薄)

6.4 The Inevitable Death (不得不诛)

6.5 Self Natural Entity (自然者)

6.6 Diagnosis of 3 Doctors (谒三医)

6.7 Better Let It Be (不如其已)

6.8 All Destiny that's (皆命也)

6.9 Characters Galore (此众态也)

6.10 To Gauge or Not To Gauge (度与不度)

6.11 Forever In-Charge (常守之)

6.12 Not Disturbed (不忧)

6.13 Effort, Destiny Enable Naturally (势,命使然也)

Summary

Chapter 6. Effort or Destiny (力命)

Introduction:

Effort and, or Destiny, that shapes the march of events, controls the experience of humanity. Here, narratives of the inevitability of denial or death of historical characters in their destinies. Discussions on the ancients lack of influence on events and their inevitable belief in Destiny. Naturally, Liezi believes in Effort for success and leaves Destiny to account for the failures !

The good is poor, the evil wealthy, such a mess is not made by Destiny, or be credited to Effort. Beigonzi was thick in virtues, thin in Destiny; Ximenzi was the reverse, so don't shame others. Yiwu's inevitable denial rested on Baoshu, his inflexibility that led to his failure in succession. Dengxi's Dual Possibility Concept inevitably clashed with Zichan, led to his 'Destined' death. Destiny, not a maker of things, not affected by anything, just allows things to happen as destined. Jiliang, a daoist with peace of mind and no indulgence, chased the doctors away and self healed. The ancients had little influence on events, thus argued, 'better let it be' and believed in Destiny. Person believing in Destiny, just acts truly, not worrying with life and death, or has other worries. Characters galore, individuals travelling together on earth, self-believing, sadly not interacting. Gauge or not gauge, similar success rate 50:50, so no advantage of knowledge, thus be at peace. Duke Jing wished forever living, forever in-charge, but then his forebears would still be around ! Dongmenwu was not troubled after his son died; this is accepting destiny and having no worries ! Effort and Destiny enable naturally, Effort accounts for success and Destiny accounts for failure.

Chapter 6. Effort or Destiny (力命)

6.1 力命 | 6.1 Effort or Destiny

01 *力谓命曰：*	***Effort to Destiny Said:***
02 "若之功奚若我哉？"	"Your Success, How can be Like Mine that's ?"
03 命曰：	Destiny Said:
04 "汝奚功于物，	"You How contribute to Success Of Matter,
05 而欲比朕？"	And Wishing to Compare with Me ?"
06 力曰：	Effort Said:
07 "寿夭、穷达、	"Longevity Premature-death, Failure Success,
08 贵贱、贫富，	Noble Humble, Poverty Wealthy,
09 我力之所能也。"	My Effort, All My Abilities, that's."
10 命曰：	Destiny Said:
11 "彭祖之智不出	"Pengzu, His Wisdom Not Exiting
12 　尧舜之上，	Above That of Yao, Shun,
13 而寿八百；	And Longevity is 800;
14 颜渊之才不出	Yanyuan, His Talent Not Exiting
15 　众人之下，	Below That of Common People,
16 而寿四八。	And Longevity 48.
17 仲尼之德不出	Zhongni, His Virtues Not Exiting
18 　诸侯之下，	Below That of The Baronage,
19 而困于陈、蔡；	But Trapped At Chen, Cai (states);
20 殷纣之行不出	Zhou of Yin, His Conduct Not Exiting
21 　三仁之上，	Above That of 3 Kind-persona,
22 而居君位。	Yet Occupy King Position.
23 季札无爵于吴，	Jizha, No Title From Wu (state),
24 田恒专有齐国。	Tianheng, Dictator Possessed (king) Qi State.
25 夷、齐饿于首阳，	Yi, Qi died of Hunger In Shouyang (mountain)
26 季氏富于展禽。	Jishu Wealthier Than Zhanqin.
27 若是汝力之所能，	If Like Your Effort, Who Is Capable,
28 奈何寿彼而夭此，	Then Why Longevity There And Premature-death here,
29 穷圣而达逆，	Failing Sage And Successful Rebel,
30 贱贤而贵愚，	Virtuous Humble And Stupid Noble,
31 贫善而富恶邪？"	Poor Good And Wealthy Evil how-is-that ?"
32 力曰：	Effort Said:
33 "若如若言，	"If Like As Said,
34 我固无功于物，	I am Certainly No Credit To Matters,
35 而物若此邪，	And Matter Like This that's,
36 此则若之所制邪？"	This Then Like What You have Created is-it-not ?"
37 命曰：	Destiny Said:
38 "既谓之命，	"As Calling It Destiny,
39 奈何有制之者邪？	Then Why Have A Creator, that's ?
40 朕直而推之，	I, if Correct Then Implement It,

195

6.1 Effort or Destiny

41 曲而任之。	Crooked Then Allow It.
42 自寿自夭，	Self Longevity Self Premature-death,
43 自穷自达，	Self Failure Self Success,
44 自贵自贱，	Self Noble Self Humble,
45 自富自贫，	Self Wealthy Self Poor,
46 朕岂能识之哉?	I, However Able to Know It, true ?
47 朕岂能识之哉? "	I, However Able to Know It, true ?"

Liezi Text Narrative
Effort to Destiny said: "Your success, how can you compare to mine ?" L2
Destiny said: "How you make the success of matters, thus wishing to compare with me ?" L5
Effort said: "Longevity/premature-death, failure/success, noble/humble, poverty/wealthy, L8
Me Effort, these are all my capabilities that's." L9
Destiny said: "Pengzu, his wisdom not above that of Yao Shun, lived to 800; L13
Yanyuan, his talents not below that of common people, and lived to only 48. L16
Zhongni, his virtues not below that of the Baronage, but got trapped at between Chen, Cai; L19
King Zhou of Yin, his conduct not above that of the 3 Kind-persona, yet occupied kingship. L22
Jizha had no title from the state of Wu, but Tainheng as dictator possessed the state of Qi. L24
Yi and Qi died of hunger on Mt Shouyang, Jishu is wealthier than Zhanqin. L26
If like Effort, you are capable, then why longevity there, premature-death here; L28
Why the sage failed and the rebel succeeded, the humble is vitruous and the noble stupid; L30
Why is the poor good and the wealthy evil, how-is-that ?" L31
Effort said, "If like as you said, I am certainly of no credit to matters; L34
And matters as they are, then these are what you have created, is-it-not ?" L36
Destiny said: "As it is called Destiny, then why have a creator that's ? L39
I, when straight then implement it, and when crooked then still allow it. L41
Self longevity, self premature-death, self failure, self success, self noble, self humble; L44
Self wealthy, self poor; I, however, am able to know it, right ? L46
I, however, am able to know it, right ?" L47

Comments:
6.1 Effort or Destiny
Effort and Destiny had an argument over whose successfully influenced matters.
Effort claimed credit for making all the possibilities like longevity/ premature-death;
Failure/success, noble/ humble, poverty/wealthy.
Destiny then raised many historical examples to ask why Effort did it all wrong, that's !
That Pengzu, not known for wisdom, lived to 800; whereas Yanyuan the talented died at age 48.
That Confucius, virtuous got trapped between Chen, Cai; but evil King Zhou inherited a kingdom.
Why did the sage fail, rebels succeeded; the poor are good and the wealthy evil, how-is-that ?
Effort countered that as he had no credit, then this mess of matters were the making of Destiny !
Interestingly, Destiny denies that a maker is needed, hence it is called Destiny !
Destiny just implemented or allowed matters to happen, whether straight or crooked.
Destiny not responsible, as it is all self-so, self longevity, self premature-death, self failure, ...

In Destiny there is no need for a maker; all matters are self-so, naturally so, true !

Chapter 6. Effort or Destiny (力命)

6.2 厚于德，薄于命　　6.2 Thick in Virtue, Thin in Destiny

01	北宫子谓西门子曰：	Beigongzi To Ximenzi Said:
02	"朕与子并世也，	"I With Sir Together in this World that's
03	而人子达；	And People allow Sir to Succeed;
04	并族也，而人子敬；	Same Clan that's, And People Respect Sir;
05	并貌也，而人子爱；	Same Look that's, And People Love Sir;
06	并言也，而人子庸；	Same Speech that's, And People Engage Sir;
07	并行也，而人子诚；	Same Conduct that's, And People Trust Sir,
08	并仕也，而人子贵；	Same Official-status that's, And People Honor Sir;
09	并农也，而人子富；	Same Farming that's, And People Enrich Sir;
10	并商也，而人子利。	Same Trade that's, And People Facilitate Sir;
11	朕衣则裋褐，食则粢粝，	My Clothe Is Brown Robe, Food Is Coarse Millet,
12	居则蓬室，出则徒行。	Residence Is Grass-hut, Travel Is Walking on Foot.
13	子衣则文锦，食则粱肉，	Sir Clothe In Fine Silk, Food Is Sorghum Meat,
14	居则连欐，出则结驷。	Residence Is Tall Mansion, Travel Is 4-horse Carriage.
15	在家熙然有弃朕之心，	At Home Happily Show Heart-feeling of Neglecting Me.
16	在朝谔然有敖朕之色。	In Court Proudly Show Appearance Of Snubbing Me.
17	请谒不相及，	Invitation Visitation No Mutual Contact,
18	遨游不同行，	Excursion Rambling Not Together Travel,
19	固有年矣。	Certainly Has been Years indeed.
20	子自以德过朕邪？"	Sir, Self Believe Virtues Exceeding Me Is-it-not ?"
21	西门子曰：	Ximenzi Said:
22	"予无以知其实。	"I, No Way to Know the Facts.
23	汝造事而穷，	Your Performance of Tasks Are Failures,
24	予造事而达，	My Performance of Tasks Are Successes,
25	此厚薄之验欤？	This The Check of Thick Thin (virtues), true-or-not ?
26	而皆谓与予并，	Yet Said All the Same With Me,
27	汝之颜厚矣。"	Your Face Thick-skin indeed."
28	北宫子无以应，自失而归。	Beigongzi Nothing To Respond, Self Lost And Returned.
29	中途遇东郭先生。	MidWay Met Teacher Dongguo.
30	先生曰：	Teacher Said:
31	"汝奚往而反，	"You Why Go-forth And Return,
32	偊偊而步，	Lonely And Slowly Walking,
33	有深愧之色邪？"	Having The Look of Deep Shame, is-it-true ?"
34	北宫子言其状。	Beigongzi Narrated The Situation.
35	东郭先生曰：	Teacher Dongguo Said:
36	"吾将舍汝之愧，	"I Will help Discard Your Shame,
37	与汝更之西门氏而问之。"	With You Change It with Ximenzi, So to Ask Him."
38	曰：	Said:
39	"汝奚辱北宫子之深乎？	"Why You Shamed Beigongzi This Deeply, right ?
40	固且言之。"	Now You Must Speak-up."
41	西门子曰：	Ximenzi Said:

6.2 Thick in Virtue, Thin in Destiny

42	"北宫子言世族、	"Beigongzi Said based on Clan Generation,
43	年貌、言行与予并,	Age Look, Speech Conduct With Me Same,
44	而贱贵、贫富与予异。	But be Lowly Noble, Poor Wealthy With Me Different.
45	予语之曰:'予无以知其实。	I Spoke to Him Said: 'I Not Know The Facts.
46	汝造事而穷,予造事而达,	You Work Tasks And Fail, I Work Tasks And Succeed,
47	此将厚薄之验欤?	This Check-out The Thick Thin (in virtues) is-it-not ?
48	而皆谓与予并,	And Everything Said, With Me Same,
49	汝之颜厚矣。'	Your Face Thick (skin) indeed.'
50	东郭先生曰:	Teacher Dongguo Said:
51	"汝之言厚薄	"You Speak Of Thick and Thin
52	不过言才德之差,	Is Just Speaking of Difference in Talent and Virtue,
53	吾之言厚薄异于是矣。	I Speak Of Thick and Thin is Other Than These that's.
54	**夫北宫子厚于德,薄于命;**	***O' Beigongzi is Thick In Virtue, Thin In Destiny;***
55	汝厚于命,薄于德。	You are Thick In Destiny, Thin In Virtue.
56	汝之达,非智得也;	You Your Success, Not Attained by Talent that's'
57	北宫子之穷,非愚失也。	Beigongzi His Poverty, Not Lost by Stupidity that's.
58	皆天也,非人也。	All from Heaven that's, Not from Human that's.
59	而汝以命厚自矜,	And You With Destiny Thick (lucky), Self Proud,
60	北公子以德厚自愧,	Beigongzi With Virtue Thick (virtuous), Self Ashamed,
61	皆不识夫固然之理矣。"	All Not Knowing the Natural Certainty Of Reason."
62	西门子曰:	Ximenzi Said:
63	"先生止矣!	"Teacher please Stop indeed !
64	予不敢复言。"	I Don't Dare to Speak Again."
65	北宫子既归,	Beigongzi Then Returned,
66	衣其裋褐,有狐貉之温;	Clothing in Brown Cloth, Had The Warmth Of Mink;
67	进其茙菽,有稻梁之味;	Eating The Coarse Millet, Had Taste Of Grain Sorghum;
68	庇其蓬室,若广厦之荫;	Covered In Grass Hut, Like Sheltered Of Big Mansion;
69	乘其筚辂,若文轩之饰。	Riding The Wooden Cart, Like The Adorned Carriage.
70	终身逌然,	Life Long Contented As Natural,
71	不知荣辱之在彼也,	Not Knowing if Honor Shame Was On Others that's,
72	在我也。	On Self that's.
73	东郭先生闻之曰:	Teacher Dongguo Heard This Said:
74	"北宫子之寐久矣,	"Beigongzi His Sleep (mis-understanding) Long indeed,
75	一言而能寤,	One Statement And Able to Awaken,
76	易悟也哉!"	Quick Learning that's, right !"

Liezi Text Narrative

Beigongzi to Ximenzi said: "I with Sir together in this world and people let you succeed; L3
Same Clan and people respect Sir; same Look and people love Sir; L5
Same Speech and people engage Sir; same Conduct and people trust Sir; L7
Same Official-status and people honor Sir; same Farming and people enrich Sir; L9
Same Trade and people facilitate Sir. L10
I wear brown clothes, eat coarse millet, reside in a grass-hut, and travel on foot. L12
Sir wears fine silk, eats sorghum meat, resides in a tall mansion, travels in a 4-horse carriage. L14
At home happily neglecting me at heart, and in court proudly snubbing me in front of others. L16

6.2 Thick in Virtue, Thin in Destiny

Certainly been years, no visitation, no mutual contact, rambling excursion, no travel together. L19
Sir, you believe your virtues exceed me, is-it-not ?" L20
Ximenzi said: "I have no way to know the facts. L22
You failed your tasks, but I succeeded in mine, this confirms our virtues, thick or thin, true ? L25
Yet say that you are all the same like me, so you are really thick-skinned in the face." L27
Beigongzi had nothing to respond, and returned like a lost soul. L28
Midway met Senior Dongguo who asked: "Why go and return alone, looking deeply ashamed. L33
Beigongzi narrated the situation; L34
Senior Dongguo said: "I will discard your shame, and we shall ask Ximenzi to change." L37
Said: "Why did you shame Beigongzi so deeply ? Now you must speak-up." L40
Ximenzi said: " Beigongzi said, on clan generation, age, look, speech, conduct, we are same; L43
But on lowliness, nobility, poverty and wealth we are different. L44
I spoke to him and said: 'I do not know the facts. L45
You failed your tasks and I succeeded mine, this proved the thick and thin in virtue, true ? L47
And everything, you said it is the same as me, your face is thick-skinned indeed.'" L49
Senior Dongguo said: "You speak of thick and thin, these differences in talent and virtue. L52
I speak of thick and thin, are other than these. L53
Beigongzi is thick in Virtue thin in Destiny; you are thick in Destiny (lucky) thin in Virtue. L55
Your success is not attained by talent that's; Beigongzi's failure, not because of stupidity. L57
All because of Heaven and not because of Humans, that's. L58
You, proud of thick Destiny; Beigongzi, ashamed of thick Virtue, both do not know logic." L61
Ximenzi said: "Teacher please stop indeed! I don't dare to speak again in this way." L64
Beigongzi then returned; clothed in brown cloth, felt the warmth of mink coat; L66
Coarse millet tasted like grain sorghum; lived in grass-hut like sheltered in a big mansion; L68
Riding the wooden cart, like the adorned carriage; L69
Life long contented as nature, not knowing if honor or shame is on others or self that's. L72
Senior Doongguo heard this, said: "Beigongzi, his sleep has been long indeed. L74
One statement and being able to be awakened, he learns quickly, is-it-not !" L76

Comments:
6.2 Thick in Virtue, Thin in Destiny
Poor Beigongzi complained to rich Ximenzi that the world had only been kind to the latter.
Though they were similar in many ways, like clan generation, look, speech, and conduct.
Same official-status, people honored Ximenzi, enriched him in farming, facilitated his trading.
Ximenzi said he was good at tasks but Beigongzi failed; a reflection of the thick or thin in virtues.
Thus the latter was thick-skinned in the face to insist that they were similar.
Insulted, Beigongzi returned deeply ashamed and midway met with Senior Dongguo.
After hearing Beigongzi, Dongguo said they can confront Ximenzi to change his thinking.
Dongguo told Ximenzi his success not by talent and Beigongzi his failure not from stupidity.
All because of Heaven, hence Ximenzi thick in Destiny and thin in Virtue shouldn't be too proud.
Whereas Beigongzi is thick in Virtues and thin in Destiny, and shouldn't be ashamed, logically.
Thick in Destiny and lucky to be born rich, Ximenzi agreed to not speak ill of Beigongzi again.
Beigongzi then returned; clothed in brown cloth, felt the warmth of mink coat;
Ate coarse millet, tasted like grain sorghum; lived in grass-hut like sheltered in a big mansion;
Dongguo one statement of logic enlightened Beigongzi, and he lived happily ever after !
Destiny is luck from Heaven, born into a rich or poor family, with good or bad consequences !

Chapter 6. Effort or Destiny (力命)

6.3 不得不薄　　　　　6.3 The Inevitable Denial

01	管夷吾、	Guanyiwu,
02	鲍叔牙二人相友甚戚，	Baoshuya 2 Persons Mutual Friendship Very Close,
03	同处于齐。	Together Residing in the State of Qi.
04	管夷吾事公子纠，	Guanyiwu Serving Prince Jiu,
05	鲍叔牙事公子小白。	Baoshuya Serving Prince Xiaobai.
06	齐公族多宠，	Duke Clans of Qi Many Favoritism,
07	嫡庶并行。	Direct and Side lineage (for kingship) Running Together.
08	国人惧乱。	Citizens Afraid of Upheaval.
09	管仲与召忽奉公子纠奔鲁，	Guanzhong With Zhaohu Supported Prince Jiu Flee to Lu,
10	鲍叔奉公子小白奔莒。	Baoshu Supported Prince Xiaobai Flee to the state of Ju.
11	既而公孙无知作乱，	Shortly Then Gongsunwuzhi Made Trouble,
12	齐无君，二公子争入。	Qi had No King, 2 Princes Contesting to Come-in.
13	管夷吾与小白战于莒，	Guanyiwu With Xiaobai Battled At Ju,
14	道射中小白带钩。	Said had Shot Hitting Xiaobai's Belt Buckle.
15	小白既立，胁鲁杀子纠，	Xiaobai When Installed, Forced Lu to Kill Prince Jiu,
16	召忽死之，管夷吾被囚。	Zhaohu Committed Suicide, Guanyiwu Got Imprisoned.
17	鲍叔牙谓桓公曰：	Baoshuya To Duke Huan Said:
18	"管夷吾能，可以治国。"	"Guanyiwu Capable, Able To Govern State."
19	桓公曰：	Duke Huan Said:
20	"我仇也，愿杀之。"	"My Enemy, that's, Wish to Kill Him."
21	鲍叔牙曰：	Baoshuya Said:
22	"吾闻贤君无私怨，	"I Heard Virtuous Duke has No Private Enmity,
23	且人能为其主，	Further Person Able to Serve His Master,
24	亦必能为人君。	Also Certainly Able to Serve The Duke.
25	如欲霸王，	If Wishing be Leader of Kings,
26	非夷吾其弗可。	Not Yiwu (Guanyiwu) That Cannot be Done.
27	君必舍之！"	Duke Certain to Give-up on Him !"
28	遂召管仲。	Then Called for Guanzhong.
29	鲁归之，	Lu Returned Him,
30	齐鲍叔牙郊迎，	Baoshuya of Qi Welcomed at Countryside,
31	释其囚。	Relieved His Shackles.
32	桓公礼之，	Duke Huan Celebrated Him,
33	而位于高国之上，	And Positioned Him Above Gao and Guo clans,
34	鲍叔牙以身下之，	Baoshuya Personally Subordinated To Him,
35	任以国政。	Appointed As State Administrator.
36	号曰仲父。	Salutation Called Father Zhong.
37	桓公遂霸。	Duke Huan Proceeded to be The Supreme (of Kings).
38	管仲尝叹曰：	Guanzhong Often Sighing Said:
39	"吾少穷困时，	"I, When Young Trapped in Poverty,
40	尝与鲍叔贾，	Often With Baoshu do Trading,

6.3 The Inevitable Denial

41	分财多自与；	Dividing Gains Gave Myself More;
42	鲍叔不以我为贪，	Baoshu Never Take Me to Be Greedy,
43	知我贫也。	Knew that I was Poor that's.
44	吾尝为鲍叔谋事	I Often For Baoshu PlannedTasks
45	而大穷困，	Had Great Limitation and Trouble,
46	鲍叔不以我为愚，	Baoshu Never Regard Me As Stupid,
47	知时有利不利也。	Knew Timing Can be Favorable Unfavorable that's.
48	吾尝三仕，	I Experienced 3 times as Officials,
49	三见逐于君，	3 Observations being Banished By King,
50	鲍叔不以我为肖，	Baoshu Never Regard Me As a Failure,
51	知我不遭时也。	Knew I have Not Encountered my Time that's.
52	吾尝三战三北，	I Experienced 3 Battles and 3 Defeats,
53	鲍叔不以我为怯，	Baoshu Never Regards Me As a Coward,
54	知我有老母也。	Knew I Had an Old Mother that's.
55	公子纠败，召忽死之，	Prince Jiu Defeated, Zhaohu Committed Suicide,
56	吾幽囚受辱；	I Got Imprisoned Suffered Disgrace;
57	鲍叔不以我为无耻，	Baoshu Never Regard Me As Shameless,
58	知我不羞小节	Knew I am Not Shy of Small Mistakes
59	而耻名不显于天下也。	But Ashamed of Name Not Shine Worldwide that's.
60	生我者父母，	Persons Created Me Father Mother,
61	知我者鲍叔也！"	Person who Knows Me Baoshu that's !"
62	此世称管鲍善交者，	This Society Praise Baoshu, Person Good in Friendship,
63	小白善用能者。	Xiaobai, Person Good in Employment of Talents.
64	然实无善交，	Naturally Truly No Good Friendship,
65	实无用能也。	Truly No Employment of Talents that's.
66	实无善交	Truly No Good Friendship
67	实无用能者，	Truly No Employment of Talented People,
68	非更有善交、	None More Having Good Friendship,
69	更有善用能也。	More Having Good Employment of Talents that's.
70	召忽非能死，	Zhaohu Not, Able to Die,
71	不得不死；	Not Able to, Not Die;
72	鲍叔非能举贤，	Baoshu Not, Able to Recommend Talented,
73	不得不举；	Not Able to, Not Recommend;
74	小白非能用仇，	Xiaobai Not, Able to Employ Enemy,
75	不得不用。	Not Able to, Not Employ.
76	及管夷吾有病，	When Guanyiwu Had Sickness,
77	小白问之，曰：	Xiaobai Asked Him, Said:
78	"仲父之病病矣，	"Father Zhong Your Illness Serious that's,
79	可不讳。	Possible No Taboo.
80	云至于大病，	Say Progressing To Big Illness (death)
81	则寡人恶乎	Then Lonely Me Has a Problem
82	属国而可？"	Entrusting State To Whom ?"
83	夷吾曰："公谁欲欤？"	Yiwu Said: "Lord, Who you Wish Truly ?"
84	小白曰："鲍叔牙可。"	Xiaobai Said: "Baoshuya Alright."

6.3 The Inevitable Denial

85	曰："不可。	Said: "Not Alright.
86	其为人也，	He As a Person that's,
87	洁廉善士也，	Clean, Incorruptible Good Scholar that's,
88	其于不己若者	With People Not Like Self
89	不比之人，	He will Not Befriend Them,
90	一闻人之过，	Once Hearing a Person's Fault,
91	终身不忘.	Life Long Not Forget.
92	使之理国，	Let Him Governs State,
93	上且钩乎君，	Above, Will Contradict The King,
94	下且逆乎民。	Below, Will Oppose The Citizens.
95	其得罪于君也，	He Having Offended The King that's,
96	将弗久矣。"	Will Not be Long-lasting indeed."
97	小白曰：	Xiaobai Said:
98	"然则孰可？"	"But Then Who Can ?"
99	对曰：	Responding Said:
100	"勿已，则隰朋可。	"Not Recovered (my illness), Then Xipeng Alright.
101	其为人也，	He As Person that's,
102	上忘而下不叛，	Above (authority) Forgets And Subordinates Not Rebel,
103	愧其不若黄帝，	Regrets He Not Like Huangdi (first legendary leader),
104	而哀不己若者。	Empathizes with People Not Like Self (sympathetic).
105	以德分人，谓之圣人；	With Virtues to Group People, Call It Sage People;
106	以财分人，谓之贤人。	With Materials to Group People, Call It Talented People.
107	以贤临人，	With Talents Confronting Others,
108	未有得人者了；	Person Never Can Win-over Others;
109	以贤下人者，	With Talents Humble-self before Others that's,
110	未有不得人者也。	Person Never Can Not Win-over Others that's.
111	其于国有不闻也，	He With State affairs, Possible Not Hearing that's,
112	其于家有不见也。	He With Family affairs, Possible Not Seeing that's.
113	勿已，则隰朋可。"	"Not Recovered (my illness), Then Xipeng Alright."
114	然则管夷吾非薄鲍叔也，	But Then Guanyiwu Not Slighting Baoshu that's,
115	**不得不薄；**	***Not Possible to Not Slighting;***
116	非厚隰朋也，不得不厚。	Not Favoring Xipeng that's, Not Possible to Not Favour.
117	厚之于始，或薄之于终；	Favored Him At Beginning, Or Slighted Him At Ending;
118	薄之于终，或厚之于始。	Slighted Him At Ending, Or Favored Him At Beginning.
119	厚薄之去来，	Favoring and Slighting Their Coming and Going,
120	弗由我也。	Not By Me (my decision) that's.

Liezi Text Narrative

Guanyiwu and Baoshuya had a very close friendship, and both resided in the state of Qi. L3
Guanyiwu was serving Prince Jiu and Baoshuya was serving Prince Xiaobai. L5
The duke clans of Qi practiced favoritism, with direct and side lineage for kingship running. L7
Citizens afraid of upheaval, Guanzhong and Zhaohu fled with Prince Jiu to the state of Lu. L9
And Baoshu with Prince Xiaobai fled to the state of Ju. L10
Shortly Gongsunwuzhi made trouble and Qi had no king; the 2 Princes contested to return. L12

6.3 The Inevitable Denial

Guanyiwu battled with Xiaobai at Ju, said to have shot and Xiaobai saved by the belt buckle. L14
Xiaobai won, forced Lu to kill Prince Jiu, Zhaohu committed suicide, Guanyiwu imprisoned. L16
Baoshuya to Duke Huan (Xiaobai) said: "Guanyiwu extremely capable, able to govern state." L18
Duke Huan said: "My enemy that's, wishes to kill him." L20
Baoshu said: "I heard that virtuous Duke has no private enmity; L22
Furthermore, a person able to serve his master, also certainly able to serve the Duke. L24
If you wish to be a Commander of Kings, cannot be done without Yiwu (Guanyiwu). L26
So my Duke, are you certain to give-up on him !" L27
Guanzhong (Guanyiwu) returned from Lu, and Baoshuya welcomed him in the countryside; L30
Relieved of his shackles, Duke Huan celebrated him with position above Gao andGuo clans. L33
As Chief administrator titled 'Father Zhong', even Baoshuya himself subordinated to him. L35
Guanzhong then assisted Duke Huan to be Commander of Kings (master, Alliance of States). L37
Sighing, Guanzhong often said: "I, when young was trapped in poverty; L39
With Baoshu often do trading, and gave myself more when came to dividing the gains; L41
Baoshu never considered me to be greedy, knowing that I was poor, that's. L43
I often planned tasks for Baoshu, had difficulties and ended in failures. L45
Baoshu never regarded me as stupid, knowing that timing can be favorable and unfavorable. L47
I experienced 3 times as officials and 3 times observed to be banished by the king. L49
Baoshu never regarded me as a failure, knowing that I had not encountered my Time, that's. L51
I experienced 3 battles and 3 times ended in defeats. L52
Baoshu never regarded me as a coward, knowing that I had an old mother, that's. L54
Prince Jiu defeated, Zhaohu committed suicide and I was imprisoned suffering disgrace. L56
Baoshu never regarded me as shameless, knowing I am not shy of small mistakes; L58
But I am ashamed of my name not shining in the world, that's. L59
Father and mother created me, but the person who knows me, Baoshu that's !" L61
This society praised Baoshu for friendship; Xiaobai, the person good at employing talents. L63
Naturally truly no good friendship, truly no employment of talents that's. L65
Truly no more of good friendship, and no more of good employment of talents. that's. L69
Not that Zhaohu was able to die, it was Zhaohu not able to, not die; L71
Not that Baoshu was able to recommend talent, it was Baoshu not able to, not recommend; L73
Not that Xiaobai was able to employ the enemy, it was Xiaobai not able to, not employ. L75
Then Guanyiwu was taken ill, and Xiaobai asking him said: L77
"Father Zhong, your illness is serious that's, so allow me to say without taboo; L79
Say progressing to the Great Illness (death), Lonely-me has a problem entrusting the state ?" L82
Yiwu said: "Lord, who do you wish, truly ?"; Xiaobai said: "Baoshuya alright."; L84
Yiwu said: "Not alright. Baoshuya as a person, clean, incorruptible, a good scholar that's. L87
He only befriends people like himself; heard of a person's fault, lifelong not forget. L91
Let him govern a state, above will contradict the King, below will oppose the citizens. L94
Then he, having offended the king that's, will not be long-lasting indeed." L96
Xiaobai said: "But then who can ?" L98
Yiwu responding said: "Not recovered (my illness), then Xipeng alright. L100
He as a person, the above authority forgets and the subordinates do not rebel. L102
He regrets he is not like Huangdi (legendary), empathizes with people not like himself. L104
With Virtues to group people, call them Sage people; L105

6.3 The Inevitable Denial

With Materials to group people, call them Talented people. L106
With Talents confronting people, a person never can win-over others; L108
With Talents humbling yourself before people, a person will always win-over others. L110
He, with frivolous state affairs not hearing, with frivolous family affairs not seeing, that's. L112
When my illness is not recovered, then Xipeng alright." L113
But then Guanyiwu was not slighting Baoshu, he was not able to, not slighting that's. L115
And Guanyiwu was not favoring Xipeng, he was not able to, not favor him, that's. LL6
Favored at the start or slighted at the end; slighted at the end or favored at the start.118
Favoring and slighting, these coming and going, not that I can decide, that's. L120

Comments:
6.3 The Inevitable Denial
This is a narrative of close friendship between two historical persons, Guanyiwu and Baoshuya.
Fearing upheaval, Guanyiwu (Guanzhong) fled with Prince Jiu and Zhaohu to the state of Lu.
Baoshu fled to the state of Ju; shortly Gongsunwuzhi made trouble and Qi had no king.
The Princes contested to return; Guanyiwu in battle shot at Xiaobai whose belt buckle saved him.
Xiaobai won, forced Lu to kill Prince Jiu, Zhaohu committed suicide, and Guanyiwu imprisoned.
Baoshu knew the great talents of Guanzhong, thus highly recommended his friend to the Duke.
Forgiving his enemy, Duke appointed Guanzhong Chief administrator, titled 'Father Zhong'.
Guanzhong soon helped Duke Huan to rise as the Commander of Kings (Alliance of States).
Guanzhong was poor, took more of the earnings in trades, and Baozhu didn't regard this as greed.
Guanzhong failed in tasks, and Baozhu didn't regard him as stupid, only unfavorable conditions.
Guanzhong, 3 times banished, and Baozhu didn't regard him as a failure, just time had not arrived.
Guanzhong, defeated in 3 battles, Baozhu didn't regard him as a coward, as he had an old mother.
Guanzhong was imprisoned, Baozhu didn't regard him as shameful as he had higher aspirations.
Guanzhong appreciatively said, "Father mother created me, but it is Baoshu who knows me !"
The world praised Baoshu for his good friendship and Xiaobai for employing his enemy.
But there's no forever friend, forever enemy, only interest determines the inevitability of events.
Baoshu, not a good administrator needing support, so inevitably recommended Guanzhong.
Xiaobai had ambition to be Master of the Alliance of States, so inevitably employed Guanzhong.
No forever friend, forever enemy, only forever interest determines the inevitability of events.

Guanzhong was taken ill, and Xiaobai asked who can be entrusted with the state after his death.
When Xiaobai suggested Baoshu, Guanzhong categorically said, "Not alright."
Baoshu, an incorruptible scholar, only befriends people like himself, never forget faults of others.
Baoshu will contradict the King above, oppose the citizens below, will not be long-lasting that's.
Guanzhong suggested Xipeng, a person the authority above forgets and subordinates not rebel.
Xipeng empathized with people, not hearing frivolity of state, not seeing frivolity in family.
Xipeng, not confrontational, but with talents humbling himself before others to win them over.
Guanyiwu was not slighting Baoshu, as his temperament is not suitable, projecting failure.
Guanyiwu was not favoring Xipeng, as his disposition is more suitable, projecting success.
However the last line is, "Favoring and slighting, these coming and going, not that I can decide."
Hence Liezi is also not certain of the inevitability of events before the events, and rightly so.
Fate, Destiny, Inevitability exists after events; only probability exists prior to events, is-it-not ?

Chapter 6. Effort or Destiny (力命)

6.4 不得不诛　　　　6.4 The Inevitable Death

01	邓析操两可之说，	Dengxi Expounded Dual Possibility Concept
02	设无穷之辞，	Set-up Endless The Argument,
03	当子产执政，	When Zichan Controlled the Government,
04	作《竹刑》。	Wrote the book *Bamboo Punishment*.
05	郑国用之，	State of Zheng Adopted Book (ideas),
06	数难子产之治。	Frequently Troubling Zichan His Administration.
07	子产屈之。	Zichan Subjugated Him.
08	子产执而戮之，	Zichan Seized And Insulted Him.
09	俄而诛之。	Shortly Then Killed Him.
10	然则子产非能用《竹刑》，	But Then Zichan Not, Able to Use *Bamboo Punishment*,
11	不得不用；	Not Able to Not Using;
12	邓析非能屈子产，	Dengxi Not, Able to Harass Zichan,
13	不得不屈；	Not Able to, Not Harassed;
14	子产非能诛邓析，	Zichan Not, Able to Kill Dengxi,
15	***不得不诛也。***	***Not Able to, Not Kill Dengxi that's.***

Liezi Text Narrative
Dengxi expounded his Dual Possibility Concept, setting up endless arguments . L2
When Zichan was in-charge of the government, Dengxi wrote the Bamboo Punishment. L4
State of Zheng implemented It, and Dengxi frequently troubled Zichan's governance. L6
Harassed by Dengxi's argument, Zichan seized him, insulted him and shortly killed him. L9
Naturally then, not that Zichan can use the Bamboo Punishment but cannot 'not use' it. L11
Not that Dengzi can harass Zichan, but he cannot 'not harass' Zichan; 13
And not that Zichan can kill Dengzi, but he cannot 'not kill' him. L15

Comments:
6.4 The Inevitable Death
Dengxi (c.545-501 BC), minister of Zheng, rhetorician and philosopher of the School of Names.
Zichan (? - 522 BC), Prime minister of Zheng, philosopher legalist, believing in the rule of law.
Dengxi championed his Dual Possibility Concept, able to set-up arguments both ways in court.
Zichan had his code of law cast on a ding, and Dengxi wrote his version on *Bamboo Punishment*.
State of Zheng implemented the rule of law, and Dengxi frequently clashed with Zichan.
Harassed by Dengxi's argument, Zichan seized him, insulted him and shortly killed him.

Implementing the rule of law, it is *inevitable* that Zichan used the revised *Bamboo Punishment*.
A clash of philosophy and character, it is *inevitable* that Dengzi frequently harassed Zichan.
To establish authority and the rule of law, it is *inevitable* that Zichan killed Dengzi shortly.
With 2 such characters in the same situation, the *inevitability* of the consequence seems fated.
Here, Liezi warned us of the *inevitability* of destiny and fate, and not be delusional of our talents.
But did Zichan kill Dengxi, as scholars today have their deaths at 522BC, 501BC respectively?
Can we read this narrative and learn to avoid the inevitability of tragedy for ourselves !

Chapter 6. Effort or Destiny (力命)

6.5 自然者   6.5 Self Natural Entity

01	可以生而生，天福也；	Able To Live And Live, Heavenly Fortune that's;
02	可以死而死，天福也。	Able To Die And Die, Heavenly Fortune that's.
03	可以生而不生，天罚也；	Able To Live And Not Live, Heavenly Punishment that's;
04	可以死而不死，天罚也。	Able To Die And Not Die, Heavenly Punishment that's.
05	可以生，可以死，	Able To Live, Able To Die,
06	得生得死有矣；	Get to Live Get to Die, Have happened, indeed;
07	不可以生，不可以死，	Not Able To Live, Not Able To Die,
08	或死或生，有矣。	May or not Die, May or not Live, Have-it indeed.
09	然而生生死死，非物非我，	But Then Live Live Die Die, Not Matter Not Self,
10	皆命也，智之所无奈何。	All Destiny that's, Talents That May Not Ever Affect.
11	故曰，	Hence Said,
12	窈然无际，	Deeply Naturally Without Boundary,
13	天道自会，	Heaven's Way Self Assemble,
14	漠然无分，	Indifferently Naturally Without Separation,
15	天道自运。	Heaven's Way Self Operational.
16	天地不能犯，	Heaven Earth Not Allowed to Trespass,
17	圣智不能干，	Sage Talent Not Allowed to Interfere,
18	鬼魅不能欺。	Devil Spirit Not Allowed to Deceive.
19	*自然者，默之成之，*	*Self Natural Entity, Quiet It Form It.*
20	平之宁之，将之迎之。	Level It Calm It, Offer It Welcome It.

Liezi Text Narrative

Able to live and live, able to die and die, Heavenly fortune that's. L2
Able to live and not live, able to die and not die, Heavenly punishment that's. L4
Able to live, able to die, and get to live, get to die, this has happened indeed. L6
Not able to live, not able to die, may or may not die, may or may not live, does happen. L8
But then, life, death, not matter not me, all destiny that's, and talents may not ever affect. L10
Hence says, deeply naturally without boundary Heaven's way self assemble. L13
Indifferently naturally without separation, Heaven's way self operational. L15
Heaven and Earth are not allowed to trespass, sage and talent are not allowed to interfere. L17
Devil and spirit are not allowed to deceive. L18
Self natural entity, quietly form it, level it calm it, offer it welcome it. L20

Comments:
6.5 Self Natural Entity
Should live and live, should die and die, normally happens and this is Heavenly fortune.
Should live and not live, should die and not die, and this is Heavenly punishment.
Not able to live but may live or die, not able to die but may live or die, also does happen.
Thus life and death, a matter of destiny, Nature's infinite way of self assembly self operation.
That human talents have no effect, Heaven Earth cannot trespass, spirits cannot deceive.

This is an ancient concept of destiny, that humanity has no influence over our own fate !

Chapter 6. Effort or Destiny (力命)

6.6 谒三医 | 6.6 Diagnosis of 3 Doctors

01 杨朱之友曰季梁。	Yangzhu His Friend Called Jiliang.
02 季梁得疾，七日大渐。	Jiliang Had Illness, 7 Days Greatly Deteriorated.
03 其子环而泣之，请医。	His Sons Around Cried for Him, Sent for Doctors.
04 季梁谓杨朱曰：	Jiliang Conversing with Yangzhu said:
05 "吾子不肖如此之甚，	"My Sons Not Smart Like This As Such,
06 汝奚不为我歌以晓之？"	Why Not You Sing For Me To Enlighten Them ?"
07 杨朱歌曰：	Yangzhu Singing Said:
08 "天其弗识，	"Heaven, It Not Knowing,
09 人胡能觉？	Humanity, How Able to be Aware ?
10 匪祐自天，	No Protection From Heaven,
11 弗孽由人。	No Evil Because of Humanity.
12 我乎汝乎！其弗知乎！	I O' You O' ! We Not Knowing O' !
13 医乎巫乎！其知之乎？"	Doctor O' Sorcerer O' ! They Know It True ?"
14 其子弗晓，终谒三医。	**His Sons Not Understood, End-up Engaging 3 Doctors.**
15 一曰矫氏，二曰俞氏，	1st Called Mister Jiao, 2nd Called Mister Yu,
16 三曰卢氏，诊其所疾。	3rd Called Mister Lu, Diagnosed His Whatever Illness.
17 矫氏谓季梁曰：	Mister Jiao To Jiliang Said:
18 "汝寒温不节，虚实失度，	"Your Cold/Hot Not Control, Empty/Full Lost Measure,
19 病由饥饱色欲。	Illness From Hunger Over-eating Sex Desires.
20 精虑烦散，	Mind Worries Stresses Dissipated
21 非天非鬼。	Not Heaven Not Devil.
22 虽渐，可攻也。"	Though Serious, Possible to Treat that's."
23 季梁曰：	Jiliang Said:
24 "众医也，亟屏之！"	"Common Doctor that's, Quick Chase Him away !"
25 俞氏曰：	Mister Yu Said:
26 "女始则胎气不足，	"You, Beginning Then Womb Air Not Enough,
27 乳湩有余。	Milk Liquid Had Excess.
28 病非一朝一夕之故，	Illness Not One Day One Night The Cause,
29 其所由来渐矣，	What Caused It been Coming Gradually indeed,
30 弗可已也。"	Not Possible to Cure, that's."
31 季梁曰：	Jiliang Said:
32 "良医也，且食之！"	"Good Doctor that's, Then Feed Him ?"
33 卢氏曰：	Mister Lu Said:
34 "汝疾不由天，	" Your Illness Not Caused by Heaven,
35 亦不由人，	Also Not Caused by Human,
36 亦不由鬼。	Also Not Caused by Devil.
37 禀生受形，	Conception of Life Reception of Form,
38 既有制之者矣，	Already Had Entity Controlling It indeed,
39 亦有知之者矣，	Also Had Entity Knowing It indeed,
40 药石其如汝何？"	Medicine Stone, How can They Help You ?"

6.6 Diagnosis of 3 Doctors

41 季梁曰：	Jiliang Said:
42 "神医也，	"God-like Doctor that's,
43 重贶遗之！"	Offer Him More Rewards !"
44 俄而季梁之疾自瘳。	Shortly Then Jiliang His Illness Self Resolved.

Liezi Text Narrative
Yangzhu's friend Jiliang was ill, 7 days deteriorated, sons cried and wanted to engage doctors. L3
Jiliang to Yangzhu said; "My sons were stupid, why not sing me a song to enlighten them ?" L6
Yangzhu singing said: : "Heaven not knowing, how humanity then is able to be aware ? L9
No protection from Heaven, no evil caused by humanity. O' you and I, we do not know ! L12
O' doctors, O' sorcerers ! They know it, truly ?" L13
The sons didn't get it, engaged 3 doctors, Mr Jiao Mr Yu and Mr Lu to diagnose his illness.L16
Mr Jiao to Jiliang said: "Your hot/cold are not controlled, empty/full lost measure. L18
Illness from hunger, over-eating, sex desires, mind with worries and stresses dissicipated. L20
Not Heaven, not devil, though serious, possible to treat, that's." L22
Jiliang said: "Common doctor, that's, quick chase him away !" L24
Mr Yu said: "You, beginning in womb air not enough, and milk liquid had excess. L27
Illness not a day or so, what causes it has been gradually coming, and not possible to cure. L30
Jiliang said: "Good doctor that's. then give him food !" L32
Mr Lu said: "Your illness is not caused by Heaven, not by humans and not by the devils. L36
Conception of life reception of form, already has the entity controlling it, knowing it indeed. L39
So herbs, medicinal stones, how can they help you ?" L40
Jiliang said: " God-like doctor, offer him more rewards !" L43
Shortly afterward, Jiliang, his illness self recovered. L44

Comments:
6.6 Diagnosis of 3 Doctors
Jiliang was seriously ill, and asked a friend to convince his sons not to bring in the doctors.
Yangzhu sang that illness has no protection from Heaven, and the evil not caused by humanity.
And so asked how would doctors, sorcerers truly know ? But the sons don't understand.
Mr Jiao said Jiliang had mistreated his body with indulgence and desires, but there was treatment.
Jiliang, a disciplined daoist, chased him away as a mediocre doctor talking rubbish.
Mr Yu said Jiliang was lacking in the womb and too much afterward, it's chronic with no cure.
Jiliang seemed to agree with what the doctor said and dismissed him with food.
Mr Lu said illness, not caused by Heaven, man or devil, nature in control, no medicine can help.
Jiliang called him God-like and rewarded him, for this is the daoist way, let nature run its course.
Yangzhu's friend, a daoist living carefree to ripe old age with sons, Jiliang self recovered shortly.
Daoist living with no indulgence and a mind at peace, the healthy body will take care of itself.

Importance of a healthy lifestyle is noted, and no delusion that doctors cure old-age illnesses.

Chapter 6. Effort or Destiny (力命)

6.7 不如其已   6.7 Better Let It Be

01	生非贵之所能存，	Life, Not Honoring It, Then Can Preserve,
02	身非爱之所能厚；	Body, Not Loving It, Then Can Strengthen;
03	生亦非贱之所能夭，	Life, Also Not Debasing It, Then Can Kill,
04	身亦非轻之所能薄。	Body, Also Not Slighting It, Then Can Weaken.
05	故贵之或不生，	Thus Honoring It May Not Live,
06	贱之或不死；	Abusing It May Not Die;
07	爱之或不厚，	Loving It May Not Strengthen,
08	轻之或不薄。	Slighting It May Not Weaken.
09	此似反也，	This Like Contradiction that's,
10	非反也；	Not Contradiction that's;
11	此自生自死，	This Self Living Self Dying,
12	自厚自薄。	Self Strengthening Self Weakening.
13	或贵之而生，	May Honor It And Live,
14	或贱之而死；	May Debased It And Die;
15	或爱之而厚，	May Love It And Strengthen,
16	或轻之而薄。	May Slight It And Weaken.
17	此似顺也，	This Like Harmony that's,
18	非顺也；	Not Harmony that's;
19	此亦自生自死，	This Also Self Living Self Dying,
20	自厚自薄。	Self Strengthening Self Weakening.
21	鬻熊语文王曰：	Yuxiong Speaking to King Wen Said:
22	"自长非所增，	"Self Lengthen Not By Increase (external),
23	自短非所损。	Self Shorten Not By Reduction (external).
24	算之所亡若何？"	Interfering It Whatever Loss How About ?"
25	老聃语关尹曰：	Old Dan (Laozi) Speaking to Guanyin Said:
26	"天之所恶，	"Heaven, That Which Dislike,
27	孰知其故？"	Who Knows The Reason ?" (Laozi, ch.73)
28	言迎天意，	Say Welcome Heaven's Wishes,
29	揣利害，	Guessing the Pros and Cons,
30	**不如其已。**	**Better Let It Be.**

6.7 Better Let It Be

Liezi Text Narrative
Life, not honoring it, then be able to preserve; body, not loving it, then be able to strengthen. L2
Life, not debasing it, then be able to kill; body, not slighting it, then be able to weaken. L4
Thus honoring it, may not live; abusing it, may not die. L6
Loving it, may not strengthen; slighting it, may not weaken. L8
This is like contradiction that's, but really not contradiction; L10
This is self living and self dying, self strengthening and self weakening. L12
May honor it and live, may debase it and die; L14
May love it and strengthen, may slight it and weaken . L16
This is harmony that's, but really not harmony. L18
This is also self living and self dying, self strengthening and self weakening. L20
Yuxiong to King Wen said: "Self lengthen self shorten, not by increase or decrease. L23
Human interference with affairs, what's lost, who knows how much ?" L24
Old Dan (Laozi) speaking to Kuanyin said: L25
"That which Heaven dislikes, who knows the reason ?" (Laozi, ch.73; Jingwei, 2012) L27
Speaking of welcoming Heaven's wishes or guessing the pros and cons, *better let it be*. L30

Comments:
6.7 Better Let It Be
Life may not be honored and survived, and life may not be abused and died.
Body may not be loved and strengthened, and the body may not be ill-treated and weakened.
This is not contradiction, it is naturally self living, self dying, self strengthening, self weakening.
Life may be honored and lived, and life may be debased and died.
Body may be loved and strengthened, and the body may be slighted and weakened.
This is not harmony, but is naturally self living, self dying, self strengthening, self weakening.

Yuxiong said to King Wen, when humans interfere in affairs we don't know how much is lost.
Laozi also says "That which Heaven dislikes, who knows the reason ?" (ch. 73, Jingwei 2012)
The march of events is unpredictable and understandably the ancients are at a loss for actions.
Thus instead of welcoming Heaven's wishes or guessing the pros and cons, better let it be.

We are less helpless today: with science we can predict the weather, contain epidemics, ..

Chapter 6. Effort or Destiny (*力命*)

6.8 皆命也 | 6.8 All Destiny that's

01	杨布问曰：	Yangbu Asking Said:
02	"有人于此,	"Has Persons At Present,
03	年兄弟也,	Age Like Brothers that's,
04	言兄弟也,	Speech Like Brothers that's,
05	才兄弟也,	Talent Like Brothers that's,
06	貌兄弟也；	Look Like Brothers that's;
07	而寿夭父子也,	But Living Dying like Father Son that's,
08	贵贱父子也,	Honor Status like Father Son that's,
09	名誉父子也,	Name Reputation like Father Son that's,
10	爱憎父子也。	Love Hate like Father Son that's.
11	吾惑之。"	I am Puzzled by These."
12	杨子曰：	Yangzi Said:
13	"古之人有言,	"Ancient-time The People Have Sayings,
14	吾尝识之,	My Experience Knowing Them,
15	将以告若。	Shall With them Inform You.
16	不知所以然而然,	Not Knowing Why It's So And Naturally,
17	命也。	Destiny that's.
18	今昏昏昧昧,	Now Faintly Ambiguously,
19	纷纷若若,	Disorderly, Seemingly,
20	随所为,	Follow What's Done,
21	随所不为。	Follow What's Not Done.
22	日去日来,	Day In Day Out,
23	孰能知其故？	Who Able to Know The Reasons ?
24	***皆命也。***	***All Destiny that's.***
25	夫信命者，亡寿夭；	O' Person Believes in Destiny, Forgets Life and Death;
26	信理者，亡是非；	Person Believes in Logic, Forgets Right and Wrong
27	信心者，亡逆顺；	Person Believes in Heart, Forgets Adversity and Accord;
28	信性者，亡安危。	Person Believes in Character, Forgets Safety and Danger.
29	则谓之都亡所信,	Thus Call This All Forget Whatever Beliefs,
30	都亡所不信。	All Forget Whatever Non-Beliefs.
31	真矣悫矣,	Truly That's Honestly That's,
32	奚去奚就？	Why Discard Why Accept ?
33	奚哀奚乐？	Why Sad Why Happy ?
34	奚为奚不为？	Why Action Why Inaction ?
35	《黄帝之书》云：	*Book of Huangdi* Says:
36	'至人居若死,	'Supreme Person Sitting Like Dead,
37	动若械。'	Motion like Machine.'
38	亦不知所以居,	Also Not Knowing Reason For Sitting,
39	亦不知所以不居；	Also Not Knowing Reason For Not Sitting;
40	亦不知所以动,	Also Not Knowing Reason For Action,
41	亦不知所以不动。	Also Not Knowing Reason For Inaction.

42	亦不以众人之观	Also Not Because The Crowd Who is Looking
43	易其情貌，	Changes His Expression and Look,
44	亦不谓众人之不观	Also Not Because The Crowd Who is Not Looking
45	不易其情貌。	Not Changes His Expression and Look.
46	独往独来，	Alone Going Alone Coming,
47	独出独入，	Alone Out Alone In,
48	孰能碍之？"	Who Able to Obstruct Him ?"

Liezi Text Narrative
Yangbu asking said: "Has persons here, age speech, talent look, are same like brothers, that's; L6
But in living/dying, honor/status, name/reputation, love/hate, are different like father and son. L10
I am puzzled, that's." L11
Yangzi (Yangzhu) said: "Ancient people have sayings, that I know and shall tell them to you. L15
Not knowing why it is so and naturally so, Destiny that's. L17
Now faintly, ambiguously, disorderly, seemingly; accordingly what's done, what is not done. L21
Day in day out, who is able to know the reasons ? All these, Destiny that's. L24
Person believes in Destiny, forgets life/death; a person believes in logic, forgets right/wrong. L26
Person believes in heart feelings, forgets opposition and agreement; L27
Person believes in character, forgets safety and danger. L28
Thus call these, all forgetting whatever believing and unbelieving. L30
Truly and honestly, what to reject/accept, what sadness/happiness, what action/inaction ? L34
The *Book of Huangdi* says: 'Enlightened person sitting like dead, moving like a machine.' L37
Also not knowing reason for sitting/not sitting; also not knowing reason for action/inaction. L41
Also not because the crowd is looking and changes his expression and look; L43
Also not because the crowd is not looking and not changing his expression and look. L45
Alone going and coming, alone out and in, then who is able to obstruct him ?" L48
Comments:
6.8 All Destiny that's
Yangbu, puzzled that there are 2 people very similar like brothers in age, speech, talent and look.
But are very different like father and son in longevity, honor status, reputation, love hate relation.
Brother Yangzi said: "The ancients say, 'Not knowing why it is so and naturally so, Destiny.'
Ambiguously, accordingly, what is done or not done, who knows the reasons, so it's all Destiny.
Person who believes in Destiny forgets life/death; believing in logic forgets right/wrong.
Person who believes in emotion forgets harmony; believing in character forgets safety/danger.
Person acts with truth, honesty, then less worry about rejection/acceptance, sadness/happiness."

Book of Huangdi describes an enlightened person as, 'sitting like dead, moving like a machine'.
Whether the crowd is looking or not looking at him, he does change or not change his expression .
Then coming and going alone, who is able to stop him ?
Such a description of an enlightened lonely person is not accurate of daoists, not acceptable !
Daoists are simple, honest, gentle, peace-loving people in any community. (p.153 Jingwei, 2012)
In Laozi's *Daodejing*, the latter presentation of daoists in several chapters is kinder and fairer.
Act with truth, honesty, the rest we can leave to Destiny, and not be troubled to know why so!

Chapter 6. Effort or Destiny (力命)

6.9 此众态也   6.9 Characters Galore

01	墨尿、单至、啴咺、憋憨	Mochi, Danzhi, Chanxuan, Biefu
02	四人相与游于世，	4 Persons Mutually Together Travelling In the World,
03	胥如志也；	All Attained own Ambitions that's;
04	穷年不相知情，	Through the Years No Mutual Knowledge of Others,
05	自以智之深也。	Self Believed The Depth of Wisdom that's.
06	巧佞、愚直、婷斫、便辟	Qiaoning, Yuzhi, Anzhuo, Bianpi
07	四人相与游于世，	4 Persons Mutually Together Travelling In the World,
08	胥如志也；	All Attained own Ambitions that's
09	穷年而不相语术，	Through the Years No Mutual Discussion of Knowledge;
10	自以巧之微也。	Self Believed The Intricacies of Skills that's.
11	(谬牙)、情露、(㵎)极、凌谇	Miuya, Qinglu, Jianji, Lingsui
12	四人相与游于世，	4 Persons Mutually Together Travelling In the World,
13	胥如志也；	All Attained own Ambitions that's;
14	穷年不相晓悟，	Through the Years No Mutual Appreciation of Others;
15	自以为才之得也。	Self Believed The Attainment of Talents that's.
16	眠娗、諈诿、勇敢、怯疑	Mianting, Zhuiwei, Yonggan, Qieyi
17	四人相与游于世，	4 Persons Mutually Together Travelling In the World,
18	胥如志也；	All Attained own Ambitions that's;
19	穷年不相谪发，	Through the Years No Mutual Enlightening of Others;
20	自以行无戾也。	Self Believed Actions No Controversies that's.
21	多偶、自专、乘权、只立	Duoou, Zizhuan, Chengquan, Zhili
22	四人相与游于世，	4 Persons Mutually Together Travelling In the World,
23	胥如志也；	All Attain own Ambitions that's;
24	穷年不相顾眄，	Through the Years No Mutual Concern for Others;
25	自以时之适也。	Self Believed The Propriety of Timing that's.
26	**此众态也。**	***This Characters Galore that's.***
27	其貌不一，	Their Looks Not One (uniform),
28	而咸之于道，	But All Inclusive In 'Dao',
29	命所归也。	The Homing of Destinies, that's

6.9 Characters Galore

Liezi Text Narrative
Mochi (pretentious), Danzhi (irascible), Chanxuan (pedantic), Biefu (impatient); L1
All 4 travelled together in this world, each attained his own ambition. L3
Through the years, no mutual knowledge of others, each believed his own depth of wisdom. L5
Qiaoning (eloquent), Yuzhi (modest), Anzhuo (stupid), Bianpi (sociable); L6
All 4 travelled together in this world, each attained his own ambition. L8
For years, no mutual discussion of knowledge, each believed the intricacy of his own skills. L10
Miuya (depressed), Qinglu (emotional), Jianji (stutterer), Lingsui (abusive); L11
All 4 travelled together in this world, each attained his own ambition. L13
For years, no mutual appreciation of others, each believed the attainment of his own talents. L15
Mianting (shy), Zhuiwei (mediocre), Yonggan (brave), Qieyi (cowardly); L16
All 4 travelled together in this world, each attained his own ambition. L18
For years, no mutual enlightening of others, each believed his actions have no controversies. L20
Duoou (deferential), Zizhuan(autocratic), Chengquan (apple-shining), Zhili (self-admiring); L21
All 4 travelled together in this world, each attained his own ambition. L23
For years, no mutual concern for others, each believed the propriety of his own timing. L25
This is characters galore that's; their looks are not uniform but all inclusive in 'Dao'. L28
The Home of Destinies, that's. L29

Comments:
6.9 Characters Galore
Mochi (pretentious), Danzhi (irascible), Chanxuan (pedantic), Biefu (impatient) together on earth.
Attained their ambition, no knowledge of the others, each believed in his own depth of wisdom.
Qiaoning (eloquent), Yuzhi (modest), Anzhuo (stupid), Bianpi (sociable) together in this world.
Attained their ambition, no mutual discussion, each believed in the intricacy of his own skills.
Miuya (depressed), Qinglu (emotional), Jianji (stutterer), Lingsui (abusive) together in this world.
Attained their ambition, no mutual appreciation, each believed in acquisition of his own talents.
Mianting (shy), Zhuiwei (mediocre), Yonggan (brave), Qieyi (cowardly) together in this world.
Attained their ambition, no mutual enlightening, each believed in his own impeccable actions.
And Duoou (deferential), Zizhuan(autocratic), Chengquan (apple-shining), Zhili (self-admiring).
Attained their ambition, no mutual concern, each believed in the propriety of his own timing.

Five groups of 4 characters travelling together in the world, and each attained individual success.
All are inclusive in the 'Dao', are Destined with different looks and with different temperament.
But each believed himself the best in the group and did not bother to interact with each other.
This 'Characters galore', their Delusional arrogance are also common in our societies today.

We may look here to identify in-born Destined faulty characters, so as to change for the better.

Chapter 6. Effort or Destiny (力命)

6.10 度与不度
6.10 To Gauge or Not To Gauge

01	佹佹成者,	That which is Almost Successful,
02	俏成也,初非成也。	Apparent Success that's, Not Start of Success that's.
03	佹佹败者,	That which is Almost Close to Failure,
04	俏败者也,初非败也。	Look-like Failure, Not Start of Failure that's.
05	故迷生于俏,	Hence, Confusion Arises From 'Apparent' (seems like),
06	俏之际昧然。	'Apparent' It's Bordering on Dawning Reality.
07	于俏而不昧然,	With 'Apparent' And Not Yet a Reality,
08	则不骇外祸,	Then Not Afraid of Disaster from Outside,
09	不喜内福;	Not Happy of Fortune from Within;
10	随时动,随时止,	Any Time Move, Any Time Stop.
11	智不能知也。	Knowledge Not Able to Know that's.
12	信命者于彼我无二心。	Believer Of Destiny With Others and Self, No 2 Feelings.
13	于彼我而有二心者,	With Others That's If Self Have 2 Feelings,
14	不若掩目塞耳,	Not Better Cover Eyes Block Ears,
15	背阪面隍,亦不坠仆也。	Back-up Wall Facing Dry-moat, Also Not Falling In.
16	故曰:	Therefore Said:
17	死生自命也,	Death Life From Destiny (fate) that's
18	贫穷自时也。	Poverty Destitute From Timing that's.
19	怨夭折者,不知命者也;	Person Blaming Early Death, Not Know Destiny that's;
20	怨贫穷者,不知时者也。	Person Blaming Poverty, Not Know Timing that's.
21	当死不惧,在穷不戚,	Imminent Death Not Afraid, In Poverty Not Grief,
22	知命安时也。	Knows Destiny at Peace with Time that's.
23	其使多智之人,	That which Causing People with Many Talents,
24	量利害,料虚实,	Measure Gain /Loss, Gauge Weakness /Strength,
25	度人情,	Assess Human Feelings,
26	得亦中,亡亦中。	Correctness Is Half, Incorrectness Also Half,
27	其少智之人,不量利害,	The Less Talented People, Not Measure Gain /Loss,
28	不料虚实,	No Gauge of Emptiness /Substance,
29	不度人情,	No Assessment of People's Feelings,
30	得亦中,亡亦中。	Correctness Also Half, Incorrectness Also Half.
31	量与不量,料与不料,	Measure And Not Measure, Gauge And Not Guage,
32	*度与不度,奚以异?*	*Assess And Not Assess, What's The Difference then ?*
33	唯亡所量,亡所不量,	So Forget What Measured, Forget What Not Measured,
34	则全而亡丧。	Then All-conserved And No Lost.
35	亦非知全,	Also Not Knowing then Conserved,
36	亦非知丧。	Also Not Knowing then Loss.
37	自全也,自亡也,	Self Conserved that's, Self Abandoned that's,
38	自丧也。	Self Lost that's.

6.10 To Gauge or Not To Gauge

Liezi Text Narrative
Almost succeed, looks succeeded, not start of success; almost fail, looks failed, not failure. L4
Hence confusion arises from 'apparent', appearance that borders on the dawn of reality. L6
'Appear' not yet a reality, then not fear tragedy from outside, nor happy with fortune inside. L9
Any time may act, any time may stop, knowledge not able to know or predict that's. L11
With others, self has 2 feelings or doubts, not better than covering eyes and blocking ears. L14
Believer in Destiny, self has no doubt; back to the wall facing the dry-moat, will not fall. L15
Therefore said: death and life from Destiny (fate) that's; poverty destitute from timing that's. L18
Person blames early death, not knowing Destiny; blaming poverty, not knowing timing that's. L20
Imminent death not afraid, in poverty not grieving, knows Destiny, at peace with the time. L22
The people with many talents, cause to measure gain/loss, gauge weakness/strength. L24
Assess people's feelings; correctness is half, incorrectness also half. L26
The people with less talents, cause not to measure gain/loss, not to gauge weakness/strength. L28
Not to assess people's feelings; correctness is half, incorrectness also half. L30
Measure and not measure, gauge and not guage, assess /not assess, what's the difference ? L32
So forget what is measured /not measured, then all be conserved and not lost. L34
Also not knowing then conserved and also not knowing then lost. L36
Self conserved that's, self abandoned that's, self lost that's. L38

Comments:
6.10 To Gauge or Not To Gauge
Appearing to succeed is not the start of success, appearing to fail is not the beginning of failure.
Not yet a Reality, have no fear of tragedy from outside, and no celebration of fortune inside.
Anytime, may act may stop, thus knowledge not able to know or predict that's.
That is to say, before the Finish-line is crossed, don't celebrate the winner.
Before the final whistle is blown, don't consider the game as lost.
Clearly Liezi warns us not to confuse apparent success and failure with Reality.
Only after the event, then the Reality is Destiny, is Fated.
That's before event finished and Reality established, there is no Destiny no Fate.

It is said: death and life from Destiny (fate) that's; poverty destitution from timing that's.
Belief in Destiny, imminent death not afraid, in poverty not griefing, at peace with the world.
Indeed Destiny does provide a reason for failure and gives solace for the sufferings.

People with many talents, measure gain/loss, assess weakness/strength, gauge people's feelings.
People with less talents, do not measure gain/loss, do not assess weakness/strength, do not gauge.
Measure and not measure, gauge and not guage, success/failure rate is half/half, no differences ?
Thus be not calculating, make the Effort to succeed, and let Destine/Fate to explain the failure.

Belief in Destiny does offer solace to the underprivileged, but badly stifles hope and progress.

Chapter 6. Effort or Destiny (力命)

6.11 常守之   6.11 Forever In-Charge

01	齐景公游于牛山，	Duke Jing of Qi Touring At Niu Mountain,
02	北临其国城而流涕曰：	Looking North At Capital City And Sobbing Said:
03	"美哉国乎！	"Beautiful O' Kingdom O'!
04	郁郁芊芊，	Peaceful and Luxuriant,
05	若何滴滴	What Reason Day by Day
06	去此国而死乎？	Leaving This Kingdom And Die O'?
07	使古无死者，	If from Ancient time No Person Die,
08	寡人将去斯而之何？"	Lonely Me Will Leave Here, Is This Possible?"
09	史孔，梁丘据皆从而泣曰：	Shikong, Liangqiuju All Follow In Crying Said:
10	"臣赖君之赐，	"Subjects Dependent on Duke's Favors,
11	疏食恶肉可得而食，	Rough Food Coarse Meat Will Have For Food,
12	驽马棱车可得而乘也，	Angry Horse Bamboo Cart Will Have To Ride,
13	且犹不欲死，	And Still Not Wanting to Die,
14	而况吾君乎？"	Then What More with Our Duke?"
15	晏子独笑于旁。	Yanzi Alone Laughing By the Side.
16	公雪涕而顾晏子曰：	Duke Dried Tears And Facing Yanzi Said:
17	"寡人今日之游悲，	"Lonely Me This Day The Tour is Sad,
18	孔与据皆从寡人而泣，	Kong And Ju All Follow Lonely Me And Cried,
19	子之独笑，何也？"	Sir You Alone Laughing, Why, that's?"
20	晏子对曰：	Yanzi Responding Said:
21	*"使贤者常守之，*	***"Enabling Wise Person Forever In-charge,***
22	则太公，桓公将常守之矣；	Then First Duke, Duke Huan Will Forever be In-charge;
23	使有勇者而常守之，	Enabling Brave Person Forever In-charge,
24	则庄公，灵公将常守之矣。	Then Duke Zhuang, Duke Ling Will Forever In-charge.
25	数君者将守之，	Several Duke Persons Will be In-charge,
26	吾君方将被蓑笠	My Duke Then Will Wear Grass-cloak Bamboo-hat
27	而立乎畎亩之中，	And Standing O' In Midst of Padi-fields,
28	唯事之恤，	Only Affairs (planting) That is Worrying,
29	行假今死乎？	What Leisure about Death Now that's?
30	则吾君	Then My Duke
31	又安得此位而立焉？	Also How Attained This position And Hold-it that's?
32	以其迭处之迭去之，	With This Alternate Occupation Alternate Vacating It,
33	至于君也，	Until Reaching Duke Yourself, that's,
34	而独为之流涕，	And Alone Because of This Crying Tears,
35	是不仁也。	This is Not Humane, that's.
36	见不仁之君，	Seeing The Duke Not Humane,
37	见谄谀之臣。	Seeing The Officials Flattering Fawning.
38	臣见此二者，	Subject Seeing These 2 Displays,
39	臣之所为独窃笑也。"	That is Why Subject Alone Secretly Laughing, that's."
40	景公惭焉，	Duke Jing Ashamed indeed,

217

6.11 Forever In-Charge

41 举觯自罚；	Held-up Goblet and Self Punished (bottom-up wine);
42 罚二臣者各二觯焉。	Punished The 2 Officials, Each with 2 Goblets (wine).

Liezi Text Narrative
Duke Jing of Qi on tour in Mount Niu, looking north at his capital city sobbing and said: L2
"What a beautiful kingdom O', all peaceful and luxuriant with woods and grassland. L4
What reason for living day by day, then leaving this kingdom to die, that's ? L6
If from ancient times there was no death, then Lonely Me will not leave this place, would I ?" L8
Shikong and Liangqiuju followed in crying, said: "Subjects dependent on Duke's favors; L10
Having vegetable and coarse meat for food, and bad horse bamboo cart for rides; L12
And still not wanting to die, so then what more with our Duke ?" L14
Yanzi alone laughed by the side. L:15
Duke dried his tears and facing Yanzi said: "Lonely Me, this day feeling sad on this tour; L17
Kong and Ju all followed me and cried, but Sir you alone laugh, why is that so ?" L19
Yanzi responding said: "Enabling the wise person to be forever in-charge; L21
Then the First Duke, and Duke Huan will forever be in-charge; L22
Enabling the brave to be forever in-charge, then it should be Duke Zhuang and Duke Ling. L24
Then my duke will be wearing a grass-cloak bamboo-hat, standing amid the padi-fields. L27
Only worry about planting affairs, and no leisure thinking about death, is-it-not true that's ? L29
Then my duke, how did you attain this position and hold it today, that's ?" L31
With this alternate occupation and alternate vacation, until reaching Duke yourself; L33
Then just for this arrangement crying tears, this is not humane that's. L35
And seeing the Duke not humane and the officials flattering and fawning. L37
Subject me, seeing these 2 displays, that is why alone is secretly laughing, that's." L39
Duke Jing ashamed indeed, raised his goblet of wine and down it in self punishment. L41
At the same time punished the two flattering officials, to drink 2 goblets of wine each. L42

Comments:
6.11 Forever In-Charge
Duke Jing of Qi was touring in Mount Niu and saw his kingdom, peaceful and luxuriant.
He was sad at the thought of getting older day by day and will have to die leaving this land.
He lamented that if only there was no death from ancient times, he could enjoy the place forever.
His officials Shikong and Liangqiuju, fawning and without thinking, agreed and cried too.

Seeing the display of ignorance, Yanzi alone laughed by the side and Duke asked him: "Why ?".
Yanzi replied that without death from ancient times, his ancestors will still be In-charge.
Like the wise First Duke and Duke Huang, and the brave Duke Zhuang and Duke Ling.
So it was with death, the alternate occupation/vacation of the In-charge that led to Duke Jing.
Else Duke Jing will be in a grass-cloak bamboo-hat amid the padi fields, worrying about crops.
Duke Jing was ashamed and punished himself with downing a goblet of wine.
He punished his 2 fawning unthinking officials with 2 goblets of wine each.

Duke Jing is delusional for thinking that there should be no death and be forever In-charge.

Chapter 6. Effort or Destiny (力命)

6.12 不忧   6.12 Not Disturbed

01	魏人有东门吴者，	Dongmenwu, Person from Wei (state)
02	**其子死而不忧。**	**His Son Died And Not Disturbed.**
03	其相室曰：	His Butler Said:
04	"公之爱子，	"Master Your Love for Son,
05	天下无有。	Beneath Heaven None Comparable.
06	今子死不忧，	Now Son Died and Not Disturbed,
07	何也？"	Why so ?"
08	东门吴曰：	Dongmenwu Said:
09	"吾常无子，	"I Previously have No Son,
10	无子之时不忧。	No Son That Time Not Disturbed.
11	今子死，	Now Son Died.
12	乃与向无子同，	Still Like the Past having No Son, Same,
13	臣奚忧焉？"	I, Why be Affected is-it-not ?"

Liezi Text Narrative

A person from the state of Wei, Dongmenwu was not disturbed when his son died. L2
His butler said; "Master, your love for your son, none can compare in this world. L5
Now your son died and you are not disturbed, why is it so ?" L7
*Dongmenwu said: "Previously I had no son, and that time without a son, not disturbed. L10
Now my son had died, still the same like the past, so why should I be distrubed, is-it-not ?" L13*

Comments:
6.12 Not Disturbed

Dongmenwuu from the state of Wei, was not disturbed when his son died.
The butler noticed his great love for the son, was surprised and asked why he was not disturbed.
Dongmenwu replied that before he had no son, and at that time then he was not disturbed.
Now that the son had died, and again he had no son like before, so why should he be disturbed !
The daoist knows that he does not even own his own body, let alone the life of his son.
Events outside our control, we learn to be stoic and not be disturbed, as life has to go on.

Dongmenwu enjoyed his son while he could, and not be disturbed when Destiny took him away.

Chapter 6. Effort or Destiny (力命)

6.13 势,命使然也   6.13 Effort, Destiny Enable Naturally

01 农赴时,	Agriculture Goes with Seasons,
02 商趣利,	Commerce Chases Profits,
03 工追术,	Effort Aspires Skills,
04 仕逐势,	Official Pursues Influences,
05 势使然也。	***Momentum (Effort) Enable Naturally* that's.**
06 然农有水旱,	Naturally Agriculture Has Floods and Droughts,
07 商有得失,	Commerce Has Gains and Losses,
08 工有成败,	Effort Has Successes and Failures,
09 仕有遇否,	Official Has Encounters and Misses,
10 命使然也。	***Destiny Enables Naturally*** that's.

Liezi Text Narrative
Agriculture goes with time of the seasons, Commerce goes where profits can be made,
Efort strives for improvement of skills, Officials pursue to collect influences.
Its human momentum (Effort) that enable these activities naturally, that's

But then Agriculture has its floods and droughts, Commerce has its gains and losses.
Effort has its successes and failures, Officials have encounters and misses.
It is Destiny that enables these uncertainties naturally, that's.

Comments:
6.13 Effort, Destiny Enable Naturally
Agriculture goes with time of the seasons, Commerce goes where profits can be made,
Effort strives for improvement of skills, Officials pursue to collect influences.
Its human momentum (Effort) that enable these activities naturally, that's
But then Agriculture has its floods and droughts, Commerce has its gains and losses.
Effort has its successes and failures, Officials have encounters and misses.
It is Destiny that enables these uncertainties naturally, that's.
So it is Effort that advances all human activities and Destiny to account for the uncertainties.

Effort in science advances our understanding, reducing the realm of uncertainties and Destiny.

Chapter 6. Effort or Destiny (力命)

Summary

6.1 **Effort or Destiny (力命):** They argue over who is more successful in human affairs.
The Mess: the good is poor, the evil wealthy,..; Effort has no credit, Destiny is not the maker.

6.2 **Thick in Virtue, Thin in Destiny (厚于德，薄于命):** Dongguo's assessment of Beigongzi.
He assessed Ximenzi as thick in Destiny, thin in Virtues, thus ought not to shame the former.

6.3 **The Inevitable Denial (不得不薄):** Yiwu and Baoshu were the best of friends for years.
Yiwu denied Baoshu's succession, as the latter's inflexibility would be an inevitable disaster.

6.4 **The Inevitable Death (不得不诛):** Dengxi's Dual Possibility Concept argued both ways.
It was inevitable that he clashed with Zichan, and also inevitable that Zichan had to kill him.

6.5 **Self Natural Entity (自然者):** Is Destiny, not affected by Heaven Earth, spirits or humans.
Destiny, not the maker of things, but just allow things to naturally happen as destined.

6.6 **Diagnosis of 3 Doctors (谒三医):** Jiliang knew they were rubbish and despatched them.
A staunch daoist with no indulgence and with a peaceful mind, his body healed by itself.

6.7 **Better Let It Be (不如其已):** As the ancients had no influence over the march of events.
But today, science has helped us immensely predicting weathers, faster communication, ...

6.8 **All Destiny that's (皆命也):** Person believing in Destiny, not obsess with life and death.
Just acts truly, honestly and less worry about rejection/acceptance, sadness/happiness, ...

6.9 **Characters Galore (此众态也):** Five groups of 4 charaters travelling together on earth.
Individuals attained success, Delusional belief himself best in the group, never interacted.

6.10 **To Gauge or Not To Gauge (度与不度):** Talented people gauge, the untalented do not.
They have similar success, no advantage with knowledge, thus accept Destiny, be at peace.

6.11 **Forever In-Charge (常守之):** Duke Jing wished he will not die, and be forever in-charge.
Yanzi reminded him that if people didn't die, his many forebears will still be in-charge !

6.12 **Not Disturbed (不忧):** Dongmenwu from Wei was not troubled after his son died.
When asked why, he said he was not disturbed before, having no son, then why now !

6.13 **Effort, Destiny Enable Naturally (势,命使然也):** In all spheres of human activities.
We make Effort to succeed and let Destiny account for the uncertainties and failures.

This chapter argues for making Effort to succeed, and lets Destiny to account for the failures.
No Destiny before the event becomes a reality, and only after the event is Destiny fated.

Chapter 7.   Yangzhu (杨朱)

Introduction

7.1 Honest Dishonest The Debate (实伪之辩)

7.2 Person's Life, What Purpose ? (人之生也奚为哉？)

7.3 Different in Life, Similar in Death (异者生, 同者死)

7.4 Purity Chastity (清贞)

7.5 Happy Living, Relaxing Body (乐生, 逸身)

7.6   The Pathways of Life Death (生死之道)

7.7 Internal And External Management (治外，治内)

7.8 Mad Man or Enlightened Man (狂人也，达人也)

7.9 And Long Life What For ? (且久生奚为？)

7.10 No Loss of One Hair (不损一毫)

7.11 Sages 4 and Evils 2 (四圣，二凶)

7.12 Great Eagle Flies High (鸿鹄高飞)

7.13 Where is the Joy of Life ? (何生之乐哉?)

7.14 Only Sage Person Can ! (唯圣人乎！)

7.15 Longevity, Honor, Power, Wealth (寿，名，位，货)

7.16 House, Clothes, Food, Sex (屋服，味色)

Summary

Liezi: World of Delusions

Chapter 7. Yangzhu (杨朱)

Introduction:

Yangzhu (395-335 BC), philosopher, early Warring States Period, Eastern Zhou Dynasty, China.
This chapter mainly covers Yangzhu's thinking on life, death and many aspects of humanity.
Of the 16 sections, 11 started with "Yangzhu said:", and 3 are responses to queries by others.

Yangzhu cited many examples of pros and cons, that Honesty is poverty, and dishonesty is wealth.
Life's a short sojourn, unshackled by fame/wealth, to enjoy life with no intrusion on others.
Different in life, king or pauper; same in death, all white bones; lets enjoy life, not worry of death.
Purity and Chastity are good virtues, but held to the extremes can result in death and no progeny.
We ought to be happy, relaxed in life; to break out of poverty, but do relax and not over-working.
Life's mutual sympathy, rest the industrious, feed the hungry; Death, mutual loss, grieve, no rites.
Premier Zichan ordered lives outside; alcoholic and womaniser brothers self ordered lives inside.
Duanmushu spent, gave away all his fortune leaving nothing for progeny, mad or enlightened !
Same order/chaos changes, would have seen all in a 100 years, thus wanting a long life for what !
Yangzhu said, "When no one needs to lose 1 hair to save the world, the world is in order."
Yangzhu detailed the life sufferings of 4 sages, the indulgence of 2 evils; what're your thoughts ?
Yangzhu may not manage his family assets well, but he has visions to play the world in his palm.
Yangzhu asked if ancient leaders had enjoyed life, as memory today cannot compensate for them.
Yangzhu said only a sage person can attain the Ultimate, publicizing body, material possessions.
Yangzhu said for longevity, honor, power, wealth, citizens not relaxed, destiny outside controlled.
Yangzhu said house, clothes, food, sex, are basic needs; people requesting more are like termites.

Chapter 7. Yangzhu (杨朱)

7.1 实伪之辩 | 7.1 Honest Dishonest The Debate

01 杨朱游于鲁，舍于孟氏。	Yangzhu Toured In Lu, Stayed With Mengshi.
02 孟氏问曰：	Mengshi Asking, Said:
03 "人而已矣，奚以名为？"	"Person Just Like This, Why For a Name, Work？"
04 曰："以名者为富。"	Said: "Person With Name For Wealth."
05 "既富矣，奚不已焉？"	"Then Wealthy Already, Why Not Stop, that's？"
06 曰："为贵"。	Said: "Work for Honor."
07 "既贵矣，奚不已焉？"	"Then Honorable Already, Why Not Stop, that's？"
08 曰："为死"。	Said: "Work for Death" (grand burial).
09 "既死矣，奚为焉？"	"Then Dead Already, Why Work, that's？"
10 曰："为子孙。"	Said: "For Children, Grandchildren."
11 "名奚益于子孙？"	"Name, How Beneficial To Children, Grandchildren？"
12 曰："名乃苦其身，燋其心。	Said: "Name Is Burdening The Body, Burning The Heart.
13 乘其名者，泽及宗族，	Person Upon The Name, Benefits Extend to Family Clan,
14 利兼乡党；	Benefits Inclusive of Village Grouping;
15 况子孙乎？"	Let Alone Children Grandchildren is-it-not？"
16 "凡为名者必廉，	"Those People Working for Name Certainly Incorruptible,
17 廉斯贫；	Incorruptible Then be Poor;
18 为名者必让，	People Working for Name Certainly are Deferential,
19 让斯贱。"	Deferential Then be Lowly."
20 曰："管仲之相齐也，	Said: "Guanzhong Assumed Premiership of Qi that's,
21 君淫亦淫，	King Lewd Also Lewd,
22 君奢亦奢，	King Extravagant Also Extravagant,
23 志合言从，	Wills Accorded Orders Followed,
24 道行国霸，	Ways Implemented Kingdom Supreme,
25 死之后，管氏而已。	Death And After, Guan Family Is Over.
26 田氏之相齐也，	Tianshi Assumed Premiership of Qi that's,
27 君盈则己降，	King Proud Then Self Humble
28 君敛则己施，	King Plundered Then Self Bestowed,
29 民皆归之，	Citizens All Submitting to Him,
30 因有齐国；	Resulted in Possession of Qi (be king);
31 子孙享之，	Children Grandchildren Enjoyed Kingship,
32 至今不绝。"	Till Now Not Ending."
33 "若实名贫，伪名富。"	"Like Solid Name, Poor; Fake Name, Wealthy."
34 曰："实无名，名无实；	Said: "Solid, No Name; Name, Not Solid (honest);
35 名者，伪而已矣。	Name Entity, Falsehood That Is indeed.
36 昔者尧舜伪以天下	Past Persons Yao, Shun Pretended With Kingship
37 让许由，善卷，	Abdication to Xuyou, Shanjuan,
38 而不失天下，郭祚百年。	And Not Lost Kingship, Dynasty maintained 100 Years,
39 伯夷，叔齐实以孤竹君让	Boyi, Shuqi Honestly With Abdication to King Guzhu
40 而终亡其国，	And Ending in Lost of The Kingdom,
41 饿死于首阳之山。	Starved to Death On The Shouyang Mountain.

7.1 Honest / Dishonest The Debate

42 *实伪之辨，*	**Honest Dishonest The Debate,**
43 如此其省也。"	Like This The Awareness that's."

Liezi Text Narrative
Yangzhu toured in Lu, stayed with Mengshi who asked: "Person work for a Name, why ?" L3
Yangzhu said: "Person needs a Name, that's a good reputation to gain wealth." L4
Mengshi asked: "With wealth already, why not stop, that's ?". L5
Yangzhu said: "Needs Honor." Mengshi asked: "Honorable already, why not stop, that's ?" L7
Yangzhu said: "Work for death, grand burial." Mengshi asked: "Dead already, why work ?" L9
Yangzhu said: "For children, grandchildren." Mengshi: "Name, how beneficial to them ?" L11
Yangzhu: "Name burdens self; benefits family, clan, and children, grandchildren, why not ?" L15
Mengshi: "For good name, a person incorruptible hence poor; also deferential hence lowly." L19
Yangzhu: "Guanzhong as premier of Qi, king lewd extravagant, also lewd and extravagant; L22
Hence able to use his plan to make the kingdom strong, his king supreme among kings. L24
But after death, the Guan family was over. L25
Tianshi was different as premier of Qi; king proud, he humble; king plundered, he bestowed. L28
Citizens submitted to him, hence took possession of Qi, and created his dynasty till this day." L32
Mengshi: " Like honest in Name becomes poor; dishonest in Name becomes wealthy." L33
Yangzhu: "Honest, no name; has name dishonest; Name entity, falsehood that's indeed. L35
Yao and Shun pretended to abdicate to Xuyou and Shanjuan, thus able to remain as leaders. L38
Boyi and Shuqi abdicated to King Guzhu, lost the kingdom and starved on Mt. Shouyang. L41
The debate of Honest and Dishonest, like this is the awareness that's." L43

Comments:
7.1 Honest / Dishonest The Debate
Yangzhu toured in Lu, stayed with Mengshi who asked why a person works for Name.
Yangzhu: with a name or good reputation, then able to gain wealth, honor, good burial on death.
Also after death, a good reputation will be beneficial to children, grandchildren, family and clan.

Mengshi: for a good name, a person incorruptible hence poor; also deferential hence lowly.
Yangzhu: King lewd, Guanzhong lewd; made kingdom of Qi great, after death Guan family done.
Yangzhu: King proud, Tianshi humble; gained citizens, became king, his dynasty still existing.
Guanzhong lewd bad name, hence ended after death; Tianshi humble good name, prosperity after.
Thus Tianshi with a good name *is not* poor and lowly, but had prosperous generations long after.

Mengshi observed: people Named for honesty are poor; Named for dishonesty are wealthy.
Yangzhu: Yao, Shun pretended to abdicate to Xuyou and Shanjuan, thus able to remain as leaders.
Yangzhu: Boyi and Shuqi abdicated to King Guzhu, lost the kingdom, starved in Mt. Shouyang.
Thus Yao, Shun pretentious remained leaders; honest Boyi and Shuqi were starved to death.
This debate of Honest and Dishonest, be aware that things work both ways, multiple factors !

Yangzhu: honest no name; has name dishonest; hence Name entity, a falsehood indeed.

7.2 人之生也奚为哉？　　7.2 Person's Life, What Purpose ?

01	杨朱曰："百年，寿之大齐。	Yangzhu Said: "100 Years, Great Level Of Longevity.
02	得百年者千无一焉。	Person Attaining 100 Years, Not 1 in 1000 that's.
03	设有一者，孩抱以逮昏老，	If Has such A Person, Childhood And In Weak Old-age,
04	几居其半矣。	About Occupying Half The time (50 years) that's.
05	夜眠之所弭，	Night Sleep That Which Resting (time),
06	昼觉之所遣，	Daylight Awaken That Which Dispatch (time),
07	又几居其半矣。	Again About Occupying Half The time (25 years) that's.
08	痛疾哀苦，	Pain Sickness Grieving Suffering,
09	亡失忧惧，	Lost Missing Troubled Afraid,
10	又几居其半矣。	Again About Occupying Half The time (12.5 years).
11	量十数年之中，	Counting In This 10 Odd Years,
12	逌然而自得	Jolly Naturally And Self Contented
13	亡介焉之虑者，	Person With Not a Bit Of Worry,
14	亦亡一时之中尔。	Also Not A Moment In There that's.
15	**则人之生也奚为哉？**	**Then Person's Living that's, What Purpose that's ?**
16	奚乐哉？	What Happiness indeed ?
17	为美厚尔，	For Beautiful (clothing) Rich (food) that's,
18	为声色尔。	For Sound (music, dance) Color (sex) that's.
19	而美厚复不可常厌足，	And Fashion Food Also Not Able Always Fully Satisfied,
20	声色不可常翫闻。	Music Sex Not Able Always be Heard and Enjoyed.
21	乃复为刑赏之所禁劝，	Then Also By Punitives Rewards That Will Restrict Warn,
22	名法之所进退；	Name Laws That Will Advance Retreat;
23	遑遑尔竞一时之虚誉，	Restively Contesting A Moment Of Flitting Celebrity,
24	规死后之餘荣；	Planning The After Death Remaining Reputation;
25	偊偊尔顺耳目之观听，	Lonely Following Ears Eyes Their Observation Listening,
26	惜身意之是非；	Mindful of Body Mind Their Good and Bad;
27	徒失当年之至乐，	In Vain Lost Life Time Of Absolute Happiness,
28	不能自肆于一时。	Not Able to Self Indulge For A Moment.
29	重囚累梏，	Heavy Confinement Double Shackling,
30	何以异哉？	What Is the Difference indeed ?
31	太古之人知生之暂来，	Most Ancient The People Know Life Is Short A-coming,
32	知死之暂往；	Knows Death Is Short A-going;
33	故从心而动，	Hence Follow Heart For Action,
34	不违自然所好；	Not Against Whatever Self Naturally Love;
35	当身之娱非所去也，	For Self Own Enjoyment, That Not Be Abandoned that's,
36	故不为名所劝。	Hence Not By Name (celebrity status) That Move.
37	从性而游，	Following own Nature To Play,
38	不逆万物所好，	Not Against All Matters Their Love (no intruding others)
39	死后之名非所取也，	After Death The Name, Not What is Wanted that's,
40	故不为刑所及。	Hence Not By Shackles That can Reach.
41	名誉先后，年命多少，	Name Reputation Before /After, Longevity More or Less,
42	非所量也。"	Not What are Considered that's."

7.2 Person's Life, What Purpose ?

Liezi Text Narrative
Yangzhu said: "100 years, a great level of longevity, and not 1 in 1000 can attain it that's. L2
If there is such a person, childhood and old-age take up about half, that is 50 years. L4
Nightly sleep resting time and daily activity time dispatch another half, that is 25 years. L7
Pain, sickness, grief, suffering, lost, missing, trouble and fear take another half (12.5 years).L10
Rest of 12.5 years, a person has hardly a moment of joy fulfilled, without a shred of worry. L14
Then a person's life that's. what purpose, what happiness indeed ? L16
For enjoyment of beautiful clothings, rich food, good music, color and romance. L18
But fashion, food also not always fully satisfied, music romance not always can be enjoyed. L20
And still be warned and restricted by social norms that reward and laws that punish. L22
Restively contesting for a moment of celebrity glory and planning for after death reputation. L24
Lonely, following eye/observation, ear/hearsay, mindful of body and mind, the good and bad.L26
Lamenting loss of absolute happiness in past years, not able to self indulge for a moment. L28
These experiences, what difference from heavy confinement and double shackling indeed ? L30
Ancient people knew that life was temporary coming, knew death was a temporary going. L32
Hence follow the heart's feeling for actions, not against whatever self naturally loves. L34
That for self enjoyment not to be abandoned that is, hence temptation for fame not be moved. L36
Following his own nature to play, but not against all matters their love (no intruding others). L38
Not wanting a name (fame) after death that's, hence will not be reached by shackles. L40
Name reputation after death, longevity long or short, all not what will be considered that's. L42

Comments:
7.2 Person's Life, What Purpose ?
Given Yangzhu analysis, not 1 in a 1000 people will attain a longevity of 100 years.
Childhood and old-age take away half the time, that's 50 years.
Sleep and work take away half the remainder, that's 25 years.
Pain, sickness, grief, loss, fear, such sufferings take away another half, that's 12.5 years.
The remaining 10 odd years, a person hardly has a moment of joy and fulfillment with no worry.

Then a person's life that's. what purpose, what happiness indeed ? L16
Life will be great if we can all enjoy fashion clothes, good food, music, art and romance.
However we may not be fully satisfied as we are restricted by social norms and punitive laws.
Choosing to contest for glory, to leave a good name after death, we must be mindful of all actions.
Thus shackled, we lament the loss of happiness and not a moment for self indulgence in the past.

Ancient people knew life and death were short sojourns, followed their natural love for actions.
Following their own nature to play without intruding on to the loves and plays of all others.
Ancient people knew that life was temporary coming, knew death was a temporary going. L32
Not be shackled by the wants of fame/wealth now and after death, and longevity long or short.

Not shackle by fame and wealth, we indulge our short sojourn here, but intruding no others.

Chapter 7. Yangzhu (杨朱)

7.3 异者生, 同者死   7.3 Different in Life, Similar in Death

01	杨朱曰：	Yangzhu Said:
02	"万物所异者生也，	*"All Matters, Whatever The Difference in Life that's.*
03	所同者死也。	*Whatever The Similarity in Death that's.*
04	生则有贤愚、贵贱，	Life Then Has Clever/Stupid, Noble/Lowly,
05	是所异也；	These The Difference that's;
06	死则有臭腐消灭，	Death Then Has Smelly Rotten Eliminated Destroyed
07	是所同也。	These The Similarity that's.
08	虽然，贤愚、	Nevertheless, Clever/Stupid,
09	贵贱，非所能也；	Noble/Lowly, Not What Able (to control) that's;
10	臭腐、消灭，	Smelly Rotten, Eliminated Destroyed,
11	亦非所能也。	Also Not Self Able (to control) that's.
12	故生非所生，	Hence Life Not Self Life,
13	死非所死；	Death Not Self Death;
14	贤非所贤，	Clever Not Self Clever,
15	愚非所愚，	Stupid Not Self Stupid,
16	贵非所贵，	Noble Not Self Noble,
17	贱非所贱。	Lowly Not Self Lowly.
18	然而万物齐生齐死，	But Then All Matters Together Live Together Die,
19	齐贤齐愚，	Together Clever Together Stupid,
20	齐贵齐贱。	Together Noble Together Lowly.
21	十年亦死，	10 Years Also Die,
22	百年亦死，	100 Years Also Die,
23	仁圣亦死，	Good Sage Also Die,
24	凶愚亦死。	Evil Stupid Also Die.
25	生则尧舜，	Alive Was Yao Shun,
26	死则腐骨；	Dead Was Rotten Bones;
27	生则桀纣，	Alive Was Jie Zhou,
28	死则腐骨。	Death Was Rotten Bones.
29	腐骨一矣，	Rotten Bones One (same) That's,
30	熟知其异？	Who Knows The Difference ?
31	且趣当生，	Lets Enjoy While Living,
32	奚遑死后？"	Why Worry Death After ?"

7.3 Different in Life, Similar in Death

Liezi Text Narrative
Yangzhu said: "All matters, differences are in Life, similarities are in Death. L3
In Life, is clever/stupid, noble/lowly, these differences that's. L5
Death is smelly, rotten, eliminated, destroyed, these similarities that's. L7
Nevertheless, clever/stupid, noble/lowly, are not self made (born with) that's. L9
Smelly, rotten, eliminated, destroyed, also are not self made (or controllable) that's. L11
Hence Life is not self enable Life, Death is not self controllable Death. L13
Clever, stupid, noble, lowly are not self made cleverness, stupidity, nobility and lowliness. L17
But then all matters have commonalities in Life and in Death. L18
Commonalities in cleverness, stupidity, nobility and lowliness. L20
Ten, or 100 years also must die; the good, the sages, the evil, the stupid, all must die. L24
While alive then was Yao, was Shun; when dead then all became rotten bones. L26
While alive then was Jie, was Zhou; when dead then all became rotten bones. L28
As rotten bones, all are the same that's; who knows their differences while alive, is-it-not ? L30
Hence let us enjoy Life while living and not worry about the after Death ?" L32

Comments:
7.3 Different in Life, Similar in Death
Yangzhu says, "All matters are different in life, but in death they are all similar."
In Life, people can be born clever or stupid, can be born into noble or lowly families.
Whereas in Death, people are all similar in being eliminated, destroyed, turn into rotten bones.
Life is not self enabled Life and Death is not self controllable Death.
All matters are together in Life and in Death, being clever or stupid, noble or lowly.
Ten to 100 years, we must all die, the good, the sages, the evils and the stupid.
The good kings Yao and Shun, the evil kings Jie and Zhou, all died and reduced to rotten bones,
Looking at their bones who can tell the difference, which belongs to the good or evil while alive.
Shall we not then enjoy Life while living and not worry about the after-Death ?"

Kings/commoners, the difference in Life; Unrecognizable bones, the similarity in Death.
So why not enjoy Life while living and not worry about Death and after !

Chapter 7. Yangzhu (杨朱)

7.4 清贞   7.4 Purity Chastity

01	杨朱曰：	Yangzhu Said:
02	"伯夷非亡欲，	"Boyi Not No Desires,
03	矜清之邮，	Valued Purity To Extreme,
04	以放饿死。	Until Starved To Death.
05	展季非亡情，	Zhanji Not No Emotion,
06	矜贞之邮，	Valued Chastity The Reason,
07	以放寡宗。	Hence Resulted in Lacking Off-springs.
08	***清贞之误善之若此！"***	***Purity Chastity, They Misled the Good Till Like This !"***

Liezi Text Narrative

Yangzhu said: "Boyi, not had no desires, overly valued purity. L2
Hence retired into the mountain, and died of hunger. L4
Zhanji, not had no emotion, just overly valued chastity. L6
Hence resulted in lacking off-springs. L7
Purity and Chastity, they misled the good people to this extent !" L8

Comments:
7.4 Purity Chastity
Boyi's father of Guzhu State appointed the prince, his brother Shuqi to be the next king.
The brother wished to abdicate to him the kingship as he was the elder one.
Boyi, pure in character, cannot accept this offer and retired himself to the hills.
When the Zhou dynasty overthrew the Shang dynasty, they also sacked the state of Guzhu.
Boyi then refused to eat the 'grain' of the Zhou dynasty and was starved to death in the hills.

Zhanji, a native of the state of Lu, learned, and respected for his upright character.
He was unperturbed when a young girl sheltered in his bosom to survive the cold in the forest.
The narrative here says that his overly valuing chastity resulted in his lack of off-springs.
And laments the extremes caused by adherence to the highest degree of Purity and Chastity.
But there are memorial sites and villages in his birth place who claimed to be his descendants !

We may not emulate these extremes of purity and chastity in character, but it is our choice !

7.5 乐生, 逸身   7.5 Happy Living, Relaxing Body

01	杨朱曰:	Yangzhu Said:
02	"原宪窭于鲁,	"Yuanxian in Poverty In Lu (state),
03	子贡殖于卫。	Zigong Trading In Wei (state).
04	原宪之窭损生,	Yuanxian His Poverty Hurt Living,
05	子贡之殖累身。"	Zigong His Trading Tired Body."
06	"然则窭亦不可,	"But Then Poverty Also Not Allow,
07	殖亦不可,	Trading Also Not Allow,
08	其可焉在?"	The Allowable Where that's?"
09	曰:	Said:
10	*"可在乐生,*	*"Allowable, On Happy Living,*
11	*可在逸身。*	*Allowable, On Relaxing Body.*
12	故善乐生者不窭,	Hence Person Good in Happy Living Not Poor,
13	善逸身者不殖。"	Person Good in Easing Body Not Trading."

Liezi Text Narrative
Yangzhu said: "Yuanxian in poverty in the state of Lu, Zigong trading in the state of Wei. L3
Yuanxian, his poverty hurting his life; Zigong, his trading tired his body." L5
Someone asked, "But then poverty not allow, trading also not allow, then what is allowable ?" L8
Yangzhu said: "Allowable to enjoy life, allowable to relax the body. L11
Hence a person good in happy living, not suffer poverty, just contented with the little he has; L12
A person good in relaxing the body, not trading (excessively), tiring out the body." L13

Comments:
7.5 Happy Living, Relaxing Body
Yuanxian, a disciple of Confucius refused to take remuneration while working under his teacher. Yangzhu is critical of Yuanxian in poverty, but is allowable if he enjoys it and not hurting his life. Zigong, a disciple of Confucius and a rich trader, worked hard to support himself and his teacher. Yangzhu is critical of Zigong trading, but is allowable if not excessive and he is relaxed in body.

Contentment and hard work are good, but we ought to be able to enjoy life, relax our body.

Chapter 7. Yangzhu (杨朱)

7.6 生死之道   7.6 The Pathways of Life Death

01	杨朱曰："古语有之：	Yangzhu Said: "Ancient Saying Has It:
02	'生相怜，死相捐。'	'Life is Mutual Sympathy, Death is Mutual Loss.'
03	此语至矣。	This Saying Extreme that's (in correctness).
04	相怜之道，非唯情也；	Mutual Sympathy The Way, Not Just Emotional that's;
05	勤能使逸，饥能使饱，	Industrious Can Enable Rest, Hungry Can Enable Full,
06	寒能使温，穷能使达也。	Cold, Can Enable Warm, Failure Can Enable Success.
07	相捐之道，非不相哀也；	Mutual Loss The Way, Not No Mutual Grieving that's;
08	不含珠玉，	Not Keep Pearl Jade (in mouth of deceased, a ritual)
09	不服文锦，	Not Clothe in Adorned Brocade,
10	不陈牺牲，	Not Display Sacrificial Animal,
11	不设明器也。"	Not Install Burial Artifacts that's."
12	晏平仲问养生于管夷吾。	Yanpingzhong Asked Healthy Living Of Guanyiwu.
13	管夷吾曰："肆之而已，	Guanyiwu Said: "Self-willed It That's It,
14	勿壅勿阏。"	Not Obstructing Not Shutting-out."
15	晏平仲曰："其目奈何？"	Yanpingzhong Said: "The Details How About ?"
16	夷吾曰：	Yiwu Said:
17	"恣耳之所欲听，	"Unrestrain Ears Their Wish To Hear,
18	恣目之所欲视，	Unrestrain Eyes, Their Wish To See,
19	恣鼻之所欲向，	Unrestrain Nose, It's Wish To Smell,
20	恣口之所欲言，	Unrestrain Mouth It's Wish To Talk,
21	恣体之所欲安，	Unrestrain Body It's Wish For Comfort,
22	恣意之所欲行。	Unrestrain Will Its Wish For Action.
23	夫耳之所欲闻者音声，	O' Ears, What Sound Voice That They Wish to Hear,
24	而不得听，谓之阏聪；	And Not Able to Hear, Call It Shut-off Hearing;
25	目之所欲见者美色，	Eyes, What Beauty Color That They Wish to See,
26	而不得视，谓之阏明；	And Not Able to See, Call It Shut-off Sight;
27	鼻之所欲向者椒兰，	Nose, What Pungent Fragrant That It Wish to Smell,
28	而不得嗅，谓之阏颤；	And Not Able to Smell, Call It Shut-off Shiver;
29	口之所欲道者是非，	Mouth, What Right Wrong That It Wish to Speak,
30	而不得言，谓之阏智；	And Not Able to Say, Call It Shut-off Wisdom;
31	体之所欲安者美厚，	Body, What Nice (dress) Rich (food) It Wish to Enjoy
32	而不得从，谓之阏适；	And Not Able to Follow, Call It Shut-off Comfort;
33	意之所为者放逸，	Will It's Whatever Action That is Free Leisurely,
34	而不得行，谓之阏性。	And Not Able to Do, Call It Shut-off Character.
35	凡此诸阏，废虐之主。	All These Shut-off Kinds, Crippling Abuses The Source.
36	去废虐之主，	Discard The Source of Crippling Abuses.
37	熙熙然以俟死，	Happily Joyously Naturally Till Upon Death,
38	一日、一月、一年、十年，	1 Day, 1 Month, 1 Year, 10 Years,
39	吾所谓养。	What I Call Living-healthy.
40	拘此废虐之主，	Restrain by This Source of Crippling Abuses,

7.6 The Pathways of Life Death

41	录而不舍，	Carved (in wood) And Not Abandon,
42	戚戚然以至久生，	Sorrowfully Naturally Till Reaching Long Life,
43	百年、千年、万年，	100 Years, 1000 Years, 10,000 Years,
44	非吾所谓养。"	Not What I Call Living-healthy."
45	管夷吾曰：	Guanyiwu Said:
46	"吾既告子养生矣，	"I Already Inform Sir Healthy Living that's,
47	送死奈何？"	Farewell in Death How About ?"
48	晏平仲曰：	Yanpingzhong Said:
49	"送死略矣，	"Farewell in Death is Simple that's,
50	将何以告焉？"	What Can I Inform, that's ?"
51	管夷吾曰："吾固欲闻之。"	Guanyiwu Said: "I Certainly Wish to Hear It."
52	平仲曰："既死，岂在我哉？	Pingzhong Said: "Already Dead, How Am I (in control)?
53	焚之亦可，沈之亦可，	Burn It Also Can, Submerge It Also Can,
54	瘗之亦可，露之亦可，	Bury It Also Can, Expose It Also Can,
55	衣薪而弃诸沟壑亦可，	Clothe with Bramble And Abandon In Gully Also Can,
56	衮衣绣裳	Brocade Embroidered Clothes
57	而纳诸石椁亦可，	And Place In Stone Tomb Also Can,
58	唯所遇焉。"	Depending on Whatever Encountered indeed."
59	管夷吾顾谓鲍叔、黄子曰：	Guanyiwu Turned and Talked to Baoshu, Huangzi Said:
60	**"生死之道，**	**"Life Death The Pathway,**
61	吾二人进之矣。"	We 2 Persons have Advanced It indeed."

Liezi Text Narrative

Yangzhu Said: "Ancient Saying has it: 'Life is mutual sympathy, Death is mutual loss.' L2
This saying is extremely correct, and the way of mutual sympathy is not just emotional. L4
Sympathy is to rest the industrious, feed the hungry, warm the cold and help the distressed. L6
Mutual Loss is grieving, but no ritual pearl in mouth of deceased, no clothe in brocade. L9
No display of sacrificial animals, no installation of burial artifacts that's. L11
Yanpingzhong asked Guanyiwu about Healthy Living. L12
Guanyiwu said: "Self-willed it, that's it, no obstructing, no shutting-off of own wishes." L14
Yanpingzhong said: "How about details ?" L15
Yiwu said: "Do not restrain the ears in hearing, the eyes in seeing, the nose in smelling. L19
Do not restrain the mouth in talking, the body in comfort and the will in actions. L22
Ears not able to hear sound voice as wished, ears blocked; L24
Eyes not able to see beauty color as wished, sight blocked; L26
Nose not able to smell pungent fragrance as wished, nose blocked; L28
Mouth not able to speak right wrong as wished, wisdom blocked; L30
Body not able to acquire beautiful clothing rich food as wished, comfort blocked; L32
The Will not able to freely and leisurely do as wished, character blocked. L34
All these numerous blockades, the source of crippling abuses. L35
Discard this source of crippling abuses, and happily naturally till upon death; L37
Be it 1 day, 1 month, 1 year, 10 years, I call it Living-healthy. L39
Restrain by this source of crippling abuses, like carved set in wood and not be abandon; L41
Sadly naturally reaching longevity of 100, 1000, 10,000 years, not what I call a healthy life." L44

7.6 The Pathways of Life Death

Guanyiwu said: "I have informed Sir on Living-healthy, now how about farewell in Death ?" L47
Yanpingzhong said: "Farewell in Death is simple, but what can I inform that's ?" L50
Guanyiwu said: "I certainly wish to hear it." L51
Yanpingzhong said: "Already dead, how am I in control ? L52
Burn it also can, submerge it also can, bury it also can, expose it also can. L54
Cover with bramble and abandon in gully also can. L55
Dress in embroidered brocade, place in a stone tomb, depending on whatever encountered." L58
Guanyiwu turned to talk to Baoshu, Huangzi and said: L59
"Life Death the pathways, the two of us have advanced their understanding indeed." L61

Comments:
7.6 The Pathways of Life Death
Ancient saying, 'Life is mutual sympathy, Death is mutual loss' is not just emotional.
Sympathy is to rest the industrious, feed the hungry, warm the cold and help the distressed.
Loss is to grieve, but no ritual pearl, brocade clothes, sacrificial animals or burial artifacts.

Guanyiwu said healthy living is, "Self-willed, no obstructing, no shutting-out of own wishes.
Ears able to hear, sound voices as wished; eyes able to see beauty color as wished.
Nose able to smell fragrance as wished; mouth able to speak right wrong as wished.
Body able to acquire comfort clothes, rich food as wished; Wills able to freely do as wished.
Living-healthy is no character blockade, living happy, be it a day, a month, a year or 10 years.
Restrained, sadly reaching longevity of 100, 1000, 10,000 years, is not Living healthy."

Yangpingzhong said, "Farewell in Death is simple, as already dead, no more in control."
Body may be burned, submerged, buried, exposed, covered with bramble, or abandoned in gully.
May dress in embroidered brocade, place in a stone tomb, depending on whatever encountered.
(note: Guanyiwu and Yangpingzhong were historic characters centuries apart.)

Living healthy for a day is better than living sad for a 100 years; after Death, posterity decides.

7.7 治外，治内 — 7.7 Internal And External Management

01	子产相郑，	Zichan as Premier of Zheng,
02	专国之政；	In-charge of Kingdom's Administration;
03	三年，善者服其化，	3 Years, Good People Submitted to His Transformation,
04	恶者畏其禁，	Evil People Afraid of His Punishment,
05	郑国以治。	Kingdom of Zheng Was Well-governed.
06	诸侯惮之。	All other Kingdoms Fearful of Zheng.
07	而有兄曰公孙朝，	But Had Elder-brother Gongsunchao,
08	有弟曰公孙穆。	Had a Young-brother Gongsunmu.
09	朝好酒，穆好色。	Chao Obsession Wine, Mu Obsession Women.
10	朝之室也聚酒千钟，	Chao His House That's Stored Wine of 1000 Vats.
11	积麴成封，	Stocks of Malted-grain Forming Piles,
12	望门百步，	Hundred Steps Looking at Door (from distance)
13	糟浆之气逆于人鼻。	Fermented Malt The Aroma Pungent In People's Nose.
14	方其荒于酒也，	When He was Famished Of Wine that's,
15	不知世道之争危，	Not Knowing World's Way Of Contest Danger,
16	人理之悔吝，	People's Understanding Of Regrets Stinginess,
17	室内之有亡，	In House What Have/Have-not,
18	九族之亲疏，	Closeness/Distance of the 9 Relationships,
19	存亡之哀乐也。	The Joy/Sadness of Life/Death that's.
20	虽水火兵刃交于前，	Though Water Fire Soldiers Crossing Swords In Front,
21	弗知也。	Not Knowing that's.
22	穆之后庭比房数十，	Mu, His Back Quarters Neighboring Rooms Several Tens,
23	皆择稚齿婑媠者以盈之。	All Filled Up With Selected Young Teeth Sensual Girls.
24	方其耽于色也，屏亲昵，	When He Indulged In Womanizing, Dismissed Relatives
25	绝交游，逃于后庭，	Severed Interactive Friendship, Fled To Behind Quarters,
26	以昼足夜；	With Days Continuing into Nights;
27	三月一出，意犹未惬。	3 Months 1 Outing, Desires Still Not Satisfied.
28	乡有处子之娥姣者，	Village Had Virgin Girls Who Were Beautiful Voluptuous,
29	必贿而招之，	Certain to Bribe And Welcome Them,
30	媒而挑之，	Go-betweens to Entice Them,
31	弗获而后已。	Not Attained Then Not Stopped.
32	子产日夜以为戚，	Zichan Day Night Troubled by This,
33	密造邓析而谋之，	Secretly Informed Dengxi And Discussing It,
34	曰："侨闻治身以及家，	Said: "I Hear that Managed Self Then Next Family,
35	治家以及国，	Managed Family Then Next Kingdom,
36	此言自于近至于远也。	This Saying From The Near To The Far that's.
37	侨为国则治矣，	Qiao (Zichan) For Kingdom Thus Managed Indeed,
38	而家则乱矣。	But Family This Chaotic Indeed.
39	其道逆邪？	The Way seems Contradictory Is-it-not?
40	将奚方以救二子？	What Method Will Save These '2 Children'?
41	子其诏之！"	Sir Your Instruction in This!"

7.7 Internal And External Management

42	邓析曰："吾怪之久矣！	Dengxi Said: "I am Surprised For a Long-time Indeed !
43	未敢先言。	Not Dared to Speak Earlier.
44	子奚不时其治也,	Sir Why Not Timing The Control that's,
45	喻以性命之重,	Explain With The Gravity of Life/Death,
46	诱以礼义之尊乎？"	Induce With The Respect of Courtesy Morality, right ?"
47	子产用邓析之言,	Zichan Used The Words of Dengxi,
48	因间以谒其兄弟,	Found Time To Visit His Elder and Young-brother,
49	而告之曰:	And Informed Them Said:
50	"人之所以贵于禽兽者,	"Human The Reason For Being Superior To Animals,
51	智虑。	Wisdom and Thinking.
52	智虑之所将者,	Wisdom Thinking, That Which They Depend,
53	礼义。	Courtesy Morality.
54	礼义成,	Courtesy Morality Formed,
55	则名位至矣。	Then Name Position Established indeed.
56	若触情而动,	If Emotionally Touched And Moved,
57	耽于嗜欲,	Indulge In Addiction Desires,
58	则性命危矣。	Then Character Life in Danger Indeed.
59	子纳侨之言,	Sirs, Accept Qiao (Zichan) My Advice,
60	则朝自悔	Then Morning Self Repent
61	而夕食禄矣。"	And Night Enjoy Employment Indeed."
62	朝、穆曰："吾知之久矣,	Chao, Mu Said: "We Know This Long-ago Indeed,
63	择之亦久矣,	Choices Made Also Long-ago Indeed,
64	岂待若言而后识之哉？	How can Wait Your Advice And Then Know, right ?
65	凡生之难遇	All Life It's Difficult to Encounter
66	而死之易及；	And Death It's Ease to Reach;
67	以难遇之生,	With The Difficult to Encounter Life,
68	俟易及之死,	Waiting for The Easy to Reach Death,
69	可孰念哉？	What Can we Think Is-it-not ?
70	而欲尊礼义	And Wishing Respect Courtesy Morality
71	以夸人,	To Boast before People,
72	矫情性以招名,	Modify Emotion Character To Invite Name (reputation)
73	吾以此为弗若死矣。	We, By This Be Considered Dead Indeed.
74	为欲尽一生之欢,	For Wishing to Complete A Life-time Of Joy,
75	穷当年之乐,	Exhausting Those Years Of Happiness,
76	唯患腹溢	Only Worry that Stomach Full
77	而不得恣口之饮,	And Not Able Indulging Mouth It's Drink,
78	力惫而不得肆情于色；	Strength Tired And Not Able for Free Emotion In Sex;
79	不遑忧名声之丑,	No Leisure Worrying The Shame of Name Reputation,
80	性命之危也。	Danger to Life that's.
81	且若以治国之能夸物,	And Like With The Ability to Govern Kingdom
82	欲以说辞乱我之心,	Wishing With Your Arguments to Confuse Our Hearts,
83	荣禄喜我之意,	Honor and Fortune to Stimulate Our Wills,
84	不亦鄙而可怜哉？	Not Also Vulgar And Be Pitied Is-it-not ?
85	我又欲与若别之。	We Also Wish With Like (arguments) to Clarify Them.

7.7 Internal And External Management

86	夫善治外者，	Person Good in Managing Outside (kingdom),
87	物未必治，	Matters Not Certain are Managed,
88	而身交苦；	And Body Interactively Suffered;
89	善治内者，	Person Good in Managing Inside (self),
90	物未必乱，	Matters May Not be Chaotic,
91	而性交逸。	And Character Interactively Relaxed
92	*以苦之治外，*	***With Suffering In Managing Externally,***
93	其法可暂行于一国，	The Laws Can Temporary Implemented In A Kingdom,
94	未合于人心；	May-not Accord With People's Heart (feeling);
95	*以我之治内，*	***With Own In Managing Internally,***
96	可推之于天下，	Can Push It To The World,
97	君臣之道息矣。	King/Subject This Path (set-up) be Abolished indeed.
98	吾常欲以此术而喻之，	We Often Wish With This Method To Advise You,
99	若反以彼术而教我哉？"	Like Reverse With Your Method To Teach Us, amazing?"
100	子产忙然无以应之，	Zichan Vaguely Lost With Nothing to Respond Them,
101	他日以告邓析。	Another Day With this Informed Dengxi.
102	邓析曰：	Dengxi Said:
103	"子与真人居而不知也，	"Sir Resides With People of Truth And Not Know that's,
104	孰谓子智者乎？	Who Says Sir is a Knowledgeable Person that's ?
105	郑国之治偶耳，	Kingdom of Zheng It's Managed, Accidental only,
106	非子之功也。"	Not Sir Your Success that's."

Liezi Text Narrative

Zichan was premier of the State of Zheng, in-charge of the Kingdom's administration. L2
In 3 years, good people submitted, evil people feared his new rules and Zheng was powerful. L5
All the other kingdoms were fearful of the State of Zheng. L6
Elder brother GongsunChao was an alcoholic, younger brother GongsunMu was a womaniser. L9
Chao, his house had a wine store of 1000 vats, stocks of malted-grain forming mounds. L11
Looking at his door a hundred steps away, the fermented malt aroma was in people's nose. L13
When he was famished for wine that's, he knew not the world's way of contest and danger; L15
Not aware of people's understanding of regrets stinginess, in-house what have/have-not; L17
Not aware of closeness/distance in the 9 relationships, the joy/sadness of life/death that's. L19
Though there were water, fire, soldiers crossing swords in front of him, he knew not that's. L21
Mu, his back quarters had tens of rooms, all filled with young-teeth sensual girls. L23
When he indulged in womanizing, he dismissed relatives, severed interactive friendships. L25
At back quarters with days continued into nights, 3 months 1 outing, desires not yet satisfied. L27
Villages had virgin beautiful voluptuous girls, certain to bribe and welcome them. L29
Had go-betweens to induce them, not attained would not stop. L31

Zichan, troubled by this day and night, secretly informed Dengxi and discussed it. L33
"I heard that the self managed then extends to family, to state, say from near to far that's. L36
I have managed the state but my family is chaotic, what has happened seems contradictory ? L39
What method will save these '2 children', Sir, your instruction for this !" L41
Dengxi said: "I was surprised for a long time but not dared to speak earlier. L43
Sir, why not find time to control them, explaining the gravity of life/death in their activities. L45
Induce them with the respect for courtesy and morality, right ?" L46

7.7 Internal And External Management

Zichan used the words of Deng, found time to visit brothers and informing them said: L49
"As humans, the reason for being superior to animals is our thinking and wisdom. L51
Thinking and wisdom, that which they depend on, are courtesy and morality. L53
Courtesy morality formed, then name position established indeed. L55
If emotionally touched and moved, indulged in addiction/desires, then lives are in danger. L58
Sirs, accept Qiao (Zichan) my advice, morning self repent, then night enjoy employment." L61
Chao, Mu said: " We know this long ago, choices made, why wait for your advice, is-it-not ? L64
Life is difficult, death is easy; a difficult life waiting for easy death, what are we thinking ? L69
Wishing for respect, practice courtesy and morality so as to boast in front of people. L71
Modify emotion and character to gain a good name, by these we may be considered dead. L73
We wish to complete a life-time of enjoyment and exhausting those years of happiness; L75
Only worry that stomach full and not able to indulge the mouth in eating and drinking; L77
Worry no strength to freely enjoy sex; no leisure to worry of reputation, danger to life that's. L80
Boasting of your ability to manage the state; wishing to confuse our hearts with arguments. L82
Using honor and fortune to stimulate our wills, you are vulgar and be pitied, true ? L84
We also wish to clarify the arguments of both sides with you. L85
Person good in managing outside (state), but matters may not be managed and self suffered. L88
Person good in managing inside (self), but matters may not be chaotic and self relaxed. L91
Suffering in managing outside, laws implemented in the state, may not accord with people. L94
With our management inside and pushed to the world, king/subjects setup may be abolished. L97
We wish to advise you on our method, but in reverse you wish to teach us yours, amazing ?" L99
Zichan was baffled and lost, not knowing what to say in response, and went to tell Dengxi. L101
Dengxi said: "Sir, you have been residing with people of 'Truth' and not knowing, that's. L103
Who says Sir, you are a knowledgeable person that's ? L104
That the State of Zheng is well managed is accidental only, not Sir your success, that's." L106

Comments:
7.7 Internal And External Management
In 3 years Zichan's new rules succeeded in making the State of Zheng strong, that others feared.
However his elder brother Gongsun Chao was an alcoholic with a wine store of 1000 vats.
When famished for wine, he forgot the world, relatives, friends, and unaware of his surroundings.
His younger brother Gongsun Mu was a womaniser, his back quarters filled with sensual girls.
With days continued into nights, appearing outside only once in 3 months, yet desired for more.
Able to administer a state but not able to control his family, Zichan was troubled day and night.
His friend Dengxi suggested he impressed brothers with the gravity of life/death in their actions.
That we are superior to animals in our thinking and wisdom, establishing courtesy and morality.
Zichan then promised his brothers to repent in the morning and enjoy employment later at night.
Chao and Mu said they knew long ago, made their choices, and were not waiting for his advice.
They accused Zichan of practicing courtesy and morality to boast in front of people.
To modify emotion and character to gain a good name; and they rather be dead than doing these.
They wished to complete a life-time of enjoyment, had no leisure to worry about name, death.
They argued that Zichan external management was self-suffering and may not accord with people.
Whereas their internal management was self-relaxing, and may be extended to the world.
Using honor and fortune to confuse them, they further accused Zichan of being vulgar and pitied.
On hearing this, Dengxi laughed at Zichan for living with people of 'Truth' and not knowing it !
Suffering for external management or relaxing in internal management, own choice really.

Chapter 7. Yangzhu (*杨朱*)

7.8 狂人也，达人也   7.8 Mad Man or Enlightened Man

01	卫端木叔者，子贡之世也。	Wei (state) Duanmushu Person, Zigong's Descendant.
02	藉其先赀，家累万金。	Based On Ancestor Assets, Family Amassed 10,000 Gold.
03	不治世故，放意所好。	Not Managed World Affairs, Indulged In Obsessions.
04	其生民之所欲为，	What The Common Citizen Wished to Do,
05	人意之所欲玩者，	What People's Will That Wished to Play,
06	无不为也，无不玩也。	None Not Do, that's; None Not Play, that's.
07	墙屋台榭，园囿池沼，	Walled House Stage Pavilion, Garden Pond Swamp,
08	饮食车服，	Drink Food Carriage Clothes,
09	声乐嫔御，	Sound Music Concubines Servants,
10	拟齐楚之君焉。	Comparable to Kings of Qi and Chu that's.
11	至其情所欲好，	To What His Emotion Wish to Like,
12	耳所欲听，	What Ears Wished to Hear,
13	目所欲视，口所欲尝，	What Eyes Wished to See, What Mouth Wished to Taste,
14	虽殊方偏国，	Though Strange Regions Isolated States,
15	非齐土之所产育者，	Not What Land of Qi Can Produced and Nurtured,
16	无不必致之；	None Not Certain to Acquire It;
17	犹藩墙之物也。	Like Things Within Fenced Walls that's (must possess).
18	及其游也，	About His Travels that's,
19	虽山川阻险，	Though Mountains Rivers Blockage Danger,
20	途径修远，	Road Path Running Faraway,
21	无不必之，	None Not Surety Itself (must access),
22	犹人之行咫步也。	Like People Walking a Few Steps, that's.
23	宾客在庭者日百住，	Friends Guests In Courtyard, Daily Numbered Hundreds
24	庖厨之下不绝烟火；	Down The Kitchen Complex, Smoke Fire Never Off;
25	堂庑之上不绝声乐。	Up The Halls Lounges, Sound Music Never Stopped.
26	奉养之馀，	Sustenance Supports Had Excess,
27	先散之宗族；	First Distributed It to Families Clans;
28	宗族之馀，	Families Clans Had Excess,
29	次散之邑里；	Next Distributed to Neighborhood;
30	邑里之馀，	Neighborhood Had Excess,
31	乃散之一国。	Then Distributed It kingdom wide.
32	行年六十，	Run-up Years 60 (age),
33	气干将衰，	Breath Body Getting Weaken,
34	弃其家事，	Abandoned His Family Affairs,
35	都散其库藏，	Distributed All His Stored Possessions,
36	珍宝、车服、	Pearls Valuables, Carriage Clothes,
37	妾媵。	Concubines Associates.
38	一年之中尽焉，	Completed Within The 1 Year that's,
39	不为子孙留财。	Not Leaving Wealth For Children Grandchildren.
40	及其病也，无药石之储；	Until His Illness that's, No Saving For Medicine;
41	及其死也；无瘗埋之资。	Until His Death that's, No Money For Burial.
42	一国之人受其施者，	People Of Whole Kingdom Who had Received His Help,
43	相与赋而藏之，	Mutually Gave Contribuutions To Bury Him.

7.8 Mad Man or Enlightened Man

44	反其子孙之财焉。	Returning Wealth To His Children and Grandchildren.
45	禽骨厘闻之，曰：	Qinguli Hearing This, Said:
46	**"端木叔，狂人也，**	**"Duanmushu, Mad Person that's,**
47	辱其祖矣。"	His Ancestors' Shame indeed"
48	段干生闻之，曰：	Duankanshang Hearing This, Said:
49	**"端木叔，达人也，**	**"Duanmushu, Enlightened Person that's,**
50	德过其祖矣。	Virtues Exceeding His Ancestors indeed.
51	其所行也，其所为也，	All His Actions that's, Whatever Their Purpose that's,
52	众意所惊，	They Surprised People's Understanding,
53	而诚理所取。	But Honestly Accorded With Reasons.
54	卫之君子	Wei's Gentlemen
55	多以礼教自持，	Mostly Self Assured with Morality Teachings,
56	固未足以得	Thus Not Enough To Attain
57	此人之心也。"	This Person's 'Heart' (feeling), that's."

Liezi Text Narrative

Duanmushu of Wei, descendant of Zigong, based on ancestral assets, amassed 10,000 gold. L2
No concern for world's affairs, indulged in his obsessions, all that citizens commonly play. L6
Walled house, stage, pavilion, garden, pond, swamp, drink, food, carriage and clothes. L8
Sound, music, concubines, servants, comparable to the kings of Qi and Chu that's. L10
For his emotional needs, what he wished to hear with ears, see with eyes, taste with mouth. L13
From isolated states far and wide, he must acquire exotic things, making them his own. L17
In travels, he must access faraway places, travel difficult mountains and dangerous rivers. L22
Daily, guests in hundreds, fire never off in the kitchens, sound music never stops in the halls. L25
Had excess, first distributed to families, clans, next to neighborhood, then kingdom-wide. L31
At age 60, his body weakened, abandoned family, and gave away all his stored possessions. L35
Valuables, carriage, clothes, and concubines, all within a year, left nothing to descendants. L39
Then he was ill and had no saving for medicine; and when he died, had no money for burial. L41
People who had received his help before returned wealth to his descendants, and to bury him. L44
Qinguli on hearing, said: "Duanmushu, a Mad person who shamed his ancestors, indeed. 47
Duankanshang said: "Duanmushu, Enlightened person, virtues exceeded his ancestors. L50
Whatever their purpose, his actions surprised people but he was honest and had his reasons. L53
In the state of Wei, gentlemen there were mostly self assured people with morality teachings. L55
Thus not enough to be able to appreciate and understand the feelings of Duanmushu, that's. L57

Comments:

7.8 Mad Man or Enlightened Man

A descendant of Zigong, Duanmushu of Wei amassed 10,000 gold based on ancestral assets.
Obsessions with house, stage, pavilion, garden, pond, swamp, drink, food, carriage and clothes.
Self indulgence in music, concubines, servants, comparable to the kings of Qi and Chu that's.
From states far and wide, he acquired exotic things; in travels, he accessed faraway places.
Daily, guests in hundreds, fire always on in the kitchens; sound of music never stops in the halls.
Had excess, first distributed to families clans, next to neighborhood, then kingdom-wide.
Enjoyed life with no harm to others, able to give out his excess; Duanmushu, an Enlightened man.
At age 60, he gave away all his possessions all within a year, leaving nothing to his descendants.
When he was ill, had no saving for medicine; and when he died, had no money for burial.
Over-charity leaving nothing to descendants to bury him with, Duanmushu is a Madman indeed.
Be warned: an over-Enlightened man can turn into a Madman; ought to strike a balance.

Chapter 7. Yangzhu (杨朱)

7.9 且久生奚为?	**7.9 And Long Life What For ?**
01 孟孙阳问杨朱曰:	Mengsunyang Asked Yangzhu, Said:
02 "有人于此,	"Has Person At Present,
03 贵生爱身,	Valued Life Loved Body,
04 以蕲不死,	With Prayer to Not Die,
05 可乎?"	Possible is-it-not ?"
06 曰:	Said:
07 "理无不死。"	"Reasonably No to Not Die."
08 "以蕲久生,	"With Prayer for Long Life,
09 可乎?"	Possible is-it-not ?"
10 曰:	Said:
11 "理无久生。	"Reasonably No for Long Life.
12 生非贵之所能存,	Life Not Valuing It Then Enable to Survive,
13 身非爱之所能厚。	Body Not Loving It Then Enable to be Privileged.
14 *且久生奚为?*	*And Long Life What For ?*
15 五情好恶,	5 Emotions Good/Bad,
16 古犹今也;	Ancient time Till Now that's;
17 四体安危,	4 Bodily Safe/Danger,
18 古犹今也;	Ancient time Till Now that's;
19 世事苦乐,	World Affairs Sad/Happy,
20 古犹今也;	Ancient time Till Now that's;
21 变易治乱,	Transform Changes Order/Chaos,
22 古犹今也。	Ancient time Till Now that's.
23 既闻之矣,	Already Heard It indeed,
24 既见之矣,	Already Seen It indeed.
25 既更之矣,	Already Changed It indeed,
26 百年犹厌其多,	100 Years Already Hated It (too) Much,
27 况久生之苦也乎?"	Especially Long Life, It's Suffering that's is-it-not ?"
28 孟孙阳曰:	Mengsunyang Said:
29 "若然,	"Like This is so,
30 速亡愈于久生;	Quick Death Better Than Long Life;
31 则践锋刃,	Then Walk Knife's Edge,
32 入汤火,	Enter Boiling-water Fire
33 得所志矣。"	Attain Whatever Wishes indeed."
34 杨子曰:	Yangzhu Said:
35 "不然;	"Naturally Not;
36 既生,	Already Living,
37 则废而任之,	Then Abandon And Let It be,
38 究其所欲,以俟于死。	Aware Whatever The Wants, To Await Till Death.
39 将死,	Soon Dying,
40 则废而任之,	Then Abandon And Let It be,
41 究其所之,以放于尽。	Aware Whatever The Process, To Let-it-be Till End.
42 无不废,无不任,	None Not Abandon, None Not Let-it-be,
43 何遽迟速于其间乎?"	Why Fear The Delay/Speed In Between is-it-not ?"

7.9 And Long Life What For ?

Liezi Text Narrative
Mengsunyang asked Yangzhu, said: "Has a person at present, values Life and loves his body. L3
With prayer, pray not to Die and to Live forever, is it possible ?" L5
Yangzhu said: "Reasonably, it is not possible to not die." L7
Mengsunyang: "With prayer for Long Life, is it possible ?" L9
Yangzhu said: "Reasonably, it is not possible to pray for a long life. L11
Life, not valuing it then enables it survival; body not loving it then enables to be privileged. L13
And Long Life, for what ? L14
Ancient times till now, the 5 emotions good/bad; 4 body-parts safety/danger (all similar); L18
Ancient times till now, worldly affairs sad/happy; transforms, changes order/chaos (similar). L22
Already heard it all, seen it all, changed it all, 100 years already having too much, hating it. L26
Furthermore, and all the suffering of Long Life, is-it-not ?" L27
Mengsunyang said: "If this is so, quick death is better than Long Life; L30
Then walk on the knife's edge, jump-into boiling water or fire to attain a quick death." L32
Yangzhu said: "Naturally not, as already living then abandon interfering and let it be. L37
While living, be aware and satisfy whatever the wants until death. L38
Soon dying, then abandon interfering and let it be, just aware of whatever process till the end. L41
Nothing more that we cannot abandon and let go, and nothing more we cannot allow to be. L42
Why rush the time process of delay/speed in between life and death ?" L43

Comments:
7.9 And Long Life What For ?
Mengsunyang, a disciple of Yangzhu.
Mengsunyang asked: "A person loves life and wishes to pray for Eternal Life, is it possible ?"
Yangzhu said: "Reasonably not possible, as we know death is inevitable for all."
Mengsunyang again asked: "Is it possible to pray for Long Life then ?"
Yangzhu said: "Reasonably, it is not possible, as valuing life does not enable its survival."
With no awareness of killer bugs, ancient people died prematurely regardless of love and care.
Since ancient times, the 5 emotions good/bad, 4 bodily safety/danger are all similar.
The worldly affairs are sad/happy; transformation and changes of order/chaos, all similar.
Everybody already seen it all, heard it all, a 100 years already having too much, and hating it.
Hence Yangzhu asked: "With all the sufferings and repetitions, a Long Life for what ?"
Mengsunyang countering, said: "If this is so, a quick death is better than Long Life;
Then we can walk on a knife's edge, or jump into boiling water or fire to end it all !"
Yangzhu disagreed: "Naturally not so, as already living, we should not interfere and let it be.
While living we should be aware and satisfy whatever the wants and needs until death.
Soon dying, we just need to let go and not interfere, allowing the natural process to proceed.
Why rush the time process of delay/speed in between life and death ?"

Which means in our time, no endless testing, no ICU admission for heroic prolonging Life.

Chapter 7. Yangzhu (杨朱)

7.10 不损一毫 — 7.10 No Loss of One Hair

01	杨朱曰：	Yangzhu Said:
02	"伯成子高不以一毫利物，	"Bochengzigao Not With 1 Hair to Benefit Matters,
03	舍国而隐耕。	Abandoned Kingdom For Concealment and Farming.
04	大禹不以一身自利，	Great Yu Not With Own Body For Self Benefit,
05	一体偏枯。	Whole Body Partially Withered.
06	古之人损一毫	The Ancient Person Lost 1 Hair to
07	利天下不与也，	Benefit The World and Not Giving that's,
08	悉天下奉一身	Knows The World will Support Whole of Self,
09	不取也。	Not Collecting that's.
10	**人人不损一毫，**	**Every Person Not (needed) to Lose 1 Hair,**
11	**人人不利天下，**	**Every Person Not (needed) to Benefit The World,**
12	**天下治矣。"**	**The World is Ordered indeed."**
13	禽子问杨朱曰：	Qinzi Asked Yangzhu, Said:
14	"去子体之一毛以济一世，	"Take from Sir's Body 1 Hair To Save Whole Society,
15	汝为之乎？"	You will Do It Is-it-not ?"
16	杨朱曰：	Yangzhu Said:
17	"世固非一毛之所济。"	"Society Certainly Not 1 Hair That Can Save."
18	禽子曰："假济，为之乎？"	Qinzi Said: "Suppose can Save, Do It or Not ?"
19	杨子弗应。	Yangzhu Not Responding.
20	禽子出语孟孙阳。	Qinzi Exited and Told Mengsunyang.
21	孟孙阳曰：	Mengsunyang Said:
22	"子不达夫子之心，	"Sir Not Comprehending Teacher's Heart,
23	吾请言之。	I Beg to Speak It.
24	有侵苦肌肤	Person Receives Invasive Injury of Muscle Skin
25	获万金者，	Gets 10,000 Gold,
26	若为之乎？"	Likely Do It, yes/no ?"
27	曰："为之。"	Said: "Do It."
28	孟孙阳曰：	Mengsunyang Said:
29	"有断若一节得一国。	"Has Break Like 1 Limb, Get 1 kingdom.
30	子为之乎？"	Sir Do It yes/no ?"
31	禽子默然有间。	Qinzi Silent Naturally For a While.
32	孟孙阳曰："一毛微于肌肤，	Mengsunyang Said: "1 Hair Smaller Than Muscle Skin,
33	肌肤微于一节，省矣。	Muscle Skin Smaller Than 1 Limb, Obviously indeed.
34	然则积一毛以成肌肤，	But Then Accumulating 1 Hair To Form Muscle Skin,
35	积肌肤以成一节。	Accumulating Muscle Skin To Form 1 Limb.
36	一毛固一体万分中之一物，	1 Hair Though is 1 Part of The Body's 10,000 Parts,
37	奈何轻之乎？"	But Why Slight It, Is-it-not ?"
38	禽子曰："吾不能所以答子。	Qinzi Said: "I Not Able With Reason to Answer Sir.
39	然则以子之言问老聃、	But Then With Sir's Words to Ask Old Dan (Laozi)
40	关尹，则子言当矣；	Guanyin, Then Sir's Words Correct indeed;
41	以吾言问大禹、墨翟，	With My Words to Ask Great Yu, Modi,
42	则吾言当矣。"	Then My Words Correct indeed."
43	孟孙阳因顾与其徒	Mengsunyang Hence Turned To His Disciples
44	说他事。	Spoke of Other Matters.

7.10 No Loss of One Hair

Liezi Text Narrative
Yangzhu said: "Bochengzigao will not lose 1 hair to save others, left the state to be a farmer. L3
Great Yu not benefiting himself but the people, fighting the Deluge, suffered partial paralysis. L5
The ancient person lost 1 hair to benefit the world and not give, that's (Bochengzigao). L7
As emperor, knew the world on offer for benefitting self, and yet not taking it (Great Yu). L9
Every single person, no need to lose 1 hair to benefit the world, the world is in order indeed."L12
Qinzi asked Yangzhu: "Take from Sir's body 1 hair to save society, will you do it, yes/no ?" L15
Yangzhu said: "Certainly, society cannot be saved with 1 hair." L17
Qinzi said: "Suppose it can be saved, you will do it, yes/no ?" L18
Yangzhu not responding. L19
Qinzi exited and told Mengsunyang. L20
Mengsunyang said: "Sir, you have not understand Teacher's heart feelings. Let me explain. L23
Person gets muscle skin injury can receive 10,000 gold, will you do it, yes/no ?" L26
Qinzi said: " Will do it." L27
Mengsunyang said: "Gets 1 Limb broken, to receive 1 kingdom, Sir will you do it, yes/no ?" L30
Qinzi remained silent naturally for a while. L31
Mengsunyang said: "1 hair smaller than muscle which in turn smaller than 1 limb obviously. L33
But then accumulating 1 hair to form muscle skin which accumulates to form 1 limb. L35
Though 1 part of the body's 10,000 parts, even 1 hair should not be slighted, is-it-not ?" L37
Qinzi said: "I am not able to answer you, but Old Dan, Guanyin will say you are correct. L40
Whereas Great Yu and Modi will say my words are correct indeed." L42
Hence Mengsunyang turned to his disciple and spoke of other matters. L44

Comments
7.10 No Loss of One Hair
Bochengzigao would not lose 1 hair to save the world, left the state for his private farming.
Great Yu would not self benefit but fought the Deluge for the people, suffered partial paralysis.
Yangzhu said: "When no person needs to lose 1 hair to save society, society is in order."

Then Qinzi asked Yangzhu if he would lose 1 hair to save society.
Yangzhu said losing 1 hair cannot save a society. Qinzi said if can, Yangzhu did not respond.
Qinzi didn't understand and went to ask Mengsunyang, Yangzhu's disciple.
Mengsunyang asked Qinzi if he let his muscle skin be injured for 10,000 gold, Qinzi said yes.
However Ginzi remained silent when asked if he was willing to lose a limb for a kingdom.
Mengsunyang explained that 1 hair accumulated to form muscle skin which joined to form limbs.
Though 1 hair, one part of 10,000 parts of the body, one should not slight it and lose it easily.
With no answer, Ginzi said old Dan and Guanyin the daoists would agree with Mengsunyang.
Whereas the Great Yu and Modi the Confucian and Moist would agree with his words.
Daoists strive for a self-sufficient world, but the non-Daoists are grateful to help and be helped.

Many have thought that Yangzhu was an unkind man who will not sacrifice 1 hair to help others.
Actually Yangzhu knows this '1 hair to save society' is a no brainer, as more hairs may be asked !
Like the philosophical trap, where to draw the line between black and white among the shades.

Yangzhu's words, "When no 1 person needs to lose 1 hair to save the world, the world is safe."

Chapter 7. Yangzhu (杨朱)

7.11 四圣，二凶   7.11 Sages 4 and Evils 2

01	杨朱曰：	Yangzhu Said:
02	"天下之美	"Beneath Heaven The Beautiful
03	归之舜、禹、周、孔，	Ascribed To Shun, Yu, Zhou, Kong (sages),
04	天下之恶	Beneath Heaven The Evil
05	归之桀纣。	Ascribed To Jie, Zhou (kings).
06	然而舜耕于河阳，	But Then Shun Farming At Heyang,
07	陶于雷泽，	Pottery-making At Leize,
08	四体不得暂安，	4 Limbs Not Getting a Moment of Rest,
09	口腹不得美厚；	Mouth Stomach Not Getting Good Rich (food);
10	父母之所不爱，	Whom The Father Mother Not Loved,
11	弟妹之所不亲。	Whom The Brothers Sisters Not Befriended.
12	行年三十，	Going-on 30,
13	不告而娶。	Not Informing (parents) Got Married.
14	乃受尧之禅，	Then Accepted Yao His Abdication,
15	年已长，	Age Had Increased,
16	智已衰。	Mind Had Deteriorated.
17	商钧不才，	Shangjun (son) Not Talented,
18	禅位于禹，	Abdicated Throne To Yu,
19	戚戚然以至于死：	Sadly Naturally To Reach Till Death:
20	此天人之穷毒者也。	This Most Suffering Person beneath Heaven that's.
21	鲧(鯀)治水土，	Gun Taming Water Earth (the Deluge),
22	绩用不就，	Results Effects Not Successful,
23	殛诸羽山。	Executed At Mount Yu (by Shun).
24	禹纂业事雠，	Yu Inherited (father Gun) Task Serving Enemy (Shun),
25	惟荒土功，	Focus on Wilderness Land Task (taming the Deluge),
26	子产不字，	Son Born Not Naming (attending),
27	过门不入；	Pass-by Door (home) Not Entering;
28	身体偏枯，手足胼胝。	Own Body Partially Paralysed, Hands Feet Callus Thick.
29	及受舜禅，	Then Accepted Shun's Abdication,
30	卑宫室，美绂冕，	Humble Palace Courts, Beautiful Ritual Attires,
31	戚戚然以至于死：	Anxiously Naturally To Reach Till Death:
32	此天人之忧苦者也。	This Most Caring Hardworking Person beneath Heaven.
33	武王既终，	King Wu Already Dead,
34	成王幼弱，	King Cheng (son) Young Weak,
35	周公摄天子之政。	Duke Zhou Assumed Governing for Son Of Heaven.
36	邵公不悦，	Duke Shao Not Happy,
37	四国流言。	4 States Spreading Rumours.
38	居东三年，	Campaigned East for 3 Years (Duke Zhou),
39	诛兄放弟，	Killed Elder-brother Banished Young-brother,
40	仅免其身，	Just Avoided Own Bodily (harm)
41	戚戚然以至于死：	Sadly Naturally To Reach Till Death:

7.11 Sages 4 and Evils 2

42	此天人之危惧者也。	This Most Threatened Terrified Person beneath Heaven.
43	孔子明帝王之道，	Kongzi Enlightened in The 'Dao' of Emperors and Kings,
44	应时君之聘，	Responding to Current Kings Their Engagements,
45	伐树于宋，	Fell Tree At state of Song (threaten),
46	削迹于卫，	Cut Trail At state of Wei (into hiding),
47	穷于商周，	Confined At Shangzhou (place),
48	围于陈，蔡，	Besieged At Chen-Cai (area between),
49	受屈于季氏，	Treated Lowly Under Jishi,
50	见辱于阳虎，	Suffered Humiliation Under Yanghu,
51	戚戚然以至于死：	Sadly Naturally To Reach Till Death:
52	此天民之遑遽者也。	This Most Frightened Worrying Person beneath Heaven.
53	凡彼四圣者，	All Those 4 Persons of Sagehood,
54	生无一日之欢，	Living with Not 1 Day Of Happiness,
55	死有万世之名。	Dead then Has Reputation Of 10,000 Generations.
56	名者，	Name (reputation) Entity,
57	固非实之所取也。	Certainly Not What is Attained In Reality that's.
58	虽称之弗知，	Though Praised Him Not Knowing,
59	虽赏之不知，	Though Rewarding Him Not Knowing,
60	与株块无以异矣。	With Wooden Block Cannot Be Differentiated indeed.
61	桀藉累世之资，	Jie With Accumulated Wealth of Generations,
62	居南面之尊，	Sat South Facing The Honor (as king),
63	智足以距群下，	Intelligence Enough To Distant the Crowd Below,
64	威足以震海内；	Power Enough To Shake Oceans Within (the lands);
65	恣耳目之所娱，	Indulging The Ears Eyes for Whatever Entertainments,
66	穷意虑之所为，	Exhausting The Mind Desires for Whatever Actions,
67	熙熙然以至于死：	Happily Naturally To Reach Till Death:
68	此天民之逸荡者也。	This Most Leisurely Swinging Person beneath Heaven.
69	纣亦藉累世之资，	Zhou Also With Accumulated Wealth of Generations,
70	居南面之尊；	Sat South Facing The Prestige (as king);
71	威无不行，	Orders None Not Implemented,
72	志无不从；	Wills None Not Obeyed;
73	肆情于倾宫，	Wanton Emotions In Upsetting Palaces,
74	纵欲于长夜；	Indulging Desires In Long Nights;
75	不以礼义自苦，	Not With Ethics Justice Restricting Self,
76	熙熙然以至于诛：	Joyously Naturally To Reach Till Execution:
77	此天民之放纵者也。	This The Most Indulgent Citizen beneath Heaven that's.
78	彼二凶也，	Those 2 Evils that's,
79	生有纵欲之欢，	Living Had Joy Of Indulgence,
80	死被愚暴之名。	Dead Blanketed With the Name of Stupidity, Violence.
81	实者，	The Reality,
82	固非名之所与也，	Certainly Not What The Name can Give that's,
83	虽毁之不知，	Though Destroying It, Not Knowing,
84	虽称之弗知，	Though Praising It, Not Knowing,
85	此与株块奚以异矣？	This With Wood Block How To Differentiate, Indeed ?

7.11 Sages 4 and Evils 2

86 *彼四圣虽美之所归,*	***Those 4 Sages Though The Praise Be Bestowed,***
87 苦以至终,	Hardships Bore Till the End,
88 同于死矣。	Similarly To Death indeed.
89 *彼二凶虽恶之所归,*	***Those 2 Evils Though The Curse Be Bestowed,***
90 乐以至终,	Happiness Enjoyed Till the End,
91 亦同归于死矣。"	Also Similarly Returned To Death indeed."

Liezi Text Narrative

Yangzhu said: "Beneath Heaven, the Beautiful ascribed to sages Shun, Yu Zhou, Kong; L3
Beneath Heaven, the Evil ascribed to King Jie and King Zhou. L5
But then Shun farming at Heyang, making pottery at Leize; L7
Four limbs not getting a moment of rest, mouth stomach not getting good rich food; L9
Father, mother, brothers, sisters did not love, going-on 30, married and parents not informed. L13
Then accepted Yao's abdication, his age had increased and his mind had deteriorated. L16
Shangjun the son was not talented, so abdicated to Yu and sadly naturally lived till death: L19
Shun is the most suffering person beneath Heaven, that's. L20
Gun was sent to tame the great Deluge with no success and Shun executed him at Mount Yu. L23
The son Yu inherited his task on the great Deluge, serving enemy Shun who killed his father. L24
Focused on taming the Deluge, he bypassed his own son's naming, bypassing home 3 times. L27
Own body partially paralysed, hands feet callus and thick, then accepted Shun's abdication. L29
Lived in humble palaces, attired beautifully only in rites, anxiously naturally lived till death: L31
Yu is the most caring hardworking person beneath Heaven, that's. L32
King Wu was already dead, the son King Cheng was very young, so Duke Zhou took charge. L35
Duke Shao was not happy, spreading rumours in 4 states that Duke Zhou usurped the throne. L37
Campaigned for 3 years in the east, killed his elder-brother, banished his younger brother. L39
Just avoided own body injury, sadly naturally lived till death: L41
Duke Zhou is the most threatened and terrified person beneath Heaven, that's. L42
Kongzi understood Emperors Kings their 'Dao', responding to current kings engagements. L44
Threatened with his tree cut at the state of Song, and fearing trouble went into hiding at Wei. L46
Confined at Shangzhou, besieged at the border of Chen-Cai, and treated lowly under Jishi. L49
Suffered humiliation under Yanghu, sadly naturally lived till death: L51
Kongzi is the most frightened worrying person beneath Heaven, that's. L52
Those 4 sage-persons, alive not 1 day of happiness, after death have a reputation forever. L55
Name (reputation) entity, certainly not what is attained in reality that's. L57
Praised him not knowing, rewarded him not knowing, no feeling like a piece of wood. L60
King Jie, with amassed wealth of generations, sat on his honorable throne facing south. L62
With intelligence far above his subjects, power to command all lands within ocean borders. L64
Indulged ears eyes for all pleasures, exhausted all mind desires for actions, happily till death. L67
King Jie is the most leisurely swinging person beneath Heaven, that's. L68
King Zhou, with amassed wealth of generations, sat on his honorable throne facing south. L70
Orders none not implemented, and wills none not obeyed; L72
Wanton emotions upsetting palaces, indulging desires into the long nights; L74
No self restriction with ethics and justice. joyously naturally lived till execution: L76
King Zhou is the most indulgent citizen beneath Heaven, that's. L77
Those 2 evils, living had joy of indulgence, after death had names for stupidity, violence. L80

7.11 Sages 4 and Evils 2

The reality, certainly not what a name can give that's. L82
Though destroyed or praised, not knowing, so how to differentiate from a piece of wood ? L85
Those 4 sages though praise be bestowed, hardships were borne to the end, till death. L88
Those 2 evils though curses be bestowed, happiness was enjoyed to the end, till death." L91

Comments:
7.11 Sages 4 and Evils 2
All beautiful praises were ascribed to sages like Emperor Shun, Emperor Yu, Duke Zhou, Kongzi. And all evils were ascribed to King Jie and King Zhou.

Shun, farming at Heyang, making pottery at Leize, not a moment's rest and no good food.
No love from parents and siblings, going-on 30, not filial married without informing parents.
Then accepted Yao's abdication, and in old age abdicated to Yu as son Shangjun, not talented.
Sadly, naturally lived till death, Sun was the most suffering person beneath Heaven, that's.
Yu was tasked to tame the Deluge after father Gun was executed by Emperor Shun for his failure.
Focused on the Deluge, bypassed home 3 times, with callus hands and feet till partially paralysed.
Accepted Shun's abdication, lived in humble palaces, attired beautifully only in performing rites.
Anxiously naturally lived till death, Yu was the most caring hardworking person beneath Heaven.
Duke Zhou took charge when King Wu died and his son King Cheng was still very young.
Duke Shao rumoured that he usurped the throne, hence he had to campaign 3 year in the East.
Killed elder brother Duke Shao and banished younger brother, thus avoiding harm to himself.
Sadly lived till death, Duke Zhou was the most threatened and terrified person beneath Heaven.
Kongzi understood the 'Dao' of kings and emperors, and responded to their engagements.
However he was threatened at Song, went into hiding at Wei and was confined at Shangzhou.
Besieged at the border of Chen-Cai, treated lowly by Jishi and humiliated by Yanghu.
Sadly lived till death, Kongzi was the most frightened and worrying person beneath Heaven.
Sages 4, suffering harsh realities in life, but not feeling the praises in name after death.

King Jie, intelligence far above subjects, power enough to command all lands within the oceans.
Indulging all the senses with pleasures, and exhausting all the mind's desires for actions.
Happily lived till death, King Jie was the most leisurely swinging person beneath Heaven, that's.
King Zhou's orders, none not implemented and wills, none not obeyed.
Indulging desires into the long nights, and with wanton emotions upsetting the palaces.
Joyously lived till execution, King Zhou was the most indulgent citizen beneath Heaven, that's.
Evils 2, kings enjoyed all the pleasures in life, not feeling the degrading names after death.

Suffer the hardships of sagehood or enjoy the indulgence of evilness, what is your choice !

7.12 鸿鹄高飞   7.12 Great Eagle Flies High

01	杨朱见梁王，	Yangzhu went to See King Liang,
02	言治天下如运诸掌。	Said Governing The World Like Playing In Palm.
03	梁王曰：	King Liang Said:
04	"先生有一妻一妾而不能治，	"Sir Has 1 Wife 1 Concubine And Not Able to Control,
05	三亩之园而不能芸；	3 Acres Of Garden And Not Able to Cultivate;
06	而言治天下如运诸掌，	And Said Governing The World Like Playing In Palm,
07	何也？"	How that's ?"
08	对曰：	Answering Said:
09	"君见其牧羊者乎？	"Your Highness Seen the Goat Herder Person right ?
10	百羊而群，	100 Goats In Herd,
11	使五尺童子荷箠而随之，	Allow 5-Foot Small Child Carry Whip To Follow It,
12	欲东而东，	Wishing East Go East,
13	欲西而西。	Wishing West Go West.
14	使尧牵一羊，	Allow Yao Leading 1 Goat,
15	舜荷箠而随之，	Shun Carry Whip To .Follow It,
16	则不能前矣。	Then Not Able Forward indeed.
17	且臣闻之：	And Subject-me Heard It:
18	吞舟之鱼，	Fish That Swallow a Boat,
19	不游枝流；	Not Swim in Branch Flow (tributary);
20	***鸿鹄高飞，***	***Great Eagles Fly High,***
21	不集洿池。	Not Gathers Stagnant Pond.
22	何则？	What Reason?
23	其极远也。	Their (vision) Absolute and Far that's.
24	黄钟大吕	Huangzhong, Dalu, (ancient temple music)
25	不可从烦奏之舞，	Not Possible Accompany Dance Of Quick Tempo,
26	何则？	What Reason ?
27	其音疏也。	The Tones Sparse that's.
28	将治大者不治细，	Person Will Govern Big, Not Govern Small,
29	成大功者不成小，	Person Achieves Big Success, Not Achieve Small,
30	此之谓矣。"	This The Explanation indeed."

7.12 Great Eagle Flies High

Liezi Text Narrative
Yangzhu went to see King Liang, and said governing the world was like play in the palm. L2
King Liang said: "Sir has 1 wife, 1 concubine cannot control; has 3 acres garden cannot weed. L5
Then you said governing the world is like playing in palm, how's that ?" L7
Yangzhu answering said: "Your Highness has seen the goat herder person, right ? L9
A herd of 100 goats, allow a 5-foot boy to carry a whip and follow them. L11
Wishing to go east, go east; wishing to go west, go west. L13
Allow Yao to lead 1 goat, Shun carrying a whip to follow, then not able to forward indeed. L16
And Subject-me heard this, fish that can swallow a boat, will not swim in tributary flow. L19
Great Eagles flying high, not gathering on stagnant ponds, reasons ? Its vision far and wide. L23
Huangzhong Dalu for ancient temple music, cannot accompany dance at a quick tempo. L25
Reasons ? The tones sparse that's. L27
Person who governs big, cannot govern small; can achieve big success but not small success. L29
This is the explanation indeed." L30

Comments:
7.12 Great Eagle Flies High
Yangzhu went to see King Liang and said governing the world was like playing it in the palm.
King Liang challenged him saying he cannot even control his wife, concubine and 3 acres of land.

Yangzhu countered saying that a little boy following can handle a herd of 100 goats with a whip.
But Emperor Yao leading a goat and Emperor Shun carrying a whip behind, cannot go forward !
That a big fish that can swallow a boat, will not swim in a small tributary river.
That great eagles flying high will not land on stagnant ponds, reasons, its vision far and wide.
Huangzhong and Dalu are for temple rites, not for quick tempo dance, reasons, tones are sparse.
Hence explained, a person who governs big cannot govern small, can achieve big but not small.

Example, a great general can plan a huge campaign but may not fight off a single assassin !

Chapter 7. Yangzhu (杨朱)

7.13 何生之乐   7.13 What's Happiness of Life

01	杨朱曰：	Yangzhu Said:
02	"太古之事灭矣，	"Most Ancient-time The Affairs Destroyed indeed,
03	孰志之哉？	Who is to Remember Them, is-it-not ?
04	三皇之事若存若亡；	3 Sovereigns Their Affairs Like Surviving Like Lost;
05	五帝之事若觉若梦；	5 Emperors Their Affairs Like Awareness Like Dreams;
06	三王之事或隐或显，	3 Kings Their Affairs Like Hidden Like Revealed,
07	亿不识一。	100-millions Not Know 1.
08	当身之事或闻或见，	May Be Personal Affairs Or Heard Or Seen,
09	万不识一。	10,000 Not Know 1.
10	目前之事或存或废，	Affairs In-front of Eyes May Keep May Abandon,
11	千不识一。	1,000 Not Know 1.
12	太古至于今日，	Most Ancient-time Reaching To This Day,
13	年数固不可胜纪。	Year Numbers Surely Not Able to Record Successfully .
14	但伏羲已来三十餘万岁，	But From Fuxi Coming-down 300,000 More Years,
15	贤愚、好丑、	Clever/Stupid, Good/Evil,
16	成败、是非，	Success/Failure, Right/Wrong,
17	无不消灭；	None Not Eliminated Extinguished;
18	但迟速之间耳。	But Sooner or Later The Timing Only.
19	矜一时之毁誉，	Valued 1 Moment Of Shame or Honor
20	以焦苦其神形，	To Burn the Spirit and Suffered the Form,
21	要死后	Chasing the After Death
22	数百年中餘名，	Residual Reputation Of Several Hundreds Years,
23	岂足润枯骨？	Where Enough to Nourish the Dry Bones ?
24	*何生之乐哉？"*	***What's Happiness Of Life , is-it-not ?"***

7.13 What's Happiness of Life

Liezi Text Narrative
Yangzhu said: "Affairs of Most ancient times are extinguished, as who is there to remember ? L3
The 3 sovereigns' affairs like survived or lost; the 5 emperors' affairs like aware or dreams; L5
The 3 kings' affairs, like hidden, like revealed; only know 1 in 100 millions . L7
May be personal affairs, or heard, or seen, only know 1 in 10,000. L9
Affairs in front of our eyes, may keep may abandon, only know 1 in 1,000. L11
Most ancient times till this day, the number of years are surely not recorded successfully. L13
But from Fuxi coming down 300,000 or more years, the clever/stupid, the good/evil; L15
The success/failure, the right/wrong, none not eliminated and extinguished; L17
Sooner or later, it's just a matter of time only. L18
Because of treasuring a moment of shame or glory, to burn the spirit and distress the body. L20
Chasing residual glory for hundreds of years after death, how able to nourish the dry bones ? L23
So what is the Happiness of Life, is-it-not ?"

Comments:
7.13 What's Happiness of Life
Yangzhu said that affairs of ancient times were all lost, as who were there to remember, record ?
 Sovereigns, 3: Fuxi (**伏羲**, c.3,000BC), Nuwa (**女娲**, c.3,000BC), Shennong (**神农**, c.3,000BC).
These 3 ancient sovereigns of Chinese mythology 5,000 years ago, their true accounts were lost.
Emperors, 5: Huangdi (**黄帝**, c.2,700BC) , Zhuan (**颛**), Hu (**喾**), Yao (**尧**, c.2,400BC), Shun(**舜**).
These 5 emperors of prehistoric Chinese culture 4,500 years ago, their accounts were like dreams.
Kings, 3: Yu (Xia dynasty, c. 2,100BC), Tang (Shang, c. 1,600BC), Wen (Zhou, c. 1,000BC).
These 3 kings of historic Chinese dynasties, their revelations, only know 1 in 100 millions.
Our own personal affairs heard or seen, only know 1 in 10,000.
Even affairs happening in front of our eyes, may retain, may forget, only know 1 in 1,000.
So, from Fuxi down, the clever/stupid, success/failure, right/wrong, all true facts lost with time.

Residual glories thousands of years after death do not nourish their dry bones, do them any good.
Liezi is in favor of enjoying Happiness in life, and not suffering to chase for glory-after-death.
Earlier, Liezi 7.11 has narrated the suffering-lives of 4 Sages and the indulgent-lives of 2 Evils.

Happiness in life can be whatever we enjoy in doing, even enjoy suffering for a good cause !

7.14 至人   7.14 Ultra Person

01	杨朱曰：	Yangzhu Said:
02	"人肖天地之类，	"Human The Best Kind of Heaven Earth,
03	怀五常之性，	Embrace The 5 Elements' Characteristics,
04	有生之最灵者也。	Has Life Of Most Spirited Kind, that's.
05	人者，	Human Kind,
06	爪牙不足以供守卫，	Claws Teeth Not Enough To Provide Guard Defence,
07	肌肤不足以自捍御，	Muscles Skins Not Enough For Self Defend Drive-off,
08	趋走不足以从利逃害，	Fast Walking Not Enough To Chase Gain, Escape Danger.
09	无毛羽以御寒暑，	No Hairs Feathers To Drive-off Cold Heat,
10	必将资物以为养，	Must Use Resource Material For Self Support,
11	任智而不恃力。	Use Wisdom And Not Depend on Strength.
12	故智之所贵，	Hence What is Valuable Is Wisdom,
13	存我为贵；	My Survival enhanced, hence wisdom Is Valued;
14	力之所贱，	Strength Its That-which is Lowly,
15	侵物为贱。	Intruding Material Hence Lowly.
16	然身非我有也，	Naturally Body Not My Possession that's,
17	既生，	Already Born-living,
18	不得不全之；	Not Allow to Not Preserve It (life);
19	物非我有也，	Material Not My Possession that's.
20	既有，	Already Possessed,
21	不得而去之。	Not Allow To Abandon Them.
22	身固生之主，	Body Certainly is Life's Master,
23	物亦养之主。	Material Also is Support's Master.
24	虽全生，	Though Preserving Life,
25	不可有其身；	Not Allow Possessing The Body;
26	虽不去物，	Though Not Abandon Material,
27	不可有其物。	Not Allow Possessing The Material.
28	有其物，	Possessing The Material,
29	有其身，	Possessing The Body,
30	是横私天下之身，	Is Perversely Privatizing The World's Body,
31	横私天下之物。	Perversely Privatizing The World's Material.
32	不横私天下身，	Not Perversely Privatizing The World's Body,
33	不横私天下物者，	Person Not Perversely Privatizing The World's Material
34	其唯圣人乎！	That Only Sage Person Capable !
35	*公天下之身，*	***Publicize The Body to The World,***
36	*公天下之物，*	***Publicize The Material to The World,***
37	*其唯至人矣！*	***That Only the Ultra Person is Capable !***
38	此之谓至至者也。"	This Is Called Achieving the Ultra Person that's."

7.14 Ultra Person

Liezi Text Narrative
Yangzhu said: "People, the best kind of Heaven Earth, embrace 5 elements' characteristics. L3
Has life of the most spirited kind that's (benevolence, justice, ethics, intelligence, trust). L4
Humankind, claws teeth not enough for defence, muscles skin not enough for self protection. L7
Speed, not enough to chase advantage or escape danger, no hairs feathers to resist cold heat. L9
Must use resource material for self support, use Wisdom and not depend on Strength. L11
Hence what is valuable is Wisdom, which enhance my survival thus is valued; L13
Strength is that which is lowly, intruding into others, thus lowly. L15
Naturally my body not my possession, as already born, not allowed not to preserve Life; L18
Material not my possession that's, but already possessed, not allowed to abandon it. L21
Body certainly is Life's master, material also is master of Life-support. L23
Life preserved, but possession not allowed; Material not abandoned, possession not allowed. L27
Possessing the material and body are perversely privatizing the world's body and material. L31
Not perversely privatizing the world's body and material, only the sage person is capable ! L34
To publicize body and material to the world, only the *Ultra Person* is capable ! L37
This is called achieving the enlightenment of the *Ultra Person* that's." L38

Comments:
7.14 Ultra Person
Heaven and Earth are made of 5 basic elements, namely Metal, Wood, Water, Fire and Soil.
Their corresponding characteristics are namely Love, Justice, Ethics, Wisdom and Trust.
Yangzhu said; "Humanity is the best kind of Heaven Earth, having the 5 elements and characters.

However human kind is weak, claws and teeth not enough for defence, no strong muscles, skin.
Speed not enough to chase advantage or escape danger, no hairs feathers to resist cold heat.
Must use resources for self support and to enhance survival must use Wisdom, hence valued.
Strength can be invasive of others, thus considered lowly, its use to be discouraged.

I own nothing, all my body and material possessions are perversely privatized from the world.
Not to perversely privatize body and material possessions from the world, only sage people can.
To publicize body and material possessions back to the world, only the Ultra Person is capable.
The Ultra Person is wise, unselfish.

Humans, weak skin, claws, teeth, strength for defence; the Ultra Person is wise, unselfish.

7.15 寿，名，位，货　　7.15 Longevity, Honor, Power, Wealth

01	杨朱曰：	Yangzhu Said:
02	"生民之不得休息，	"Living Citizens They Not Able to Rest Relax,
03	为四事故：	For 4 Matters or Reasons:
04	*一为寿，二为名，*	*1 For Longevity, 2 For Name (honor)*
05	*三为位，四为货。*	*3 For Status (power), 4 For Commodity (wealth)*
06	有此四者，	Have These 4 Reasons,
07	畏鬼，畏人，	Fear Devils, Fear People,
08	畏威，畏刑，	Fear Power, Fear Punishment,
09	此谓之遁民也。	These Called Them Escapist Citizens that's.
10	可杀可活，	Able be Killed Able to Survive,
11	制命在外。	Control of Destiny On the Outside.
12	不逆命，何羡寿？	Not Opposing Destiny, Why Envy Longevity ?
13	不矜贵，何羡名？	Not Valuing Honor, Why Envy Name ?
14	不要势，何羡位？	Not Desiring Power, Why Envy Status ?
15	不贪富，何羡货？	Not Greedy of Wealth, Why Envy Possession ?
16	此之谓顺民也。	These Are Called Natural Citizens that's.
17	天下无对，	Heaven Beneath No Equals (undefeated)
18	制命在内，	Control of Destiny On the Inside,
19	故语有之曰：	Thus Sayings Have This, Said:
20	'人不婚宦，	'People No Marriage Officialdom ,
21	情欲失半；	Emotions Desires Lost Half;
22	人不衣食，	People Not Clothe Eating,
23	君臣道息。'	King/Subjects Way Terminated.'
24	周谚曰：	Zhou Proverb Said:
25	'田父可坐杀。'	'Farming Elder Possible Sitting to Death.'
26	晨出夜入，	Dawn Out Evening Return,
27	自以性之恒；	Self Realise Characteristic Is Permanent
28	啜菽茹藿，	Sipping Soya-milk, Eating Beans,
29	自以味之极；	Self Thought Taste Is Best;
30	肌肉粗厚，	Muscle Flesh Tough and Thick,
31	筋节腾急，	Tendons Joints Tense and Prominent,
32	一朝处以柔毛绨幕，	One Morning Lying On Soft Down in Woven Tent,
33	荐以粱肉兰橘，	Offered With Sorghum Meat Fragrant Orange,
34	心痞体烦，	Heart Sick, Body Irritated,
35	内热生病矣。	Internal Heat Giving-rise to Sickness that's.
36	商鲁之君与田父侔地，	Shang Lu Their Kings With Farmer Elder Same Position,
37	则亦不盈一时而惫矣。	Then Also Not Fully Two Hour Will Tired-out indeed.
38	故野人之所安，	Hence Outdoor Person Whatever His Comfort,
39	野人之所美，	Outdoor Person Whatever He Admires,
40	谓天下无过者。	Call-it Heaven Beneath None Exceeding It.
41	昔者宋国有田夫，	Previously, State of Song Has Farmer Person,

7.15 Longevity, Honor, Power, Wealth

42	常衣缊<麻黂>,	Often Clothe in Hemp Coat,
43	仅以过冬。	Barely To Survive Winter.
44	暨春东作,	Early Spring Planting Season,
45	自曝于日,	Self Exposed Under Sun,
46	不知天下	Not Knowing Heaven Beneath
47	之有广厦隩室,	There Is Spacious Mansion Warm Rooms,
48	绵纩狐貉。	Fine Silk Mink Fur.
49	顾谓其妻曰:	Turning and Talking to His Wife Said:
50	'负日之暄,	'Bearing Sun Its Warmth
51	人莫知者;	People None Knowing This;
52	以献吾君,	To Offer Our King,
53	将有重赏。'	Will Get a Big Reward.'
54	里之富室告之曰:	Village The Wealthy Family Informed Him Said:
55	'昔人有美戎菽,	'Formerly Person Had Nice Wild Soya,
56	甘枲茎芹萍子者,	Sweet Stem Celery Duckweed Kinds,
57	对乡豪称之。	Recommending Them To Village Wealthy.
58	乡豪取而尝之,	Village Wealthy Took And Tasted Them,
59	蜇于口,	Stinging In Mouth,
60	惨于腹,	Suffering In Stomach,
61	众哂而怨之,	Crowd Laughed And Cursed Him,
62	其人大惭。	That Person Greatly Ashamed.
63	子此类也。'"	Sir, This Type that's.' "

Liezi Text Narrative

Yangzhu said: "Citizens are not able to relax for 4 reasons: longevity, glory, status, wealth. L5
For these 4 reasons, citizens fear devils, fear people, fear power, fear punishment. L8
These are escapist citizens, can be killed, can survive, and control of destiny is from outside. L11
Not opposing destiny, why envy Longevity ? Not valuing Honor why envy Name ? L13
Not desiring power, why envy Status ? Not greedy for Wealth, why envy possession ? L15
These are natural citizens, Heaven beneath undefeated, and control of destiny from within. L18
*Hence these sayings: 'People no marriage no officialdom, emotions desires are half lost; L21
People not clothed, not eating, the king/subjects relationship will be terminated.' L23*

Zhou Proverb said: 'Farming elders can die sitting (bored to death).' L25
Dawn out evening return, self considered this characteristic is permanent; L27
Sipping soya-milk, eating beans, self thought taste is the best; L29
Muscle flesh tough and thick, tendons joints tense and prominent. L31
One morning lying on soft down in woven tent, being offered sorghum meat, fragrant orange; L33
Will feel heart sick, body irritated and internal heat rising to cause sickness that's. L35
Kings of Shang and Lu, in the position of elder farmer, will be tired-out within 2 hours indeed. 37
Outdoor person's whatever comfort or admiration, thought cannot be exceeded in the world. L40

7.15 Longevity, Honor, Power, Wealth

The state of Song had a farmer, often clothed in hemp coat, barely able to survive winter. L43
Spring planting season, self exposed under sun, not known world has mansion, warm rooms. L47
Not knowing fine silk mink fur, to wife said: 'Bearing sun its warmth, people do not know. L51
With this information to offer our King, will get a big reward.' L53
The village wealthy family informed him said: 'Formerly, a person had nice wild soya; L55
Sweet stem celery duckweed kinds, and recommending them to the village wealthy people. L57
Village wealthy people took and tasted them, resulting in a stinging mouth, bad stomach. L60
The crowd laughed and cursed him; that person was greatly ashamed. L62
Sir, and you are this kind that's.'" L63

Comments:
7.15 Longevity, Honor, Power, Wealth

Yangzhu says that citizens cannot relax as they strive for: Longevity, Honor, Power and Wealth.
And to achieve them, citizens fear evils, fear other people, fear power and fear punishment.
These are escapist citizens, as to survive or be killed, the control of their destiny is from without.
Not envious for Longevity, not envious for Name, not envious for Status, not envious for Wealth.
These are natural citizens and they are undefeatable, as control of their destiny is from within.
Be relaxed natural citizens, not striving for Longevity, Honor, Power, Wealth; destiny in our hands.

Zhou Proverb: "Farming elders can die sitting."; bored to death if not working !
Worked at dawn, returned at night, sipping soya-milk eating beans, feeling them the best of taste.
If offered sorghum meat in woven tent lying on soft down, his internal heat rises causing illness.
In contrast Kings of Shang and Lu will be tired out within 2 hours working like the farmer elders.
Therefore indoor or outdoor, people's different comforts are not comparable in their own world.

Strive for Longevity, Honor, Power, Wealth, then control of our destiny is from without !

Chapter 7. Yangzhu (杨朱)

7.16 屋服，味色   7.16 House Clothes, Food Sex

01	杨朱曰：	Yangzhu Said:
02	*"丰屋美服，*	*"Luxurious House Beautiful Clothes,*
03	*厚味姣色，*	*Rich Taste (food) Pretty Color (sex)*
04	有此四者，	Having These 4 Things,
05	何求于外？	What Else To Request ?
06	有此而求外者，	People Having These And still Request More,
07	无厌之性。	Never Dislike (always greedy) This Character.
08	无厌之性，	Never Dislike (wanting ever more) This Character,
09	阴阳之蠹也。	The Termites of Yin Yang (Nature) that's.
10	忠不足以安君，	Loyalty Not Enough To Calm King,
11	适足以危身；	Suitable Enough To Endanger Self;
12	义不足以利物，	Righteousness Not Enough To Benefit Matters,
13	适足以害生。	Suitable Enough To Harm Lives.
14	安上不由于忠，	Saving Above (king) Not Due To Loyalty,
15	而忠名灭焉；	Then Loyalty Name Dies indeed;
16	利物不由于义，	Benefiting Matters Not Due to Righteousness,
17	而义名绝焉。	Then Righteousness Name Dies indeed.
18	君臣皆安，	King Ministers All Safe,
19	物我兼利，	Matters and I Together Benefiting,
20	古之道也。	Ancients' Way that's.
21	鬻子曰：	Yuzi Said:
22	'去名者无忧。'	'Person Abandons Name No Worries.'
23	老子曰：	Laozi Said:
24	'名者实之宾。'	'Name Entity, Guest of Reality (the master).'
25	而悠悠者趋名不已。	But Long-time People Chasing Name Not Stopping.
26	名固不可去？	Name Certainly Not Allow Losing ?
27	名固不可宾邪？	Name Certainly Not Allow Subjugating, Is-it-not ?
28	今有名则尊荣，	Now Having Name Then Respected Honored,
29	亡名则卑辱。	No Name Then Lowly and Disgraceful.
30	尊荣则逸乐，	Respected Honored Then Relax Happy,
31	卑辱则忧苦。	Lowly Disgraceful Then Worrying Sad.
32	忧苦，	Worries Sadness,
33	犯性者也；	These Against Character (nature) that's;
34	逸乐，	Relaxation Happiness
35	顺性者也，	Accordant with Character (nature) that's,
36	斯实之所系矣。	That is What Reality Is Connected indeed.
37	名胡可去？	Name Why Allow Abandoning ?
38	名胡可宾？	Name Why Allow Subjugating ?
39	但恶夫守名而累实。	But Evil Person Guarding Name And Tiring Reality.
40	守名而累实，	Guarding Name And Tiring Reality,
41	将恤危亡之不救，	Will be Aware of Danger Loss And Not Saving,
42	岂徒逸乐	Why Chase Relaxation Happiness
43	忧苦之间哉？"	In Among Worries Sadness Is-it-not ?"

7.16 House Clothes, Food Sex

Liezi Text Narrative
Yangzhu said: "Luxurious house, beautiful clothes, rich food, pretty color (sex). L3
Having these 4 things, what else to request ? L5
People having these and still request for more, are greedy in character. L7
Greedy people are like termites of nature, destructive that's. L9
Loyalty, not enough to save the king, but suitable enough to endanger self; L11
Righteousness not enough to benefit matters, but suitable enough to harm lives. L13
Saving the King not due to loyalty, then the name of loyalty dies indeed; L15
Benefiting matters not due to righteousness, then the name of righteousness dies indeed. L17
King and Ministers all safe, matters and I together benefit, this the ancients' way that's. L20
Yuzi said: 'Person who abandons name or celebrity, has no worries.' L22
Laozi said: 'Name (fame) entity, guest of reality (the master).' L24
But for a long time, people have been chasing fame non-stop. L25
Name (fame) certainly not allow to be lost, and also not allow to be subjugated, is-it-not ? L27
Now having name (fame) then get respected, honored, no name then is lowly and disgraced. L29
Respected honored then relaxed and happy, else lowly and disgrace then worrying and sad. L31
Worries and sadness, these are against our character that's; L33
Relaxation and happiness, in accord with our character, are what we needed in our reality. L36
Name or fame, why allow to be abandoned, to be subjugated ? L38
But the fierce person in guarding his name or fame, tired-out in reality, not enjoying life. L39
Guarding name till exhausting the reality, like knowing the danger yet not saving ourselves; L41
Why chase the relaxation and happiness in among the worries and sadness, right ?" L43

Comments:
7.16 House Clothes, Food Sex
Yangzhu said we all need nice housing, nice clothes, rich food and pretty wives.
Requesting more are greedy characters, and these people are like termites of nature, destructive.
So have our needs for housing, clothes, food and sex, and not be greedy for more.

Loyalty cannot save the king, righteousness cannot benefit matters but harm lives.
Loyalty, righteousness all dead; the ancient way, king/ministers all safe, matters/I together benefit.
When nobody is greedy, no need for loyalty, justice; king/minister/matters/I, together benefit.

Yuzi said: 'Person who abandons name or celebrity, has no worries.'
Laozi said: 'Name (fame) entity, guest of reality (the master).'
Relaxing happiness is in accord with our character; worries and sadness are against our nature.
In reality, having fame get respected and honored; and having no fame is lowly and insulted.
We ought to be happy and relax in life, so why allow fame be abandoned and subjugated ?
For a long time, people have been chasing fame non-stop till exhausted, not able to enjoy life.
So we have a dilemma, chasing happiness in among the worries and sadness, is-it-not ?
Celebrity is an exhaustive business; so abandon name, have no worries; enjoy more life.

Liezi: World of Delusions

Chapter 7. Yangzhu (杨朱)

Summary

7.1 Honest Dishonest The Debate (实伪之辩): Mengshi:the honest poor, the dishonest wealthy. Yangzhu cited many examples for and against honesty and dishonesty, thus true, and not true.

7.2 Person's Life, What Purpose ? (人之生也奚为哉?): Life is a short sojourn here on earth. Not shackle by wants of fame and wealth, follow our nature to play without intruding others.

7.3 Different in Life, Same in Death (异者生, 同者死): King/pauper in life, all bones in death. Thus shall we not then enjoy Life while living and not to worry about Death and thereafter.

7.4 Purity Chastity (清贞): These are good virtues and are the aspiration of many good people. But when held to the extreme, resulted in death for Boyi and lack of off-springs for Zhanji.

7.5 Happy Living, Relaxing Body (乐生, 逸身): We ought to live happy and relaxing lives. Yuanxian contented in poverty, no happy life; Zigong tired in heavy trading, no relaxed life.

7.6 The Pathways of Life/Death (生死之道): Life is mutual Sympathy, Death is mutual Loss. Sympathy is to rest the industrious, feed the hungry; Loss is to grieve, no rites, no sacrifices.

7.7 Internal, External Management (治外, 治内): Premier Zichan had 2 indulgent brothers. While Zichan labored outside, the alcoholic and womaniser brothers enjoyed lives inside.

7.8 Mad Man or Enlightened Man (狂人也, 达人也): Duanmushu had huge ancestral assets. He indulged in food, wine, music, travels, gave away what was left, nothing for his children.

7.9 And Long Life What For ? (且久生奚为 ?): 100 years would have seen it all, and hating it. Repetitions of the same suffering of emotions, bodily dangers, order/chaos, since ancient era.

7.10 Not Losing One Hair (不损一毫): To save the world is not selfish, just a logic position. Yangzhu said: " When no one needs to lose 1 hair to save the world, the world is in order."

7.11 Sages 4 and Evils 2 (四圣, 二凶): Yangzhu detailed their life sufferings and indulgence. Suffering the hardships of sagehood or enjoy the indulgence of evilness in life, your choice !

7.12 Great Eagle Flies High (鸿鹄高飞): It had vision, far and wide, Yangzhu told King Liang. Thus Yangzhu may not manage his family assets well, but can play the world in his palm.

7.13 Where is the Joy of Life ? (何生之乐哉?): Of our ancient sovereigns, emperors and kings. Scant records and faint memories of their glory are no compensation for their sufferings.

7.14 Only Sage Person Can ! (唯圣人乎 !): Acquires the attributes of an Ultimate person. Not privatizing his body and material possessions, but makes public, shares with the world.

7.15 Longevity, Honor, Power, Wealth (寿, 名, 位, 货): For these reasons, citizens not relaxed. These escapist citizens, destiny outside control; be natural citizens, destiny self control.

7.16 House, Clothes, Food, Sex (屋, 服, 味, 色): These are the basic 4 needs of all people. People having these and still request for more, are greedy, termites of nature, destructive.

Yangzhu says, life's a short sojourn, ought to relax, enjoy life without intruding on others. Yangzhu actually says, "If nobody needs to lose a hair to save society, society will be in order." Accusers of Yangzhu having a 'hedonistic philosophy' may have missed exactly what he says !

260

Chapter 8.   Charming Talks (説符)

Introduction
8.1 Watching The Shadow (顾若影)
8.2 Discerning the Reason Why So (察其所以然)
8.3 Difficulty in Government (治国之难)
8.4 Jade-Made Mulberry Leaf (玉为楮叶)
8.5 Minister Not Personally Know Me (君非自知我)
8.6 Principles Not Always Right (理无常是)
8.7 Also Had An Admirer (亦有招之者)
8.8 State of Jin Suffered Banditry (晋国苦盗)
8.9 Loyalty, Trust and Honesty (忠信诚)
8.10 Can People be Trusted with Secrets ? (人可与微言乎？)
8.11 Down 2 Cities in A Day (一朝而两城下)
8.12 A Kind and Righteous Family (好行仁义者)
8.13 King In Happy Mood (寡人有欢心)
8.14 Bole Assessment of Horses (伯乐相马)
8.15 Never: Self Chaotic, State Ordered (未闻身乱而国治)
8.16 People Have 3 Complaints (人有三怨)
8.17 This Land Is Bad (此地不利)
8.18 Bandits Have No Mercy ? (为盗仁将焉在？)
8.19 Disaster Falling From Heaven (飞鸢适坠其腐鼠)
8.20 Not Eating Bandit's Food (食为盗而不敢食)
8.21 Perverse Hatred (怼以忘其身者)
8.22 Enmity (ill-will) Brings Disaster (怨往者害来)
8.23 Many Branching Paths (多歧路)
8.24 Don't Blame The Dog ? (岂能无怪哉？)
8.25 Caution Doing Charity (慎为善)
8.26 'Dao' Of Life Everlasting (不死之道)
8.27 Liberating Life (放生)
8.28 Humanity Made For Mosquitoes Gnats (为蚊蚋生人)
8.29 No Shame Exceeds Begging (辱莫过于乞)
8.30 Perversely Wealthy (得人遗契者)
8.31 Withered Sycamore Tree (枯梧树)
8.32 No Actions Not Like Axe-Thief (无为而不窃鈇也)
8.33 Beigongsheng Pondering Rebellion (白公胜虑乱)
8.34 See Nobody Only Gold (不见人, 徒见金)
Summary

Liezi: World of Delusions

Chapter 8. Charming Talks (説符)

Introduction:
Miscellaneous charming talks on individuals' conduct, interaction with others, birds and animals. Also serious talks on difficulties in government, benefits of being virtuous, and life uncertainties. Discussion on life-everlasting and on whether humanity is made to feed mosquitoes and gnats !

Shadow moves depend on the body, to learn humility to follow; without respect, we are Animals.
Learning the reasons and principles for success and failure is more important; a tenet of Science.
Leaders, self virtuous not enough, need to engage other virtuous people to assist in Government.
Making a jade mulberry leaf has limited benefits; the sage uses 'Dao' to help transform People.
Liezi was wise to decline the minister he didn't know; Ziyang killed by rebels, Liezi not faulted.
Principles, not always right when situations changed and timing not right, thus fates not the same.
Man flirting with a woman in front, turned to find that his wife was also engaged with an admirer.
State of Jin suffered banditry, a great bandit-catcher was killed, Wenzi deployed civic education.
Man shot rapids, whirlpool with 'loyalty, trust', Confucius believed water can know loyalty, trust!
Kongzi said: "Absolute actions unselfish, no secrets."; Beigong schemed rebellion and was killed.
Taken 2 cities in a day, the great Xiangzi heard the good news and worried if this was sustainable.
Virtuous family, father and son had sudden blindness, spared conscription, recovered after war.
Performer found the King happy, awarded gold; next performer not so lucky, arrested and jailed.
Bole's friend Jiufanggao, found a black stallion he called yellow mare, a fine world class horse !
Zhanhe to King Zhang of Chu said: "The ruler self chaotic, and the state ordered, never happen."
People had 3 complaints, Sunshuao's solutions, be humble, be less ambitious and be generous.
Sushuao advised son to choose Qinqiu, a bad land that nobody wanted, for keeping it long term.
Bandits have no mercy; scholar Niuque, Yan people were killed for their threatening potentials.
Disaster falling from heaven when a flying eagle dropped its rotten rat on a line of swordsmen.
Aijingmu perversely refused to eat food from bandit Qiu, regurgitated till he died by the wayside.
Zhulishu, perversely returned to sacrifice for the duke to spite the latter for not appreciating him.
Yangzhu: "Hatred forth, disaster cometh."; goodwill begets goodwill, ill-will brings disaster.
Yangzhu was sad, not for loss of a goat, but scholars who lost focus over many branching paths.
Yangzhu asked his brother Pu, how he felt if his white dog went out and came back a black dog!
Yangzhi said: "Doing charity is not to make a name, but reputation, benefits, rivalry will follow."
Debate on whether the 'Dao' of life-everlasting can be passed on; No, as death is inevitable.
Jianzi rewarded citizens for bringing him doves; guest said, kinder to ban citizens catching them.
Top of the food chain, is humanity made for the mosquitoes and gnats; today, Covid19 says it all.
No shame exceeds begging; any work for food and lodging, ought to be respected.
Person perversely wealthy after collecting outdated contracts ! Lost sanity for wealth obsession.
Withered sycamore tree not auspicious, neighbor said; then asked for firewood after tree was cut.
Neighbor's son acted like an axe-thief; when the axe was recovered, his actions appeared normal.
Beigongsheng pondering rebellion, unaware his jaw was pierced, tripping, hitting head on poles.
"See nobody, only gold", the person said; obsession with gold causing delusion, illusion, crime.

Can you find a semblance of yourself reflected in the narratives, realise the fault and repent ?

Chapter 8. Charming Talks (*說符*)

8.1 顾若影

8.1 Watching The Shadow

01	子列子学于壶丘子林。	Teacher Liezi Under Tutelage of Huqiuzilin
02	壶丘子林曰：	Huiqiuzilin Said:
03	"子知持后，	"Sir Knows 'Keep Back' (humility),
04	则可言持身矣。"	Then Can Talk 'Keep Body' (life) that's.
05	列子曰：	Liezi Said:
06	"愿闻持后。"	"Willing to Hear 'Keep Back'."
07	曰：	Said:
08	*"顾若影，*	***"Watch The Shadow,***
09	则知之。"	Then Knows It."
10	列子顾而观影：	Liezi Watched And Observed the Shadow:
11	形枉则影曲，	Form (body) Crooked Then Shadow Curved,
12	形直则影正。	Form (body) Straighten Then Shadow Upright.
13	然则枉直随形而不在影，	But Then Crooked Straighten Follow Body Not Shadow,
14	屈申任物而不在我，	Bend Stretch Depended on Matter And Not On Self,
15	此之谓持后而处先。	This Is Called 'Keep Back' And be Positioned in Front.
16	关尹谓子列子曰：	Guanyin Told Teacher Liezi Said:
17	"言美则响美，	"Words Beautiful Then Echo Beautiful,
18	言恶则响恶；	Words Evil Then Echo Evil;
19	身长则影长，	Body Long Then Shadow Long,
20	身短则影短。	Body Short Then Shadow Short.
21	名也者，	Name Entity that's,
22	响也；	Echo that's;
23	身也者，	Body Entity that's,
24	影也。	Shadow that's.
25	故曰：	Hence Said:
26	慎尔言，	Careful Your Words,
27	将有和之；	Will Have Their Resonance;
28	慎尔行，	Careful with Your Actions,
29	将有随之，	Will Have Their Followers,
30	是故圣人见出以知入，	Thus Sage Person Saw Exiting To Know what Entered.
31	*观往以知来，*	*Observed the Past To Know the Coming (future),*
32	此其所以先知之理也。	This Is The Reason For Whatever Prior Knowing that's.
33	度在身，	Regulate By Self,
34	稽在人。	Check By People (others).
35	人爱我，	People Love Me,
36	我必爱之；	I Certainly Love Them;
37	人恶我，	People Hate Me,
38	我必恶之。	I Certainly Hate Them.
39	汤武爱天下，	Tang, Wu Loved The World,
40	故王；	Hence be Kings;

8.1 Watching The Shadow

41	桀纣恶天下，	Jie, Zhou Hated The World,
42	故亡，	Hence Perished,
43	此所稽也。	This was What had been Checked that's.
44	稽度皆明而不道也，	Checked Regulated All Clear And Not Ethical that's,
45	譬之出不由门，	Example of This like Exiting Not Through Door,
46	行不从径也。	Walking and Not Following Paths that's.
47	以是求利，	With This Aspiring for Gain,
48	不亦难乎？	Not Also Difficult right ?
49	尝观之神农有炎之德，	Often Observed It in Shennong Youyan Their Virtues,
50	稽之虞、夏、商、周之书，	Checked It in Yu, Xia, Shang, Zhou Their Books,
51	度诸法士贤人之言，	Assess Those Law Scholars Virtuous People Their Words,
52	所以存亡废兴	Reasons For Survival, Death, Abandonment, Prosperity
53	而非由此道者，	And That Not Through This 'Dao' Entity,
54	未之有也。"	Never Ever Happened that's."
55	严恢曰：	Yanhui Said:
56	"所为问道者为富，	"Reason For Person Enquiring of 'Dao' is For Wealth,
57	今得珠亦富矣，	Now Having Pearls Also Wealthy that's
58	安用道？"	Why the Need for 'Dao' ?"
59	子列子曰：	Teacher Liezi Said:
60	"桀纣唯重利而轻道，	"Jie, Zhou Because Favored Wealth And Slighted 'Dao',
61	是以亡。	Henceforth Perished.
62	幸哉余未汝语也！	Lucky Indeed I have Not Spoken to You that's !
63	人而无义，	Humans Having No Righteousness,
64	唯食而已，	Just for Food That Is,
65	是鸡狗也。	Are liken to Chickens, Dogs that's.
66	强食靡角，	Fighting for Food Locking Horns,
67	胜者为制，	Victorious People Set Rules,
68	是禽兽也。	Are like Birds, Animals that's.
69	为鸡狗禽兽矣，	As Chickens, Dogs, Birds, Animals indeed,
70	而欲人之尊己，	Then Wishing from People Their Respect for Us,
71	不可得也。	Not Possible to Attain that's.
72	人不尊己，	People Not Respecting Us,
73	则危辱及之矣。"	Then Danger Insults Coming to Us indeed."

Liezi Text Narrative

Teacher Liezi was under the tutelage of Huqiuzilin who said: L2
"Sir knows 'keep back' (deference) then can talk of 'keep body' (living life) that's. L4
Liezi said: "Willing to hear 'keep back' principle." L6
Huqiuzilin said: "Watch the Shadow, then know it." L9
Liezi watched and observed the Shadow; the form (body) crooked then Shadow curved. L11
Form (body) straightened then Shadow upright; all moves followed the body, not Shadow. L13
Bend stretch depended on matter and not Shadow itself; this is 'keep back' and be fronted. L15
Guanyin told teacher Liezi said: "Words beautiful then echo beauty, evil words echo evil; L18

8.1 Watching The Shadow

Body long then Shadow long, body short then Shadow short. L20
Name (reputation) is just an echo that's; body entity is just a Shadow (not independent). L24
Hence: Careful with words, they have resonance; careful with actions, they have followers. L29
Thus Sage saw what exit to know what entered, observing the past to know the future. L31
This is the reason for prior knowledge, that's. L32
Regulation is by self, checking by others. L34
People love me, I certainly love them; people hate me, I certainly hate them. L38
Tang, Wu loved the world, and be kings; Jie, Zhou (evil kings) hated the world, hence died. L42
They were checked, clearly not ethical, like exiting not through doors, walking not on paths. L46
Not ethical and not regulated, with this conduct and aspiring for gain also difficult, is-it-not ? L48
Often observed Virtues of Shennong, Youyan, checked in the books on Yu, Xia, Shang Zhou. L50
Assessing scholars, virtuous people their words, for reasons of the rise and fall of dynasty. L52
And that not through this selfless 'Dao' of Shadow, never ever happens." L54
Yanhui said: "Reason for people enquiring about 'Dao' is to acquire wealth, that's. L56
Now people having pearls are also wealthy, so why do they have the need for 'Dao'. ?" L58
Teacher Liezi said: "Jie, Zhou, kings who favored wealth and slighted 'Dao', hence perished. L61
Humans with no righteousness, just existing for food, are liken to chickens and dogs that's. L65
Locked horns fighting for food, victorious people setting rules, are like birds and animals. L68
As chickens, dogs, birds, animals indeed, and wishing for the respect of others, **not** *possible. L71*
When people do not respect us, then danger and insults are coming our way indeed." L73

Comments:
8.1 Watching The Shadow
Liezi's teacher Huqiuzilin told him to know 'keep back' before discussing 'keep life'.
Liezi was willing to learn but how, and so Huqiuzilin asked him to watch his Shadow.
Liezi observed that Shadow bended, straightened following the body, was behind in all actions.
Recognising that life is just like Shadow, dependent on outside matters, so be humble to follow.

Our reputation is an echo of our words good or evil, and our body is a Shadow cast long or short.
Hence we must be mindful with our words and actions, as they affect others for good or evil.
The sage studies the past in anticipation of the future, and deduces what entered from what exited.
Thus study and deduction are the reason for prior knowledge, not some sorcery of 'Dao'.

I love people and people love me; hence we regulate ourselves and are checked by others.
Tang, Wu loved the world and were made kings; Jie, Zhou hated the world and were overthrown.
Scholars observed the virtues of Shennong, Youyan, checked the books on Yu, Xia, Shang, Zhou.
The rise and fall of dynasties are never outside the need to practice unselfish 'Daoism'.

Yanhui: had pearls no need for 'Dao'; Liezi: Jie, Zhou favored wealth, slighted 'Dao', perished.
Humans without righteousness or 'Dao', just existing for food, are like chickens and dogs.
Locked horns fighting for food, victorious people setting rules, and winning no respect of others.
With no respect from others, danger and insults are coming our way !
Humans without righteousness, are just like birds and animals fighting for food, that's. L65

Chapter 8. Charming Talks (説符)

8.2 察其所以然   8.2 Discerning the Reason Why So

01	列子学射中矣，	Liezi Learning, Shot On-target that's,
02	请于关尹子。	Consulted With Guanyinzi.
03	尹子曰：	Yinzi Said:
04	"子知子之所以中者乎？"	"Sir, You Know The Reason For Hitting Target, yes/no ?"
05	对曰：	Answering Said:
06	"弗知也。"	"Not Knowing that's."
07	关尹子曰：	Quanyinzi Said:
08	"未可。"	"Not Ready."
09	退而习之。	Retreat And Practice It.
10	三年，	3 Years,
11	又以报关尹子。	Again Reported To Quanyinzi.
12	尹子曰：	Yinzi Said:
13	"子知子之所以中乎？"	"Sir, You Know The Reason For Hitting-target, yes/no ?
14	列子曰：	Liezi Said:
15	"知之矣。"	"Know It indeed."
16	关尹子曰：	Quanyinzi Said:
17	"可矣；	" Ready indeed;
18	守而勿失也。	Guard And Not Lose that's
19	非独射也，	Not Only in Shooting that's,
20	为国与身，	For State And Body (self)
21	亦皆如之。	Also All Like This.
22	故圣人不察存亡，	Thus Sage Person Not Concern with Survival or Loss,
23	**而察其所以然。"**	**But with Discerning The Reason Why So."**

Liezi Text Narrative
Liezi learned to shoot, hit the target, and then consulted with Guanhyinzi. L2
Yinzi said: " Sir, you know the reason for hitting the target, yes/no ?" L4
Liezi responding said: "Not knowing that's." L6
Quanyinzi said: "Not ready." L8
Liezi retreated to practice, and 3 years later, again reported to Quanyinzi. L11
Yinzi said: "Sir, you know the reason for hitting the target, yes/no ?" L13
Liezi said: "Know it indeed." L15
Quanyinzi said: "Ready indeed; guard the skill and not lose it that's. L18
Not only in shooting that's, also in actions for the state and for self, also all like this. L21
Thus sage person not concerned with results but with discerning the reason why so." L23

Comments:
8.2 Discerning the Reason Why So
Liezi shot on target but did not know the reason for success, so Guanyinzi said he wasn't ready.
Liezi practiced another 3 years and knew the reason for success, so Guanyinzi said he was ready.
Quanyinzi warned Liezi not to lose the skill, to apply it in all actions for the state and himself.
Thus sage person was not concerned with success/failure but with discerning the reason why so.
Knowing reason(s) behind each success or failure is more important, reproducibility ensured.

Chapter 8. Charming Talks (說符)

8.3 治国之难   8.3 Difficulty in Government

01	列子曰：	Liezi Said:
02	"色盛者骄，	"Countenance Robust Person Proud,
03	力盛者奋，	Strength Robust Person Restive,
04	未可以语道也。	Not Possible With Words to Guide that's.
05	故不班白语道失，	Hence No Spots of White (hairs) Words Guiding Lost,
06	而况行之乎？	Let Alone Acting It Is-it-not ?
07	故自奋则人莫之告。	Hence Self Restive Then People None will Inform Him,
08	人莫之告，	People None will Inform Him,
09	则孤而无辅矣。	Then Alone And No Help Indeed.
10	贤者任人，	Virtuous Person Appoints People,
11	故年老而不衰，	Hence Years Old And Not Weaken,
12	智尽而不乱。	Intellect Exhausted And Not Chaotic.
13	*故治国之难 在于*	***Hence The Difficulty of Governing State Is In***
14	*知贤而不在自贤。"*	***Know the Virtuous And Not In being Self Virtuous."***

Liezi Text Narrative
Liezi said: "Countenance robust person is proud, strength robust person is restive; L3
Not possible with words to guide him that's. L4
Without spotting white hairs (old enough), guiding words are lost, let alone action, is-it-not ? L6
Hence a self restive person, no others will inform him, then he is alone with no help indeed. L9
Virtuous person appoints other virtuous people to help, hence even in old age, not inefficient. L11
In old age when intellect is exhausted, the person with help does not become chaotic. L12
Hence the difficulty in government is in knowing the virtuous, not just being self virtuous." L14

Comments:
8.3 Difficulty in Government
Liezi says young person robust in color and strength are proud and restive, not able to guide.
Without spotting white hairs when old enough, guiding words are lost, let alone with actions.
Hence a self restive person, nobody will advise, and he will be left alone with no help indeed.
A virtuous person will appoint other virtuous, thus even in old age, will remain efficient.
A virtuous person will engage other virtuous, thus when intellect exhausted will not be chaotic.

A governing leader is to engage other virtuous people, not enough to be self virtuous alone.

Chapter 8. Charming Talks (説符)

8.4 玉为楮叶　　8.4 Jade-Made Mulberry Leaf

01	宋人有为其君	Song People Had For The King
02	*以玉为楮叶者，*	**Person who Made a Mulberry Leaf With Jade,**
03	三年而成。	3 Years Then Completed.
04	锋杀茎柯，	Prominent Vein-net Stalk Handle,
05	毫芒繁泽，	Micro Hairs Luxuriant Growth,
06	乱之楮叶中	Mixed It Among Mulberry Leaves
07	而不可别也。	And Not Able to Differentiate that's.
08	此人遂以巧	This Person Henceforth With Skill
09	食宋国。	Employed by Song State.
10	子列子闻之，	Teacher Liezi Heard This,
11	曰：	Said:
12	"使天地之生物，	"Enabling Heaven Earth The Living Things,
13	三年而成一叶，	3 Years To Produce 1 Leaf,
14	则物之叶者寡矣。	Then Those Things Their Leaves Rare indeed.
15	故圣人恃道化	Hence Sage Person Holds 'Dao' to Transform
16	而不恃智巧。"	And Not Hold Cleverness Skill."

Liezi Text Narrative
People of Song had a person who made a mulberry leaf with jade for the king. L2
It was completed after 3 years, with prominent vein-net, stalk, and luxuriant micro hairs . L5
Mixed it among mulberry leaves, and was not able to differentiate it apart, that's. L7
This person with the skill henceforth was employed by the state of Song. L9
Teacher Liezi heard this and said: "Enabling the living things of Heaven Earth, L12
To produce 1 leaf in 3 years, then those things with leaves are a rarity indeed. L14
Hence, Sage person holds 'Dao' for transformation and not holds cleverness and skill." L16

Comments:
8.4 Jade-Mulberry Leaf
A person from Song was able to make a jade mulberry leaf for his king in 3 years.
It cannot be differentiated apart from the real thing with prominent vein-net and micro hairs.
It was a rare achievement but it benefited only the king and himself with employment in court.
The sage person rather holds 'Dao' that can transform and benefit the masses for better lives.

Cleverness and skill benefit a rare few, whereas teaching of 'Dao' better lives of the masses.

8.5 君非自知我 — 8.5 Minister Not Personally Know Me

01	子列子穷,	Teacher Liezi Poor,
02	容貌有饥色。	Face Countenance Had Color of Hunger.
03	客有言之郑子阳者曰:	Guest Had Spoken This to Person Zhengziyang Said:
04	"列御寇盖有道之士也,	"Lieyukou Is Reputedly A Daoist Scholar that's,
05	居君之国而穷。	Residing In the Minister's Kingdom And in Poverty.
06	君无乃为不好士乎?"	Minister Not Likely Be Not Loving Scholar is-it-not?"
07	郑子阳即令	Zhengziyang Instantly Ordered
08	官遗之粟。	Official Bestowed Him Millet.
09	子列子出,	Teacher Liezi came Out,
10	见使者,	Met with Envoy,
11	再拜而辞。	Repeatedly with Hands-in-worship And Declining.
12	使者去。	Envoy Returned.
13	子列子入,	Teacher Liezi Entered.
14	其妻望之而拊心曰:	His Wife Watched Him And Patting Heart Said:
15	"妾闻为有道者之妻子,	"Concubine-me Heard, As Wife Of Person With 'Dao',
16	皆得佚乐,	Always Attain Relaxation and Happiness,
17	今有饥色,	Now Having Color of Hunger,
18	君过而遗先生食。	Minister Visited And Bestowed Teacher Food.
19	先生不受,	Teacher Not Accepting,
20	岂不命也哉?"	How can it be Not Destined, is-it-not?"
21	子列子笑谓之曰:	Teacher Liezi Laughingly Told Her, Said:
22	*"君非自知我也。*	*"Minister Not Personally Knows Me that's*
23	以人之言而遗我粟,	With Words of People And Bestowed Me Millet.
24	至其罪我也,	When He Fault Me that's,
25	又且以人之言,	Also Is With Words Of People,
26	此吾所以不受也。"	This Is Why I Not Accepting, That's."
27	其卒,	The Ending,
28	民果作难,	Citizens Did Made Trouble,
29	而杀子阳。	And Killed Ziyang.

8.5 Minister Not Personally Know Me

Liezi Text Narrative
Teacher Liezi was poor, and face countenance had the color of hunger. L2
Guests who had spoken of this to Zhengziyang, said: "Lieyukou is reputably a daoist scholar. L4
He is living in poverty in your kingdom; it is likely Your Highness loves a scholar, is-it-not ?" L6
Zhengziyang instantly ordered an official to go, bestowing him with millet. L8
Teacher Liezi came out, met with the envoy, and repeatedly with Hands-in-worship, declined. L11
Envoy returned and Teacher Liezi entered; his wife watched him and patting her heart said: L14
"Concubine-me heard, as wife of person with 'Dao', always attain relaxation and happiness; L16
Now suffering in hunger, the prime minister had visited and bestowed Teacher with food. L18
Teacher you have not accepted, how can this be our Destiny, is-it-not ?" L20
Teacher Liezi laughingly told her, said: "Minister not personally know me. L22
He bestowed me millet on the words of others, likewise will fault me on words of others. L25
This is why I am not accepting." L26
In the end, citizens did make trouble and killed Ziyang. L29

Comments:
8.5 Minister Not Personally Know Me
In the state of Zheng, Liezi was living in poverty with hunger showing in his face.
Guests told the prime minister, Zhengziyang of this, as he was a lover of daoist scholars.
Instantly he ordered an envoy to bring millet to Liezi who repeatedly declined.
The wife lamented his none acceptance and questioned that it was their destiny to suffer hunger.
To which Liezi laughingly explained that Zhengziyang did not know him personally.
On the words of others he was offered help; likewise on the words of others he will be faulted.
In the end, citizens did make trouble and killed Ziyang; and Liezi was not faulted.

Liezi is wise to decline Ziyang, knowing the danger in accepting help from unfamiliar sources.

Chapter 8. Charming Talks (說符)

8.6 理无常是　　8.6 Principles Not Always Right

01	鲁施氏有二子，	Lu (state), Family of Shi Had 2 Sons,
02	其一好学，	One of Them Loved Scholarship,
03	其一好兵。	One of Them Loved Warfare.
04	好学者以术干齐侯；	Person Loved Scholarship With Art Engaged Duke of Qi;
05	齐侯纳之，	Duke of Qi Accepted Him
06	以为诸公子之傅。	To Be All Princelings Their Teacher.
07	好兵者之楚，	Person Loved Soldiering Went to Chu (state)
08	以法干楚王；	With Strategies Engaged King of Chu;
09	王悦之，	King Happy with Him,
10	以为军正。	To Be Army Administrator
11	禄富其家，	Remuneration Enriched The Family
12	爵荣其亲。	Titles Honored The Relatives.
13	施氏之邻人孟氏，	Shi Family Their Neighboring People Meng Family,
14	同有二子，	Similarly Had 2 Sons,
15	所业亦同，	Whatever Studies Also Similar,
16	而窘于贫。	And Distressed In Poverty.
17	羡施氏之有，	Envious of Shi Family Their Possession,
18	因从请	Hence Following Requested for
19	进趋之方。	The Forward Progress Formula.
20	二子以实告孟氏。	2 Sons With Facts Informed the Meng Family.
21	孟氏之一子之秦，	Meng Family His 1 Son Went to Qin (state)
22	以术干秦王。	With Art Engaged King of Qin.
23	秦王曰：	King of Qin Said:
24	"当今诸侯力争，	"Presently Now All Dukes Contesting with Strength,
25	所务兵食而已。	What is Required, Army Food That's It.
26	若用仁义治吾国，	If Using Kindness Righteousness to Manage My State,
27	是灭亡之道。"	Is The Way to Destruction Loss (of state)."
28	遂宫而放之。	Chased out of Palace And Banished Him.
29	其一子之卫，	His 1 Son (the other) Went to Wei (state)
30	以法干卫侯。	With Strategies Engaged Duke of Wei.
31	卫侯曰：	Duke of Wei Said:
32	'吾弱国也，	"My Weak Kingdom that's,
33	而摄乎大国之间。	And Sandwiched O' In Between Big States.
34	大国吾事之，	Big States I Serve Them,
35	小国吾抚之，	Small States I Help Them,
36	是求安之道。	Is Aspiring for Peace, The Way.
37	若赖兵权，	If Relying on Military Power,
38	灭亡可待矣。	Destruction Loss Possibly Awaiting indeed.
39	若全而归之，	If Whole And Return You,
40	适于他国。	Association With Other States.
41	为吾之患不轻矣。"	Will Be My Trouble, Not Light indeed."

271

8.6 Principles Not Always Right

42	遂刖之，	Then Nose-cut Him (punishment),
43	而还诸鲁。	And Returned To Lu (state)
44	既反，	Already Returned,
45	孟氏之父子	Meng Family, The Father and Sons
46	叩胸而让施氏。	Beat Chests And Complained with the Shi Family.
47	施氏曰：	Shi Family Said:
48	"凡得时者昌，	"Those Attain Accord in Timing Prosper,
49	失时者亡。	Those Lost Timing Perish.
50	子道与吾同，	Your Way And Mine Same,
51	而功与吾异，	But Effectiveness With Mine Different,
52	失时者也，	Yours Lost Timing that's
53	非行之谬也。	Not Actions Are Absurdity that's.
54	***且天下理无常是，***	*And Heaven Beneath Principles Not Always Right,*
55	***事无常非。***	*Affairs Not Always Wrong.*
56	先日所用，	Previous Days What in Use,
57	今或弃之；	Now Maybe Abandoning It;
58	今之所弃，	Now What Is Abandoned,
59	后或用之。	Afterward Maybe Using It.
60	此用与不用，	This Using And Not Using,
61	无定是非也。	Not Confirming Right Wrong that's.
62	投隙抵时，	Find the Opening Arrive at Timing,
63	应事无方，	Responding to Affairs No Formula,
64	属乎智。	Belong O' to the Intellect.
65	智苟不足，	Intellect Careless Not Enough,
66	使若博如孔丘，	Even Like Knowledgeable As Kongqiu (Confucius),
67	术如吕尚，	Artful As Lushang,
68	焉往而不穷哉？"	How to Go-forth And Not Failed, right ?"
69	孟氏父子	Meng Family Father Sons
70	舍然无愠容，	Abandoned Naturally, No Angry Face,
71	曰：	Said:
72	"吾知之矣，	"We Know It Already,
73	子勿重言！"	Sir Don't Say Again !"

Liezi Text Narrative

In the state of Lu, the Shi family had 2 sons, one loved scholarship, one loved warfare. L3
With arts, the scholar engaged the Duke of Qi who made him teacher of the princelings. L6
With strategies, the soldier engaged with King of Chu who made him run the army. L10
Remunerations enriched the family, and titles honored the relatives. L12
The Shi family had neighbors, the Meng family who had 2 sons with similar studies. L15
The Meng family was distressed in poverty, envious of the Shi family for their possession. L17
The Shi family was approached for the success formula, and was honestly told all the facts. L20
Meng family's scholar son similarly went to Qin, and with his arts engaged with the King. L22
King of Qin said: "Presently all dukes are contesting strength, requiring soldiers and food. L25
To use kindness and righteousness to manage my state is the way to destruction of the state." L27
So chased him out of the palace and banished him. L28

8.6 Principles Not Always Right

The son who studied warfare went to Wei and with strategies engaged the Duke of Wei. L30
Duke of Wei said: "My kingdom is weak, that's sandwiched O' in between big states. L33
The big states I serve them, the small states I help them, only aspiring for peace this way. L36
If I rely on military power, destruction and loss are possibly awaiting for me indeed. L38
If you are to return whole and you associate with other states, my troubles are not light." L41
Thus punished him by cutting-off his nose and returned him to the State of Lu. L43

The Meng family, father and sons beat their chests and complained to the Shi family. L46
The Shi family said: "Those that accord with timing prosper, those lost timing perish. L49
Your way and mine are the same, but effectiveness with mine is different. L51
Yours is a loss of timing that's, and not that your actions are absurdities, that's. L53
And beneath Heaven, principles are not always right, affairs are not always wrong. L55
Previous days what is in use, may now be abandoned; what is abandoned may be used later. L59
This used and not used, are not for confirming right or wrong that's. L61
*Find the opening, arrive in time, responses to affairs have no formula, a matter of intellect. L64
Intellect careless and not enough, even like knowledgeable as Kongqiu (Confucius), L66
Artful as Lushang, how to go forth and not to fail, right?" L68*
Meng family, father and sons gave up naturally, and with no more angry faces said: L71
"We know all already, Sir, don't say any more !" L73

Comments:
8.6 Principles Not Always Right
The state of Lu had the Shi family, with a son studied in Confucianism, another in warfare.
The scholar impressed the Duke of Qi and was made tutor of the many princelings.
The strategist went to the King of Chu and was made to manage the army.
The neighboring Meng family also had 2 sons who were similarly studied.
Envious of the Shi, they went to ask for the formula for success and were told the facts honestly.
The Meng scholar-son went to the King of Qin who said, all the dukes are contesting each other.
Hence presently soldiers and food were needed, not kindness and righteousness, so banished him.
The Meng strategist-son went to Duke of Wei who was weak, sandwiched between big states.
Duke of Wei cannot rely on military power, else destruction and loss of kingdom awaits him.
Believing the son a danger if he goes to other states, he punished him by cutting off his nose.

The Meng family complained, and the Shi family explained thus:
 *Actions similar but results differ, it's all about right timing (prosper), wrong timing (disastrous).
And beneath Heaven, principles are not always right, affairs are not always wrong.
Used yesterday, abandoned today, used or not used cannot confirm right or wrong that's.*

Find the opportunity, arrive in time, response to affairs have no formula, a matter of intellect.
L62-4

Chapter 8. Charming Talks (說符)

8.7 亦有招之者   8.7 Also Had An Admirer

01 晋文公出会，	Jin (state) Duke Wen,
02 欲伐卫，	Wished to Attack Wei,
03 公子锄仰天而笑。	Prince Chu Looked Skyward And Laughed.
04 公问何笑。	Duke Asked Why Laughed.
05 曰：	Said:
06 "臣笑邻之人	"Subject-me Laughing At Neighbor Person
07 有送其妻适私家者，	Who Was Sending His Wife to Visit Relative's Home,
08 道见桑妇，	Wayward Saw Mulberry Woman (feeding silkworms),
09 悦而与言。	Happy And Talked With (her).
10 然顾视其妻，	Naturally Turned to Look at His Wife,
11 亦有招之者矣。	***Also Had a Person Engaging Her Too.***
12 臣窃笑此也。"	Subject-me secretly Laughing at This that's"
13 公寤其言，	Duke Awakened to His Words,
14 乃止。	Then Stopped (attack).
15 引师而还。	Led Army And Returned.
16 未至，	Before Arriving (home),
17 而有伐其北鄙者矣。	And Had State Attacking His Northern Border Indeed.

Liezi Text Narrative
Duke Wen of Jin State wished to attack Wei, and Prince Chu looked up skyward and laughed. L3
Duke asked why he laughed. L4
Said: "Subject-me laughing at a neighbor who was sending his wife to visit a relative's home. L7
On the way he saw a mulberry woman (feeding silkworms), happy and talked with her. L9
Naturally turned to look at his wife, and found that she also had a person beckoning her too. L11
Subject-me is secretly laughing at this, that's." L12
Duke awakened to his words, then stopped his attack on Wei, and led his army to return. L15
And before arriving home, had the neighboring state attacking his northern border indeed. L17

Comments:
8.7 Also Has An Admirer
Duke Wen of Jin wished to attack Wei.
Prince Chu laughed and Duke asked him why.
Prince told the parable of a neighbor sending his wife on a visit to a relative's home.
On the way he saw a woman feeding silkworms, happy and engaged in talk with her.
On looking back, he also found his wife talking with an admirer.
Then Duke, awakened to the consequences, stopped his campaign and led his army back.
Indeed before reaching home, he found his northern border being attacked by a neighboring state.

Beware, when we scheme on others, others are also scheming on us.

8.8 晋国苦盗   8.8 State of Jin Suffered Banditry

01	*晋国苦盗,*	*Jin State Suffered Bandits,*
02	有郄雍者,	Had Person Queyong,
03	能视盗之貌,	Able to See Bandit's Countenance,
04	察其眉睫之间	Detected In Between His Brows and eye-lashes
05	而得其情。	And Obtained The Information.
06	晋侯使视盗,	Duke of Jin Employed him to Scrutinise for Bandits,
07	千百无遗一焉。	Thousands Hundreds Not Missed 1 Indeed.
08	晋侯大喜,	Duke of Jin Greatly Pleased,
09	告赵文子曰:	Informed Wenzi of Zhou, Said:
10	"吾得一人,	"I Acquired 1 Person,
11	而一国盗为尽矣,	And Whole State Banditry Is Extinguished indeed,
12	奚用多为?"	Why Use More Actions?"
13	文子曰:	Wenzi Said:
14	"吾君恃伺察而得盗,	"My Lord Uses Observations Checks To Catch Bandits,
15	盗不尽矣,	Banditry Not Ending Indeed,
16	且郄雍必	And Queyong Certainly
17	不得其死焉。"	Not Getting His natural Death indeed."
18	俄而群盗谋曰:	Shortly The Crowd of Bandits Scheming, Said:
19	"吾所穷者郄雍也。"	"Person Who Impoverished Us, Queyong that's."
20	遂共盗而残之。	Hence Bandits Combined And Killed Him.
21	晋侯闻而大骇,	Duke of Jin Heard And Greatly Shocked,
22	立召文子而告之曰:	Instantly Summoned Wenzi To Inform Him, Said:
23	"果如子言,	"Rightly As You Said,
24	郄雍死矣!	Queyong Dead Already!
25	然取盗何方?"	So Resolving Banditry What Method?"
26	文子曰:	Wenzi Said:
27	"周谚有言:	"Zhou Proverb Has Saying:
28	察见渊鱼者不祥,	Observed Fish In-depth Person's Misfortune,
29	智料隐匿者有殃。	Intelligent Guessing Hidden Secrets, Person Has Trouble.
30	且君欲无盗,	And Lord Wishing No Banditry,
31	莫若举贤而任之;	None Like Raising the Talented And Appoint Him;
32	使教明于上,	Ordered to Teach Civility at the Top,
33	化行于下,	Civilised Conduct at the Bottom,
34	民有耻心,	Citizens Having Shame at Heart,
35	则何盗之为?"	Then Why To Be Bandits?"
36	于是用随会知政,	Therefore Employed Suihui In-charge of Government,
37	而群盗奔秦焉。	And Bandit Hordes Scrambled to Qin (state) Indeed.

8.8 State of Jin Suffered Banditry

Liezi Text Narrative
State of Jin suffered bandits, and Queyong by looking at faces was able to identify the bandits. L3
Obtaining the information by detecting them in between the brows and eye-lashes. L5
Duke of Jin employed him to scrutinise bandits, and in thousands hundreds, missed not one. L7
Duke of Jin greatly pleased, informed Wenzi from state of Zhou and said: L9
"I have got a person and the whole state's banditry is resolved, why take more actions?" L12
Wenzi said: "My Lord uses observations to catch bandits, and banditry does not end indeed. L15
And Queyong certainly will not die a natural death surely." L17
Shortly the crowd of bandits scheming said: "Person who impoverished us, Queyong that's." L19
Hence bandits combined and killed him. L20
Duke of Jin heard this and was greatly shocked, instantly called Wenai to inform him, said: L22
"Rightly as you said, Queyong was killed ! So resolving banditry, what method to use ?" L25
Wenzi said: "Zhou has a proverb saying: L27
"Person able to observe fish in the depth, ominous; person able to guess secrets, in danger. L29
And Lord, wishing no banditry, nothing better than to raise the talented with an appointment. L31
Order him to teach enlightenment at the top, and civility conduct at the bottom. L33
Citizens having a sense of shame at heart, then why do they need to be bandits ?" L35
Thus Suihui was put in charge of the government, and the bandit horde scrambled to Qin. L37

Comments:
8.8 State of Jin Suffered Banditry
State of Jin suffered bandits, and Queyong was able to identify them by looking them in the face.
Duke of Jin boasted to Wenzi that he had the person employed to resolve the state's banditry.
Wenzi predicted that banditry will not end here and Queyong will die an unnatural death.
Person able to observe fish depth, ominous; a person able to guess another's secret is in danger.
Shortly the bandits banded together and killed Queyong to the great astonishment of the Duke.
The Duke of Qin hence consulted Wenzi for a method to stop banditry.

Zhou proverb: "Person able to observe fish in the depth, ominous; to guess secrets, in danger.
Wenzi advised, to engage a talented person to enlighten the top and teach civility at the bottom.
The rationale is to teach all citizens a sense of shame at heart for banditry, and they will not do it.
Suihui was put in charge of the government, and the bandit horde scrambled to the state of Qin.

Shame only drove banditry from Jin to Qin, hence the ultimate solution is rooting out poverty.

Chapter 8. Charming Talks (**説符**)

8.9 忠信诚	**8.9 Loyalty Trust and Honesty**
01 孔子自卫反鲁，	Kongzi From Wei Returned to Lu,
02 息驾乎河梁而观焉。	Resting Carriage On River Bridge And Viewing that's,
03 有悬水三十仞，	Had Water Fall 30 Ren (Zhou meter),
04 圜流九十里，	WhirlPool 90 Li (Zhou mile)
05 鱼鳖弗能游，	Fish Turtle Not Able to Swim,
06 鼋鼍弗能居，	Sea-turtle Water-lizard Not Able to Inhabit,
07 有一丈夫方将厉之。	Had An Elder Man About To Cross It.
08 孔子使人并涯止之，	Kongzi Asked People Along Riverside to Stop Him,
09 曰：	Said:
10 "此悬水三十仞，	" This WaterFall 30 Ren (Zhou meter),
11 圜流九十里，	WhirlPool 90 Li (Zhou mile),
12 鱼鳖弗能游，	Fish Turtle Not Able to Swim that's,
13 鼋鼍弗能居也。	Sea-turtle Water-lizard Not Able to Inhabit that's.
14 意者难可以济乎？"	Meaning That's Difficult, Possible To Cross yes/no ?"
15 丈夫不以错意，	Elder Man No Wish to Be Concerned
16 遂度而出。	Hence Crossed And Exit.
17 孔子问之曰：	Kongzi Asking Him Said:
18 "巧乎？	"Incidental True ?
19 有道术乎？	Have 'Dao' Technique True ?"
20 所以能入而出者，	Therefore Able to Enter And Exit That's,
21 何也？"	Which, that's ?"
22 丈夫对曰：	Elder Man Answering Said:
23 "始吾之入也，	"Initially I My Entry that's,
24 以忠信；	With Loyalty Trust;
25 及吾之出也，	Till I My Exit that's
26 又从以忠信。	Again Followed With Loyalty Trust.
27 忠信错吾躯于波流，	Loyalty Trust Bended My Body With Waves and Flow,
28 而吾不敢用私，	And I Not Dared Use Selfishness,
29 所以能入而复出者，	Therefore Able Entry And Again Exit that's
30 以此也。"	With This that's."
31 孔子谓弟子曰：	Kongzi Addressing Disciples Said:
32 "二三子识之！	"Two Three Disciples Recognize This !
33 水且犹可以	So Water Also Able With
34 ***忠信诚身亲之，***	***Loyalty Trust Honesty Be Closely Intimated***
35 而况人乎？"	Let Alone with People Right ?"

8.9 Loyalty Trust and Honesty

Liezi Text Narrative
Kongzi returned to Lu from Wei, resting his carriage on the river bridge, enjoying the scenery. L2
Had a waterfall, 30 ren (meter) tall, and whirlpool 90 li (mile) long. L4
Fish turtles not able to swim, sea-turtle water-lizards not able to inhabit. L6
Had an elder man about to cross, and Kongzi asked people along the riverside to stop him. L8
Said: "This waterfall is 30 meter tall, whirlpool is 90 li long. L11
Fish turtles are not able to swim, sea-turtle and water-lizards are not able to inhabit, that's. L13
Meaning that's difficult, possible to cross truly ?" L14
Elder man no wish to be concerned, hence crossed and exited. L16
Kongzi asking him said: "Incidental, true ? Have 'Dao' technique, true ?" L19
Therefore able to enter and exit, which is true ?" L21
Elder man answering said: "Initially I entered with Loyalty and Trust; L24
Till I exit, again following with Loyalty and Trust. L26
Loyalty and Trust bended my body with the waves and flow, not daring to be selfish. L28
Therefore able to enter and again exit, with this that's. L30
Kongzi addressing disciples said: "You disciples listen to this ! L32
Water also able to respond, with Loyalty Trust and Honesty water can be closely intimated. L34
Let alone with people, right ?" L35

Comments:
8.9 Loyalty Trust and Honesty
Kongzi was returning to Lu from Wei, resting his carriage on the river bridge, enjoying the scene.
There was a waterfall, 30 ren (meter) tall, and a whirlpool 90 li (mile) long.
Fish turtles were not able to swim, sea-turtle water-lizards were not able to inhabit.
An elder man was about to cross, and Kongzi asked people along the riverside to stop him.
Warning him of the difficulty, but the man unconcerned crossed and exited.
Kongzi asked him whether it was incidental or that he had the power of 'Dao', which is true ?
Elder man answered that he entered with Loyalty and Trust.
Until he exited, he followed through with Loyalty and Trust, and not daring to be selfish.
In short, the man went with the flow with trust, not daring to be selfish to swim against the flow.
Kongzi noted that even water responds to Loyalty, Trust and Honesty !

Liezi's satire on Confucians' dogmatism, even water responds to Loyalty, Trust and Honesty !

Chapter 8. *Charming Talks (説符)*

8.10 人可与微言乎?　　8.10 Can People be Trusted with Secrets ?

01	白公问孔子曰：	Beigong Asking Kongzi Said:
02	**"人可与微言乎？"**	***"People Possible With Micro (secret) Words True ?"***
03	孔子不应。	Kongzi Not Responding.
04	白公问曰：	Beigong Asking Said:
05	"若以石投水，	"Like With Stone Cast into Water,
06	何如？"	How About ?"
07	孔子曰：	Kongzi Said:
08	"吴之善没者能取之。"	"People of Wu Good at Diving Able to Retrieve it."
09	曰：	Said:
10	"若以水投水何如？"	"Like With Water Cast into Water How About ?"
11	孔子曰：	Kongzi Said:
12	"淄、渑之合，	"Li (river), Yin (river) Their Combining,
13	易牙尝而知之。"	Yiya Tastes And Knows Them."
14	白公曰：	Beigong Said:
15	"人故不可与微言乎？"	"People Certain Not Able With Micro Words, Right ?"
16	孔子曰：	Kongzi Said:
17	"何为不可？	"Why Can Not be Done ?
18	唯知言之谓者乎！	Only Person Knows What Words are Saying, Right !
19	夫知言之谓者，	He who Knows What the Words are Saying.
20	不以言言也。	Not With Words Saying that's.
21	争鱼者濡，	Person Catching Fish got Wet,
22	逐兽者趋，	Person Catching Animals got (sweat) Chasing,
23	非乐之也。	Not Loving It (getting wet or sweat chasing) that's.
24	故至言去言，	Hence Absolute Words Abandon Words.
25	至为无为。	Absolute Action No Action (unselfish).
26	夫浅知之所争者，	O' Shallow Knowledge, That Is What is Contested,
27	末矣。"	Tip Only."
28	白公不得已，	Beigong Not Getting It,
29	遂死于浴室。	Hence Died In the BathRoom.

8.10 Can People be Trusted with Secrets

Liezi Text Narrative
Baigong asking Kongzi said: "People possible with micro (secret) words, be Trusted ?" L2
Kongzi not responding; L3
Baigong asking, said: "Like with a stone cast into water, how about ?" L6
Kongzi said: "People from the state of Wu, good at diving are able to retrieve it." L8
Baigong said: "Like with water cast into water, how about ?" L10
Kongzi said: "Zi (river) and Zhu (river) their combining, Yiya tastes and knows them." L13
Baigong said: "People certainly are not able to trust micro (secret) words, right ?" L15
Kongzi said: "Why can't it be done? L17
Only with people who know what the words are saying, right ! L18
He who knows what the words are saying, then no need to say it out, that's. L20
People caught fish got wet, people caught animals got sweat chasing, not that they love it. L23
Hence absolute words (secret) abandon words; absolute action (secret) unselfish. L25
O' those shallow knowledge that is contested, no depth just at the tip only." L27
Baigong did not understand Kongzi's warning, schemed to rebel and died in the bathroom. L29

Comments:
8.10 Can People be Trusted with Secrets ?
Baigong asked Kongzi if people can be trusted with secret words, and the latter did not respond. Baigong persisted with asking, "How about if a stone with a written secret casted into water ?"
Kongzi said: "People from the state of Wu, good at diving are able to retrieve it."
Baigong further persisted with, "How about mixing water with water ?"
Kongzi said: "Mixing water from Zi River and Zhu River, Yiya can taste and know it."
Baigong finally said: "So people cannot be scheming and be trusted with words, right ?"
Kongzi said: "Why can't it be done ?
Those people who know what the words are saying, then no need to say it out with words.
The evidence said it, like people who caught fish got wet, people who caught animals got sweat.
Absolute secrets don't use words, and absolute actions are unselfish and are not secrets."
Baigong or Baigongsheng, a senior minister of Chu, did not heed Kongzi's warning of no secrecy. He later plotted rebellion, got defeated and died in the bathroom.

All actions leave evidence behind, hence actions ought to be unselfish and no secrecy is needed.

Chapter 8. Charming Talks (說符)

8.11 一朝而两城下 | 8.11 Down 2 Cities in A Day

01	赵襄子使新稺穆子攻翟，	Zhaoxiangzi Ordered Xinzhimuzi to Attack the Di (clan),
02	胜之，取左人中人；	Won Them, Took-down Zuoren, Zhongren (2 cities);
03	使遽人来谒之。	Sent Messenger Coming to Report It.
04	襄子方食而有忧色。	Xiangzi Was Eating And Had Color of Worries.
05	左右曰：	Left Right (attendants) Said:
06	*"一朝而两城下，*	***"One Day And 2 Cities Down (taken),***
07	此人之所喜也；	This What Made People Happy that's;
08	今君有忧色，	Now Lord Had Color of Worries,
09	何也？"	Why that's ?"
10	襄子曰：	Xiangzi Said:
11	"夫江河之大也，	"O' Lakes and Rivers So Big that's
12	不过三日；	Not More than 3 Days (flooding);
13	飘风暴雨不终朝，	Flash Wind Torrential Rain Not Lasting a Day,
14	日中不须臾。	Sun Zenith Not A Moment (momentarily).
15	今赵氏之德行，	Now Clan of Zhao Its Virtues and Conduct,
16	无所施于积，	None That was Bestowed And Accumulated,
17	*一朝而两城下，*	1 Day And Took-down 2 Cities,
18	亡其及我哉！"	Is Disaster Upon Me, Right !"
19	孔子闻之曰：	Kongzi Heard This, Said:
20	"赵氏其昌乎！	"Clan of Zhao Their Prosperity, Indeed !
21	夫忧者所以为昌也，	O' Worrying Person, Reason For Being Prosperous that's,
22	喜者所以为亡也。	Happy Person, Reason For Being Lost that's.
23	胜非其难者也；	Victory Not the Difficult Part that's;
24	持之，其难者也。	Sustaining It, The Difficult Part that's.
25	贤主以此持胜，	Talented Master With This Sustained Victory,
26	故其福及后世。	Hence The Fortune Reaching Future Generations.
27	齐、楚、吴、越皆尝胜矣，	Qi, Chu, Wu, Zhao All Tasted Victory Before,
28	然卒取亡焉，	Naturally Finally Attained Extinction indeed,
29	不达乎持胜也。	Not Attained Sustainable Victory that's.
30	唯有道之主为能持胜。"	Only The Master Has 'Dao', Then Able Sustain Victory."
31	孔子之劲，	Kongzi His Strength,
32	能拓国门之关，	Able to Lift City Gate The Bolt,
33	而不肯以力闻。	But Not Willing By Strength be Known.
34	墨子为守攻，	Mozi Planning Defence Attack,
35	公输般服，	Gongshuban Submitted (as good)
36	而不肯以兵知。	But Not Willing By Strategy be Known
37	故善持胜者	Hence People Good Sustaining Victory
38	以强为弱。	With Strength As Weakness.

8.11 Down 2 Cities in A Day

Liezi Text Narrative
Zhaoxiangzi ordered Xinzhumuzi to attack the Di clan, won and took down Zuoren, Zhongren. L2
A messenger was sent with the news, and Xiangzi was eating, showing the color of worries. L4
Left and right attendants said: "One day and 2 cities taken, news makes people happy, that's. L7
Now the Lord has the color of worries. why is that ?" L9
Xiangzi said: "O' Seas and rivers so big, yet flooding not lasting more than 3 days. L12
Flash winds, torrential rains not lasting a day, and sun at zenith lasting only a moment. L14
Now clan of Zhao, its virtues and conduct, none was bestowed and accumulated. L16
Took down 2 cities in a day, so unbelievable I worry that disaster is soon upon me, right !" L18

Kongzi heard this, said: "Clan of Zhao, they will prosper indeed ! L20
A worrying person, the reason for prosperity; a happy person, the reason for failure that's. L22
Because victory is not the difficult part, it is sustaining victory that is the difficult part that's. L24
The virtuous master can sustain victory, hence his fortune can pass on to future generations. L26
Qi, Chu, Wu, Zhao tasted victory but all finally extinct, as they had no sustainable victory. L29
Only the master who has 'Dao' then able to sustain victory," L30
Kongzi his strength, able to lift the bolt of the city gate, yet no wish be known by strength. L33
Mozi built defences/attacks that Gongshuban admired, also no wish be known by strategy. L36
Hence people good at sustaining victory, does not show off their strength but appear weak. L38

Comments:
8.11 Down 2 Cities in A Day
Xiangzi of Zhao ordered Xinzhumuzi to attack the Di clan, and he took Zuoren and Zhongren.
When a messenger brought the good news, Xiangzi looked worried and the attendants asked why.
Xiangzi said, big rivers flooding not lasting 3 days, winds and torrential rain won't last a day.
Sun at zenith last but a moment, hence good news of winning 2 cities in a day may not last.

Kongzi heard this, said Zhao will prosper, as a person knows worry is the reason for prosperity.
Because victory is not the difficult part, it is the sustainability of victory that is the difficult part.
Qi, Chu, Wu, Zhao had tasted victory, but were finally extinct as they had no sustainable victory.
Only the master who has 'Dao' is able to sustain victory and pass fortune to future generations.

People good at sustaining victory, does not show off their strength but appear weak. L37

Chapter 8. Charming Talks (説符)

8.12 好行仁义者 　　　　8.12 A Kind and Righteous Family

01 宋人有好行仁义者，　　*Song People Had Person Loved Doing Kind, Righteous,*
02 三世不懈。　　　　　　3 Generations Without Neglect.
03 家无故黑牛生白犊，　　Family No Reason Black Cow Reproduced a White Calf,
04 以问孔子。　　　　　　With this Asked Kongzi.
05 孔子曰：　　　　　　　Kongzi Said:
06 "此吉祥也，　　　　　 "This Auspicious Harmony that's,
07 以荐上帝。"　　　　　 With-it Offerings Emperor Above."
08 居一年，　　　　　　　Stayed 1 year,
09 其父无故而盲，　　　　The Father No Reason Went Blind,
10 其牛又复生白犊。　　　The Cow Then Again Reproduced a White Calf.
11 其父又复令其子问孔子。The Father Then Again Ordered The Son to Ask Kongzi.
12 其子曰：　　　　　　　The Son Said:
13 "前问之而失明，　　　 "Previously Asked Him Then Lost Sight,
14 又何问乎？"　　　　　 So Why Ask, Right ?"
15 父曰：　　　　　　　　Father Said:
16 "圣人之言先迕后合。　 "Sage Person His Words First Contradicts Later Accord.
17 其事未究，　　　　　　The Affairs Prior Settlement,
18 姑复问之。"　　　　　 Just Again Ask Him."
19 其子又复问孔子。　　　The Son Then Again Asked Kongzi.
20 孔子曰：　　　　　　　Kongzi Said:
21 "吉祥也。"　　　　　　"Good Fortune that's."
22 复教以祭。　　　　　　Again Instructed Make Offerings.
23 其子归致命。　　　　　The son Returned Transmitted Instruction (of Kongzi).
24 其父曰：　　　　　　　The Father Said:
25 "行孔子之言也。"　　　"Implement Kongzi His Instruction that's."
26 居一年，　　　　　　　Stayed 1 Year,
27 其子无故而盲。　　　　The Son No Reason Went Blind.
28 其后楚攻宋，　　　　　Then Afterward, Chu Attacked Song,
29 围其城；　　　　　　　Besieged The City;
30 民易子而食之，　　　　Citizens Exchanged Children To Eat Them,
31 析骸而炊之；　　　　　Broke Bones To Burn Them;
32 丁壮者皆乘城而战，　　Male Strong People All On City-wall To Fight,
33 死者大半。　　　　　　Dead People Greater than Half.
34 此人以父子有疾皆免。　This Person As Father Son Had Sickness All Exempted
35 及围解而疾俱复。　　　Until Siege Relieved And Sickness Totally Recovered.

8.12 A Kind and Righteous Family

Liezi Text Narrative
Song had a person who loved to do good righteous acts, and for 3 generations without neglect.L2
For no reason, family's black cow gave birth to a white calf, and so went to ask Kongzi.L4
Kongzi said: "This is auspicious harmony that's, to make offerings to the Emperor Above." L7
Stayed a year, the father for no reason went blind, and the cow again reproduced a white calf.L10
Asked to consult Kongzi, his son said; "Before, consulted him then lost sight, so why ask ?" L14
Father: "Sage person's words first contradict later accord, affairs not settle, just ask again." L18
The son went to ask again and Kongzi said: "Auspicious Harmonious that's." L21
Kongzi again said to make offerings, and the son returned to report Kongzi's instruction. L23
The father said: "Implement Kongzi's instructions, that's. L25
Another year, the son for no reason went blind. L27
Then afterward, the state of Chu attacked the state of Song, besieging the city; L28
Citizens exchanged children as food, and broke the bones to burn for fire. L31
All strong males were enlisted to fight on the city wall, and more than half the people died. L33
This family father and son had sickness and were exempted. L34
After the siege was lifted, their sicknesses were totally recovered. L35.

Comments:
8.12 A Kind and Righteous Family
Song State had a family who loved to do good, kind and righteous deeds for 3 generations.
For no reason, the family's black cow gave birth to a white calf, and Kongzi said: "Auspicious".
Another year, the father for no reason went blind, and the cow again reproduced a white calf.
Again Kongzi said, "Auspicious, and to make offerings", and they did.
Another year the son went blind, and the state of Chu went to war with the state of Song.
The city besieged, citizens of Song exchanged children as food, and burnt bones for fire.
Strong males were enlisted to fight on the city walls, and more than half died.
And after the siege was lifted, the family recovered from all their sickness.

Goodwill begets goodwill on Earth, and Heaven protects the kind and righteous family.

Chapter 8. Charming Talks (說符)

8.13 适值寡人有欢心　　8.13 When King In Happy Mood

01	宋有兰子者，	Song Had Performer Person,
02	以技干宋元。	With Skills Engaged Songyuan (king).
03	宋元召而使见，	Songyuan Summoned To Watch His Skills,
04	其技以双枝，	His Skills With 2 Sticks,
05	长倍其身，	Length Double His Height,
06	属其胫，	Tied to His Shins,
07	并趋并驰，	Coordinated Brisk-walking Coordinated Running,
08	弄七剑迭而跃之，	Playing 7 Swords, Stacking And Throwing Them,
09	五剑常在空中。	5 Swords Often In The Air,
10	元君大惊，	King Yuan Greatly Surprised,
11	立赐金帛。	Instantly Awarded Gold and Silks.
12	又有兰子	Again Had Performer
13	又能燕戏者，	Also a Person Capable in Acrobatic Skills,
14	闻之，	Heard This,
15	复以干元君。	Likewise Wishing to Engage King Yuan.
16	元君大怒曰：	King Yuan Greatly Angered, Said:
17	"昔有异技	"Formerly Had Strange Skills
18	干寡人者，	Person Engaged Lonely-me,
19	技无庸，	Skills No Usefulness,
20	**适值寡人有欢心，**	***Suitably When Lonely-me Had Joyous Heart,***
21	故赐金帛。	Hence Bestowed Gold Silks,
22	彼必闻此而进，	He Certainly Heard This And coming Forward,
23	复望吾赏。"	Again Hoping I will Reward."
24	拘而拟戮之，	Arrested And Intended to Kill Him,
25	经月乃放。	Past a Month Then Released.

Liezi Text Narrative
Song had a performer person with skills, who wished to perform for Songyuan the King. L2
Songyuan summoned him to watch his skills. L3
His skills was with 2 sticks, double his height, tied to his shin, coordinated walking, running; L7
Playing 7 swords, stacking and throwing them, with 5 swords often in the air. L09
King Yuan, greatly surprised, instantly awarded him with gold and silks. L11
Another performer capable of acrobatic skills heard this, also wanted to perform for King. L15
King Yuan was angry, said: "Formerly a strangely skilled person performed for Lonely-me; L18
Skills have no use, but suitably when Lonely-me was happy, hence bestowed with gold silks. L21
You certainly heard of this and are coming forward, again hoping I will be rewarding you." L23
So arrested him and intended to kill him, and a month passed before releasing him. L25
Comments:
8.13 When King In Happy Mood
Similarly skilled, two performers wished to perform for Songyuan, king of the State of Song.
Having the king in a joyou mood, the first performer was awarded with gold and silks.
Having the king in an angry mood, the second performer was arrested, and held for a month.
Skills are not the only factor that matters in success/failure, outside forces equally important.

285

Chapter 8. Charming Talks (説符)

8.14 伯乐相马   8.14 Bole Assessment of Horses

01	秦穆公谓伯乐曰：	Qin, Duke Mu Asking Bole, Said:
02	"子之年长矣，	"Sir Your Years Advanced (old) Indeed
03	子姓有可使求马者乎？"	Sir's Clan Has Person For Sending to Acquire Horses ?"
04	**伯乐对曰：**	***Bole Answering Said:***
05	**"良马可形容筋骨相也。**	***"Good Horse Assessment, in Form Look Sinews Bones.***
06	天下之马者，	The World-class Horse That's
07	若灭若没，	Like Extinct, Like Submerge (nondescript),
08	若亡若失，	Like Dead, Like Lost,
09	若此者绝尘弭辙。	Like This Kind, raises No Dust leaves No Trail.
10	臣之子皆下才也，	Subject-me My Sons All Lowly Talents that's,
11	可告以良马，	Able to Inform About Good Horses,
12	不可告以天下之马也。	Not Able to Inform About The World-class Horses that's.
13	臣有所与共	Subject-me Have Close Associate
14	担纆薪菜者，	Person Collecting Firewood Carrying on Shoulder-pole,
15	有九方皋，	He is Jiufanggao,
16	此其于马，	This His (knowledge) In Horses,
17	非臣之下也。	Not Below (level) Of Subject-me that's.
18	请见之。"	Please See Him."
19	穆公见之，	Duke Mu Saw Him,
20	使行求马。	Sent on Trip to Find Horse (world-class).
21	三月而反，	3 Months Then Returned.
22	报曰：	Reporting Said:
23	"已得之矣，	"Already Acquired It (horse) indeed,
24	在沙丘。"	On the Sand Hillock."
25	穆公曰：	Duke Mu Said:
26	"何马也？"	"What Horse, that's ?"
27	对曰：	Answering Said:
28	"牝而黄。"	"Mare And Yellow."
29	使人往取之，	Sent Person Forth to Collect It,
30	牡而骊。	Stallion And Black (horse).
31	穆公不说，	Duke Mu Not Speaking,
32	召伯乐而谓之曰：	Summoned Bole And Addressed Him, Said:
33	"败矣，	"Failure Indeed,
34	子所使求马者！	Sir, Person You Sent to Acquire Horse !
35	色物、	Color Horse,
36	牝牡尚弗能知，	Female/Male Also Not Able to Know,
37	又何马之能知也？"	Then How Able to Know The Horse that's ?"
38	伯乐喟然太息曰：	Bole Sighed Naturally a Primal Breath, Said:
39	"一至于此乎！	"Uniquely Till This Level Truly !
40	是乃其所以千万	This Is Why He Is Thousand Ten-thousand
41	臣而无数者也。	Exceeding Subject-me And Countless that's.
42	若皋之所观，	Like Gao What He Observed,
43	天机也，	Heavenly Secret that's,

8.14 Bole Assessment of Horses

44	得其精而忘其粗，	Attaining The Essence And Forgetting The Coarse,
45	在其内而忘其外；	On The Inside And Forget The Outside;
46	见其所见，	Sees What He Sees,
47	不见其所不见；	Not See What He Not See;
48	视其所视，	Discerned What He Discerned,
49	而遗其所不视。	And Lost What He Not Discerned.
50	若皋之相者，	Like Gao His Assessment Skill,
51	乃有贵乎马者也。"	Also Has More Value Beyond The Horse, that's."
52	马至，	Horse Arrived,
53	果天下之马也。	Certainly A World-class Horse that's.

Liezi Text Narrative

Duke Mu of the State of Qin asking Bole, said: " Sir, your years are advancing indeed. L2
Sir's family has a person to send to source for horses ?" L3
Bole answering, said: "Good horses, able to assess base on the form, look, sinews, bones. L5
The world-class horses, like extinct, nondescript, dead, lost, but raise no dust, leaves no trail. L9
My sons are lowly talented, able to source for good horses but not for world-class horses. L12
Subject-me have a close associate, a firewood collector, carrying loads on a shoulder-pole. L14
He is Jiufanggao, his knowledge of horses not below my level that's, so please see him." L18
Duke Mu saw him and sent him on a trip to source for the world-class horse. L20
After 3 months returned, reporting said: "Already acquired the horse, on the sand hillock."L24
Duke Mu said: "What horse that's ?"; Jiufanggao, answering said: "Mare and yellow." L28
A person was sent forth to collect the horse, a stallion and black. L30
Duke Mu was not speaking, summoned Bole and addressing him, said: L32
"Failure indeed, Sir, the person you sent to source for the horse ! L34
Color of horse, female or male, also not able to know, then how to know the horse that's ?" L37
Bole sighing a naturally primal breath, said: "Uniquely reaching this level truly ! L39
This is why he is ten thousand times exceeding subject-me and countless more that's. L41
Like Gao, what he observed is a heavenly secret, that's. L43
Attaining the essence and forget the coarse; on the inside and forget the outside; L45
Seeing what he observed and not seeing what he has not observed; L47
Discerning what he discerned and lost what he has not discerned. L49
Like Gao his assessment skill, also has more value beyond the horses, that's. L51
The horse arrived, certainly a world-class horse, that's. L53

Comments:

8.14 Bole Assessment of Horses

Duke Mu noted Bole's advanced age, so asked if his family members can help source for horses.
Bole said his sons were lowly talented, able to source for good horses, not the world-class kind.
The world-class horses, like extinct and nondescript, but in speed raise no dust and leave no trail.
But he had a close associate named Jiufanggao, a woodcutter who had better knowledge of horses.
Then Duke Mu sent Jiufanggao on a trip to source for the world-class horse.
After 3 months he returned, reporting said: "Already acquired the horse, a mare and yellow."
Duke Mu saw it was a black stallion and told Bole it was a total failure, in sex and color !
However Bole was elated when the horse arrived, certainly a world-class horse indeed.
Gao had observed a heavenly secret, attained the inner essence and forgot the coarse outside.
Bole's assessment of inner strength and not superficial traits, may extend beyond horses. L51

Chapter 8. Charming Talks (說符)

8.15 未闻身乱而国治   8.15 Never: Self Chaotic, State Ordered

01	楚庄王问詹何曰：	King Zhuang of Chu (state) Asked Zhanhe Said:
02	"治国奈何？"	"Administration of State How About?"
03	詹何对曰：	Zhanhe Said:
04	"臣明于治身而	"Subject-me Understand The Ordering of Self But
05	不明于治国也。"	Not Understand The Ordering of State, that's."
06	楚庄王曰：	King Zhuang of Chu (state) Said:
07	"寡人得奉宗庙社稷，	"Lonely-me Need to Support Family Temple and Society,
08	愿学所以守之。"	Willing to Learn Whatever To Preserve Them."
09	詹何对曰：	Zhanhe Answering, Said:
10	"臣未尝闻身治	"Subject-me Never Ever Heard Self Ordered
11	而国乱者也，	And Person made the State Chaotic, that's,
12	*又未尝闻身乱*	*Also Never Ever Heard Self Chaotic*
13	*而国治者也。*	*And Person made the State Ordered, that's.*
14	故本在身，	Hence Basically On Self,
15	不敢对以末。"	Not Dare Answer In Details."
16	楚王曰：	King of Chu Said:
17	"善。"	"Excellent."

Liezi Text Narrative

King Zhuang of Chu asking Zhanhe said: "Administration of state, how about?" L2
Zhanhe said: "Subject-me clear about ordering of self but not about ordering of state, that's. L5
King Zhuang said: "Lonely me has to support family temple and society. L7
So willing to learn whatever necessary to preserve them." L8
Zhanhe answering, said: L9
"Subject-me never ever heard, a person self ordered will make the state chaotic, that's. L11
Also never ever heard, a person self chaotic can make a state ordered, that's. L13
Hence basically depends on the self and I do not dare to answer in detail." L15
King of Chu said: "Excellent." L17

Comments:
8.15 Never: Self Chaotic, State Ordered
King Zhuang of Chu asked about administration of a state.
Zhanhe said he was clear about ordering himself but not about ordering a state.
King Zhuang persisted that he was willing to learn to preserve the family temple and society.
Zhanhe said he never ever heard, a person self ordered will make the state chaotic, that's.
And also never ever heard, a person self chaotic can make a state ordered.
Zhanhe finally said, basically it all depends on the ruler himself and said no more.
King of Chu said, "Excellent".

Truly, to put a state in order, a ruler must first put himself in order.

Chapter 8. Charming Talks (說符)

8.16 人有三怨   8.16 People Have 3 Complaints

01	狐丘丈人谓孙叔敖曰：	Huqiu Elder Person Telling Sunshuao Said:
02	*"人有三怨,*	*"People have 3 Complaints,*
03	子知之乎？"	Sir, Know Them or Not ? "
04	孙叔敖曰：	Sunshuao Said:
05	"何谓也？"	"What Saying that's ?"
06	对曰：	Answering Said:
07	"爵高者人妒之，	"Nobility High Person, People Envy Him,
08	官大者主恶之，	Official-status Big Person, Master Hates Him,
09	禄厚者怨逮之。"	Remuneration Thick Person, Complaints Catch Him."
10	孙叔敖曰：	Sunshuao Said:
11	"吾爵益高，	"My Nobility More Higher,
12	吾志益下；	My Wishes More Lower (humble);
13	吾官益大，	My Official-status More Bigger,
14	吾心益小；	My Ambition More Smaller;
15	吾禄益厚，	My Remuneration More Substantial,
16	吾施益博。	My Giving More Broadly.
17	以是免于三怨，	Therefore Exempt From the 3 Complaints,
18	可乎？"	Possible, Right ?"

Liezi Text Narrative
Elder Huqiu telling Sunshuao said: "People have 3 complaints. L2
Sir, do you know them ?" L3
Sunshuao said: "What are you talking about, that's ?" L5
Elder Huiqiu said:
"High nobility, people envy; Big official-status, master hates; salary fat, people complain." L9
Sunshuao said: L10
"High nobility, lower wishes; big office, reduced ambition; fat salary, broader giving." L16
Therefore can be exempted from the 3 complaints, this is possible, right ?" L18

Comments:
8.16 People Have 3 Complaints
Elder Huiqiu told Sunshuao the 3 common complaints that people have:
Envious of nobility, master hates subordinates of high office, and complaints of fat remuneration.
Sunshuao solutions are:
Of high nobility, be humble; of high office, be less ambitious; with fat salary, be generous.

Simple solutions offered here to gain exemption from the 3 common complaints of people.

8.17 此地不利   8.17 This Land Is Bad

01 孙叔敖疾将死，	Sunshuao Sick And Dying,
02 戒其子曰：	Warning His Son Said:
03 "王亟封我矣，	"King Repeatedly Confers Me Indeed,
04 吾不受也，	I Never Accepted that's,
05 为我死，	If I die,
06 王则封汝。	King Then Confers You.
07 汝必无受利地！	You Certainly Don't Accept Favorable Land !
08 楚越之间有寝丘者，	Chu Yue In Between Has Qinqiu Land,
09 *此地不利而名甚恶。*	***This Land Not Favorable And Name Rather Bad.***
10 楚人鬼而越人(礻 几)，	People of Chu Bedevil And People of Yue Prayerful,
11 可长有者唯此也。"	Possible for Prolong Possessing It Only Here, that's."
12 孙叔敖死，	Sunshuao Died,
13 王果以美地封其子。	King Really With Good Land Conferred His Son.
14 子辞而不受，	Son Declined And Not Accept,
15 请寝丘。	Requested Qinqiu.
16 与之，	Given Him,
17 至今不失。	Till Now Not Lost.

Liezi Text Narrative
Sunshuao was sick and dying, and warning his son, said: L2
"King has repeatedly conferred on me and I never accept. L4
When I die, King will confer on you. L6
You surely should not accept favorable land ! L7
Between the State of Chu and the State of Yue has a land called Qinqiu (Sleepy Hillock). L8
This land is not favorable and has a bad name. L9
People of Chu are bedeviled and people of Yue prayerful with regard to it. L10
Possible for prolong possession, this is the only place, that's. L11
Sunshuao died, and sure enough, King conferred his son with good land. L13
Son declined and did not accept, but did request for Qinqiu. L15
He was given the land, and till now the land was not lost. L17

Comments:
8.17 This Land Is Bad
Sunshuao was sick and dying, hence warned his son and said:
"King frequently confers on me and I never accept.
When I die, King will confer on you, and you must not accept favorable land.
Qinqiu (Sleepy Mound), the land between the states of Chu and Yue is not favorable.
This land has a bad name.
People of Chu are bedeviled with it and people of Yue are prayerful with it.
So this is the only place that nobody wants, that can be possessed for a long time."
Indeed, after Sunshuao died, the king conferred his son with a good piece of land
As instructed by father, the son declined, and instead requested for Qinqiu.
His wish was granted, and till now the land was still with the family. L17

A poor piece of land that nobody will contest, and you can keep it long-term.

8.18 为盗仁将焉在?

01	牛缺者，	Niuque Person
02	上地之大儒也，	Shangde's Great Scholar that's,
03	下之邯郸，	Down To Handan,
04	遇盗于耦沙之中，	Met Bandits In The Ousha Region,
05	尽取其衣装车，	Completely Took His Clothes Belongings Carriage,
06	牛步而去。	Niu Walked And Left.
07	视之欢然无忧(又弘)之色。	He Looked Joyous No Worry Stingy The Color.
08	盗追而问其故。	Bandits Chased And Asked The Reason.
09	曰：	Said:
10	"君子不以所养	"Gentleman Not Letting What is Supporting
11	害其所养。"	Harms What is Supported."
12	盗曰：	Bandits Said:
13	"嘻！贤矣夫！"	"Hee ! Virtuous Indeed Right !"
14	既而相谓曰：	Then And Together Discussing, Said:
15	"以彼之贤，	"Person With His Virtues,
16	往见赵君，	Ventures to See King of Zhao,
17	使以我为，	Send To (stop) My Actions,
18	必困我。	Certain To Trap Us.
19	不如杀之。"	Nothing Better than to Kill Him."
20	乃相与追而杀之。	Hence Together Banded Chased And Killed Him.
21	燕人闻之，	Yan People Heard This,
22	聚族相戒，	Gathered Clan people Mutually Warning,
23	曰：	Said:
24	"遇盗，	"Meeting Bandits,
25	莫如上地之牛缺也！"	Don't be Like Niuque Of Shangde that's !"
26	皆受教。	All Accepted Teaching.
27	俄而其弟适秦，	Shortly And The Young-brother Traveled to Qin,
28	至关下，	Reached Border-pass Below,
29	果遇盗；	Did Met Bandits;
30	忆其兄之戒，	Remembering The Brother His Warning,
31	因与盗力争；	Hence With Bandits Strongly Contested;
32	既而不如，	As Such No Match,
33	又追而以卑辞	Again Chased And With Lowly Words
34	请物。	Begged Possessions (be returned).
35	盗怒曰：	Bandits Angrily Said:
36	"吾活汝弘矣，	"We let You Live, Great Indeed,
37	而追吾不已，	And Chasing Us Not Stopping,
38	迹将著焉。	Also Will Expose us Too.
39	***既为盗矣，***	***Already Be Bandits Indeed,***
40	***仁将焉在?"***	***Mercy Where Can be Found ?"***
41	遂杀之，	Proceeded to Kill Him.
42	又傍害其党	Also Besides Killed His Associates
43	四五人焉。	4, 5 People Too.

8.18 Bandits Have No Mercy ?

8.18 Bandits Have No Mercy ?

Liezi Text Narrative
Niuque, a great scholar of Shangde, went to Handan and met with Bandits in the Ousha region.L4
Completely relieved of his clothes, belongings, carriage, Niu just walked off and left. L6
He looked joyous, not worried or stingy in color, so bandits chased up and asked the reason. L8
Niu said: "Gentleman not letting what is supporting to harm what is supported." L11
Bandits said: "Hee ! Virtuous indeed, right !" L13
Then together discussing, said: "Person with his virtues, ventures to see the King of Zhao. L16
If he is sent to stop our action, certainly will trap us, then we better kill him." L19
Hence banded together, chased and killed him. L20

People of Yan heard this, gathered clan people, mutually warning said: L23
"Meeting with bandits, don't be like Niuque of Shangde, that's !"; and all accepted teaching. L26
Shortly, the young-brother traveled to Qin, and did meet the bandits below the border-pass. L29
Heeding the brother's warning, he strongly contested with the bandits, but was no match. L32
He again chased up and with humble words begged to get back his possessions. L34
Bandits angrily said: "We release you alive, already great indeed, yet chasing us none stop. L37
You will be exposing us too, therefore already as bandits, where can you find mercy ?" L40
They proceeded to kill him, and besides all his associates, 4 or 5 people in all. L43

Comments:
8.18 Bandits Have No Mercy ?
Niuque, great scholar of Shangde went to Handan and met with bandits at Ousha region
Relieved of all his belongings and carriage, he walked away quite joyous and unaffected.
Bandits asked and he said: "Gentleman do not let what is supporting to harm what is supported."
Bandits suspected he would meet King of Zhao, would come back to trap them, and so killed him.
Thus over-display of virtues and potentials threatened the bandits and cost Niuque his life.

Yan people heard it, and the clan was warned not to be like Qiuque when meeting with bandits.
Shortly, the young-brother travelled to Qin and met with bandits below the border-pass.
So unlike Niuque, he contested the bandits, and chased after them to get back his possessions.
Bandits were angry as his none stop chasing exposed them, thus killing him and his associates.

Bandits are merciless when they feel threatened, so don't mess with them.

Chapter 8. Charming Talks (説符)

8.19 飞鸢适坠其腐鼠　　8.19 Disaster Falling From Heaven

01	虞氏者，	This Yu Clan,
02	梁之富人也，	Wealthy People of Liang (state) that's,
03	家充殷盛，	Family Fully Substantial Prosperous,
04	钱帛无量，	Money Silk Not Measurable,
05	财货无訾。	Wealth Commodities Not Estimable
06	登高楼，	Ascended Tall Club-Building,
07	临大路，	Upon Big Thoroughfare,
08	设乐陈酒，	Set-up Music Displayed Wine,
09	击博楼上，	Playing Gambling Up Stairs,
10	侠客相随而行，	Swordsmen Together Walking In Line,
11	楼上博者射，	Up Stairs Gambling People Casting (dices),
12	明琼张中，	Clearly Hitting The Jackpot,
13	反两㲉鱼而笑。	Repeated Twice Winning And Laughing.
14	**飞鸢适坠**	***Flying Eagle Coincidentally Dropped***
15	**　其腐鼠而中之。**	***　Its Rotten Rat And Hit Him (leader).***
16	侠客相与言曰：	Swordsmen Together In Conversation Said:
17	"虞氏富乐之日久矣，	"Yu Clan Rich and Happy Their Days been Many indeed,
18	而常有轻易人之志。	And Often Had The Wish of Slighting Despising People.
19	吾不侵犯之，	I have Not Infringed Offended Them,
20	而乃辱我以腐鼠。	And Still Insulted Me With Rotten Rat.
21	此而不报，	This And Not Retaliated,
22	无以立慬于天下。	Nothing To Stand Brave Here Beneath Heaven.
23	请与若等戮力一志，	Imploring With All Comrades, Kill Strength One Will,
24	率徒属	Leading Our Followers
25	必灭其家为等伦。"	Certain to Extinct The Family To Even the Score."
26	皆许诺。	All Gave Promise.
27	至期日之夜，	Till Appointed Day That Night,
28	聚众积兵，	Gathered the People Accumulated the Weapons,
29	以攻虞氏，	To Attack Clan of Yu,
30	大灭其家。	Totally Extinguished The Family.

8.19 Disaster Falling From Heaven

Liezi Text Narrative
The Clan of Yu, wealthy people of the state of Liang, that's. L2
Family fully prosperous, had an immeasurable amount of money, silk and commodities. L5
Ascended tall club-building built upon big thoroughfare, had live music, fine-wine dining. L8
Playing games. gambling upstairs, while swordsmen together in file walking pass below. L10
Upstairs gambler casting dice, playing jackpot, had repeated twice winning and laughing. L13.
Coincidentally, an eagle flying by, dropped its rotten rat and hit the swordsmen leader. L15

Swordsmen conversing together said: "Clan of Yu, been rich and happy for too many days. L17
And often have the habit of slighting and despising people. L18
I have not infringed and offended them, and yet have insulted me with this rotten rat. L20
If this incident is not retaliated, we have nothing with which to stand brave beneath heaven. L22
I implore that we join strength, and with one will, extinguish this family to even the score." L25
All gave promise, and at the appointed day that night, gathered together followers, weapons. L28
They attacked the Clan of Yu and totally annihilated the family. L30

Comments:
8.19 Disaster Falling From Heaven
State of Liang had this Clan of Yu, people with immeasurable amounts of money and silk.
On top of a tall club house built upon big thoroughfare, they had live music and fine dining.
Casting dice gambling, playing jackpot, with repeated twice winning and hilarious laughing.
Coincidentally, an eagle flew by, dropped its rotten rat, hit a swordsman who passed below.
Swordsmen conspired, the Clan of Yu had been rich for too long, becoming intolerably arrogant.
The swordsmen leader had not offended them, yet he was insulted with this rotten rat.
The incident must be retaliated, else they had nothing with which to stand brave beneath Heaven.
To even the score, they must join force and with one will, to exterminate the family.
On the night of action day, they gathered forces and weapons, and totally wipe-out the family.

Arrogant, clan of Yu suffered retribution from Heaven when eagle dropped rat on swordsmen.
Today, Covid19 pandemic is a disaster from Heaven as thousands die for not wearing masks.

Chapter 8. Charming Talks (說符)

8.20 食为盗而不敢食 | 8.20 Not Eating Bandit's Food

01	东方有人焉，	The East Had Person that's,
02	曰爰旌目，	Named Aijingmu,
03	将有适也，	Had Planned Travels that's,
04	而饿于道。	Was Hungry (faint) By the Way.
05	狐父之盗曰丘，	Bandit of Hufu (region) Named Qiu,
06	见而下壶餐以餔之。	Saw And Down Water-bottle Food To Feed Him,
07	爰旌目三餔而后能视，	Aijingmu 3 Feeds And Then Able to See,
08	曰：	Said:
09	"子何为者也？"	"Sir What are You Doing that's ?"
10	曰：	Said:
11	"我狐父之人丘也。"	"I, Person of Hufu, Name Qiu that's."
12	爰旌目曰：	Aijingmu Said:
13	"譆！汝非盗耶？	"Hee ! Aren't You a Bandit ?
14	胡为而食我？	Indiscriminately Acting And Feeding Me ?
15	吾义不食子之食也。"	I Righteously Not Eating, Sir Your Food that's."
16	两手据地而欧之，	Two Hands Braced on Floor And Vomiting It,
17	不出，	Not Coming-out,
18	喀喀然遂伏而死。	Ka' Ka' Sounding, Then Prostrated And Died.
19	狐父之人则盗矣，	The Person of Jufu Was Bandit indeed,
20	而食非盗也。	But Food Not Bandit that's.
21	以人之盗，	Because Person Is Bandit,
22	**因谓食为盗而不敢食，**	***Hence Said Food Is Bandit And Not Dare to Eat,***
23	是失名实者也。	Is Losing Fact and Name that's.

Liezi Text Narrative

From the East, Aijingmu who had planned travels, fainted by the way from hunger. L4
From the Hufu region, bandit Qiu saw him, took down a water-bottle and food to feed him. L6
Aijingmu was able to see after 3 feeding, said: " Sir, what are you doing, that's ?" L9
Bandit Qiu said: "I, a person from Hufu, name Qiu that's." L11
Aijingmu said: "Hee ! Aren't you a bandit ? Indiscriminately feeding me ? L14
I righteously not eating, Sir, your food that's." L15
Bracing two hands on the ground and trying to throw out food, but not coming-out. L17
Ka' ka' sounding, until prostrated and died. L18
Person from Hufu is indeed a bandit, but food is not banditry, that's. L20
Person a bandit, hence his food is banditry and not dare to eat, is a loss of reality in names. L23

Comments:

8.20 Not Eating Bandit's Food

Aijingmu on travels fainted from hunger, and bandit Qiu revived him with water and food.
Aijingmu asked, "Sir, what are you doing ?"; Bandit Qiu said: "I am from Hufu, name Qiu that's."
Aijingmu said: "Hee ! aren't you a bandit ? I righteously not eating, Sir, your food that's."
Sounding ka' ka', he tried hard to throw out but failed and died prostrated on the ground.
Person a bandit, hence his food is banditry and not dare to eat, is a loss of reality in names.

Arrogant and perceived prejudice only harm oneself, but it is a matter of individual choice

Chapter 8. Charming Talks (說符)

8.21 怼以忘其身者   8.21 Perverse Hatred

01	柱厉叔事莒敖公，	Zhulishu Served Duke Juao,
02	自为不知己，	Self Thought (Duke Juao) Not Knowing Self,
03	去，居海上。	Left, Living By the Sea.
04	夏日则食菱芰，	Summer Days Then Eating Water Chestnut,
05	冬日则食橡栗。	Winter Days Then Eating Oak Chestnut,
06	莒敖公有难，	Duke Juao Had Troubles,
07	柱厉叔辞其友	Zhulishu took Leave of His Friend
08	而往死之。	And Go-forth to Sacrifice for Him (Duke Juao)
09	其友曰：	His Friend Said:
10	"子自以为不知己，	"Sir, Self Thought That (Duke Juao) Not Know Self,
11	故去。	Hence Left (Duke Juao).
12	今往死之，	Now Go-forth to Sacrifice for Him,
13	是知与不知无辨也。"	Is Knowing/Not Knowing, No Discrimination, that's."
14	柱厉叔曰：	Zhulishu Said:
15	"不然；	"Not True;
16	自以为不知，	Self Thinking Not Knowing (by Duke Juao),
17	故去。	Hence Left.
18	今死，	Now Sacrificing,
19	是果不知我也。	Is Proof Not Knowing Me, that's (by Duke Juao).
20	吾将死之，	I Shall Sacrifice for Him (Duke Juao),
21	以丑后世之人主	To Shame Future Generations, Those Masters of People
22	不知其臣者也。"	Those Not Knowing Their Subjects, that's."
23	凡知则死之，	Normally, Know Then Sacrifice for Master,
24	不知则弗死，	Not Know Then No Sacrifice,
25	此直道而行者也。	This The Straight Way For Action, that's.
26	**柱厉叔可谓怼以**	**Zhulishu, Possible to Say Hatred Until**
27	**　忘其身者也。**	**　Overlooking Own Body (life), such a Person that's.**

Liezi Text Narrative

Zhulishu served Duke Juao, self realised not being appreciated, so left, and lived by the sea. L3
Summer days eating water chestnuts, and winter days eating oak chestnuts. L5
Duke Juao had troubles, Zhulishu took leave of friend to go-forth, ready to sacrifice for Duke. L8
His friend said: "Sir self thought Duke not appreciative, hence left. L11
Now go-forth to sacrifice for him, so knowing and not knowing, no discrimination. that's." L13
Zhulishu said: "Not true; self thought not being appreciated, hence left. L17
Now going forth to sacrifice is proof that Duke did not know me. L19
I sacrifice for Duke, to shame later generations of masters, unappreciative of their subjects." L22
Usually, knowing then sacrifice for master, not knowing no sacrifice, is the direct way to act. L25
Zhulishu, this is to say his hatred overlooked his own body (life), just such a person that's. L27

8.21 Perverse Hatred

Comments:
8.21 Perverse Hatred
Zhulishu served Duke Juao, realised not being appreciated, left and lived on chestnuts by the sea. Duke Juao in trouble, so Zhulishu took leave of friend to go-forth, ready to sacrifice for Duke. Friend questioned his indiscriminate action, as generally, no appreciation means no sacrifice. Zhulishu said this is proof of his loyalty and also to shame future unappreciative masters ! *Zhulishu was a person who allowed his hatred to overlook his own safety and life.*

Perversely, Zhulishu chose to die to prove his loyalty, to spite all future unappreciative masters!

Chapter 8. Charming Talks (說符)

8.22 怨往者害来   8.22 Enmity (ill will) Brings Disaster

01 杨朱曰：   Yangzhu Said:
02 "利出者实及，   "Whatever Benefit Given-out, Solid (goodwill) Returnth,
03 怨往者害来。   **Whatever Hatred Go-forth, Disaster Cometh.**
04 发于此而   Project From Here (self) Then
05   应于外者唯请：   Responses From Outside People are Only Feelings :
06 是故贤者慎所出。"   Therefore Wise Person Mindful Whatever Given-out."

Liezi Text Narrative
Yangzhu said: "Whatever benefit is given out, solid goodwill returns. L2
Whatever hatred go-forth, disaster cometh. L3
Project from self, then responses from outside people are only feelings: L5
Therefore a wise person mindful of whatever given out." L6

Comments:
8.22 Enmity (ill will) Brings Disaster
Yangzhu believes, benefits given out gets goodwill in return, hatred given out will bring disaster. Projection from self will get responses from others, so it is all a matter of feelings. *Therefore a wise person is always mindful of what he projects.*

It seems logical and fair to expect, goodwill begets goodwill, and ill-will can bring disaster.

8.23 多歧路   8.23 Many Branching Paths

01 杨子之邻人亡羊，	Yangzi His Neighbor Lost a Goat,
02 既率其党，	Instantly Led His Party,
03 又请杨子之竖追之。	Also Requested Yangzi His Servant to Find It.
04 杨子曰：	Yangzi Said:
05 "嘻！	"Hee !
06 亡一羊何追者之众？"	Lost A Goat, Why, A Crowd of People Chasing ?"
07 邻人曰：	Neighbor Said:
08 "多歧路。"	"Many Branching Paths."
09 既反，问：	Already Returned, Asked:
10 "获羊乎？"	"Caught Goat Already ?"
11 曰："亡之矣。"	Said: "Lost It indeed."
12 曰："奚亡之？"	Said: "Why Lost It ?"
13 曰：	Said:
14 **"歧路之中又有歧焉。**	***"Branching Paths Therein Also Has Branching, that's.***
15 吾不知所之，	I Not Know Where It is,
16 所以反也。"	Therefore Return that's."
17 杨子戚然变容，	Yangzi Suddenly Sadden Naturally Change Countenance,
18 不言者移时，	Not Speaking That's for Some Time,
19 不笑者竟日。	Not Laughing That's for a Whole Day.
20 门人怪之，	Disciples Were Surprised,
21 请曰：	Enquiring Said:
22 "羊贱畜，	" Goat Lowly Animal,
23 又非夫子之有，	Also Not Teacher Your Possession,
24 而损言笑者何哉？"	And Lost Speech Laughter That's Whatever For ?"
25 杨子不答。	Yangzi Not Answering.
26 门人不获所命。	Disciples Not Catching His Teaching.
27 弟子孟孙阳出，	Disciple Mengsunyang Exited,
28 以告心都子。	To Tell Xindouzi.
29 心都子他日与孟孙阳偕入，	Xindouzi Another Day With Mengsunyang Both Entered,
30 而问曰：	And Asking Said:
31 "昔有昆弟三人，	"Formerly Had Elder, Younger-brothers 3 Persons,
32 游齐，鲁之间，	Travelling in Qi, Lu Those Regions,
33 同师而学，	Same Teacher For Learning,
34 进仁义	Entered Love Justice
35 之道而归。	These Paths And Return.
36 其父曰：	The Father Said:
37 '仁义之道若何？'	'Love Justice These Paths Like What ?"
38 伯曰：	Bo (elder-brother) Said:
39 '仁义使我爱身而后名。'	'Love Justice Lets Me Love Life Then After Name.'
40 仲曰：	Zhong (second-brother) Said:
41 '仁义使我杀身以成名。'	'Ethics Justice Lets Me Sacrifice Life To Make a Name.'

8.23 Many Branching Paths

42	叔曰：	Shu (third-brother) Said:
43	'仁义使我身名并全。'	'Love Justice Lets Me Preserve Both Life and Name.'
44	彼三术相反，	Their 3 Tactics Mutually Contradicting,
45	而同出于儒。	And Similarly Emerging From Confucianism.
46	孰是孰非邪？"	Who's Right Who's Wrong That's ?"
47	杨子曰：	Yangzi Said:
48	"人有滨河而居者，	"Had The Person Living By River Side,
49	习于水，	Practiced In Water,
50	勇于泅，	Brave In Diving,
51	操舟鬻渡，	Managing Boat Plying the Crossing,
52	利供百口。	Earnings Support 100 Mouths (people).
53	裹粮就学者成徒，	Bringing Supplies To Learn, People Forming Droves,
54	而溺死者几半。	And Drowning Death, People About Half.
55	本学泅，	Originally to Learn Diving,
56	不学溺，	Not to Learn Drowning,
57	而利害如此。	And Gain/Loss Like This.
58	若以为孰是孰非？"	How To Think What's Right, What's Wrong ?"
59	心都子嘿然而出。	Xindouzi Quietly Naturally Came Out.
60	孟孙阳让之曰：	Mengsunyang Complaining to Him Said:
61	"何吾子问之迂，	"Why my Sir Asking So Tortuously,
62	夫子答之僻？	Teacher Answering So Weirly ?
63	吾惑愈甚。"	My Confusion More Deep."
64	心都子曰：	Xindouzi Said:
65	"大道以多歧亡羊，	"Great Paths With Many Branching Lost Goat,
66	学者以多方丧生。	Scholars With Many Methods Lost Lives.
67	学非本不同，	Learning, Not Originally (intention) Not Same,
68	非本不一，	Not Originally (intention) Not One,
69	而末异若是。	But Ending Different Like This.
70	唯归同反一，	Only Return to Same, Back to One (original intention),
71	为亡得丧。	To Cut The Loss.
72	子长先生之门，	Sir, Senior in Teacher's Tutelage
73	习先生之道，	Practicing Teacher's Way ('Dao'),
74	而不达先生之况也，	And Not Know Teacher His Condition that's,
75	哀哉！"	Sad Indeed !"

Liezi Text Narrative

The neighbor lost a goat, led a party in search, even requesting Yangzi's servant.to help. L3
Yangzi said: "Hee ! Lost a goat, why need a crowd of people to help recovery ?" L6
Neighbor said: "Many branching paths." L8
Already returned, Yangzi asked: "Caught the goat ?" L10
Neighbor said: "Lost it indeed."; Yangzi asked: "Why lost it ?" L12
Neighbor: "Branching paths therein more branching, I do not know where it is, so return. L16
Yangzi sadden, countenance changed, not speaking for a while, not laughing for a whole day. L19
Disciples were surprised, enquiring said: "Goat lowly animal, and not teacher, your property. L23
And you lost speech and laughter that's whatever for ?"; Yangzi did not answer. L25

8.23 Many Branching Paths

The disciples didn't understand him and Mengsunyang disciple exited to tell Xindouzi. L28
One day, Xindouzi with Mengsunyang both entered Yangzi's room and asking said: L30
"Formerly had elder brother and young brothers, 3 persons travelling in Qi, Lu regions. L32
They learned from the same teacher, the paths of Love and Justice, before returning. L35
The father asked: 'Love and Justice these paths like what ?' L37
Bo, the elder brother said: 'Love and Justice lets me love life first and put the name behind.' L39
Zhong, the second brother said: 'Love and Justice lets me sacrifice life to make a name.' L41
Shu, the third brother said: 'Love and Justice lets me preserve both life and name.' L43
Their 3 tactics are mutually contradicting, and similarly evolved from the same teacher. L45
Who's right and who's wrong, that's ?" L46
Yangzi said: "Had the person living by the river side, practiced in water, brave in diving. L50
Managing the boat plying the crossing, earning enough to support 100 mouths (people). L52
Bearing supplies, people in droves came to learn, and about half of them died from drowning.L54
Originally to learn diving, not to learn drowning, the gain/loss like this, so different. L57
How to think what's right and what's wrong ?" L58
Xindouzi quietly came out, and Mengsunyang complaining to him said: L60
"Why is Sir asking so tortuously and teacher answering so weirdly ?; I am deeply confused." L63
Xindouzi said: "The great paths with many branchings, lost a goat. L65
Scholars with many methods lost lives. L66
Learning, originally the same one intention, but the ending so different such as this. L69
Only by returning to originally the same and one intention, to cut the loss. L71
Sir, senior in teacher's tutelage, and practicing teacher's 'Dao'. L73
And not knowing the teacher's disposition, that's sad indeed !" L75

Comments:
8.23 Many Branching Paths
Neighbor lost a goat, led a party in search, even requesting the help of Yangzi's servant boy.
Yangzi asked why he needed a host of people to help, and neighbor said there were many paths.
Later Yangzi asked if the goat was found; the neighbor said no because of more branching paths.
Yangzi was sad as he thought of scholars in quest of truth, lost in the branching paths ahead.

Not understanding his sadness, Xindouzi and Mengsunyang went in, asking in a tortuous way.
Said there were 3 brothers, learning benevolence and righteousness from the same teacher.
Hence one loves life ahead of name; second will sacrifice life for a name; third will preserve both.
Three contradicting tactics learned from the same teacher, so who is right and who is wrong that's.
Yangzi, not answering directly, but weirdly told another story.
A person brave in diving was plying the river crossing and earning enough to support 100 people.
Thus bearing supplies, people in droves came to learn, and about half of them died, drowning.
So how to think what's right and what's wrong ?"
Xindouzi explained that branching paths lost a goat, and with many tactics scholars lost lives.
So to cut loss, keep focus and return to the same, first, original intention for action (不忘初衷).

Goat lost over many branching paths, scholars lost over forgetting the first, original intention.

Chapter 8. Charming Talks (說符)

8.24 岂能无怪哉?   8.24 Don't Blame The Dog ?

01	杨朱之弟曰布,	Yangzhu His Brother Called Bu,
02	衣素衣而出。	Clothed in Plain (white) Clothing And Out.
03	天雨,	Heaven Rained,
04	解素衣,	Took-down Plain (white) Clothing,
05	衣缁衣而反。	Clothed in Black Clothing And Returned.
06	其狗不知,	His Dog Not Knowing
07	迎而吠之。	Greeting With Barking at Him.
08	杨而怒,	Yang Was Angry,
09	将扑之。	Going to Attack It.
10	杨朱曰:	Yangzhu Said:
11	"子无扑矣!	Sir No Attacking Indeed !
12	子亦犹是也。	Sir Also Like This that's.
13	向者使汝狗白而往,	Just Then Let Your Dog White And Go-forth,
14	黑而来,	Black On Return,
15	***岂能无怪哉?"***	***How Possible No Surprise, Right ?"***

Liezi Text Narrative
Yangzhu, his brother named Bu, was clothed in white clothing when he went out. L2
Heaven rained, so he took off his white clothing, changed into black clothing before returning. L5
His dog did not know this and so greeted him with barking. L7
Bu was angry and was going to attack it. L9
Yangzhu said: "Sir no attacking indeed ! Sir also will behave like this, that's. L12
Just then let your dog go out, be seen as white; then be seen as black in return. L14
How possible not to be surprised, right ?" L15

Comments:
8.24 Don't Blame The Dog ?
Yangzhu's brother, Bu went out in white clothing, met with rain and changed into black clothing.
On his return, his dog barked at him; he was angry with it and was going to attack it.
Yangzhu stopped him by saying he will behave the same way under the same circumstance.
Like, when his dog was seen as white dog going out, then seen as a black dog coming back !

It is fair to empathize with the dog, with all living things and with the environment.

Chapter 8. Charming Talks (說符)

8.25 慎为善   8.25 Caution Doing Charity

01 杨朱曰：	Yangzhu Said:
02 "行善不以为名，	"Doing Charity Not To Make a Name,
03 而名从之；	And Name Follows It;
04 名不与利期，	Name has No Appointment With Benefits,
05 而利归之；	But Benefit will Return to It;
06 利不与争期，	Benefit has No Appointment With Contest,
07 而争及之：	But Contest will Reach It:
08 *故君子必慎为善。"*	***Hence Gentleman Must be Careful Doing Charity.***

Liezi Text Narrative

Yangzhu said: "Doing Charity is not to make a name, but name or reputation will follow you. L3
Name or reputation has no appointment with benefits, but benefits will follow you. L5
Benefits have no appointment with rivalry, but rivalry will reach you. L7
Hence gentlemen must be careful when doing charity." L8

Comments:
8.25 Caution Doing Charity

Doing charity is not to make a name, yet reputation, benefits, and rivalry will find you.
Hence Yangzhu said, gentlemen ought to be careful when doing charity

True charity seeks no name, no return benefits and no competition.

8.26 不死之道 — 8.26 'Dao' Of Life Everlasting

01	昔人言有知	*Formerly Person Said Had Knowledge of*
02	不死之道者，	*The 'Dao' of Life Everlasting,*
03	燕君使人受之，	King of Yan Sent Person to Learn from Him,
04	不捷，而言者死。	No Success, The 'Said Person' Died.
05	燕君甚怒其使者，	King of Yan Very Angry of His Envoy Person,
06	将加诛焉。	Going to Confer Death-sentence Indeed.
07	幸臣谏曰：	Favored Official Opposing Said:
08	"人所忧者	"People Whatever Worry About
09	莫急乎死，	None More Urgent than Death,
10	己所重者	Self Whatever Serious About
11	莫过乎生。	None More Than Life.
12	彼自丧其生，	Person Himself Lost Own Life,
13	安能令君不死也？"	How Possible to Enable my King to Not Die, That's ?"
14	乃不诛。	Hence No Death-sentence.
15	有齐子亦欲学其道，	Qizi Also Wish to Learn The 'Dao' (of Life Everlasting),
16	闻言者之死，	Heard 'Said Person' His Death
17	乃抚膺而恨。	Then Banging Chest And Lamenting.
18	富子闻而笑之曰：	Fuzi Heard And Laughing at Him Said:
19	"夫所欲学不死，	"What You Wish to Learn is Life Everlasting,
20	其人已死而犹恨之，	That Person Already Dead And Still Lamenting for Him,
21	是不知所以为学。"	This Not Knowing What Is For Learning."
22	胡子曰：	Huzi Said:
23	"富子之言非也。	"Fuzi His Words Incorrect that's.
24	凡人有术	Generally People Have Art
25	不能行者有矣，	Not Able to Enact, such People there Are indeed,
26	能行而无其术者	People Able to Enact And Have-not The 'Dao'
27	亦有矣。	Also there Are indeed.
28	卫人有善数者，	People of Wei Had Person Good at Numbers,
29	临死，	Upon Dying,
30	以诀喻其子。	With Trick-of-trade Informed His Son.
31	其子志其言而不能行也。	The Son Memorized His Words But Not Able to Enact.
32	他人问之，	Another Person Asked Him,
33	以其父所言告之。	With Whatever His Father had Said Informed the Person.
34	问者用其言	Enquiring Person Used The Information
35	而行其术，	And Enacted The 'Dao',
36	与其父无差焉。	With His Father's No Difference that's.
37	若然，	Like Naturally,
38	死者奚为	Dead Person Why That's
39	不能言生术哉？"	Not Able to Speak the 'Dao' of Life, Right ?"

8.26 'Dao' Of Life Everlasting

Liezi Text Narrative
In the past, a person said he had knowledge of the 'Dao' of Life Everlasting. L2
King of Yan sent a person to learn from him, but before success the 'said person' died. L4
King of Yan was very angry with his envoy person and prepared to put him to death, indeed. L6
His favored official opposing said: " People worried about death and most serious about life. L11
Person himself lost his own life, so how is it possible to enable my King to not die, that's ?" L13
Hence death-sentence retracted. L14
Qizi also wished to learn the 'Dao' of Life Everlasting, heard 'said' person's death, lamented. L17
Fuzi heard and laughingly said: "What you wished to learn is the 'Dao' of Life Everlasting. L19.
That person is already dead and still lamenting, Qizi is not knowing what he wishes to learn." L21
Huzi said: "Fuzi, his words are incorrect that's. L23
Generally, people who have 'Dao' and are not able to enact, there are such people indeed . L25
Also people who are able to enact but not have the 'Dao', there are also such people. L27
People of Wei had a person good at Numbers, and upon dying passed his son trick-of-trade. L30
The son memorized his words but was not able to enact. L31
A person asked, and the son informed the person whatever his father had said to him. L33
The person used the information, and was good at Numbers, no difference from the father. L36
Likewise a dead person, why is he not able to speak the 'Dao' of Life Everlasting, right ?" L39

Comments:
8.26 'Dao' Of Life Everlasting
A person said he had the 'Dao' of Life Everlasting and the king of Yan sent an envoy to learn it. Before succeeding, the 'said person' died, and the king was angry, sentencing the envoy to death. An official asked how the 'said person' be able to help the king to not die, when he himself died ! The envoy's life was spared.

Qizi also wished to learn the Art of Life Everlasting, and lamented when the 'said person' died. Fuzi laughing said: "Lamenting death of the 'said person', Qizi does not know what he wants."

However, Huzi said Fuzi was incorrect.
People of Wei had a person good at Numbers, and on his death passed the 'Dao' to the Son.
The son cannot use it, but a person who acquired the 'Dao' or way, can use it like his father.
Hence a dead person can also pass on his 'Dao' of Life Everlasting, right ?

Wrong ! Death is inevitable; anything can pass on, but not the 'Dao' of Life Everlasting.

Chapter 8. Charming Talks (説符)

8.27 放生   8.27 Liberating Life

01	邯郸之民,	Handan Its Citizens,
02	以正月之旦献鸠于简子,	On First Month First Day Offer Doves To Jianzi,
03	简子大悦,	Jianzi Greatly Joyous,
04	厚赏之。	Hugely Rewarded Them.
05	客问其故。	Guest Asked The Reason.
06	简子曰:	Jianzi Said:
07	***"正旦放生,***	***"First-month First-day Liberating Lives,***
08	示有恩也。"	Display Having Kindness that's."
09	客曰:	Guest Said:
10	"民知君之欲放之,	"Citizens Know King Your Wish to Liberate Them,
11	故竞而捕之,	Hence Contesting To Catch Them,
12	死者众矣。	Those Died Multitude indeed.
13	君如欲生之,	King If Wishes to Liberate Them,
14	不若禁民勿捕。	May Be Banned Citizens Not to Catch.
15	捕而放之,	Catch And Liberating Them,
16	恩过不相补矣。"	Kindness Harm Not Mutually Balanced indeed."
17	简子曰:	Jianzi Said:
18	"然。"	"Naturally."

Liezi Text Narrative

Handan, its citizens offered doves to Jianzi on the first month first day of the year. L2
Jianzi, greatly joyous, rewarded them hugely. L4
Guest asked why, and Jianzi said: "First day of the year, liberating lives to display kindness." L8
Guest said: "Citizens know King wishes to liberate them, contest to catch and many died. L11
If our King wishes to liberate them, then better to ban citizens from catching them. L14
Catching and liberating doves, kindness and harming not mutually balanced, indeed." L16
Jianzi said: "Naturally." L18

Comments:
8.27 Liberating Life

Citizens of Handan offered Jianzi doves on the first day of the year, and King rewarded them well.
Guest asked and Jianzi explained, liberating doves on the first day of the year to show kindness.
Guest said citizens knew King wished to liberate doves, so they contested to catch and many died.
The guest suggested that it was better for King to ban citizens catching them in the first place.
The liberating and harming of doves did not mutually balance out indeed.
Jianzi said: "Naturally."

Practice of Liberating Lives persists in some religious quarters today, and ought to be banned.

Chapter 8. Charming Talks (**説符**)

8.28 为蚊蚋生人	**8.28 Humanity Made For Mosquitoes Gnats**
01 齐田氏祖于庭，	Qi (state), Clan of Tian held Ancestral-feast In the Hall,
02 食客千人。	Feasting Guests Thousand People.
03 中坐有献鱼雁者，	Among Those Seated Had Offered Fish Geese
04 田氏视之，	Clan of Tian Saw Them,
05 乃叹曰：	Then Sighing, Said:
06 "天之于民厚矣！	"Heaven Bestows To Citizens Substantial indeed !
07 殖五谷，	Growth of 5 Cereals.
08 生鱼鸟，	Production of Fish Birds,
09 以为之用"	For Them To Use."
10 众客和之如响。	All Guests Agreed with Him Like Echos.
11 鲍氏之子年十二，	Clan of Bao, His Son Years 12 (age),
12 预于次，	Attending And Seated,
13 进曰：	Standing-up Said:
14 "不如君言。	"Not Like King Words.
15 天地万物与我并生，	Heaven Earth Myriad Things With Us Together Living,
16 类也。	Kinds (different) that's.
17 类无贵贱，	Kinds, None Noble none Lowly,
18 徒以小大智力	Just By Small Big (size) and Intellectual Strength
19 而相制，	Thus Mutually Restricting,
20 迭相食；	Alternately and Mutually Eating;
21 非相为而生之。	Not Mutually Working To Enliven Ourselves.
22 人取可食者而食之，	People Take Whatever Can be Eaten And Eat Them,
23 岂天本	How can it be Heaven Originally
24 　为人生之？	For Humans (consumption) Produced Them ?
25 且蚊蚋嘈肤，	Then Mosquitoes Gnats Biting Skin,
26 虎狼食肉，	Tigers Wolves Eating Meat,
27 **非天本**	***Is-it-Not Heaven Originally***
28 　**为蚊蚋生人、**	***For Mosquitoes Gnats (to feast) Produced Humans ,***
29 虎狼生肉者哉？"	Tigers Wolves Produced Meat (humans) that's, right ?"

8.28 Humanity Made For Mosquitoes Gnats

Liezi Text Narrative

Qi State, Clan of Tian held an ancestral feast in the hall, and had guests of a thousand people. L2
Some among the seated had offered fish and geese, Clan of Tian saw them and sighing, said: L5
"Heaven has bestowed citizens greatly, growth of 5 cereals, production of fish birds as food." L8
All guests agreed with him like echos, except the 12-year-old son of Mr Bao. L11
He stood up and said: "King's words are not correct. L14
Heaven Earth and the myriad things living together with us, are different in kinds, that's. L16
All kinds are similar, none noble and none lowly. L17
Just by being small/big and intellectual strength, mutually restricting and eating each other; L20
Not mutually working to enliven each other. L21
People taking whatever can be eaten and eating them. L22
How can it be that Heaven originally produced them for human consumption ? L24
Now mosquitoes/gnats biting skin and tigers/wolves eating meat. L26
Then Heaven originally produced humans for mosquitoes and gnats to feast on. L28
Produced humans as meat for tigers and wolves, is-it-true ?"

Comments:
8.28 Humanity Made For Mosquitoes Gnats

State of Qi, Clan of Tian (king) held an ancestral feast in the hall, attended by a thousand guests.
King was grateful that Heaven bestowed us with 5 cereals, production of fish and birds for food.
All the guests echoed in agreement, except for the 12-year-old son of Mr Bao.
He held that the myriad things living with us are kinds, but similar in being not nobler or lowlier.
Being small/big and intellectually different, we contested each other to eat and be eaten.
So how could it be that Heaven originally produced them for human consumption ?
Mosquitoes and gnats feast on our skin, and tigers/wolves eat our flesh when they have a chance.
Then could it also be said that Heaven originally produced humans for their consumption ?

COVID19 pandemic exposes our lack of nobility and immunity in front of other living things.

Chapter 8. Charming Talks (説符)

8.29 辱莫过于乞　　8.29 No Shame Exceeds Begging

01	齐有贫者，	State of Qi Had a Poor Person,
02	常乞于城市。	Often Begging At City Market.
03	城市患其亟也，	City Market Troubled by Him Repeatedly that's,
04	众莫之与。	People None Giving Him.
05	遂适田氏之厩，	Hence Joined Tianshi's Stable (king's),
06	从马医作役，	Followed Horse Veterinarian As Servant,
07	而假食。	For Food and Lodging.
08	郭中人戏之曰：	People From City Ridiculed Him Said:
09	"从马医而食，	"Following Horse Veterinarian For Food,
10	不以辱乎？"	Not Being Shameful, Right ?"
11	乞儿曰：	Beggar Said:
12	**"天下之辱莫过于乞。**	***"Heaven Beneath, All Shames None Exceeds A Beggar.***
13	乞犹不辱，	Begging Also Not Ashamed,
14	岂辱马医哉？"	Why Ashamed as a Horse Veterinarian, right ?"

Liezi Text Narrative
State of Qi had a poor person who often begged at the city market. L2
City market was thus repeatedly troubled by him, and none of the people were giving him. L4
Hence he joined Tianshi's (king) stable, helping the vet as a servant for food and lodging. L7
City people ridiculed him and said: "Following horse vet for food, aren't you ashamed ?" L10
Beggar said: "Heaven beneath, all shames none exceeded begging. :12
As a beggar I am not ashamed, why then be ashamed to help a horse veterinarian, right ?" L14

Comments:
8.29 No Shame Exceeds Begging
State of Qi had a poor person begging often at the city market, and soon nobody gave him.
Then he joined Tianshi's (king) stable, helping the veterinarian for food and lodging.
People ridiculed him for this job, and he replied that he was more ashamed to go begging.

Working at whatever job for food and lodging, is certainly less shameful than begging.

Chapter 8. Charming Talks (說符)

8.30 得人遺契者　　8.30 Perversely Wealthy

01	宋人有游于道，	State of Song, Had Person Wandering The Streets,
02	***得人遺契者，***	***Pick-up People's Abandoned Contracts,***
03	归而藏之，	Returned And Stored Them,
04	密数其齿。	Secretly Counting The Stamps.
05	告邻人曰：	Telling Neighboring People Said:
06	"吾富可待矣。"	"My being Wealthy Can be Expected indeed."

Liezi Text Narrative
State of Song had a person wandering the streets, picking up people's abandoned contracts. L2 *Returned home and stored them, and secretly counted the stamps (number of contracts). L4 Then telling neighbors said: "I shall be wealthy, may soon be expected, indeed." L6*

Comments:
8.30 Perversely Wealthy
State of Song had a person who wandered the streets collecting abandoned outdated contracts. *The person had lost his sanity and was delusional to tell the neighbors he would soon be rich.*

Be contented, not to be too obsessive and delusional with wealth, as to lose our sanity.

Chapter 8. Charming Talks (說符)

8.31 枯梧树　　　　　　　8.31 Withered Sycamore Tree

01 人有枯梧树者，	Person Who Had Withered Sycamore Tree,
02 其邻父言	His Neighbor's Father Said
03 　枯梧之树不祥。	Withered Sycamore The Tree Not Auspicious.
04 其邻人遽而伐之。	The Person With Urgency Cut It.
05 邻人父因请以为薪。	Neighbor's Father Then Requested It For Firewood.
06 其人乃不悦，	The Person Certainly Not Happy,
07 曰：	Said:
08 "邻人之父徒欲为薪，	"My Neighbor, His Father Only Wishes For Firewood,
09 而教吾伐之也。	And Teaches Me to Cut It that's.
10 与我邻，	With My Neighbor,
11 若此其险，	Like This So Dangerous,
12 岂可哉？"	How Possible, Right ?"

Liezi Text Narrative

A Person had a withered sycamore tree, and his neighbor's father said it was not auspicious. L3
The person then with urgency cut it and the father then requested it for firewood. L5
The person certainly not happy, said: "The father only wishes for firewood and advised me. L9
As my neighbor, like this is so dangerous, how possible, right ?" L12

Comments:
8.31 Withered Sycamore Tree
Neighbor's father said the withered sycamore tree was not auspicious, and the person cut it down.
Then the father requested it for firewood, and the person was not happy.
The father's advice was based on a wish to have firewood, thus such a neighbor is dangerous !

Always be alerted to advice given with ulterior motives, especially from close quarters.

Chapter 8. Charming Talks (説符)

8.32 无为而不窃鈇也　　8.32 No Actions Not Like Axe-Thief

01	人有亡鈇者，	Person Who Had Lost Axe,
02	意者邻之子，	Suspected Thief was Neighbor's Son,
03	视其行步，	Looking at His Movement Steps,
04	窃鈇也；	Stolen Axe that's;
05	颜色，	Facial Look,
06	窃鈇也；	Stolen Axe that's;
07	言语，	Words Speech,
08	窃鈇也；	Stolen Axe that's;
09	*动作态度*	*Motion Work Attitude*
10	*无为而不窃鈇也。*	*No Action And Not like Stolen Axe that's.*
11	俄而抇其谷而得其鈇，	Shortly In Digging His Field And Retrieved His Axe,
12	他日复见其邻人之子，	Another Day Again Observed The Neighbor's Son,
13	动作态度，	Motion Work Attitude,
14	无似窃鈇者。	None Like a Person Stolen Axe.

Liezi Text Narrative

A person lost his axe and was suspicious of the neighbor's son. L2
Watching his every movement and steps, like having stolen the axe that's; L4
Facial expression like having stolen the axe; words speech also like having stolen the axe; L8
Working attitude and all actions, none not like having stolen the axe that's. L10
Shortly, while digging in the field, the person found his axe. L11
Next day, again he observed the neighbor's son. L12
Every move and working attitude, none like a person who had stolen the axe. L4

Comments:
8.32 No Actions Not Like Axe-Thief

A person lost his axe and suspected his neighbor's son had taken it.
Watching the son's every move and steps, facial expression, none not like having taken the axe.
Shortly, digging in the field, he recovered his axe.
Next day, observing the son's every move, steps and working attitude, none like an axe-thief!

Be ever mindful that our suspicions and prejudices distort our observations and perceptions.

Chapter 8. Charming Talks (說符)

8.33 白公胜虑乱　　8.33 Beigongsheng Pondering Rebellion

01 白公胜虑乱,	***Baigongsheng Pondering Rebellion,***
02 罢朝而立,	Court session Ended Still Standing (in place),
03 倒仗策,	Inverted Staff Goad (for horses),
04 鐓上贯颐,	Sharp-end Upward Piercing Jaw (lower),
05 血流至地而弗知也。	Blood Flowing To Floor And Not Knowing that's.
06 郑人闻之曰:	People of Zheng Heard This, Said:
07 "颐之忘,	"Face Can Forget,
08 将何不忘哉?"	Then Whatever Cannot Forget, Right ?"
09 意之所属著,	Attention On Whatever Concerned so Focused,
10 其行足蹶株埳,	He Walking, Leg Tripped on Roots Threshold,
11 头抵植木,	Head Hitting Tree Pole,
12 而不自知也。	And Not Self Knowing that's."

Liezi Text Narrative
Baigongsheng pondering rebellion, court session ended, still standing in place. L2
Inverted goad (probe for horses), sharp-end piercing jaw and blood flowed without knowing. L5
People of Zheng heard this, said: "Face can forget, then whatever cannot forget, right ?" L8
Attention to whatever concerned so focus, that in walking he tripped over roots. L10
His head hitting a tree pole, and not self knowing that's. L12

Comments:
8.33 Beigongsheng Pondering Rebellion
Baigongsheng was absorbed pondering rebellion that he still stood in place after court adjourned
With inverted goad piercing jaw and blood flowing unaware, people said he even forgot his face.
With attention so focus he was unaware of tripping over tree roots, and hitting his head on poles.

Absent-mindedness causes lives, like preoccupation with the hand phone, even while driving !

312

Chapter 8. Charming Talks (說符)

8.34 不见人, 徒见金   8.34 See Nobody Only Gold

01	昔齐人有欲金者,	Formerly, People of Qi Had Person who Wished for Gold,
02	清旦衣冠而之市,	Early Dawn Dressed and Capped Then To Market,
03	适鬻金者之所,	Went to Place Where Person Retailing Gold,
04	因攫其金而去。	Hence Grabbed The Gold And Escape.
05	吏捕得之,	Official Successfully Arrested Him,
06	问曰:	Asking, Said:
07	"人皆在焉,	"People All Present that's,
08	子攫人之金何?"	Sir Grabbed People's Gold, Why ?"
09	对曰:	Answering Said:
10	"取金之时,	"Taking Gold That Moment,
11	**不见人,**	***Not Seeing People,***
12	**徒见金。"**	***Only See Gold."***

Liezi Text Narrative

Formerly, people of Qi had a person who wished for gold. L1
Early dawn, he dressed capped, then went to the market place where the person retailed gold. L3
He grabbed the gold and escaped; Official successfully arrested him. L5
Asking, said: "People all present that's, Sir grabbed people's gold, Why ?" L8
Answering, said: " Taking gold at that moment, not seeing people, only seeing gold." L12

Comments:
8.34 See Nobody Only Gold
People of Qi had a person who was obsessed with gold.
One day he grabbed gold from a shop when many people were present and was caught.
When asked why he did what he did, he said at that moment he did not see people, only see gold!

Obsession creates delusion, illusion and crimes, especially at the bottom of society.

Chapter 8. Charming Talks (說符)

Summary

8.1 Watching The Shadow (顾若影): dependent, behind in all actions, i.e. be humble to follow. Learn the past to know the future; lose virtues, lose dynasty; without respect, we are animals.

8.2 Discerning the Reason Why So (察其所以然): is more important than success and failure. Knowing the principles behind ensures reproducibility, and adaptability with extended usage.

8.3 Difficulty in Government (治国之难): With leaders, self virtuous alone, not enough. Need to recognise others who are virtuous, engage them for support, continuity to govern.

8.4 Jade-Made Mulberry Leaf (玉为楮叶): A leaf for the king, required 3 years in the making. Skill of limited benefits; rather, sage uses the principle of 'Dao' to transform, help people.

8.5 Minister Not Personally Know Me (君非自知我): Minister didn't know Liezi in person. Liezi was wise to decline; when citizens rebelled and killed Ziyang, Liezi was not faulted.

8.6 Principles Not Always Right (理无常是): when situations are different and timing wrong. Meeting kings of different states, sons of the Shi and Meng families met with different fates.

8.7 Also Had An Admirer (亦有招之者): behind talking to wife while man flirted with woman. Prince Chu's narrative alerted Duke Wen to abort his campaign in time to defend his borders.

8.8 State of Jin Suffered Banditry (晋国苦盗): Queyong good at catching bandits, was killed. Wenzi taught the shame of banditry only drove it from Jin to Qin. (poverty is the root cause)

8.9 Loyalty, Trust and Honesty (忠信诚): man said virtues made him able to brave the rapids. Confucius concluded that water can appreciate loyalty and trust (a satirical narrative).

8.10 Can People be Trusted with Secrets? (人可与微言乎?): Beigong scheming rebellion. Kongzi said: "Absolute actions are unselfish, no secrets." Beigong killed in the bathroom.

8.11 Down 2 Cities in A Day (一朝而两城下): Xiangzi was worried hearing the good news. Thus Kongzi predicted prosperity for the State of Zhao, for those who worried, do well.

8.12 A Kind and Righteous Family (好行仁义者): father and son suffered sudden blindness. The city was besieged, they were spared the call to defend, survived to recover their sights.

8.13 King In Happy Mood (寡人有欢心): Circus performer was rewarded with gold and silk. Next circus performer caught the king in a bad mood, was arrested and jailed for a month.

8.14 Bole Assessment of Horses (伯乐相马): Old Bole recommended Jiufanggao to Duke Mu. Jiufanggao found a black stallion he called yellow mare, and it was a world class horse.

8.15 Never: Self Chaotic, State Ordered (未闻身乱而国治): Zhanhe said to King Zhuang. King of Chu said: "Excellent."; to put a state in order, the ruler must be self ordered first.

8.16 People Have 3 Complaints (人有三怨): Envy nobility, hate high status, complain fat pay. Sunshuao's solutions: be humble, be less ambitious and be generous with a fat salary.

8.17 This Land Is Bad (此地不利): Qinqiu, land that people of Chu and Yu doesn't want. Sunshuao died, the king conferred land; as instructed, son chose it, and family still held it.

8.18 As Bandits What is Mercy? (为盗仁将焉在?): When threatened, bandits were sure to kill. Niuque may return with a posse, killed; Yan people chased bandits exposing them, killed.

8.19 Disaster Falling From Heaven (飞鸢适坠其腐鼠): Flying eagle dropped its rotten rat. Swordsmen below took the hit as an insult and avenged by killing the arrogant Clan of Yu.

Chapter 8. Charming Talks (説符)

Summary

8.20 Not Eating Bandit's Food (食为盗而不敢食): Hungry, Aijingmu fainted by the wayside.
Qiu revived him; on learning that Qiu was a bandit, he regurgitated all the food and died.

8.21 Perverse Hatred (怼以忘其身者): Unfavored by Duke, Zhulishu left to live on chestnuts.
Duke had trouble, he was ready to return to sacrifice, to show his loyalty and to spite Duke!

8.22 Enmity (ill-will) Brings Disaster (怨往者害来): Yangzhu: "Hatred forth, disaster cometh."
It seems logical and fair to expect, goodwill begets goodwill, and ill-will can bring disaster.

8.23 Many Branching Paths (多歧路): Neighbor lost a goat over many branching paths.
Yangzhu was sad linking this to scholars who progressed on many paths, lost original focus.

8.24 Don't Blame The Dog ? (岂能无怪哉?): Pu out in white, changed in rain, returned black.
Pu was angry when his dog barked; Yangzhu asked, what if the black dog came back white!

8.25 Caution Doing Charity (慎为善): Yangzhu said: " Doing charity is not to make a name."
Nonetheless, name, reputation, benefits, rivalry, and unknown problems will follow you.

8.26 'Dao' Of Life Everlasting (不死之道): Much debates that this 'Dao' can be passed on.
Anything that can be passed on, not the 'Dao' of life everlasting, for death is inevitable.

8.27 Liberating Life (放生): Is display of kindness, thus Jianzi rewarded citizens for the doves.
Guest said, catching and liberating doves; better, ban citizens from catching as many dead.

8.28 Humanity Made For Mosquitoes/Gnats (为蚊蚋生人): We are not above the food-chain !
The COVID19 pandemic truly exposes our lack of nobility in front of other living things.

8.29 No Shame Exceeds Begging (辱莫过于乞): Thus beggar went to work in the king's stable.
Working at whatever job for food and lodging, is certainly less shameful than begging.

8.30 Perversely Wealthy (得人遗契者): Person wandered the city collecting outdated contracts.
He told neighbors he will soon be rich; be contented, obsession with wealth will lose sanity.

8.31 Withered Sycamore Tree (枯梧树): Neighbor said was not auspicious, advised to cut it.
After which the father asked for the firewood; such neighbors are dangerous to have !

8.32 No Actions Not Like Axe-Thief (无为而不窃鈇也): Suspecting neighbor's son stole it.
The axe was recovered, son's action all seems normal; prejudices truly distort perceptions.

8.33 Beigongsheng Pondering Rebellion (白公胜虑乱): Unaware inverted staff pierced his jaw.
He tripped over tree roots, hitting head on poles; oft seen today with focus on handphones.

8.34 See Nobody Only Gold (不见人, 徒见金): Said person, caught grabbing gold from shop.
Obsession can cause delusion, illusion and crimes; **or** sign of unfair distribution of wealth.

This chapter reveals our delusions, perversions, prejudices, obsessions and lack of empathy.

316	**Discussion**
317	*Authorship and Dating*
318	*Is Liezi a Mystic ?*
319	*Is Liezi a Scientific ?*
320	*On Life Purpose*
321	*On Death and After*
322	*Natural Daoism*
323	*All Lives Matter*
324	*Humanity, Birds and Animals*
325	*Awareness, Dreams and Minds*
326	*Confucius and Sagehood*
327	*Liezi and Confucians*
328	*Effort and Destiny*
329	*Yangzhu (杨朱, c.395-335BC)*
330	*World of Delusions*
331	*Leadership*
332	*Freedom*
333	*Concept of 'Dao'*

NB:

References to the Liezi text are made for evidence presented in the Discussion.
Read the referred sections to enhance understanding of the points made.
And the readers may yet discover more interesting points for themselves.

Discussion

Authorship and Dating

Liezi (c.450-375BC) came before Zhuangzi (庄子, c.369-286BC), was much quoted by the latter. Liezi did exist, a person named Yukou (圉寇) as quoted in *Book of Han.Art Literature Records*. However scholars down the centuries believed the book *Liezi* in its present form was a 'forgery'. It was believed to be compiled by Zhang Zhan (張湛, 317-420AD), a scholar of East Jin Period. There are also many who insisted that the book was a product initiated before the Qin Dynasty. And there are insertions and additions by individuals who later edited and annotated the book. Inclusion of Gongsunlong (公孙龙 c.320-250BC) who came after Liezi, attested to this (ch.4.13). Nonetheless, a 20th century scholar Qian Zhongshu (錢钟書,1910-1998) had pointed out, quote: "Even if the *Liezi* is truly a fabrication, we may not diminish the *Liezi* but respect Zhang Zhan."

Liu Xiang (刘向, 77-6BC) in his *Liezi new book catalogue* (列子新书目录) listed 8 chapters. Zhang Zhan mentioned 8 chapters in the *Liezi Preface (列子序)*, said Liezi was much quoted. However the *Historic Records (史記)* lists Laozi and Zhuangzi but makes no mention of Liezi ! Chapter 4 is named Zhongni (alias Confucius), and '孔子' appeared more than 80x in the text. Confucius asked elder if he had 'Dao' picking cicada; elder said no, 6 months practice. (ch.2.10) Children asked if Sun is nearer in the morning than at noon, Confucius cannot answer. (ch.3.7) Though personally liberated, Confucius was sad, as still worried for society and states. (ch.4.1) Confucius asked swimmer if he had 'Dao' braving rapids; swimmer said it's Loyalty, Trust. (8.9) Many satirical narratives put Confucius and disciples in a bad light, like with a certain disrespect. Subtly suggesting that confucians are not on the level of daoist liberty, hence Liezi was alienated. And Sima Qian (司馬迁, c.145-87BC) a true confucian, leaves out Liezi in his *Historic Records*. Altogether, the then dominant confucians seem to succeed in almost blocking Liezi in existence. Narratives like *Kuafu Chased the Sun (夸父追日)*, and *Qiren Worried Sky A-falling (杞人忧天)*. Like *Stupid Grandpa moved mountains (愚公移山)* that has long been taught in primary classes. These wonderful stories have come from Liezi, yet few people know this or even heard of Liezi.

Liezi (列子), the name occurs in the text more than 50x, confirming Liezi as a person did existed. The text began with Liezi at Zhengpu, had many disciples but was unknown for 40 years. (ch.1.1) Liezi had a huge following, and was fearful his fame might alert the king to engage him.(ch.2.14) Once he led 40 disciples on a discovery visit with hermit Nankuazi who talked to win! (ch.4.5)

Laozi (老子, c.580 BC) occurs in the text 4x, and there is no mention of Zhuangzi (庄子). That is, Liezi has quoted Laozi his predecessor, and later came Zhuangzi who is unknown to him. Thus we may accept Liezi as the main author of the *Liezi* text, albeit with some corruptions later. And that it was written after Laozi and before Zhuangzi, around the early 4th century BC.

Discussion

Is Liezi a Mystic ?

The *Zhuangzi* (ch.1) first introduced Liezi: "enjoyed riding on wind for 15 days, then returned". Ever since, people have been directed to a metaphysical interpretation of Liezi and Daoism. However, careful study of the text suggests that Liezi is actually against teaching transcendence.

商丘开曰："吾亡道。	Shangqiukai Said: "I have No Dao. (ch.2.6.72)
请问蹈水有道乎？"	May Ask Treading Water Has 'Dao' Is-it-not ?" (2.9.21)
曰："亡，吾无道。	Said: "No, I have No 'Dao' (swimmer shooting rapids).
"子巧乎！有道邪？"	"Sir Skillful Indeed ! Have 'Dao' is-it-not ?" (ch.2.10.05)
曰："我有道也。	Said: " I Have 'Dao' that's (elder picking cicada).
五六月，	Five Six Months (practice),

Confucius asked individuals if they had 'Dao' when they performed seemingly impossible feats. The performers' answers clearly reflect Liezi's objections to the transcendental power of 'Dao'.

列子师老商氏，	Liezi Studied under Laoshangshi, (ch.2.3.01)
九年之后，	And Nine Years After, (ch.2.3.38)
横心之所念，	Unbridle Heart Whatever The Thoughts,
横口之所言，	Unbridle Mouth Whatever The Speech,
亦不知我之是非利害欤，	Also Not Know My Own Right Wrong, Good or Evil,
亦不知彼之是非利害欤；	Also Not Know Others' Right Wrong, Good or Evil;
竟不知风乘我邪？	Somehow Not Know If Wind is Riding on Me ? (2.3.53)
我乘风乎？	Or I am Riding on Wind ?

Liezi under-studied Laoshangshi (fictitious) for 9 years meditating on right/wrong, good/evil. Then returned not knowing if 'Liezi rides on wing' or 'wind rides on Liezi'! Liezi is teaching the virtues of Daoism, rather than promoting the transcendental power of 'Dao'.

揖御寇而进之。	Greets Yukou And Offered Arrow (Bohunwuren). (2.5.18)
御寇伏地，	Yukou Prostrated on Ground,
汗流至踵。	Sweat Drained To Heels.

Bohunwuren asked Liezi to demonstrate his archery standing on a cliff 100 meters above abyss. Liezi humbly admitted he prostrated on the ground with fear, having no power to 'ride on wind'!

老成子学幻于尹文先生，	Laochengzi Learned Illusions With Yuwen Senior,(3.2.01)
"吾与汝亦幻也 (尹文先生)，	"I With You Also Illusions that's, (Yuwen Senior) (3.2.22)
奚须学哉？"	Why Need to Learn (be illusionist) is-it-not ?"
老成子归，	Laochengzi Returned, (ch.3.2.24)
用尹文先生之言深思三月，	Using Yuwen Senior's Words Deep Thinking 3 months,
终身不箸其术，	Till Death Not Show-off His Skills, (ch.3.2.30)
故世莫传焉。	Hence in Society None Transfer (his skills) that's.

Yuwen Senior told Laochengzi that they were both 'illusions', so why the need to learn illusions? Laochengzi returned, never showing his skills; thus, Liezi exposes the falsehood of illusions.

The Liezi text consistently refutes expectation that daoists have transcendental power of 'Dao'. Hence Liezi is far from being a mystic but the rare voice and embodiment of natural Daoism.

Discussion

Is Liezi Scientific ?

Scientific method: identify a problem, gather relevant data, formulate a hypothesis to be tested.
Problem: How does the universe come to exist? To seek the Ultimate Reality like Laozi.
(Jingwei, 2012)

Liezi's Hypothesis of self-Creator initiating creation of all things, is no better than Laozi's 'Dao'.

其言曰：有生不生，	His words said: has Creator not created (self-Creator) (ch.1.1.13)

But to Liezi's credit, he rejects all claims of evidence for the transcendental power of 'Dao'.

竟不知风乘我邪？	Somehow Not Know If Wind is Riding on Me ? (ch.2.3.53)
我乘风乎？	Or I am Riding on Wind ?
商丘开曰："吾亡道。	Shangqiukai Said: "I have No 'Dao'. (ch.2.6.72)
曰："我有道也，五六月	Said: " I Have 'Dao', that's Five Six Months (practice) (ch.2.10.06)

Skull is Evidence of inescapable death, but no evidence if 'I' still exists when spirit/body parted.

从者见百岁髑髅，	Followers saw 100-year-old Dead-man Skull. (ch.1.4.02)
"精神入其门,骨骸反其根	"Spirit Enter Its Door, Skeleton Revert to Its Roots (ch.1.5.30)
我尚何存？"	Am I Still Existing ?"

Liezi wants *no empty talk;* says, 'Emptiness' is emptiness, better embrace quietude and humility.

列子曰："虚者无贵也。"	Liezi Said:"Emptiness Entity No Value that's"(ch.1.10.3)
莫如静，莫如虚。	Not Better than Quietude, Not Better than Humility.

To discuss Problems, Liezi brings in various people, like on the collapse of Heaven and Earth.

杞国有人忧天地崩坠，	Qi State Had Person Worried Collapse of Heaven Earth.(ch.1.10.1)
晓之者亦舍然大喜。	Informer-Person Also Relieved Naturally, Very Happy. (ch.1.10.26)
长庐子闻而笑曰：	Zhangluzi Heard And Laughing, Said: (ch.1.10.27)
子列子闻而笑曰：	Teacher Liezi Heard And Laughing, Said: (ch.1.10.44)

Liezi is Observant of Nature, attributes of humanity, ecosystem, environmentals.

列子见百岁髑髅	Liezi and the Dead-man Skull (ch.1.4)
众态也，自以为才之得也。	Characters Galore, Self Believes Attainment of Talents. (ch.6.9)
貉逾汶则死矣。	Fox Go-beyond Wen (river) Then Die indeed. (ch.5.1.170)
故竞而捕之，死者众矣。	Hence Contesting To Catch Them, Those Died Multitude. (8.27.11)

Liezi (alias, Yukou), with Humility and Honesty, did not cover-up when he failed to perform.

御寇伏地，汗流至踵。	Yukou Prostrated on Ground, Sweat Drained To Heels. (ch.2.5.19)

A tenet of science: It is more important to know the Reasons behind, than the success/failure.

故圣人不察存亡，	Thus Sage Person Not Concern with Survival or Loss, (ch8.2.22)
而察其所以然。"	But with Discerning The Reason Why So."

In writing, Liezi gives credit where credit is due with proper reference to source of information.

《黄帝书》曰：	Huangdi Text Said: (ch.1.1.26)
'谷神不死，	'Valley-spirit (of fertility) never die,
古者谓死人为归人。	The Ancients Called Dead People As Returnee People. (ch.1.9.29)

Liezi's observational study of nature and humanity is compassionate, in depth, evidence based.
Liezi's writing is not plaigerism with quoting sources; he inherits the wisdom of past sages.

Discussion

On Life

It is only natural for all living things to seek comfort and enjoyment, and to avoid sufferings. What advice does Liezi have to help us achieve happiness and prosperity in our lives?

Human life from birth till death, there are 4 major transformations. (ch.1.06)
03	婴孩也，少壮也，	Baby Child that's, Youth Strength that's,
04	老耄也，死亡也。	Old Feeble that's, Death Loss that's.

Subtle changes never paused a moment, our decline from birth to old-age. (ch.1.11)
19	皮肤爪发，	Skin Claws Hairs,
20	随世随落，	Anytime Growing Anytime Drop-off,

Be happy and count our blessings like Rongqiqi, and we may achieve longevity. (ch.1.07)
10	而吾得为人，	And I Able Be Human,
15	吾既得为男矣，	Since I Able Be Male indeed,
19	吾既已行年九十矣，	I Since Already been Through 90 Years indeed,

Like centurion hermit Linlei, always relaxed, contented and with no fear of death. (ch.1.08)
24	"吾之所以为乐，	"I, The Reasons For Being Happy,
25	人皆有之，	Every Person Has Them,
26	而反以为忧。	But in Contrast They Cause Worries to others.

Zichan suffered serving the state or like brothers indulging themselves, individual choice. (ch.7.07)
92	以苦之治外，	With Suffering In External Management,
95	以我之治内，	With Self In Internal Management,

Duamushu spent his ancestral fortune leaving nothing to progeny, mad or enlightened ? (ch.7.08)
03	不治世故，放意所好。	Not Manage World Affairs, Indulge What Will's Loved
39	不为子孙留财。	Not Leaving Wealth For Children Grandchildren.

Life is a cycle of the same order/ chaos, a 100 years is enough to see it all. (ch.7.09)
14	且久生奚为？	And Long Life What For ?
27	况久生之苦也乎？"	Especially Long Life Suffering that's, is-it-not ?"

Harvesting Heaven and Earth by our labor is allowed, taking from others is criminal. (ch.1.14)
38	然吾盗天而亡殃。	Naturally I Rob Heaven And have No Misfortune.
43	若盗之而获罪，	Like Robbing Them (people) And Get Convicted,

We are no different from dogs and pigs if we are dependent and don't earn our keeps. (ch.4.11)
11	受人养而不能自养者，	Receive Others Feed And Not Able Self Sustain People,
12	犬豕之类也；	Dogs Pigs Those Kinds that's;

And begging is the most shameful; any work for food and lodging is respectable. (ch.8.29)
12	"天下之辱莫过于乞。	"Heaven Beneath, All Shames None Exceeds A Beggar.

Liezi is a libertarian, no condemnation of indulgence if Not built on the misery of others.
A 100 years can see it all, Liezi sees no need for life-everlasting, unlike the pseudo-daoist.
Be happy, relax, count your blessings, with no fear of death to achieve longevity of 100 years.

Discussion

On Death

We wonder, does the individual 'I' still exist after death, and then what kind of After-life ?
Pseudo-daoists claiming possession of 'Dao' possible, ever trying to achieve life-everlasting !

The skull is evident that all living things emerge from nature, go back to nature. (ch.1.4)

59	万物皆*出于机*,	All Matters Always Emerging From Ji (Primal-source),
60	皆入*于机*。"	Always Entering Into Ji (Primal-source, or Yi, or Dao !)."

When the spirit disperses in Heaven and the body returns to Earth, do 'I' still exist ? (ch.1.5)

30	"精神入其门,	"Spirit Enters Its Door (in Heaven),
31	骨骸反其根,	Skeleton Returns to Its Root (on Earth),
32	*我尚何存?"*	*Am I Still Existing ?"*

Zigong weary of learning wished to rest, and Confucius says there is rest only in death ! (ch.1.09)

11	坟如也,鬲如也,	Cemetery Like that's, Tomb Like that's,
12	则知所息矣。"	Then Know Places for Resting, that's."

Yangzhu cried on Jiliang's death, and sang on Suiwu's death, all in accord with 'Dao'. (ch.4.09)

21	隶人之死,	Common People Their Death,
22	众人且歌,众人且哭。	The People They Sing, The People They Cry.

Jiliang rejected 3 doctors, he healed naturally, a daoist at peace with no fear of death. (ch.6.06)

44	俄而季梁之疾自瘳。	Shortly Then Jiliang His Illness Self Resolved.

In Death we are similar, all turn into white bones and return to dust (ch.7.3)

28	死则腐骨。	Death Then Rotten Bones.
29	腐骨一矣,熟知其异?	Rotten Bones One (same), Who Knows The Difference ?

Path after death is easy, as already dead, no rites, no sacrifices, any burial does not matter. (ch.7.6)

52	平仲曰:"既死,岂在我哉?	Pingzhong Said: "Already Dead, How Am I (in control)?
53	焚之亦可,沈之亦可,	Burn It Also Can, Submerge It Also Can,

An eagle dropped a rat on swordsmen who killed family, like death from Heaven, e.g. Covid19.

28	聚众积兵,	Gathered the People Accumulated the Weapons, (ch.8.19)
29	以攻虞氏,大灭其家。	To Attack Clan of Yu, Totally Extinguished The Family.

'Dao' for everlasting life never exists, as death is inescapable and inevitable. (ch.8.26)

12	彼自丧其生,	Person Himself Lost Own Life,
13	安能令君不死也?"	How Possible to Enable my King to Not Die, That's ?"

Confucians, conscientious people working for the welfare of states, tired, will find rest in death!
Daoists, sing or cry in the natural course of events, enjoy life while it lasts, fear not of death.
Pseudo-daoists, cultivating 'Dao' for life-everlasting in vain, are also reduced to white bones.

Discussion

Natural Daoism

Liezi entertains no 'emptiness' talk, refutes his transcendental power with 'wind riding on him'. A joyful and relaxed daoist, he thinks no evil, speaks no evil, naturally protected with no foes.

Liezi says no value in valuing 'emptiness', better to practice quietude and humility. (ch.1.10)
06 "非其名也，   "Unimportant The Name that's,
07 莫如静，莫如虚。   Not Better than Quietude, Not Better than Humility.

Liezi meditated 9 years, thought /spoke no evil, enlightened with 'wind riding on him'! (ch.2.3)
53 竟不知风乘我邪？   Somehow Not Know If Wind is Riding on Me ?
54 我乘风乎？   Or I am Riding on Wind ?

Daoist, joyous, relaxed, heaven protects; like a fallen drunkard, relaxed, no broken joints. (ch.2.4)
26 夫醉者之坠于车也，   Like Drunken Person His Fall From Carriage that's
27 虽疾不死。   Though Injured Not Dead.

Liezi admitted he can't shoot at the edge of a high cliff, a self display of great humility. (ch.2.05)
19 御寇伏地，   Yukou (alias, Liezi) Prostrated on Ground,
20 汗流至踵。   Sweat Drained To Heels.

The sorcerer can't predict the teacher's death; enlightened, Liezi returned to feed pigs. (ch.2.13)
78 为其妻爨，   Helped The Wife in Cooking,
79 食豨如食人，   Feeding Pigs Like Feeding People (with respect),

Gentleness will triumph, thinking of others as superior, thus no offence, no misfortune. (ch.2.17)
13 先出于己者，   First (think) People Superior To Self,
14 亡所殆矣。   No Such Misfortune indeed.

Liezi loves to travel to observe; Huqiuzi says beware, you are also being observed. (ch.4.7)
36 物物皆游矣，   All Matters All Travelling that's,
37 物物皆观矣，   All Matters All Observing that's,

Person has knowledge but not emotional, has ability but not selfish, is a true daoist. (ch.4.15)
26 知而忘情， 能而不为，   Knows And Forget Emotion, Capable And Not Selfish,
27 真知真能也。   True Knowledge True Capability.

Skill to make exquisite jade leaf for king; better, teaching Daoism to transform people. (ch.8.4)
15 故圣人恃道化   Hence Sage Person Holds 'Dao' to Transform
16 　而不恃智巧。"   And Not Hold Cleverness, Skill."

Liezi teaches humility, respect, gentleness, and self-discipline, not emotional and not selfish.
Natural Daoism has no transcendental power, is not little skill and cleverness to win favors.
Natural Daoism, a natural extension of Laozi's pacific Daoism for all mankind. (Jingwei 2012)
Daoism is self-cultivation of primal virtues, not dependent on conventional virtues of others.

Discussion

All Lives Matter

Liezi has many references to other life forms of nature, and with sympathetic understanding.
We are like birds and animals with similar instincts for survival, love and kindness.

Starling birds kept away, sensitive to the boy's ill intention to catch them for his father. (ch.2.11)
07 汝取来，吾玩之。"   You Bring Here, I Play with Them."
09 沤鸟舞而不下也。   Starling Birds Dancing But Not Coming Down that's.

Birds, animals and humans have the same natural instincts for love, unselfish kindness. (ch.2.18)
55 小者居内，壮者居外；   Small Members Stay Inside, Strong Members Stay Outside;
57 饮则相携，食则鸣群。   Drinking Then Mutually Helping, Feeding Then Calling the Herd.

Actually, the monkeys were wise to choose 4 for the morning, safer with more in hand. (ch.2.19)
15 朝四而暮三，足乎？"   Morning 4 Then Evening 3, Enough Right ?"
16 众狙皆伏而喜。   Monkey Crowd All Prostrated And Happy.

If we are lazy and don't labor to earn our keeps, we are no different from dogs and pigs. (ch.4.11)
11 受人养而不能自养者，   Receive Others Feed And Not Able Self Sustain People,
12 犬豕之类也；   Dogs Pigs Those Kinds that's;

Similarly we call greedy people who request more after basic needs, termites of nature. (ch.7.16)
08 无厌之性，   Never Dislike (wanting ever more) This Character,
09 阴阳之蠹也。   The Termites of Yin Yang (Nature)that's.

Humans fighting for food, have no righteousness, win no respect and danger cometh. (ch.8.01)
66 强食靡角，   Fighting for Food Locking Horns,
67 胜者为制，是禽兽也。   Victorious People Set Rules, Are like Birds, Animals that's.

Goat lost at branching paths; Scholar confused by diverse disciplines lost original focus. (ch.8.23)
65 "大道以多歧亡羊，   "Great Paths With Many Branching Lost Goat,
66 学者以多方丧生。   Scholars With Many Methods Lost Life.

Yangzhu urged brother Pu to empathize; imagined your white dog came back, black! (ch.8.24)
13 向者使汝狗白而往，   Just Then Let Your Dog White And Go-forth,
14 黑而来，岂能无怪哉？   Black On Return, How Possible No Surprise, Right ?"

Jianzi: liberating life is a display of kindness; Guest: citizens catching doves, many died.(ch.8.27)
10 "民知君之欲放之，   "Citizens Know King His Wish to Liberating Them,
11 故竞而捕之，死者众矣。   Hence Contesting To Catch Them, Those Died Many indeed.

If animals are made for us as food, are humans made for mosquitoes, tigers/wolves ? (ch.8.28)
27 非天本为蚊蚋生人、   Is-it-Not Heaven Firstly For Mosquitoes Gnats Produced Humans,
29 虎狼生肉者哉？"   Tigers Wolves Produced Meat (humans) that's, right ?"

***Nature has made all living-things for each other, including humans as Covid-19 has shown.
We ought to behave, unselfish with more empathy, fairness and respect, for* All Lives Matter.**

Discussion

Awareness, Dreams and Minds

Experience in the day affects our dreams at night, thoughts in the mind affect emotion presently. Knowing the interactions between awareness and the mind, then we are able to handle our fear.

Awareness has 8 signs, dreams have 6 states; know the connections, and not be alarmed. (ch.3.03)
15	识感变之所起者，	Know The Rising Cause of Feeling Changes,
16	事至则知其所由然。	Affair Arrive Then Know the Reason That Causes.
17	知其所由然，	Know The Reason That Causes,
18	则无所怛。	Then No Whatever Fear.

The states of Gumang, Middle and Fuluo show different reality perceptions. (ch. 3.04)
03	名古莽之国，	Name State Of Gumang,
	五旬一觉.	Five Xun (10-days) One Awakening.
13	谓中央之国，	Call-it State Of Center Middle,
	故一昼一夜.	Hence One Day One Night.
31	曰阜落之国.	Call-it State Of Fuluo,
	常觉而不眠.	Always Awake And Not Sleep.

Yinshi, very harsh, had labored dreams; Stoic servant had sweet dreams after labor. (ch.3.05)
27	昔昔梦为人仆，	Night after Night Dreaming As Somebody's Servant,
21	夜为人君，其乐无比。	Nightly As People's King, The Joy No Comparison.

Woodcutter's mix-up dream and reality with a deer he killed; had to share it with Finder.(ch.3.06)
32	"若初真得鹿，妄谓之梦；	"Like Initially, Really Got Deer, Rashly Call It Dream;
33	真梦得鹿，妄谓之实。	Really Dream of Got Deer, Rashly Call It True.

Huazi lost memory, lived a carefree life; a confucian cured him, anxieties came back ! (ch.3.07)
39	"曩吾忘也，荡荡然	"Formerly I Forgetful that's, Swinging Free Naturally
48	好恶之乱吾心如此也.	Good /Evil They Confuse My Heart Like This Ye'.

The son had delusion, seeing white as black; Laozi: "Son maybe right, we are wrong!" (ch.3.08)
21	"汝庸知汝子之迷乎？	"How You Know Your Son is Delusional, is-it-not ?
22	今天下之人皆惑于是非	Today The World's People All Confuse in Right/Wrong

Yanren had little emotion at his hometown; emotion was released earlier at 'hometown'. (ch.3.09)
24	真见先人之庐冢，	Truly Sees the Cemetery and Tombs of Ancestors,
25	悲心更微。	Griefs of Heart further weaken.

Know interactions between minds and dreams; Yinshi stressed his servant less and slept better. It is nice to keep good memories like the woodcutter and to discard bad memories like Huazi. Yanren released his emotion at 'hometown' pointed at earlier, had little left on final arrival. We ought be aware of all the chaos caused by evil people with 'fake news' in the world, today.

324

Discussion

Confucius and Sagehood

Confucius (孔子 alias 孔丘, 551-479 BC) has been honored a sage for millennia in China.
What is sagehood and what makes many virtuous and talented people willing to serve Confucius?

Confucius, happy with Heaven, accepted destiny; but still worried for the world/society. (ch.4.01)
17	汝徒知乐天	You Disciples Knows Happy with Heaven
18	知命之无忧，	Knows Destiny And No Worry.
19	未知乐天知命	Not Know Happy with Heaven Knows Destiny
20	有忧之大。	Has Worry That's Big.

Sage has no supernatural power, like see with ears; but intelligent, sensitive to danger. (ch.4.02)
22	"传之者妄。	"Person Transmitting It (information) is Mistaken.
24	不能易耳目之用。"	Not Able Exchange Ears Eyes Their Usage."

Confucius says he is no sage; ancient kings also not sages, merely did their duties. (ch.4.03)
04	"圣则丘何敢，	"Sage Then Qiu (丘, Confucius) How Dare (claiming),
05	然则丘博学多识者也。"	But Then Qiu is All Studies Much Knowledge Person."
09	"三王善任智勇者，	"3 Kings Good at Appointing Talented Brave People,
13	"五帝善任仁义者，	"5 Emperors Good at Appointing Kind Upright People,

Confucius, not best in specific talents, but had many talents, able to teach flexibilities. (ch. 4.04)
05	子曰："赐之辨贤于丘也。"	Teacher Said: "Ci's Debate Better Than Qiu that's."
07	子曰："由之勇贤于丘也。"	Teacher Said: "You's Bravery Better Than Qiu that's."
14	赐能辨而不能讷，	Ci Able to Debate But Not Able be Quiet,
15	由能勇而不能怯，	You (alias, Zilu) Able be Brave But Not Able be Afraid,

Longshu can resist all temptations, but feeling self not self ! Delusional with sagehood ! (ch.4.08)
10	视生如死；	Look at the Living Like the Dead;
11	视富如贫；	Look at the Wealthy Like the Poor;
12	视人如豕；	Look at People Like the Pigs;
13	视吾如人。	Look at Self Like another Person.

Yangzhu: only a sage can be the ultra person; shares his body and possession with the world. 7.14
35	公天下之身，	Publicize The Body to The World,
36	公天下之物，	Publicize The Material to The World,
37	其唯至人矣！	That Only the Ultra Person is Capable !

Confucius has many talents, not the best in each talent, but may teach disciples flexibilities.
Longshu was probably obsessed with cultivation of virtues and sagehood, became illusional !
Sage has no super power, just a person who can share body and possessions with the world.

Discussion

Liezi and Confucians

The text *Liezi* is regarded as one of the 3 writings that form the basics of philosophical Daoism. Liezi was unknown until quoted by Zhuangzi; Sigma Qian left him out of his *Historic Records* . What has caused his sanction in the world of confucianism, and his neglect extending to this day?

Confucius was depicted as naive in asking the swimmer if he had 'Dao'. (ch.2.9)
21	请问蹈水有道乎？"	May Ask, Treading Water Has 'Dao' Is-it-not ?"
22	曰："亡，吾无道。	Said: "No, I have No 'Dao'.

Confucius asked the elder if he had 'Dao' picking cicada, and was rebuked. (ch.2.10)
04	仲尼曰："子巧乎！有道邪？"	Zhongni said: "Sir Skillful Indeed ! Have 'Dao' right ?"
06	曰："我有道也。五六月，	Said: " I Have 'Dao' that's. Five Six Months (practice),
27	修汝所以，	Revise Your Whatever For (discipline),
28	而后载言其上。"	And Then Come to Speak of The Above."

Duke Weiwen asked if Confucius can move in metal and rocks, Zixia's answer is 'yes'! (ch.2.12)
36	子夏曰：	Zixia Said:
37	"夫子能之而能不为者也。"	"Teacher Able To, But Able to, Not Do, that's."

Confucian scholar was chased away for helping Huazi to recover his memories (ch.3.7)
34	华子既悟，乃大怒，	Huazi With Realization, Thereupon Greatly Angered,
35	黜妻罚子，	Expels Wife Punish Son,
36	操戈逐儒生。	Grasp Axe to Chase-out Confucian Scholar.

Liezi liberates confucian's *happy with Heaven/Destiny* to daoist's *no joy no knowledge*. (ch.4.1)
15	此吾昔日之言尔，	This My Former Days' Words to You,
16	请以今言为正也。	Please Take Present Words As Correct that's.
44	无乐无知，是真乐真知；	Not Happy Not Knowing, Is Real Happy Real Knowing;
45	故无所不乐，无所不知，	Thus None What Not Happy, None Whatever Not Know,
47	无所不忧，无所不为。	None Whatever Not Worry, None Whatever Not Do.

Confucius was exposed as ignorant by two little children ! (ch.5.7)
19	孔子不能决也。	Kongzi Not Able to Decide that's.
20	两小儿笑曰：	Two Little Children Laughing, Said:
21	"孰为汝多知乎？"	"Who Says You're Very Knowledgeable ?"

And Confucius even believes that in-animate objects can appreciate virtues like humans ! (ch.8.9)
33	水且犹可以	So Water Also Able With
34	忠信诚身亲之，	Loyalty Trust Honesty Be Closely Intimated
35	而况人乎？"	Let Alone with People Right ?"

Liezi has been harsh with Confucians, exposing them disrespectfully in numerous narratives. Dominant, confucians ostracized him, and he was 'covered' till first mentioned by Zhuangzi. And Sima Qian, a staunch confucian, even failed to list Liezi in his 'Historic Records'.

Discussion

Queries of Limits

Given leisure, humanity naturally seeks to find limits of the universe and of human experiences.

Tang queried his minister Xiage on limits of the universe; the minister answered honestly.(ch. 5.1)
176 吾何以识其巨细?   I, How To Know The Big and Small ?

Grandpa to move mountains with his progeny; a legend, querying resilience in difficulty. (ch.5.2)
41 子子孙孙，无穷匮也，   Sons Grandsons, No End no Lacking that's,
42 而山不加增，   But Mountain No Adding Increasing,
Kuafu chased Sun to where it set; a legend celebrating those who died in quest of truth. ch. 5.03)
03 逐之于隅谷之际。   Chased It To It to the Boundary of Yugu.

Yu: Creations by gods, spirits, sages; Xiage: Creations by nature (Dao); how do we think?(ch.5.4)
22 其道自然，   The Way (Dao) Self Natural,
Query bizarre customs like eating the first born to get more, most extreme of superstition. (ch.5.6)
10 其长子生，则鲜而食之，   The Elder Son Born, Then Offer To Be Consumed,

Query if sun is nearer in the morning or at noon; a sign that children are curious thinkers. (ch.5.7)
05 "我以日始出时去人近，   " I Think Sun First Emerges Nearer To People,
07 一儿以日初出远，   One Child Thinks Sun First Emerges Is Further,

Shiwen queried his music for 3 years; had a break, then played with feelings/characters.(ch. 5.10)
30 及冬而叩徵弦以激蕤宾，   Till Winter To Hit Zheng String To Arouse Ruibin (tune),
31 阳光炽烈，坚冰立散。   Sun Shine Glowing Fierce, Hard Ice Instantly Disperse.

Hane, the legendary singer who sang and still can be heard 3 days after she left ! (ch.5.11)
16 既去而餘音绕梁欐，   Then Left And Remnant Sound Lingered in Rafter,

Zhongziqi a good player, Boya a good listener; a legend, the limit of soulmate in music. (ch.5.12)
24 志想象犹吾心也。   Aspiration Thinking Like My Heart feelings that's.

Yanshi's artificial performer winked at court ladies; a legendary limit in automation ! (Ch. 5.13)
29 倡者瞬其目而招王   Performer Blink Its Eyes To Teasing King
30 之左右侍妾。   His Concubines Servant on Left and Right.

Zaofu: must first walk stable on raised piles, then learn charioteering; a training legend. (ch.5.15)
12 汝先观吾趣。   You First Observe My Brisk-walk.
Prince denied reality of the Kunyu sword and fire-cloth; the limit in arrogance. (ch.5.17)
13 皇子以为无此物，   The Prince Believes No Such Materials,

Reasons behind successes/failures are more important; a tenet of science and queries. (ch.8.2)
22 故圣人不察存亡，   Thus Sage Person Not Concern with Survival or Loss,
23 而察其所以然。"   But with Discerning The Reason Why So."

Liezi queries limits of the universe, and sets standards with legendary high performers.
These legendary limits are often quoted for comparison or praises for today's performers.

Discussion

Effort or Destiny

Is Destiny fated, and is it possible for an individual to make an effort to change Destiny ?
It has been said that Liezi preached fatalism, is this true ?

The good is poor, the evil is wealthy, Destiny is not a maker of this mess, and so ? (ch.6.1)
31 贫善而富恶邪?"   Poor Good And Wealthy Evil how-is-that ?"
38 "既谓之命,   "As Calling It Destiny,
39 奈何有制之者邪?   Then Why Have The Creator, that's ?
Dongguo's assessment of Beigongzi for being poor, thick in Virtues but thin in Destiny. (ch.6.2)
54 夫北宫子厚于德, 薄于命;   Fu' Beigongzi is Thick In Virtue, Thin In Destiny;
58 皆天也, 非人也。   All from Heaven that's, Not from Human that's.
Baoshu's inflexibility Destined him for denial by best friend Yiwu in his advancement. (ch.6.3)
87 洁廉善士也,   Clean Incorruptible Good Scholar that's,
93 上且钩乎君, 下且逆乎民。   Above, contradict the King, below, oppose the citizens.
Dengxi's Dua Possibility concept Destined him to clash with Zichan, inevitable death. (ch.6.4)
01 邓析操两可之说,   Dengxi Expounded Dual Possibility Concept
02 设无穷之辞,   Set-up Endless The Argument,

Destiny, unaffected by spirits and humans, let everything naturally so, ancient fatalism. (ch.6.5)
10 皆命也, 智之所无奈何。   All Destiny that's, Talents That May Not Ever Affect.
"Better let it be", Destiny of the ancients with little influence over the march of events. (ch.6.7)
01 生非贵之所能存,   Life, Not Honoring It, Then Can Preserve,
03 生亦非贱之所能夭,   Life, Also Not Debasing It, Then Can Kill,
29 揣利害, **不如其已**。   Guessing the Pros and Cons, Better Let It Be.

Ancient person believing in Destiny, not troubled with life/death, happiness/sadness. (ch.6.8)
16 不知所以然而然, 命也。   Not Knowing Why It's So And Naturally, Destiny that's.
25 夫信命者, 亡寿夭;   O' Person Believes in Destiny, Forgets Life and Death;

Looks failing is not failure, that's not admitting failure until failed, this is no fatalism ! (ch.6.10)
03 佁佁败者,   That which is Almost Close to Failure,
04 俏败者也, 初非败也。   Look-like Failure, Not Start of Failure that's.

Naturally then, we make Effort to succeed, and leave Destiny to account for the failures. (ch.6.13)
04 仕逐势, 势使然也。   Official pursues influences, Effort enables naturally that's.
09 仕有遇否, 命使然也。 Official has favors/disfavors, Destiny enables naturally that's.

Performers rewarded or punished, depended on king's mood; fate, luck or destiny ! (ch.8.13)
20 适值寡人有欢心,   Suitably When Lonely-me Had Joyous Heart,
21 故赐金帛。   Hence Bestowed Gold Silks,

***Clash of concepts destined for bad results; performers reward depending on the king's mood.
No forever friend, forever enemy, only forever interest determines the inevitability of events.
Many factors affecting Fate; hence make efforts to succeed, leave after failures to Destiny.
Probability exists prior to events; Fate, Destiny, Inevitability exist only after events, is-it-not ?***

Discussion

Yangzhu (楊朱, c.395-335 BC)

It has been said that Yangzhu teaches Hedonism, and that chapter 7 is an abnormality in the *Liezi*. But Liezi does embrace Yangzhu, quoting him in more than 10 sections, in 6 of the 8 chapters.

Honest-poor, dishonest-wealthy: in all fairness, Yangzhu cited examples, pros and cons. (ch7.1)
36 昔者尧舜伪以天下　　　　Past Persons Yao, Shun Pretended With Kingship
37 让许由，善卷，　　　　　Abdication to Xuyou, Shanjuan,

Life is a short sojourn, 'no' to fame and wealth, enjoy play without harming others.(ch7.2)
31 太古之人知生之暂来，　　Most Ancient The People Know Life Is Short A-coming,
37 从性而游，　　　　　　　Following own Nature To Play,
38 不逆万物所好，　　　　　Not Against All Matters Their Love (no intruding others)

Good/Evil, different in life; all bones, same in death; to enjoy life, not to worry of death. (ch.7.3)
25 生则尧舜，死则腐骨；　　Alive Was Yao Shun, Dead Was Rotten Bones;
27 生则桀纣，死则腐骨。　　Alive Was Jie Zhou, Death Was Rotten Bones.

Purity, Chastity are virtues; but held to extreme, caused Boyi's death, Zhanji's suffering. (ch.7.4)
03 矜清之邮，以放饿死。　　Valued Purity The Extreme, Hence Retired and Starved to Death.
06 矜贞之邮，以放寡宗。　　Valued Chastity The Reason, Resulting in Lacking Off-springs.

Yuanxian ought to be happy in poverty, Zigong ought to relax in trade. (ch.7.5)
12 故善乐生者不窭，　　　　Hence Person Good in Happy Living Not Poor,
13 善逸身者不殖。"　　　　　Person Good in Easing Body Not Trading."

In Life, rest the worker, feed the hungry; In Death, grieve but no rites, no sacrifices. (ch.7.6)
06 寒能使温，穷能使达也。　Cold, Can Enable Warm, Failure Can Enable Success.
09 不服文锦，不陈牺牲，　　Not Clothe in Adorned Brocade, Not Display Sacrificial Animal,

Zichan tried in vain to correct his brothers who indulged in wine/women, harmed nobody.(ch.7.7)
09 朝好酒，穆好色。　　　　Chao Obsession in Wine, Mu Obsession in Women.
83 荣禄喜我之意，　　　　　Honor and Fortune to Excite Our Wills,
Duanmushu, indulgent, generous, spending away ancestral fortune, enlightened or mad ? (ch.7.8)
39 不为子孙留财。　　　　　Not Leaving Wealth For Children Grandchildren.
46 "端木叔，狂人也，　　　"Duanmushu, Mad Person that's,

Yangzhu said: "When no one needs to lose 1 hair to save society, the world is in order." (ch7.10)
10 人人不损一毫，　　　　　Each Person Not (needed) to Lose 1 Hair,
11 人人不利天下，　　　　　Each Person Not (needed) to Benefit The World,
12 天下治矣。"　　　　　　 The World is Ordered indeed."
Yangzhu warns: wishing Longevity, Honor, Power, Wealth, Destiny not self-control. (ch.7.15)
01 杨朱曰："生民之不得休息，Yangzhu Said: "Citizens They Not Able to Rest Relax,
10 可杀可活，制命在外。　　Be Killed To Survive, Control of Destiny On the Outside.

Life's a short sojourn, we ought to be happy and relaxed, not be shackled by fame and wealth.
"Life, rest the worker, feed the hungry; Death, grieve but no sacrifices", words of a hedonist !?
"When no one needs to lose a hair to save society, the world is in order", words of a hedonist!?

329

Discussion

World of Delusions

Pseudo-daoists suffer the Delusion of possessing 'Dao' for super feats, even for life-everlasting !
Individuals often suffer Delusions of self-importance, arrogance, being the best among others !

We cannot not die, and know not where we are going; possession of 'Dao' is a Delusion.(ch.1.13)
03 曰："汝身非汝有也，　　　　Said: "Your Body Not Your Possession that's,
04 汝何得有夫道？"　　　　　　You However Acquire and Possess O' Dao ?"

Laozi: "Broad Virtues like deficient"; lifted Yangzhu's arrogance that kept people away. (ch.2.15)
19 "而睢睢而盱盱,　　　　　　"Like Looking Proud, Like Looking Up,
20 而谁与居？　　　　　　　　So Who will Stay With (you) ?

Beautiful wife's Delusion of self-importance needed attention; innkeeper ostracized her.(ch.2.16)
09 其美者自美,　　　　　　　　" The Beautiful Person Self Beautiful,
10 吾不知其美也；　　　　　　 I Don't Know Her Beauty that's;

Jishengzi's satire on swordsmen who had the Delusion that being emotionless will win. (ch.2.20)
16 已无变矣。　　　　　　　　Already No Changes that's.
17 望之似木鸡矣,　　　　　　　Look At It Like Wooden Cock indeed,

Characters galore, each self-belief the best, no interaction, each living his Delusion. (ch.6.09)
04 穷年不相知情,　　　　　　　Through the Years No Mutual Knowledge of Others,
05 自以智之深也。　　　　　　Self Believes Own Depth of Wisdom that's.

Duke Delusional, be forever in-charged; Yanzi said his forebears would have done so.(ch.6.11)
21 "使贤者常守之,　　　　　　"Enabling Wise Person Forever In-charge,
22 则太公，桓公将常守之矣；　Then First Duke, Duke Huan Will Forever be In-charge;

Dongmenwu was not sad before birth and after the death of his son; is he Delusional ? (ch.6.12)
11 今子死,　　　　　　　　　　Now Son Died.
12 乃与向无子同,　　　　　　　Still Like the Past having No Son, Same,

Delusional hatred; Aijingmu rather be dead than take food/water from Qiu the bandit. (ch.8.20)
14 胡为而食我？　　　　　　　Indiscriminately Acting And Feed Me ?
15 吾义不食子之食也。"　　　　I Righteously Not Eating, Sir Your Food that's."

Delusional hatred; Zhulishu to die for the Duke who rejected him, to spite the latter! (ch.8.21)
18 今死,　　　　　　　　　　　Now Sacrificing,
19 是果不知我也。　　　　　　Is Proof Not Knowing Me, that's (by Duke Juao).

Delusional wealth; insane person obsessed with wealth, collecting outdated contracts. (ch.8.30)
05 告邻人曰：　　　　　　　　Telling Neighboring People Said:
06 "吾富可待矣。"　　　　　　 "My being Wealthy Can be Expected indeed."

Delusional possession; the person grabbed gold from a shop, oblivious to people there. (ch.8.34)
10 "取金之时,　　　　　　　　"Taking Gold That Moment,
11 不见人，徒见金。"　　　　　Not Seeing People, Only Seeing Gold."

Delusions arising from arrogance, self-importance and obsessions cause illusions, even crimes.
Characters galore highlight the prevalence of Delusion among us, lack of true self knowledge.

Discussion

Leadership

Good leaders are self-disciplined, able to use other talents for support and able to abdicate power. Not self-serving but serving citizens, solving problems like alleviating poverty, creating peace.

Huangdi dreamt of land with no leader, led with non-interference, won citizens' love. (ch. 2.1)
30　其国无帅长, 自然而已。　　　The State No Teacher/Elder, Self Naturally That Is.
65　百姓号之, 二百余年不辍。　　Citizens Lamented for Him, 200 More Years None Stop.

Good Spirit in control, nice weather, good harvest, no fear, no disease, imaginary utopia !(ch.2.2)
02　山上有神人焉,　　　　　　　Mountain Top Has Spirit Person that's,
11　字育常时, 年谷常丰；　　　　Procreation Ever Timely, Year Harvest Ever Plentiful.

Fictitious satire on the gullibility of Duke, i.e. ruling class. (ch. 2.12)
37　"夫子能之而能不为者也。"　　"Teacher Able To, But Able to Not Do (restrained) that's."
38　文侯大说。　　　　　　　　　Duke Wen was Very Happy.

Huiang debated King Kang of Song, extolled kindness and justice for the government. (ch.2.21)
42　其贤于孔, 墨也远矣。　　　　In Virtues more Than Confucius, Far-ahead of Mozi.
48　客之以说服寡人也！"　　　　Guest, With This Speech Convinced Lonely Me that's !"

The Sorcerer helped King Mu to enjoy astro-travels, left citizens to prosper in peace. (ch.3.01)
133　犹百年乃徂,　　　　　　　　Till a 100 years then died, (King Mu)
134　世以为登假焉。　　　　　　　Society believed he had ascended Fairyland, that's.

Legendary Yao (c.2,350BC) abdication, peaceful transfer of power to Shun is laudable. (ch.4.14)
26　尧还宫, 召舜,　　　　　　　　Yao Returns to Palace, Summon Shun,
28　因禅以天下。　　　　　　　　Reason, to Abdicate The World.

Zhanhe's bizarre fishing technique; to show balance and equality are good governance. (ch.5.08)
01　均,　　　　　　　　　　　　Fairness (balance, uniformity, even distribution)
02　天下之至理也,　　　　　　　Heaven Beneath (the world) The Most Logical that's,

Leaders, self virtuous not enough, need to recognize virtuous-talented for support. (ch.8.03)
13　故治国之难 在于　　　　　　Hence The Difficult of Governing State Is In
14　　知贤而不在自贤。"　　　　Know the Virtuous And Not In being Self Virtuous."

Wenzi advised teaching morals to eradicate banditry; truly the root cause is poverty. (ch. 8.08)
34　民有耻心,　　　　　　　　　Citizens Having Shame at Heart,
35　则何盗之为？"　　　　　　　Then Why To Be Bandits ?"

Zhanhe said to King Zhuang, "A self-disciplined person will not disorder a state." (ch.8.15)
10　"臣未尝闻身治　　　　　　　"Subject-me Never Ever Heard Self Ordered
11　　而国乱者也,　　　　　　　And Person made the State Chaotic, that's,

Good rulers do not trouble with conquests, building palaces, no interference with citizens' life.
Good governance embraces the virtuous-talented, kindness and justice, equality and fairness.

Discussion

Freedom

Are all humans born with inalienable rights of absolute and total freedom ?

Self-Creator cannot not continue creations and transformations naturally, not by design. (ch.1.1)

35	自生自化，自形自色，	Self created self transformed, self formed self colored,
36	自智自力，自消自息。	Self intellect self action, self death, self life (naturally).

Creator selflessly created all matters, and all created matters have specific selfless duties. (ch.l.3)
There is no claim of selfish ownership by the creator, all matters are created equal and free.

28	生之所生者死矣，	Creator, Its Whatever Created Entity Died that's,
29	而生生者未尝终；	But Creator of the Created Entity Never Ever Perish;
17	**宜定者不出所位。**	*Purpose Intended Entity Not Exceeding Purpose Position.*
38	**皆无为之职也。**	*All Selfless These Duties that's.*

What's life's purpose ? (ch.7.2)
Life: a short sojourn on earth, to follow our nature to play without intruding the rights of others.

15	则人之生也奚为哉?	Then Person's Living that's, What Purpose that's ?
31	太古之人知生之暂来，	Most Ancient The People Know Life Is Short A-coming,
37	从性而游，	Following own Nature To Play,
38	不逆万物所好，	Not Against All Matters Their Love (no intruding others)

Guanyiwu said, "Sorrowfully living till 10,000 years is not what I call living healthy." (ch.7.6)

42	戚戚然以至久生，	Sorrowfully Naturally Till Reaching Long Life,
43	百年、千年、万年，	100 Years, 1000 Years, 10,000 Years,
44	非吾所谓养。"	Not What I Call Living-healthy."

Zichan's brothers, their indulgences are their choice, as not built on the misery of others. (ch.7.7)

01	子产相郑，	Zichan as Premier of Zheng,
09	朝好酒，穆好色。	Chao Obsession Wine, Mu Obsession Women.
95	以我之治内，	With Our Own Management Internally,

But Duanmushu splashed all ancestral wealth leaving nothing to posterity is rather mad ! (ch.7.8)

01	卫端木叔者，子贡之世也。	Wei (state) Duanmushu Person, Zigong's Descendant.
03	不治世故，放意所好。	Not Manage World Affairs, Indulge What Will's Loved.
39	不为子孙留财。	Not Leaving Wealth For Children Grandchildren.

Yangzhu says, citizens are shackled by following 4 concerns and are not able to relax. (ch.7.15)

02	"生民之不得休息，	"Living Citizens They Not Able to Rest Relax,
04	一为寿，二为名，	1 For Longevity, 2 For Name (honor)
05	三为位，四为货。	3 For Status (power), 4 For Commodity (wealth)

The creator selflessly created, and all matters have selfless duties; thus all matters are free.
Not be shackled by conventions, we are free to choose enjoyment with no intrusion on others.

332

Discussion

Concept of 'Dao'
A Western perception (negative words italicized):
Lieh-tzu (Pinyin Liezi, Micropedia, Encyclopedia Britannica, 2002.)
"As in earlier Taoist classics, emphasis in the Lieh-tzu centres on the *mysterious* Tao (Way) of Taoism, a great unknowable cosmic reality of incessant change to which *human life should conform*...The 'Yang Chu' chapter of the classic gives the Lieh-tzu a particular interest, for this chapter acknowledges the *futility of challenging* the *immutable and irresistable* Tao; it concludes that *all man can look forward to* in this life is sex, music, physical beauty, and material abundance, and *even* these goals are not always satisfied. Such *'fatalism'* implies a life of *radical 'self-interest'* (a new development in Taoism), according to which a person *should not sacrifice so much as a single hair* of his head for the benefit of others."

Liezi's perception:
'Dao', the primal entity with no beginning, never be depleted, postulated to create all matters.
01 无所由而常生者, 道也。 No Whatever Origin And Ever Existing Entity,'Dao' that's (ch.4.9)
25 疑独其道不可穷。 Focus Unique The 'Dao' Can Not be Depleted. (ch.1.1)
The attributes of 'Dao' is like water conforming, like mirror reflecting and like echo responding.
04 其动若水, 'Dao' Flow Like Water (conforming), (ch.4.15)
05 其静若镜, 'Dao' Silent Like Mirror (reflecting),
06 其应若响。 'Dao' Respond Like Echo (authentic).
Its other attributes are quietude, humility, and other primal virtues.
08 静也虚也, 得其居矣 Quietude, Humility that's, Enter The Abode (of Dao); (ch.1.10)
'Dao' is all accommodating, accepting everybody, not threatening anybody, good or bad.
26 此众态也。 *This Characters Galore that's. (ch.6.9)*
27 其貌不一, Their Looks Not One (uniform),
28 而咸之于道, But All Inclusive In 'Dao',
Confucius, enlightened in the virtues of 'Dao', was requested to help in managing states.
43 孔子明帝王之道, Kongzi Enlightened in The 'Dao' of Emperors and Kings, (ch.7.11)
44 应时君之聘, Responding to Current Kings Their Engagements,
Evil Kings, Jia and Zhou not embracing the virtues of 'Dao' in their administrations, perished.
60 "桀纣唯重利而轻道, "Jie, Zhou Because Favor Wealth And Slight 'Dao', (ch.8.1)
61 是以亡。 Henceforth Perished.
Pseudo-daoists claimed they *can acquire 'Dao'* to look into Heaven, and achieve life-everlasting !
22 "夫至人者, 上窥青天 "O' That Dao-attained Person, Above, Peering into Heaven (ch.2.5)
01 昔人言有知 Formerly Person Said Had Knowledge of (ch.8.26)
02 *不死之道者,* *The 'Dao' of Life Everlasting,*
Liezi is adamant that the *acquisition of 'Dao'* is falsehood, as we cannot even own our body !
02 "道可得而有乎? " "Dao Possible to Acquire And Possess, True ?" (ch.1.13)
03 曰："汝身非汝有也, Said: "Your Body Not Your Possession that's,
04 汝何得有夫道? " You However Acquire and Possess O' Dao ?"

'Dao' is a primal hypothesis of Laozi to explain creation of all matters (Jingwei, 2012).
'Dao' is perceived as having primal virtues like quietude/humility, conforming/accommodating.
'Dao' is an idea, not a real mystical entity that demands conformation, and never was feared.

Conclusions

All Lives Matter

Effort or Destiny

Enjoy Life

Fear not Death

Government for the People

Know your Delusions

Minds and Dreams

Natural Daoism

Queries and Curiosity

Reject Transcendentals (no 'Dao')

Selfless Duties

Strive for Excellence

Liezi: World of Delusions

Conclusions

Translations of the *Liezi* are few, and often they are biased in mystical interpretation.
Tutored in both the East and West traditions, the author has a new perspective to share.
It has been said Daoism is hard to comprehend and difficult to apply in everyday life !
When one is not looking for transcendental experience, practicing Daoism is actually simple.
The 139 narratives are revealing of our common faults, delusions, pride and prejudices.
Daoism is self-cultivating primal virtues, like humility, honesty, respectful, gentleness, unselfish.

All Lives Matter

To survive, animals and humans have natural instincts for kindness and selfishness. (ch.2.18)
We are no different from dogs and pigs if we are dependent and don't earn our keeps. (ch. 4.11)
Humans, weak skin claws teeth strength for defence; Ultra person, wise, unselfish. (ch.7.15)
Have housing, clothes, food and sex, people wanting more are like termites of nature. (ch7.16)
Humans without righteousness, are just like birds and animals fighting for food, that's. (ch.8.1)
As Yangzhu urges, we ought to empathize with all our animals that help and feed us. (ch.8.24)
Like plants and animals, humans are not above the food chains; ask Covid19. (ch.8.28)
We should not catch doves for 'kind' liberation as many died, for All Lives Matter. (ch.8.27)

Effort or Destiny

The good is poor, the evil wealthy; Effort has no credit, Destiny not a maker of this mess. (ch.6.1)
Dongguo's assessment of poor Beigongzi, thick in Virtues but thin in Destiny ! (ch.6.02)
Baoshu's inflexibility Destined him for denial by Yiwu and failure in his advancement. (ch.6.3)
Dengxi's Dua Possibility Concept Destined for inevitable clashes and death by Zichan. (ch.6.4)
Destiny, unaffected by Heaven, Earth, spirit, not the maker as everything is naturally so. (ch.6.5)
The ancients with little knowledge on the march of events, can only believe in Destiny. (ch.6.07)
Belief in Destiny, be blessed and not be obsessed with life/death, happiness/sadness. (ch.6.8)
Often, calculating pros and cons makes no difference, thus accept Destiny, be at peace. (ch. 6.10)
Naturally then, we make Effort to succeed, and leave Destiny to account for the failures. (ch.6.13)
Honest, poor; dishonest, wealthy; Yangzhu cited examples for both the pros and the cons. (ch.7.1)
Crave for Longevity, Honor, Power, Wealth, then Destiny will be controlled by others. (ch.7.15)
Principles not right in all situations, thus Shi and Meng families met different fates. (ch.8.6)
Circus performers rewarded or punished, depending on king's mood; Effort or luck ! (ch.8.13)
Fate is not fated until the finish-line is crossed, failure may be a blessing in disguise, be positive !

Enjoy Life

Humans go through 4 stages of transformation, childhood, youth, old-age and death. (ch.1.6)
Rongqiqi born a human, a male, counted his blessings and was happy, achieved longevity.(ch.1.7)
Linlei happy as a hermit, relaxed with no stress of Life commitments, achieved longevity.(ch. 1.8)
Harvest Heaven Earth by timing and labor is allowed; robbing from others is criminal. (ch.1.14)
Unshackled by fame/wealth, we may *indulge in our sojourn* here, without harming others.(ch.7.2)
Contentment and working hard is good, but also ought to enjoy life, relax the body. (ch.7.5)
Life: rest the worker, feed the hungry; happy for a day, better than sad for 100 years; (ch.7.6)
Premier Zichan external control of state; brothers' indulgence, internal control of selves! (ch.7.7)
Duanmushu: spent ancestral fortunes, left progeny nothing, mad or enlightened ? (ch.7.8)
Life's a repetition of order/chaos since the ancient era; in 100 years, we see it all. (ch.7.9)
Yangzhu says, "When *no one needs* to lose 1 hair to save society, the society is in order." (ch.7.10)
Liezi favors enjoying Happiness in life, and not suffering to chase for glory-after-death. (ch.7.13)
Strike a balance between exhaustion in guarding our fame, and relaxing to enjoy life. (ch.7.16)
We are products of random meetings of sperms and eggs, so let's respect each other and enjoy life.

Conclusions

Fear not Death

The hundred-year skull reminds us that all lives emerge from nature, return back to nature.(ch.1.4)
When spirit disperses in Heaven and body returns to Earth, does the entity 'I' cease ? (ch.1.5)
Zigong weary of learning and wishing to rest; Confucius says, only in Death we rest ! (ch.1.9)
Yangzhu cried on Jiliang's death, and sang on Suiwu's death, for Death may be a relief. (ch.4.9)
Jiliang rejected all 3 doctors; a true daoist at peace, fear not Death, his body healed itself. (ch.6.6)
King/pauper, different in life; all bones in death; so enjoy life, not to worry of Death. (ch.7.3)
Death: grieve the loss with no rites, no sacrifices; after Death, posterity decides.(ch.7.6)
Retribution: Arrogant clan of Yu was killed when an eagle dropped its rat on swordsmen.(ch.8.19)
'Dao' of Life Everlasting never existed, can never be passed on, for Death is inevitable. (ch.8.26)

Gongsunlong and Logic (公孙龙, c.320-250 BC)

Gongsunlong's logic: "A white horse is a white horse, not a black horse, not a horse !" (ch.4.13)
Matters push to the limit, will revert; oppressing the people to the limit, gets a rebellion. (ch.4.10)
Gongyibo, frail and unable to bear weight, was well known for logical use of strength. (ch.4.12)
Gongsunlong with his interesting arguments in logic, came after Liezi (列子, c.450-375 BC).
Thus Gongsunlong is a corrupt insertion by recent scholars who edited and annotated the Liezi.

Government for the People

Huangdi dreamt of land with no leader, governed with non-interference, citizens loved. (ch.2.1)
Fairyland with Good Spirit, nice weather, good harvest, no fear, no disease, nice fantasy! (ch.2.2)
Odd man of rocks and fire, a fictitious satire on the gullibility of Duke, the ruling class. (ch2.12)
Huiang debated King Kang, extolled the practice of kindness, justice in government. (ch.2.21)
Sorcerer helped King Mu to enjoy astro-travels, hence left citizens to prosper in peace. (ch.3.1)
Legendary Yao's abdication, and peaceful transfer of power to Shun is laudable. (ch.4.14)
Legend of Zhongbei, no rain, no animals, all play, no work; Liezi called it an absurd state.(ch.5.5)
Zhanhe fishing with a hair-line; to show balance and equality are good for governance. (ch.5.8)
Reasons for the rise and fall of dynasties, never outside the need for the selfless Daoism. (ch.8.1)
Leaders self virtuous not enough, must enlist the virtuous-talented for support, continuity. (ch.8.3)
Wenzi taught ethics only drove banditary from Jin to Qin; best solution, alleviate poverty. (ch.8.8)
Zhanhe: "Self in disorder, and able to order a state, can Never happen !" (ch. 8.15)
Equality, justice, good governance, abolish poverty, a good Government for the People.

Know your Delusions

We cannot not die, know not where we are going, thus possession of 'Dao' is a Delusion.(ch.1.13)
Laozi:"Broad Virtues like deficient"; Yangzhu shed his Delusion of arrogance. (ch.2.15)
With the Delusion that beauty will gain her everything, the beautiful wife was disliked. (ch.2.16)
Jishengzi's cocks is a satire on swordsmen, the Delusion of non-emotion equals success.(ch.2.20)
Nankuazi spoke to the last of Liezi disciples, aiming to win; truly a Delusional hermit. (ch.4.5)
Characters galore, each self-belief the best, thus no interaction, living self Delusion. (ch.6.9)
Duke Jing was Delusional wishing forever-in-charged; for then his forebears came first. (ch.6.11)
Dongmenwu was not sad before birth and after the death of his son, living in Delusion. (ch.6.12)
Liezi rejected the offer, as was not Delusional with Ziyang who was later killed by rebels.(ch.8.5)
Tale of flirting man; Duke heard, shed Delusion of warring, returned to defend his border.(ch.8.7)
"Person able to guess secrets, in danger"; Queyong recognised bandits, died by bandits.(ch.8.8)

Conclusions

Complaints of nobility, high status, fat pay; then be humble, be generous, less ambitions.(ch.8.16)
Sunshuao, not Delusional, chosed the bad land Qiuqiu that family can keep long-term.(ch.8.17)
Bandits have no mercy, kill when threatened; Don't be Delusional, argue/provoke them. (ch.8.18)
Delusional, upright Aijingmu rather die than to take food offered by Qiu the bandit. (ch.8.20)
Delusional, Zhulishu wished to die for the Duke who had rejected him, to spite the latter!(ch.8.21)
Delusional, charity to make a name, but benefits, rivalry, unknown problems will follow. (ch.8.25)
Delusional, a person collected outdated contracts and declared himself wealthy, insane ! (ch.8.30)
Delusional neighbor said withered sycamore not auspicious, then asked for its firewood! (ch.8.31)
After recovery of the lost axe, conduct of neighbor seems all normal, Delusion at work. (ch..8.32)
Delusional rebel Beigongshen, unaware of his goad piercing jaw, tripping on tree roots.(ch.8.33)
Delusional person grabbed gold from a shop, saw only gold and no people in a robbery. (ch.8.34)
These narratives reveal many pitfalls that we may face daily in our human relationships in society.
A person's arrogance, obsessions, perverse thinking may cause illusions, Delusions, even crimes.
Characters galore (ch.6.09) highlights our Delusion as individuals, lack of true self-knowledge.

Minds and Dreams

Awareness has 8 signs, dreams have 6 states; know the connections, and not be alarmed. (ch.3.3)
Tales of 3 states, Gumang, Middle and Fuluo, be aware of different reality perceptions. (ch.3.4)
Advised, Yinshi lightened the workload of his stoic servant, and slept better at night. (ch.3.5)
Woodcutter's mix-up dreams and reality with a deer he killed; had to share it with Finder. (ch.3.6)
Huazi lost memory, led a carefree life; a confucian cured him, brought back his anxieties! (ch.3.7)
Satire of a son's illusion, seeing white as black; Laozi:"Son maybe right, we are wrong!"(ch.3.8)
Yanren released emotion at 'hometown' pointed at earlier, had little left on final arrival.(ch.3.9)
Today, we ought to be aware of all the chaos caused in the world by evil people with 'fake news'.

Natural Daoism

Liezi says to value 'emptiness' is empty talk; better, to practice quietude and humility. (ch.1.10)
Daoist gentle, relaxed, heaven protects; like a fallen drunkard, no tension, none the worst.(ch.2.4)
Liezi admitted he cannot shoot at the edge of a high cliff, a self display of great humility. (ch.2.5)
The sorcerer cannot predict the teacher's death; enlightened, Liezi returned to feed pigs.(ch.2.13)
Gentleness will triumph, first thinking of others as superior, no offence, no misfortune. (ch.2.17)
Liezi, 9 years thinking/speaking no good/evil, liberated the mind, and body light in steps. (ch.4.6)
Liezi loved travels; Huqiuzi says, to observe changes inside, not just outside yourself. (ch.4.7)
Guanyinxi: "Enlightened, unselfish, but has no knowledge, no ability, not a true daoist." (ch.4.15)
Purity and Chastity held to extreme, caused Boyi's death, no progeny for Zhanji; worth it!(ch.7.4)
Yangzhu detailed the sufferings of 4 sages, indulgences of 2 evils; be a sage or not to be!(ch.7.11)
Life is just like Shadow, dependent on outside matters, so be humble to follow. (ch.8.1)
Skill for making an exquisite jade leaf is not enough; better, teaching people Daoism. (ch.8.4)
Beigong: can people be trusted with secrets; Confucius: "Actions unselfish, no secrets." (ch.8.10)
Goodwill begets goodwill on Earth, and Heaven protects the kind and righteous family. (ch.8.12)
Yangzhu: "Hatred forth, disaster cometh."; better, extending goodwill begets goodwill. (ch.8.22)
Begging, most shameful; any work for food and lodging is acceptable, to be respected. (ch.8.29)
Liezi attained enlightenment after 9 years meditation, thought spoke no good/evil, no right/wrong.
Liezi, natural Daoism is practicing quietude, humility, be gentle, unselfish with self examination.
Confucius: "Actions unselfish, no secrets."; Unselfish, no secrecy, no pride, no prejudice, no sins.

Conclusions

Queries and Curiosity
Qiren worried sky a-falling, ancient learning about nature; we worry of meteor strikes. (ch.1.12)
KingTang had an enquiring mind, queried the inside and outside limits of the universe. (ch.5.1)
Kuafu chased the sun to where it set; a legend, celebrating those who quest for truth. (ch.5.3)
Creations by gods, spirits, sages; or Creations by nature (Dao); raises more queries. (ch.5.4)
Querying bizarre customs of faraway lands, like eating the first born to get more children.(ch.5.6)
A query if sun is nearer in the morning or at noon; a sign that ancients are curious thinkers. (5.7)
Prince denied the Kunyu sword and fire-cloth; the arrogant limit, not querying for truth. (ch.5.17)
A key tenet of science, importance of reasons behind success/failure is being stressed (8.2).
'Qiren's Worries' and these many queries attested to enquiring minds among the ancient Chinese.

Reject Transcendentals (no 'Dao')
Liezi meditated 9 years, thought/spoke no evil, enlightened, with 'wind riding on him'! (ch.2.3)
Shangqiukai entered fire/water; having no 'Dao', cannot repeat after knowing the danger. (ch.2.6)
Liangyang kept tigers, said he knew their nature, no power of 'Dao' in taming the wild. (ch.2.7)
Ferryman, god-like handling the ferry, said a diver can handle prior to training, not 'Dao'. (ch.2.8)
Swimmer said to Confucius, "I have no 'Dao'; live by water, safe by water, naturally so." (ch. 2.9)
Elder picking cicada from trees said, "I have no 'Dao', just months of practice." (ch.2.10)
Laochengzi meditated on 'You and I are illusions'; an illusionist, *never showed his skill* ! (ch.3.2)
Study and deduction are the reason for prior knowledge, not some sorcery of 'Dao'. (ch.8.1)
Swimmer: virtues helped brave the rapids; Confucius believes water appreciates virtues! (ch.8.9)
Liezi rejects transcendental, says there is no 'Dao' superpower through ferryman, elder, others.
In contrast, Liezi depicts Confucius as ignorant, going around asking people if they have 'Dao'.
Liezi thus alienated all confucians, and even Sima Qian left him out of his "Historic Records".

Selfless Duties
Self-Creator and Self-Transformer were postulated to initiate creations/transformations. (ch.1.1)
Describing the formation stages of the universe, introducing the concepts of Yin/Yang. (ch.1.2)
Selfless creation of Heaven, Earth, Sages and all matters, each with specific selfless duty. (ch.1.3)
Liezi postulates the Self-Creator and Self-Transformer to explain the origin of the Universe.
Details do not really enhance the description of Dao (Ultimate Reality) by Laozi (Jingwei, 2012).

Strive for Excellence
Grandpa to move mountains with his progeny; a legend, showing resilience in difficulty. (ch.5.2)
Bianque strived for balance in temperament with exchange of hearts, and had problems. (ch.5.9)
Shiwen strived for 3 years in music; *rested*, then played with feelings of the 4 seasons. (ch.5.10)
Hane's singing still lingered 3 days after she left; a legend, setting the power in music. (ch.5.11)
Zhongziqi a good player, Boya a good listener; a legend, the limit of soulmate in music. (ch.5.12)
Yanshi's artificial performer able to wink at court ladies; legendary limit in automation. (ch.5.13)
Feiwei dueled to kill Jichang; a legend, querying the limit in teacher/student relation. (ch.5.14)
Zaofu first to balance on raised piles before charioteering; a legend of limits in training. (ch.5.15)
Laiden avenged his father with an imaginary sword; a legendary limit in imagination. (ch.5.16)
Bole's friend in assessing horses, focused on their inner traits, and forgot their looks. (ch.8.14)
With these many legendary characters, Liezi sets us to strive for higher standards of excellence.
In no way can I see Liezi as promoting transcendentals, and encouraging illusional practices.

In short:
Liezi: we are not above the food-chain, so cast out our Pride and Prejudice, All Lives Matters.
We ought to make Effort to succeed, and Destiny does not exist before the Finish-line is crossed.
That Life is a short sojourn, it's our nature to Enjoy life, not to spread Hatred, Wars and Misery.
Zichan's brothers, their indulgence caused no misery to others, Hedonism itself is not criminal.
Death is inevitable, life everlasting never existed, no after-life, we rest in Death, Fear Not.
Gongsunlong and his logics came after Liezi, thus he is a Corruption inserted later by scholars .
Government for the People stresses on Fairness, Justice, Good Governance, Abolition of Poverty.
Liezi's legends and stories are Reflective of our many Delusions, we ought to take note and repent.
To Know the Interactions between our minds, dreams and emotions, and Not Be Alarmed.
Liezi's natural Daoism is Quietude, Humility, Gentleness, Unselfish, all Primal Virtues of Self.
Like King Tang we query the limits of the Universe, and like Kuafu, braved in seeking the Truth.
Like Liezi we Reject Transcendental beliefs, but ought to respect Confucius and Confucianism.
Self-Creator, Self-Transformer, and All Matters of Nature in the Universe, have Unselfish Duties.
Like Hane, Shiwen, Yanshi, Zaofu, Bole, we strive for Excellence in our separate endeavors.
Thus from Liezi, we cannot hope to learn the superpower of 'Dao' for feats or life-everlasting.
And Yangzhu truly says, "When nobody needs to lose 1 hair to save society, society is in order."
It is clear, Liezi and Yangzhu are promoting natural Daoism and not a hedonistic philosophy.
NB:
Exhaustive appreciation of the *Liezi text* will extend the study to a huge volume of 2,000 pages.
To facilitate further study, the Full Chinese Text and English translation have been presented.
There are many interesting points that I missed, and readers may discover more for themselves.

Lookig Forward

Many stories are well known, but often we do not know that they are from the *Liezi* text.
Stories like *Qiren worried the Sky Falling (ch.1.12), Zaofu Learned Charioteering (ch.5.15)*
Tales like *Grandpa Moved Mountains (ch.1.2), Kuafu Chased The Sun (ch.5.3), many others.*

Laozi, Zhuanghzi and *Liezi* are now recognized as the 3 pillars of philosophical Daoism.
It has been lamented that these texts are difficult to access for Daoism in practice.
With Laozi, I have made it easier with *Laozi: Quest for the Ultimate Reality* (Jingwei, 2012).
Hopefully, this monograph *Liezi: World of Delusions* will be helpful for understanding Liezi.
The new perspective is: reading *Liezi* for revelations of Delusional states for self correction.
And Not be Delusional to read *Liezi* for achieving supernatural and transcendental power.

Stories in the Liezi are often simple, exciting and easy to understand.
Many such stories have long been taught in primary school like *Grandpa Moved Mountains*.
So I am looking forward to having more readings of *Liezi* to be conducted in secondary classes.
And more studies of the natural Daoism of Liezi to be initiated in the universities.
It is important to know our Delusions and repent for a happier life, and peace with others.

After Thoughts

Lieh-tzu *(Pinyin Liezi, Micropedia, Encyclopedia Britannica, 2002.)*
"As in earlier Taoist classics, emphasis in the Lieh-tzu centres on the mysterious Tao (Way) of Taoism, a great unknowable cosmic reality of incessant change to which human life should conform...The 'Yang Chu' chapter of the classic gives the Lieh-tzu a particular interest, for this chapter acknowledges the futility of challenging the immutable and irresistable Tao; it concludes that all man can look forward to in this life is sex, music, physical beauty, and material abundance, and even these goals are not always satisfied. Such 'fatalism' implies a life of radical 'self-interest' (a new development in Taoism), according to which a person should not sacrifice so much as a single hair of his head for the benefit of others."

Above is a typical sample of the negative appreciation of Daoism from a Western perspective. From a religious tradition, most Westerns seem to seek and find mystical Daoism in the East ! With strong contradictory evidence, Richard Dawkins wrote *The God Delusion* in 2006. Hawking and Mlodinow said the Universe needs no designer in *The Grand Design* (2010). Tutored in the biological science tradition, me too is an atheist, believing in gradual evolution. And Laozi's quest for the Ultimate Reality has not been answered to this day (Jingwei,2012).

More than 2000 years ago, Laozi and Liezi may seem mystical with their imaginative writings. Reading without prejudice, 'Dao' is a vague hypothetical exploration with amusing expressions. Thus we may ignore the tortuous descriptions of the Yi, the primal Dao, the self-Created, ...
The *Yijing* teaches Confucian hierarchy, love, justice, order and public service. (Jingwei, 2018).
The *Laozi* teaches primal virtues like gentleness, no-contesting, unselfish, respect (Jingwei, 2012).
The *Liezi* rejects transcendence with revelation of our pride, prejudice and Delusions (this study).

The Book of Lieh-tzu *(AC Graham transl. 1960.Columbia U. Press, NY, p.II)*
"The Taoist, it will already be clear, cannot be a philosopher, in the Western sense, establishing his case by rational argument; he can only guide us in the direction of the Way by aphorisms, poetry and parable."
'Rational argument' of the West gives us universal 'Democracy', that 49% ought to obey 51% !!!
Universal 'Freedom of Speech' that bears no responsibility for the truth, creating havoc today !!
I prefer simple gentleness, humility, unselfish sharing, respect, and *No* to 'endless arguments' !

People with primal universal values will not harm or seek to dominate over others.
True universal, primal values that people of all colors can accept and live together in harmony.

Universal Basic Income (UBI)
Recently a presidential candidate for 2020, Andrew Yang revitalizes this idea of UBI in America. Each adult age 18 and above, is to be given $1000/- monthly, cash for life with no string attached. A similar plan to alleviate poverty was proposed by Thomas Paine (1817) in the *Agrarian Justice*. Advanced automation has increasingly made jobs redundant, pushing more people out of work. To help the masses, the urgency of such a scheme is acutely felt at the moment, the world over.

The concept
When a nation is attacked, it is every citizen's duty to come forward to defend it.
In peace time logically, it is the responsibility of the nation to take care of each and every citizen. Thus no one citizen ought to drop below the poverty line at any one time in his whole existence. A UBI in cash paid monthly into an individual's account, from birth till death, is a neat solution.
Financing
The only problem is getting enough money to finance this scheme, and it is not impossible.
A rough estimate of money needed is huge, and would be equivalent to about 10% of the GDP.
Every citizen inherits the nation's land on the day of his birth.
Paine's plan for the Nation Fund, thus was from duties payable for usage of all the nation's land.
Every citizen owns the huge benefits that automation brings.
Yang's plan is to raise funds from every transaction with a Goods and Service Tax (GST).
From online discussions on YouTube, it seems UBI may actually pay for itself to a large extent !
UBI abolishes poverty, can have huge savings from terminating the many complex aid-schemes.
UBI raises the well-being of people, reduces insecurity and anxiety, resulting in less crimes.
Thus there will be more savings in reducing the police force and the costs for running jails.
UBI cash is largely spent locally resulting in a trickle-up economy and increased tax revenue.
The UBI cash is significant, this trickle-up economy is significant, consistently recycling itself.
Justification
UBI actually does more than help the homeless and eradicate poverty.
The average families will feel more secure with a guaranteed basic income for an emergency.
The population will be happier, resulting in less quarrels, less crimes and a safer environment.
The UBI creates a more equal society where women working at home now have values.
The UBI also gives value to the old and feeble, the sick and handicapped, and can pay for help.
Furthermore, the UBI gives strength to the weak and gentle, to stand up to bullies around us.
Lastly, UBI may promote birth rates, reverse the ageing problem that plagues many nations.
Administration
This is very simple when cash is to be given directly without qualifications or strings attached.
In Singapore, the Post Office Saving Bank (POSB) is set up to serve the people and not for profit.
All citizens have an account, and government pay-out can be directly transferred to each account.
After the system is linked-up, the administration cost is almost zero and is negligible.
Conclusion
Every morning, I never fail to see birds busy foraging to fill their stomachs, to live for the day.
Hopefully the UBI will lift all humanity above the animal level of subsistence.

Bibliographies

Publications in English

Clearly, Thomas (1993). *I Ching*. Shambhala, Boston & London. ISBN 978-0-87773-661-5.
Coutinho, Steve (not dated). *Liezi*. Internet Encyclopedia of Philosophy. (site visited, June 2020)
Dawkins, Richard (2006). *The God Delusion*. ISBN 9780618918249.
Graham, A.C. (1990). *The Book of Lieh-tzu*. Columbia University Press. ISBN 0-231-07236-8.
Hawking, S.W., Mlodinow L. (2010). The Grand Design. A Bantam Book, London. ISBN 9780553819229
Jingwei (2012). *Laozi: Quest for the Ultimate Reality*. Self-publication. Print-on-demand, Lightning Source, UK. ISBN 978-981-07-3758-0.
Jingwei (2018). *Yijing: Wisdom of 4 Sages*. Self-publication. Print-on-demand by Lightning Source, UK, ISBN 978-981-14-0204-3.
New Encyclopedia Britannica (1988). *Lieh-tzu*. Vol. 28, 5th ed., Encyclopedia Britannica Inc. Chicago USA.
Paine, Thomas (1817). Agrarian Justice. W.T. Sherwin Printed. London.
Pearson, Margaret J. (2011). *The Original I Ching*. North Clarendon, U.S.A., Tuttle Publishing. ISBN 978-0-8048-4181-8.
Stein, Jess (1984). *Random House College Dictionary*. Revised Edition. Random House, USA. ISBN 0-394-43600-8.
Seymour-Smith, Martin (1998). *The 100 most influential books ever written: the history of thoughts from ancient times to today*. Secaucus, N.J. : Carol Publ. Group. ISBN 978-0806520001.
The Bible Societies (1976). *Good News Bible*. Collins. UK. Bible Society. ISBN 0-564-00311-5.
Wikipedia (2018). *I Ching*. https://en.wikipedia.org/wiki/I_Ching.
Wikipedia (2020, last edited May 31). *Liezi*. https://en.wikipedia.org/w/index/title=Liezi.
Wong Eva (2001). Lieh-Tzu: A Taoist Guide to Practical Living. Boston: Shambhala. ISBN 1-57062-899-8.

Publications in Chinese

Chen, Caijun, Gu Shumei, An Rui (2012). Annotate. *Liezi Complete Work*. Beijing, Haichao Publishing House. (陈才俊，谷淑梅，安睿 (2012). 注译.《列子全集》北京，海潮出版社). ISBN 978-7-5157-0032-8.

Liu, Sibai (Qing) (1985). *Zhou Yi Simply Explain*. Taipei, Tian Long Publishing House. Republic of China, Year 74. Taiwan Publishing Office. Record No. 2483. (劉思白 著.《周易話解》. 台北, 天龍出版社. 中華民國74年. 局版台業字第2483號).

Lou, Fei (2006). Annotated. *Laozi, Zhuangzi*. Beijing, Beijing Publishing House. (楼霏 (2006). 编.《老子，庄子》. 北京. 北京出版社). ISBN 7-200-06509-9.

Luo, Zhaojin (1985). Annotated. *Liezi*. Hongkong. Po Yi Group Pte. Ltd. Book No. CC8513. (羅肇錦 (1985). 編撰.《列子》. 香港. 博益出版集團有限公司. 出版書號CC85013.)

Mao, Peiqi, Li Zefeng (1989). Edit. *Of History, Mountains and Rivers: Chinese History in Pictures*. Shanghai Ancient Books Publishing House. (毛佩琦，李泽奉 (1989). 主编.《歲月山河: 图说中国历史》.上海, 古籍出版社). ISBN 7-5325-0591-X /K.54.

Sima Qian (c.145-87BCE). *Historic Records*. In: Wang, Jun (2007). Compiled. *Shi Ji (Sima Qian,Han)*. Beijing Zhonghua Book Company. (王軍 (2007). 编.《史記 (司馬迁,漢)》. 北京, 中华書局). ISBN 978-7-101-05146-9.

Xu, Shen (Han, 206BCE-220CE). *Words Explain*. Tianjin City, Antiquarian Bookshop printed. 1994.(許慎 (漢).《說文解字》. 天津市古籍書店影印. 1994.)

Ye, Beiqing (2016). Annotate. *Liezi*. Beijing, Zhonghua Bookstore. (叶蓓卿 (2016). 译注.《列子》. 北京, 中华书局). ISBN 978-7-101-11358-7.

Yu Haidi, Li Na, Li Cuixiang, Li Peng, Zhou Shuiqin (2011). Eds. *General Knowledge of National Studies that Chinese Nationals Ought to Know, the Complete Work*. Beijing, NewChinese Bookshop. (于海娣，黎娜，李翠香，李鵬，周水琴 (2011). 编委.《中國人應知國学常识大全集》. 北京, 新華書店). ISBN 978-7-5113-0809-2.

Zhang, Xiuping, Wang Xiaoming (1993). Ed. *100 Books which have affected China*. Nanning City, Guangxi People's Publishing House. (張秀平，王曉明 (1993). 主编.《影响中国的100書》. 南宁市, 广西人民出版社). ISBN 7-219-02339-1 /K.

Zhang, Jiawen (1994). Ed. *Book of Phraseology*. Taipei, Zhongwen Publishing House. (张嘉文 (1994). 主编.《辭海》. 臺北，鐘文出版社). ISBN 957-0488-23-9.

Zhou, Bingjun (2001). Annotate. *Book of History*. Hunan Changsha City, Yuelu Bookstore. (周秉鈞 (2001). 譯注.《尚書》. 湖南長沙市, 岳麓書社). ISBN 7-80665-093-8.

Zhu, Xi (1130-1200, Song). Annoted. *Zhou Yi Original Meaning*. In: Scholars (Song, 960-1279CE; Yuan, 1271-1368CE). Annotated. *The 4 Books and 5 Classics*. Tianjin City, the Ancient Shop printed, 1988. (朱熹 注.《周易本義》. In: 宋元人 (960-1278CE; 1271-1368CE). 注《四書五經》.天津市, 古店影印, 1988.)

344 Appendices

345   Acknowledgements

346   List of Important Dates

347   Glossary

348   Self-Publishing

349   Copyrights and Disclaimer

350   Back-cover

Appendices

Acknowledgements

Firstly, I like to register my highest respect for Liezi, and feel much privileged to translate him. A big thank you to all the authors and contributors listed and not listed in the Bibliographies. And particularly grateful to Ye Beiqing (2016) annotation which I have heavily relied upon.

Also am most grateful to the National Library Singapore for the complimentary ISBN and CIP.

And many thanks to Lightning Source UK. for facilitating the print-on-demand (POD) setup, Online distribution through Ingram International.

And lastly to my sister Rita, a big thank you for a favorable feed-back on this work. Much effort has been exercised with the honest use of facts and figures in this monograph. My deepest apologies for any errors and omissions that remain.

Appendices

List of Important Dates	In Chronological Order
Stone age (石器時代)	600,000 - 4,000 BC
Bronze age (石器時代)	2,100 - 771 BC
Fuxi (伏羲)	c.3000 BC (legendary sovereign of ancient China)
Suiren (燧人)	c.3000 BC (legendary sovereign of ancient China)
Shennong (神農)	c.3000 BC (legendary sovereign of ancient China)
Huangdi (黄帝)	c.2700 BC (legendary ruler of ancient China)
Emperor Yao (尧帝)	c.2400 BC (legendary ruler of ancient China)
Emperor Shun (舜帝)	c.2300 BC (legendary ruler of ancient China)
Emperor Yu (禹帝)	c.2200 BC (legendary ruler of ancient China)

Dynasties

Xia Dynasty (夏朝)	2,100 - 1,600 BC (China. 1st dynasty, with no written language)
Shang Dynasty (商朝)	1,600 - 1,066 BC (China. 2nd dynasty, writing on shells, bones)
Zhou Dynasty (西周)	1,066 - 771 BC (China. 3rd dynasty, with written history)
Zhou Dynasty (東周)	770 - 221 BC (China. 3rd dynasty, with capital moved eastward)
Spring Autumn (春秋)	770 -476 BC (numerous vassal states coalesced into 7 majors)
Warring States (战國)	475 - 221 BC (7 major vassal states fighting for supremacy)
Qin Dynasty (秦朝)	221 - 206 BC (China. 4th dynasty, unified all states and languages)
Han Dynasty (漢朝)	206 BC - 220 CE (China. 5th dynasty, consolidation, prosperity)

Books

Yijing (易經)	c.1066 BC (*Book of Changes*, byFuxi,KingWen, Zhougong,Kongzi)
Liji (礼記)	c.1066 BC (*Rites of Zhou*. author Zhougong, Duke of Zhou)
Shangshu (尚書)	c.500 BC (*Book of History*. records of Xia, Shang, Zhou dynasties)
Shijing (詩經)	c.500 BC (*Book of Poems*. records of Xia, Shang, Zhou dynasties)
Shiji (史記)	c.100 BC (*Historic Records*. author Sima Qian. Han Dynasty)

People

King Zhou (纣王)	c.1105 -1046 BC (Shang. last evil king who lost the dynasty)
King Wen (文王)	c.1096 BC (Zhou. father of King Wu, co-author of *Yijing*).
King Wu (武王)	c.1046 BC (Zhou. founder-king of Zhou Dynasty)
Zhougong (周公)	c.1046 BC (Zhou. brother of King Wu, co-author of *Yijing*)
Laozi (老子)	c.580 BC (Zhou. SpringAutumn period.Chinese philosopher, sage)
Kongzi (孔子)	551 - 479 BC (Zhou.SpringAutumn.Chinese philosopher, sage)
Liezi (列子)	c.450 -375 BC (Zhou, Warring States, Chinese philosopher, sage)
Yangzhu (楊朱)	c.395 - 335 BC (Zhou, Warring States, Chinese philosopher, sage)
Zhuangzi (庄子)	c.369 - 286 BC (Zhou, Warring States, Chinese philosopher, sage)
Gongsunlong (公孙龙)	c.320 - 250 BC (Zhou, Warring States, Chinese philosopher, sage)
Sima Qian (司馬迁)	145 - 87 BC (Han. *author of Historic Records*, 史記)
Liu Xiang (刘向)	77 - 6 BC (Western Han, historian, imperial librarian, compiler)
Xu Shen (許慎)	58 - 147 AD (Han. author of *Words Explain*, 説文解字)
Zhang Zhan (張湛)	317-420 AD (Eastern Jin, Chinese writer, scholar, philosopher)
Zhu Xi (朱熹)	1130 -1200 AD (Song. writer, politician,Chinese philosopher, sage)
Liu Xiang (刘向)	77 - 6 BC (Western Han, historian, imperial librarian, compiler)
Zhang Zhan (張湛)	317-420 AD (Eastern Jin, Chinese writer, scholar, philosopher)

Appendices

Glossary
Dao (道)	Path, Laozi's Ultimate Reality, Confucian's Moral Principles
Delusion	False, especially psychotic beliefs
Junzi (君子)	Gentleman, virtuous cultured person, king, noble, respectable
Lonely-me (寡人)	Humble Self-address of emperors and kings
Subject-me (臣)	Humble Self-address of ministers before the emperors and kings

People
King Zhou (纣王)	c.1105 -1046 BC (Shang. last evil king who lost the dynasty)
King Wen (文王)	c.1096 BC (Zhou. father of King Wu, co-author *of Zhouyi*)
King Wu (武王)	c.1046 BC (Zhou. founder-king of Zhou Dynasty)
Kongzi (孔子)	551 - 479 BC (Zhou.SpringAutumn. Chinese philosopher, Sage)
Laozi (老子)	c.580 BC (Zhou. SpringAutumn period. Chinese philosopher,Sage)
Liezi	c.450 - 375 BC (Zhou. Warring States. Chinese philosopher, Sage)
Liu Xiang (刘向)	77 - 6 BC (Western Han, historian, imperial librarian, compiler)
Sima Qian (司馬迁)	145 - 87 BC (Han. *author of Historic Records, 史記*)
Xu Shen (許慎)	58 - 147 AD (Han. author of *Words Explain, 説文解字*)
Zhang Zhan (張湛)	317-420 AD (Eastern Jin, Chinese writer, scholar, philosopher)
Zhougong (周公)	c.1046 BC (Zhou.brother of King Wu, co-author *of Zhouyi*)
Zhu Xi (朱熹)	1130 -1200 AD (Song. writer, politician,Chinese philosopher, Sage)
Zhuangzi	c.369 - 286 BC (Zhou. Warring States. Chinese philosopher, Sage)

Pre-historic leaders
Fuxi (伏羲)	c.3000 BC (legendary sovereign of ancient China)
Suiren (燧人)	c.3000 BC (legendary sovereign of ancient China)
Shennong (神農)	c.3000 BC (legendary sovereign of ancient China)
Huangdi (黄帝)	c.2700 BC (legendary ruler of ancient China)
Emperor Yao (尧帝)	c.2400 BC (legendary ruler of ancient China)
Emperor Shun (舜帝)	c.2300 BC (legendary ruler of ancient China)
Emperor Yao (禹帝)	c.2200 BC (legendary ruler of ancient China)

Dynasties
Xia Dynasty (夏朝)	2,100 - 1,600 BC (China. 1st dynasty, with no written language)
Shang Dynasty (商朝)	1,600 - 1,066 BC (China. 2nd dynasty, writing on shells, bones)
Zhou Dynasty West (西周)	1,066 - 771 BC (China. 3rd dynasty, with written history)
Zhou Dynasty East (東周)	770 - 221 BC (China. 3rd dynasty, with written history)
Spring Autumn period (春秋)	770 -476 BC (numerous vassal states coalesced into 7majors)
Warring States period (战國)	475 - 221 BC (7 major vassal states fighting for supremacy)
Qin Dynasty (秦朝)	221 - 206 BC (China. 4th dynasty, unified all states and languages)
Han Dynasty (漢朝)	206 BC - 220 CE (China. 5th dynasty, consolidation, prosperity)

Books
Yijing (易經)	c.1066 BC(*Book of Changes* by Fuxi,KingWen,Zhougong,Kongzi)
Daodejing (道德經)	c.580 BC (*The Primal and Virtue Classic*. by Laozi, Zhou, sage)
Shiji (史記)	c.100 BC (*Historic Records*. author Sima Qian. Han Dynasty)

Self-Publishing

These days when one has something to say, self-publishing a book is not difficult.
Do-it-yourself all the way will cost less than SD1000/- with self-editing, self-assessment.
However as a self-publisher, you have to do your own promotion of the book to readers!
To help avoid the Vanity Press, my simple experience to share is as followed:

Manuscript
Have the full script between covers all completed, format digitally in a doc.pdf for print.

Optional
Kirkus Reviews (online)
For a 250-word review in 6 weeks, UDS550 (~SD850/-).
(my first book *Laozi: Quest for the Ultimate Reality*, 206 pages in 2016)

Accounting and Corporate Regulatory Authority (ACRA)
As a self-publisher, I need to register an account with the above authority.
First registration on site, cost SD68/- in 2012, subsequently yearly fee SD20/-.
Require a registered Office address (home address, $5/- annually, HDB authority)

National Library Board Legal Deposit Office (online)
In Singapore these are complimentary services and take about a week.
First apply for an International Standard Book Number (ISBN).
Then apply for Cataloguing in Publication (CIP) -
(require to submit title page, title page verso, copyright page, table of contents, preface and introduction).

Local Printer
Ultra Supplies, Queensway Shopping Centre, Singapore.
Have a book cover design for about SD100/-.
Print the First test copy with perfect binding for about SD30/- (paperback, 300 pages).
Confirmed that the book product is in order, and print more as required.

Lightning Source UK (online)
Set-up fee GBP42 (~SD84/-) for Print-on-demand (POD).
Market Distribution fee GBP7 yearly(~SD14/-) for distribution worldwide to online retailers.

Liezi: World of Delusions
by Jingwei, 2020 December
email: jjingwei11@gmail.com

Copyright © 2020
All rights reserved.
Copying is allowed for individual private use.
Copying is *not* allowed for commercial trade.

Disclaimer:
Every precaution has been taken in the preparation of this monograph.
The publisher and author apologize for any errors or omissions that may remain.
The publisher and author assume no liability whatsoever for damages suffer from its usage.

Other Publications by Jingwei:

Laozi: Quest for the Ultimate Reality (2012.non-fiction.204 pp.)ISBN978-9810737580
(listed among the "Indie Books Worth Discovering", 15 May 2017 Kirkus Reviews)

Yijing: Wisdom of 4 Sages (2019. non-fiction. 312 pp.) ISBN 978-981-14-0204-3
(a guide-book for understanding the *Yijing*, a DIY-book for practical Divination)

email: jjingwei11@gmail.com
Title Availability:
Print-on-demand (POD) by Lightning Source, UK
Distribution through Ingram International
Order online (world-wide)
The Book Depository.co.uk (with free delivery worldwide)
Amazon.com
Espresso Book Machine

back-cover

Liezi, together with Laozi and Zhuangzi, are the 3 pillars of philosophical Daoism. Liezi was not mentioned by Sima Qian in his *Historic Records*, and is much neglected. The Liezi text includes 139 short amusing stories, teaching morality easily and simply. Tales, *Kuafu Chased Sun* and *Yukong Moved Mountains* are taught in primary school. Liezi favors enjoy life, fear not death; rejects transcendentals like "riding on wind". His stories are vivid, full of marvels, often humorous, and reflective of our Delusions.

Liezi: World of Delusions:
Full Chinese Text Presentation and English Translation
Chapter 1. Heavenly Signs (天瑞)
Chapter 2. Huangdi (黃帝)
Chapter 3. King Mu of Zhou (周穆王)
Chapter 4. Zhongni (Confucius, 仲尼)
Chapter 5. Tang's Queries (汤问)
Chapter 6. Effort or Destiny (力命)
Chapter 7. Yangzhu (杨朱)
Chapter 8. Charming Talks (說符)
Discussion
17 topical analyses
Conclusions
All Lives Matters
Effort or Destiny
Enjoy life
Government for the People
Know your Delusions
Minds, Dreams and Emotions
Natural Daoism
Queries and Curiosity
Reject Tanscendentals
Selfless Duties
Strive for Excellence
After Thoughts
Universal Basic Income (UBI)
Bibliographies

Jingwei (景維) 1945-, a research-biochemist retired in 2007, first self-published in 2012 with 1. *Laozi: Quest for the Ultimate Reality* (ISBN 978-981-07-3758-0), 206 pp, nonfiction. 2. *Yijing: Wisdom of 4 Sages* (ISBN 978-981-14-0204-3), 2019, 311 pp. All books are available print-on-demand (POD) by Lightning Source UK, offered on Espresso Book Machine, Amazon.com, online stores. Email: jjingwei11@gmail.com

www.ingramcontent.com/pod-product-compliance
Lightning Source LLC
Chambersburg PA
CBHW021801220426
43662CB00006B/141